"The Bloody Fifth"

The 5th Texas Infantry Regiment,

HOOD'S TEXAS BRIGADE,

Army of Northern Virginia

Vol. 2: Gettysburg to Appomattox

John F. Schmutz

SB

Savas Beatie
California

Library of Congress Cataloging-in-Publication Data

Names: Schmutz, John F., 1947- author.
Title: The Bloody Fifth": The 5th Texas Infantry Regiment, Hood's Texas Brigade, Army of Northern Virginia, vol. 1: Secession to the Suffolk Campaign / John F. Schmutz.
Description: First edition. | El Dorado Hills, CA: Savas Beatie LLC, 2016. |
Includes bibliographical references and index.
Identifiers: LCCN 2015028122| ISBN 9781611213348 (alk. paper) |
ISBN 9781611212051 (ebk.)
Subjects: LCSH: Confederate States of America. Army. Texas Infantry Regiment, 5th. | Texas—History—Civil War, 1861-1865—Regimental histories. |
United States—History—Civil War, 1861-1865—Regimental histories. |
United States—History—Civil War, 1861-1865—Campaigns.
Classification: LCC E580.5 5th .S36 2016 | DDC 973.7/464—dc23
LC record available at http://lccn.loc.gov/2015028122

First Edition, First Printing

SB
Published by
Savas Beatie LLC
989 Governor Drive, Suite 102
El Dorado Hills, CA 95762

Phone: 916-941-6896
(web) www.savasbeatie.com
(E-mail) sales@savasbeatie.com

Proudly published, printed, and warehoused in the United States of America.

MIX
Paper from responsible sources
FSC www.fsc.org FSC® C011935

This book is dedicated to the officers and men of the 5th Texas Infantry Regiment who fought above and beyond the call of duty for nearly four years, enduring untold hardships, all in furtherance of a cause that was sacred to them.

Table of Contents

Table of Contents (continued)

Preface

The "Bloody Fifth" represents the first comprehensive study of the 5th Texas Regiment, a narrative I found long overdue and greatly in need of telling. While I was quite familiar with Hood's Texas Brigade prior to my immersion in this work, I acquired a much deeper appreciation for the individual fighting men as I prepared this manuscript for publication. These uncommonly brave soldiers joined an army fighting for independence and for their own state's right to control its own destiny. They believed deeply in a cause they were willing to die for to preserve.

The 5th Texas was one of only three infantry units from Texas to fight in the Eastern Theater as part of the Army of Northern Virginia. Serving more than 1,300 miles from home created particular hardships not experienced to the same degree by other troops, particularly after the Mississippi River was firmly in Federal hands and Southern ports more effectively blockaded. The supply of food, clothing, sundries, and even letters from home became increasingly scarce. While the men grumbled, as all soldiers are prone to do, the regiment maintained its morale and fighting edge. These Texans were always prepared to fight to the last measure, a fact that led Robert E. Lee to proudly proclaim that "the Texans are always ready."

Volume 2, *Gettysburg to Appomattox*, commences where the first volume left off, in the spring of 1863 with the Union army having been defeated at Chancellorsville and General Lee's army preparing to carry the war north. It follows the 5th Texas on its fateful march into Pennsylvania. The narrative, rich in detail about the men themselves, carries the "Bloody Fifth" through the bloody defeat at Gettysburg and the retreat back into Virginia. Two months later the Texans moved westward by rail to North Georgia and the grand tactical victory fighting with the Army of Tennessee at Chickamauga. The frustrations of the quasi-siege of Chattanooga followed, as did the dismal winter campaign against Union-held Knoxville, Tennessee. The verdant fields of Virginia welcomed the Texans once more in the spring of 1864, their return all-too-soon followed by the horrors of the Wilderness, Spotsylvania, Cold Harbor, and the stagnation of Petersburg's trenches. Heavy fighting followed, including New Market Heights and Darbytown Road. With the lines finally broken around Richmond and

Petersburg, all that was left was the hard road to Appomattox and the long journey home.

* * *

As with the first volume, there are many people to thank for making this book possible. Please see the Acknowledgments noted in the first installment, and I extend my thanks once more to my publisher, Savas Beatie, for its faith in my work and this history of the 5th Texas Infantry.

John F. Schmutz
San Antonio, TX

Chapter 1

Gettysburg: Gathering Storm

On May 24, having missed the fight at Chancellorsville, the Texas Brigade held a regular review in an open field about 600 yards from its camp. A number of ladies in mourning dress watched the proceedings on horseback. (One Texan estimated that "more than *two-thirds* of the women in the Confederacy" were in black by then.) Four days later, the men departed camp at 8:00 a.m. for a five mile march to participate in a "grand Division Review," in a clearing behind Hood's headquarters, with the public invited. Hood relished the opportunity to show off his veterans. The brigades of Anderson, Law, Robertson, and Benning drew up in a mile long line of battle. The division, formed into companies, preceded by about 20 artillery pieces, passed in review before their beaming commander. The 4th Texas band and those of the three other brigades provided a variety of stirring marching tunes.[1]

Following the formal review, a mock battle was staged for the dignitaries and what one participant described as an "immense crowd of citizens." Smither wrote his mother that, "[w]e also had a sham Artillery duel and an Infantry charge, it was a very grand affair throughout, the 'Old 5th' was just in front of Hood, and coming up at a doublequick with fixed bayonets, and arriving within 50 yds of the General we raised the 'Old Texas Yell'"that the entire brigade quickly and loudly took up. "You have no idea how terrific it sounds to hear a line of 10,000 men yelling like mad," Smither exclaimed.[2]

1 West, *Texan in Search of a Fight*, 53-55, 63.

2 Mark Smither to Elizabeth Smither, May 30, 1863, in SHSU.

Afterward, the regiment bided its time until May 31, when the brigade trudged 14 miles through heavy dust back toward Fredericksburg, bivouacking on the Fredericksburg Road two miles closer to the town than their encampment of the previous year. Remaining on alert throughout the night, it then returned back to its camp near Raccoon Ford. The subsequent 28 mile trek with full packs through the dusty, hot sun was thoroughly exhausting, especially on new recruits—one reporting himself "pretty tired" with "very much blistered" feet. While Lee mulled the prospect of launching another major offensive, he ordered a number of feigned movements and demonstrations such as this one to confuse the enemy about his intentions.[3]

Following its victory at Chancellorsville, Lee's army was positioned halfway between Richmond and Washington along the Rapidan-Rappahannock basin. The high command faced a critical decision: should the army be sent west to reinforce Confederate forces facing Grant and Rosecrans, or should Lee invade the North again? Disagreeing with several of his generals, Lee favored a thrust northward into Pennsylvania. While such an invasion presented significant logistical issues, it had considerable merit. President Davis and his war department wanted to keep Lee's army in the East, and the advantages accruing from a victory on Northern soil were undeniable. So they backed Lee's proposed course of action.[4]

Lee reorganized the Army of Northern Virginia for a third time on May 30, dividing it into three corps, replacing the previous two. Longstreet retained command of First Corps. Two new lieutenant generals, Richard S. Ewell and Ambrose Powell Hill, took command of the other two corps. Ewell's Second Corps absorbed the majority of Jackson's old corps, while the new Third Corps under Hill comprised divisions transferred from the other two. Hood's Division, of about 8,000 effectives, remained under Longstreet. "So high-wrought was the pride and self-reliance of . . . [these] troops," Hood wrote, with pride "they believed they could carve their way through almost any number of the enemy's lines, formed in the open field in their front."[5]

Beginning on June 3, Lee slowly began withdrawing his army from the Rapidan-Rappahannock line toward the Shenandoah Valley and the designated rally point at Culpeper Court House. McLaws' Division of Longstreet's Corps left Fredericksburg first. Ewell's three divisions proceeded north on June 4-5, while Lee

3 Cobb Diary, May 31, June 1, 1863, in SHC/UNC; West, *Texan in Search of a Fight*, 54-57.

4 Foote, *Civil War Narrative*, 2:430-31; James Longstreet, "Lee's Invasion of Pennsylvania," in *B&L*, 3:245-46; Reichardt, *Forever the Cause*, 51.

5 *OR* 25, pt. 1, 4; Hood, *Advance and Retreat*, 53; West, *Texan in Search of a Fight*, 57-58, 71; Stevens, *Reminiscences*, 102; Foote, *Civil War Narrative*, 2: 434-36; James Longstreet, "Lee's Invasion of Pennsylvania," in *B&L*, 3:245.

himself left Fredericksburg on the 6th. Meanwhile, A. P. Hill's Third Corps remained near Fredericksburg to counter any potential Federal advance toward Richmond, as well as to deceive the Yankees about Lee's actual intentions. Hooker did indeed remain largely uncertain about what Lee was doing.[6]

On June 3, the brigade prepared for its move to Culpeper Court House. The men cooked three days' rations and were ready to move out early the following morning. Early on June 4 they set out, waded the Rapidan at Raccoon Ford, and marched 15 miles, finally bivouacking three miles south of the town, where they had camped the prior November. Even during their short stay, the Texans were still ordered out of camp twice, once to attend a review of Stuart's cavalry and again as a planned misdirection.[7]

Along with the rest of Longstreet's Corps, the regiment departed camp at 1:00 p.m. in a heavy rain storm on June 6, heading northeast toward Rappahannock Station, plodding through the mire until 10:00 p.m. that evening. They bivouacked a few feet off the road, and slept under dripping trees on the wet ground "like so many tired hounds." "It was a novel sight," a Texan recalled, "to see or rather to hear 20,000 or 30,000 men rushing into the woods on the side of the road to . . . secure a place to lie down." After a light breakfast on June 7, the men formed ranks at dawn and marched 16 miles back to their Culpeper campsite. "This marching and countermarching," one later noted, "is what the military authorities call making a demonstration." It was "a tiresome and monotonous business, but if it accomplishes the purpose for which I left home I will be satisfied." Lee was in fact using Longstreet to feign a movement east of the Blue Ridge Mountains toward Washington, while Ewell's Corps marched through the Shenandoah Valley and into Pennsylvania.[8]

Stuart, perhaps seeking to top Hood's recently successful review, held his own on June 8 near Brandy Station, halfway between Culpeper and the Rappahannock. Invited to attend with his "people," i.e., his staff, Hood arrived instead with his entire division. "There were 8,000 or 10,000 horsemen covering an immense area," an astonished Texan later reported. The infantry watched the horsemen's maneuvers from [a] railroad embankment, and the Texans considered it awe inspiring. Admonished by from both Fitzhugh Lee and Wade Hampton, all the men were on their best behavior. "As brigade after brigade, in the bright sun, with shining rifles

6 *OR* 27, pt. 2, 293; West, *Texan in Search of a Fight*, 58; Foote, *Civil War Narrative*, 2:436-37; Longstreet, "Lee's Invasion of Pennsylvania," *B&L*, 3:245.

7 West, *Texan in Search of a Fight*, 57, 74-75; Winkler, *Confederate Capital*, 135; Foote, *Civil War Narrative*, 2:436-37.

8 West, *Texan in Search of a Fight*, 69, 74-75; Cobb Diary, June 7 and 8, 1863, in SHC/UNC.

marched by followed by thousands of prancing cavalry, and battery after battery of artillery, it seemed a world of arms."[9] At the conclusion of the review, the Texans trudged seven miles back to their camp.

On June 9, Hooker ordered his cavalry commander Maj. Gen. Alfred Pleasanton, to reconnoiter across the Rappahannock River to ascertain what Lee was up to. Near Brandy Station, Pleasanton's force of 11,000 men, and 3,000 infantry surprised Stuart's force, resulting in the largest cavalry engagement of the entire war. The battle itself ended in a stalemate when Pleasanton withdrew across the Rappahannock, having accomplished his mission. The Federals were now certain that the Confederate army had left Fredericksburg and was headed north, preparing for a major movement. Lee now had to accelerate his movements. To forestall Hooker from moving on Richmond while he marched north, Lee ordered Ewell from Culpeper to the Shenandoah Valley, to destroy the Union garrisons at Martinsburg and Winchester. He belived this would cause Lincoln to pull Hooker back toward Washington, thus nullifying any threat to Richmond. Ewell advanced rapidly up the Valley and had overrun the Federal garrisons by June 15. Two days later, he began crossing his force over the Potomac into Maryland.[10]

Lee's strategy worked as intended—Hooker pulled back from the Rappahannock, concentrating around Centreville, between Lee and the Federal capital. A. P. Hill now marched his corps from Fredericksburg toward Culpeper, and subsequently followed Ewell up the Valley into Maryland. On June 15, Longstreet's Corps also embarked to the North from Culpeper, but stayed east of the Blue Ridge Mountains, protecting the passes into the Shenandoah Valley and hoping to confuse Hooker about Lee's actual objective, Washington or Pennsylvania. Stuart's cavalry's first mission was to screen Longstreet's movements and help guard passes and then cross the Potomac and screen Ewell's march into Pennsylvania.[11]

The 5th Texas left Culpeper Court House on June 13 moving five miles west and bivouacking on a familiar spot—the Cedar Mountain battleground of the previous August. Some of the men walked the still-ghastly battlefield with its many "unburied skeletons" as well as one small ditch containing 49 skulls. Here and there, a grisly hand or foot protruded from the ground. Mark Smither, the regimental sergeant major, remembered camping there previously. Much looked the same, except "more Yankee

9 West, *Texan in Search of a Fight*, 58; Freeman, *Lee's Lieutenants*, 3:1-4.

10 Longstreet, *Manassas to Appomattox*, 288-89; Foote, *Civil War Narrative*, 2:437-39, 441; Winkler, *Confederate Capital*, 135; Mark Smither to John Smither, June 14, 1863 in SHSU; Freeman, *Lee's Lieutenants*, 3:8-13.

11 *OR* 27, pt. 2, 295-96; Mark Smither to Elizabeth Smither, June 14, 1863, in SHSU; Freeman, *Lee's Lieutenants*, 3:20-22, 47; Simpson, *Lee's Grenadier Guard*, 246-47.

bones where the farmers have planted their crops" were visible. "There are a couple of leg bones lying on the desk beside me," he wrote, "which one of the boys pulled out a pair of blue Yankee breaches yesterday."[12]

The Texans continued marching north on June 15 under a blazing sun, climbing the east side of the Blue Ridge Mountains toward Ashby's Gap. The grueling trek, led "by that unmerciful driver, our beloved General Hood . . . who simply strikes a trot," John West later wrote, "and is satisfied that the Texas Brigade at least will camp with him at nightfall." The regiment marched nearly 25 miles this day, as far as Gaines' Cross Roads, a costly journey, as over 500 men fell out by the roadside from exhaustion, and a number died where they fell. The last 10 miles, under "a clear starlit sky," were lined with exhausted soldiers, causalities of the grueling march, the heat, plus lack of adequate hats and serviceable shoes. "It was frightful indeed to see so many men falling by the roadside," a Texan recalled. "Under every shade tree men were lying senseless, overcome by the heat."[13]

On June 16, the 5th Texas marched yet another 20 miles, again with many stragglers, as far as Markham Station on the Manassas Gap Railroad, finally camping in a field of clover. The following day they made another 14 miles, camping in a magnificent grove of oak and hickory trees one mile from Uppersville. Traveling west on June 18, they traversed the mountains through Ashby's Gap and up into the Valley, crossing to the west bank of the Shenandoah and camping near Millwood. The river, cold and deep, reached nearly to their armpits as the men crossed, fully clothed per orders, holding rifles and cartridge boxes over their heads. The next day the Texans marched north along the river 10 miles to Berryville, crossed over it again proceeding east and finally stopping on a mountain adjacent to Snicker's Gap. They camped two miles from the river and constructed breastworks. Stevens reported that the men tried to form their blankets into tents to keep everything dry, "but it was no use—the underside of the tent was as wet as the upper side—everywhere the air could penetrate the cloud was there, too. Even the inside of our cartridge boxes were wet." The regiment remained near the mountain top over three days, guarding the gap. On the night of June 19, the men experienced the hardest wind and rain storm many of them ever saw when "the cold and rain, like the two-edged sword of holy writ, penetrated to the very joints and marrow." The steady incessantly rainy wind blew down tents and thoroughly soaked the men, and conditions remained woeful the entire time the Texans stayed on the heights. Then, on June 23, they finally withdrew from their

12 Mark Smither to John Smither, June 14, 1863, in SHSU; West, *Texan in Search of a Fight,* 59-60 74-75, 89; Cobb Diary, June 10, 13 & 15, 1863, in SHC/UNC.

13 West, *Texan in Search of a Fight,* 75-76 , 89; Muster Rolls, Field, Staff and Band 5th Texas Infantry, April 30—June 30, 1863, in TSA; Sims, "Recollections of the Civil War."

mountain perch, crossed again to the river's west bank, returning to Millwood to block any enemy movement in their rear.[14]

On June 24, the regiment marched steadily from Millwood once again, through Berryville until evening, camping about a mile south of Smithfield and two miles north of the Winchester and Potomac Railroad near Summit Point (approximately 15 miles northeast of Winchester). The following day, the men covered another grueling 25 miles and finally bivouacked eight miles from Martinsburg. They reached the ford of the Potomac River opposite Williamsport at around 7:00 a.m. the next day and began crossing the cold, swift stream around noon. Most of the infantry had to wade the 300-yard wide river, as artillery and wagon trains clogged the solitary pontoon bridge. The men, with clothes, rifles, and cartridge boxes held overhead had reached the Maryland shore.[15]

While the men crossed, a group of Maryland ladies buggy-bound for Virginia, unable to turn back in the narrow approach to the ford, had to ride alongside the endless, half-naked line; they passed by the soldiers as quickly as possible. One of Longstreet's officers wryly observed that "50,000 men without their trousers on cannot be passed in review every day of the week." As the bulk of the brigade reached the north bank, it started to rain hard once again.[16]

The crossing had several other lighter moments. Stevens recalled a newly-promoted lieutenant, dazzling in his gold-laced new uniform, who was decidedly averse to the thought of subjecting it to river water. He offered a private $5 to carry him across on his back. Apparently the whole regiment knew what was coming, save for the hapless lieutenant. All went well till mid-stream, where the private "lost his footing" in waist deep water and "down they came, under they went, both private and lieutenant." A boisterous Rebel yell filled the air, to the young officer's exquisite embarrassment.[17]

The brigade's bands had forded the river first and serenaded their comrades with "the inspiring strains of 'Dixie'" as they climbed up the bank onto Maryland's shore.

14 Stevens, *Reminiscences*, 103; Cobb Diary, June 18 and 19, 1863, in SHC/UNC; West, *Texan in Search of a Fight*, 75-76, 90; Polley, *Hood's Texas Brigade*, 146; Simpson, *Lee's Grenadier Guard*, 248-49; Freeman, *Lee's Lieutenants*, 3:52-55; Longstreet, "Lee's Invasion of Pennsylvania," *B&L*, 3:289.

15 Cobb Diary, June 20, 22, 24, 25 and 26, in SHC/UNC; Stevens, *Reminiscences*, 105; Reichardt, *Forever the Cause*, 53; Polley, *Hood's Texas Brigade*, 146; West, *Texan In Search of a Fight*, 81; Foote, *Civil War Narrative*, 3:440-42; Winkler, *Confederate Capital*, 135.

16 *OR* 27, pt. 1, 358; Cobb Diary June 24, 25, and 26, 1863, in SHC/UNC; Mark Smither to Elizabeth Smither, June 28, 1863, in SHSU; Polley, *Hood's Texas Brigade*, 126; Freeman, *Lee's Lieutenants*, 3:47-48.

17 Stevens, *Reminiscences*, 105-106; Fletcher, *Rebel Private*, 71.

Brig. Gen. Jerome Bonaparte Robertson
Texas Historical Baptist Museum, Independence, TX

"Never before, nor since," explained General Hood, had he "witnessed such intense enthusiasm as that which prevailed throughout the entire Confederate Army" that memorable day. Once the entire brigade was across, Brig. Gen. Jerome Robertson marched his men a short distance where they stacked rifles and built fires to cook their rations. Soon the aroma of coffee and frying bacon suffused the air. In high spirits, the Texans were ready to "fight, forage or drink," whichever occasion first presented itself.[18]

Actually, "liquid fortification" became available almost immediately following the crossing. A large store of Federal whiskey had been confiscated near Hagerstown. Always mindful of morale, Hood requested and received a sizeable number of barrels for his thirsty division. Each soldier received a ration of a one gill (a quarter-pint). It was, recalled Col. Powell, "the first and only time I ever knew it done in the Confederate army." As far as Powell was concerned, it "was better than Virginia 'apple jack.'" The sizeable number of non-drinkers cheerfully drew their prescribed ration and bestowed it upon their fellow comrades. Unfortunately, a few strong shots of whiskey combined with the hard march, a hot day, empty stomachs, and the anticipation of the upcoming campaign in Yankeedom proved disastrous.

According to Stevens,

> inside of half an hour there was more drunk men in Williamsport than I think I ever saw in my life. Either before or since—they were drunk all over—through and through, up and down, side edge and bottom, fore and aft, sideways and edgeways, some laughed, some cried, some hooped and yelled, some cussed and swore, others ripped and tore and called for gore. It kept the sober boys busy to keep the drunk ones from killing each other. Soon some fell by the wayside, helpless and were

18 Hood, *Advance and Retreat*, 54; Polley, *Hood's Texas Brigade*, 146; Lasswell, *Rags and Hope*, 176; Fletcher, *Rebel Private*, 71.

> dumped into wagons and ambulances, and hauled the balance of the day. Some others were not seen for 15 hours afterwards, and when they caught up with their commands, they were quite sober, and their eyes looked like two burnt holes in a blanket.

Polley of the 4th Texas recalled that the amount of available whiskey "was amply sufficient to put fully half the Brigade not only in a boisterously good humor, but in such physical condition that the breadth of the road over which they marched that evening was more of an obstacle to rapid progress than its length." Another recalled that a least one-third of the men "got pretty tight and . . . many of them slipped down and rolled in the mud."[19]

Fighting broke out in companies where imbibing was the heaviest. Fletcher recalled a fellow private, Taylor of Company F, grabbing a stack of rifles with fixed bayonets and "attacking" his unsuspecting comrades, leading to an officer being cut on the cheek. Just as this happened, the long roll sounded recommencing the march, and the lucky miscreant's deed was soon forgotten. Commanders used various techniques to sober up the heavy drinkers. Colonel Van Manning of the 3rd Arkansas, a strict disciplinarian, ordered the drunks in his regiment dunked in a nearby stream until he was satisfied the individual could continue reasonably unimpaired.[20]

With order restored, the regiment trudged approximately seven miles through Hagerstown, bivouacking near Greencastle, Pennsylvania. That day, the regiment ate breakfast in Virginia, lunch in Maryland, and supper in Pennsylvania, a singular feat for only Hood's Division during the war. Hillsboro, Texas, native W. A. Culbertson of the 9th Georgia credited the men with having been in *four* states that June 26th, including "the state of intoxication!" Longstreet, to stifle any further trouble, ordered all whiskey found along the march be "destroyed."[21]

19 Stevens, *Reminiscences*, 105-06; Polley, *Letters to Charming Nellie*, 121; Reichardt, *Forever the Cause*, 53; West, *Texan in Search of a Fight*, 91, 106; Smith, *Reminiscences*, 35. Simpson, *Lee's Grenadier Guard*, 251. Some company commanders reportedly totally ignored Hood's order of one gill per man, and observers reported whiskey being issued "by the cupful." "I don't suppose the oldest man living in America ever saw as many drunk at any one time," said one. J. M. Polk, *The North and South American Review* (Austin, TX, 1912), 22.

20 Polley, *Hood's Texas Brigade*, 147; Collier, *They'll Do To Tie To*, 127; Fletcher, *Rebel Private*, 71-72. The soldier involved remains unidentifiable, as there were then three Taylors in the company: H. L., Thomas W., and William M. See Simpson, *Compendium*, 216.

21 *OR* 51, pt. 2, 729-30; Muster Rolls, Cos. A and B, 5th Texas Infantry, April 30-June 30, 1863, in TSA; Reichardt, *Forever the Cause*, 53; Stevens, *Reminiscences*, 106-07; Mark Smither to Elizabeth Smither, June 28, 1863, in SHSU; Moore, *Men of the Bayou City Guard*, 68; Cobb Diary, June 26, 1863, in SHC/UNC. Maryland is only seven miles wide measured directly north from

Surveying the lush Pennsylvania countryside, prospects for foraging were never far from the men's thoughts. Col. Powell admired the land's ample bounty: "white cottages embowered in groves of trees laden with fruit . . . fields of wheat like restless seas of emerald. The evidences of prosperity, happiness and comfort were all in striking contrast to the dismal, mourning, half populated land we had just left over the river." Fletcher and his Company F mess mates immediately began inspecting the countryside for food, bribing camp guards that evening with the promise of a share of their loot. The first house they encountered, occupied by three females, royally "entertained and fed them." Soon thereafter, the enterprising crew came upon a large bee hive. Tying a rope to it, the Texans started off on a "sweeping trot." When the bees had flown away, the demolished hive yielded an abundance of "golden sweet gum ready for satisfying the inner man," according to Fletcher. With no containers to transport a portion of the "take" back to the guards, Fletcher's group felt "required" to consume it all. A milk house provided a cool nightcap to the evening's festivities.[22]

Though now quite late, the foragers were determined to secure chickens before returning. Sighting a coop, the most agile of the group, "Tobacco Boy," the soldier who had earlier taught Fletcher the appropriate procedures of chicken thievery, was detailed as the break-in man. Fletcher posted himself near the door of the coop to retrieve the fruits of Tobacco Boy's labor, while the others took strategic positions around the farmhouse, watching carefully for the owner, watchdogs, or other foragers. After a long wait with no word from inside, Fletcher called out "Why in the H— ain't you killing and throwing them out?" Immediately, a dull thump sounded at the front door, followed by others. Fletcher then

> felt and found some warm but lifeless large chickens. I remained squatting by the pile and at short intervals there would be another thump, and that went on for some time, and as I felt no small chickens, I said: 'Enough large ones; want some frying size.' So the thumps of less sound continued a sufficient length of time, to fill the order. I said, 'Enough.'. . . We soon found that we had an all night's job unfeathering our fryers and expended a good deal of strength to pluck one feather; and after trying them all we concluded that they were old bantams and left them. I have often wondered since if a bantam ever sheds its feathers.

Williamsport. The regiment actually would have traveled at least 12 miles on the route it took through the state. Stevens, *Reminiscences*, 106.

22 Fletcher, *Rebel Private*, 73; Robert M. Powell, "With Hood At Gettysburg, The Experiences of a Texas Officer in One of the Charges at Little Round Top," *Philadelphia Weekly Times*, December 13, 1884; Reichardt, *Forever the Cause*, 53.

With no more bounty for their nocturnal foraging, the men crept back to camp, carefully eluding the thoroughly duped, expectant guards.[23]

The 5th Texas seemed to be the brigade's most active foragers that first evening in Pennsylvania. Company K was assigned to guard Hood's headquarters, near a large mansion just outside town surrounded by outbuildings, orchards, and gardens. Hood told the men reporting for duty to set up camp near his tent. "Boys, you are now on enemy's soil, stack your arms and do pretty much as you please. [Just] stay close by and prevent any stranger from coming here to kill me." Interpreting their instructions liberally, they soon scattered in all directions, invading the summer kitchen, smoke house, spring house, garden, and poultry yards. Stevens related that within five minutes, all were "as empty as a last year's bird nest, and there was not a single thing left in that garden that could be eaten, either cooked or raw." Finally, the owner of the house left her third floor haven, approached Hood asking him to restrain his men. Hood smiled, and in a tone "modestly as a little girl," replied that he was aware of the men's activity, but that "my men are hungry for chickens. Your people have killed every chicken, and nearly everything else, in Virginia, and I guess your people ought to have a little teaching of what war means."[24]

Hood's men were soon "about shoe mouth deep" in chicken, turkey, and duck feathers, and every pot and cooking vessel that could be scavenged bubbled on fires full of cooking fowls, "baked, stewed, fried, roasted, smothered, and in fact, cooked in every way and style known to the cuisine art of camp life." Stevens later reminisced that, "[o]f all the eating that you ever saw a lot of men do I reckon we done it there that night."[25]

The following morning, June 27, the anniversary of the victory at Gaines' Mill, the Texans resumed marching north with regimental bands playing martial airs. Passing through Greencastle, they continued up the Cumberland Valley toward Chambersburg through acres of well-kept orchards, heavy fields of grain, fat livestock, and deep green hills. The many macadamized roads presented a marked contrast to the dusty, deep-rutted dirt roads of Virginia. The men were amazed at all the substantially built, neatly kept barns and houses. They all "appeared to be models," to Stevens. John West admitted not seeing "a barn in the last three days that was not more substantially and carefully built and fitted out than any house . . . in the country

23 Fletcher, *Rebel Private*, 74-75; Robert M. Powell, *Recollections of a Texas Colonel at Gettysburg*, Gregory A. Coco, ed. (Gettysburg, PA, 1990), 7.

24 Stevens, *Reminiscences*, 107; Nabours, "Active Service of a Texas Command," *CV*, 24:70.

25 Stevens, *Reminiscences*, 105, 107.

of Texas," and all of them seemed "more tastily built than two-thirds of the houses in Waco. . . [and indeed] "as fine as . . . anywhere."[26]

The entire Confederate army was now north of the Potomac River. When he learning this, Hooker concentrated his forces around Frederick, Maryland, in order to maintain a position between Lee and Washington, DC. As his forces massed, Hooker, in a tiff with Maj. Gen. Halleck in Washington over disposition of his troops, offered his resignation as commander of the Army of the Potomac. To his great surprise, Lincoln quickly accepted it and replaced him with Major General George Gordon Meade.[27]

Late that afternoon, the 5th Texas entered Chambersburg, a sizable and important town in south-central Pennsylvania. It "had the appearance of a city of banners," Col. Powell observed. "A Union flag surrounded every house, pole and post." Lt. Col. James Fremantle, a British army observer, commented on the "scarecrow" appearance of "Hood's Ragged Jacks" as they proudly marched into town that day. Noting their reputation as fighters, Fremantle described the Texans as a "queer lot to look at. They carry less than other troops," he wrote, and "many of them have only got an old piece of carpet or rug as baggage; many have discarded their shoes in the mud; all are ragged and dirty, but full of good humor and confidence in themselves." "[W]hen a citizen wearing a "desirable hat approached too near . . . [the marching Texans'] lines, . . . he was certain to become a participant in a hat exchange, receiving one in return, which had no value except for its antiquity, honorable scars or as a fragmentary relic."[28]

Along the march, Private Nabours of Company G recalled an old lady hailing one of his comrades in the column, inquiring how he came into possession of the knapsack on his back. The soldier replied that he had retrieved it from a dead Yankee after Chancellorsville. The side of the knapsack was imprinted with the name of its former owner, along with a regiment and company designation in large, bold letters. "That was my son," the old lady said, and the Texan stopped at once, retrieved his

26 Ibid., Muster Rolls, Cos. A and B, 5th Texas Infantry, April 30-June 30, 1863, in TSA; Cobb Diary, June 27, 1863, in SHC/UNC; Sorrel, *Confederate Staff Officer*, 168; West, *Texan in Search of a Fight*, 81, 91-92.

27 *OR* 27, pt. 2, 297-99, 313-16; West, *Texan in Search of a Fight*, 105. Boatner, *Civil War Dictionary*, 333.

28 James A. Fremantle, *The Freemantle Diary: Being the Journal of Lieutenant Colonel James Arthur Lyon Fremantle, Coldstream Guards on His Three Months in the Southern States*, Walter Lord, ed. (London, 1956), 190-91; Reichardt, *Forever the Cause*, 54; Polley, *Hood's Texas Brigade*, 147.

personal effects from the pack, and respectfully gave the bag to the woman, "who seemed to appreciate it very much."[29]

Smither thought Chambersburg "the prettiest place I ever saw, laid out with regular Dutch precision, the girls (and they were beauties) in town, were Union to the back bone and had capital sport at our shabby and unmilitary appearances," he continued, "but as a general thing our boys took it good humoredly and marched by in silence." The locals were rather astonished at the size of the Confederate force, for they were under the misconception that their Union army had nothing but "a disorganized handful of rebels to contend with." While he generally felt exulted, Smither reported that, "looking on every side . . . and seeing nothing but unfriendly looks from the whitehaired sires down to the child I confess it made me feel very badly."[30]

The Chambersburg women came out in full force, lining front yard fences, and leaning from upper story windows, observing the ragged Confederates as they passed. Another Texan wrote home that these women

> did not say anything, they just looked. Did you ever see a woman look mad and look with all her might and just keep looking tigers and wildcats and yet say nothing with her mouth but with her eyes she is hurling great sluices of burning, sizzling, blazing sulphur at you? This gives you a very feeble idea of how they looked. . . . I'll never forget how those women looked.[31]

Smither, when asked what troops were passing, proudly identified the men as "the Texas brigade." At this, one woman declared to her companions, "They are the ones who have killed so many of our soldiers." Many of these women had miniature U.S. flags or red, white, and blue badges or ribbons pinned to their dresses in defiance of the invading Confederate army, and some wore clothes that displayed the national colors to excellent advantage. One such woman stood boldly in her front door with a large American flag draped across her ample bosom, all the while boldly manifesting her contempt for the Southerners as Hood's men tramped past. One Texan, in a solemn voice heard above the tramping feet, loudly remarked, "Take care, Madam, for Hood's boys are great at storming breastworks when the Yankee colors is on them."

29 Nabours, "Active Service in a Texas Command," *CV*, 24:70.

30 Mark Smither to Elizabeth Smither, June 28, 1863, in SHSU.

31 Stevens, *Reminiscences*, 109.

Fremantle, witnessing this exchange, noted that the "buxom beauty" beat a "precipitate retreat."[32]

"The people here," noted West, "have quite a chagrined and subdued look as we march through these towns and villages." Some hurled derisive remarks at the Texans as they passed. "Thank God, you will never come back here alive," yelled one local bystander, and West, the recruit from Waco, quickly issued a retort to his tormentor, responding pithily: "No, as we intend to go to Cincinnati by way of New York." That night, the Texans camped "in a grove of magnificent timber" a mile north of Chambersburg near a crystal clear stream. Here they stayed until the afternoon of June 30, foraging and recuperating from the excruciating march. Grim, bloody work soon lay ahead.[33]

General Lee was unalterably opposed to indiscriminate foraging, preferring to pay for necessary supplies, impressing them only when absolutely necessary. General order No. 73, written June 27, spelled it out. Besides warning his army to "abstain with most scrupulous care from unnecessary or wanton injury to private property," and to respect the status of non-combatants, he charged officers to "arrest and bring to summary punishment" anybody who violated the orders. Powell noted that the very next day, many locals came forward to claim their horses, "which the boys had borrowed the day before."[34]

Lee's directive was well-intended, but unrealistic. His army had been deprived of so much for so long that the temptations of plunder in a bountiful country were next to irresistible for his ragged, ill-fed army. Thus, many soldiers ignored Lee's order and continued foraging in the towns and farmland of the Cumberland Valley. Quartermasters and commissary officers continued to pay for all items they requisitioned from the area, but they did so in Confederate promissory notes or script.[35]

32 Mark Smither to Elizabeth Smither, June 28, 1863, in SHSU; Fremantle, *Freemantle Diary*, 190-91; W. C. Ward, "Incidents and Personal Experiences on the Battlefield at Gettysburg," *CV* (1900), 8:346; West, *Texan in Search of a Fight*, 109.

33 Polley, *Hood's Texas Brigade*, 147. Mark Smither to Elizabeth Smither, June 28, 1863, in SHSU; West, *Texan in Search of a Fight*, 82; Cobb Diary, June 27, 28 and 30, 1863, in SHC/UNC.

34 *OR* 27, pt. 2, 297-98, 727-28, *OR* 27, pt. 3, 912, 942-43; Mark Smither to Elizabeth Smither, June 28, 1863, in SHSU; Powell, *Recollections of a Texas Colonel*, 9; Polley, *Hood's Texas Brigade*, 147-48; Stevens, *Reminiscences*, 109. Lee's General Order No. 73 was precipitated by the depredations committed by the Texas Brigade and Evander Law's Brigade, among others, immediately after they crossed the Potomac River. Powell, *Recollections of a Texas Colonel*, 9. This supplemented a prior general order issued June 21 to the same effect. See *OR* 27, pt. 3, 1863, 912.

35 Davis, *Gray Fox*, 218; Simpson, *Lee's Grenadier Guard*, 259.

In their stay north of Chambersburg, the Texans took full advantage of the prosperous land to supplement their rancid bacon and musty flour. "The delirious fumes of coffee and frying bacon were an earnest of the good things in this land of plenty," Col. Powell noted. "Poor beef and sour flour were henceforth to be only memories of the past." Smither wrote his mother about eating "many large, ripe, Blackheart Cherries as I could stand up to with Apple Butter & milk ad infinitum dont you wish you were an Invader?" Feeling guilty later in the same letter, Smither beseeched his mother "to pray [to] God to make me a better man, as the army had presented so many temptations that I can see no chance of becoming any better until I am out of it."[36]

On Tuesday, June 30, the regiment headed east from Chambersburg at 8:00 a.m. following A. P. Hill's advance of the previous day down the Chambersburg Pike toward Cashtown, some eight miles west of the next town up ahead, Gettysburg. The men started late and proceeded only about five miles before setting up a bivouac a half-mile from the village of Fayetteville that evening. Stevens guarded a private house that night occupied by a "typical Pennsylvania Dutchman" and his family. Pleasant duty, this, because the protected family generally fed their guards—a vast improvement from soldiers' fare. But the approach of the Texans so surprised the Dutchman and his family that they were paralyzed with fear. Stevens, as commander of the guard, reassured them that no mistreatment would befall them, and that the Texans were there to protect them and their property from any "depredations" by any of our men who might try to injure their property. Soon seven hungry rebels "were seated to one of the finest old Pennsylvania Dutch dinners you ever saw."[37]

Little did the men of the 5th Texas realize how their respite in this comparatively idyllic setting was soon to change into one of the most horrific bloodlettings they were to encounter in the entire war. Within the next two days, they would lose half their ranks, most of whom were gone for the rest of the war. The impending battle was probably the most detrimental of the entire war for the regiment.

With still no word from Jeb Stuart, General Lee grew increasingly frustrated at the paucity of intelligence about the Union army's movements. He had granted Stuart wide discretion to conduct another grand raid, reminiscent of the "Ride Around McClellan" during the Seven Days' campaign, providing that he kept in contact with Ewell's right during the advance north. But Stuart had failed to establish contact with any portion of the Confederate army and had written only one dispatch during his

36 Mark Smither to Elizabeth Smither, June 28, 1863, in SHSU; Reichardt, *Forever the Cause*, 53.

37 Mark Smither to Elizabeth Smither, June 28, 1863, in SHSU; Cobb Diary, June 30, 1863, in SHC/UNC; Stevens, *Reminiscences*, 112-13; Reichardt, *Forever the Cause*, 54-55; Polley, *Hood's Texas Brigade*, 147.

absence. Lee was thus deprived of his "eyes and ears" deep in enemy territory, with no knowledge of his enemy's strength or location. Stuart would have severely chastised himself had he but known how anxious Lee was for such news and how crippling his lack of intelligence was becoming.[38]

The Federals had pursued the Rebels northward, though at a cautious distance. They crossed the Potomac at Edward's Ferry on June 25-26, about the same time the Texans crossed at Williamsport. Without cavalry to probe and screen, Lee was unaware of this event until June 28, whereupon he ordered his army to concentrate at Gettysburg, a college town east of South Mountain, just a few miles north of the Maryland border. On June 30, Longstreet followed A. P. Hill's Corps east from Chambersburg with the bulk of his corps through South Mountain toward Gettysburg, marching five miles to Fayetteville. Lt. Gen. Richard Ewell's three divisions had moved to the north and northeast, two in Carlisle (Rodes and Johnson), and the third in York (Early). When Lee ordered a return, Early and Rodes marched to the vicinity of Heidlersburg, 11 miles northeast of Gettysburg, while Maj. Gen. Edward Johnson moved to within four miles northeast of Chambersburg.[39]

For days General Meade had slowly but relentlessly marched his 100,000-plus man Army of the Potomac north, stalking Lee's army. Both armies moved methodically, and fate would bring them together in southwest Pennsylvania in what most historians consider the turning point of the Civil War. Without question, the meeting resulted in the bloodiest encounter ever fought in the Western Hemisphere, and what came to called "the high water mark of the Confederacy."[40]

On June 30, Major General Henry Heth's Division of A. P. Hill's Corps was encamped near Cashtown, about eight miles from Gettysburg. Brig. Gen. James J. Pettigrew's Brigade advanced toward Gettysburg, only to find it already occupied by what appeared to be a sizable Federal force. Not wishing to precipitate a general

38 Powell, *Recollections of a Texas Colonel at Gettysburg*, 9; Freeman, *Lee's Lieutenants*, 3:68. Stuart finally rejoined the army at Dover on the morning of July 1. Not until the afternoon of July 2 that Stuart, riding ahead of his columns, reached his anxious and frustrated chief on Seminary Ridge. Lee apparently noted "Well, General Stuart, you are here at last," and left it at that. Freeman, *Lee's Lieutenants*, 3: 71-72, 136-40.

39 *OR* 27, pt. 2, 307, 358, 428; Allen C. Guelzo, *Gettysburg: The Last Invasion* (New York, 2013), 127-28; Cobb Diary, June 29 & 30, 1863, in SHC/UNC; Polley, *Letters to Charming Nellie*, 133; Polly, *Hood's Texas Brigade*, 150-51.

40 Simpson, *Lee's Grenadier Guard*, 262-63.

engagement on a foraging mission, Pettigrew fell back to Cashtown and duly reported conditions to Heth.[41]

Neither Lee nor Meade envisioned Gettysburg as a field of battle. However, with Lee himself still miles away, A. P. Hill decided to take the initiative. The following morning, well before daylight, Hill sent a strong force down the Chambersburg Pike toward Gettysburg to confirm Pettigrew's observations of the previous day. Heth's Division was in the lead, followed by Maj. Gen. William Dorsey Pender's. Near Herr and McPherson's Ridges along Willoughby Run to the west of Gettysburg, Heth threw out a line of skirmishers, and almost immediately, gunfire announced the unlikely inception of the great battle. Heth's Division began trading shots with Brig. Gen. John Buford's troopers west of the town. Faced with superior numbers, Buford was forced to give ground, albeit grudgingly, quickly sending for reinforcements as he fell back toward the town. Meade quickly forwarded Reynold's I Corps and Oliver O. Howard's XI Corps to Buford's assistance. The Federals put up a stiff resistance on the ridges west of Gettysburg, but by late afternoon, two divisions of Ewell's Corps had moved into the city from the north. The Federals, thus caught in the Confederates' pincer movement from the west and north, were forced to fall back in considerable disorder through the streets of the town to a series of ridges to the south and east. By dawn of July 2, the better part of five Union corps had arrived on the field and extended the Federal line southwards along an outcropping called Cemetery Ridge.[42]

Meanwhile, near Fayetteville, some 18 miles to the northeast, the regiment received urgent orders to march immediately toward Gettysburg, as the fighting had begun. "Every man was in his marching and fighting attire," Col. Powell recalled, "and as quickly as the order could be given, 'right face, forward march!' we were on the way to the general meeting of the armies." Longstreet had ordered his corps to be at Gettysburg by sunup on July 2. But according to one Texan, the Texas Brigade moved "lazily and plethorically " in column toward Gettysburg. Excruciatingly slowly, in fact, with the column advancing "a hundred yards or so . . . [only to] stop and stand still . . . not to sit down for five, ten or twenty minutes at a time." The march was significantly delayed when Johnson's Division and his wagon train cut across the road on its way to Cashtown from Shippensburg. After midnight, the Texans had reached the vicinity of Cashtown, where they stacked arms and lay down on the bare ground, and fell asleep.

41 Henry, *Story of the Confederacy*, 275; Simpson, *Lee's Grenadier Guard*, 263; Mark Smither to Elizabeth Smither, July 29, 1863 in SHSU. Pettigrew encountered troopers of Brigadier General John Buford's cavalry division, then screening the movements of Meade's army.

42 A. H. Belo, "The Battle of Gettysburg," *CV* (1900), 8:165; Hood, *Advance and Retreat*, 57; Stephen W. Sears, *Gettysburg* (Boston, MA, 2003), 160-65.

After a two-hour respite they were on the road again. Before long, the men passed a field hospital where many of the wounded from the first day's fighting reposed. One of the Texans observed that men "were mangled and bruised in every possible way, some with their eyes shot out, some with their arms, or hands, or fingers, or feet or legs shot off, and all seeming to suffer a great deal." The column finally stopped where Marsh Creek crossed the Chambersburg Pike after 1:00 a.m. on July 2.[43]

When the regiment finally approached the site of the July 1 clash, Powell reflected upon the gruesome scene whose "melancholy evidences of its results were not calculated to evoke cheerful reflections or give assurances to those about to participate in the same kind of entertainment. To the right and to the left among the wounded and dead we recognized comrades with whom we had exchanged greetings two days before." The Texans reached Lee's headquarters west of town and south of the pike an hour before sunrise on July 2. By 7:00 a.m., they could see the ground of the coming engagement. Powell waxed poetic. It was, he observed:

> already quick with events which were to give it historical interest and value when the actions were forgotten. . . . Coming over the mountains, moving along the valleys, deploying on the plains with flying banners and glittering arms, music calling from every crest and hilltop an echo to swell the chorus, was the grand pageant of the gathering armies.

After several hours awaiting further orders, the regiment relocated about one mile southwest to the valley of Willoughby Run, behind Seminary Ridge, with readily available water and wood. There the men cooked breakfast and enjoyed a brief rest before marching to their assigned battle position on Lee's right.[44]

Longstreet had met with Lee late in the afternoon of July 1 as the Confederates were driving the Federals through the streets of Gettysburg toward Cemetery Hill. Lee surprised him by indicating he intended to attack Meade's army on the heights the next

43 West, *Texan in Search of a Fight*, 84; Glenn W. LaFantasie, *Twilight at Little Round Top: July 2, 1863–The Tide Turns at Gettysburg* (New York, NY, 2007), 23; *OR* 27, pt. 2, 358; "John Bell Hood's Post-War Recollections of Gettysburg." Accessed June 12, 2010: http://vcwsg.com/PDF%20Files/John%20Bell%20Hood's%20Post%20War%20Recollestions%20of%20gettysburg%20.pdf; Coddington, The Gettysburg Campaign, 195. Longstreet reported that Hood stopped at Marsh Creek, four miles from Gettysburg; Cobb related the same in his diary. Cobb Diary, July 2, 1863, in SHC/UNC.

44 Cobb Diary, July 2, 1863, in SHC/UNC; LaFantasie, *Twilight at Little Round Top*, 24; Guelzo, *Gettysburg: Last Invasion*, 229, 236; John Martin, "Accurate Historic Records," *CV*, 12:114; Polley, *Hood's Texas Brigade*, 154-55; Stevens, *Reminiscences*, 113; Coddington, *The Gettysburg Campaign*, 369; Powell, *Forever the Cause*, 55.

morning. Old Pete reminded Lee that this would be contrary to the original invasion plan—which prescribed a defensive campaign. "If the enemy is there to-morrow, we must attack him," Lee replied. Longstreet pressed Lee to turn Meade's left instead, interposing the Confederate army between Meade and Washington, thus threatening his communications and forcing him to attack the Confederates on their own ground. Lee, however, opined that Meade could still play "a waiting game," that would render the Confederate position impossible to maintain in open country.[45]

Lee believed a battle necessary, given the circumstances as he saw them. He reasoned that if a battle did have to take place, the sooner the better. His army was almost all present, and further delay would not improve his position. But it would, however, aid his enemies, since large portions of Meade's army were still not in place on July 2. So influenced more by "cold calculations than hot blood," Lee decided to accept an unplanned for battle at Gettysburg by taking the offensive. After carefully examining the Union positions on and about Cemetery Ridge and Culp's Hill, he decided to attack the left of the Union line with Longstreet's Corps the following morning.[46]

Longstreet was up at 3:00 a.m. on the morning of July 2 to again try dissuading Lee from his proposed attack. Finding him on Seminary Ridge while it was still dark, Longstreet argued against an assault on a fortified position and pressed anew for turning Meade's left on ground more suited to the defensive. Lee judiciously considered the proposal, but uncertain as to the enemy strength and lacking a cavalry screen for the maneuver, he vetoed it again. He remained determined to strike the Federal lines as soon as he could gain a better sense of the enemy's current deployment and strength.[47]

At sunrise Lee could see that the Federals had assumed a strong position on the high ground south of town and along the prominent ridge which ran to the base of the

45 James Longstreet, "Second Day at Gettysburg," in *B&L*, 3:293; Harry W. Pfanz, *Gettysburg: The Second Day* (Chapel Hill, NC, 1987), 26-29; Foote, *Civil War Narrative*, 2:479-80; Coddington, *The Gettysburg Campaign*, 360-61; Sears, *Gettysburg*, 234, 237-38. Longstreet and his defenders embellished his objections to Lee's plan over the intervening years. Clearly, he never voiced "that the outcome . . . would be anything but a certainty.'" See Guelzo, *Gettysburg: Last Invasion*, 230-31.

46 Oliver Wilcox Norton, *The Attack and Defense of Little Round Top: Gettysburg, July 2, 1863* (New York, 1913), 253; James Longstreet, "General James Longstreet's Account of the Campaign and Battle," *SHSP* (1878), 5:60-61; LaFantasie, *Twilight at Little Round Top*, 19-20; Coddington, *The Gettysburg Campaign*, 365; Guelzo, *Gettysburg: Last Invasion*, 229-30.

47 *OR* 27, pt. 2, 308; James Longstreet, "Lee's Right Wing At Gettysburg," in *B&L*, 3:340; LaFantasie, *Twilight at Little Round Top*, 28-29; Freeman, *Lee's Lieutenants*, 3:106-107, 112-18; Pfanz, *Gettysburg Second Day*, 104-105: Coddington, *The Gettysburg Campaign*, 371.

Round Tops. Little Round Top is situated approximately three and a half miles south of town, an extension of Cemetery Ridge. It rises 150 feet above the valley to its west and dominates the ground around it. Covered with boulders up to the size of small houses, its crest is a position difficult to ascend and easy to defend. Open to the north and west, dense woods covered the south and east of the prominence. Just 600 yards to the south lies its larger counterpart, Big Round Top, over 120 feet taller and far more massive, but entirely covered with thick woods, rendering Little Round Top the strategic key to the area.[48]

To obtain a clearer picture of the Federal dispositions to the south, Lee dispatched Captain Samuel R. Johnson, a staff engineer, to scout the Union left. While awaiting his return and report, Generals Hood, Heth, and Hill soon joined Longstreet and Lee with their staffs near the Texans' bivouac area. They sat on a fallen tree with Longstreet and Hood whittling sticks to while away the time. Fifth Texas troops still awake after breakfast got to witness this meeting of the renowned generals right in front of them. Lee paced back and forth under the trees, halting from time to time to train his binoculars on the Union lines. When Hood inquired about the enemy's current deployment, Lee responded "The enemy is here, and if we do not whip him, he will whip us." Lee told his generals he intended to retain the initiative that day—to strike before the Federals could get all their seven corps into battle line.[49]

Returning from his reconnaissance mission of the Federal left flank, supposedly all the way to the Round Tops, Johnson reported seeing no Federal troops in the area. Given Johnson's report, Lee ordered Longstreet to conduct the day's primary attack: that being an oblique thrust up the Emmitsburg Road against the Federal left. However, only two of his divisions, Hood's and McLaws', were on the field at that point; Pickett was still en route from Chambersburg. Anderson's Division of Hill's Corps was therefore ordered to support Longstreet's attack, while Ewell's and the rest of Hill's Corps launched diversionary thrusts against the Union right and center as Longstreet struck Meade's left flank. Lee thereby hoped to roll up the Federal left, seize Cemetery Ridge, and thereby force the Federals to fight on less favorable ground to the south, perhaps destroying that portion of Meade's army.[50]

48 Garry E. Adelman, *Little Round Top: A Detailed Tour Guide*, Gettysburg, PA (2000), 7; E. M. Law, "The Struggle For 'Round Top,'" & Hunt, "The Second Day At Gettysburg," in *B&L*, 3:318-19, 3:295; Foote, *Civil War Narrative*, 2:479.

49 Hood, *Advance and Retreat*, 57; Polley, *Hood's Texas Brigade*, 155; LaFantasie, *Twilight at Little Round Top*, 28-30; Simpson, *Gaines' Mill to Appomattox*, 137.

50 As it turned out, Johnson was mistaken. Had he gone the entire distance required, he would have encountered approximately18,000 Federal troops. Yet, on the basis of Johnson's report, Lee assumed there were no Federal troops on the far left. Longstreet, "Lee's Right Wing At Gettysburg," in *B&L*, 3:340-41; Pfanz, *Gettysburg: Second Day*, 106-107; Guelzo, *Gettysburg: Last*

Lee's plan called for Longstreet to attack to the northeast up the Emmitsburg Road, striking the Union left flank on Cemetery Hill at an angle. McLaws would spearhead the attack, with Hood next and finally Anderson, all attacking *en echelon*. In this manner, the Federals would receive increasingly more pressure as the Confederates moved from the south to north, thereby gathering strength as the movement progressed. Meanwhile, Ewell would vigorously attack the Federal right flank, preventing Meade from shifting reinforcements to his threatened left. Old Pete was told that his attacks would take place over easily-traveled fields, allowing him to employ the weapon of speed his men so frequently used with devastating effect. Further, according to Lee's scouting report, the Federal left flank was exposed, and with no enemy present on that part of the field.[51]

When Lafayette McLaws subsequently arrived at headquarters, Lee pointed on his map to a line drawn perpendicular to the Emmitsburg Road where he wished McLaws to position his men. Longstreet then indicated a line *parallel* to Emmitsburg Road, stating that was how *he* wanted McLaws' Division formed. Lee demurred. "No, General, I wish it placed just perpendicular to that." Immediately after this correction in front of his subordinate, Longstreet seemingly turned sullen, and McLaws sensed a strain between the two commanders, indicating to him that "only Lee seemed entirely clear about what he expected to be accomplished in the impending battle."[52]

In addition to his general reluctance for mounting an offensive, Longstreet was doubly apprehensive about attacking with two of his best units, Law's Brigade and Pickett's Division, still absent from the field, in spite of Lee's assurance that he could borrow Anderson's Division of A. P. Hill's Corps. Although both were currently on their way, neither had arrived by mid-morning of July 2. Old Pete persisted in waiting for the arrival of these absent units. He remained reluctant to attack, confiding to Hood, "I never like to go into battle with one boot off;" that boot, in this case, being Pickett's division of 5,000 Virginians. As General Lee anxiously awaited the movement's commencement, Longstreet lounged with Hood "near the trunk of a tree," and at one point, casually explained to Hood that Lee was "a little nervous this

---

Invasion, 238; Sears, *Gettysburg*, 253-54; LaFantasie, *Twilight at Little Round Top*, 30; Coddington, *The Gettysburg Campaign*, 374.

51 *OR* 27, pt. 2, 308; Mark Smither to Elizabeth Smither, July 29, 1863, in SHSU; Freeman, *Lee's Lieutenants*, 3:112-18; Longstreet, "Lee's Right Wing At Gettysburg," in *B&L*, 3:340; Foote, *Civil War Narrative*, 2:499-501.

52 McLaws, "The Battle of Gettysburg," Philadelphia *Weekly Press*, (April 21, 1886); Lafayette McLaws to James Longstreet, June 12, 1873, Lafayette McLaws Papers, 1836-1897, #472, *Southern Historical Collection*, The Wilson Library, SHC/UNC; LaFantasie, *Twilight at Little Round Top*, 30; McLaws, *A Soldier's General*, 39; Sears, *Gettysburg*, 254-55.

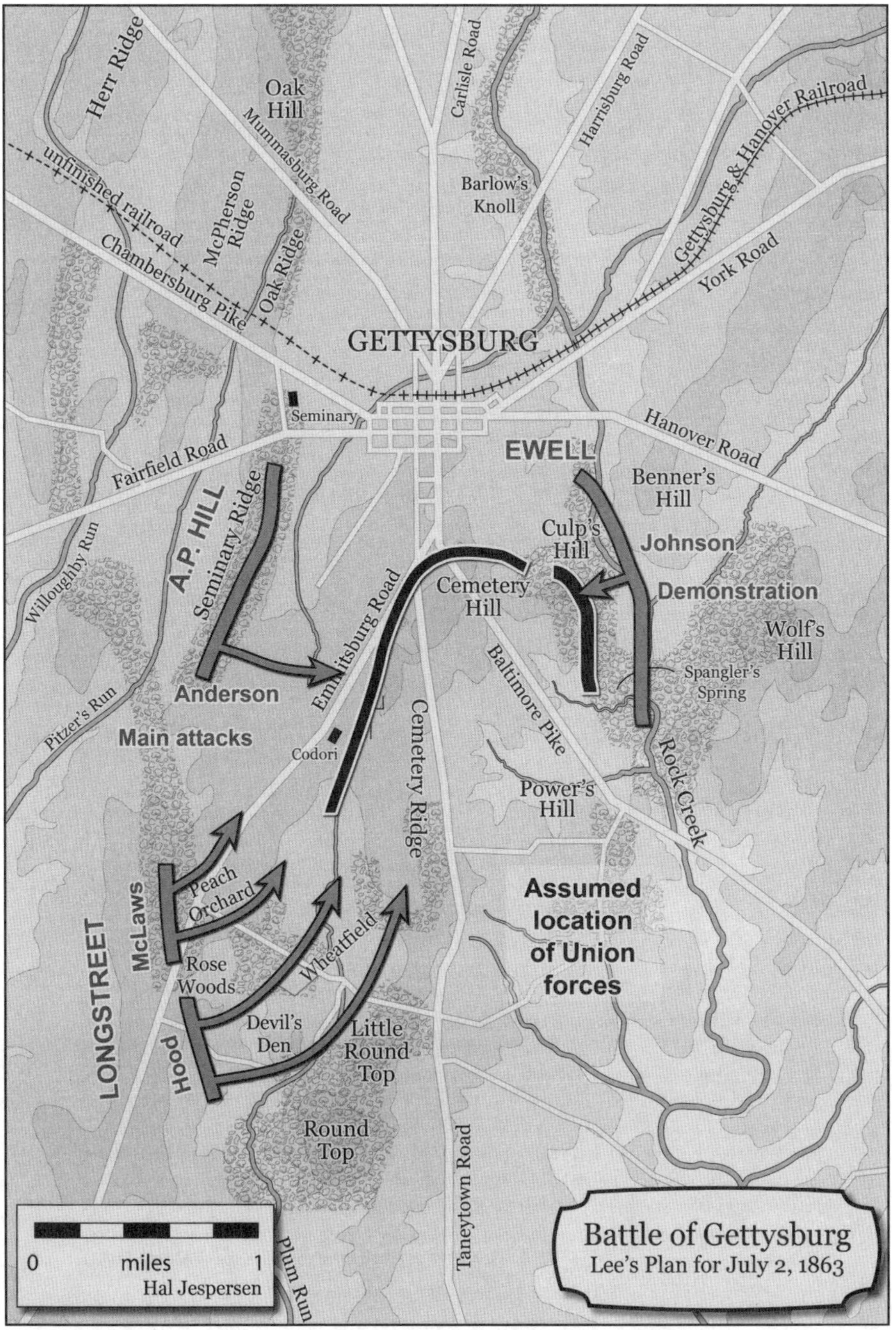

Battle of Gettysburg
Lee's Plan for July 2, 1863

morning; he wishes me to attack." Lee "ordered the movement" at 11:00 a.m., telling Longstreet "I think you had better move," but then relented to persuasion, allowing Longstreet to await Law's arrival, but not Pickett's.[53]

Around noon, Law's Brigade finally arrived from New Guilford after marching more than 23 miles in fewer than nine hours. McLaws stepped off somewhere between noon and 1:00 p.m., and after forming up with Hood's Division in the vicinity of Willoughby Run, the men loaded their guns without capping them while they moved. Even after the march began, Longstreet, after his encounters with Lee, remained sullen. "There was apparent apathy in his movements," recalled his chief-of-staff Moxley Sorrel. "They lacked the fire and point of his usual bearing on the battlefield." Still in a petulant mood, he began to "put on a display of pettiness of heroic proportions," by pretending to believe that he could not direct his own troops. Lee had assigned Capt. Johnson, who scouted in the area that morning, to assist Old Pete on the march. Longstreet took the position that Johnson, as "Lee's man on the spot," was really in command of the march. This tragicomic affair unfolded without Johnson even knowing that he was "the stalking horse for the pouting commander." Johnson later stated that Longstreet "did not move off very promptly—nor was our march at all rapid. It did not strike me that Genl Longstreet was in a hurry to get into position. It might have been that he thought hurry was unnecessary."[54]

Following many narrow roads and farm lanes, the column traversed countryside that Alexander with his artillery had earlier avoided by cutting across fields, providing a better screen for his caissons. Under a blazing hot sun, it marched past the Black Horse Tavern, until McLaws turned from Fairfield Road onto a narrow farm road running southeast toward the Pitzer Schoolhouse. As the column climbed a hill on the Emmitsburg Road, it became apparent they were in clear view of the signal station

53 *OR* 27, pt. 2, 308; Robert K. Krick, "'If Longstreet . . . Says So, It Most Likely Is Not True,' James Longstreet and the Second Day at Gettysburg," Gary Gallagher, ed., *The Second Day At Gettysburg: Essays on Confederate and Union Leadership* (Kent, OH, 1993), 69-71; Hood, *Advance and Retreat*, 57; Sears, *Gettysburg*, 255-57; Coddington, *The Gettysburg Campaign*, 378-79; Guelzo, *Gettysburg: Last Invasion*, 236-38. Lee apologists have long argued that he expected a dawn attack by Longstreet. If this is what he expected, "he displayed suspiciously little anxiety about it." In point of fact, he still had to await a reconnaissance of the intended battleground. Porter Alexander later wrote that he did not get the impression Lee "thought there was any unnecessary delay going on," at that time, although Sears writes that Lee was said to be exasperated that Longstreet had not earlier begun his preparations for the march. Guelzo, *Gettysburg: Last Invasion*, 235, 238; Sears, *Gettysburg*, 257; see also Glenn Tucker, "Longstreet-Culprit or Scapegoat," *Civil War Times* (1962), 1:5-7, 39-44.

54 Krick, "'If Longstreet . . . Says So, It Most Likely Is Not True,'" *Second Day at Gettysburg*, 69-71; Todd, *Sketch of History*, 15; Allan, "Reply to General Longstreet," in *B&L*, 3:355; Coddington, *The Gettysburg Campaign*, 378-79; Sears, *Gettysburg*, 258.

atop Little Round Top, and so the march was quickly halted. Longstreet, in the rear riding with Hood, then made it clear that he was "impatient" with the "delay."[55]

Alexander, who had already moved his artillery around the far edge of this knoll, was shocked that the infantry not only failed to do likewise, but halted in clear view of the signal tower, thereby endangering both the mission's speed and secrecy. Longstreet then agreed that an alternative route be identified and ordered a countermarch. To save time, he instructed Hood to push his division forward and take a position on the right of McLaws But the two divisions got hopelessly entangled, resulting in a huge traffic jam. Longstreet then suggested that Hood take the lead in order to break the logjam, but McLaws would have none of it, since Lee himself had presumably given him that honor. The column thus continued to move with "unwanted sluggishness." Meanwhile, Longstreet further demonstrating his apathy, decided to assume direct command over Hood's Division, but not McLaws'.[56]

The column moved all the way back to where the march began on Herr Ridge. Then it moved down the valley of the then dry Willoughby Run, and along a farm lane to a schoolhouse behind the Pitzer's farm. The countermarch proved particularly grueling, with rough terrain full of ditches and fences to negotiate. "The day was hot, and we were thirsty and had not stopped to rest or drink," one of the veterans later recalled. The detour delayed the planned attack by at least another hour.[57]

Up to this point, there was no Southern intelligence about Maj. Gen. Daniel E. Sickles moving his entire corps forward from Cemetery Ridge to the Peach Orchard on the eastern side of Emmitsburg Road, over a half mile forward from his assigned

55 Ward, "Incidents and Personal Experiences on the Battlefield at Gettysburg," *CV*, 8:346; Polley, *Hood's Texas Brigade*, 160; Sears, *Gettysburg*, 258; Coddington, *Gettysburg Campaign*, 379.

56 LaFantasie, *Twilight at Little Round Top*, 52-53; Reichardt, *Forever the Cause*, 56; Joseph B. Kershaw, "Kershaw's Brigade at Gettysburg," in *B&L*, 3:331-32; William M. Abernathy, *Our Mess: Southern Gallantry and Privations* (McKinney, TX, 1977), 31; Krick, "If Longstreet . . . Says So, It Most Likely Is Not True," in *Second Day at Gettysburg*, 69-74; Coddington, *The Gettysburg Campaign*, 380. While Lee left Longstreet alone on the march, he did become impatient with him, especially when he learned of Sickles' advance to the Emmitsburg Road.

57 Ward, "Incidents and Personal Experiences on the Battlefield at Gettysburg," *CV*, 8:346; Lafayette McLaws, "Gettysburg," *SHSP*, (1879), 7:69; LaFantasie, *Twilight at Little Round Top*, 52-53; Reichardt, *Forever the Cause*, 56; Joseph B. Kershaw, "Kershaw's Brigade at Gettysburg," in *B&L*, 3:331-32; Wert, *General James Longstreet*, 269; William M. Abernathy, *Our Mess: Southern Gallantry and Privations* (McKinney, TX, 1977), 31; Krick, "If Longstreet . . . Says So, It Most Likely Is Not True," 69-71, 72-74. A veteran of Law's Brigade recalled: "We had already marched twenty-four miles, and were still marching two or three miles farther in view of the Federal Army crouching along the mountain ridge." Ward, "Incidents and Personal Experiences on the Battlefield at Gettysburg," *CV*, 8:346. While Lee left Longstreet alone on the march, he did become very impatient with him, especially when he learned of Sickles' advance to the Emmitsburg Road.

position in the general line. Sickles' line ran from Emmitsburg Road to Devil's Den, 1000 yards south of the Peach Orchard. He began the movement a little after 1:00 p.m. and completed it between 2:00 and 3:00 p.m. Two full divisions—Humphreys on the right along the Emmitsburg Road with his left near the Peach Orchard, and Birney's, from the Peach Orchard all the way to the rocks of Devil's Den were now positioned where Longstreet least expected to find any enemy forces.[58]

Longstreet, unaware of Sickles' massive salient, had advised McLaws that his division would be deployed on the Federal left flank, with no enemy in his front Thus misinformed, McLaws decided to continue in columns of companies, and upon forming at the jump-off point, he would then face left and advance on the enemy. However, when the head of his column arrived at the proposed jump-off point around 3:00 p.m., it was apparent that the Confederate attack, if it was to proceed as ordered, would expose the troops up Emmitsburg Road to a raking fire from their right flank and rear as they advanced.[59]

Emerging from the woods, McLaws arrived at an open field fronting a stone wall which extended east all along Flaherty's farm then past Slyder's farm. They were in full view of the Federal position, which by then appeared to extend from Little Round Top with its wagging signal flags as far as they could see to the left. McLaws appeared astonished at the size of this Federal force; its position seemed impregnable, according to Kershaw. Deepening the quandary, Longstreet's force had already been sighted by the signal station atop Little Round Top. With the element of surprise totally gone, Longstreet's chances of complete success were proportionately diminished.[60]

It quickly became apparent that the Confederates had never truly understood the enemy's location. Initially, Lee—relying upon Johnson's faulty reconnaissance—believed the Union left rested on Cemetery Ridge just south of the soon-to-be famous copse of trees on its crest. His plan had therefore called upon McLaws, supported by Hood, to form a battle line out of view of the Federals, behind a swale south of the Peach Orchard, and then to drive up the road, "partially enveloping the enemy's left." However, McLaws would now be forced to attack *perpendicular* to the Emmitsburg

58 Hunt, "Second Day At Gettysburg," in *B&L*, 3:301-302; Edward J. Stackpole, *They Met At Gettysburg* (New York, NY:, 1956), 193-94; Norton, *Attack and Defense*, 253; Longstreet, *Manassas to Appomattox*, 310-11. Sickles later claimed to be the hero of the day for this move. LaFantasie, *Twilight at Little Round Top*, 63; Sears, *Gettysburg*, 249, 252.

59 LaFantasie, *Twilight at Little Round Top*, 63; Pfanz, *Gettysburg: Second Day*, 150-51; Coddington, *The Gettysburg Campaign*, 381.

60 *OR* 27, pt. 2, 425; Hood, *Advance and Retreat*, 57; Law, "The Struggle for Round Top," in *B&L*, 3:320; E. P. Alexander, "The Great Charge and Artillery Fighting at Gettysburg," in *B&L*, 3:359; Sears, *Gettysburg*, 260.

Road, as opposed to parallel. Given the current situation, it would have courted disaster to stick with the original plan.[61]

As Hood's men filed out from behind the tree line on Seminary Ridge, anticipating a deployment across Emmitsburg Road supporting McLaws' attack, they, too, discovered that the Federals were not in the anticipated position. Hood immediately recognized that he could not position his troops to McLaws as intended, but that his men would be required to scramble through fields and meadows to a point considerably farther south, crossing the Emmitsburg Road more than 600 yards below the Peach Orchard. Thus, he had to shift his whole division to McLaws' right, which remained where it had originally been positioned, but now opposite Sickles' force. Hood became Longstreet's outflanking division. The new maneuver stretched the Confederate battle line considerably farther to the south in order to cover the Federal line which stretched all the way to Devil's Den.[62]

Once Meade detected the Confederate force to his left, he quickly began directing reinforcements, including several artillery batteries, to Little Round Top, Houck's Ridge, and Devil's Den, the three prominent defensive positions on that portion of the Federal line, to bolster Sickles' advanced troops. Sickles' men, in battle position in the Wheat Field, the Peach Orchard, and stretching to the rocks at Devil's Den, braced themselves for the spine-tingling Rebel yell and the shock of the infamous Confederate infantry.[63] They would not wait long.

An increasingly impatient Lee finally set off to personally confer with Longstreet over the delay. Apprised of the new situation, Lee had to quickly alter his planning by extending his front southward nearly three-fourths of a mile. He now proposed to attack the Federals on the Emmitsburg road ahead, drive them out of the way, then execute the intended long curve to Cemetery Hill. Under his amended battle plan, Hood on Longstreet's right would proceed first, heading eastward toward the stony ridges and Round Tops, following the direction of the Emmitsburg Road toward Cemetery Ridge, with Hood's left, guiding as well as possible along the road. McLaws' Division, following Hood, would assault the Peach Orchard. This advance would begin as soon as Longstreet fixed upon positions to serve as guiding points against which his men could march. Old Pete, some thought, was frustrated and agitated by

61 *OR* 27, pt. 2., 318; LaFantasie, *Twilight at Little Round Top*, 63, 65; McLaws, "Gettysburg," *SHSP*, 7:69-70; Reichardt, *Forever the Cause*, 57-58; Sears, *Gettysburg*, 254-55.

62 *OR* 27, pt. 2., 318; Kershaw, "Kershaw's Brigade At Gettysburg," in *B&L*, 3:331-32; LaFantasie, *Twilight at Little Round Top*, 63 Reichardt, *Forever the Cause*, 57-58.

63 Hunt, "Second Day At Gettysburg," in *B&L*, 3:307.

the circumstances of this assault and appeared to some to have "more the look of gloom" than ever noticed before.[64]

Longstreet's two divisions were in position by about 3:30 p.m. The Confederate line of battle occupied a partially wooded ridge with a valley intervening between it and the heights held by the Federals to their front. Hood's four brigades constituted the right flank, with McLaws' Division to Hood's left and Anderson's Division of Hill's Corps positioned on McLaws' left. Hood deployed his division in a double line of brigades. The first line was composed of the Texas and Law's Brigades, with the Texans on the left. Two hundred yards behind this front line were Hood's two Georgia brigades—Benning's supporting Law, and Anderson's, behind the Texans.[65] The Federal left wing, now fully in view, was "one of the most formidable it had ever been the fortune of any troops to confront." Little Round Top guarded the Federal left flank, with spurs and ridges trending off to the north of it, affording unrivaled positions for artillery. A thick wood covered much of Big Round Top's sides and the adjacent hills, concealing most of its rugged ground.[66]

In his revised battle orders, Hood was to attack the Federals *en echelon* as originally planned, but with the Texas Brigade driving at right angles to the Emmitsburg Road, while holding the Federals in place in Devil's Den. Meanwhile, on the Division's right, Law would swing across Little Round Top in order to turn the Federal left flank. Hood's mission was now what Lee intended for McLaws—"to smother the enemy's flank and start to roll it up. Once that process was begun, McLaws and then . . . Anderson would take up the task" Hood's four brigades would now be moving eastward, instead of northeast. And his division would sweep down the Federal lines in a curving direction toward Cemetery Hill. Kershaw was ordered to attack as soon as Hood became engaged, swinging around toward the Peach Orchard and establishing contact with Hood on his immediate right.[67]

Before reaching his pre-assigned position on the Confederate right, Hood had dispatched a number of his "picked Texas scouts" to determine exactly where the

64 Longstreet, "Lee's Right Wing At Gettysburg," ibid., 341; LaFantasie, *Twilight at Little Round Top*, 65; Guelzo, *Gettysburg: Last Invasion*, 253-55; Coddington, *The Gettysburg Campaign*, 384. Longstreet intended McLaws to attack first, but a late change was made in the plan.

65 Law, "Struggle for Round Top," in *B&L*, 3:320; Longstreet, *Manassas to Appomattox*, 312; Pfanz, *Gettysburg: Second Day*, 158.

66 *OR* 27, 2:391, 835; Alexander, "The Great Charge and Artillery Fighting at Gettysburg," in *B&L*, 3:359; Law, "Struggle for Round Top," in *B&L*, 3:320-21.

67 Kershaw, "Kershaw's Brigade At Gettysburg," in *B&L*, 3:331-32; Pfanz, *Gettysburg: Second Day*, 152-53; LaFantasie, *Twilight at Little Round Top*, 65; Sears, *Gettysburg*, 265; Coddington, *The Gettysburg Campaign*, 382.

Federal left flank actually ended, search the woods, and act as videttes. These scouts actually climbed Big Round Top, and from there they could view the whole two-and-a-half miles of Cemetery Ridge, all the way into Gettysburg. There they could see behind the ridge, along Taneytown Road masses of the wagon "trains of the Union Army, its artillery, and thousands of its troops huddled together, not suspecting the enemy was so near." The scouts also reported that the Federal left was in the air with nothing between it and the enemy trains. The scouts told Hood that he could easily march his division "through an open woodland pasture around [Big Round Top] and assault the enemy in flank and rear." As Hood weighed this new intelligence, he ordered his artillery to open fire on the Federals.[68]

The scouts' startling new information convinced Hood a Confederate victory was all but assured if the hanging Federal left flank could be turned and attacked from the rear. Recognizing that the Federal line extended farther south than expected, but still dangled amorphously around the vaguely defined region north of Big Round Top, he dispatched a staff officer seeking Longstreet's permission to shift the impending attack and instead skirt around the Round Tops and into the Federal flank and rear. Such a maneuver had already been proposed and rejected the previous day, came Longstreet's prompt response, and Lee's orders remained "to attack up the Emmitsburg road." Longstreet seemed to abdicate his role as on-scene commander in the active alignment of his troops, insisting instead that Lee's obviously stale plan and never more than a general guide anyway, be rigidly honored regardless.[69]

Hood, the smell of victory in his nostrils, was not so easily dissuaded, and persisted in questioning Longstreet's attack order. He soon dispatched another staff officer to Longstreet, this time declaring that he "feared nothing could be accomplished by [the proposed] attack" and renewing his request "to turn Round Top." Longstreet repeated his refusal: "Gen'l Lee's orders are to attack up the Emmitsburg road."[70]

68 Hood, "Letter From General John B. Hood," *SHSP*, 4:148; Foote, *Civil War Narrative*, 2:499; LaFantasie, *Twilight at Little Round Top*, 62-65.

69 Hood, "Letter From General John B. Hood," *SHSP*, 4:145; LaFantasie, *Twilight at Little Round Top*, 67; Pfanz, *Gettysburg: Second Day*, 164-65; Coddington, *The Gettysburg Campaign*, 382.

70 J. O. Bradfield, "At Gettysburg, July 3," *CV*, (1922) 30:225; John Purifoy, "The Lost Opportunity at Gettysburg," *CV*, (1923) 31:214-18; Law, "Struggle for Round Top," in *B&L*, 3: 321-27; Krick, "If Longstreet Says . . . It Most Likely Not True," *Second Day at Gettysburg*, 75-76. "John Bell Hood's Post-War Recollections of Gettysburg," http://vcwsr.com/PDF%20Files/John%20Bell%20Hood's%20Post%20War%20Recollections%20of%20gettysburg%20.pdf. Some have strongly advocated that Longstreet's motivation for strict compliance with Lee's "plan" was based upon a desire to prove his commander wrong.

Hood remained passionate for the alternative plan. Attacking up the Emmitsburg Road, pursuant to current orders meant first driving off the advance line of Federals and then confronting the immense stone boulders at the base and along the slope of the ridge packed so closely together his ranks would inevitably break apart and scatter. All the while his division would be exposed to heavy fire from the main line of the enemy firmly positioned on the crest of the high ridge ending at the Round Tops, not to mention destructive fire in flank, rear, and front given the concavity of the Federal main line. Under such circumstances, it was next to impossible to put the Federals to flight in that area, or, even if the impossible were accomplished, Hood later wrote, "it must be at a most fearful sacrifice of as brave and gallant soldiers as ever engaged in battle."[71]

Armed with his own intelligence on the exposed Federal left flank, Evander Law sought out Hood on the ridge near the Texas Brigade's formation and quickly made the same case; while Hood obviously concurred with Law's views, he indicated his orders were nonetheless to attack in front when the left of the corps got into position, and that those orders "must be obeyed." Law thereafter entered a detailed protest against this direct attack. At this point Hood called over his staffer, Capt. James Hamilton, and requested Law to repeat his protest and its grounds. This done, he then ordered Hamilton to seek out Longstreet as quickly as possible and deliver the protest, and add his full endorsement to it. Hamilton returned within ten minutes accompanied by one of Longstreet's own staff officers who instructed Hood that "General Longstreet orders you to begin the attack at once." Hood dejectedly turned to Law: "You hear the order?"[72]

Despite Hood's impassioned requests, Longstreet refused to inspect the field for himself or to even consider alternatives. "To do so would have been to exercise corps command, and he was not yet ready to climb off his high horse," a Texas veteran later

71 Hood, *Advance and Retreat*, 58; Hood, "Letter From General John B. Hood," *SHSP*, 4:145; Law, "Struggle for Round Top," in *B&L*, 3:230-21.

72 Law, "Struggle for Round Top," 3:320-21, 332; Pfanz, *Gettysburg: Second Day*, 163; Norton, *Attack and Defense*, 254-55; Krick, "If Longstreet Says.... It Most Likely Not True," *Second Day at Gettysburg*, 75-76. Soon after Hood had dispatched his scouts, Maj. Gen. Law had sent out some of his own on a similar mission to ascertain how far the Federal line extended up toward Little Round Top. Law's scouts went to the top of Big Round Top and did not encounter so much as a picket line. They could see the entire Federal wagon train with scout guards and nothing in its way. One of Law's commanders also sent out a detail that captured several Union prisoners near the Emmitsburg Road. The captives related that the Union anticipated little danger in the area, and of a road off of his right which led to the area where the Federal wagon train was located. It was perfectly clear to Law that Confederates' true focal point was Big Round Top, from which the Confederate right wing could be extended toward the Taneytown and Baltimore Roads, on the Federal left and rear.

wrote. Hood sought out Lieutenant Colonel Moxley Sorrel of Longstreet's staff and "begged . . . [him] to look at" his division's plight. Sorrel complied, riding back to Longstreet with Hood's plea, only to receive the same response from Old Pete, still seemingly abdicating the role of a crops commander. Sorrel expressed surprise at Longstreet's attitude that day. He detected an "apathy in his movements" and the lack of "fire and his usual bearing on the battlefield."[73]

Hood next conferred with Major John W. Fairfax, Longstreet's assistant adjutant and inspector general. Fairfax, a scion of one of Virginia's founding families, had only recently brought Hood the revised order to attack. He listened intently to Hood's arguments and suggested that Hood delay his advance until he could confer with Longstreet about the alternative opportunity. Hood agreed, requesting that Fairfax bring Longstreet to observe the arena for himself. Fairfax sought out Longstreet with the information; however, Old Pete yet again responded "It is General Lee's order, the time is up—attack at once!" Fairfax hurried back and gave Hood the final message.[74]

In desperation, Hood dispatched his adjutant general, Major William "Harry" Sellers, well known to Longstreet, to repeat the request for the third time and file a formal protest, the only time in his entire military career he ever did. "Go as fast as your horse can carry you," he admonished, "and explain all this to General Longstreet, and ask him to permit me to move by the right flank, so as to be able to envelope that knob." Sellers quickly returned with Longstreet's message: "You will execute the orders you have already received." Close on Sellers' heels, Old Pete himself arrived, and Hood pleaded yet again for the alternative plan of attack. Unmoved, Longstreet replied, "We must obey the orders of General Lee." A resigned Hood then surprisingly replied "Very well; when we get under fire I will have a digression."[75]

73 Pfanz, *Gettysburg: Second Day*, 165; Krick, "If Longstreet Says . . . It Most Likely Not True," in *Second Day at Gettysburg*, 75-76; Hood, "Letter From General John B. Hood," *SHSP*, 4:146; LaFantasie, *Twilight at Little Round Top*, 67-68; Sorrell, *Recollections of a Confederate Staff Officer*, 169 ; "Hood's Brigade at Gettysburg," in Chilton, *Hood's Texas Brigade*, 338-39; Law, "Struggle for Round Top," in *B&L*, 3:320. While Lee was opposed to a strategic move interposing the army between Washington and Gettysburg at the time, he had not offered comment on moving against the Federal tactical left on the battlefield. He had always left the means of committing a corps on the battlefield up to its commander.

74 Krick, "If Longstreet Says ...It Most Likely Not True," *Second Day at Gettysburg*, 76-77; Sorrel, *Confederate Staff Officer*, 169; Longstreet, *Manassas to Appomattox*, 381; Pfanz, *Gettysburg: Second Day*, 163-65; Law, "Struggle for Round Top," in *B&L*, 320-21. McLaws was so revolted by Longstreet's behavior that he could not abide his further patronage (up to that point he had been one of Old Pete's favorites). He remained at loggerheads with Longstreet thereafter.

75 Samuel W. Floca, Jr., "Hood's Protest," *CV*, (1898) 6:27; Polley, *Hood's Texas Brigade*, 162; Chilton, *Hood's Texas Brigade*, 339; Hood, "Letter From General John B. Hood," 150.

Cemetery Ridge followed a line running close to north-south as far as the J. Weikert's house. There, the line got lost in a large body of rocks, hills, and woods lying athwart a direct line to the Round Tops, and forcing a bend to the east toward Taneytown Road. This rough place extends out for a quarter mile west toward Plum Run. Toward the south, it then sinks into a low, marshy ground which reaches to the base of Little Round Top about half a mile from Weikert's house. Woods covered the western side of this ground, and between the woods and Plum Run a clearing, approximately 300 yards wide continuing the open country in front of Cemetery Ridge. Plum Run flowed southeasterly, toward Little Round Top, then made a bend where it received another small stream from Seminary Ridge. Angled between these two streams stood Devil's Den, a bald, rocky height, steep on its eastern face and prolonged as a ridge to the west, some 500 yards due west of Little Round Top and about 100 feet lower. Huge rocks and boulders, forming innumerable crevices and holes, formed its northern extremity. Marshy Plum Run valley was also strewn with large boulders, as were the slopes of Little Round Top.[76]

A little over a mile to the west, Hood's Division formed a line north to south, facing east along Warfield Ridge, a southeasterly extension of Seminary Ridge, and south of the Slyder farm. Law's and the Texas Brigade stood in the front, supported by Benning's and Anderson's Georgia brigades 200 yards to their rear. Both stood in the prescribed two ranks, backed by a third, partial rank of file closers, noncommissioned officers and lieutenants in position where they could superintend the men. The Texas Brigade formed its line in a large clearing some 200 yards behind a wooded area fronting on Emmitsburg Road and the Bushman farm lane. The 3rd Arkansas and the 1st Texas stood north of the road, and the 4th and 5th Texas south of it. Law's Brigade of Alabamians was to its immediate right, with the 5th Texas connecting to the 4th Alabama on its right; Kershaw's North Carolina brigade was to the Brigade's left. Hood decided to attack *en echelon* as originally planned, but with the Texas Brigade moving straight ahead to hold the Federals in place in Devil's Den, while Law's Brigade on the right would swing across Big Round Top to turn the Federal left flank. The Texans were ordered to move east, instead of northeast. Law's and Robertson's men were to step off first, the right of the 5th Texas staying in contact with Law's men and the left of the 3rd Arkansas staying in contact with the Emmitsburg Road. The

76 Hunt, "Second Day At Gettysburg," in *B&L*, 3:294-95; *OR* 27, pt. 2, 414; Law, "Struggle for "Round Top,"" in *B&L*, 3:320-21; Pfanz, *Gettysburg: Second Day*, 160.

movement was to proceed on an easterly tack, and then pivot to the northeast in order to hit the massed Federal line in its flank per Lee's orders.[77]

The wooded area in which they had formed up partially screened the 5th Texas troops from Federal observation. From their vantage point the Texans studied the route of their upcoming advance. They could see through the trees to Devil's Den, and to its rear, a large, heavily wooded hill known as Little Round Top. Finally positioned for the assault, though exhausted and parched from a total lack of water, the regiment now stood ready. Just before the signal gun, Hood rode up to Col. Powell, commanding the regiment, pointed to Big Round Top as the direction for him to take with the 5th Texas, "whose flag," he said, "should be the leader for the brigade." "Before us stood in serried, rugged defiance Great Round Top," Powell related, "with Little Round Top leaning against it."[78]

Maj. Mathis W. Henry's battalion of artillery directly supported Hood's Division. Although it consisted of four batteries, there was room for only two on Hood's immediate front—Reilly's North Carolina Battery, six guns, posted on the ridge crest in front of Hood's right wing, and Captain Alexander C. Latham's battery of five pieces in front of the brigade near the Bushman farm lane. Reilly's Napoleons, 10-pounder Parrots, and 3-inch rifles, were positioned hub-to-hub on a slight rise of ground at the edge of the woods. The Tarheel gunners had frequently supported the Texans in the past, and on this July 2, these units would face one of their toughest tests of the entire war.[79]

Law's pioneer corps quickly passed to the front and began felling trees in front and to the right of the 5th Texas. Soon the men were able see the Stars and Stripes waving at them on the hills to their left. The engagement opened with a Confederate artillery barrage against the Union positions in front of the Round Tops. Federal batteries positioned along the slopes and ridges a mile to the east, as well as those around Devil's Den, immediately answered Longstreet's artillery. And the rows of Confederate infantry soon felt the effects "as rounds whistled over them or exploded into deadly metal fragments above their heads," in a "hideous dialogue of flame and smoke and unnerving noise." The Federal barrage soon took its toll on the idle Texans. The second or third shells, bursting in on the rightmost company of the 5th Texas, killed three men and wounded a number of others. A following shell killed 15

77 Pfanz, *Gettysburg: Second Day*, 158; OR 27, pt. 2, 397, 414; Law, "Struggle for Round Top," in *B&L*, 3:318-30.

78 Chilton, *Hood's Texas Brigade*, 339. Reichardt, *Forever the Cause*, 58-59.

79 *OR* 27, pt. 2, 407, 410-11; Polley, *Hood's Texas Brigade*, 167; Collier, *They'll Do To Tie To*, 138-39; Law, "Struggle for 'Round Top,'" in *B&L*, 3:320; Stevens, *Reminiscences*, 113; Pfanz, *Gettysburg: Second Day*, 159-60.

men in the 4th Texas. The "infernal machines came tearing and whirring through the ranks with a most demoralizing tendency," John West commented. At the height of this frightening barrage, a private stood up and moved to the front of the 5th Texas, offering a brief prayer. Seeing the brutal impact of the cannon fire, Robertson soon ordered his troops to move back to a less vulnerable position, and to lie down to minimize casualties until the advance started. A veteran Texan commented that it was "very trying upon men to remain still and in ranks under a severe cannonading. . . . The men are all flat on the ground, keeping their places in ranks, and as a shell is heard, generally try to sink themselves into the earth." As Reilly's battery commenced rapid fire on the Federals, Stevens remembered that "Gens Longstreet, Hood and Pickett were all sitting on their horses just in front of us. . . . These generals were directing the fire . . . [of the] guns, all of which lead our men to the conclusion that we . . . [were] very near to the enemy's infantry line." This bombardment started at approximately 3:30 p.m. and lasted half an hour, until about 4:00 p.m. The curtain was about to rise on the second act of Gettysburg's bitter, bloody drama.[80]

80 West, *Texan in Search of a Fight*, 93 ; Ward, "Incidents and Experiences on the Battlefield at Gettysburg," *CV*, 8:347; Chicoine, *Confederates of Chappell Hill*, 92; Norton, *Attack and Defend*, 255; Bradley M. Gottfried, *Brigades at Gettysburg: The Union and Confederate Brigades at the Battle of Gettysburg* (New York, NY, 2002), 438; Stevens, *Reminiscences*, 113; Collier, *They'll Do To Tie To*, 138-39.

Chapter 2

Gettysburg: High Tide and Low

Time slithered by for the Confederates awaiting the signal gun to charge across the Emmitsburg Pike toward the Federal position. Just after 4:00 p.m., a solitary Confederate artillery signal shot sounded. As it reverberated across the valley of Plum's Run and the hills beyond, Hood's Division sprang to the attack. Hood ordered his division to advance through the woods, past its gun positions, forming in a company front on the fringe of the woods. With capped guns, the Texans moved a little further in the woods and finally out into the open field in front of Reilly's guns. The stilled Confederate batteries once again sprang to life, this time with a rolling barrage over the heads of the infantry to assist in clearing their way. Peering through the trees, the Texans were able to glimpse the formidable Federal position to their front—the two Round Tops—looking quite foreboding even from over a mile away.[1]

Hood assumed his favorite position in front of the Texas Brigade. For one last time from the crest overlooking the Bushman and Slyder farms, he pressed Longstreet to swing around the Union left, repeating his protest in person and begging him to reconsider. Longstreet insisted "We must obey the orders of General Lee," and then quickly rode back towards McLaws' position as limbs of trees cascaded all around him. Captain Goree, a member of the regiment and one of Longstreet's staff, soon approached Hood with Old Pete's compliments and the order to attack the enemy.

1 *OR* 27, pt. 2, 407, 410-12; Chilton, *Hood's Texas Brigade*, 339; Law, "Struggle for 'Round Top,'" in *B&L*, 3:323; Sorrel, *Confederate Staff Officer*, 159; Pomeroy, "War Memoirs," 52; West, *Texan In Search of a Fight,* 86; Sims, "Recollections of the Civil War," 10.

Capt. Thomas J. Goree
Newton Gresham Library, Sam Houston State University, Huntsville, Texas

After meeting with Hood, Goree rode down the line of his comrades informing them that "possession of Little Round Top—pointing to its ragged heights—was necessary. The Texans were expected to take it. 'We'll do it!' was the enthusiastic reply." In a booming voice Hood then gave a brief speech that "Stentor might have envied," then rising up in his stirrups shouted, "Fix bayonets, my brave Texans. Forward and take those heights!" His thrilling words passed down the line like an electric shock. Immediately thereafter, Col. Work of the 1st Texas pointed his regimental flag at the objective, exclaiming, "Follow the Lone Star Flag to the top of the mountain!"[2]

Following the initial *en echelon* movements of Law's Brigade on its right, particularly the 4th Alabama upon which the 5th Texas was to guide, the regiment pushed forward into the open fields to the east. Word passed down the line to proceed "Quick, but not double quick." The Texans and Law's adjacent brigade advanced with bayonets fixed and the sound of the Rebel yell emanating all along the line. Regardless of the command, the troops advanced rapidly, with officers initially keeping the lines in good order. Encountering a rail fence aside Emmitsburg Road, Robertson called for men to throw it down. "We're going in there, men. . . . Grab it by the bottom rail and heave." With the obstruction gone, the men swept across the road. The Texans

2 Powell, *Recollections*, 11-14; Chicione, *Confederates of Chappell Hill*, 92; West, *Texan In Search of a Fight*, 92, 94; Sims, "Recollections of the Civil War," 10; Chilton, *Hood's Texas Brigade*, 339, 350; LaFantasie, *Twilight at Little Round Top*, 75-76; Gottfried, *Brigades at Gettysburg*, 438; Pfanz, *Gettysburg: Second Day*, 168. The time of the advance varies among sources: Chilton and Oliver Norton have it commencing at 4:00 p.m.; Law, Lasswell, and Gottfried at 5:00 p.m. The "Official Reports of the Battle of Gettysburg" at 4:30 p.m. Given the amount of fighting which ensued, I believe the assault had to have begun by about 4:00 p.m. See Chilton, *Hood's Texas Brigade*, 350; Norton, *Attack and Defense*, 155; Gottfried, *Brigades at Gettysburg*, 438; Law, "Struggle for Round Top," in *B&L*, 3:323; Lasswell, *Rags and Hope*, 179. Hood's exact exhortation to his troops has varied among different sources. West claimed he shouted "Forward-steady!-Forward!" Chilton believes he said "Forward my Texans, and win the battle or die in the effort." Regardless of the exact words spoken by the Texans' beloved leader, as Chilton pointed out, "The ball had opened." Chilton, *Hood's Texas Brigade*, 339, 350.

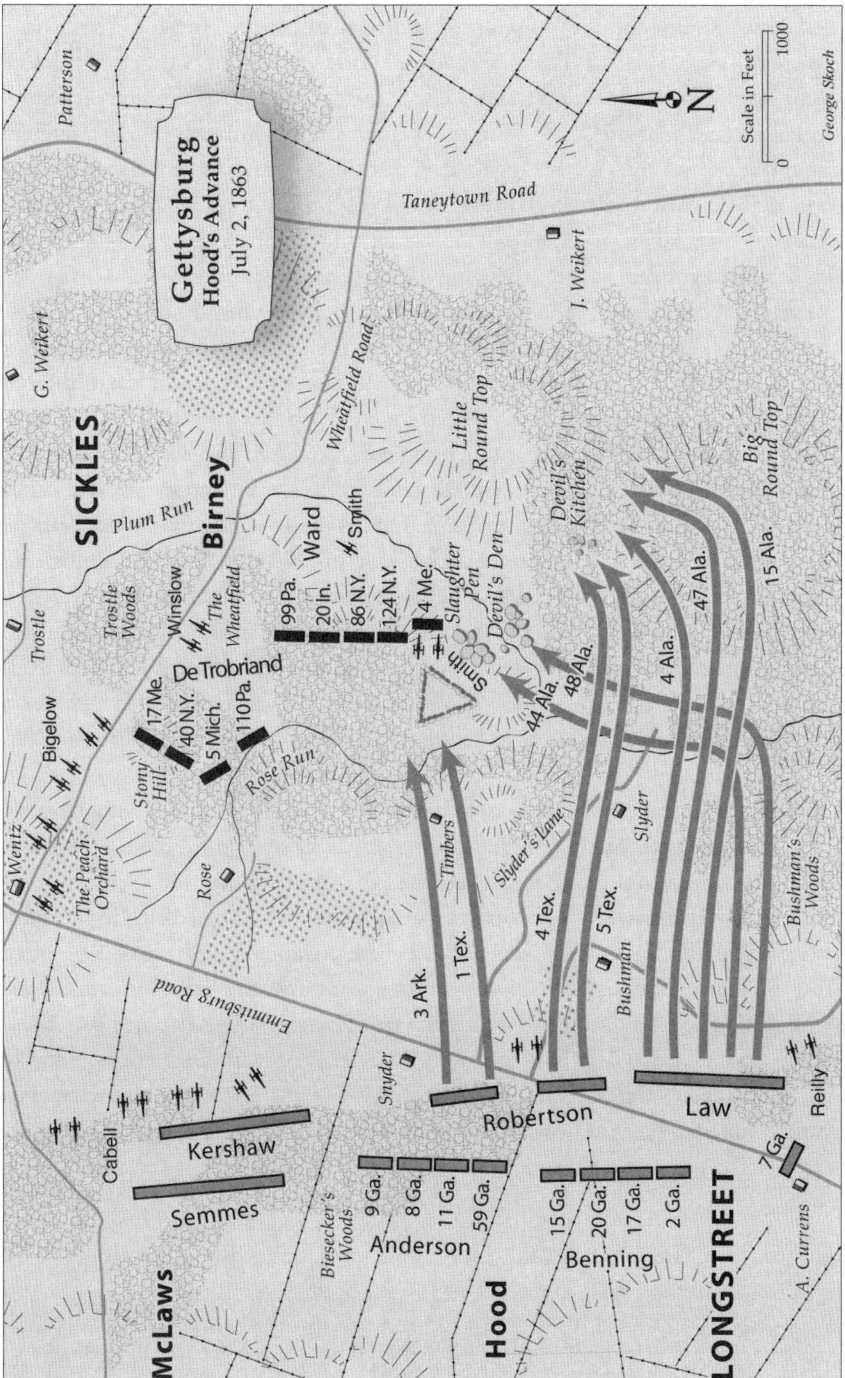

Gettysburg
Hood's Advance
July 2, 1863
Scale in Feet
0
1000
N
George Skoch
Patterson
Taneytown Road
J. Weikert
G. Weikert
Wheatfield Road
Little Round Top
Big Round Top
Devil's Kitchen
Devil's Den
Slaughter Pen
SICKLES
Plum Run
Birney
Ward
Smith
99 Pa.
20 In.
86 N.Y.
124 N.Y.
4 Me.
Trostle
Trostle Woods
Winslow
The Wheatfield
De Trobriand
17 Me.
40 N.Y.
5 Mich.
110 Pa.
Bigelow
Stony Hill
Rose Run
Wentz
The Peach Orchard
Rose
Timbers
Slyder's Lane
Slyder
44 Ala.
48 Ala.
4 Ala.
47 Ala.
15 Ala.
3 Ark.
1 Tex.
4 Tex.
5 Tex.
Bushman
Bushman's Woods
Emmitsburg Road
Snyder
Robertson
Law
Reilly
7 Ga.
Cabell
Kershaw
Semmes
McLaws
Biesecker's Woods
9 Ga.
8 Ga.
11 Ga.
59 Ga.
Anderson
Hood
15 Ga.
20 Ga.
17 Ga.
2 Ga.
Benning
LONGSTREET
A. Currens

spilled across Emmitsburg Pike behind Robertson and dashed toward Plum Run and the Round Tops. The 5th Texas immediately drew fire from the Federal batteries plowing up the ground around them. Devil's Den, with a Federal battery interposed between the regiment and Little Round Top, was still a half mile away. Fletcher, after moving out, noted that to the regiment's front, less than a mile off, "the country looked well elevated and from barren spots I took it to be rocky." As the regiment advanced, "[s]moke from either side rolled in billows," Powell observed, "meeting and writhing in conflict in the valley midway the engaging armies."[3]

The rugged terrain of swales and ditches soon threw the attack into confusion, with the Confederates struggling to maintain their lines as they encountered additional fences and stumbled over rock outcroppings. As Law's men moved down the ridge, they picked up speed, and soon a gap opened up between the two brigades. Consequently, the Texans broke into a double-quick to keep up with the Alabamians to their right. Robertson later contended that Law had prematurely ordered a charge "a full mile from the enemy's line of battle." One of the 4th Alabama officers urged his men to emulate the 5th Texas, remarking "how orderly they were marching to the charge." Instead, one of the Alabamians cheered his regiment on by yelling "Come on, boys; come on! The Fifth Texas will get there before the Fourth!" Meanwhile, various buildings of the Bushman and Slyder farms stood directly in the Texans' path, and their lines rapidly broke up as they passed around these obstacles. This widened the gap between the two brigades considerably—a harbinger of even greater chaos yet to come.[4]

Hood had ordered Robertson to keep his right well closed on General Law's left, while at the same time keeping his left resting on the Emmitsburg Road. As the Texas Brigade advanced, Robertson quickly realized the Emmitsburg Road "[bore] sharply to the left . . . while Law on my right bore to the right." His single brigade was far too small to cover the intervening space. So, before advancing 200 yards, Robertson's right was already straining to keep up with Law's fast moving brigade as it continued veering farther to its right. Obviously Robertson needed to violate orders either by breaking contact with Law's Brigade on his right, or with the road on his left. Robertson and Col. Manning of the 3rd Arkansas, designated to maintain contact with the road, came to the same conclusion—they must break with the road rather than

3 *OR* 27, pt. 2, 411-12; Reichardt, *Forever the Cause*, 59; Law, "Struggle for 'Round Top,'" in *B&L*, 3:323; Fletcher, *Rebel Private*, 78.

4 William C. Oates, *The War between the Union and the Confederacy: History of the 15th Alabama Regiment*, (New York, NY, 1905), 207-08; LaFantasie, *Twilight at Little Round Top*, 78; Pfanz, Gettysburg: *Second Day*, 168, 172; Ward, "Incidents and Personal Experiences on the Battlefield at Gettysburg," *CV*, 8:347.

Law. To do otherwise would create a dangerous gap in the division's front. As soon as McLaws' command advanced on their left, it could cure any problems developing along the road. Robertson thus "abandoned the pike out of necessity," and tried instead to close with Law.[5]

The 1st Texas and 3rd Arkansas on the Texas Brigade's left continued hurriedly forward under Robertson's supervision in an effort to align with the troops on their right. The 3rd Arkansas went in at a "brisk gait," sometimes double-quick, while exposed to artillery fire from the vicinity of the Peach Orchard, as well as from Capt. James E. Smith's 4th New York Battery in Devil's Den. As the men advanced, they could hear the charges of canister "passing over . . . [them] with the noise of partridges in flight." The advance had been reasonably free of obstacles for the first 400 yards after traversing Emmitsburg Road, but now two clumps of wood south of the Timbers house and then the steep slope down into the rocky valley of Plum Run combined to retard further progress. Here, Robertson attempted to close right with his 4th and 5th Texas regiments, while his left wing was receiving fire from Federal troops in the woods to his left. He had become aware that McLaws had not yet advanced on his left and thus had to send back for reinforcements.[6]

Robertson was likewise cognizant that the gap between his two wings was widening. The 1st Texas and 3rd Arkansas were headed toward Houck's Ridge and Devil's Den, while the 4th and 5th Texas were then inclining right, closing on Law, and making for the Slyder farm and the small gap between the boulders of Devil's Den and the low ridge forming the northwestern base of Big Round Top. Recognizing that he could not eliminate the gap by closing his left wing upon his right, Robertson sent orders for the right wing to shift left. However, the officer carrying this order could not reach either the 4th or 5th Texas. While Robertson reported later the "separation of my regiments . . . was remedied as promptly as the numerous stone and rail fences would allow," in reality, the two wings would end up fighting independently for the remainder of the day.[7]

With the battle plan rapidly unraveling by this time, the continuing guidance of an experienced division commander was essential. Hood had initially remained with Robertson; then he left and rode to the peach orchard west of the Bushman

5 *OR* 27, pt. 2, 404, 407; Gottfried, *Brigades at Gettysburg*, 438; Pfanz, *Gettysburg: Second Day*, 172; LaFantasie, *Twilight at Little Round Top*, 75.

6 Pfanz, *Gettysburg: Second Day*, 173; LaFantasie, *Twilight at Little Round Top,* 86; Norton, *Attack and Defense*, 255-56.

7 *OR* 27, pt. 2, 404, 407, 411-12; Pfanz, *Gettysburg: Second Day*, 172-73, Norton, *Attack and Defense*, 255-56; LaFantasie, *Twilight at Little Round Top*, 86; Ward, "Incidents and Personal Experiences on the Battlefield at Gettysburg," in *CV*, 8:347.

outbuildings. In this spot he would be at the center of his division, able to observe its progress and in position to direct reinforcements as needed. Doubtless, he witnessed the attack beginning to falter under the Federals' merciless fire, and the impact of the treacherous terrain. Then in an instant, a shell burst 20 or 30 feet overhead, sending red hot shrapnel flying in all directions. Some of it shattered Hood's left arm from bicep to wrist. Nearly falling from the saddle in shock, he was "eased down by his aides who instantly had dismounted," recalled Col. Work of the 1st Texas. Hood was transported to the rear, experiencing "deep distress of mind and heart at the thought of the inevitable fate of . . . [his] brave fellow-soldiers." The day's assault was just underway, and the Confederate's key division commander was already out of the action.[8]

Meanwhile, troops from the 2nd U.S. Sharpshooters, positioned behind fences, stone walls, and other cover near the foot of Big Round Top and the woods on Houck's Ridge, as well as in the Slyder farmyard, had opened up a scathing fire on the advancing Texas line. The Plum Run valley became a storm of bullets whining through the advancing gray line. The 5th Texas also became easy targets for Capt. Smith's battery on Devil's Den. When Confederate artillery fire had slackened to avoid hitting their own advancing forces, the Federal artillery seized its chance.[9]

The regiment charged through the valley toward Plum Run "yelling and whooping," but its lines soon became severely broken and confused. The Texans maintained their "wild, reckless, unhesitating rush towards the [enemy]" while shells, grape shot, canister, and Minié balls slashed through their ranks. As the men of the 5th Texas struggled forward, Powell remembered one Texan joking as he admonished Walter Keenan of Company D not to "shoot in the top of the trees. I bet you two dollars you will; there, you did, give me the two dollars!" The fire from Federal sharpshooters and a large number of artillery pieces finally became so intense that the brigade could not remain exposed to the murderous spray of lead and iron. Men were falling in every direction. The Rebel Lines were becoming so jumbled and the ranks so

8 Hood, "Letter Form General John B. Hood," *SHSP*, 4:150; Pfanz, *Gettysburg: Second Day*, 172-73; LaFantasie, *Twilight at Little Round Top*, 88; Polk, *North and South American Review*, 28; Chicoine, *Confederates of Chappell Hill*, 92. General Law succeeded Hood as acting division commander. Little is known of when or how he learned of Hood's wounding, or the manner in which he exercised his new command. Law, apparently, never appointed a successor as acting commander of his own brigade. Jerome Robertson learned that Law was in command of the division only after he was fully engaged and had sent back a message to Hood seeking reinforcements. Interestingly, he then made the request to Longstreet and Anderson, not Law. *OR* 27, pt. 2, Oates, *The War Between the Union and the Confederacy*, 210-12; Pfanz, *Gettysburg: Second Day*, 173.

9 *OR* 27, pt. 2, 404; Pfanz, *Gettysburg: Second Day*, 177; Reichardt, *Forever the Cause*, 61; LaFantasie, *Twilight at Little Round Top*, 87.

split apart that the regiments "lapped over each other," and the advancing lines became hopelessly tangled.[10]

In the midst of this disintegrating assault, Law discovered that his brigade had veered too far to the right. He decided to close the gap by marching the two regiments on his extreme right, the 44th and 48th Alabama, behind the advancing lines of the 15th, 47th and 4th Alabama, as well as the 4th and 5th Texas, and swinging them into position to bridge the gap between the left of the 4th Texas and the right of the 1st Texas. Not only was a movement this complex quite difficult to accomplish under fire, but this one had been undertaken without the knowledge of Col. William Oates, commanding the 15th Alabama.

Law now informed Oates that his regiment constituted the extreme right of the Confederate line, ordering him to hug the foot of Big Round Top on the west side, pass up the valley between the two hills, and turn the Union left. Meanwhile, the 44th and 48th Alabama quickly got into position to the left of the 4th Texas and made ready for an assault at Devil's Den. Amazingly, Law's quick action had closed the gap between the brigades, and Hood's front was now largely restored. It constituted an essentially unbroken line across the slope of Big Round Top and in front of Devil's Den.[11]

However, confusion still bedeviled the Confederate lines. Brigadier General Benning obeyed Hood's order to follow Law's Brigade into the attack, while maintaining a distance of 400 yards behind. Benning quickly saw that the line ahead of him was in trouble, and he ordered his brigade forward in support. Not until much later in the fighting, however, did he discern that he had been following Robertson's left wing, the 1st Texas and 3rd Arkansas, into the battle, rather than Law's Alabamians. Brigadier General "Tige" Anderson, observing Benning's movements, then came to the aid of the hard-pressed 1st Texas and 3rd Arkansas; the Georgians

10 Powell, *Recollections*, 14-16; Robert M. Powell to F. Charles Hume, November 8, 1913, in Reichardt, *Forever the Cause*, 134-36 ; LaFantasie, *Twilight at Little Round Top*, 87; West, *Texan In Search of a Fight*, 86, 94; Decimus et Ultimus Barziza, *The Adventures of a Prisoner of War, 1863-1864*, R. Henderson Shuffler, ed. (Austin, TX, 1964), 45. According to Powell, the speaker of the warning not to shoot into the trees was Lewis Mass of Company D. However, Mass had been killed in action at Second Manassas in August of 1862. For more on Private Keenan, see Appendix D.

11 *OR* 27, pt. 2, 393, 396, 404-05; Oates, *The War*, 228; Pfanz, *Gettysburg: Second Day*, 174; Reichardt, *Forever the Cause*, 61; Edward G. Longacre, *Joshua Chamberlain: The Soldier and the Man* (Cambridge, MA, 2004), 132. The confusion was so great at this point that Company I of the 4th Texas became separated from the regiment, and instead of moving around Devil's Den with its own formation, advanced with the right wing of the 1st Texas. Scott Bowden, *Last Chance for Victory: Robert E. Lee and the Gettysburg Campaign* (New York, 2003), 395n12.

passed through a wheat field and into some woods, and quickly became engaged with Brig. Gen. J. H. Ward's brigade of Sickles' III Corps.[12]

The 4th and 5th Texas regiments were situated to the left of the 4th, 47th, and 15th Alabama of Law's Brigade. Informed that these Texas regiments could not be moved without greatly injuring Law's line, Robertson requested Law "to look to them," and for the rest of the day, these Texans fought as part of Law's Brigade. The two regiments forded the Plum Run, wheeled left, and reached the foot of Big Round Top thoroughly exhausted and disorganized. They had moved in tandem through the broken ground of the Plum Run valley and into the thicket and woods between Devil's Den and Big Round Top, passing east of the Slyder farm buildings, and surged into the woods while still under a withering fire. The two regiments had attempted to maintain a semblance of order, while remaining tightly closed upon Law's left. They had lost all contact with the brigade's other two regiments on the left, and their own lines had been shredded by the unrelenting fire of Federal sharpshooters and artillery. Men were "tumbling out of the ranks at every step," Smither reported, "knocked over by the Enemy's sharpshooters who lined the side of the mountain." As they moved into the woods, the trees and boulders increasingly broke their lines apart, making it impossible to identify exactly where the Texas lines ended and the Alabama lines began. It was, a Texan later exclaimed, "a badly mixed crowd."[13]

The 5th Texas continued moving toward the base of Big Round Top, all the while veering more to the right to maintain linkage with Law. The 44th and 48th Alabama had by then moved to their left behind them. From a stone wall at the hill's base, the 2nd U. S. Sharpshooters hit the regiment with a withering fire. The men moved directly at the sharpshooters, soon convincing them that they would be not be stopped. The march to the stone wall from Plum Run covered over 400 yards, through the heat, trees, underbrush and "large boulders, from the size of a wash pot to that of a wagon bed." All had badly fragmented the regiment's forward advance.[14]

As the 4th and 5th Texas pushed through the rugged valley east of Devil's Den, they could hear the din of battle raging to their left rear in that vicinity. Brigadier General J. H. Hobart Ward's brigade was desperately attempting to hold back the 3rd

12 *OR* 27, pt. 2, 414-15, 421, 424; Norton, *Attack and Defense*, 158; LaFantasie, *Twilight at Little Round Top*, 94; Pfanz, *Gettysburg: Second Day*, 175-76.

13 *OR* 27, pt. 2, 301, 405, 411-12; Reichardt, *Forever the Cause*, 61; Mark Smither to Elizabeth Smither, July 29, 1863, in SHSU; Pfanz, *Gettysburg: Second Day*, 215; Ward, "Incidents and Personal Experiences on the Battlefield at Gettysburg," *CV*, 8:349; Stevens, Reminiscences, 114.

14 Stevens, *Reminiscences*, 114; West, *Texan in Search of a Fight*, 87; Gottfried, *Brigades at Gettysburg*, 440; LaFantasie, *Twilight at Little Round Top*, 96-97; Reichardt, *Forever the Cause*, 61-62.

Arkansas and 1st Texas in a fight lasting well over an hour. As the 3rd Arkansas engaged in its firefight with the 86th New York, the 1st Texas forged ahead through dense thicket and dark woods and dislodged the Federal line holding Houck's Ridge. Each time Robertson felt his men had finally broken through, however, "another fresh [Federal line] would present itself." He later reported that the enemy reinforced "his lines in our front from his reserves to our right and front, and from his lines to our left." The resultant carnage here was "frightful," according to one Texan.[15]

As Hood's embattled front line was reforming, Benning's Georgians arrived in support of Robertson, immediately pouring a terrific fire into the Union lines. The 44th and 48th Alabama, now positioned to Smith's left, only added to this pressure. The horrific casualties here in the open rocky area east of Plum Run and Devil's Den earned the area the sobriquet the "Slaughter Pen." Smith's position soon became untenable and he finally retreated, taking the firing mechanisms from his three guns. The 1st Texas seized Smith's three Parrotts after driving off the remaining Federals from the southern tip of Houck's Ridge. Meanwhile, Benning's men swept forward past the 44th Alabama and engaged the wilting Federal line. Smith's remaining two Parrotts, spewing canister into the surging Confederates, continued exacting considerable damage on the gray and butternut line. Soon, the 40th New York came up, forcing the Georgians and the 48th Alabama back toward Devil's Den. Smith removed his remaining two guns to the Wheatfield and then left the field with his wounded. Although they had lost the fight for Houck's Ridge and Devil's Den, the Federals succeeded in making the victors too exhausted to assist in the ongoing fight for Little Round Top.[16]

Despite the heat and the massive boulders in their path, the 4th and 5th Texas and the 4th Alabama had driven away the remnants of the Federal sharpshooters from behind the stone wall. While they tried to maintain some semblance of order, the extremely rocky terrain had broken their lines apart almost as effectively as enemy canister. The regiment found itself caught in a *cul de sac* or depressed basin, surrounded

15 *OR* 27, pt. 2, 405-406; LaFantasie, *Twilight at Little Round Top*, 102-103; Pfanz, *Gettysburg: Second Day*, 187, 191.

16 *OR* 27, pt. 2, 405, 426; Hamilton, *History of Company M*, 30; LaFantasie, *Twilight at Little Round Top*, 102-03; Polk, *North and South American Review*, 28; Polley, *Hood's Texas Brigade*, 169; Chilton, *Hood's Texas Brigade*, 340; Ken Allers, "Compliments In Such A Damned Place As This: The Trans-Mississippi Units At Gettysburg," reprinted from *Trans-Mississippi News*, www.gdg.org/Research/Authored Items/allers.html accessed May 12, 2009; Norton, *Attack and Defense*, 158. Later, the Georgians claimed that they had taken Smith's battery, to which the Texans took great exception. Benning soon settled the matter, indicating to his men, "Ah, boys, those Texans had captured this battery before you were in a quarter of a mile of here." Sims, "Recollections of the Civil War," 10; Sears, *Gettysburg*, 271; Hunt, "The Second Day at Gettysburg," in *B&L*, 3:311; John Martin, "Accurate Historic Records," *CV*, (1904) 12:114.

on three sides by projecting or shelving rocks, surmounted by a stone fence, later referred to as the "Devil's Kitchen." Captain John S. Cleveland, commanding Company H, "with a voice heard above the din of battle," offered a purse of $50 to the first man over the stone wall. Almost immediately, Sgt. Madison Ross sprang forward to earn the reward, but Cleveland quickly ordered him back to his post. "Back to your place Sergeant Ross! File closers not included." Numerous men soon rushed up to the stone wall and dropped to one knee to fire a volley. Moving over the wall, they scattered the Federals who fled up the slope of Little Round Top. Stevens noted that "to preserve anything like a line of battle, was impossible," as the Texans surged forward in the face of stiff fire against their front and left flank.[17]

Under increasing Federal pressure, some Texans gave up their lines altogether, taking cover behind the massive boulders to shield themselves from the hurricane of flying lead. These men began operating as snipers, picking off Federals on Houck's Ridge and Little Round Top. Their remaining comrades soon stormed a rail fence behind which they believed hid the enemy, only to discover it totally undefended. As the exhausted Texans and Alabamians swept across the heavily wooded shoulder of Big Round Top, the trees provided welcomed shade from the scorching sun. One veteran recalled also how the dead trees "formed a natural abatis, through which passage was difficult," especially for the Texans attempting to move at the double-quick. The boulders presented even greater impediments to rapid movement. They created "a natural breastwork over and through . . . [which the] line had to mount." Scaling these boulders shattered any chance of an orderly advance. But the two Texas regiments nonetheless continued to curve relentlessly around the northeast shoulder of Round Top, until arriving at the north edge of a wood.[18]

As the 4th and 5th Texas passed through this woods and into the saddle between the Round Tops, emerging into the bright, merciless sunlight, they observed a

17 Stevens, *Reminiscences*, 144; Reichardt, *Forever the Cause*, 61-62; Mark Smither to Elizabeth Smither, July 29, 1863, in SHSU; Polly, *Hood's Texas Brigade*, 173-74. Some sources identify "Sergeant Ross" as J. B. Ross, but he died in Richmond during the winter of 1861-62. The individual referred to must be Sergeant Madison Ross, who was present at Gettysburg. In a follow-up to this incident, Benjamin LaBree in *Camp Fires of the Confederacy* related that Privates Stones and Settler were the first over the stonewall that day. LaBree remarked that "[a]fterward they claimed the . . . [reward], but I don't know whether they got it or not." Benjamin LaBree, *Camp Fires of the Confederacy: a volume of humorous anecdotes, reminiscences, deeds of heroism, thrilling narratives, campaigns, hand-to-hand fights, bold dashes, terrible hardships endured, imprisonments . . . etc.* (Louisville, KY, 1898), 366. For more on Joseph Stone, see Appendix B, Volume 1.

18 Reichardt, *Forever the Cause*, 62; Ken Discorfano, *They Saved the Union at Little Round Top: Gettysburg—July 2, 1863* (Gettysburg, PA, 2002), 50; Stevens, *Reminiscences*, 114; Robert Powell to F. Charles Hume, November 8, 1913, in Reichardt, *Forever the Cause*, 135-36; West, *Texan in Search of a Fight*, 86-87; LaFantasie, *Twilight at Little Round Top*, 116-17.

majestic, yet intimidating sight. Little Round Top's steep slope loomed directly in front of them, strewn with gigantic boulders from top to bottom. And the enemy were everywhere, posted behind ledges and brush, wedged into the crevasses formed by the rocks and trees. Although only 170 feet above the floor of Plum Run valley, the promontory "rose sharply halfway up its slopes, leaving a more gradual ridgeline" running nearly from the banks of the stream to "a cluster of boulders and rock outcroppings along a vertical ledge about twenty-five yards" below the summit. The Texans observed Federals recently driven from the woods scrambling up the hill to unite with a solid line of Col. Strong Vincent's 1,000-man brigade, which slanted across the hill in the Texans' front. The men on the left probably saw Federal signalmen atop the hill, as well as the ominous appearance of cannon arriving to greet their approach.[19]

Meanwhile, Col. Oates, now leading the 15th and 47th Alabama, disregarded Law's order to wheel left after crossing Plum Run, instead directing his regiments to wheel right toward the crest of Big Round Top, with the 47th Alabama holding his left. Thus, while three of Law's regiments on the division's right swung directly toward Little Round Top, the two rightmost units continued ahead uphill toward the summit of Big Round Top itself pursuing fleeing 2nd U. S. Sharpshooters. The 15th Alabama indeed did reach that summit, while the 47th Alabama traversed the eminence lower down on its slope.[20]

Already worn out and parched from lack of water from the day's long ordeal—a 25-mile march from New Guilford, the approach march and countermarch, and the assault—the Alabamans deemed a brief rest just about mandatory. During this brief respite, Oates finally learned that Law had taken over command of the division. A courier from the general reminded Oates there were no Confederates on his right, and that he had to press on, turn the exposed Union left flank, and capture Little Round Top. Oates was to "do all the damage he could to the enemy" all without any further delay.

For his part, Oates vehemently protested his orders. His current position was impregnable, higher than the other hill, and commanded the entire field. However, he followed his orders, reluctantly leading his men down the hill's north slope. When his two regiments reached the saddle between the hills, they observed the Federal line on an irregular ledge of rocks parallel to the 47th Alabama, but bent back somewhat from

19 *OR* 27, pt. 2, 412; LaFantasie, *Twilight at Little Round Top*, 118; West, *Texan in Search of a Fight*, 98; Pfanz, *Gettysburg: Second Day*, 219; Sears, *Gettysburg*, 271.

20 LaFantasie, *Twilight at Little Round Top*, 116; Pfanz, *Gettysburg: Second Day*, 217-18.

the 15th Alabama's right. There, they were soon to be welcomed with what Oates later characterized as "the most destructive fire I ever saw."[21]

Colonel Strong Vincent, commander of the Third Brigade, First Division of Sykes's V Corps, while awaiting orders as the battle raged around him, learned that orders had been issued for his division commander to dispatch a brigade to occupy Little Round Top. Vincent immediately ordered Col. James C. Rice of the 44th New York to move his brigade (Vincent's) up the hill, while he went up the prominence himself to position his troops there. Vincent and Rice formed the brigade in an arc beginning on the southern slope and stretching round to its rocky western face. After some adjustments, the 20th Maine, under Col. Joshua Chamberlain assumed the extreme left. Vincent stressed to Chamberlain that "[t]his is the left of the Union line, you are to hold this ground at all costs." The 83rd Pennsylvania and the 44th New York stood to its right. The 16th Michigan held the extreme right, where it occupied a pile of boulders and outcroppings along the western face of the hill. The brigade's line was "nearly that of a quarter circle," with its right "forward somewhat to the front of the ledge of rocks," more exposed than other points of the line. Vincent had been in place less than 15 minutes when the Confederates opened fire on him. If the Federal movement had happened five minutes later, Pvt. Charles Salter of the 16th Michigan later wrote, "the enemy would have gained the ridge we were on, and turned our left flank, and it would have been very hard to drive them from it." Simply by moving its artillery up to its summit, the Rebels would then have been in a position to enfilade Meade's entire line, making it impossible for him to remain anywhere on Cemetery Ridge. From their extreme right, Rice and Chamberlain were able to observe the Confederates overrunning Devil's Den, as well as the those directly below them then "pressing past the base of the Round Tops," looking as if it were "rolling toward us in tumultuous waves." Returning to their lines, the two commanders then prepared for the "waves," which would soon come crashing onto the rocks of Little Round Top with a brutal vengeance.[22]

21 *OR* 27, pt. 2, 392; Oates, *The War*, 207, 211-12, 214, 221, 586; Powell, "With Hood At Gettysburg, The Experiences of a Texas Officer in One of the Charges at Little Round Top," Philadelphia *Weekly Times*, December 13, 1884"; Law, "Struggle for Round Top," in *B&L*, 324-25; Russell C. White, ed., *The Civil War Diary of Wyman S. White, First Sergeant of Company F, 2nd United States Sharpshooter Regiment, 1861-1865*, (Baltimore, MD, 1993), 165. It has been suggested that when the 15th and 47th Alabama executed their flanking movement, halting for some ten minutes on the crest of Big Round Top for a rest, proved fatal to the Confederates' undertaking, as it enabled Vincent's brigade to consolidate on Little Round Top. H. S. Melcher, "The 20th Maine At Little Round Top," *B&L*, 3:315.

22 Norton, *Attack and Defense*, 264-65; Oliver W. Norton, *Army Letters, 1861-1865: Being Extracts from Private Letters to Relatives and Friends from a Soldier in the Field During the Civil War, With*

Meanwhile, the ragged but still relentless Confederate line scattered the remaining Federal sharpshooters, who yielded ground slowly and reluctantly. Showing little concern for an enemy almost literally crawling up their backs, the Federal sharpshooters hustled up through the wooded saddle the Round Tops and entered the lines of the 83rd Pennsylvania, which dipped down close to the floor of the valley.[23]

The 5th Texas, accompanied by the 4th, continued forward, but suddenly a new line of skirmishers ordered up by Vincent appeared in their front. These skirmishers, from the 83rd Pennsylvania and 44th New York, gave the Texans a "sharp contest," resisting the surge of the oncoming gray line with a vicious volley which temporarily halted the Texans. The men quickly regained their composure, however, and responded to the Federal volley with a terrific fire of their own that broke apart the Union skirmish line almost immediately. Colliding with the rear ranks of the fleeing Federals, the Texans collected a number of prisoners, while the rest of the Yankees found safety in the rocks and ledges of Vincent's lines. The Texans, and the 4th Alabama, having advanced to that point in columns of four, now reformed into a battle line with the 4th Texas on the left, the 5th Texas in the center, and the 4th Alabama on the right.[24]

Powell noted his men had rushed on "through Devil's Den, blazing with infernal fire, crushing and destroying opposing forces at the foot of the mountain, onward and upward they struggled over precipitous rocks, where the enemy, lying in ambush, was surprised." But at this point, the commander of the 4th Texas as well as his immediate successor fell severely wounded in a matter of minutes. Additionally, the regiment discovered that maintaining its newly adjusted battle lines was next to impossible among the boulders at the base of Little Round Top in this "Valley of Death." The huge rocks formed defiles "which not more than 3 or 4 men could pass abreast" at a time, according to Lt. Col. King Bryan of the regiment, breaking up the regiment's "alignment . . . [and] rendering its reformation impossible." A forward advance without firepower had no future: the Texans found it nearly impossible to fire up the hill while they continued to stumble amongst the boulders and rocks at the base of the

---

an Appendix Containing Copies of Some Official Documents, Papers and Addresses of Later Date (Chicago, IL, 1903), 165; LaFantasie, *Twilight at Little Round Top*, 108-112; Reichardt, *Forever the Cause*, 63; Philander Platt, "On Little Round Top," *National Tribune*, April 11, 1907; LaFantasie, *Twilight at Little Round Top*, 111; Belo, "Battle of Gettysburg," *CV*, 8:168; Eugene A. Nash, *A History of the Forty-Fourth Regiment New York Volunteer Infantry in the Civil War, 1861-1865* (Chicago, IL, 1911), 154; *OR* 27, pt. 1, 616-17, 623.

23 LaFantasie, *Twilight at Little Round Top*, 118-19; Pfanz, *Gettysburg: Second Day*, 214.

24 *OR* 27, pt. 2, 391, 411-12; Ward, "Incidents and Personal Experiences on the Battlefield at Gettysburg," *CV*, 8:349; Stevens, *Reminiscences*, 114; LaFantasie, *Twilight at Little Round Top*, 118-19; Pfanz, *Gettysburg: Second Day*, 214.

slope. This brutal uphill climb, Powell later wrote, "was so difficult as to forbid the use of arms." Smither noted that the rocks presented a considerable barrier to their movement. "We could hardly have gone over them," he wrote his mother, "if there had been no Yankees there."[25]

The Federal line erupted in another blaze of fire, killing and wounding many of the Confederates attackers. William Fletcher saw the regiment's colors fall at least five times during this struggle. Color Sgt. T. W. Fitzgerald of Company A, the last remaining color-bearer, pressed "gallantly forward . . . [until] badly wounded." The flag was quickly taken up by Color Corp. J. A. Howard of Company B, who was instantly killed. As the colors fell for the last time, a shell deflected a piece of the staff, striking Fletcher in the face while flying between his legs, causing him to lose his balance. He instinctively gave the staff "a kick," cursed, and passed on. First Sgt. W. S. Evans of Company F then bravely bore the colors for the remainder of the fight. Ultimately, he "planted them defiantly in the face of the foe during the remainder of the fight, always advancing promptly to the front when the order was given."[26]

One Texas veteran quickly learned that scaling the rocks was probably possible for someone without accouterments; however, soldiers could barely make headway encumbered by all their gear. Many in the regiment were wounded "passing over the space between the Round Tops," according to Lt. Col. Byran. "[A] mountain goat would have reveled" at the sight of such harsh, rocky terrain, John West observed, considering his personal struggles to advance up the harsh slope amid the heavy smoke and deafening noise of battle. It reminded him of a particular alliteration from his childhood: "Round the rude rock the ragged rascal ran." However, few Texans that day, including West, succeeded in running around these "rude" rocks, many of which by some accounts were "as large as a meeting house."[27]

The din of battle soon grew so loud the Texans could not hear the orders shouted by officers in the forward lines. The deafening sounds of battle simply wiped out most speech. "Private soldiers," a Texan later wrote, "gave commands as loud as the officers . . . Nobody paid any attention to either." Another Texan observed "[e]very

25 *OR* 27, pt. 2, 405, 412-413; Reinhardt, *Forever the Cause*, 61-65; Mark Smither to Elizabeth Smither, July 29, 1863, in SHSU. Lt. Col. B. F. Carter, who succeeded Col. J. C. G. Key, died from his wounds. West, *Texan In Search of a Fight*, 102; Lasswell, *Rags and Hope*, 178; Polley, *Hood's Texas Brigade*, 184.

26 *OR* 27, pt. 2, 412-13; Fletcher, *Rebel Private*, 80-81; Powell, "With Hood At Gettysburg," Philadelphia *Weekly Times*, "Official Reports of the Battle of Gettysburg," 192; Reichardt, *Forever the Cause*, 62, 64-65; Chilton, *Hood's Texas Brigade*, 341.

27 *OR* 27, pt. 2, 412; West, *Texan in Search of a Fight*, 98; LaFantasie, *Twilight at Little Round Top*, 120.

Major Jefferson Carroll Rogers
Milam County Historical Commission

fellow was his own general" at this stage of the advance. To make matters even more hellish, the Confederate artillerymen to the rear were mistakenly cutting fuses too short, so friendly fire was bursting behind the Texans, in treetops, over and all around them. "Nothing demoralizes troops quicker than to be fired into by their friends," said a Texas veteran at the time. Unable to run from the short rounds, the troops began taking considerable casualties from their own guns.[28]

Lieutenant Colonel Bryan likened the Federal fire at the regiment's front to "being showered like hail upon us." The ground was "strewn with the dead and dying—the warm blood yet pouring from them." In the middle of this cacophony, Maj. Jefferson C. Rogers heard Powell yell out "Swing up the left, Major Rogers." Rogers immediately shouted back, "I'll do it, Colonel, by jingo." "For some reason it became [suddenly] very quiet in the instant of Roger's reply and the words 'by Jingo' sounded loudly, clearly, and ludicrously over the Fifth's part of the field." The incongruous exclamation prompted a hearty round of laughter from all the remaining members of the regiment.[29]

In spite of the dire conditions in the midst of this conflagration, the men of the 5th Texas continued inching forward, pulling each other up and over the rocks. As he dodged bullets and climbed rocks, Rufus Felder concluded that Lee "must have been mad" to order this particular assault. He "came very near loosing his whole army by it," he later wrote his mother. John West agreed the attack was "pure folly," but asserted that "Lee never would have attacked the enemy in their position on the

28 Foote, *Civil War Narrative*, 2:501; Lasswell, *Rags and Hope*, 180; Pfanz, *Gettysburg: Second Day*, 219-20. It has been asserted that Confederate artillery was mishandled in the fight by not moving forward to a position more accurately to fire on Vincent's brigade on Little Round Top. Nonetheless, it still performed outstanding service. Bowden, Last Chance for Victory, 293; Pfanz, Gettysburg: Second Day, 160, 168, 553n9.

29 Powell, *Recollections*, 16; LaFantasie, *Twilight at Little Round Top*, 120; Pfanz, *Gettysburg: Second Day*, 219-20; Mark Smither to Elizabeth Smither, July 29, 1863, in SHSU. For more on Rogers, see Appendix B, Volume 1.

mountain side except for the splendid condition of his army, and his confidence in its ability to accomplish anything he chose to attempt." Smither also wrote home following the fight bemoaning the Texans' plight, but blamed "Bullhead Longstreet" for this "reckless assault on a fortified position."[30]

A ledge of boulders on the lower terrace of Little Round Top brought the advance to a halt. Fletcher later recalled that as they struck the foot of the hill, it was "rough and rocky, with large boulders now and then, so our lines were not at all times well closed. We soon were near enough the enemy's line for them to open fire. We had but poor chance to retaliate with much effect." John Stevens related that "[a]s we start up the mountain we got a plunging volley from the enemy . . . not more than 25 to 30 steps away and well protected behind the rocks, while we . . . [were] exposed to their fire. Their first volley was most destructive to our line. Every line officer of my regiment is shot down except one man—the major."[31]

Men everywhere sought the shelter of any boulder large enough to crouch behind, fighting individually and firing with some accuracy. Col. Bryan recalled "small clusters of rocks far below the elevated position of the enemy, which gave us partial protection." From here, he said, the Texans could "fire for the first time with accuracy." Smither noticed Powell had been urging his men forward by "waving his sword and cheering." At his side, Lt. R. Thomas Harper of Company E was hit and staggered, but Powell quickly caught him and eased him to the ground. Then a bullet hit Powell in the left side and passed out of his back. Smither quickly caught him and was able to drag him to temporary cover behind a boulder.[32]

At this moment, Bryan decided that the 5th Texas could advance no farther without reinforcements, and went searching for Powell for further orders. Toward the center of the regiment's line, Bryan passed "many officers and men who had fallen, having discharged their whole duty like true soldiers." Finally, he located his commander, now wounded and prostrate on the ground behind the center of the 5th Texas' lines. As he approached Powell, a ball struck him in the left arm. Despite this own wound, Bryan still examined Powell closely enough to discover a hole in his coat where the bullet had exited his body. Although still alive, Powell appeared mortally wounded. By then, however, Bryan could not arrest the flow of blood from his own

30 Rufus Felder to Mother, July 9, 1863, in CRC ; Mark Smither to Elizabeth Smither, July 29, 1863, in SHSU; West, *Texan in Search of a Fight*, 98.

31 Stevens, *Reminiscences*, 114; Fletcher, *Rebel Private*, 79.

32 Chicoine, " . . . Willing Never To Go in Another Fight," SHQ, 106:585; Mark Smither to Elizabeth Smither, July 29, 1863, in SHSU; Reichardt, *Forever the Cause*, 66; OR 27, pt. 2, 413.

wound and left the field after turning over command of the regiment to Major Rogers.[33]

The 5th and 4th Texas along with the 4th, 15th, 47th, and 48th Alabama pushed back the skirmish line, and hit the Union lines with a great blast of gunfire. Vincent's troops saw the Confederates swinging out in battle formation and advancing on them, and could hear the dreaded Rebel Yell, "the shiver-provoking howl which seemed . . . a cross between a fox yelp and the cry of the banshees." One member of the 83rd Pennsylvania thought it sounded "as if all pandemonium had broken loose and joined in the chorus of one grand, universal war whoop."[34]

The Texans soon struck the center of Vincent's line in front of the 44th New York and the 83rd Pennsylvania. A thick, blinding smoke enveloped the hillside and men on each side strained to distinguish their targets, often firing blindly into the smoke in hopes of hitting a foe. The Federals observed the Texans zigzagging among the trees below their position. At first Vincent's brigade seemed to hold them in check, but they were soon swarming along the slopes of the hill, edging northwards. From atop a rock behind the 83rd Pennsylvania, Vincent could see almost his whole line except the right flank of the 16th Michigan, which lay hidden around a bulge of the hillside. And though the Texans seemed to falter some 40 or 50 yards beneath the Union line, they still seemed determined to force their way up regardless of the obstacles before them. Vincent promptly petitioned for reinforcements, reporting: "the enemy are coming against us with an overwhelming force."[35]

Maj. Rogers, now commanding the 5th Texas, assumed a position on a log behind the regimental color guard, and imparted a brief patriotic speech exhorting his Texans to aim carefully. The 5th Texas "continued to advance until the first line came to within about 40 yards of our line," reported Lt. Col. Freeman Conner of the 44th New York. Then "we opened a heavy fire upon them, which was continued until they were compelled to retreat." The Federals were close enough, Fletcher later wrote, that "with good aim we could have been shot in the top of the head, either standing or kneeling." The injured Powell, from his vantage point on the ground, likened the scene to "a devil's carnival." Fletcher noted that "we stopped advancing, without

33 *OR* 27, pt. 2, 405, 412; Evans, *Confederate Military History*, 11:219; Reichardt, *Forever the Cause*, 65; Fletcher, *Rebel Private*, 79; Mark Smither to Elizabeth Smither, July 29, 1863, in SHSU; LaFantasie, *Twilight at Little Round Top*, 121; *New York Times*, July 3, 1913; Pfanz, *Gettysburg: Second Day*, 220; Stevens, *Reminiscences*, 114.

34 LaFantasie, *Twilight at Little Round Top*, 131-33.

35 *OR* 27, pt. 1, 616-17, 623; Amos M. Judson, *A History of the Eighty-Third Regiment, Pennsylvania Volunteers* (Erie, PA, 1865), 66-68, 126; Gottfried, *Brigades at Gettysburg*, 247; LaFantasie, *Twilight at Little Round Top*, 133-34.

orders as far as I was concerned as I had heard none." The troops "immediately took shelter, Indian fashion, behind rocks and trees," Smither related, "and commenced popping away at the Yankees wherever they showed their heads." And they were answered with "volley after volley down on us with frightful effect." The situation appeared utterly hopeless. The Texans could not advance, and raising their heads invited having them blown off. Stevens recalled that "for the first time in the history of the war, our men began to waver. We [were] suffering terribly."[36]

Through the dense smoke and deafening noise, Rogers suddenly realized the 4th Texas to his left had fallen back, and the 4th Alabama to his right had not yet emerged from the woods, which left the 5th Texas completely isolated on the steep slopes of the hill. He thus ordered an immediate withdrawal "to an open space about 50 yards in rear." Fletcher later described how, when the order came to fall back, he "had no fear of the enemy charging and capturing the retreating forces for they had ample dead and wounded to satisfy them, if all parts of our line were as badly butchered as at the point I went in and out." Ripped and battered, the regiment retired in good order until it reached the position where the Federal sharpshooters had previously hidden, and there halted with other units to reform. As his men moved under cover, Rogers learned that close to two-thirds of the regiment was down, either killed or wounded. By this point, the Texans had been fighting approximately an hour, and the totally spent men needed a respite from combat. Sgt. William Henry Matthews of Company K wrote of a fatigue so debilitating "that when we reached the enemy's line we were all exhausted, and could go no further." Rogers reported that due to this "exhausted condition of the men, it was . . . necessary to remain. . . . [there] for a few moments"[37]

36 Mark Smither to Elizabeth Smither, July 29, 1863 in SHSU; Stevens, *Reminiscences*, 113-14; Reichardt, *Forever the Cause*, 68; Lasswell, *Rags and Hope*, 180; Fletcher, *Rebel Private*, 79.

37 *OR* 27, pt. 2, 413; Fletcher, *Rebel Private*, 79; Barziza, *Adventures*, 47; Reichardt, *Forever the Cause*, 66, 68-69; Yeary, *Reminiscences of the Boys in Gray*, 2:471-472. The 4th Alabama was pinned down in the woods near the saddle in between the Round Tops, caught in an enfilading fire which stopped them cold. Sgt. William Ward was one of the many Alabamians falling at this point, shot through both legs. The regiment's commander had dropped from exhaustion soon after crossing Plum Run; his successor, retracting his lines and established a rallying point in the rocks, yelled to his troops "Halt here, boys, and let us make a stand at this place." Ward, "Incidents and Personal Experiences on the Battlefield at Gettysburg," in *CV*, 8:347-48; Reichardt, *Forever the Cause*, 65. Major Rogers indicated in his report of July 8 that the initial order to fall back came "from [an] unknown source," although after looking right and left he deemed it necessary to follow the same. *OR* 27, pt. 2, 413. During this trying time, Capt. John S. Cleveland, commander of Company H, led the right wing of the regiment, and was later commended by Maj. Rogers for his skillful leadership under fire. Similarly, Capt. Tacitus T. Clay managed the left wing. Evans, *Confederate Military History*, 11:219; *OR* 27, pt. 2, 413. For more on W. H. Matthews, see Appendix B, Volume 1.

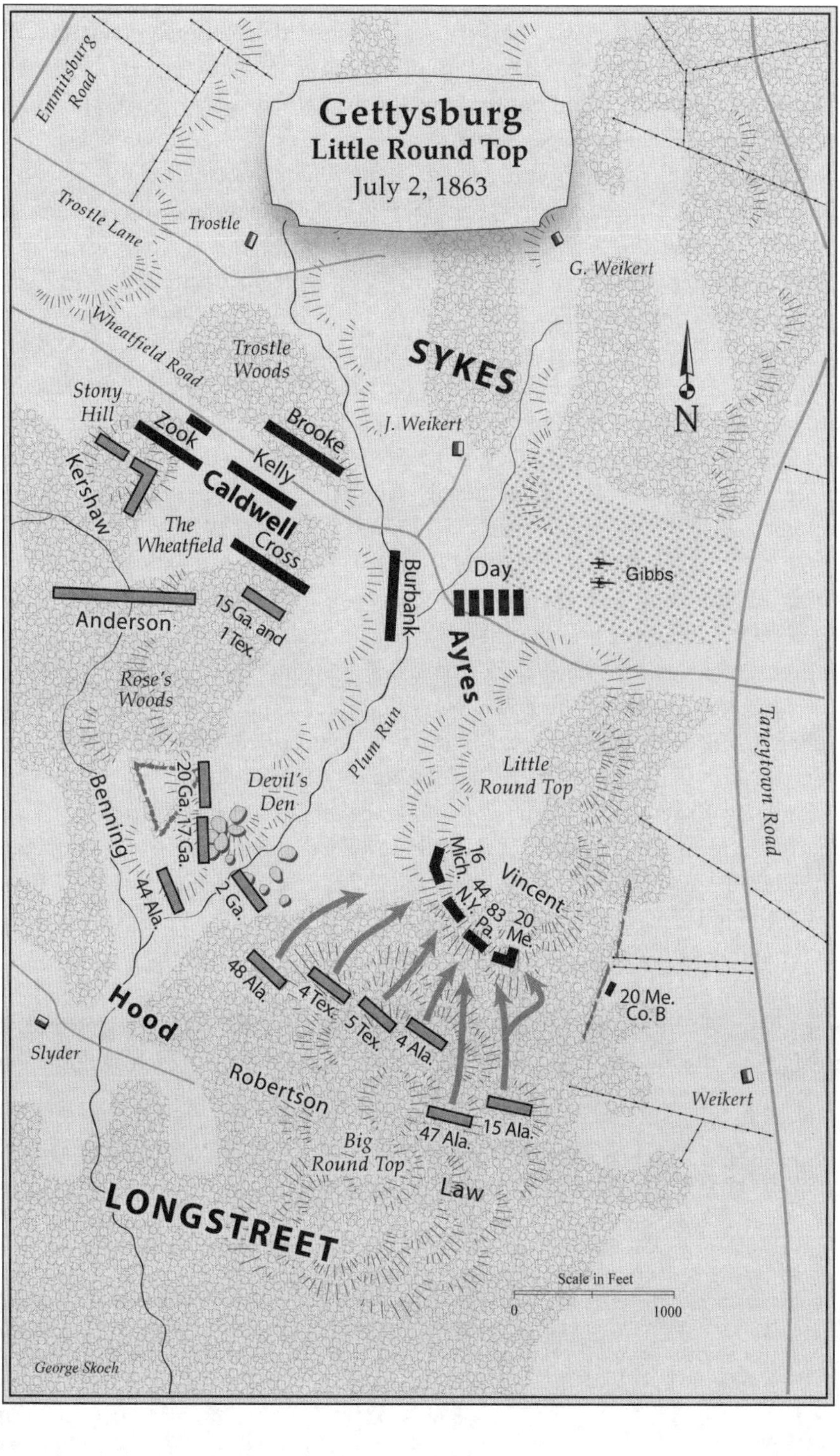
Gettysburg
Little Round Top
July 2, 1863
Emmitsburg Road
Trostle Lane
Trostle
G. Weikert
Wheatfield Road
Trostle Woods
SYKES
Stony Hill
Zook
Brooke
J. Weikert
N
Kershaw
Kelly
Caldwell
The Wheatfield
Cross
Burbank
Day
Gibbs
Anderson
15 Ga. and 1 Tex.
Ayres
Rose's Woods
Plum Run
Taneytown Road
Little Round Top
Devil's Den
Benning
20 Ga.
17 Ga.
16 Mich.
44 N.Y.
83 Pa.
20 Me.
Vincent
44 Ala.
2 Ga.
48 Ala.
4 Tex.
5 Tex.
4 Ala.
20 Me. Co. B
Hood
Slyder
Robertson
Weikert
47 Ala.
15 Ala.
Big Round Top
Law
LONGSTREET
Scale in Feet
0
1000
George Skoch

It is not entirely clear as to how the second Confederate assault got started. The seriously wounded Powell believed it originated spontaneously in response to someone in the ranks yelling out that the Texans should charge again. Maj. Rogers later indicated he had received orders to advance again, although never identifying who had given the order or how it came to be delivered. Nonetheless, the 4th and 5th Texas did advance again, the men shouldering their way around the boulders and between trees near the base of Little Round Top, positioning themselves yet again under the blazing guns of the enemy. In the brief interim, a battery of four Parrott guns under the command of Lt. William Hazlett, had been literally manhandled to the summit of Little Round Top. And while they could not be lowered sufficiently to blast the oncoming Texans, the presence of the guns atop the hill certainly discouraged the Confederates struggling mightily to ascend amidst the natural obstacles and horrific small arms fire. And even if the Texans succeeded in gaining the Federal main line, a further advance would place them directly within the line of fire of these devastating cannon.[38]

The Texans and Alabamians found themselves moving up the slope they had only recently abandoned, picking their way between boulders and using them to their advantage by hiding until ready to shoot at the Federals above them. However, these same rocks precluded the new attack from gaining any momentum. Groups of Texans inched their way between the boulders trying to get a foothold on the slope which would allow a lunge at the Federal line at the appropriate time with some power behind it. But the Federals succeeded in keeping the Texans at a good distance, forcing them to remain in clumps or to take cover behind the rocks then "heavily pocked and creased" by the blizzard of Minié balls that had ricocheted off them. So disorganized was this second assault that there was little or no coordination between the 4th and 5th Texas, and none at all with the 4th Alabama.[39]

A number of soldiers from Company K never withdrew from the first assault and, consequently, eagerly awaited the return of the rest of the regiment as they reformed for another attack. These men stood their ground on the slope, taking horrible casualties as the bullets flew all around them. Troops separated from their own

38 *OR* 27, pt. 2, 413, Mark Smither to Elizabeth Smither, July 29, 1863, in SHSU; Fletcher, *Rebel Private*, 80; Pfanz, *Gettysburg: Second Day*, 221.

39 LaFantasie, *Twilight at Little Round Top*, 124-25 ; Stevens, *Reminiscences*, 114. Mark Smither wrote that Law ordered the second advance, although it is unlikely he would have personal knowledge of this fact. See Mark Smither to Elizabeth Smither, July 29, 1863, in SHSU. Maj. Rogers reported he ordered both the second and third assaults, and implied that both Texas regiments received such an order, while not indicating who gave the orders. It was certainly not Robertson, who was then heavily engaged in front of Devil's Den. See Pfanz, *Gettysburg: Second Day*, 509n50-51.

companies and regiments soon joined them, and one soldier from the 5th Texas recalled that the balls flew so thickly that "a man could hold out a hat and catch it full." Some of the Texans there were not even aware another assault was underway; others found themselves behind the same rocks where they had sheltered before. Upon reflection after the war, many veteran Texans related that, for them, the subsequent assaults seemed to run together into one, single, continuous charge—"one seamless episode in bloodletting, one black and endless nightmare."[40]

Vincent's Yankees were holding their own, slapping down the Texans in this second assault without mercy or let up. The blue line laid down a terrifying "a sheet of smoke and flame." Capt. Amos M. Judson of the 83rd Pennsylvania later wrote: "The enemy had everything to gain if they carried the position; everything to lose if they failed."[41]

Similarly, Vincent's men had everything to lose by failing to stem the Confederate attack. Despite their commanding position, their status as the day's victors was far from assured. But the terrain of the hill worked to their great advantage, keeping them in position as they defended the slopes. The scattered rocks and boulders provided cover while at the same time making it possible to maintain the semblance of a battle line formation—a shoulder-to-shoulder defense in the face of the enemy's more diffused and fragmented assaults. By then, the second Confederate assault had progressed to within 40 yards of the main Union line, with bullets flying like a swarm of angry wasps. The Confederates "poured in a deadly fire upon our troops," Capt. Judson reported. Pvt. Salter recalled that it was "the most desperate fighting I ever saw."[42]

The Confederates, desperately clambering uphill in their second assault, had advanced "like an endless swarm of bees," according to Judson. However, Vincent's troops held steady in their shelter of the rocks and boulders while laying down a concentrated fire that "laid the rebels in heaps" upon the slope as the Federals "fought like demons." Hazlett's guns were in full blaze, hammering the Confederates across the valley with shot and shell, their racket seemingly shaking Little Round Top to its core. With their ammunition slackening, the Federals, as had their enemies, began combing the dead and wounded for replenishment. Firing from above, the defenders possessed a decided advantage in ascertaining their targets, while the Texans on the

40 Stevens, *Reminiscences*, 114; Pfanz, *Gettysburg: Second Day*, 221.

41 *OR* 27, pt. 1, 616-17, 632; Judson, *A History of the Eighty-Third Regiment,* 126-27; Platt, "On Little Round Top," *National Tribune*, April 11, 1907; LaFantasie, *Twilight at Little Round Top*, 135.

42 LaFantasie, *Twilight at Little Round Top*, 144; Judson, *History of the Eighty-Third Regiment*, 127.

slope tended to aim high sending many slugs whizzing over the heads of Vincent's men.[43]

All order and discipline had apparently vanished in the thick smoke still hugging the ground in this second assault. Then "[t]he men," Fletcher reported "about faced near as if ordered and marched back." The 5th Texas's officers initially desperately attempted to halt the retreat, but their commands were ignored. Just as the men of the 5th Texas wheeled about, a lieutenant near Fletcher wailed in pain when a ball cut off his big toe, and Fletcher noted that he "made more racket than I ever heard from one wounded man."[44]

Rogers desperately attempted to hold the regiment's second advance together, even as his men grudgingly began to turn to their rear under the merciless barrage of Federal lead. Rogers knew the minds of these troops: they knew as well as he that bravery and resoluteness alone would not pierce an impregnable Federal position. The regiment had already accomplished much more than reckoned humanly possible. His report would laud their "coolness and determination" which proved "equal to the occasion." But at the moment the courage and resoluteness of his soldiers did not negate the unassailable fact that the 5th Texas had again been left alone on the slope, devoid of any support. Fearful of being flanked, Rogers reluctantly ordered his troops to retire. In actuality, a spontaneous retreat was already underway regardless of Rogers actions. The veterans of the 5th Texas had already discerned that without reinforcements, they could no longer face the withering fire and continuous hurricane of lead and grape. As a result, most were were already back-stepping their way down the slope.[45]

With depleted ranks and battered bodies, the Texans commenced back-stepping down the slope, panting for breath, to the protection of the thick woods along the shoulder of Big Round Top. There they hoped to reorganize their lines yet again while enjoying a brief respite from the firestorm around the crest of Little Round Top. But they still endured heavy musket fire even as they rested and reformed. These premier shock troops of Lee's army of stellar and unstained combat reputation had received their own shock late that afternoon—for, try as they might, they had utterly failed at

43 Norton, *Army Letters*, 161; Nash, *History of Forty-Fourth Regiment*, 145; James R. Rice, "The Rebel Invasion of Pennsylvania: The Truth Regarding Some Important Historical Facts," *New York Times*, November 28, 1863; LaFantasie, *Twilight at Little Round Top*, 143-47.

44 Fletcher, *Rebel Private*, 80-81; Lasswell, *Rags and Hope*, 180; LaFantasie, *Twilight at Little Round Top*, 128.

45 *OR* 27, pt. 2, 413; Lasswell, *Rags and Hope*, 180-81; LaFantasie, *Twilight at Little Round Top*, 128-29; Braziza, *Adventures*, 48-49.

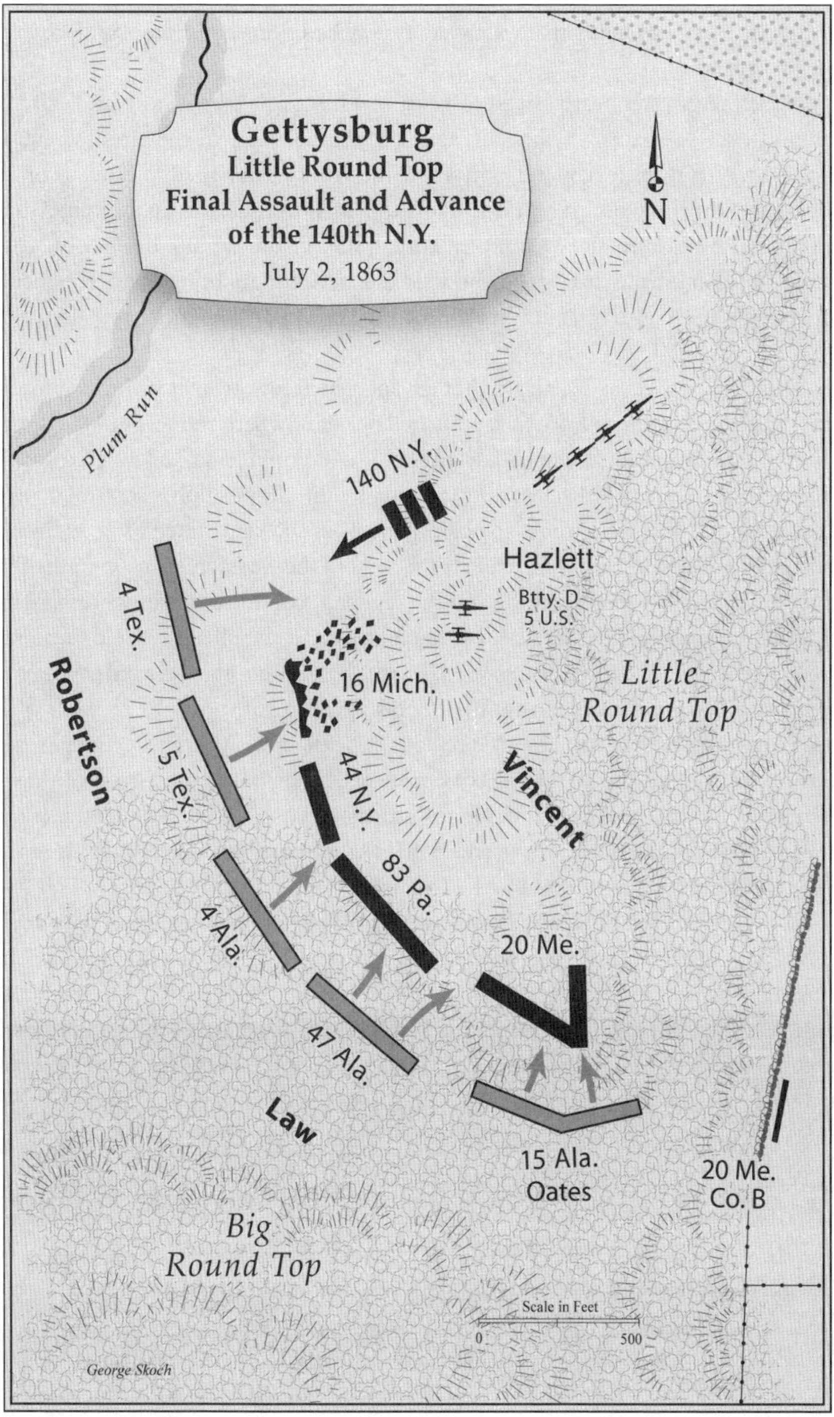
Gettysburg
Little Round Top
Final Assault and Advance
of the 140th N.Y.
July 2, 1863
N
Plum Run
140 N.Y.
Hazlett
Btty. D
5 U.S.
4 Tex.
Robertson
16 Mich.
Little
Round Top
5 Tex.
44 N.Y.
Vincent
83 Pa.
4 Ala.
20 Me.
47 Ala.
Law
15 Ala.
Oates
20 Me.
Co. B
Big
Round Top
Scale in Feet
0
500
George Skoch

driving the fortified enemy from the field as they had so many other occasions in the past two years.[46]

Nevertheless, this hearty breed of Texans "with rowdy dispositions and stubborn beyond belief" remained willing, if not enthusiastic, to give the dreaded hill yet another try. Off to their right, beyond where the 4th Alabama tried to catch its breath, they could hear the noise of battle as the 15th and 47th Alabama finally joined in the fight along the eastern slope of the exploding hill. In the waning day's light, as the setting sun behind them dimmed the field and reduced its brutal heat, the men of Robertson's and Law's brigades braced themselves for yet one more brutal effort to take Little Round Top.[47]

While the 5th Texas began another advance, bent low by enemy fire as if leaning into a hard rain, a courier from Law appeared out of nowhere and found Maj. Rogers. Saluting, he announced: "General Law presents his compliments, and says to hold this place at all hazards." Rogers, furious with the imposition, screamed back: "Compliments, hell! Who wants any compliments in such a damned place as this! Go back and ask General Law if he expects me to hold the world in check with the Fifth Texas Regiment!" Nonetheless, he and the regiment continued pushing forward into frightful punishment: its dead and wounded blanketed the hillside. "Cold, heat, rain, fatigue and danger are alike disregarded," Capt. Braziza wrote afterwards, "and even God himself is, for the time, forgotten." This advance got to within 25 yards of the Federal line, closer than the Texans' previous two attempts. With the regiment's color guard already obliterated, Sgt. Evans of Company F again rallied the men forward with the regimental flag, up a rough defile toward the exposed right flank of the enemy. With superhuman fortitude, these amazing Texans scrambled up through the rocks, closer and closer to the foreboding Federal lines.[48]

As this third assault hit the now formidable Federal defenses, its impact at first seemed no different from the previous two attempts to capture the coveted hill. Crippling volleys from the Federals behind the ledges slowed the Texans' steady progress. Oncoming Confederates again fell dead in massive heaps. However, Vincent's men noticed that the focus of this latest assault had shifted from the center of their line—the ledges defended by the 83rd Pennsylvania and the 44th New

46 LaFantasie, *Twilight at Little Round Top*, 128-29; Oates, *The War*, 214; Pfanz, *Gettysburg: Second Day*, 234-35.

47 OR 27, pt. 1, 628, pt. 2, 413; Lasswell, *Rags and Hope*, 180-81; Braziza, *Adventures*, 48-49; LaFantasie, *Twilight at Little Round Top*, 128-29; Oates, *The War*, 214.

48 Chilton, *Hood's Texas Brigade*, 342; Braziza, *Adventures*, 48-49; LaFantasie, *Twilight at Little Round Top*, 129. By this time, a veteran of the 4th Texas witnessed members of several regiments crowded around Rogers. Lasswell, *Rags and Hope*, 181.

York—to Vincent's much more vulnerable flanks. The 4th and 5th Texas, with the 48th Alabama, had swerved to the far right of the Union line, scrambling over rocks and bushes, relentlessly climbing the western slope of Little Round Top and fiercely striking the exposed flank of the 16th Michigan just where its line had been refused into a salient. Three refused Michigan companies faced north with their right resting at the foot of large rocks that formed the crest of a ridge. The 16th Michigan, already the smallest regiment in Vincent's brigade, had deployed its two largest companies as skirmishers to the line of defenders holding Devil's Den. Without these men and accounting for casualties, the remainder of the regiment numbered barely 150 men. These brave survivors clung desperately to their precarious hillside perch, determined to deny the high ground to the enemy.[49]

As Captain William T. Hill of Company D, a 5th Texas regimental staff officer, went down with a severe wound in the foot, his last image was of Maj. Rogers waving his sword over his head, "bravely leading the men to the battle." Lt. Campbell Wood of Company D, the regimental adjutant, also suffered a foot wound. Smither, W. R. Campbell, and J. M. Green quickly assisted him in mounting Law's horse to ride back down the slope. For a while, it appeared the Texans might achieve the impossible. Just above, they could see the Union lines begin to splinter and waver. The right of Vincent's line was crumbling. Through the thick smoke, it appeared the Federal troops holding the extreme right flank were beginning to fall back, breaking apart. The Texans had opened a crack in the Union line, and by exploiting it, "the Butternuts could sweep the Federals from the hill." They charged on, climbing with an iron will and saving their shots for the struggle which would occur on the crest above them in the event of a breakthrough. Amazingly, as these Lone Star State warriors willed themselves forward beyond all human endurance with their last reserves of courage and energy in the twilight, it appeared victory was finally within their grasp.[50]

The Texans had converged in mass without firing until they achieved the Union line, then engaged in hand-to-hand combat with the Michigan defenders, who soon started to fall back in disorder. They seemed to have gathered all their energies for this final assault. The colors were ordered back up the hill as Col. Welch, the color guard and a significant number of men quickly left the battle line for safer ground to the rear. Vincent, spotting the 16th Michigan's flag and its officers falling back, and the extreme

49 LaFantasie, *Twilight at Little Round Top*, 146-47; Chilton, *Hood's Texas Brigade*, 343; Discorfano, *They Saved the Union at Little Round Top*, 60-63; Sears, *Gettysburg*, 292.

50 *OR* 27, pt. 2, 396, 416; Chilton, *Hood's Texas Brigade*, 342-43; LaFantasie, *Twilight at Little Round Top*, 129-30, 133-34; Discorfano, *They Saved the Union at Little Round Top*, 58-60. For more on William Hill and Campbell Wood, see Appendix B, Volume 1.

right of his line crumbling, immediately rushed over to rally its remaining defenders. Once there he was immediately shot down with a mortal wound.[51]

Just when a Confederate breakthrough appeared assured, Federal reinforcements arrived: the 140th New York under Colonel Patrick H. O'Rorke from Weed's brigade of Ayres' division had been rushed forward at an angle up the east slope of Little Round Top in column of fours. O'Rorke drew his saber and yelled" Down this way, boys!" The column scrambled down the hill in disorder until it drew abreast of the 16th Michigan's right, less than 40 feet from the panting Texans. A Confederate ball soon killed O'Rorke, and his apparent shooter was found after the battle with 17 holes in his body. In a fierce exchange of fire, a significant number of Federals on the extreme right fell. However, the 500 fresh troops tipped the scales in the defenders' favor. "The Texans were within our lines for a few moments when the timely arrival of the One Hundred and Fortieth New York and their charge down the slope, caused the enemy to retire, and our line was re-established," Rice later reported.[52]

The fight was now being contested at close quarters. Company K of the 5th Texas worked to within less than 20 yards of the Federal line but could move no farther. Lieutenant James E. Cobb of Company F noted that the lines at that point were no more than "20 to 30 paces apart." It was a wonder, given the intensity of the fire, that

51 *OR* 27, pt. 1, 624, pt. 2, 396; LaFantasie, *Twilight at Little Round Top*, 129-30; William Harley Gandy, *A History of Montgomery County, Texas*, University of Houston 1952, accessed July 7, 2008, http://www.countygenweb.com/txmontgomery/gandy_a_history_of_montgomerycounty.htm; Sears, *Gettysburg*, 292; Randy Chadwick, "CSA General Hood's Texans & The 140th New York," The American Civil War: The Battle of Gettysburg, www.brotherswar.com/Gettysburg-2t.htm; Chilton, *Hood's Texas Brigade*, 342. Other veterans have disputed whether there was ever a clear potential for victory on that hill. Maj. W. M. Robbins, acting major of the 4th Alabama that day, confided 25 years later that "[w]e were very near victory several times, but I have concluded that God Almighty did not intend it. . . .We whipped the devil in his den, but Round Top ran up too much toward heaven, and we didn't seem to make quite as good progress in that direction." However, he believed they would have taken the hill had they not been "so fagged out by our long, forced march on that broiling July day, and, moreover . . . [having] to climb over the steep and ragged spur of Big Round Top before reaching the foot of Little Round Top." Belo, "The Battle of Gettysburg," *CV*, 8: 167, 168. Some Texans' accounts indicate their line was finally stopped 25 yards away from the enemy. Others claim some Texans managed to get within 10-15 yards. What is certain is that this last great surge of the two Texas regiments, along with the 4th Alabama, nearly crumpled the right flank of the Union lines on Little Round Top, which would have dramatically altered the day's outcome. Chilton, *Hood's Texas Brigade*, 342. Oliver Norton later found Welch and 40 or 50 men of the regiment well behind the lines. Welch claimed he had orders to pull back up the hill to a more defensible spot. Sears, *Gettysburg*, 292; Disconfano, *They Saved the Union at Little Round Top*, 58-60, 63-64.

52 Norton, *Strong Vincent*, 9, 11, 53 ; Lafantasie, *Twilight at Little Round Top*, 151-54; Norton, *Army Letters, 1861-1865*, 37 ; Pfanz, *Gettysburg: Second Day*, 226-28, 230-31. Weed's brigade came up following the 140th New York and extended the line to its base and held there until the end of the battle.

Lt. James E. Cobb
Alabama Dept. of Archives and History

anyone survived the barrage. The overwhelmed Texans soon had to fall back. Two twin brothers from Company G, W. C. and G. A. Jones, inseparable throughout their military service, had somehow worked their way into Company K's line. When a bullet hit one, his brother caught him, lowering his dead body gently to the ground. Before he stand up, however, he, too was shot and killed. The two remained together there. "This was a very affecting scene," wrote a witness, "—those two boys were twin brothers, so much alike that you could hardly tell them apart. They had both passed safely through all the previous battles unhurt—now they die together." Moments later, Frank Fitzgerald of Company H, whom Stevens had known "from the cradle," was shot dead right in front of his friend. In all, six men who had become separated from their own respective commands congregated where Stevens was standing and began firing, and "the entire six were left dead at . . . [his] feet" within minutes.[53]

Capt. Robert W. Hubert futilely called for his Company K to stand fast, but by then only three officers and eight enlisted men were left to respond. Stevens continued firing on the Federal line from behind a boulder, and even though so many of his comrades had fallen around him, he felt little fear from the Yankees. Rather, he worried about friendly fire from his fellow Confederates behind him. While he saw his comrades pulling out, he was certain they would soon return and waited for them. Meanwhile Yankees came up a gorge off to his rear. Suddenly, while he was still firing, a sword blade slapped him across the back and an order came "like a thunderstorm" for him to throw down his gun and behave himself, as he was now a prisoner.[54]

53 Cobb Diary, July 2, 1863, in SHC/UNC; Stevens, *Reminiscences*, 114-15; Scott, "Battle Flags of Hood's Texas Brigade," in Chilton, *Hood's Texas Brigade*, 353.

54 Stevens, *Reminiscences*, 114-15; Lasswell, *Rags and Hope*, 182; Cobb Diary, July 2, 1863, in SHC/UNC. See Michael A. Dreese, *Torn Families: Death and Kinship at the Battle of Gettysburg* (Jefferson, NC: McFarland Publishing Company, 2007), 179-80; Abner Doubleday, *Chancellorsville and Gettysburg*, (New York, 1882), 168. Yet another set of 5th Texas brothers also came to

After a fire fight lasting another few more minutes, a sizeable number of Texans raised their hands in surrender; the rest risked a shot in the back as they bounded down the slope to relative safety. Officers concluded that further attacks were futile, as their men were by then thoroughly exhausted, their ranks decimated, and the Federal position all but impregnable and being reinforced. Soon, many of these too were overwhelmed, dropped their arms and surrendered, or were shot while retreating.[55]

Darkness was now rapidly closing in on the combatants. The Texans had done all that could humanly be expected of them—in actuality more, and they knew it. One of them later lamented that "for the first time in its history, the Fifth Texas recoiled in the slaughter pen and yielded the field." Cobb reported that the regiment's left flank had finally been turned and compelled to hastily fall back, noting "I was captured upon the field." At someone's order, the regiments pulled back and reformed on Big Round Top's shoulder southeast of Devil's Den. Powell was so grievously wounded he had to be left behind. An eerie silence then descended, prompting Powell to raise his head to see what was happening. He observed Sgt. Ross of Company H walking down the slope, stopping, and leisurely picking up a ramrod leaning against a rock, then continuing into the cover of the woods. Several minutes thereafter, Union soldiers appeared, searching for wounded. By then it was almost dark.[56]

While the Texans were contending with Vincent's right, the 15th and 47th Alabama moved along the foot of Big Round Top to the right of the 4th Alabama, came into line, and advanced against the 20th Maine on Vincent's extreme left. Soon there was desperate fighting on the slope as the Alabamians charged repeatedly. Colonel Joshua Chamberlain, the 20th Maine's commander, met this movement by

---

grief that day. Sergeant Theophilus Meece and his brothers, Private J. P. Meece and Calvin Wood Meece were all wounded and captured in the battle. Theophilus cared for his badly wounded brother J. P., who died a few days later. Calvin ultimately died of his wounds at Ft. Lookout, Maryland on June 15, 1864. Dreese, *Torn Families*, 168; Yeary, *Reminiscences of the Boys in Gray*, 2:510. For more on Hubert and Meece, see Appendix B, Volume 1.

55 Samuel R. Hazen, "'Fighting the Good Fight,': the 140th New York and Its Work on Little Round Top," *National Tribune*, September 13, 1894; Chilton, *Hood's Texas Brigade*, 342; Reichardt, *Forever the Cause*, 68. One soldier in the 140th New York shared his impressions with a member of Hood's Brigade, recalling that as they "reached the apex we saw the Texans coming up. It was a hard climb for you, but you Johnnies were coming fast. Then our officers ordered a bayonet charge, leading the charge themselves with unsheathed swords. You kept a-coming, and soon we had it hard and heavy, hand-to-hand clubbing and bayoneting. You didn't get up there, but you were mighty close to it and made a desperate fight." *New York Times*, July 3, 1913.

56 Mark Smither to Elizabeth Smither, July 29, 1863, in SHSU; Cobb Diary, July 2, 1863, in SHC/UNC; Powell, *Recollections*, 16; Reichardt, *Forever the Cause*, 70; James G. Scott, "The Texans at Gettysburg," Galveston *Daily News*, July 1913.

putting the right wing of the regiment into a single rank, and then bent back his five left companies at a right angle. With only 308 men, the 20th Maine was outnumbered three to one. After 130 men had fallen, and every remaining man had gone through the allotted 60 rounds carried into the fight, the situation called for desperate measures. Chamberlain ordered his men to fix bayonets and charge down the hill, executing a right wheel with the left of the line moving first and closing with the Confederates. Oates' men were forced to retreat, and a considerable number of them surrendered to avoid being shot from behind. The 20th Maine's charge ended the fighting in Vincent's front that evening, ensuring that Little Round Top, the key to Meade's line on Cemetery Ridge, remained safely in his hands.[57]

"The angel of death had done fearsome work at Little Round Top that day," as night finally descended into the valley. Confederate sharpshooters still occupied the rocks at Devil's Den and the woods near Big Round Top. Meanwhile, the Federals had their hands full preparing breastworks, caring for the wounded, and burying the dead. Bodies were everywhere. Rufus Felder wrote home that: "Our regiment suffered severely having charged up within thirty yards of the enemy four successful times & having to fall back as many times two hundred yards from the enemy's works." Following the withdrawal, the respective lines remained quite close, while the chaplains were busy caring for the wounded and dying in the rear. "White-winged peace didn't roost at Little Round Top that night!" Val Giles noted. "There was not a man there that cared a snap for the golden rule, or that could have remembered one line of the Lord's Prayer. Both sides were whipped, and all were furious about it."[58]

Powell was later placed with a severely wounded Lt. White of the 2nd Minnesota, still clutching the colors he had refused to relinquish to the Confederates that day. White told Powell of a Texas soldier he killed fighting for the flag. Noting the overall bravery of the Texans, he recalled that "[e]very bullet from the Texans did its execution." Powell told Capt. Amos M. Judson of the 83rd Pennsylvania: "you have peppered us pretty badly . . . but you'll get the worst of it before it's over!" Eventually,

57 *OR* 27, pt.1, 624; Norton, *Attack and Defense*, 260-61; Melcher, "The 20th Maine at Little Round Top," in *B&L*, 3:315; Longacre, *Joshua Chamberlain*, 134-38; Mark Nesbitt, *Through Blood and Fire: Selected Civil War Papers of Major General Joshua Chamberlain* (Mechanicsburg, PA, 1996), 81-83, 91, 98-99. The 15th Alabama regiment contained 644 men and 42 officers at the time. The 47th Alabama had 200 men, but 50 were detailed to capture the Union wagon train. "Oates claimed to have fired not only into the front of one wing of the 20th Maine . . . [but also] on the rear of the 83rd Pennsylvania and 44th New York. Present day historians have upheld his contention." Longacre, *Joshua Chamberlain*, 137-38; Melcher, "The 20th Maine at Little Round Top," *B&L*, 3:315.

58 Chicoine, *Confederates of Chappel Hill*, 93; Lasswell, *Rags and Hope*, 183; LaFantasie, *Twilight at Little Round Top*, 200-01.

a Union surgeon treated Powell for his wounds. The doctor told him he would soon succumb from his injury, but he defied the odds and recovered, and spent the next 18 months as a prisoner of war.[59]

The regiment had not moved far after falling back a third time, reforming east of Devil's Den. One Texan recalled that the men of the 5th Texas were lying down, taking advantage of the available cover, with only Maj. Rogers and one other officer standing. The Texans built a wall for protection against counterattack on the line across the west slope of Round Top about halfway up from Plum Run. The Texans clung to a perpendicular wall of gray limestone where they laid that night with "the devil in command of both armies." The thoroughly shot up and exhausted 4th and 5th Texas rested on their arms that evening. One Texas recruit spent an uncomfortable night, thinking about the "slaughter of our men." He had requested before the battle that his friends safeguard his Bible and a treasured tin cup keepsake in the event that he was to fall. After retrieving those items after the fight, John West wrote his wife that he had "started from Texas to find a fight, and I have made a success of it." As darkness finally descended, Lt. Pugh Fuller of Company A shared picket duty with J. M. Polk, an old friend from the 1st Texas. And although medical attention and even water arrived slowly for the men that night, crushing fatigue brought most quickly to sleep.[60]

Devil's Den was "a dismal mausoleum of glory-crowned Texas heroes," where "the sunburst veteran from the verdure clad steppes of the Brazos and the pale faced boys from the frozen lakes of Minnesota make one common funeral pile." Fletcher reflected on his unfortunate wounded comrades suffering that night in the open. He confessed to being "on the dark side of life's thoughts . . . in a depressed condition." Another Texan wrote that "Alexander Dumas says the devil gets in a man seven times a day, and if the average is not over seven times, he is almost a saint. At Gettysburg that night, it was about seven devils to each man." Curses mingled in the air with the wails and groans of the wounded, while sporadic musket fire broke the occasional silence. The darkness and its hideous sounds simply aggravated the bedeviling

59 Chilton, Hood's *Texas Brigade*, 342; Reichardt, *Forever the Cause*, 71; Powell, *Recollections of a Texas Colonel*, 16, 48; Judson, *History of the Eighty-Third Regiment, Pennsylvania Volunteers*, 70. Powell was officially taken prisoner by Capt. David R. Rodgers of the 83rd Pennsylvania, who immediately confiscated his field glasses and Colt revolver. Nearly 29 years later, Rodgers returned the revolver to Powell, with the dates of his capture and the return of the pistol engraved on its handle grips. Reichardt, *Forever the Cause*, 72-74; LaFantasie, *Twilight on Little Round Top*, 200-201.

60 West, *Texan In Search of a Fight*, 88; Fletcher, *Rebel Private*, 82-83; LaFantasie, T*wilight at Little Round Top*, 203, 209; Pfanz, *Gettysburg: Second Day*, 427-28.

uncertainty and fear in the soldiers who against all their instincts had to remain on the wretched battlefield.[61]

Most of the fallen Texans lay in "no-man's land," out of reach of their comrades who were forced to listen to their groans and pleas for help throughout this night. "I could see men lying around in every direction and in all attitudes," Powell recalled. Twilight faded into night before "the victors came to gather the spoils and take charge of the wounded," and "the slightly wounded were the most earnest in their appeals to be left to die where they lay, insist[ing] that it was wanton cruelty to subject dying men to the unnecessary torture of removal and so on. They [actually] hoped to be able to escape under cover of darkness and be ready to fight another day."[62]

As the cries of the gravely wounded grew fainter, a Texan noted the men knew "their lives were fast passing away." Throughout the long night, the Federals sent out burial parties to bury their own dead and retrieve the wounded. Often, captured Confederate prisoners were impressed for that dangerous work, where snipers on both sides fired into the darkness, without knowing what their projectiles would hit. The Confederate dead were left where they lay. Overhead, the moonlight flickered through the trees and cast an eerie light on the gray rocks of Little Round Top. It was a long night. "Stern duty," a Texan remarked, "bids the survivor to forget," although forgetting friends was never altogether possible.[63]

The seriously wounded commander of the 5th Texas still lay on the field, conscious but unable to move. His men believed him dead. Pvt. William H. Lewis of Company D related in a letter to his mother that "Colonel Powell was left on the field as we thought dead or mortally wounded." However, Powell was considerably stronger than any of his men realized. When Union troops found him, he was lying on the western slope of the hill surrounded by many of the regiment's wounded and dead.[64]

Among the first Federal soldiers to come upon Powell was none other than Joshua Chamberlain, who recalled:

61 *OR* 27, pt. 2, 409; Lasswell, *Rags and Hope*, 183; Chilton, *Hood's Texas Brigade*, 342; Fletcher, *Rebel Private*, 82; LaFantasie, *Twilight at Little Round Top*, 203, 209-10; West, *Texan in Search of a Fight*, 86, 88, 96; Chilton, *Hood's Texas Brigade*, 342.

62 LaFantasie, *Twilight at Little Round Top*, 200-01; Powell, *Recollections of a Texas Colonel*, 16-17.

63 LaFantasie, *Twilight at Little Round Top*, 216-17; Brown, "On Gettysburg Field," Philadelphia *Weekly Times*, May 26, 1883: Braziza, *Adventures*, 49.

64 Reichardt, *Forever the Cause*, 71; Powell, *Recollections of a Texas Colonel*, 16; LaFantasie, *Twilight at Little Round Top*, 200; Judson, *History of the Eighty-Third Regiment, Pennsylvania Volunteers*, 70; Discorfano, *They Saved the Union at Little Round Top*, 81.

> We were taking prisoners by scores—more than we could hold or send to the rear, so that many made [a] final escape up Great Round Top. Half way down to the throat of the vale I came upon Colonel Powell of the . . . [5th Texas] a man of courtly bearing, who was badly wounded. I sent him to the Eighty-third Pennsylvania, nearest to us and better able to take care of him than we were.

Powell was soon transported with other wounded from the rocks where he had fallen and spread on the ground in an open field, where they all lay "forlorn, wretched, ragged and battered." Then it began to rain; Powell and his fellow prisoners shivered without blankets or other protection, undoubtedly many suffering from severe shock.[65]

Most of the wounded Texas prisoners were carried from the immediate Federal rear to the 102-acre Weikert farm at Little Round Top's eastern base, converted into a large field hospital for the V Corps. Corporal James R. Campbell of the 140th New York from Rochester, New York, visited the field hospital that evening to speak with his boyhood friend Benjamin Simpson of the regiment's Company A. Simpson told to Campbell that his New York regiment had been "the only Regiment that ever defeated them." Simpson went on to say that he hoped that "our Regiment may never meet his again, but that if it does . . . [he would] turn over and fire the other way."[66]

Confederate casualties on this day were staggering, especially for the Texas Brigade. Next to Tige Anderson's, it suffered the highest loss in Hood's whole Division. Of the brigade's 1,729 effectives entering the battle that afternoon, 602 were killed, wounded, or missing, 35 percent of the force. Robertson, along with three of his regimental commanders, and two of *their* successors were wounded, one, B. F. Carter, of the 4th Texas, fatally. The 5th Texas suffered more severely than any regiment in the brigade, attacking that afternoon with 409 men and losing 211 during the battle, nearly *52 percent.* Fifty-five men were killed or mortally wounded, and another one soon thereafter. At least 45 men returning to the regiment's lines were seriously wounded, and 112 had been captured. Thus, 168 of the regiment were gone from the ranks, almost none of whom would be seen again before the war's end. Several company commanders were killed or wounded; every officer of Company K

65 LaFantasie, *Twilight at Little Round Top*, 200-01; Powell, *Recollections of a Texas Colonel*, 16-17; Reichardt, *Forever the Cause*, 71; Powell, *Recollections of a Texas Colonel*, 16; Judson, *History of the Eighty-Third Regiment, Pennsylvania Volunteers*, 70; Discorfano, *They Saved the Union at Little Round Top*, 81.

66 Barziza, *Adventures*, 49; Brown, "On Gettysburg Field"; Reichardt, *Forever the Cause*, 72-73. Simpson was an original member of Company A, joining at Galveston in 1861. Powell, *Recollections*, 49-50n14; Simpson, *Compendium*, 180.

had been taken prisoner. Joe Joskins' company entered the battle with 27 men, and returned to Virginia with but five! When Joskins rejoined his company following the battle, only one of his six messmates were left. "Many of my intimate friends found a resting place upon the soil of Pennsylvania," he lamented. Smither reported that Company D went into the fight with 50 men and lost 32. He later wrote home that his company "was ahead as usual, it is a given up fact that it is the best fighting the best looking and more gentlemen in it than any other company in the Regt." It was fair to say, another veteran observed, that "the Brigade never really recovered from the slaughter at Gettysburg."[67]

Both sides exhibited instances of compassion during the bloody battle. In the bitter fighting on the rock and tree studded slope of Little Round Top, Private John H. Roberts of Company E was in the advance pressing the Federals up toward the summit. Reinforced by fresh troops, and protected by rock barriers, the Federals turned on their tormentors, pouring a horrific fire into the Texans as they struggled mightily to gain the crest. Roberts, both legs shattered by the massive fire, fell helpless just a short distance in front of the Union barricade. Several Federal soldiers ventured out into the deadly fire wrought by both sides, crawling from their relatively safe position, and piled a protective wall of stones around Roberts' broken body, no doubt saving his life.[68]

Confronted with the reality of the day's bloodletting, some of the regiment's common soldiery grappled to understand it. Fletcher experienced deepening discouragement as the night wore on. In his estimation, "it looked as though our officers were blind." Why had they not attempted to outflank the Union left? "Why were we fighting an impregnable position?—[w]as it ignorance? I guess so. It was a very unfortunate condition for the right of an army with true and tried men being shot

67 *OR* 27, pt. 2, 339-40, 404-405; Joskins, "A Sketch of Hood's Texas Brigade," 121-26; Mark Smither to Elizabeth Smither, July 29, 1863, in SHSU; Chicoine, *Confederates of Chappel Hill*, 94; Simpson, *Lee's Grenadier Guard*, 286; Robertson, *Touched With Valor*, 75-76, 92-93. While the casualty rate of the 5th Texas was shockingly high, the 11th Georgia went into battle with 310 men, and came out with only 109, suffering a casualty rate close to 65 percent. The 5th Texas suffered grievously. At the commencement of the campaign, it consisted of 409 officers and men. Smither placed the 5th Texas casualties at 215 out of 342. Mark Smither to Elizabeth Smither, July 29, 1863 in SHSU. The Texas Brigade casualties were are follows: 87 killed, 329 wounded, 416 total. Initial reports show considerably fewer casualty figures. Later numbers reflect more accurate POW counts and those soldiers who soon died of their wounds. See LaFantasie, *Twilight on Little Round Top*, 210; Reichardt, *Forever the Cause*, 70; Robertson, *Touched With Valor*, 92-93; Coco, *Reflections of a Texas Colonel*, 4-5, 43; Simpson, *Compendium*, 535.

68 Byran *Eagle*, June 27, 1925; Calvert *Picayune*, June 27, 1912; Simpson, *Lee's Grenadier Guard*, 286; John H. Roberts, April 28, 1915, *Texas Confederate Collection*, Haley Memorial Library and Museum Collection, Midland, TX. For more on John Roberts, see Appendix B, Volume 1.

down like dogs." Fletcher occupied a rock pile on the extreme right of the Federal outpost, where he felt relatively safe as the night wore on as long as he avoided raising his head. It was, however, far from a heartening place to be, after that bloody day. Another Texan later wrote that, "[a]t Gettysburg we suffered defeat, bloody, terrible and disastrous defeat." And another vented that even as a private, "I could see it in this one. Our brigade as I have been told, was ordered to fall back, but had we been supported at the right time we could have captured or deposed of their line of battle, and would have gained the day at Gettysburg."[69]

Robertson later reported that the day's fight had been among the "[h]ardest fought battle of the war in which I have been engaged, all, both officers and men, as far as my observation extended, fully sustained the high character they have heretofore made." He spoke with immense pride and sadness that "the Fourth and Fifth Texas, under the command of Maj. J. B. Bane and Capt. J. C. Rogers, continued to hold the ground of their original line, leaving the space over which they had made their successive charges strewn with their wounded and dead comrades." General Longstreet himself later wrote that the action of Hood's and McLaws' divisions constituted "the best three hours of fighting ever done by any troops on any battlefield."[70]

During the night, Robertson took advantage of darkness and the relative lull in fighting to unite his command. Around 1:00 a.m. on July 3, the 1st Texas and 3rd Arkansas were ordered"[i]n silence, by the right flank forward" to move around Benning's Brigade, which had filled the gap between them and the 4th and 5th Texas. After the former two regiments wound around and over huge boulders in the darkness, the brigade was again reunited in a semicircle around Big Round Top, midway between its base and apex. Here the men closed ranks and adjusted as much as the darkness permitted, in the area where they had done "their bloody work the day before." At daybreak, the unified brigade occupied a sector along Plum Run in between Devil's Den and Big Round Top along the main Confederate defensive lines. The men could see and hear little of the helpless wounded at this point, as they lay now

69 LaFantasie, *Twilight at Little Round Top*, 210-11; Fletcher, *Rebel Private*, 81-82, 84; Powell, *Recollections*,17-18; Smith, "Reminiscences," 38; Joskins, "A Sketch of Hood's Texas Brigade," 121-26; Mark Smither to Elizabeth Smither, July 29, 1863 in SHSU; Yeary, *Reminiscences of the Boys in Gray*, 2:472. To fight off sleep from the sheer exhaustion under which he was laboring, Fletcher finally applied tobacco juice to his eyes, a remedy that worked "so long as the pain is greater than the desire to sleep."

70 *OR* 27, pt. 2, 406; Chadwick, "CSA General Hood's Texans & The 140th New York"; Polk, "Memories of the Lost Cause," 17; Pfanz, *Gettysburg: Second Day*, 425; James Longstreet, "Lee in Pennsylvania," in *Annals of the War* (Philadelphia, PA, 1879), 440.

well to the front and out of sight. The regiment stayed in this position throughout the day of July 3.[71]

The men spent the morning and early afternoon of July 3 dodging a thick hail of bullets from Federal sharpshooters who succeeded in wounding a number of the regiment's members. Throughout the day, the Texans held their ground, making unsuccessful sallies and lightly skirmishing. One veteran remarked years later: "[w]e Alabamians and our Texas comrades lay on the western slope of Big Round Top all day July 3, and the breastwork of stone which the boys with their own hands threw up there is standing yet [25 years later]."[72]

At 1:07 p.m., a massive artillery barrage opened along the entire line "and such thundering and crashing and roaring surely was never heard." Truly, "Milton's account of the great battle between the combined forces of good and evil, which originated in the same question of secession, gives some faint idea of this artillery duel." All along the line a "sulphuric kind of odor filled the air, caused by the great amount of black powder burned in the ongoing battle. Maybe it was the fumes of old Satan as he pulled out that morning leaving the row to be settled by Lee and Meade." Although the brigade was relatively safe during this particular artillery barrage, the infantry just above them still kept things unpleasant. Any man who raised his head risked being instantly killed.[73]

In reserve, the regiment, with the rest of Hood's entire division, witnessed the charge of Pickett's men into the center of the massed enemy. Powell likewise listened to the fighting on July 3 from the Weikert house as a prisoner. "[H]ope rose high as Pickett's men, like the rush of many waters, lashed with storming fury the enemy's solid and bristling front. Then despair expelled hope when they receded, broken and bleeding. We were grief-stricken, sick at heart and wearied with the tumultuous emotions of the battle's storm." He noted afterward that "[t]his was a gloomy night and we wished we were lying in the valley with our dead."[74]

That same afternoon, during the Pickett-Pettigrew-Trimble charge, Federal cavalry under Brig. Gen. Elon J. Farnsworth of Brig. Gen. Judson Kilpatrick's division

71 *OR* 27, pt. 2, 406; Longstreet, *Manassas to Appomattox*, 316; Chilton, *Hood's Texas Brigade*, 340; Sims, "Recollections," 12; Collier, *They'll Do To Tie To*, 145; Leon County Genealogy Society, *Leon County*, 56-57; Fletcher, *Rebel Private*, 80-81.

72 Belo, "Gettysburg," *CV*, 8:167-68; West, *Texan in Search of a Fight*, 95; LaFantasie, *Twilight at Little Round Top*, 235, 238.

73 Lasswell, *Rags and Hope*, 183-85; West, *Texan in Search of a Fight*, 95, 97; Sears, *Gettysburg*, 396; Coddington, *The Gettysburg Campaign*, 493; Polley, *Hood's Texas Brigade*, 194-95.

74 Powell, *Recollections of a Texas Colonel*, 19-20; Reichardt, *Forever the Cause*, 73; Todd, *A Sketch of History*, 16.

attempted to outflank the Confederates. Law accordingly withdrew the 1st Texas from the division's main line and placed it in position on the extreme right behind a stone fence, midway between the Round Tops and Emmitsburg Road. The 1st Texas repulsed the initial charge, but eventually the Union horsemen were able to move around the Texans' left flank. Col. Oates quickly called for the 4th Alabama to close the gap, and they did so.[75]

Having been attended to himself, Powell thought continually of the unfortunate Confederates still lying on the battle field on the night of July 3. "Many died during this interval who might have been saved. I knew one man who slew himself rather than endure further torture and suffering." Late in the evening, the regiment, with the rest of Hood's Division, withdrew three-fourths of a mile from their forward position to a line near the Emmitsburg Road on the crest of a ridge near where it began the advance the previous day. There, the men were finally allowed to "unsaddle," stripping off their accoutrements and spreading their blankets, according to Fletcher. The brutal battle of Gettysburg was finally over.[76]

Rapid, continuous volleys all along the Federal line heralded dawn on July 4. The 5th Texas had orders to hold its position at all costs. Considerable firing occurred between the respective skirmish lines. Rations that day were distributed only once, toward nightfall. Fortunately, "a majority of the men had their haversacks pretty well filled with good old Pennsylvania grub when we went into the fight," one of the men confessed. Late that afternoon and evening, Lee began withdrawing to the southwest, toward the Potomac and Virginia. As night fell that 4th of July, the Confederates loaded the wounded into wagons and began their retreat toward the Potomac.[77]

The thousands of wounded men and a majority of the supply trains proceeded on a safer road west of South Mountain to Hagerstown, by way of Cashtown and Chambersburg. Guarded by Brig. Gen. John D. Imboden's cavalry brigade of some 2,000 troopers, the column stretched for 17 miles. The main body of the army, plus 4,000 prisoners, took the road to Hagerstown via Fairfield. Longstreet's I Corps was in the center of this line of march behind Hill's Corps. As General Lee passed down the line, the men began to wave their hats and cheer him, a Texan recalled. "He simply

75 Law, "Struggle for Round Top," *B&L*, 3:327, 330; Alexander, *Military Memoirs*, 434; "Official Reports of the Battle of Gettysburg," 194; H. C. Parsons, "Farnsworth's Charge and Death at Gettysburg," *B&L*, 3:307; W. T. White, "First Texas Regiment at Gettysburg," *CV*, 30:185; West, *Texan in Search of a Fight*, 94-96.

76 *OR* 27, pt. 2, 406, 411; Law, "Struggle for Round Top," in *B&L*, 3: 330 "Official Reports of the Battle of Gettysburg," 194; Reichardt, *Forever the Cause*, 73; Jeffry D. Wert, *Gettysburg: Day Three* (New York 2001), 252-53; Fletcher, *Rebel Private*, 86-87.

77 *OR* 27, pt. 2, 309-311; Lasswell, *Rags and Hope*, 188.

raised his hat, rode along, and said nothing. . . . We all wanted to show to him that we had not lost confidence in him, and he understood it that way."[78]

Heavy rains, high winds, and the deeply rutted roads slowed the regiment's march considerably. The men continued to struggle through the muck and mire in the early hours of July 5. While on the march that same day, still only a few miles from Gettysburg, the men learned of the fall of Vicksburg. The news caused them to become quite "gloomy and dispirited," magnifying the depths of their failure at Gettysburg, "for every intelligent soldier knew that these two events would give encouragement to the North and cast gloom over the South." Indeed, some felt these losses might well be "the handwriting on the wall" for their cause.[79]

The regiment continued its southwestward march through Maryland, reaching Hagerstown in late afternoon of July 6, where it bivouacked southeast of town on the Sharpsburg Road. Here it remained until July 10 to "clean up and rest," a desperately needed rest from fighting, marching, or standing on alert, as had been the case the last six days—a period in which the men of the regiment had little to eat, almost no rest, and had been thoroughly soaked from a heavy rainstorm that hit Gettysburg on July 4. During the first six days of July, most of the men never even shed their accoutrements. The rocks and heavy brush had been extremely hard on uniforms and shoes. Fletcher lamented the shoddy condition of his old shoes and clothes. "My pants were frazzled and split up to the knees, so I cut them off just below the knees, and thought if I looked like I felt, I was a fright. Short sleeves worn to near point of the elbow, no socks or drawers, and knee breeches."[80]

Soon Fletcher lost the sole on one shoe, which he discarded completely and continued on with one bare foot. While it was only 40 miles to Falling Waters, where Longstreet's Corps was to cross the Potomac, the army took 10 days to complete the trek. For many veterans, this indicated the army not as badly whipped as many may have thought. William A. Nabours noted the regiment received no "special trouble" from the Federals during the march. While Meade had days to reorganize his army and follow up his great "victory," the Federals did not initiate a serious confrontation until

78 *OR* 27, pt. 2, 309, 311, pt. 2361; John D. Imboden, "The Confederate Retreat From Gettysburg," in *B&L*, 3:422-28; Simpson, *Lee's Grenadier Guard*, 286-87; J. M. Polk, *Memories of the Lost Cause; Stories and Adventures of a Confederate Soldier in General R. E. Lee's Army, 1861 to 1865; and Ten Years in South America, Its Resources, Trade and Commerce, and Business Intercourse With Other Countries* (Austin, TX, 1905), 17-18; Lasswell, *Rags and Hope*, 188.

79 *OR* 27, pt. 2, 361; Lasswell *Rags and Hope*, 188; Polley, *Hood's Texas Brigade*, 196. That same day, July 5, Surgeon William P. Powell of the regiment was captured at Cashtown while taking care of the wounded. Simpson, *Compendium*, 169.

80 Fletcher, *Rebel Private*, 87; West, *A Texan in Search of a Fight*, 87-88.

all of Lee's army, except two of Longstreet's brigades, had crossed back into Virginia. Lieutenant Benjamin I. Franklin of Company I, absent due to his wounds from Second Manassas, finally caught up with his comrades in Hagerstown on July 9. He reported to his wife that the weather was hot and the marching exhausting. He was emphatic that the army "was not whipped and the Yankeys were afraid to attack us."[81]

While the regiment was resting at Hagerstown, Lee and his staff had reached the Potomac on July 7, finding it badly swollen from the recent rains. Although Meade had stalked Lee's columns, it had been at a respectful distance. Unable to cross the surging river, the army formed a defensive crescent from above Williamsport to below Falling Waters, guarding its the two potential crossings. By the evening of July 10, all three corps were positioned on this defensive perimeter, with Hill in the center, Ewell and Stuart's cavalry on the left, and Longstreet the right, behind Marsh Creek, south of Falling Waters. The pontoon bridge at Falling Waters, partially destroyed by rising water, had to be reconstructed. Thanks to Meade's cautiousness, the army remained safely in this somewhat precarious position until the waters subsided and the pontoon bridge could be rebuilt. By July 13, a bridge once again spanned the river and the army commenced crossing to the south side that evening. By 1:00 p.m. the next day, Lee's entire army had crossed safely back into Virginia.[82]

The regiment itself had departed Hagerstown on July 10 to its defensive position on the north bank of the Potomac. On its way, the troops passed through Funkstown, crossed Antietam and Marsh Creeks, and arrived near Falling Waters that same evening. There the men fortified their position on July 11, remaining there until the night of July 13. It rained all evening on July 13-14 as they moved slowly through the dense night toward the bridge. The downpour made the road next to impassible, and it was dawn therefore before the Texans finally reached the stream. By then, the rain had ceased, and a heavy mist hung over the valley on the Maryland side of Falling Waters.[83]

The slowly pursuing Federals finally reached the Confederate front on July 12 between Williamsport and Falling Waters. Federal cavalry had been shadowing the Texans, and on the morning of July 14, as Longstreet began his crossing, their artillery began to roar from the Maryland hills, two miles away. Consequently, Brig. Gen.

81 Nabours, "Active Service of a Texas Command," 70; Lasswell, *Rags and Hope*, 188-89; Benjamin Franklin to Mary Franklin, August 8, 1863, Benjamin I. Franklin Papers, 1863-1865, Peace Civil War Collection, Navarro College, Corsicana, TX, hereinafter NC. For more on Benjamin Franklin, see Appendix B, Volume 1.

82 *OR* 27, pt. 2, 309-11; Mark Smither to Elizabeth Smither, July 29, 1863, in SHSU. The supply and hospital columns had reached the river late on July 6 without serious loss.

83 Lasswell, Rags and Hope, 189-90; Sims, "Recollections," 16; *OR* 27, pt. 2, 310; Mark Smither to Elizabeth Smither, July 29, 1863, in SHSU.

James Pettigrew about-faced his brigade and "stood like a stone wall" between the Federals and Longstreet's corps, as a long stream of regiments continued to cross the rickety old pontoon bridge. Lee sat astride Traveler on the Maryland side anxiously scanning his rear as he spoke in a low, pleasant tone, reminding the men to fall into two ranks and keep on the middle of the bridge. As the brigade passed him, "each soldier bared his head. There was no salute, no cheer and no word was spoken as the men marched silently by." The 4th Texas band struck up "Dixie," enlivening the Texans' steps onto the pontoon bridge. This heavy tramp of the men caused the bridge to vibrate so violently the men "were all on the verge of shipwreck, until the officers began to yell 'Halt! Halt! Go slow! Break the step!'" During the crossing, some of men laid down to rest and got temporarily lost, and were ultimately captured by Federal cavalry before they could locate their comrades. Once the Texans were across the Potomac, the bridge was quickly dismantled.[84]

Back on Virginia soil, the regiment would never again cross the Potomac during the war. The great Northern invasion was over, with Lee's army badly damaged both by the staggering loss of men and a concomitant loss of morale. The two major invasions of 1862 and 1863 had ultimately ended in failure, and the grand plan for winning the war stymied. Henceforth, the Confederates would be fighting on their own land, under adverse conditions, in a desperate effort to avoid ultimate defeat. "Our invasion of the North had failed, and all hope of the foreign recognition we needed so desperately was gone. But we plodded on in rags and hope, believing we were right and would finally win," a Texan sadly noted.[85]

The next day, the army marched through Martinsburg to Bunker Hill and camped there for several days. Badly needed clothing and shoes awaited the men when the regiment arrived and made camp. Joe Joskins finally caught up with his company after recuperating from Second Manassas wounds at Frederick Hall in Louisa County, Virginia. He arrived just in time to view the Texans marching by looking "dirty, ragged, barefooted and dispirited." While the regiment recuperated, a foraging party located a cache of whiskey hidden in a straw stack. "Word of this discovery spread rapidly through the camp, and soon every pot, canteen and kettle was reportedly filled with the liquid, so much so that some of the men were going around offering a canteen

84 *OR* 27, pt. 2, 406-10; Tacitus Clay to Bettie Clay, July 16, 1863, in MSU; Lasswell, *Rags and Hope*, 190-91; Sorrell, *Confederate Staff Officer*, 165-66. Brigadier General James Pettigrew was wounded in the Pickett-Pettigrew-Trimble Charge, but continued leading his men during the retreat. He was directing his troops in a skirmish with Union cavalry at Falling Waters, Maryland, when he was shot at close range. He died three days later at Bunker Hill.

85 *OR* 27, pt. 2, 310, 361; Alexander, *Military Memoirs*, 439; Sorrel, *Confederate Staff Officer*, 165; Sims, "Recollections," 16; Simpson, *Lee's Grenadier Guard*, 289; Lasswell, *Rags and Hope*, 190-91.

of liquor for a 'drink of water'." Texans were lying drunk all along the side of the road; but, as Joskins pointed out, who could blame them? True, they had been "defeated and dispirited by the defeat at Gettysburg." However, the primary reason for the low morale was the "news since—that on the 4th of July 63 'Vicksburg' had fallen and with it fell the hope and spirits of many brave men—[if] *only* for awhile."[86]

While recuperating at Bunker Hill, Capt. Clay wrote his wife of the 5th's arrival there. He had visited Lt. C. A. Graham of his company, who was at a private home in Brucetown dying of his Gettysburg wounds. Before the regiment left the area, the Yankees captured Madison Ross of Company H on July 17.[87]

The Texans left Bunker Hill on July 20 and subsequently moved down the Blue Ridge Mountains by way of Chester's Gap. Longstreet's orders were to block the middle passes into the Shenandoah—Manassas Gap and Chester Gap. On the difficult march from Bunker Hill, men fainted from the heat along the way every 200-300 yards. Joskins, unable to keep up with his company due to his wound, was left to fend for himself. Passing Millwood early on July 21, the 5th Texas continued south through Stone Bridge and Cedarville. The men had to wade through waist deep waters of the Shenandoah and North Fork rivers in current so swift they had to link arms five or six together for support. A number of men who tried to venture across unaided got seized by the current and had to be rescued by their comrades.[88]

The regiment bivouacked near Chester Gap that evening, where its scouts had a brush with Federal cavalry the next day in a gap to the east side of the mountain. Once on the other side, its men marched through Sandy Rock as far as Washington, Virginia, and camped there the evening of July 23rd. They moved on to Culpeper Court House on July 24 and remained there for a week before marching to Fredericksburg. The brave remnants of the 5th Texas, though shaken to its core by the horrific bloodletting at Gettysburg, would subsequently recover, put their memories of the terror that July 2 wrought behind them, and live on to fight and gain glory yet again and again.[89]

86 *OR* 27, pt. 2, 406-407; Joskins, "A Sketch of Hood's Texas Brigade," 128-29. Joskins was shot in the leg at Second Manassas and taken to Warrenton. On October 9, 1862, he was furloughed to Texas until April 6, 1863, after which he rejoined the regiment. However, his wound worsened, and he was again given a 60-day furlough to Frederick Hall. He thus missed Gettysburg altogether. Joskins, "A Sketch of Hood's Texas Brigade," 110-20.

87 Tacitus Clay to Bettie Clay, July 16, 1863, in MSU; Gary Willson, "Madison Ross Letter; 5th Texas Infantry vs 5th NY Zouaves," www.nycivilwar.us/ross.html; Simpson, *Compendium*, 232.

88 *OR* 27, pt. 2, 324, 362, 428-29; Joskins, "A Sketch of Hood's Texas Brigade," 128-29.

89 *OR* 27, pt. 2, 324, 362, 428-29; Muster Rolls, 5th Texas, June 30-Aug. 31, 1863 in TSA; Joskins, "A Sketch of Hood's Texas Brigade," 128-29.

Chapter 3

The Battle of Chickamauga

The battle and march-weary regiment remained at Culpeper Court House until July 31. While there, the Texans rested, drew supplies and equipment, and corresponded with loved ones about their failed venture into Pennsylvania. Many of the men had not changed clothes since Gettysburg, and their disintegrating clothing had become a haven for lice. Many were also barefooted, a source of significant medical problems.[1]

Despite their setback and the grim news from Vicksburg, the men remained in good spirits. Never considered to be the best disciplined soldiers in Lee's army, however, they often griped about inadequate quartermaster support, poked fun at officers, indulged in drinking exhibitions when the opportunity arose, and continued extensive, unapproved foraging. Their behavior approached the mutinous stage only once, however, when a member of the 4th Texas was convicted and sentenced to wear a ball and chain. A number of men from the brigade attempted to free the felon, and mutiny charges were preferred against the participants. Before matters escalated, however, all the miscreants were cleared through Lee's good offices. No further record appears of a member of the Texas Brigade ever being sentenced to a ball and chain again.[2]

On July 31, the regiment left Culpeper, starting east toward Fredericksburg to thwart a potential Federal movement there. Hood's Division, now under the Law's

1 West, *Texan in Search of a Fight*, 89, 99; Tacitus Clay to Bettie Clay, August 17, 1863, in MSU.

2 William Lewis to Mother, August 11, 1863, in Parker, *Touched by Fire*, 70; Simpson, *Lee's Grenadier Guard*, 293.

command, led the First Corps advance. The regiment broke camp on the 31st, moved southeast to Sommerville Ford on the Rapidan River, bivouacking there that night. The next day, it crossed the Rapidan marching south another nine miles to Rapidan Station on the Orange and Alexandria Railroad. The leisurely march to Rapidan Station covered only 21 miles in four days. The tempo of the eastward march was accelerated considerably, however, when word was received Meade was approaching the Rappahannock at Fredericksburg. The regiment went from Rapidan Station to Fredericksburg, a distance of 32 miles, "in a day and a half, arriving . . . at 12 o clock," according to Smither, after camping upon the Chancellorsville battlefield the prior evening. The regiment entered the historic city only one hour before the advanced units of the Federal force appeared on the opposite bank of the Rappahannock.[3]

The regiment remained in the Fredericksburg area for close to one month, relaxing and refitting while guarding the fords of the Rappahannock. Hood's Division was assigned a picket line extending from United States Ford above Fredericksburg, to a point one mile below the town. While in Fredericksburg, many of the men received sorely needed care packages containing clothing, shoes, and jackets—a delightful sight after months of fighting which left their uniforms in raggedy and threadbare, with some unfortunates with nothing but their underwear. The men also collected several months' pay, and some a $50 enlistment bonus. Within a short time, blankets and cards were retrieved from haversacks and the poker games commenced in earnest.[4]

Ewell's and A. P. Hill's corps and Stuart's cavalry maintained the picket line along the upper reaches of the Rappahannock and along the Rapidan—the left and center of Lee's defensive line. Federal probes kept the Confederate picket line on constant alert. Many of the Texans felt they had been poorly supported at Gettysburg by Ewell and Hill. Indeed many blamed the other corps for the army's failure at Gettysburg and thus took delight in the daily skirmishing they were currently enduring. "Let 'em fight, let 'em fight," was the cry, "it's high time they were doin' it, durn 'em. . . . Let 'em fight—it's not our funeral."[5]

The regiment, anticipating a lengthy stay around Fredericksburg, established a semi-permanent camp just south of the town. Captain Clay wrote of his frequent dinners with General Robertson, indicating his commander and close personal friend "dispenses every thing, as he so well knows how to, in a generous and bountiful

3 Mark Smither to James Smither, August 7, 1863, in SHSU; *OR* 27, pt. 2, 429.

4 Polley, *Hood's Texas Brigade*, 197.

5 *OR* 27, pt. 2, 429; Polley, *Hood's Texas Brigade*, 197; Joskins, "A Sketch of Hood's Texas Brigade," 128-29; Mark Smither to James Smither, August 7, 1863, in SHSU.

manner, but I fancy that his Cook would just as soon I make my visits less frequent and not be such a drain upon his hospitality." Clay also poked some fun at the frequent military reviews prevalent while the army was in camp:

> [O]ur officers have in truth as much tinsel & occasionally as much traps—as any bedizened King or Queen that ever trod the boards, or flaunted its magisterial robes before the gaping multitude. Well, a grand review of the well appointed and disciplined army is well enough for one to see once in a life time—but for my part I am willing to dispense with these shows (Military) with one exhibition—And when this War is over, and settled to our satisfaction, I do not care if I never see another brass button or shoulder strap.

The "Army is in fine spirits," Clay continued, "and is receiving accessions to it every day." In Fredericksburg, the men were said to be living "in clover." They were happy, eating well, and many sported new uniforms from the Richmond depots and blockade-run shoes from England. Moxley Sorrel, years later, reflected on this time with nostalgia, exclaiming, "Ah! Those were lovely days; that short rest amid such environments."[6]

These pleasant days on the Rappahannock soon ended, however. On September 2, Law ordered Robertson to prepare three day's rations and move the brigade some 20 miles below Fredericksburg to Rappahannock Academy near Port Royal. A sizable Federal force had been sighted near the fords in that area, and Robertson was cautioned to place pickets at all river crossings and report any enemy movement. The regiment remained down at Rappahannock Academy with the brigade until September 7, in an area known locally as Northern Neck. There, to the regiment's delight, the foraging was good, "the people wealthy," the women pretty, and their duties light. Too soon, however, it received orders to break camp and move to Milford Station, where it would board cars on the Richmond, Fredericksburg and Potomac Railroad destined for Richmond. Another major campaign was in the offing![7]

In the western theater, the fight for possession of Chattanooga had raged for some time. Chattanooga, situated on the Tennessee River as it passed through the Cumberland Mountains, was referred to as the "Key to East Tennessee," or the "Gateway to the Deep South." A major railroad center, with four lines radiating from

6 Sorrel, *Confederate Staff Officer*, 175; Joskins, "A Sketch of Hood's Texas Brigade," in UTSA 128-29; Tacitus Clay to Bettie Clay, August 17, 1863, in MSU.

7 *OR* 29, pt. 2, 706; Robertson, *Touched With Valor*, 48; Smith, "Remembrances," 40; Muster Rolls, Field, Staff and Band, 5th Texas, Aug. 3–Oct. 31, 1863, in TSA; Joskins, "A Sketch of Hood's Texas Brigade," in UTSA 128-29; Campbell, *Lone Star Confederate*, 76.

town in the four principal directions, its possession was was vital to the Confederacy, and, thus a coveted objective of the Federals. Lincoln encouraged Maj. Gen. William S. Rosecrans, commander of the Army of the Cumberland, that "[i]f we can hold Chattanooga and East Tennessee, I think the rebellion must dwindle and die." General Braxton Bragg, commander of the Confederate Army of Tennessee, established headquarters there during the summer of 1863, after having been pushed out of Tullahoma, Tennessee by Rosecrans. Thereafter, the two armies were relatively stationary for some time, with the Union army occupying a line from Winchester to McMinnville, 60 miles southeast of Nashville. Despite urgings from Washington, Rosecrans had refused to initiate any further movement until August 16, 1863, when he finally moved toward the Tennessee River and Chattanooga.[8]

By September 4, the Army of the Cumberland had safely crossed this great barrier, thus posing Bragg, who had left the crossings below the city practically undefended, a severe threat. He therefore decided abandon Chattanooga and retreat southward, a decision which sat poorly with many of the officers and men.[9] However, Bragg did not withdraw as far south as Rosecrans had at first believed—instead halting behind Pigeon Mountain, near Lafayette, Georgia, concentrating his army there, and awaiting reinforcements. Fresh troops soon began arriving: Maj. Gen. Simon Buckner's corps from Knoxville, and a pair of divisions and brigades from Gen. Joseph E. Johnston's Army of Mississippi.

Following the losses at Gettysburg and Vicksburg, the Confederate high command determined that it had to assume the offensive to win the war. They reviewed a number of locations and possibilities for such action. Most promising appeared to be an attack on Rosecrans in Tennessee. Longstreet supported such a movement and agreed wholeheartedly with the suggestion that he be detached from the Army of Northern Virginia in a fast, secret movement to northern Georgia, to reinforce Bragg's grand assault.[10]

Initially Lee balked about detaching a significant portion of his army hundreds of miles away while Meade still probed his defenses. He finally acceded to pressure from above and reluctantly supported the proposal. The plan called for Longstreet's Corps to deal a crushing blow to Rosecrans, by traveling by rail through western Virginia and

8 Peter Cozzens, *The Battle of Chickamauga: This Terrible Sound* (Urbana, IL 1992), 21-22; *OR* 30, pt. 2, 27. See Gilbert E. Govan and James W. Livingood, *The Chattanooga County, 1540-1976: From Tomahawks to TVA* (Knoxville, TN, 1977), 167-68.

9 *OR* 29, pt. 2, 699; Cozzens, *This Terrible Sound*, 48-51, 53, 59-60; Thomas Lawrence Connelly, *Autumn of Glory: The Army of Tennessee, 1862-1865* (Baton Rouge, LA, 1971), 152-53; James R. Sullivan, *Chickamauga and Chattanooga Battlefields*, (Washington, DC, 1956), 9-10.

10 Longstreet, *Manassas to Appomattox*, 371-74; Freeman, *Lee's Lieutenants*, 3:220-21.

eastern Tennessee to Georgia, and follow up the anticipated a victory with a vigorous pursuit of the Federals all the way back to the Ohio River. If the plan succeeded, it would forestall a Federal drive through the heart of Dixie and relieve some of the pressure on Lee in the East, not to mention stirring up a mild panic in states above the Ohio.[11]

This plan, aptly named "Westward Ho," finally approved by the Confederate war department, called for the bulk of Longstreet's Corps to execute a rapid, secret movement by rail through western Virginia and eastern Tennessee to northern Georgia, ultimately augmenting Braxton Bragg's Army of Tennessee considerably. Transferring these troops from Virginia would prove to be an outstanding logistical achievement for the Confederacy. No troop movement of such magnitude had ever even been attempted to date, a measure of the hopes the Confederate war department placed in the success of the impending offensive.[12]

The plan called for Hood's and McLaw's Divisions, together with 26 guns of Col. E. Porter Alexander's Artillery Battalion, to join Bragg, all under Longstreet's command. Once the movement began, Brig. Gen. Micah Jenkins's South Carolina Brigade was also added to the force (although it did not arrive in time for the battle).[13]

The actual movement proved neither fast nor secret, however. The estimated distance of the intended route was 540 miles, a trip anticipated to take four days. However, just prior to departure, the railroads in East Tennessee fell into Federal hands. This necessitated a much more circuitous route through the Carolinas, into southern Georgia, and then back up through that state to the Tennessee border. Almost overnight, new routes were selected and coordinated by Confederate quartermaster-general Brig. Gen. Alexander Lawton and Maj. Frederick W. Sims, Chief of the Railroad Bureau. The new routes required a trip of somewhere between 800-900 miles in length, 260-360 miles more than the original plan. Moreover, in addition to the scarcity of reliable rolling stock, the rail systems of the Deep South, were far from uniform, thus necessitating considerable off and on loading. And as if these major problems were not enough, there was also a major intelligence leak. The *New York Herald* reported the detachment of Longstreet's Corps from Lee's army on September 9, accurately identifying the planned route and organizations involved in its movements south. With secrecy eliminated, the element of surprise cancelled, and the

11 Freeman, *Lee's Lieutenants*, 3:221, 223; Longstreet, *Manassas to Appomattox*, 371-74; Foote, *Civil War Narrative*, 2:708-09.

12 Longstreet, *Manassas to Appomattox*, 374-75; Foote, *Civil War Narrative*, 2:709.

13 Alexander, *Military Memoirs*, 448; Foote, *Civil War Narrative*, 2:709-10, 838; *OR* 29, pt. 2, 720-21.

enemy cognizant of their whole strategy, the Confederates had to scramble to avoid an attack on Bragg before Longstreet's arrival.[14]

The regiment boarded trains at Milford Station on the night of September 8, arriving in Richmond the following morning. As the Texans passed through the town on their way to the Richmond & Petersburg Railroad depot, the men were still unaware of where they were going. A popular rumor had them headed to Charleston, South Carolina. Many of the men spent what little free time they had in the local saloons, preparing for a hard ride. As the men assembled to board the trains south, General Hood, his arm was still swathed in bandages from his severe wounding at Gettysburg, unexpectedly arrived at the station to visit with the officers and address the men. The men of the brigade accorded him a tumultuous welcome and implored him to accompany them to Georgia. Though only partially recovered from this serious wound, Hood could not resist the entreaties of his men, as well as a petition signed by the division's officers. The emotional impulse to accompany the men proved too great when he saw that his "old troops, with whom I had served so long, were thus to be sent forth to another army—quasi, I may say, among strangers." He, therefore, had his favorite horse, "Jeff Davis," placed on one of the trains early the following morning, and together, the pair followed his division south to Georgia.[15]

The regiment commenced its rail odyssey on September 9 south through North Carolina from Weldon to Wilmington, then on to Florence and Kingsville, South Carolina, then to Augusta, Atlanta and Dalton, Georgia, before finally terminating at Catoosa Station, near Ringgold, Georgia. Every type of rolling stock imaginable, from boxcars, flat cars, coal cars, passenger cars, baggage cars, gondolas and cabooses, were impressed into service along this circuitous route. Traveling conditions in route were, to say the least, austere, with the men cramped and uncomfortable in the ragtag trains. Some shared spaces with the horses, while others spent the whole trip standing. Others climbed on top of the boxcars and flatbeds, exposing themselves not only to weather, soot, smoke, and dust, but also overhanging branches and other obstacles, which naturally produced sicknesses as well as some serious injuries. Those in boxcars began tearing apart their wooden surroundings down to the frame with bayonets, knives, axes, and swords to provide some relief from the Southern heat, and catch

14 *OR* 29, pt. 2, 198-99, 719-20; Kyle J. Foley, "John Bell Hood's Division in the Battle of Chickamauga: A Historical Analysis," *U. S. Army Command and General Staff College*, Fort Leavenworth, KS, 2003, 25; Longstreet, *Manassas to Appomattox*, 436-37; John Coxe, "Chickamauga," *CV* (1922), 30:291.

15 Skoch, *Lone Star Confederate*, 96; Simpson, *Gaines' Mill to Appomattox*, 152; Robertson, *Touched With Valor*, 47; Lasswell, *Rags and Hope*, 196; Hood, *Advance and Retreat*, 55 , 61-64; Simpson, *Lee's Grenadier Guard*, 300. See Connelly, *Autumn of Glory*, 322; Winston Groom, *Shrouds of Glory: From Atlanta to Nashville* (New York, 1995), 104-08.

unobstructed views of the countryside. In all, the regiment traveled approximately 900 miles on eight different railroad systems, enduring eight major transfer points on the way. The journey took nine days: a remarkable feat given the logistical difficulty involved.[16]

Although the men knew they were on their way to participate in yet another bloody contest, the journey south took on a carefree, almost carnival-like atmosphere. An officer commented that "never before were such crazy cars . . used to carry such good soldiers." In one car, a soldier played a fiddle while in another one played a horn. "All were happy lords," a member of the brigade commented, "yet knowing at the same time that we were going right into another big killing and that many of us would go to our long homes." All along the route, the men were greeted with ovations, and at each rest stop, a cheering crowd eager to catch sight of Lee's famous veterans. Baskets of food and jugs of cold water, as well as much more potent beverages made their way to the troops, often followed by plentiful kisses from "enthusiastic women who combined sentiment with patriotism." "Rags and dirt seemed to be a recommendation," one lowly veteran observed, "where gilt and brass failed to excite attention." At Kingsville, South Carolina, Mary Chestnut wrote of personally witnessing this movement south:

> I caught a glimpse of Longstreet's Corps going past. It was a strange sight. What seemed miles of platform cars, soldiers rolled in their blankets lying in rows with their heads all covered, fast asleep. In their gray blankets packed in regular order, they looked like swathed mummies. One man nearby was writing on his knee. He used his cap for a desk, and he was seated on a rail.[17]

At some stops, flowers showered the soldiers, and many towns contributed articles of handmade clothing, tossing them aboard the slow moving trains. Bonfires along roadbed lighted the men on their way. The whole trip was one enthusiastic

16 Skoch, *Lone Star Confederate*, 96; Polley, *Hood's Texas Brigade*, 198-99; Foley, "John Bell Hood's Division," 30; Robert C. Black III, *Railroads of the Confederacy*, (Chapel Hill, NC, 1952) 187. Other brigades of Hood's Division followed a slightly longer route through Raleigh and Charlotte, NC, and Columbia, SC, then on to Augusta, GA, after which they followed the same route as the brigade. Black, *Railroads of the Confederacy*, 191; Simpson, *Lee's Grenadier Guard*, 300; Foley, "John Bell Hood's Division," 28. Eight separate railroads transported the troops: The Richmond, Fredericksburg and Potomac; The Richmond and Petersburg; The Petersburg, Wilmington and Weldon; The Wilmington and Manchester; The South Carolina; The Georgia; and The Western and Atlantic. Simpson, *Lee's Grenadier Guard*, 301.

17 Mary Boykin Chesnut, *A Diary From Dixie* (New York, 1906), 241; Sullivan, *Chickamauga*, 12-13; Sorrell, *Confederate Staff Officer*, 180; Polk, *North American Review*, 27; West, *Texan in Search of a Fight*, 111.

ovation of handkerchief and flag waving, as the trains rumbled southward. At Sumter, South Carolina, a spread of food was laid out for all the men, and the train stopped for 15 minutes while the men feasted at long tables "spread with goodies," and even some cigars. Carrying what they could not devour in the allotted time, the men climbed back aboard their transportation and were soon again on their way.[18]

The Texans were involved in one noteworthy "incident" along their way. During a 24-hour layover at Wilmington, North Carolina, a sizable group ventured into "Paddy Hollow," the city's seamy waterfront section. Fortified with drink, many became rather "boisterous, obnoxious and abusive." The local police force, consisting primarily of elderly citizens, was soon summoned to contain the unruly soldiers. The booze-addled Texans believed the blue clad police were Yankee soldiers, promptly formed a battle line, raised the Rebel Yell, and charged. Several peace officers were beaten, and one stabbed before the force retreated from the waterfront. Ultimately, no arrests were made, and the Texans quietly left town early the next morning, heading west.[19]

The men also found at least one opportunity to practice their superior foraging skills. Troop trains were given the right of way on the westward movement. Civilian trains were required to pull onto a siding to allow the troop transports passage. In such cases, it was customary for the civilians to stick their heads out of the windows to cheer the soldiers on as the trains slowly passed one another. Several times, the Texans seized this proximity to snag hats from the heads of unsuspecting well-wishers. Given the frequency of such incidents, it is safe to assume that a good portion of the 5th Texas went into battle in Georgia with non-military, but stylish headgear.[20]

Rosecrans had now determined exactly where Bragg was concentrated, and that his enemy's divided force was extremely vulnerable. He dispatched Maj. Gen. Gordon Granger's Reserve Corps from Bridgeport, Alabama, to Chattanooga and Maj. Gen. Thomas L. Crittenden's XXI Corps to a position at Lee and Gordon's Mill on Chickamauga Creek, some 12 miles south of Chattanooga. He also ordered Maj. Gen. George H. Thomas's XIV Corps to strike out northward toward Crittenden as soon as Maj. Gen. Alexander McDowell McCook's XX Corps could join him. McCook soon withdrew from Alpine, Georgia, crossed Lookout Mountain and then up Lookout Valley. Confusion in McCook's marching orders required him to change his route of

18 Lasswell, *Rags and Hope*, 198; Joskins, "A Sketch of Hood's Texas Brigade," in UTSA 131-33; Sorrell, *Confederate Staff Officer*, 182.

19 Polley, *Hood's Texas Brigade*, 198; Glen Tucker, *Chickamauga* (New York, 1961), 95.

20 Sorrel, *Confederate Staff Officer*, 180; Simpson, *Lee's Grenadier Guard*, 302-04; Joskins, "A Sketch of Hood's Texas Brigade," in UTSA 131-33; Lasswell, *Rags and Hope*, 196-97; Simpson, *Gaines' Mill to Appomattox*, 153; West, *Texan in Search of a Fight*, 111.

march, and it took him five days, until September 17, to complete this convoluted movement. Rosecrans, expecting McCook to follow the shorter route on top of Lookout Mountain or the roads through McLemore's Cove much sooner, was justifiably upset, albeit without knowledge of what had actually happened. Meanwhile, Bragg made no attempt to prevent this concentration of Federal forces, and during the night of September 17, the three Federal corps were well within supporting distance of one another. The Federal left extended west and south from Lee and Gordon's Mill through McLemore's Cove to Stevens Gap and through Lookout Mountain.[21]

To seize the initiative Bragg ordered a change of position. Turning northward, he planned a major offensive against Crittenden, then at Lee and Gordon's Mill, who had been trailing his rear since the evacuation of Chattanooga. Bragg moved his army northward along the east side of Chickamauga Creek so as to seize the crossing north of Lee and Gordon's Mill, which would in turn gain him possession of the roads leading to Chattanooga. He would thereafter continue pressing Crittenden, either crushing his corps or driving it back into the Federal concentration at McLemore's Cove by flanking the Federal left, thereby interposing his army between Chattanooga and the Yankees. This movement would require Rosecrans to fight to regain the city, or fall back across the Tennessee River to protect his supply line.[22]

Bragg worked late that evening at his headquarters at Lee's Mill and Tan Yard on a revised battle plan. Early on September 18, he issued new orders. The new plan called for Hood's and Brig. Gen. Bushrod Johnson's divisions to cross Chickamauga Creek at or near Reed's Bridge, turn left (west) and sweep up the creek toward Lee and Gordon's Mill. Simultaneously, Maj. Gen. William H. T. Walker's Reserve Corps would cross at Alexander's Bridge south of Reed's Bridge, and push the Federal flank and rear in the same direction. Meanwhile, Maj. Gen. Simon B. Buckner's Corps would cross further south at Tedford's Ford and join the movement to the left, thereby putting pressure on the enemy then fronting Lt. Gen. Leonidas Polk at Lee and Gordon's Mill. Polk, in turn, was to hurry his corps up to Lee and Gordon's Mill, cross there, "and [then] join in the attack where ever the enemy may be." Lt. Gen. D. H. Hill would cover the left flank against any advance of the Federals to the south, and

21 Sullivan, *Chickamauga*, 13-14; Cozzens, *This Terrible Sound*, 87. Thomas told McCook to take the route over Lookout Mountain, fearing otherwise the Confederates could strike at his flanks. A frustrated Rosecrans ordered him to march by way of Lookout Valley. McCook's testy reply on the conflicting orders caused Rosecrans to relent, and he instructed McCook to proceed through the valley, while leaving a detachment to watch the gap and oversee the baggage trains over the mountain. *OR* 30, pt. 3, 628-29, 648.

22 Thomas Robson Hay, "The Campaign and Battle of Chickamauga," *Georgia Historical Quarterly*, hereinafter GHQ (1923), 7:224; Cozzens, *This Terrible Sound*, 89.

then attack their flank in the event they tried to reinforce the Union force at Lee and Gordon's Mills.[23]

While some writers have considered this to be Bragg's best plan, "its hasty conception was evident." He envisioned an early crossing by his forces, and yet unfortunately, he set no hour for the movement to begin. The plan required Walker and Buckner to use the same road to reach their respective crossing sites, and an inevitable entanglement resulted. Consequently, it was early afternoon before the Confederate forces even neared Chickamauga Creek.[24]

In the past this entire area had been home to a fierce band of Cherokee Indians, runaway slaves, fugitive Tories, and dispossessed Creeks, all of whom ambushed river traffic along the Tennessee and murdered venturesome pioneers who ventured into its rugged country. Frightened settlers, to distinguish these cutthroats from the more passive elements of the Cherokee, called them "Chickamaugas," the name of the stream along which their villages stood. "Chickamauga" loosely translated from Cherokee meant "River of Death."

While the Chickamaugas and Cherokees were ultimately driven out of these environs in 1838, few improvements came to the area, which was inhospitable to regular agriculture. Only two structures of any consequence graced the region. One was the John Ross house, around which the small village of Rossville grew. Raised a Cherokee, Ross had been recognized as the head of that nation for 40 years. The second sizable building was the Gordon-Lee mansion, a 12-room, two story brick structure, with a smokehouse and six slave cabins. When the Cherokees ceded their land to the government in 1836, James Gordon and James Lee purchased a 2,500 acre tract and set up a milling and sawmill operation on Chickamauga Creek. Directly in front of this mansion percolated Crawfish Springs, the best source of crystal clear, cold water for miles around.[25]

On September 13, an anxious Bragg learned of the Texans' progress toward Catoosa Station via Resaca. On the afternoon of Thursday, September 17, the 1,300-man contingent of Texas soldiers finally began arriving at the station, two miles east of Ringgold, Georgia, ending their arduous nine-day journey. The Texas Brigade was first to arrive, followed hours later by Benning's and Law's brigades. The 5th Texas unloaded its equipment, basically little more than troops' rifles and 40 cartridges of ammunition per man, and moved into a bivouac site for the night near Ringgold, about a mile and a half from the station. That evening, the men prepared four days'

23 *OR* 30, pt. 2, 30-31.

24 Cozzens, *This Terrible Sound*, 103; Connelly, *Autumn of Glory*, 197.

25 Cozzens, *This Terrible Sound*, 91-92; Govan, *Chattanooga County*, 75-97.

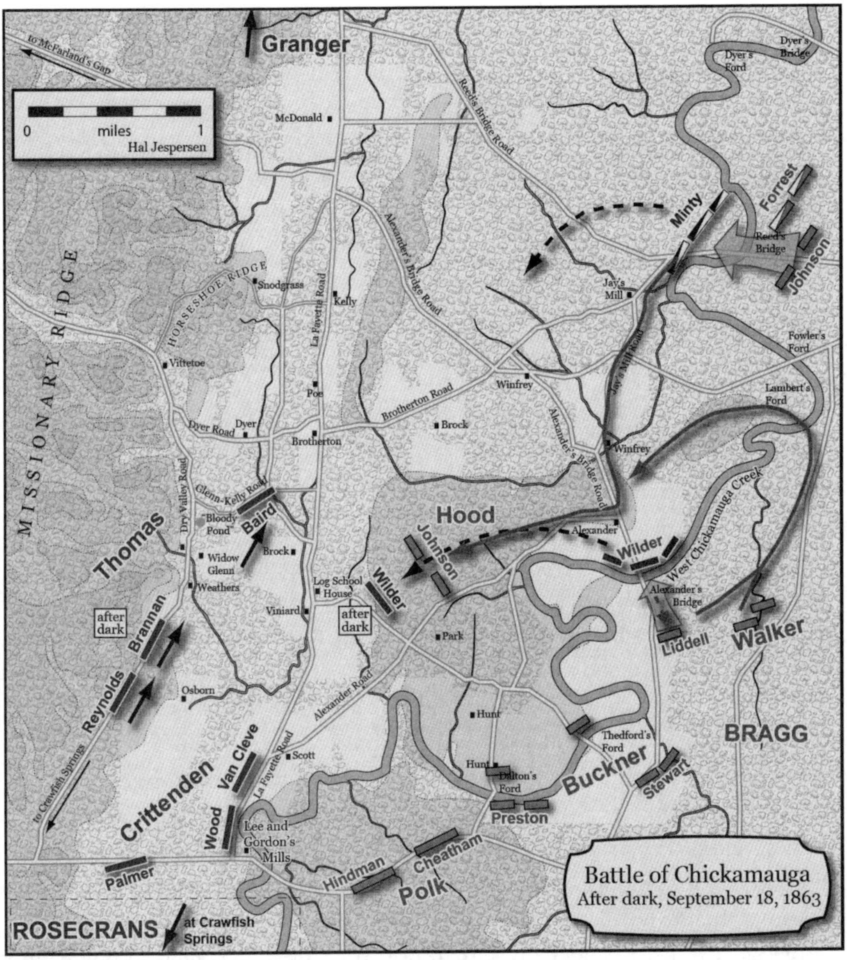

Battle of Chickamauga
After dark, September 18, 1863

rations, wolfed down their supper, and concluded final preparations for the upcoming battle.[26]

26 *OR* 30, pt. 4, 652; Foley, "John Bell Hood's Division," 32; Muster Rolls, Co. C, 5th Texas, Aug. 31-Oct. 31, 1863, in TSA; Coxe, "Chickamauga," *CV*, 30:292; Joskins, "A Sketch of Hood's Texas Brigade," in UTSA, 134-35. In the convoy from Virginia, Benning's Brigade had preceded the Texans. Benning reached Atlanta first, but remained there to draw rations and shoes. The Texans left Atlanta on September 14, Benning and Law following on the evening of September 15. *OR* 30, pt. 4, 652; Simpson, *Gaines' Mill to Appomattox*, 154. Only three brigades of Longstreet's force (Texas Brigade, Law's and Benning's), out of nine, arrived in time for the first day's fighting at Chickamauga; another two arrived in time for the second day's fight. The remaining four, as well as Porter Alexander's artillery, unfortunately did not arrive until long after the battle. Simpson, *Gaines' Mill to Appomattox*, 154.

Ringgold, less than six miles from Bragg's headquarters, served as the designated rendezvous point for all the Confederate reinforcements from Johnston and Lee. In Bragg's haste to move men to the front to secure the bridges to the west, regardless of where they originated, the Texas Brigade was assigned to a temporary division under command of the most senior brigadier then present, Bushrod R. Johnson. Thus, the Texas Brigade, along with Johnson's brigades under Brig. Gens. John Gregg and Evander McNair, and Johnson's old brigade under Col. John S. Fulton, were all combined into a "Provisional Division" on the evening of September 17 near Ringgold. Under orders, Johnson moved his force south along the road toward Bragg's headquarters at Leet's Tan Yard, and then to the west to join Walker's force at Alexander's Bridge.[27]

At 5:00 a.m. on September 18, Johnson's division marched south. Bragg, however, soon learned the enemy was actually located near Reed's Bridge, and thus redirected Johnson northwest towards that place to dislodge the Federals from Chickamauga Creek. Three miles out when he received the new orders, Johnson reversed his columns and started back toward Ringgold, but without Brig. Gen. Nathan Bedford Forrest's cavalry, which had been ordered to screen his front and right flanks, as Forrest had not received the orders. Reed's Bridge was approximately eight miles to the west, and now Johnson received supplemental orders. Once across Reed's Bridge, he was to turn south and sweep along the creek toward Lee and Gordon's Mill, uniting with Walker and Buckner's forces in the process. In other words he would now lead the attack on the Federal left. While in route toward the bridge with Johnson, the 5th Texas passed a column of the 8th Texas Cavalry, known as Terry's Texas Rangers, under command of Lt. Col. Gustave Cook. The encounter precipitated warm greetings between the two forces from Texas; it was the first time in the war that the men of the brigade would fight alongside other fellow Texans.[28]

Forrest eventually caught up with Johnson's force, and their combined force proceeded west toward Pea Vine Creek late that morning, encountering a stream of civilian refugees moving eastward with all their household possessions. Continuing along Ringgold Road, stiff resistance from Col. Robert H. G. Minty's Union cavalry brigade compelled Johnson to form a line of battle and fight his way through. The 5th Texas served as a part of the reserve force as the Confederates drove the Federals

27 *OR* 30, pt. 4, 652; Muster Roll, Co. C, 5th Texas, Aug. 31-Oct. 31, 1863; in TSA Joskins, "A Sketch of Hood's Texas Brigade," in UTSA, 134-35; Robertson, *Touched With Valor*, 77-78; Foley, "John Bell Hood's Division," 35; Skoch, *Lone Star Confederate*, 96.

28 *OR* 30, pt. 2, 17, 451; Cozzens, *This Terrible Sound*, 101-03; Foley, "John Bell Hood's Division," 36-37. The 7th Texas Infantry, commanded by Colonel Hiram D. Granbury, was in Gregg's Brigade, also assigned to Johnson's Provisional Division.

across Pea Vine Creek, first from a strong position on a hill west of the stream, and thereafter from a hastily prepared position east of Reed's Bridge over Chickamauga Creek. By mid-afternoon, Johnson was in position to force a crossing at Reed's Bridge.[29]

Hood himself arrived at Catoosa Station from Virginia a little after noon on September 18, and immediately received orders from Bragg to assume command of the Provisional Division. Hood, arm sling and all, mounted his horse, leapt from the train to the sound of the guns seven miles distant, and about 3:00 p.m. joined the troops, then in line of battle. A tremendous, enthusiastic roar rose from the Texans as he approached them and quickly made his way to the head of the column. There, he found Johnson, and after a brief conversation, formally took over command of the Provisional Division. He immediately took steps to secure a crossing of the Chickamauga: sending skirmishers to the front to support Forrest's cavalry, ordering Maj. Felix H. Robertson's Artillery Battalion forward and unlimbered, and dispatching flanking parties across the creek above and below Reed's Bridge.[30]

Federal infantry and cavalry disputing the creek's crossing soon gave ground, and Hood's force crossed the bridge and advanced to Jay's Steam Saw Mill, a quarter of a mile beyond. The Federals fell back along Brotherton Road, without stopping until they reached Lee and Gordon's Mill. At the saw mill, Hood turned his columns southwest and led them down the west side of the Chickamauga along Alexander's Bridge Road toward Lee and Gordon's Mill.[31]

About two-and-a-half miles down the road, in the rapidly falling darkness, Hood's troops encountered stiff Federal resistance some 800 yards east of the Viniard House on Lafayette Road, near the destroyed Alexander's Bridge. Armed with

29 Cozzens, *This Terrible Sound*, 102-103; Polley, *Hood's Texas Brigade*, 199-200; Hood, *Advance and Retreat*, 61.

30 *OR* 30, pt. 1 447, 922-23, *OR* 30, pt. 2, 45; "Organizations of the Army of Tennessee, General Braxton Bragg, Confederate States Army Commanding, at the Battle of Chickamauga," *SHSP* (1884), 12:157; Simpson, *Gaines' Mill to Appomattox*, 154-55; Campbell, *Lone Star Confederate*, 96; Cozzens, *This Terrible Sound*, 110-12; Polley, *Hood's Texas Brigade*, 201. Felix H. Robertson was the son of Brig. Gen. Jerome Roberetson, commander of the Texas Brigade. Since Alexander's artillery battalion from the Army of Northern Virginia was not yet on the field, Bragg ordered Maj. Robertson, then commanding the Reserve Artillery for the Army of Tennessee, to support Hood. The younger Robertson later became a general and commanded a cavalry brigade in the Army of Tennessee. The Robertsons were the only father-son generals to fight in the Civil War, with the exception of Robert E. Lee and two of his sons, and he was also the Confederacy's only Texas born general. Felix also had the distinction of being the last Confederate general to die on April 28, 1928, in Waco. Felix H. Robertson, "Service with the Reserve Artillery," *CV* (1920), 28:251.

31 *OR* 30, pt. 2, 452-53; Cozzens, *This Terrible Sound*, 111-14; Foley, "John Bell Hood's Division," 39-41.

Spencer repeating rifles, Col. John T. Wilder's brigade of mounted Union infantry delivered volleys so precise and continuous that the two-mile long Confederate column had to deploy in line of battle to meet the threat. Wilder's force was the only unit at Chickamauga equipped with these seven-shot repeating rifles. Minty's cavalry from Reed's Bridge, as well as regiments from Crittenden's XXI Corps soon reinforced him.[32]

With Crittenden's 14,000-man corps only several hundred yards west of his isolated division, Hood was in a precarious situation. Gregg's Brigade then moved out towards La Fayette Road, while McNair's and Fulton's Brigades quickly followed, falling in on his right flank. The Texans continued forward. When the advance lines of Hood's force got within 50 yards of the enemy, Wilder's soldiers fired another salvo into them, driving them back 200 yards. By now, 9:00 p.m., darkness enveloped the field. Hood, surprised by the volume of fire, decided to disengage and fall back an additional 600 yards. Unfamiliar with the local terrain, and unwilling to fight with such a handicap in total darkness, he decided his men had done enough and ordered temporary breastworks constructed, forming a defensive position facing south and west, with the Texas Brigade facing northwesterly. Works facing in three directions were thrown up approximately 800 yards east of the Viniard House, and by 10:00 p.m., the regiment was ready for some much needed sleep.[33]

The Texans faced the La Fayette-Chattanooga Road, the main thoroughfare on which Rosecran's army was moving north. A third of the men remained on duty through the night, while the rest were allowed to sleep with their arms. Throughout the night, the men could hear the work of axes and rumbling of artillery as the Federals constructed breastworks and moved their guns into new positions. One Texan on guard that evening, within sight and hearing of these preparations, confidently expected that a "wool-tearing" would occur the next morning.[34]

The sun rose blood red the morning of September 19, with two powerful armies eyeing each other along a several mile front with dense undergrowth along Chickamauga Creek. Battle formations would prove to be impossible in this wilderness. The dense woods, flush with tangled undergrowth, brambles, and cedar thickets, prevented both easy movement and adequate observation. Thus, neither

32 *OR* 30, pt. 2, 453; Hood, *Advance and Retreat*, 61; West, *Rebel Private*, 112. Hood's was the only division west of the creek at nightfall on the 18th.

33 Cozzens, *This Terrible Sound*, 113-14; Simpson, *Lee's Grenadier Guard*, 310; Polley, *Hood's Texas Brigade*, 201; Foley, "John Bell Hood's Division,"40-41.

34 *OR* 30, pt. 2, 452-53; Cozzens, *This Terrible Sound*, 111-14; Foley, "John Bell Hood's Division," 39-41; West, *A Texan in Search of a Fight*, 112; Hood, *Advance and Retreat*, 61-62; Robertson, "Service with the Artillery Reserve," 251.

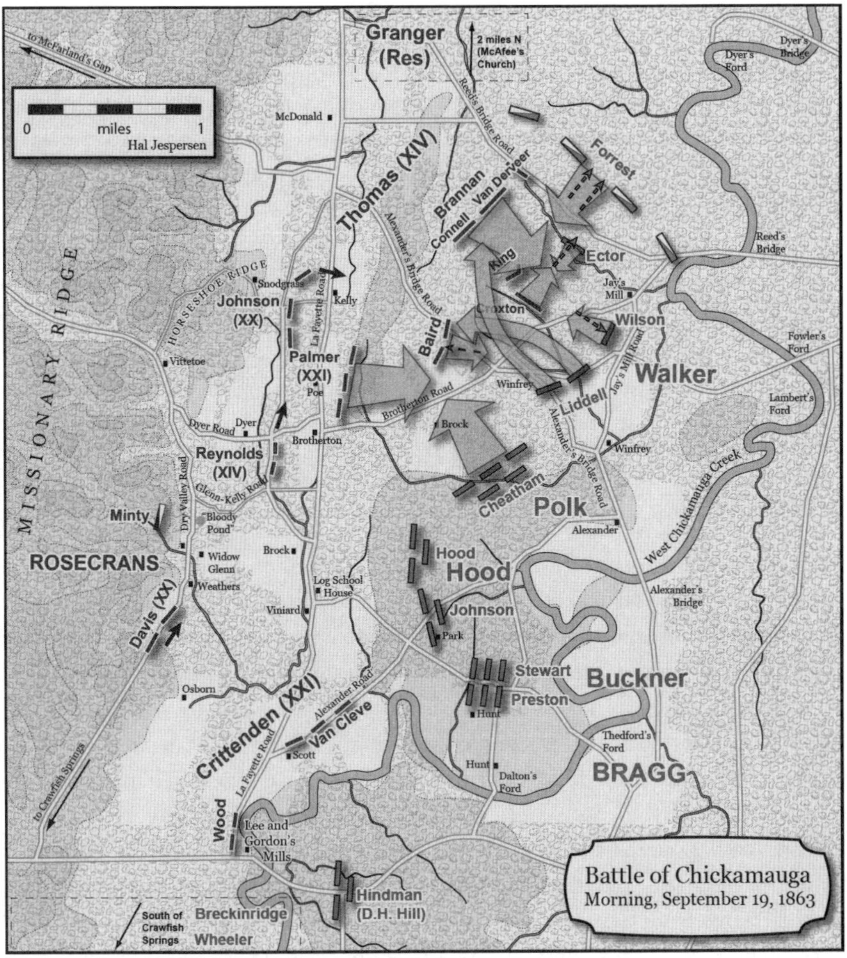

Battle of Chickamauga
Morning, September 19, 1863

army knew the precise location of their opponent as they continued pre-dawn maneuvering for position. Commanders had trouble even remaining in continuous contact with their own commands. Nonetheless, the armies were so close at this point, sometimes separated by only a few hundred yards, that a desperate clash was imminent.[35]

During the night, all Confederate forces except three divisions were moved and in position west of the creek from Reed's Bridge on the north to near Dalton's Ford and Lee and Gordon's Mill on the south. Forrest's cavalry held the right flank at Reed's

35 Sullivan, *Chickamauga*, 15-18; Daniel H. Hill, "Chickamauga—The Great Battle of the West," in *B&L*, 3:649.

Bridge; from there toward the left (south) were Maj. Gen. W. H. T. Walker's Corps, Maj. Gen. Benjamin F. Cheatham's Division of Polk's Corps, Longstreet's Corps, and Buckner's Corps. On the east side of the stream, forming the Confederate right: Maj. Gen. Patrick R. Cleburne's Division of Hill's Corps, about to cross to the west at Tedford's Ford, Maj. Gen. Thomas C. Hindman's Division of Polk's Corps near Lee and Gordon's Mill, and Maj. Gen. John C. Breckinridge's Division, forming at the far left, opposite Glass's Mill. Meanwhile, Maj. Gen. Joseph Wheeler's cavalry anchored the left flank along the upper fords of the Chickamauga. The Federal army under the command of Maj. Gen. George Thomas, following a long night's march, occupied a line west of and nearly parallel to Bragg's forces.[36]

The Texans were reunited early that morning with Law's Alabamians and Benning's Georgians, both having arrived from Ringgold. Law, the senior brigadier, took command of Hood's Division, as Hood, in Longstreet's absence—still on his way from Virginia—had assumed command of his corps. This corps now consisted of Law's (Hood's) and McLaws' divisions (with only Kershaw's Brigade present at the time), along with Johnson's Brigade, temporarily placed under Hood's jurisdiction.[37]

Serious fighting started around 7:00 a.m., when "Old Pap" Thomas ordered Brig. Gen. John M. Brannan's division to destroy what he perceived as a small Confederate force which had "inadvertently" crossed to the west side of Chickamauga Creek. The fight was joined when some of Forrest's dismounted cavalry on the Confederate right at Jay's Mill, near Reed's Bridge blindsided Brannan. While Col. John T. Croxton's Brigade initially drove Forrest back, he was forced to retreat when Confederate reinforcements arrived. Both sides soon recognized a major engagement was was underway, and poured more troops into the conflict, with the fight ebbing and flowing, as one side, and then the other, gained the advantage. Rosecrans forced marched troops from Crawfish Springs into the battle. Meanwhile Bragg ordered the remaining divisions of his left wing to cross to the west side of the creek.[38]

After 10:00 a.m., the 5th Texas, with the rest of the division, had marched about a mile and a half south and formed a line of battle with the Alabama Brigade under Col. James Sheffield, posted on the right. The brigade formed from the left to right with the 3rd Arkansas, 1st Texas, 4th Texas, and 5th Texas in line. As the battle began to define itself, the Texas Brigade occupied the extreme left of the Confederate line. And here the Texans remained a half mile east of La Fayette Road and northeast of the

36 Boatner, *Civil War Dictionary*, 151; Sullivan, *Chickamauga*, 17-18.

37 Cozzens, *This Terrible Place*, 120; Hood, *Advance and Retreat*, 62; *OR* 30, pt. 2, 453.

38 Daniel H. Hill, "Chickamauga—The Great Battle of the West," in *B&L*, 3:650-51; Henry, *Story of the Confederacy*, 310; Cozzens, *This Terrible Sound*, 128-33; Sullivan, *Chickamauga*, 11-19.

Viniard House while the battle raged on the Confederate right. The immediate terrain consisted largely of an undulating plain, covered with thick woods of oak trees, pine and underbrush so dense in places that the various regiments were often hidden from one another. By noon, the Confederate line was formed with Buckner's left resting on the Chickamauga, approximately one mile below Lee and Gordon's Mills. To the right of Buckner's Corps stood Hood's Division, now including Johnson's Division and Walker's Corps on the extreme right, together with Cheatham's Division in reserve. The general direction of the line of battle was a little east of north. By mid-afternoon, fighting had spread along a jagged line a full three miles in length. Both armies had built up heavy concentrations near the Viniard and Widow Glen houses, north of Lee and Gordon's Mill.[39]

By 11:00 a.m., Bragg had ordered Cheatham to the right of Hood's Division in support of Liddell's Division of Walker's Corps. An opening in the line eventually developed between Cheatham and Hood, where Maj. Gen. Alexander P. Stewart's Division of Buckner's second line was thrown in to the right in support, and the fighting became hotly contested there.

Then, about 2:00 p.m., Federal infantry, supported by artillery, advanced from the Viniard House, driving in the Confederate pickets. Fighting on the defensive, with stubborn skirmishing and well-served batteries, Johnson was eventually able to halt this Union advance force. Subsequently, at 2:30 p.m., Hood ordered Johnson's Division to advance, and the Confederates crashed through the underbrush into cleared fields east of La Fayette Road, where they almost immediately encountered the troops of Brig. Gen. Jefferson C. Davis' Division. In desperate, fierce fighting, both sides stood their ground, blowing holes in each other's lines at short range. Hood rode by on his horse to the cheering of the troops as his division formed. The general acknowledged the acclaim, tipping his hat and hollering: "Remember boys, we are here to whip them." Hood soon threw in his other divisions in a desperate effort to crush this Federal counterassault.[40]

The 5th Texas had lain in line of battle for over an hour while Union shells burst all around them. Rumors from the front told of opposing forces simply standing erect in lines 200 yards apart, firing into each other. This was definitely not the Texans' style of fighting. By this time, with a sense of resignation about their fate, they had developed their own unique fighting style. They much favored a quick charge to

39 Simpson, *Gaines' Mill to Appomattox*, 156-57; Polley, *Hood's Texas Brigade*, 205-206; *OR* 30, pt. 2, 423; I. B. Webster, "Chickamauga: Going Into Action with Hands Full of Bacon and Coffee," *National Tribune*, July 2, 1891.

40 Lasswell, *Rags and Hope*, 201; Polley, *Hood's Texas Brigade*, 210-11; Foley, "John Bell Hood's Division," 44, Cozzens, *This Terrible Sound*, 204-206.

determine matters as soon as possible. Soon the brigade was ordered into the fight to aid the hard-pressed troops of General Johnson. Fletcher had to be awakened from a deep sleep, later writing home "I was shaken and ordered to rise," to charge the Federals. The brigade moved forward in its established battle line. As they moved westward toward the Viniard House and the front, they met many stragglers from Johnson's Division hurrying the other way. Some men from Gregg's Brigade shoved their way past the oncoming Texans in great haste, one exclaiming:

> 'You fellers'll catch hell in thar,' one of them shouted as he came near us; 'them fellers out thar" you ar goin' up again, ain't none of the blue-bellied, white-livered Yanks an 'sassidge-eatin' forrin hirelin's you have in Virginny that'll run at the snap of a cap—they are Western fellers, an' they'll mighty quick give you a bellyful o'fightin'.

As the Texans passed by one of Stewart's Tennessee regiments, torn and bloody from their brief penetration of the Union lines, an enthusiastic Texan shouted out to them, "Rise up, Tennesseans, and see the Texans go in!" Too weary to reply, let alone follow, Stewart's battle weary troops simply lay there watching Hood's men sweep by—the pride of the Army of Northern Virginia.[41]

The Texans advanced less than 200 yards before rifle fire crackled in earnest from beyond their left. Robertson sent word to charge and the men emerged from the woods and underbrush a few hundred yards east of La Fayette Road and north of the Viniard House. The Texas advance took pressure off Brig. Gen. John Gregg's Brigade, but it immediately drew the attention of Col. Hans C. Heg's brigade of McCook's XX Corps. As the regiment advanced some 500 yards into the clearing of the Viniard farm, Federals concealed in a nearby ditch covered with underbrush attacked them from the left. The 3rd Arkansas began taking significant fire. Upon cresting a ridge, Robertson discovered an additional two regiments from Heg's brigade, the 25th Illinois and the 15th Wisconsin, were also bearing down on the brigade's left.[42]

Robertson immediately halted, requesting a change of front from Law. Law approved but kept Benning and Sheffield on course, which separated the brigade somewhat, creating a gap in the division's line. Robertson shifted his line "forward on the left battalion" to confront Brig. Gen. William P. Carlin's brigade of the XX Corps. The Texans had turned against Union troops massed in a ravine lying and squatting in

41 *OR* 30, pt. 2, 514; Polley, *Hood's Texas Brigade*, 209; Cozzens, *This Terrible Sound*, 203-05; Foley, "John Bell Hood's Division," 48; Smith, *Reminiscences*, 40.

42 J. T. Hunter, "Hard Fighting of the Fourth Texas," in *CV*, (1906), 14:22. Foley, "John Bell Hood's Division," 44-52; Cozzens, *This Terrible Sound*, 203-205.

the bushes and underbrush. At the double-quick and with the Rebel yell, the Texas regiments advanced across the recently plowed field to engage this hidden foe. The Federals fired one heavy volley, then bolted the ravine, streaming back across La Fayette Road toward the Viniard House. But the Texans now came under frontal fire from Heg's infantry, supported by the 38th Illinois and from the right by Hotchkiss' 2nd Minnesota Light Artillery battery, discharging double-shotted canister at 200 yards.[43]

The Texans continued their rush forward towards La Fayette Road and the Viniard House, with the 4th and entire 5th Texas fighting on their own, having driven back what remained of Heg's 15th Wisconsin, the 25th Illinois and Carlin's 38th Illinois. The right-hand companies of the 4th Texas and the 5th Texas continued forcing the Federals back through the woods, and Robertson soon lost sight of them. These two regiments fought largely on their own for the remainder of the afternoon that often involved savage hand-to-hand combat before the Federals eventually gave way.[44]

As they continued forward, the Texans soon encountered General Gregg lying in the field between the lines, shot through the neck and dragged by his horse's reins toward the brigade. Some Federals were about to pilfer Gregg's spurs and sword when the Texans had charged forward, driving off the scavengers and rescuing the general and his horse, and carrying him back to his lines.[45]

The fighting then shifted toward the Viniard House itself, where the Federals had beaten back Johnson's previous attacks, though at considerable cost. Bluecoats from Indiana, Illinois and Ohio fell back across the road as the Texans charged, taking refuge behind fences, trees, and farm buildings around the Viniard farm, and in a ditch in the west field on the crest of the hill to the north. In this position the Federals gained the additional support of several Federal artillery batteries and, thus enhanced, they were soon pouring a deadly fire into the ragged ranks of Robertson's advancing

43 Foley, "John Bell Hood's Division," 48-52; Cozzens, *This Terrible Sound*, 202-207; Hamilton, *History of Company M*, 52.

44 *OR* 30, pt. 1, 516, 529, pt. 2, 413-14, 430, 511, 516; "Colonel Robert C. Trigg, of Virginia," in *CV*, (1909), 17:65; Cozzens, *This Terrible Sound*, 205-06; Foley, "John Bell Hood's Division," 48-50.

45 *OR* 30, pt. 1, 454-55. Little did the men of the brigade realize that the officer they had so bravely rescued would soon be in command their brigade, leading them into battle at Darbytown Road near Richmond in early October, 1864, dying as a hero. Simpson, *Lee's Grenadier Guard*, 320-21. Cozzens suggests Gregg's wounding came later in the afternoon, after 5:00 p.m. Cozzens, *This Terrible Sound*, 260. However, Bushrod Johnson's report of the day's events places Gregg's wounding occurring before the brigade reached La Fayette Road the first time. See *OR* 30, pt. 2, 454-55.

Texans. A long and desperate, vicious struggle ensued, including hand-to-hand combat with clubbed rifles and bayonets. It was "impossible for one in the ranks to see what was happening to right or left," Polley observed. A man could not worry about his flanks: "he could only look straight before him, and tackle the foe immediately facing him." Individual actions were magnified in this kind of personal combat. "No fighting that day was more bitter or less organized than that around the Viniard farm." Divisions were irrelevant, brigades unraveled and even regiments splintered in the whirlwind of battle.

The battle had exacted a considerable price from Heg's and Carlin's troops, with their ranks sorly depleted. However, the Federals were not about to fold easily. Brig. Gen. Thomas J. Wood had already ascertained that Davis needed support and directed Col. George Buell's brigade to form a battle line on La Fayette Road behind Carlin. To confront Hood's advance, Buell deployed in two lines parallel to La Fayette Road, holding the ground north and west of the Viniard farm, with its ideal open fields of fire for engaging the Rebel advance. Buell brought up four guns from Wood's divisional artillery for support, positioning them in the center of the formation.[46]

With almost no breeze that day, choking smoke from dozens of cannon and thousands of muskets hung low above the ground, "so dense it was almost stifling." The Texans charged Heg's and Carlin's positions near a log school house a second time. In the woods north of the Viniard field, the 4th and 5th Texas had Heg up against the road, while the rest of the brigade pushed Carlin toward a slight rise on the western edge of the field. The regiment, with helpful support from the survivors of the 50th Tennessee on the right, now fought Heg's men to within 50 yards of the La Fayette Road. Well-drilled in skirmish tactics, taking advantage of obstacles, "seeking cover wherever it might present itself, " the 5th Texas used every tree, sapling, and stump in their advance. The Federals also had good protection for a while, as the road itself was more gully than actual road.[47]

The 13th Michigan got only as far as the fence on the east side of the farm before running into the 5th Texas. As the 4th Texas then worked its way around the Michiganders' left flank, these Yankees fell back into the crowded ditch on the side of the road. Members of the 58th Indiana and the 26th Ohio got farther than all the rest of Buell's brigade with a bayonet charge. But as they neared the farmhouse and stables, several companies blundered across the road to within yards of the 5th Texas, lying in the ditch below the rise. The Texans stood up and opened fire, and the small Federal

46 Polley, *Hood's Texas Brigade*, 210. Cozzens, *This Terrible Sound*, 202-04; Simpson, *Gaines' Mill to Appomattox*, 158-59.

47 Robert Campbell to Father, September 29, 1863, in Skoch, *Lone Star Confederate*, 99; Lasswell, *Rags and Hope*, 203; Cozzens, *This Terrible Sound*, 218.

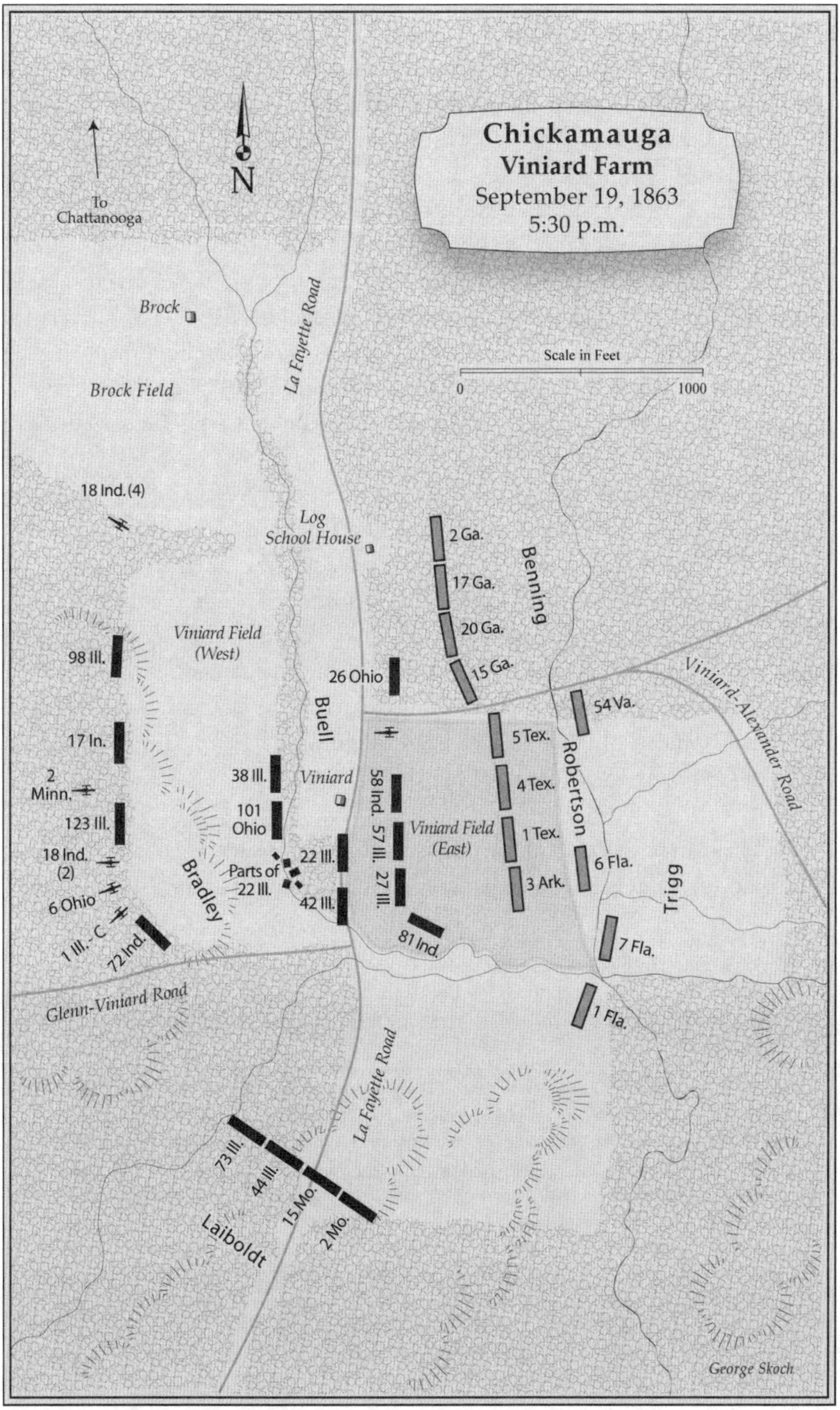
Chickamauga
Viniard Farm
September 19, 1863
5:30 p.m.
To Chattanooga
N
Brock
Brock Field
La Fayette Road
Scale in Feet
0
1000
18 Ind. (4)
Log School House
2 Ga.
17 Ga.
20 Ga.
15 Ga.
Benning
Viniard Field (West)
98 Ill.
26 Ohio
Buell
54 Va.
Viniard-Alexander Road
17 In.
5 Tex.
Robertson
2 Minn.
38 Ill.
Viniard
58 Ind.
4 Tex.
101 Ohio
123 Ill.
57 Ill.
Viniard Field (East)
1 Tex.
18 Ind. (2)
22 Ill.
Parts of 22 Ill.
27 Ill.
3 Ark.
6 Fla.
Trigg
6 Ohio
Bradley
42 Ill.
81 Ind.
7 Fla.
1 Ill.-C
72 Ind.
Glenn-Viniard Road
1 Fla.
La Fayette Road
73 Ill.
44 Ill.
15 Mo.
2 Mo.
Laiboldt
George Skoch

command quickly melted away in the smoke. The Viniard farm began to resemble some horrid abattoir, with Federal soldiers squeezed in like sheep desperately attempting to flee the carnage in the yard. Eventually, the Texans forced the majority of Heg's and Carlin's troops to flee west to the protective fire of Wilder's Spencer repeating rifles.[48]

The Texans' last assault had been bold, but costly. Within a short time, the regimental commanders of the 1st, 4th, and 5th Texas regiments fell wounded. Major Jefferson C. Rogers, then commanding the regiment, toppled with a severe wound in the left side, and command of the regiment passed to Capt. J. S. Cleveland of Company H. Robert Campbell was struck down with wounds in his arm and leg while pursuing fleeing Yankees. Smither also took a wound that he reported "stays sore longer than any flesh wound ever inflicted on a rebel soldier." Or so he told his mother.[49]

In their hasty retreat, the Federals abandoned four pieces of artillery and fell back to a line of timber a quarter mile west of the La Fayette Road. However, the sheer numbers of Federals and their firepower concealed in the breastworks to the west soon forced the Texans to withdraw from their advanced position back toward their main line. As they fell back from the ditch and farmyard, they again came under accurate, heavy artillery fire as well as hot fire from the repeating rifles of Wilder's men who pursued them during the retreat. In desperation, the brigade turned about and repelled the Federals from their barricaded position for the second time. Lt. Benjamin Franklin of Company I wrote home after the fight that:

> The Yanks fought well but we charged them and they gave way when our lines on the right and left of our Brigade give way we were forced to retire a short distance when

48 *OR* 30, pt. 1, 654, 662; Cozzens, *This Terrible Sound*, 217-18; Robert Campbell to Father, September 29, 1863, in Skoch, *Lone Star Confederate*, 99; "The 26th Ohio Veteran Volunteer Infantry," accessed January 23, 2009, www.geocities.com/ovi26th/onehundredfortyyearsagojan63.html.

49 *OR* 30, pt.1, 654, 662; Mark Smither to Elizabeth Smither, November 3, 1863, in SHSU; Evans, *Confederate Military History*, 11:177-78; Cozzens, *This Terrible Sound*, 217-18; Skoch, *Lone Star Confederate*, xvii; "The 26th Ohio Veteran Volunteer Infantry," accessed January 23, 2009, www.geocities.com/ovi26th/onehundredfortyyearsagojan63.html. Campbell was furloughed to recuperate, first in Richmond, then Selma, Alabama. He later sought reassignment out of the infantry, which recommendation ultimately reached President Davis with a favorable endorsement from Hood. Skoch, *Lone Star Confederate*, xvii; 98-100. Instead, he became a brigade courier upon his return to duty. Smither recuperated in the Welch household near Marietta, Georgia, where he informed his mother that he was having a "splendid time," being cared for by Mr. Welch's three daughters. The Welches had two nephews in Company D, likewise wounded at Chickamauga, recuperating there as well. Mark Smither to Elizabeth Smither, November 3, 1863, in SHSU.

> we reformed and again charged them they resisted stubbornly and we came to close quarters punishing them severely and driving them in confusion before us but I am sorry to say with considerable loss ourselves.[50]

Robertson, now desperately desiring to hold the only high ground on the Viniard farm, sent for artillery and infantry support. Unfortunately, he received no artillery assistance , but he did get infantry support at about 4:00 p.m. from Benning's brigade. Law directed Benning to advance 200 yards in support of the Texas Brigade against what remained of Davis's and Buell's troops defending the ground parallel to the western side of La Fayette Road.[51]

In this action, Fletcher watched the Yankees crowd against a fence blocking their retreat. He fired two shots into the crowd, all the while lamenting , "oh, for a shot-gun loaded with buck shot!" As he moved past the corner of the Viniard House for a better shot, a piece of shrapnel ripped across his left foot, and he tumbled backwards into a hole beside a chimney. As he got up, he discovered the heel of his left shoe had been shot off and his heel badly mangled. With the fight raging over the ground where he lay, Fletcher deemed it prudent under the circumstances to hop to the rear and safety. After about 75 yards, he fell against an oak tree to catch his breath. Under the tree was a wounded Yankee, sitting down for protection from the bullets of his own regiment. "Pain here struck me and I felt faint," Fletcher recounted, "so with a hop or two I was at the Yank's side, and as there was not room enough for two, I gave him a shove, saying: 'The day is ours.'"

Soon Fletcher gathered his strength and continued hopping towards the rear until pain "blinded" him. But not completely. Upon encountering a dead Yankee, he refused to miss this opportunity to gather his "fair share" of battlefield plunder. "Wounded though he was," he quickly went through the dead man's possessions. "He was a poor corpse and it was a poor haul," Fletcher observed. "[H]is knapsack was good but was light and as I did not have time to make an honorable exchange, I had it off and on my shoulders, over mine, in quick time." Fletcher soon found the Confederate main lines and an ambulance. As he bounced toward the field hospital, he opened the knapsack and found several "well written sweet letters" from a "sweet girl stuck on" the dead enemy. In the letters, the sweetheart anticipated a happy meeting and "fulfillment of vows, when the 'Rebs' were whipped and the cruel war was over."

50 Benjamin Franklin to wife, October 2, 1863, Peace Civil War Collection, Navarro College, Corsicana, TX.

51 *OR* 30, pt. 1, 667 & pt. 2, 511, 513-14, 516, 518; Dave Dameron, *Benning's Brigade: A History and Roster of the Fifteenth Georgia* (Spartanburg, SC, 1997), 1:56-57; Foley, "John Bell Hood's Division," 50-51; Cozzens, *This Terrible Sound*, 212, 221.

Fletcher expressed he felt no guilt about "being a party to breaking up that match." The inexorable logic of war had prevailed. "She wanted me whipped— she got that; I wanted dead Yankees—I got that. So both at least got part of their wants satisfied."[52]

Meanwhile, the Texas Brigade remained heavily pressed. Four separate Union artillery batteries had now joined the seemingly eternal Spencer rifle fire on Fletcher's comrades. In the northwest corner of the field, Capt. Eli Lilly's 18th Indiana Battery had four guns raking the Texans' right flank. In the southwest corner, Lilly positioned the remaining section of the 18th Indiana and the 6th Ohio Battery, left behind by Col. Charles G. Harker when he retreated north, all pouring double-shotted canister into the Texans' left flank. In between, the 2nd Minnesota Light Artillery and Capt. George Estep's 8th Indiana Battery blasted the men from the front. Benning advanced forward to within 100 yards of the Viniard House, moving to support the Texans' last assault on the left flank. This combined force crossed the road through brutal fire, taking cover in the western ditch of La Fayette Road. In fierce combat and dense smoke, the Confederates finally rolled over the Federals, securing the field around the Viniard House, and establishing defensive positions to ward off counterattacks. The remnants of Heg's troops withdrew to positions behind Wilder's brigade. Near the Viniard House, Robertson and Benning continued to beseech artillery support and additional reinforcements, but none came.[53]

Without reinforcements and under unbearable cannon bombardment, the high ground Benning and the Texans occupied could not be held. Lilly's 18th Indiana Battery proved exceptionally effective in stopping the Texans. Its raking canister fire

52 Fletcher, *Rebel Private*, 97-110. Fletcher arrived at the infirmary after dark and was placed on some straw near the operating table. One of Fletcher's comrades from Company F came in, shot through the side of his face and nose. Though terribly disfigured, his wounded comrade said that at least he could turn away his disfigured side in public, whereas Fletcher would not be able to hide his "wooden leg." This suggestion of amputation, which the comrade claimed he had overheard from one of the surgeons, disturbed Fletcher considerably. After watching another soldier's foot being amputated, Fletcher decided he would be having none of it. During the surgeon's examination, Fletcher shoved him with his good leg. "I will leave you alone," declared the harried doctor, "without treatment." Which was fine with Fletcher. The next evening he was transported to Augusta, quartered in a church, and carefully attended by the Sisters of Charity (to whom he was grateful the rest of his life). After a painful recovery, including gangrene and a broken ankle, he healed and rejoined the 5th Texas in East Tennessee. While there, he was granted a transfer to the 8th Texas Cavalry, known as Terry's Texas Rangers.

53 *OR* 30, pt. 2, 518; Dameron, *Benning's Brigade*, 57; Foley, "John Bell Hood's Division," 52-54. Unfortunately, Porter Alexander's guns had not arrived on the field as yet, and Bragg's Reserve Artillery was not available due to other requirements. The 18th Indiana Light Artillery, under Captain Eli Lilly, had six three inch ordnance rifles and four mountain howitzers in its arsenal that day. Steve Cameron, "In Defense of the Mountain Howitzer," *The Artilleryman*, (2003), 24:2003, 1-2.

up and down the ditch providing their cover compelled them to retreat. "The ditch was literally full of dead and wounded and proved to be a self made grave for hundreds of them," wrote one of the Indiana gunners. Wilder confirmed that Lilly fired 200 rounds of double-shotted canister at ranges of between 75 and 350 yards. "At this point it actually seemed a pity to kill men so," he said. "They fell in heaps, and I had it in my head to order the firing to cease, to end the awful sight."[54]

Benning was forced back across La Fayette Road, with staggering losses, including 17 of his 23 officers in the 20th Georgia alone. The 5th Texas, with the rest of the brigade, and Benning's Brigade, fended off repeated assaults from Heg's and Buell's troops for another two hours. The Texas and Benning's Brigades held their positions until 6:00 p.m., as the sun was setting, with men by then completely exhausted and severely bloodied. Meanwhile, troops of the 27th Illinois and 58th Indiana succeeded in pulling the four recently recaptured guns of Estep's 8th Indiana Battery back to their line, along with the fallen colors of the 21st Illinois.[55]

Following a third, unanswered request for artillery support, Law ordered the two battered brigades to withdraw under the cover of darkness 150 yards east of La Fayette Road where they lay in line of battle for the night, within earshot of the groans and cries of the Viniard House slaughter pen. As the weary regiment retired back through the woods where it had earlier encouraged Stewart's bloodied troops to "rise up . . . and see the Texans go in," the Tennesseans, still on the field licking their wounds, taking advantage of the opportunity, greeted them with pointed mockery: "Rise up, Tennesseans, and see the Texans come out." Both Robertson and Benning later wrote bitterly that they could have secured and held the field had the repeatedly requested support been provided. Hood's entire division bivouacked a half mile northeast of the Viniard House and La Fayette Road, building temporary breastworks and maintaining a "one-third security" for the night. The regiment, hungry and weary after the bloody fighting, rested on its arms as the men prepared biscuits from a ration of rice flour.[56]

The first full day's fighting at Chickamauga, with brutal combat all along the line and staggering casualties on both sides, produced scant gain for either. Bragg failed to

54 John Rowell, *Yankee Artillerymen: Through the Civil War With Eli Lilly's Indiana Battery* (Knoxville, TN, 1975), 117.

55 Cozzens, *This Terrible Sound*, 227-29.

56 *OR* 30, pt. 1, 448, 595, & pt. 2, 518; Cozzens, *This Terrible Sound*, 225, 227-29; Foley, "John Bell Hood's Division," 53, 59; Foote, *Civil War Narrative*, 2:721; J. Gary Laine and Morris M., *Law's Alabama Brigade in the War Between the Union and the Confederacy* (Shippensburg, PA, 1996), 156. The tangled, wooded terrain and the confusion and chaos of battle most likely account for the fact that General Robertson's couriers were unable to contact Maj. Robertson for artillery support. Robertson, "With the Reserve Artillery," 251; Simpson, *Lee's Grenadier Guard*, 320.

either gain possession of La Fayette Road (although the brigade had temporarily held a section of it) or isolate the Yankees from Chattanooga. Rosecrans, in turn, failed to drive the Southerners across Chickamauga Creek and back to Dalton. During the night, the Federals built breastworks to protect their position on La Fayette Road, and assumed a more compact defensive arrangement through shortening their lines to about three miles. That evening Longstreet, with two brigades of McLaw's Division, finally arrived from Virginia.[57]

Bragg now divided the army into two wings, assigning Longstreet to command the newly-formulated left wing and Polk, the right. Bragg's army formed a line more or less parallel with the La Fayette Road, facing west. On the Federal side, McCook's Corps faced La Fayette Road in the center, with Crittenden on the right, slightly withdrawn, west of the road. Nothing that cold night made more of an impression on the soldiers of both sides than the horrible wails of the wounded. Alva Griest of the 72nd Indiana wrote of the plaints and pleadings from thousands of wounded between the lines in agonizing pain and thirst. "Oh, if yet I must sleep in spite of it all," he jotted in his journal.[58]

Bragg met with his commanders and formulated a plan for renewing the battle in the morning. It was virtually devoid of any creativity. Polk received oral instructions to attack at daylight on the extreme right with his right wing. Because of the dense forest and limited visibility, each brigade would begin moving only after the left flank of the unit to its right started forward. The left wing thus had to await the attack from the right, with the whole line, once engaged, pushing "vigorously and persistently against the enemy throughout its extent." Bragg was actually retaining his original plan of turning the Union left, pushing Rosecrans south into McLemore's Cove. Unaware of the meeting, Hood arrived late, just before Polk departed. There he found a rather

57 Longstreet's train arrived at Ringgold at approximately 2:00 p.m. As he and his staff disembarked, they were taken aback that no one from Bragg's staff was there to greet them, not even a guide to assist them to the front. So Longstreet had to wait two hours for the train carrying the group's horses to arrive. It was well after dark before they made it to the east bank of Chickamauga Creek, and from there they then had to find a safe passage to Bragg's headquarters. With Federal pickets accosting them periodically along the way, they did not reach Bragg's headquarters until around 11:00 p.m. that night. *OR* 30, pt. 2, 287; Longstreet, *Manassas to Appomattox*, 438; Sorrell, *Confederate Staff Officer*, 193; Cozzens, *This Terrible Sound*, 299, 301.

58 *OR* 30, pt. 2, 32-33, 287-88; Cozzens, *This Terrible Sound*, 283; Sullivan, *Chickamauga*, 19. Bragg offered no credible explanation for the sudden restructuring. Such a move midway through a battle "not only was imprudent, but was also bound to create further ill will in the high command." Polk and D. H. Hill were both lieutenant generals, as was Longstreet. Dividing the army into two wings relegated Hill to a corps commander under Polk—a position tantamount to no job at all. Cozzens, *This Terrible Sound*, 300.

"detached" group of commanders. Among them was Maj. Gen. John C. Breckinridge, a childhood friend, sitting listless on a tree root, a slouch hat covering his face, unwilling to engage in conversation. Hood began "rambling on alone" about the battle, expressing his sincere belief that they would rout the Yankees in the morning. "My dear Hood, I am delighted to hear you say so," Breckinridge exclaimed, springing to his feet. "You give me renewed hope; God grant it may be so." With that, Breckinridge rode off with Polk, and Hood approached Bragg for his new orders.[59]

Polk returned to headquarters before issuing written orders for the next day. His plan called for D. H. Hill to initiate the attack at daylight. Orders to that effect, however, carried by a member of Polk's headquarters escort, were never delivered, and the erstwhile courier did not even report his failure. Consequently Hill was totally unaware that he was to lead the morning's attack.[60]

Hood had arrived in Georgia with nothing beyond what he brought with him on the train. His men lacked even a single wagon or ambulance for conveying their wounded. "They were destitute of almost everything," Hood later recalled, "except pride, spirit, and forty rounds of ammunition to the man." Soon he chanced upon Col. J. Stoddard Johnson of Buckner's staff, who invited Hood to his bivouac. While the conditions there were still Spartan, the company was good. Hood was soon asleep on a pile of leaves beside Johnson, the two sharing a blanket. Meanwhile, Longstreet finally got to Bragg's headquarters after 11:00 p.m.; Bragg was awakened from a sound sleep, and the two talked for over an hour. Afterwards, a seemingly satisfied Longstreet bedded down right there, without contacting his own command, or communicating at all with Hood or Buckner.[61]

At sunup on September 20, the 5th Texas formed in battle line with the brigade about three quarters of a mile northeast of the Viniard House and La Fayette Road. Soon thereafter, the Texans were ordered north and right approximately a half mile to their new attack position some 500 yards east of La Fayette Road and the Brotherton field, "the stronghold of the enemy," as Hood later described the position. The regiment remained there, lying down at 10:00 a.m. to allow Polk's Corps to pass over them to the front—a movement that never took place. Meanwhile the regiment was taking "spirited fire" from both left and right. Longstreet's wing had Stewart's, Johnson's, Hindman's, and Preston's divisions in its front. Johnson and Hindman

59 Cozzens, *This Terrible Sound*, 301; Hood, *Advance and Retreat*, 62-63; William C. Davis, *Breckinridge: Statesman, Soldier, Symbol* (Baton Rouge, LA, 1973), 370-71.

60 Hill, "Chickamauga," in *B&L*, 652-53; Cozzens, *This Terrible Sound*, 302-03; *OR* 30, pt. 2, 140. Connelly, *Autumn of Glory*, 213.

61 *OR* 30, pt. 2, 287-88; Hood, *Advance and Retreat*, 62-63; J. Stoddard Johnson, "General J. B. Hood and Chickamauga," *CV* (1905), 13:552; Longstreet, *Manassas to Appomattox*, 376.

each had one brigade in their rear as a reserve, comprising a second line. Hood's Division, under Law's command, was deployed with two brigades forward and one back in reserve to the rear and east of Johnson, thereby forming a third and fourth line of the wing. When McLaws' Division finally arrived from Ringgold, Kershaw and Humphreys' Brigades were deployed behind Hood's in yet a fifth line. Thus, Longstreet had a masked column five brigades deep occupying a front about a quarter mile wide.[62]

Events were not progressing as Bragg expected—there was no dawn attack because of confusion within Polk's right wing command. Hill, who was supposed to lead the assault had been absent from the previous night's meeting and did not receive his orders until 6:00 a.m. and even then he remained "indifferent" about the need for haste. He received further orders at 8:00 a.m., this time delivered personally by an enraged Bragg. Another delay ensued getting the troops moved into line of battle. At around 9:30 a.m., Breckinridge finally advanced, followed by Cleburne's men. The left of the Union line quickly fell back from the attack, but the Confederate advance was soon retarded by heavy fire from the Union breastworks. Neither side made any appreciable gain on this sector of the field. Equally matched, neither Thomas nor Polk could demonstrate any appreciable gains the entire morning. Bragg's patience finally gave out: at 11:00 a.m. he ordered a general attack all along the line. Consequently, Longstreet ordered the advance of his left wing, choosing to move forward with a "column of brigades at half distance," a masterpiece tactic.[63]

The Federal center, Longstreet's focus of attack, was held by Brig. Gen. Thomas J. Wood's division of the XXI Corps. To Wood's immediate left was Brannan's Division, and on Brannan's left, that of Maj. Gen. Joseph J. Reynolds. As Longstreet made his final preparations, a devastating blunder occurred on the Union side. Capt. Sanford C. Kellogg, Maj. Gen. Thomas's aide-de-camp and nephew, inaccurately reported Brannan's division out of line, thus exposing Reynolds' division on the flank. Without substantiating this intelligence, Rosecrans immediately ordered Wood to close up and support Reynolds. To accomplish this, Wood had to pull his entire division out of line and cross behind Brannan's division in order to reach Reynolds. The departure of Wood's division to close a non-existent gap in fact created one in the Union line where none previously existed. Wood's movement behind Brannan's force

62 *OR* 30, pt. 2, 511, 516; Foley, "John Bell Hood's Division," 63-65; J. T. Hunter, "Lieut. Gen. John B. Hood," *CV* (1916), 24:258; Laine, *Law's Alabama Brigade*, 157.

63 *OR* 30, pt. 1, 277, pt. 2, 209; Connelly, *Autumn of Glory*, 220; Cozzens, *This Terrible Sound*, 307-09, 319-22; Hill, "Chickamauga—The Great Battle in the West" in *B&L*, 653.

was well underway when Longstreet's five advancing divisions struck this gaping breach in the line.[64]

Longstreet, as was his custom, had massed his force five brigades deep to aim at a single point for a concentrated effort, in this case the Brotherton cabin. He selected this objective based upon the advice of his "secret weapon"—Tom Brotherton, a Confederate officer who had lived in that particular cabin before the war and was intimately familiar with the local topography. The cabin provided an ideal target for a breakthrough: no adjacent high ground, nor any streams or rivers impeded an advance. The presence of some rudimentary roads would allow Confederate wagons to the front. Moreover, the cabin stood just short of a mile in front of Widow Glenn's house, which Rosecrans currently occupied as his field headquarters.[65]

Longstreet's hordes hit Wood's and Brannan's divisions on their exposed right flank and drove them from the field of battle. On the other side of this 300 yard-wide gap, the onrushing Confederates struck Davis's division, then in the process of marching up to replace Wood in the line, as well as the flank of Maj. Gen. Philip H. Sheridan's division of the XX Corps. Brannan tried to stabilize the Federal troops at the breakthrough, calling on Col. John T. Croxton's brigade for assistance. Croxton slowed the gray juggernaut to a degree, harassing Benning's Georgians as they advanced, but Croxton soon went down, and his force retreated northward. Crittenden also attempted to organize a line of battle, but he, too, soon withdrew to a ridge in the rear. In short order, the entire Federal right flank had crumbled and was being driven from the field. Wilder's Brigade on its extreme right stood valiantly for a few minutes, but nothing, even repeating rifles, could arrest this Confederate onslaught, and Wilder was soon forced to withdraw as well, to avoid being cut off.[66]

Eight Confederate brigades, including those of Hood's Division, poured rapidly through the half mile gap in the enemy line as a result of the Federal blunder. Hood's

64 *OR* 30, pt. 1, 635, 983; William Lamers, *The Edge of Glory: A Biography of William S. Rosecrans, U. S. A.* (New York, 1961), 343; Cozzens, *This Terrible Sound*, 350-63; Sullivan, *Chickamauga*, 20-21. Wood knew when he read the order that Brannan was in position, and that no vacancy existed. However, he had been twice upbraided by profanity-laced, written reprimands for failing to obey orders promptly. Additionally, 90 minutes before, he was dressed down in front of his entire staff. Thus, Wood indicated to the dumbfounded messenger that he would "move at once," indicating the "meaning of the order 'was clear and undoubted,'" and that he was glad the order was in writing "for future reference," telling his staff: "Gentlemen, I hold the fatal order of the day in my hand and would not part with it for five thousand dollars." Cozzens, *This Terrible Sound*, 362-63; *OR* 30, pt. 1, 983-84.

65 *OR* 30, pt. 1, 448, 462, 548; Gates P. Thurston, "The Crisis at Chickamauga," in *B&L*, 3:664; Cozzens, *This Terrible Sound*, 316; Sullivan, *Chickamauga*, 21-22.

66 *OR* 30, pt. 2, 288, 503; Cozzens, *This Terrible Sound*, 368-75; Connelly, *Autumn of Glory*, 222; Sullivan, *Chickamauga*, 21-22.

lead column, followed by his own division marching three brigades deep, began advancing at 11:10 a.m., with the brigades of Kershaw and Humphreys as additional support. He personally led the advance by divisions in column forward, toward La Fayette Road. Law, following in furtherance of Hood's orders, ordered Hood's Division to move forward at a steady pace. He arranged the division in a triangular formation, with his own brigade, now under Colonel Perry in front, and Robertson's and Benning's to the left and right, respectively, some 300 to 400 yards behind Perry.[67]

As the movement began, Capt. Cleveland, previously commanding Company H, but now commanding the regiment after the wounding of Maj. Rogers, delivered an encouraging "valedictory" to the men and placed himself in front of the colors as the regiment started forward. "[O]n they came like an angry flood." McCook and Davis, with the remaining three brigades of XX Corps, executed a gallant but futile resistance as the Confederates swarmed their flanks, striking Wood's last brigade as it was pulling out. The regiment crossed La Fayette Road just south of the Brotherton cabin and advanced for some distance through the broken, timbered country before encountering small arms fire. During the movement, the Texans suffered casualties when hit by shrapnel from massed Federal batteries to their front. After advancing a mile under this artillery fire, the men tangled with Union cavalry of considerable strength, supported by artillery positioned on a wooded hill to their right front. The Texans immediately wheeled to the right, moving directly toward the smoke-shrouded hill. In so doing, with the rest of Hood's force, they reached Dyer Field.

The combined brigades of Fulton, Sugg, McNair, Perry, and Robertson charged from the woods into Dyer field at 11:45 a.m. "It was a triumph of rare splendor," writes historian Peter Cozzens. "All who witnessed the movement were deeply moved." No one captured the exhilaration better than Bushrod Johnson:

> Our lines now emerged from the forest into open ground on the border of long, open fields, over which the enemy was retreating . . . . The scene now presented was unspeakably grand. The resolute and impetuous charge, the rush of our heavy columns sweeping from the shadow and gloom of the forest into the open fields flooded with sunlight, the glitter of arms, the onward dash of artillery and mounted

67 *OR* 30, pt. 1, 402, 635, 1070, pt. 2, 303, 363, 392, 457, 511; Cozzens, *This Terrible Sound*, 340, 368-72; Laine, *Law's Alabama Brigade*, 161. Col. Sheffield, commanding Law's Brigade, was thrown from his horse and seriously injured his back, forcing him to quit the field on the afternoon of September 19; Col. William Frank Perry of the 44th Alabama assumed command of the brigade. Some authorities place Sheffield back in command the next day; however, Perry led the brigade on September 20. See DiNardo and Nofi, *James Longstreet*, 125, 156; Foley, "John Bell Hood's Division," 65-68.

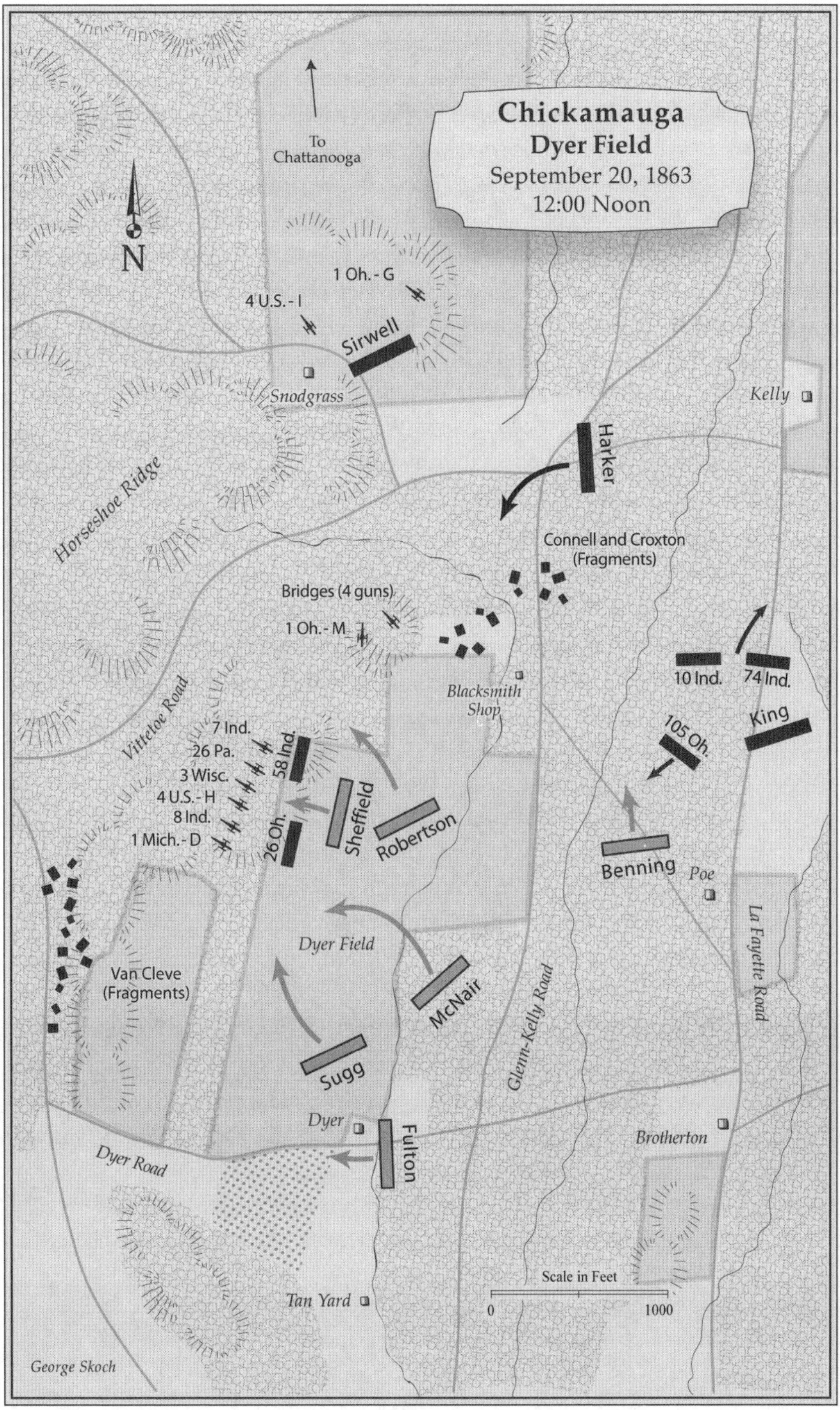
Chickamauga
Dyer Field
September 20, 1863
12:00 Noon
To
Chattanooga
N
1 Oh. - G
4 U.S. - I
Sirwell
Snodgrass
Kelly
Harker
Horseshoe Ridge
Connell and Croxton
(Fragments)
Bridges (4 guns)
1 Oh. - M
Blacksmith
Shop
10 Ind.
74 Ind.
King
105 Oh.
Vittetoe Road
7 Ind.
26 Pa.
3 Wisc.
4 U.S. - H
8 Ind.
1 Mich. - D
58 Ind.
26 Oh.
Sheffield
Robertson
Benning
Poe
La Fayette Road
Dyer Field
Van Cleve
(Fragments)
McNair
Glenn-Kelly Road
Sugg
Dyer
Fulton
Brotherton
Dyer Road
Scale in Feet
0
1000
Tan Yard
George Skoch

> men, the retreat of the foe, the shouts of the hosts of our army, the dust, the smoke, the noise of fire-arms—of whistling balls and grape-shot and of burning shell—made up a battle scene of unsurpassed grandeur.

Hood soon interrupted Johnson's reverie. Much remained to be done before congratulations were in order. First, the 6th Ohio Battery from Rosecrans's previous headquarters, as well as the massive batteries of Maj. John Mendenhall, XXI corps' chief of artillery, located on a ridge 1,000 yards away, needed to be silenced. To this end, Hood directed Johnson to "Go ahead, and keep ahead of everything."[68]

While the disorganized Federals fled back through the field near Widow Glenn's house, Rosecrans, with Crittenden and McCook, were caught up in the breakthrough, and fled the field. Assistant Secretary of War Charles Dana, sleeping from sheer exhaustion near the Widow Glenn cabin, awoke at 11:00 a.m. with a start by what he later described as "the most infernal noise I ever heard." As he shook the cobwebs of sleep away, he observed devout Catholic Rosecrans crossing himself. "[I]f the general is crossing himself," he thought, "we are in a desperate situation." He then witnessed the Federal line "break and melt away like leaves before the wind." The routed troops withdrew to the northwest through McFarland's Gap to Rossville. This exodus, which included army commander Rosecrans, left Thomas in command of all remaining Union forces in the field.[69]

Moving forward, the Confederates took a terrific pounding. The converging fire of Mendenhall's massed artillery and Battery M, of the 1st Ohio, limited their penetration beyond the Dyer field. The Texans advanced northwesterly against Battery M, located on a small knoll. Perry moved diagonally across Dyer field against the northern tip of the ridge, while Benning felt his way south, paralleling La Fayette Road. Perry's men soon overran the 26th Pennsylvania Light Artillery and the 7th Indiana Battery, capturing three guns. To the south, Sugg's Brigade of Georgians hit the 8th Indiana Battery, which fled, leaving six guns. On the left, the 4th U. S. Artillery lost one gun. In all, Crittenden's Corps lost a total of 15 out of its 26 guns.[70]

The Texans entered Dyer field from the south. Kellogg, Thomas's aide-de-camp, observed a large force moving into an open cornfield to the rear of Reynold's position "advancing cautiously with skirmishers deployed." As he rode closer to verify their

68 *OR* 30, pt. 2, 303, 363, 457, 511, 516-18; Cozzens, *This Terrible Sound*, 374-75; Thurston, "Crisis at Chickamauga," in *B&L*, 3:663-64.

69 Cozzens, *This Terrible Sound*, 380; Charles Dana, *Recollections of the Civil War* (New York, 1898), 115; Lamers, *Edge of Glory*, 351; Sullivan, *Chickamauga*, 21-22.

70 *OR* 30, pt. 1, 622-23; Cozzens, *This Terrible Sound*, 400-03.

identity as friend or foe, it fired on him. This unidentified force was actually the Texas Brigade. And for the first and only time in its storied and heroic history, the it earned laurels for its attractive appearance. Most of Hood's men had drawn new uniforms in route to Georgia. Their new garb, however, consisted of dark blue shell jackets and light blue trousers. The first impression of an observer from Cheatham's Division "was that they were Yankees," partly by the color of their uniforms, but more by its uniformity, and the superior style of their equipment, in haversacks, canteens and knapsacks. The contrast between them and General Bragg's motley, ragged troops was arresting. "They were certainly superior to the troops of the Army of Tennessee in dress."[71]

The Texans' objective was the small knoll to their north where Battery M of the 1st Ohio stood, still booming away. If taken, the knoll opened the way to Negley's batteries, then Snodgrass Hill. Seize Snodgrass Hill and Thomas' entire Kelly Field line would immediately be in dire jeopardy. As the Texans stepped into the cornfield, Robertson ordered them to wheel to the right, to take the knoll from the flank. The Texans angled almost due north against this battery which occupied a rise of ground northwest of a small field abutting the northern end of Dyer field. The brigade's right flank swung around to within 300 yards of Brig. Gen. Wood's division of Crittenden's corps, who immediately ordered up Col. Charles G. Harker's brigade to check their advance.[72]

The Texas Brigade "in full and plain view in the open fields" evidently "far outnumbered mine," Wood later erroneously reported. Harker's men opened fire on the brigade before Robertson realized what had happened. The smoke from 50 cannons and 10,000 muskets completely enveloped the Texans. The Texas lines quickly became broken and irregular, making it difficult for men to recognize their leaders. Companies, even regiments, were soon overlapping each other. Before Robertson could restore order, Harker attacked, and a fierce and bloody confrontation followed. "That was the meanest, most unsatisfactory place I struck during the whole war," a member of the 4th Texas later recalled. Soon, the 4th Texas began to recoil in disorder, having absorbed the brunt of the heavy flanking fire. Meanwhile, the 1st Texas and the 3rd Arkansas fought their way to the crest, only to find that Battery M had already been withdrawn.[73]

71 Cozzens, *This Terrible Sound*, 406-408; Todd, *First Texas Regiment*, 18.

72 S. P. Snider, "Reminiscences of the War," *Glimpses of the Nation's Struggle," MOLLUS, Minnesota Commandery*, 242; *OR* 30, pt. 2, 1863, 636-37, 514; Cozzens, *This Terrible Sound*, 407-09.

73 *OR* 30, pt. 1, 636, pt. 2, 512, 514; Lasswell, *Rags and Hope*, 203-04, 207-208; DiNardo & Nofti, *James Longstreet*, 125; Cozzens, *This Terrible Sound*, 408-09.

The Texans had advanced so far so rapidly to the front and right that they were now well ahead of the rest of the army. Robertson had unsuccessfully requested support for both his flanks before assaulting the hill. And now that he possessed it, his position was untenable, totally isolated from the rest of the army and under heavy assault. Suddenly he was taking fire from both rear flanks—musketry later believed to have come from other Confederate forces. With his line thrown into confusion, isolated, and under fire now from three directions, Robertson had no recourse but to escape the fatal crossfire and take cover in a section of nearby woods while reforming.[74]

While the rest of the brigade was moving up the knoll, however, the 5th Texas was moving in a different direction because Capt. Cleveland obeyed an order to fall back, moving the regiment 100 yards to the rear. Word soon came from Robertson, however, to press forward, and the regiment again moved out and helped capture a Federal battery to its left. As the regiment subsequently moved across Dyer field to rejoin the brigade, its right flank came under fire from Federals in the woods. The regiment immediately made a right half-wheel, firing a volley into its tormentors that "proved so fatal that they scattered and fled." Cleveland took the regimental flag with a portion of the regiment, and moved off to rejoin the brigade. Upon reaching the woods on the heights, though, the brigade began falling back, recrossing the Dyer field. While giving the order to withdraw, Cleveland took a severe wound in the thigh.[75]

When Cleveland started back to rejoin the brigade, he had left Capt. Clay and 25 or 30 men of the regiment to hold the enemy in check. Clay's men were successful in their mission, driving the Federals from their breastworks and prompting them to set fire to the works and provisions. During the movements, Sgt. John Calhoun Cox of Company C fell carrying the colors. The flag was quickly retrieved, but Cox was seriously wounded in the middle of his lower back by a lead ball that cut through his rectum and before striking the pubic bone and finally coming to rest close to his femoral artery. Lt. Samuel S. Streetman, who was then commanding Company G, fell mortally wounded during the last advance that day by the Texans. The regiment captured a number of prisoners and three pieces of Federal artillery, which it retained until the 8th South Carolina stepped forward to claim the guns. Clay's portion of the

74 *OR* 30, pt. 1, 402, 636, *OR* 30, pt. 2, 512, 514-15; Lasswell, *Rags and Hope*, 203-04, 207-08; Cozzens, *This Terrible Sound*, 408-409; Polley, *Hood's Texas Brigade*, 210; Foley, "John Bell Hood's Division," 70.

75 Joskins, "A Sketch of Hood's Texas Brigade," in UTSA, 142-43; Cozzens, *This Terrible Sound*, 408-410; *OR* 30, pt. 2, 515-16.

5th Texas, left behind to hold the enemy back, was ordered to rejoin the balance of the brigade.[76]

Once Robertson yielded his position, the Confederates poured back down the slope of the knoll into the Dyer field. Having been thrown into the battle early in the initial breakthrough, the brigade was not involved in subsequent major assaults against Sheridan and Davis, or the turning movement behind the Federal center and its futile thrashing against Thomas on Snodgrass Hill. Hood had been directing the battle on the Confederate left from a ridge some 300 yards behind where Robertson's men had just made their hasty retreat. Animated by the sight of his old command retiring from the field in obvious confusion, he galloped over to the woods to where the Texans were reforming for another assault. He rode amongst the disorganized Texans, encouraging, exhorting them to stand their ground. While he and Robertson conversed in front of those woods, a bullet struck Hood in the upper thigh, shattering bone. Some men of his old brigade caught him as he fell. Several witnesses thought the shot had come from friendly fire—maybe from the same troops who had fired on the brigade previously. Incapacitated once more, Hood's command devolved upon Bushrod Johnson.[77]

Hood's latest wounding wreaked incalculable harm to the Confederate cause. His presence at the height of the breakthrough was critical. Success depended on rapid exploitation of the breach, and no other commander in Bragg's army had that special type of reckless self-assuredness so appropriate for such moments. His absence threw

76 *OR* 30, pt. 2, 511-17; Hood, Advance and Retreat, 63; Joskins, "A Sketch of Hood's Texas Brigade," 142-43; "John Calhoun Cox," accessed March 13, 2008, www.gennotes.150m.com/batflag.html; "Uncle John Cox," *Nolan County Recorder*, February 15, 1894. Cox was previously wounded at Sharpsburg, where he lost a finger, and again at Gettysburg. He carried this souvenir of Chickamauga in his body for over 30 years, finally having it removed in 1894, carrying the bullet in a velvet bag made by his wife. After the surgery, Cox exclaimed "Now, more than ever, I am ready to make peace with the Yankees." At a reunion of Hood's Brigade on June 26-27, 1903 in Marlin, Texas, an unnamed veteran recalled the fate of so many who carried the colors of the 5th Texas into battle. "I don't know how many men were killed or disabled carrying the flag, but I can count fourteen who were killed under it. In one battle alone, the Wilderness, we lost seven color bearers in less than an hour. The only man living now who ever held that flag in battle is J. C. Cox of Tyler, and he is all shot to pieces." "John Calhoun Cox," accessed March 13, 2008, www.gennotes.150m.com/batflag.html; "Uncle John Cox," *Nolan County Recorder*, February 15, 1894. Cozzens ascribes the friendly fire which hit the Texans' left flank and rear just as Harker's Federals opened on their right as coming from Brig. Gen. Evander McNair's Brigade. Cozzens, *This Terrible Sound*, 409. For more on Cox and Streetman, see Appendix B in Volume 1.

77 *OR* 30, pt. 2, 512; Hood, *Advance and Retreat*, 64; Cozzens, *This Terrible Sound*, 412-13; Foote, *Civil War Narrative*, 2:730.

the command structure into utter chaos. Though unaware of it at the time, the Texans would not see Hood again during the war. The Fates had other plans for him.[78]

Following a long convalescence in Georgia and then Richmond, Hood was promoted to lieutenant general. In February 1864, he was assigned a corps in the Army of Tennessee under Johnston, and several months later, took command of the Army itself, where he remained almost until the end. As a tribute to the admiration and esteem in which his men held Hood, soon after the battle, the brigade took up a collection for "the best" artificial limb then available, since his leg had to be amputated.[79]

Meanwhile, the short pause while the Confederates reorganized gave Thomas just enough time to form a new defensive line (with Brannan's division and portions of three others) further to the north on Snodgrass Hill, almost at right angles with the Union left. Thereafter Thomas met the onslaught of Longstreet's troops "with such stubborn and determined resistance" that he earned the name "Rock of Chickamauga." Longstreet assaulted this line repeatedly, and nearly succeeded in enveloping Brannan's right. At the crucial moment reinforcements finally reached Thomas' position. Maj. Gen. Gordon Granger, without awaiting orders, followed the sound of battle and delivered two brigades of his Reserve Corps to Thomas just in time to impede the Confederates from finally enveloping Brannan's right. Following a fierce fight, the Rebels were forced from the crest of the hill.[80]

Later, Longstreet tried and failed again to carry Snodgrass Hill with McLaws', Hindman's, and Johnson's Divisions. Bragg refused him reinforcements after this. But still determined to make one final attempt to take the hill, Old Pete formed a column of troops he was able to put together for one final assault. The desperate fighting lasted until nightfall, the Federals at one point with their ammunition exhausted repulsing their enemies with bayonets. At length, Longstreet shoved Brig. Gen. James B. Steedman's division of Granger's corps back to the rear ridge and occupied the ground to Brannan's front. But then Thomas pulled away. Thomas who by then had assumed command of all Union forces remaining on the field, received a dispatch at 4:30 p.m. from Rosecrans ordering him to "assume a threatening attitude at

78 Winkler, *Confederate Capital*, 143; Cozzens, *This Terrible Sound*, 412; Dyer, *The Gallant Hood*, 238.

79 Rufus Felder to Mother, October 12, 1863, in Chicoine, *Confederates of Chappel Hill*, 121; Cozzens, *This Terrible Sound*, 412; Dyer, *The Gallant Hood*, 238. The artificial limb, made of cork, likely helped Hood maintain his balance when riding and he kept a spare strapped to his saddle on a second mount. When walking, he preferred using crutches. Wright, *A Southern Girl In '61*, 161.

80 *OR* 30, pt. 2, 457-58; Cozzens, *This Terrible Sound*, 412.

Rossville," some seven miles north of the battlefield. At first, Thomas balked at the thought of leaving the field, believing it would "ruin the army to withdraw it now," instead of awaiting darkness. Soon thereafter, however, he gave orders for a general withdrawal.

The 5th Texas saw no further action at Chickamauga after Hood's wounding. Robertson, recognizing that he could not retake the knoll without considerable support, reformed the brigade in the timber where it had previously taken cover and reported to Law for instructions. Around 3:00 p.m., the Texans received orders to move to the left of Hood's Division and to erect a barricade of logs and rails in their immediate front. Captain Clay took formal command of the regiment, which soon moved to the right, where it remained under desultory artillery fire until 5:00 p.m. Thereafter, it moved forward to its left in the vicinity of Snodgrass Hill. There, the brigade took possession of the heights, relieving Brig. Gen. Archibald Gracie's Brigade in the front lines, and remained on the alert there until the last of the Federal forces had retreated to Chattanooga. Here the regiment was able finally to bivouac for the night.[81]

After some initial bothersome Confederate interference with their withdrawal to Rossville, the Union forces accomplished it in relatively good order. The road back was "a melancholy one" for the Federals: their wounded, having "lain down by the roadside to die," littered the route of march for miles. Disorganized and unruly, the erstwhile "army" that better resembled a mob reached Rossville by about 11:00 p.m. Despite the challenge of reforming the plethora of mixed commands, Thomas succeeded in placing these forces at Rossville Gap and along Missionary Ridge in preparation for any further attacks. By the morning of September 21, the Army of the Cumberland had been more or less reorganized and was largely unmolested in its new position. On the evening of September 21, the Army of the Cumberland was entrenched around Chattanooga.[82]

If the sun at Chickamauga rose red on September 19, it went down much redder on September 20. The great battle for the west—what was later termed the "Gettysburg of the West"—had ended, with total casualties approaching 35,000, second only to Gettysburg. The overall losses on both sides were appalling. Both armies lost approximately 28 percent of their forces. The Federals suffered a total of 16,170 casualties, including 1,657 dead, out of a total of 58,222 engaged. The Confederates had 18,454 total casualties, including 2,312 dead, out of 66,326 engaged.

81 Previous paragraphs based upon *OR* 30, pt. 2, 417, 505, 512, 514-15, 517; Coxe, "Chickamauga," *CV*, 30:294; Simpson, *Lee's Grenadier Guard*, 326.

82 *OR* 30, pt. I, 254-55; Cozzens, *This Terrible Sound*, 476-77, 490, 492-93, 495, 508, 511-12, 520-21; Alfred Hough, *Soldier in the West: The Civil War Letters of Alfred Lacey Hough* (Philadelphia, PA, 1952), 150-52; Lamers, *Edge of Glory*, 366-67; Sullivan, *Chickamauga*, 22-24.

Rufus King Felder
Historical Research Center, Hill College

And for all this blood, the battle was inconclusive in the end. The Confederates had won the field, but Rosecrans had still been allowed to slip away.[83]

The Texans suffered a huge casualty toll. Of the 1,300 men who traveled from Virginia, 570, or close to 44 percent, were casualties. The 5th Texas, the only regiment to officially report its casualties, suffered: 17 killed (initial report said 13), 87 wounded, and 12 missing, 116 total. The loss of brigade officers was especially damaging—the 4th and 5th Texas both lost their commanders and their respective seconds in command. John West wrote home that "The Old Texas Brigade is fearfully cut up. There are not more than 150 in any regiment. The Fifth numbers about 100 and the First about the same." Franklin informed his wife that he and his friend got through the battle unscathed. "Clay got a bullet through his coat sleeve my clothes were not even touched but we lost some of our bravest and best men."[84]

While in route to Georgia, Rufus Felder had obtained a pass to visit family at the old Felder hometown at Orangeburg, South Carolina, while the regiment continued its journey southward. He discovered that the war had ravaged the city and its people. He made a point to visit their old homestead. "I went to the back door & looked out. Everything looked so natural. I did not wish to carry my inspection any farther." Felder was still in South Carolina while his 5th Texas comrades were charging into the inferno along Chickamauga Creek. Having missed one of the biggest battles of the war, Felder wrote, "After I left Orangeburg I heard of the battle that was raging at

83 Sullivan, *Chickamauga*, 24; Richard C. Drum, *Battle of Chickamauga, Ga., September 19-20, 1863* (Washington, DC, 1889), 24; Cozzens, *This Terrible Sound*, 534; West, *Texan in Search of a Fight*, 109; Simpson, *Gaines' Mill to Appomattox*, 164-65. The Confederates did manage to capture an impressive amount of equipment. Longstreet's wing alone captured 40 pieces of artillery, 17,646 small arms, 1,130 sets of accouterments, 393,000 rounds of ammunition, and 10 regimental colors.

84 *OR* 30, pt. 1, 515; Benjamin Franklin to Mary Franklin, October 2, 1863, in Pearce Museum, Navarro College, Corsicana, TX; West, *Texan in Search of a Fight*, 109; Cozzens, *This Terrible Sound*, 534; Simpson, *Gaines' Mill to Appomattox*, 164-65.

Chicamauga. Having seen that our division was seriously engaged, my curiosity was excited to the highest pitch to know who of our devoted band were made victims of the ruthless invaders. I met thousands of wounded between Atlanta & Ringold." Felder soon discovered that his brother-in-law, Thomas Elliott, 24th Texas Cavalry, had been in the fight, and, sadly, was among the dead.[85]

The regiment spent September 21-22 on the battlefield burying its dead, as well as foraging for equipment, clothing, and valuables discarded by the Federals in their hasty retreat. The Texans were buried in a trench long enough to accommodate the number of dead, six feet wide and twenty inches deep. with articles of clothing and blankets placed on the bottom of the trench, and the corpses laid therein "tenderly side by side." Then more clothing and blankets were placed over the dead, and they were covered with red clay Georgia soil.[86]

While Hood's Division was still engaged in the gruesome work of burial detail, together with the more pleasant task of foraging on the battlefield, Brig. Gen. Micah Jenkins' South Carolina Brigade joined them. Jenkins had been assigned to the Division while the trains were traveling to Georgia; however, transportation difficulties prevented his brigade from arriving in time for the fighting. Jenkins outranked Law, so on arrival, he promptly assumed command of the Division, much to the consternation of the Texans, who considered Law the "logical successor of General Hood." Law, after all, had commanded the Division both times Hood was injured—at Gettysburg and again at Chickamauga—and had performed commendably. The Texans placed a "high estimate on his courage and ability," so Jenkins' assumption of command set off a major controversy that festered all through the winter of 1863-64, with major repercussions for the Texans' future.[87]

With the dead finally buried and knapsacks filled with the pickings of the battlefield, the regiment marched north to Rossville on September 23. The men cooked breakfast early on September 23 in their captured pots and pans, then continued their march north to the Confederate lines investing Chattanooga. The regiment crossed Chickamauga Creek and bivouacked for the evening in woods east of Lookout Mountain. The next morning, the men reached the Confederate siege line

85 Rufus Felder to Mother, October 12, 1863, in Chicoine, *Confederates of Chappel Hill*, 112-13; Felder wrote that his father-in-law was going to send for his son's remains. Unfortunately, they were never found.

86 Simpson, *Lee's Grenadier Guard*, 330-31; Hanks, *History of Captain Benton's Company*, 26-27.

87 Polley, *Hood's Texas Brigade*, 213-14; Hamilton, *History of Company M*, 34; Hanks, "History of Captain Benton's Company," 26. Special Orders 216 and Longstreet's directive of September 12, 1863, replaced Anderson's Brigade with Jenkins' Brigade. Jenkins was a particular favorite of Longstreet. *OR* 29, pt. 2, 713.

south of Chattanooga, moving to its assigned post on the left of that line. Private Franklin wrote his wife that "[o]ur lines extend from the river below to the river above completely shutting them [the Federals] in on this side of the river." The Texans occupied a sector of the left flank of the Confederate siege line, about a mile and a half east of the northern point of Lookout Mountain. Here, the regiment built formal breastworks, the first they had ever constructed, and then pitched camp behind this strong defensive line. The Texans would camp here for the next month, performing picket duty, playing plenty of poker, and grousing about the usual things—the quality and quantity of food, the shortage of clothing, and the abominable weather.[88]

While Chickamauga had been a tactical victory, Bragg's failure to pressure his demoralized foe hard turned the victory somewhat pyrrhic. B. A. Nabours of Company G wrote later of laying on the field all day on that Monday following the battle, and thinking that "for the want of energy on the part of our commander [Bragg] we lost nearly all of the fruits of an important victory, which cost many lives." By September 22, the Federals were safely entrenched at Chattanooga. The opportunity for the Confederates to retake Tennessee and Kentucky and invade north into Ohio had vanished. "That 'barren victory'," Lt. Gen. D. H. Hill later wrote, "sealed the fate of the Southern Confederacy."[89]

88 Muster Roll, Co. C, 5th Texas, Aug 31–Oct. 31, 1863, in TSA; Polley, *Hood's Texas Brigade*, 214; Benjamin Franklin to Mary Franklin, October 2, 1863, in Pearce Museum, Navarro College, Corsicana, TX ; Winkler, *Confederate Capital*, 145-46.

89 Hill, "Chickamauga," in *B&L*, 3:662; Nabours, "Active Service of a Texas Command," *CV*, 24:70. For the best treatment of this campaign, see the recently completed trilogy by David A. Powell, *The Chickamauga Campaign* (Savas Beatie, 2014-2016).

Chapter 4

Chattanooga, Knoxville, and East Tennessee, 1863-1864

After the disaster at Chickamauga, Rosecrans withdrew to Chattanooga, preparing as best he could to hold the city from Bragg's inevitable investment of it. Washington had responded to the crisis by sending him substantial reinforcements from Virginia under Maj. Gen. Hooker and Mississippi under Maj. Gen. William T. Sherman. Advance elements of Hooker's large force arrived on September 30 at Bridgeport, Alabama, 30 miles from Chattanooga. Within a week, Bragg had established a strong siege line around the city, with both flanks resting on the Tennessee River and firmly in control of the overlooking heights of Lookout Mountain and Missionary Ridge Longstreet's command—Walker's Corps and Hood's (Jenkins) and McLaws' divisions—held the left flank of this siege line. Breckinridge's Corps held the center, and Hardee's Corps the right. Porter Alexander's artillery batteries, atop Lookout Mountain, commanded the city and its immediate approaches. Law's Brigade, detached from Hood's Division, patrolled west along the river toward Bridgeport while Forrest's and Wheeler's cavalry patrolled east of the city.[1]

On the south bank of the Tennessee River, Chattanooga sits at the northern end of the five to six-mile wide Lookout Valley which encompasses Chattanooga Creek.

1 Boatner, *Civil War Dictionary*, 141-43; Simpson, *Lee's Grenadier Guard*, 333-34; Mark Smither to Elizabeth Smither, November 3, 1863 in SHSU; Simpson, *Lee's Grenadier Guard*, 334; Chicione, *Confederates of Chappell Hill*, 114; Longstreet, *Manassas to Appomattox*, 463-64. Men from the 5th Texas, including B. A. Nabours of Company G, formed part of the detachment which prepared Alexander's batteries atop Lookout Mountain. Nabours, "Active Service on a Texas Command," *CV*, 24:70. For more on Nabours, see Appendix B, Volume 1.

Missionary Ridge, rising some 500-800 feet above that creek, stands to the east. Lookout Mountain, some 2,200 feet above the water, is on the southwestern side of the valley. The river turns south just below the town running toward the base of Lookout Mountain. The Nashville and Chattanooga Railroad passes at this point, the northern end, where the mountain stands nearly perpendicularly for a considerable distance, before assuming a more gentle slope of cultivated fields to near its summit, where it ends in a rocky palisade 30 feet high. South Chickamauga River runs east of Missionary Ridge; Lookout Creek runs west of Lookout Mountain, with Raccoon Mountain farther west yet.[2]

The 5th Texas under the temporary command of Lt. Col. King Bryan, part of Hood's Division, anchored Bragg's left flank on the river. The position was about a mile and a half east of the northern foot of Lookout Mountain, near where Chattanooga Creek empties into the Tennessee River. Here, the Texans built the most extensive series of breastworks and rifle pits they had constructed thus far in the war. The entire brigade remained behind this defensive line for the next month whiling away time scouting and picketing, playing cards, and sightseeing. Aside from scout and sharpshooter details, by and large the regiment remained inactive for weeks and performed no significant duties during this lull. Smither noted as much when he wrote home that he and his comrades were "in line . . . doing nothing, the enemy is occasionally shelling" us.[3]

The lines between the armies were quite close at points, sometimes less than 100 yards. Just as at Fredericksburg last December, this proximity encouraged considerable unauthorized fraternization between pickets. They exchanged newspapers, coffee, and tobacco regularly, as well as friendly chatter and good-natured bantering. The Texans ignored official policy altogether, arranging truces with Federal pickets along their section of the line. They agreed not to shoot at one another—so as not to waste powder and shot and force the inconvenience of a round-the-clock alert on anyone. Jenkins' South Carolinians, posted to the immediate left of the Texans, had no such truce with the Federals. Thus the peculiar sight of Carolinians hiding in their rifle pits or behind trees, while not more than 50 feet away,

2 Ulysses S. Grant, "Chattanooga," in *B&L*, 3:685.

3 Polley, *Hood's Texas Brigade*, 214; West, *A Texan in Search of a Fight*, 115; Winkler, *Confederate Capital*, 146; Mark Smither to Elizabeth Smither, November 3, 1863, in SHSU; Simpson, *Lee's Grenadier Guard*, 338. Col. Powell, captured at Gettysburg and a prisoner at Johnson's Island in Sandusky, Ohio, was still on the rolls as commander of the 5th Texas at the time. *OR* 31, pt. 1, 452.

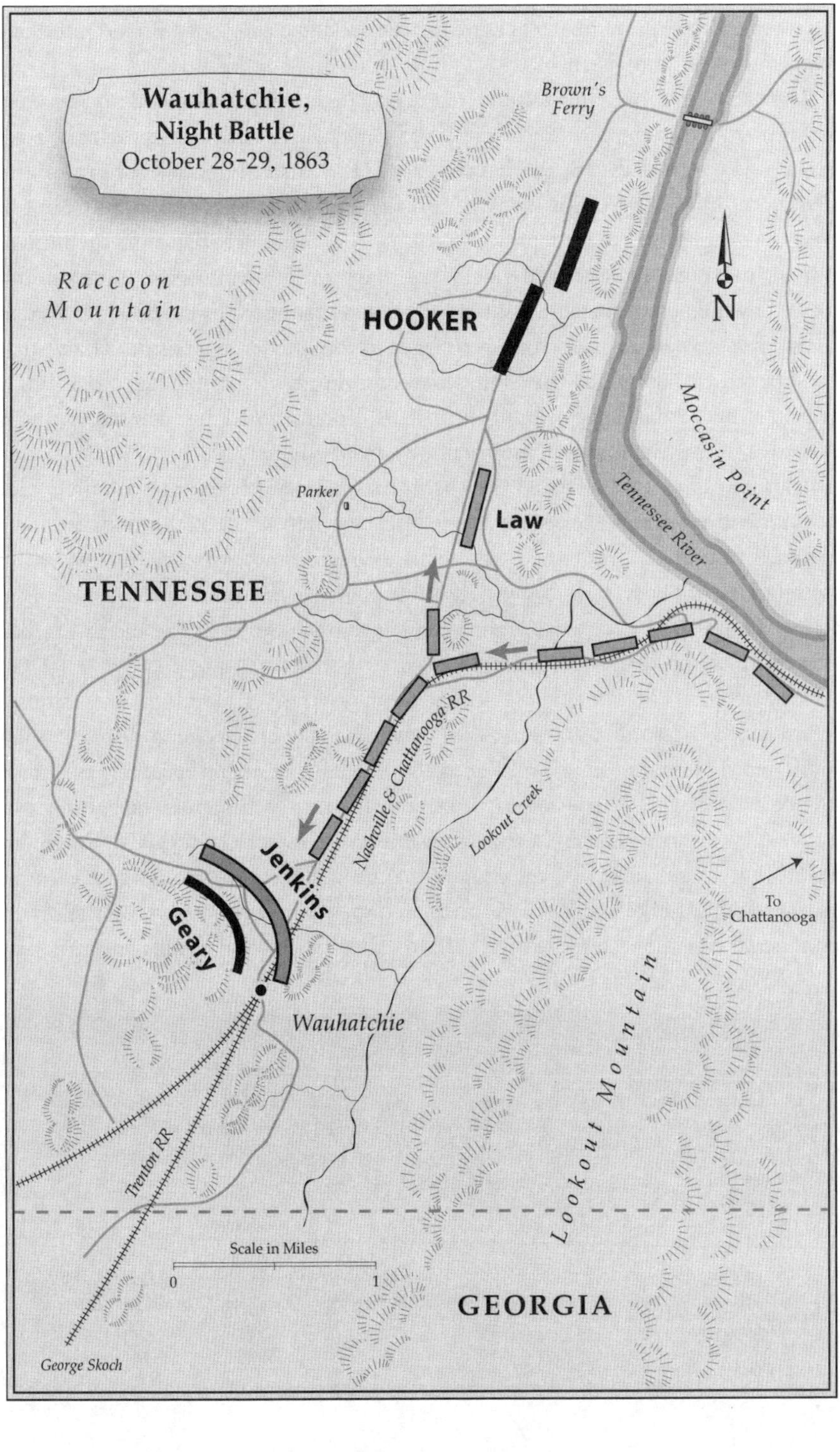
Wauhatchie,
Night Battle
October 28-29, 1863
Brown's Ferry
Raccoon Mountain
HOOKER
N
Moccasin Point
Tennessee River
Parker
Law
TENNESSEE
Nashville & Chattanooga RR
Lookout Creek
Jenkins
Geary
To Chattanooga
Wauhatchie
Lookout Mountain
Trenton RR
Scale in Miles
0
1
GEORGIA
George Skoch

Texans stretched out on blankets enjoying the sunshine or playing poker in the open, within 100 yards of their enemy.[4]

Unfortunately, by mid-October, the Confederates suffered food and provision shortages similar to those of the beleaguered Federals. The creaky Confederate supply system also contended with the havoc wrecked by the continuous autumn rains. A quagmire of mud bogged down roads, slowing transportation of supplies to an ooze. Local foraging in this mountainous region of few farms left the unfortunate Rebel troops almost completely dependent on the army's commissary system. Food supplied by the commissariat was often unpalatable, sometimes inedible. Often damp and moldy ears of corn yielded cobwebs three to four inches long inside. The regiment also suffered contaminated drinking water, and the resultant, inevitable diarrhea. At one point, the Texans went without almost any food for four days, without the chance of foraging in this "exhausted, mountainous, poor country."[5]

Clothing shortages persisted also. Most of the Texans had deposited their winter clothing in the various Texas regimental storage depots in Richmond, and many became embittered over their lack of warm clothing, and the failure of the Confederate supply system to alleviate their plight. Cold weather came early in the mountains of Tennessee: frost often in early October. Some of the men were being offered $75 for a used, woolen blanket.[6]

One major, albeit intangible, consolation to the regiment's plight during its investment of Chattanooga was the magnificent local scenery. With Lookout Mountain, Missionary Ridge, and Raccoon Mountain all within relatively easy hiking distance, many of the men—utterly unaccustomed to such picturesque countryside, discovered mountain climbing a rewarding experience. From Lookout Mountain, they could see the extensive Federal encampment and defensive works and with field glasses could observe the soldiers at their duties and ease. Views of the looping Tennessee River sequestered within rolling valleys and wooded hills and mountains

4 Ulysses S. Grant, *Memoirs and Selected Letters*, Mary McFeeley and William S, McFeeley, eds. (New York 1990), 421; West, *Texan in Search of a Fight*, 117; Polley, *Letters to Charming Nellie*, 144-46. John West told his children about discussions with Federal pickets: "They are very tired of the war, and want to go home as badly as we do."

5 West, *A Texan in Search of a Fight*, 120; Simpson, *Gaines' Mill to Appomattox*, 188, Simpson, *Lee's Grenadier Guard*, 336-37; Polley, *Hood's Texas Brigade*, 214. The Yankees, on half rations, suffered as well. No artillery or even forage wagon could be moved because over 10,000 pack animals starved to death in Chattanooga during October and early November. Grant, "Chattanooga" in *B&L*, 3:683.

6 West, *Texan in Search of a Fight*, 124.

presented a beautiful scene that many Texans noted in diaries and described in letters home.[7]

Across the river, in addition to reinforcements, the Federal war department had provided new leadership. It placed Maj. Gen. Ulysses S. Grant in command of the now-combined departments of the Tennessee, the Cumberland, and the Ohio. Grant, in turn, replaced Rosecrans as commander of the Army of the Cumberland with Thomas, who was ordered to hold out in Chattanooga "at all hazards" until help arrived. His answer was: "we shall hold it until we starve."[8]

To relieve their starving troops inside Chattanooga, by stealthy amphibious operations and a spirited action on October 27, the Federals forced open a supply line from the city to the nearest railhead at Bridgeport, Alabama. In the meantime, that same day, the Confederates had completely missed a march by Hooker and a mixed force of 10,000 troops from Bridgeport up Lookout Valley and through a pass at Raccoon Mountain to near Wauhatchie Station. Hooker proceeding north to Brown's Ferry, joined the other Federals the following day, detaching Maj. Gen. Geary's division at Wauhatchie, one mile south from where Lookout Creek flows into the Tennessee, to protect his line of communications to the south, as well as the road to Kelley's Ford to the west.[9]

Early on October 28, from atop Lookout Mountain, Longstreet and a shocked Bragg helplessly watched as the Federals poured into the valley from Bridgeport, while 10,000 more climbed up the road from Kelly's Ferry. Bragg ordered Longstreet to mount an attack, promising his support. Normally opposed to such spontaneous attacks, a Federal wagon train at Wauhatchie Station, caught Old Pete's eye. Besides other advantages of attacking, these lightly guarded rations for his underfed and poorly outfitted troops could not be ignored.[10]

The subsequent night attack carried out solely by Micah Jenkins' division under the command of Col. John Bratton was little short of a fiasco. Longstreet's plan called for Law's and the Texas Brigades, under Law's command, to hold the high ground along the Wauhatchie-Brown's Ferry Road and intercept any reinforcements from Hooker's main body while Bratton assailed the Yankees at Wauhatchie, three miles to the south. Law, who claimed to have heard nothing about an offensive movement

7 Winkler, *Confederate Capital*, 146; Simpson, *Lee's Grenadier Guard*, 337; West, *A Texan in Search of a Fight*, 116, 124.

8 *OR* 30, pt. 1, 404.

9 Joseph S. Fulleerton, "The Army of the Cumberland at Chattanooga," in *B&L*, 3:720-21.

10 Cozzens, *Shipwreck of Their Hopes*, 79-80.

when Jenkins issued instructions, estimated the plan's chance of success at "close to zero."[11]

After supper on October 28, the 5th Texas vacated the siege line, along with the remainder of the brigade, and marching west eventually formed a line of battle along the eastern side of Lookout Creek. Law's troops also moved out and ascended the tangled, heavily wooded slope of the hill he had been ordered to hold.[12]

At 10:00 p.m., Robertson had moved across Lookout Creek, reporting to Law with the Texas Brigade; Law told him to hold his command in the open field behind the hill as a reserve and to cover the gap between Law's right and the river. Jenkins then ordered the 3rd Arkansas and the 1st Texas to Law's left. The enemy was believed to be on or near the road, in the edge of a woods near the open field. Robertson so notified Law, who ordered the 5th Texas placed in an open field near the upper bridge, where it could cover that bridge in his rear. He also threw a picket line forward to the base of the hill in the field, and from this picket, vedettes thrust further out to watch the approaches along the river bank. The 5th Texas was ordered to hold its position around the upper bridge crossing Lookout Creek "at every hazard."[13]

Law, who had learned of the proximity of more Yankee reinforcements, then went to persuade Jenkins to call off the enterprise. Jenkins merely reiterated that his orders were to proceed. All the supporting players—Longstreet, Law, and the Texas Brigade—now awaited Bratton's attack. Bratton however wasn't in position to launch his attack until 11:30 p.m. And then he did so before McLaws' division had arrived to assist. Longstreet, who assumed Jenkins knew McLaws had not come up, assumed also that it should have been apparent to Jenkins the battle could not go forward without McLaws. Jenkins, however, soon returned to Wauhatchie and at 11:30 p.m. ordered Bratton ahead.[14]

Bratton had no idea of the fate awaiting his men. He advanced with only a portion of his brigade, feeling obligated to detach a third of his force to guard the ground to

11 Ibid., 81-82 ; Longstreet, *Manassas to Appomattox*, 405-406; Alexander, *Military Memoirs*, 469. Law's objections to the plan are in "Opening the Cracker Line: The Battle of Wauhatchie Junction October 29, 1863," *TAC News*, May-June 2009, accessed July 22, 2010, www.ghqmodels.com/newsletters/mayjun2009.pdf, 3.

12 *OR* 31, pt. 1, 226; Winkler, *Confederate Capital*, 147; Cozzens, *Shipwreck of Their Hopes*, 81; Simpson, *Lee's Grenadier Guard*, 339.

13 *OR* 31, pt. 1, 226. 234 , 52, pt. 1, 89; Cozzens, *Shipwreck of Their Hopes*, 82; Polley, *Hood's Texas Brigade*, 216; Alexander, *Military Memoirs*, 469.

14 *OR* 31, pt. 1, 98, 218-21, 226-227; Alexander, *Military Memoirs*, 469-70; Longstreet, *Manassas to Appomattox*, 405-406, 470; Cozzens, *Shipwreck of Their Hopes*, 82; "Georgia's Blue and Gray Trail Presents America's Civil War," accessed July 23, 2010, www.blueandgraytrail.com/event/Battle_of_Wauhatchie; Freeman, *Lee's Lieutenants*, 2:282-83.

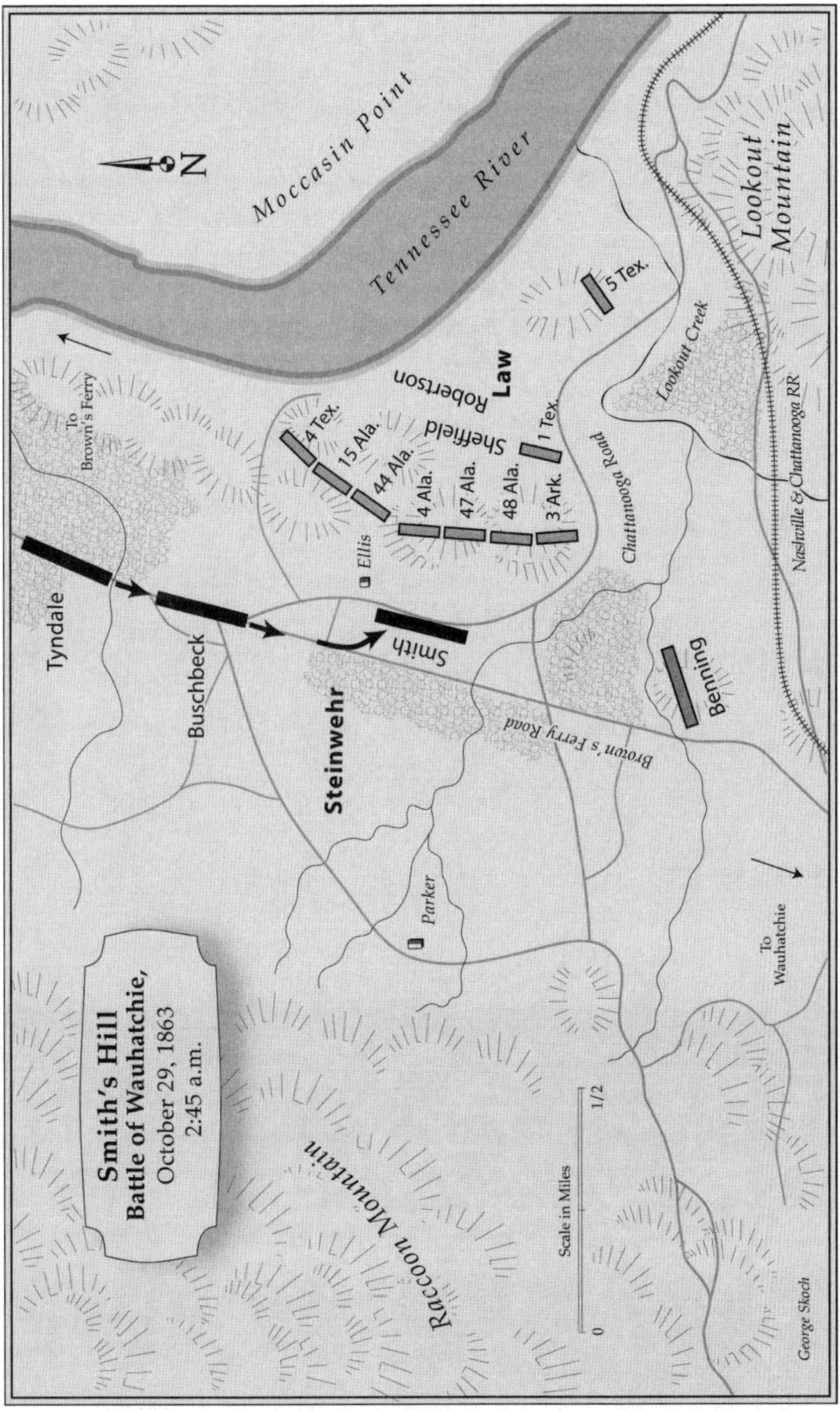
Smith's Hill
Battle of Wauhatchie,
October 29, 1863
2:45 a.m.
N
Moccasin Point
Tennessee River
Lookout Mountain
Lookout Creek
Nashville & Chattanooga RR
Chattanooga Road
Brown's Ferry Road
To Brown's Ferry
To Wauhatchie
Raccoon Mountain
Tyndale
Buschbeck
Steinwehr
Smith
Ellis
Parker
Law
Robertson
Sheffield
4 Tex.
15 Ala.
44 Ala.
4 Ala.
47 Ala.
48 Ala.
3 Ark.
1 Tex.
5 Tex.
Benning
Scale in Miles
0
1/2
George Skoch

Law's left until Benning's brigade arrived. With his remaining force, Bratton drove up the road toward Wauhatchie, initially raining bedlam on Geary's unprepared encampment. The roar of battle alerted Maj. Gen. O. O. Howard, two miles away, who quickly began organizing a counterattack when he received a message from Hooker to push two divisions into the battle to the south. After a three-hour fight at Wauhatchie, the arrival of these reinforcements tipped the balance, and Jenkins ordered Bratton to break off the attack.[15]

Meanwhile to the north, Maj. Gen. Law had already repulsed one Yankee attack when he learned of Bratton's withdrawal. Robertson soon reported a strong Union force moving over the next hill to Law's right, approaching a triangular opening to his immediate rear, adjacent to the river bank. Under a second Union assault, Law's line gave way, and he ordered his command to retire to the hill where it had first formed, and thence onto the road and back across the bridge. The 1st Texas joined the 5th, already posted on an open hill between the bridge and where the enemy was moving on Law's right. Law quietly executed the movement, and the Federals did not pursue him. Law later contended he had already received word of Bratton's retreat and was at the bridge when he ordered withdrawal of his troops, believing he had accomplished his mission. No one, however, mentioned any of this to the 4th Texas.[16]

After midnight, an eerie silence fell and these Texans, blissfully ignorant of their solitude, dropped to the ground "to take their ease." Suddenly, a burst of gunfire to their left rattled, followed by volleys on all sides. Scouts quickly confirmed no friendly troops anywhere. Skirmishers rapidly fell back, shouting about the strong force approaching. Then the cry "we are flanked" prompted the 4th Texas to begin giving way (the only time in the war that a Texas Brigade regiment was routed in the face of the enemy). Small groups, then more, faced about, breaking pell-mell for the safety of the bridge they had passed over earlier. The men of the 4th raced down the ridge slope a lot faster than they had gone up. Off to the "Raccoon Races . . . splitting underbrush and moonshine wide open," according to one Texan. The rush down the steep slope could not be halted. Brambles and thorns, branches and tree limbs so disfigured many 4th Texas soldiers during the rush, they were later recognizable only by their voices. The Federals advanced only to the deserted hogbacks and awaited daylight. At dawn, the 4th Texas reformed and made its way across the upper bridge, still guarded by the

15 *OR* 31 pt. 1, 97-98, 216-18, 231, 52, pt. 1, 89; Cozzens, *Shipwreck of Their Hopes*, 83; Foote, *Civil War Narrative*, 2:809-10.

16 *OR* 31, pt. 1, 106-107, 225-26, 234; Polley, *Hood's Texas Brigade*, 214-16; Simpson, *Lee's Grenadier Guard*, 340. Fullerton, "Army of the Cumberland," in *B&L*, 3:720; [E. M. Law] "Lookout Valley, October 28, 1863," in *SHSP*, (1876), 8:502-05; *OR* 31, pt. 1, 226-28; Cozzens, *Shipwreck of Their Hopes*, 96-98.

5th Texas. Bratton's Brigade, south of the 5th Texas, was the last of Longstreet's troops to return to the east side of Lookout Creek. Casualties had been light in both Law's and Robertson's brigades.[17]

Known by several names, the 5th Texas called it the battle of Raccoon Mountain. From the Confederate standpoint, by whatever name, it was a mess, the result of petty jealousies, a confused battle plan, and failed vertical communications. Jenkins and Law issued conflicting orders to the brigades of Hood's old division. The battle plan was not devised until hours before its execution; forces promised were never committed, and commanders never briefed on their expected roles in the assault. Bragg indicated McLaws would be available for support, and at the last minute withdrew this offer—too late, however, to halt the attack. A successful day-time assault in this terrain would have been difficult. At night it was next to impossible.[18]

On the day following the Wauhatchie affair, the 5th Texas was positioned in the "shady recesses" of some woods on the west side of Lookout Mountain to check any attack Hooker might undertake.. The remainder of Jenkins' force occupied the front along Lookout Creek. A small scare arose on October 30 sending the brigade up Lookout Mountain and into a position under a line of cliffs which encircled the top. A member of the 5th Texas light-heartedly confided to a 4th Texas friend that "Aunt Polly" (Robertson) made the decision, as he

> heard of the speed you fellows made night before last in that stampede down-hill, and he has got an idea from it that he wants to test. If the Yankees line up anywhere below us, he is going to order the brigade to charge them. He calculates, I reckon, that the force of gravity and the momentum we acquire will combine with our bravery to make the downset —it'll be no onset, you know — absolutely irresistible, and that we'll knock the Yankees, guns and all, into Lookout Creek, and there let the last one of 'em drown.

On Lookout Mountain that night, the regiment bivouacked in battle line on ground so steep and loosely covered with rocks they could only keep from rolling downhill after

17 *OR* 31, pt. 1, 93-95, 227-28; Joseph Polley, "A Battle Above the Clouds," *CV*, 5:105; *OR* 31, pt. 1, 234; Polley, *Hood's Texas Brigade*, 218-20; Cozzens, *Shipwreck of Their Hopes*, 92-93, 98-99, 100-02; Fullerton, "Army of the Cumberland," in *B&L*, 3:720; Lasswell, *Rags and Hope*, 214-15; Robertson, *Touched With Valor*, 48-50. Bratton had 31 killed, 286 wounded, and 39 missing, while Federal losses were placed at 420.

18 *OR* 31, pt. 1, 104-107, 216-35; Polley, *Hood's Texas Brigade*, 219-20; Lasswell, *Rags and Hope*, 215-16; Longstreet, *Manassas to Appomattox*, 474-75; Connelly, *Autumn of Glory*, 261; Ulysses Grant, "Chattanooga," in *B&L* 3:690. The battle also had various other names: battle of Wauhatchie, of Wauhatchie Junction, Smith's Hill, Brown's Ferry, or Lookout Valley.

carefully bracing their feet against trees. The next day, the men moved around Lookout Point to the east side of the mountain.[19]

Furious with the results of the night attack, Longstreet unleashed his frustration on Robertson. He had already complained to Bragg about Robertson's fitness for command after Chickamauga; following the failure at Wauhatchie, Jenkins supported him in this assessment. "This officer has been complained of so frequently for want of conduct in time of battle," Jenkins wrote Bragg, "that I apprehend that the abandonment by his brigade of its position of the night of the 28th may have been due to his want of hearty co-operation." Robertson immediately denied the charge: "my Brigade did not 'abandon its position.' It came out under orders, the object for which it went in having, according to my understanding, been accomplished." Nonetheless, special orders no. 284, on November 2, relieved Robertson from duty pending proceedings of the examining board. But when Longstreet's Corps moved to East Tennessee soon thereafter, its commander was surprised to find Robertson still leading the Texas Brigade. By special orders no. 290, on November 8, apparently without consulting with Longstreet, Bragg changed his mind.[20]

After the battle, a despondent Bragg telegraphed President Davis insinuating a "disobedience of orders and slowness of movements" on Longstreet's part, urging Davis to allow another housecleaning, or to relieve Longstreet. Davis orchestrated an entirely different solution, ordering Bragg to dispatch Old Pete into East Tennessee with two divisions to confront Burnside, who was inching south toward Chattanooga to aid the besieged Federals. Bragg thus ordered Longstreet's divisions, Alexander's and Maj. A. Leyden's artillery battalions, and four brigades of cavalry under Maj. Gen. Joseph A. Wheeler off to check this advance. Bragg was convinced a strong move toward Knoxville would relieve the pressure on his army along the Tennessee and that a quick victory would allow Longstreet's return to the city long before Grant could mount a major offensive on his weakened force.[21]

Plans called for Longstreet's army to move by rail from Chattanooga to Sweetwater, Tennessee, some 40 miles from Knoxville, to arrive no later than

19 Polley, *Hood's Texas Brigade*, 220-22.

20 *OR* 31, pt. 1, 466-67; Robertson, *Touched With Valor*, 48. Since the movement of troops had suspended the proceedings of the examining board, Bragg ordered that "Brigadier-General Robertson will rejoin his command until the board can renew its session."

21 *OR* 31, pt. 1, 544-56; Alexander, *Military Memoirs*, 472, 480; E. Porter Alexander, "Longstreet at Knoxville," in *B&L*, 3:746. Longstreet's command consisted of 15,000 men and 47 guns, including 5,000 cavalry troopers with 12 pieces of artillery. Alexander Mendoza, "Machinations in the Confederate High Command: Gen. Braxton Bragg and His Campaign to Discredit Lt. Gen. James Longstreet," *North & South*, (2009), 11:44. Longstreet considered his force only half what was needed for the mission. Freeman, *Lee's Lieutenants*, 3:286.

November 8. Jenkins' Division would march to the tunnel through Missionary Ridge on November 5, and board trains there. Unfortunately, the gross inefficiencies in the Confederate transportation and supply systems, together with the total lack of cooperation from Bragg's command, completely botched the beginning phase of this movement. The regiment received its operational orders on November 4, each man receiving ten days' rations of fresh beef and corn meal to be cooked immediately. However, all cooking utensils had already been dispatched, and the men had to bake their bread "in the ashes." By sundown on November 5, the brigade left its position near Lookout Mountain in a driving rainstorm, marching east parallel to the East Tennessee and Georgia Railroad, toward Missionary Ridge. On the way, many of the men threw away their playing cards. Without knowing whether they would survive the next encounter, they did not "want to be killed with [cards] in their possession."[22]

The 5th Texas was supposed to board the trains for East Tennessee at the railroad tunnel through Missionary Ridge. Unfortunately, upon its arrival no trains awaited, so they were forced to continue on to Tyner's Station, approximately 10 miles farther west. Trudging all night on the half-frozen road in a sleet storm, the men reached the station early on November 6. This rather ominous inception of the East Tennessee campaign only mildly presaged what lay in store for Longstreet's veterans.[23]

Cold, hungry, and therefore unhappy, the 5th Texas remained at Tyner's Station another three days awaiting railroad cars. On November 8, with no prospects for the promised rail transportation in sight, the regiment marched the 20 miles to Cleveland, arriving the next day. There, the trains finally caught up with the men. Elated to be rid of the frozen mud, the men climbed aboard the dilapidated railroad cars. If the rolling stock which carried Longstreet's men to Georgia was pitiable, the railroad transportation for the move to East Tennessee bordered upon ludicrous, "comical in [its] inefficiency." Whenever trains came to a hill, the cars had to be emptied for the engine to negotiate the grade. Men would spring like ants out from platforms, roofs, windows, and doors, leaving the cars and then reboarding the train again on the downgrade. A scarcity of water reservoirs and watersheds along the way compounded

22 *OR* 31, pt. 1, 455-56, 524; Longstreet, *Manassas to Appomattox*, 410-12, 480-81; Freeman, *Lee's Lieutenants*, 3:286-87; Alexander, *Military Memoirs*, 473, 480-81; Simpson, *Lee's Grenadier Guard, 346 ; Winkler, Confederate Capital*, 149-51; Boatner, *Civil War Dictionary*, 144-47. Before leaving, the Texans were at least heartened by news of the affair at Sabine Pass, Texas, where the small Confederate garrison with about 200 men had resisted five Federal gun boats, ultimately capturing them, 200 prisoners, and 15 heavy guns. While the Federals reportedly had 50 casualties, the Confederates did not lose a man. This disaster caused Banks to abandon the elaborate expedition he had envisioned against Texas.

23 *OR* 31, pt. 1, 534; Longstreet, *Manassas to Appomattox*, 412-13; Sorrel, *Confederate Staff Officer*, 201.

the inconvenience. The men often had to bail water from local streams and cut up fences to keep the engines going. Longstreet later ascribed all these problems completely to Bragg. Due to these blunders in train scheduling, the last of his command did not arrive at Sweetwater until November 12—four full days behind schedule.[24]

The 5th Texas left the railroad cars at Sweetwater on November 10 and spent the next two days there. It then marched toward Loudon, where it confronted a want of wagons to transport the pontoons required to cross the Tennessee River at this narrow, perilous point. As the infantry moved down to the river, a small force of Federal scouts and skirmishers disputed their advance. The men were kept back from the river until the pontoons arrived by rail and could be offloaded. To deceive Burnside as the exact point of crossing, Longstreet had the pontoons brought to the river bank at Huff's Ferry, near Loudon, after dark. Engineers built the bridge at Loudon on the night of November 13 without significant Federal opposition. It was a rickety affair largely because of the force of the current and its being constructed in the dark. Instead of straight across the river, the bridge formed an "S" that swayed and bucked with the current. The regiment gingerly made its way across late on November 14, along with most of Jenkins' Division, and proceeded to construct breastworks to guard the bridge.[25]

Consolidating his forces north of the Tennessee, Longstreet began steadily pressing the Federals back toward Knoxville. Old Pete advanced from Loudon in two columns, with McLaws' Division taking the road to the left and the regiment, a part of Jenkins' Division, on the right, following the rail line to Lenoir's Station, approximately 20 miles southwest of Knoxville. Confronting and chasing off Federal skirmishers prevented the column reaching Lenoir's that day. Muddy ground and the steep hills likewise prevented the Confederates from getting into position before nightfall. The following morning, Confederates found Lenoir's Station deserted.[26]

The two forces clashed at Lenoir's Station on November 15 and again at Campbell's Station nearer Knoxville on November 16. The Confederates both times attempted unsuccessfully to outflank the Federals, cutting them off from their Knoxville base. Following parallel routes, Longstreet and Burnside raced for a vital road junction about a mile southwest of Campbell's Station, a small town some 11

24 *OR* 31, pt. 1, 456; Longstreet, *Manassas to Appomattox*, 483; Alexander, "Longstreet at Knoxville," in *B&L*, 3:746; West, *Texan in Search of a Fight*, 130.

25 *OR* 31, pt. 1, 456-57, 524; Chicoine, *Confederates of Chappell Hill*, 114; Longstreet, *Manassas to Appomattox*, 415.

26 Orlando M. Poe, "The Defense of Knoxville" in *B&L*, 3:733.

miles from the city: Longstreet intended to force Burnside to fight outside his earthworks, while the latter to preserve his supply train, and indeed, his entire command. Burnside's men ultimately won the race by a forced march. About 15 minutes later, Longstreet appeared and immediately attempted a double envelopment. McLaws' Division struck the Union right so forcefully the Federals had to redeploy, but they ultimately held their ground. Meanwhile, Jenkins' Division, with the 5th Texas, maneuvered ineffectively as it advanced and proved unable to turn the Federal left. Burnside ordered his two divisions astride the Kingston Road to withdraw three-quarters of a mile to a ridge in their rear. From there, he easily continued his retrograde movement to Knoxville. On November 16, Jenkins' Division, with the 5th Texas, tried to turn the Federal left flank, while McLaws held the front and right, and was repulsed. The next day Burnside withdrew to the safety of his defensive perimeter on the hills surrounding Knoxville, and on the 18th Longstreet encircled the city and began siege operations. It appeared that not only was Knoxville, but also Burnside's entire army of 12,000 penned-in men were in Longstreet's grasp.[27]

Longstreet recalled the Texas Brigade to Loudon on November 16, concerned with a potential Union cavalry attack against his line of communications. The Texans' mission was to "[k]eep things in order there and take charge of the bridges." Three days later they rejoined the rest of Jenkins' Division in front of Knoxville and were placed on the siege line north of the Holston River and west of the city.[28]

The Confederate siege line formed a semi-circle around the city with both flanks resting on the Holston River. Its center was located near the railroad north of the city. The Federal line was anchored by Fort Sanders on the west, Fort Huntington Smith on the east and Fort Comstock to the north. South of the river, on high ground, Burnside erected Forts Stanley to the east, Dickerson in the center, and Higley to the west. The forts' garrisons to the south linked with Burnside's main body by a pontoon bridge across the Holston.[29]

27 Longstreet, *Manassas to Appomattox*, 419-20; Alexander, *Military Memoirs*, 481; Polley, *Hood's Texas Brigade*, 222; Alexander, "Longstreet at Knoxville," in *B&L*, 3:746-47; *OR* 31, pt. 1, 457-58, 498; Poe, "The Defense of Knoxville," *B&L*, 3:738; Sorrell, *Confederate Staff Officer*, 202.

28 *OR* 31, pt. 1, 462, 525; Alexander, "Longstreet at Knoxville," in *B&L*, 3:750; Robertson, *Touched With Valor*, 49-50; West, *A Texan in Search of a Fight*, 130-32. The Holston River system rises in southwestern Virginia, flowing southwest to the north of Bays Mountain until reaching the confluence of the French Broad River just east of Knoxville. This confluence is considered the start of the Tennessee River. In the nineteenth century, the Holston River terminated some 51 miles downstream from Knoxville at Lenoir City, where the Little Tennessee River entered that stream.

29 *OR* 31, pt. 1, 459; Poe, "The Defense of Knoxville," in *B&L*, 3:735-36; Simpson, *Lee's Genadier Guard*, 351-52; Alexander, *Military Memoirs*, 484.

Soon thereafter, Longstreet became convinced "that the true key to the enemy's position was by the heights on the south side of the Holston." Captain William Parker's four-gun 6th Virginia Artillery Battery had already been positioned on Cherokee Heights, a 360-foot prominence to the west of Fort Higley. The move was intended to allow the Confederate artillery to dominate Federal lines to the north by firing from high ground south of the river. Longstreet further believed if the Federals could be driven from their high fortress at Fort Higley, a well-timed assault across the pontoon bridge could perhaps breach the Union line from the rear, rendering all Federal positions in Knoxville untenable. Thus, on November 21, the Texas Brigade, supported by the 10th Georgia, and Law's Brigade, was ordered across the Holston on flatboats. The Texans and Georgians landed about a mile and a half west of Fort Higley. The Texas Brigade, with the 5th Texas on its extreme left, next to the river, moved slowly eastward along the Holston's south bank, driving in the Federal pickets before it.[30]

Troops of the XXIII Corps manned the Federal position there; a brigade under the command of Col. Daniel Cameron, consisting of the 103rd Ohio, 24th Kentucky, and three other regiments invested the forward skirmish line on the western slope of Armstrong's Hill, rising along the river between Cherokee Heights and Fort Higley. On November 18, the green troops of the 103rd Ohio, who had seen little action, moved from what its men thought was their winter quarters to the vicinity of Armstrong's Hill, west of Fort Higley. There, one of its companies began chopping down trees for breastworks and abatis on the western slope of the hill.[31]

A cleared 10-acre field lay between Armstrong's Hill and Cherokee Heights, bordered by a rail fence running along the wood's edge at the slope of Armstrong's Hill, turning to enclose a road running across the field's southern edge to the foot of Cherokee Heights. Between the slopes north of the road stood a two-story log cabin. A dense, 60-yard-wide thicket along the river bank sheltered the field from view. Cameron's pickets and sharpshooters found good protection in the dense thicket with its rocky outcroppings, as well as in the woods behind the fence line at the base of

30 *OR* 31, pt. 1, 459; Digby Gordon Seymour, *Divided Loyalties: Fort Sanders and the Civil War in East Tennessee* (Knoxville, TN, 1990), 261-62; Robert K. Krick, *Parker's Virginia Battery, C.S.A.* (Berryville, VA, 1975), 208-209; Alexander, *Military Memoirs*, 484.

31 103rd OVI Memorial Foundation, *Personal Reminiscences and Experiences by Members of the One Hundred and Third Ohio Volunteer Infantry: Campaign Life in the Union Army from 1862 to 1865* (Sheffield Lake, OH, 1984), 163; Seymour, *Divided Loyalties*, 261-62. Armstrong's Hill did not bear that name at the time. Its name came later by virtue of being a part of the vast real estate holdings of Drury Armstrong, a wealthy local landowner.

Armstrong's Hill. To its east, Armstrong's Hill was separated from Fort Higley by a steep, treacherous ravine.[32]

The Confederates soon discovered only two companies of the 103rd Ohio guarded the vulnerable pontoon bridge. Observing this new Yankee position, Robertson and Law believed that they could advance their lines through the dense woods and there, await the 103rd letting down its guard and stacking arms. They would then push forward on the river bank toward the pontoon bridge. Even better, the batteries at Forts Higley and Dickerson, set to fire in the opposite direction, could not support the 103rd.

Around noon on November 25, the bulk of the 103rd Ohio crossed the saddle between the heights, marching up the slope to the crest of Armstrong's Hill. A heavy barrage of Confederate artillery promptly opened on them from Cherokee Heights, "tearing up trees and earth as if a cyclone had started on its mission of death," a member of the 24th Kentucky observed. Then the Ohioans heard the ear splitting Rebel yell and witnessed a Confederate battle line two columns deep emerging from the woods, moving rapidly toward them. This attack commenced with the Texas Brigade on the left near the river and Law's Alabamians on the right.[33]

The Texans rapidly traversed the 200-plus yards of open ground, only to be slowed by close-range volleys from the veteran 24th Kentucky and 65th Illinois regiments as they advanced up the slope to a rail fence bordering the wood line. Meanwhile Law's Brigade met with more initial success. With considerably less ground to traverse, the Alabamians surged up the slope and on into the woods, meeting the 103rd Ohio at the crest, and forcing them off toward the deep ravine in their rear.[34]

In their current precarious position the Federals would soon be slaughtered or forced to surrender, opening passage across the pontoon bridge and the city of Knoxville to the Confederate forces. In apparent desperation or heedless courage, someone yelled out "Forward!" and "Charge bayonets!" and thus launched a courageous Federal counteroffensive, which soon drove the Texans back to the base

32 Geoffrey R. Walden, "The Battle of Armstrong Hill: The Sideshow of the Big Shoe," Accessed June 6, 2008, www.rootsweb.ancestry.com/~tnkcwr/KCWRT/Civil War History files/ARMSTRONG.pdf; Seymor, *Divided Loyalties*, 264-65.

33 103rd OVI Memorial Foundation, *Personal Reminiscences*, 223-41; Geoffrey R. Walden, "The Battle of Armstrong's Hill: The Sideshow of the Big Show," accessed June 6, 2008, www.rootsweb.ancestry.com/~tnkcwr/KCWRT/Civil War History files/ARMSTRONG.pdf; Longstreet, *Manassas to Appomattox*, 490.

34 Seymour, *Divided Loyalties*, 264-65; Walden, "The Battle of Armstrong's Hill," John A. Joyce, *A Checkered Life* (Chicago, IL, 1883), 93-95.

of Cherokee Heights. Law fell back soon thereafter, leaving pockets of resistance along the rail fence and at the log cabin. As the Texans fell back, the 24th Kentucky followed them across the field and began scaling Cherokee Heights, only to be driven back by the depressed guns of Parker's artillery raking them with shell and canister. The field changed hands several times during the fighting. Moving back, some of the Texans managed their way into the thicket bordering the river, maintaining a hot crossfire with their comrades in the log cabin and along the rail fence. As dusk fell over the valley, Cameron, supported by a Federal cavalry brigade, flushed the Confederates out of the thicket and the log cabin and back to Cherokee Heights. The entire engagement had lasted approximately two hours.[35]

The Texans maintained a steady fire against this strong position for the next two days but could not drive the Federals out. Longstreet then halted further action there to preserve his limited supply of ammunition. The 5th Texas and rest of the brigade remained in this position until the siege of Knoxville lifted, continually exchanging sniper fire with the Federals at Fort Higley, as well as with those from across the river.[36]

Food and clothing soon dwindled for the besiegers as well as the penned-up Federals. The southerners relied primarily on foraging (both authorized and not) to acquire a sufficient food supply. Uniforms were mostly threadbare and nondescript in color, size, and material. Many Texans still wore the blue blouses, trousers, and caps acquired en route to Chickamauga. Shoes too were a major problem with many in the ranks barefooted. Longstreet had attempted to remedy this crucial problem on the march to East Tennessee by permitting his men to exchange footwear with their prisoners. He made it a rule, however, that the Confederate soldier must have something to trade, so as not to leave a prisoner totally barefooted. While honored in spirit, many Federal prisoners ended up wearing hats, bits of canvas, and pieces of blankets on their feet. Reportedly, most of the Yankee prisoners accepted these irregular exchanges philosophically, believing that "when a man is captured his shoes are captured too."[37]

35 Joyce, *A Checkered Life*, 95-98; Seymour, *Divided Loyalties*, 264-66; 103rd OVI Memorial Foundation, *Personal Reminiscences*, 223-41.

36 Poe, "The Defense of Knoxville," in *B&L*, 3:734-35; *OR* 31, pt. 1, 459; Simpson, *Lee's Grenadier Guard*, 352-53. Company D's muster roll for this period indicates the regiment crossed to the south side of the Holston on November 24. Longstreet reported the crossing as having taken place on November 21. A diarist of the 3rd Arkansas, however, wrote in his journal that his unit crossed on November 23. Simpson, *Lee's Grenadier Guard*, 352; Polley, *Hood's Texas Brigade*, 222.

37 Polley, *Letters to Charming Nellie*, 176; Alexander, "Longstreet at Knoxville," in *B&L*, 3:750.

The Confederates made one more serious effort to break through the Federal line at Knoxville. Longstreet selected Fort Sanders, the key locale on the western perimeter of the Federal line, as the one point the Confederates might assault with a potential for success. It was located on a hill that fell off to the northwest, so a large force could be marched under cover to within 200 yards of its walls without being seen. Initially set for November 22, the assault was postponed until November 25, and then further delayed until November 29. The subsequent attack failed dismally. The original plan called for the artillery to soften Fort Sanders for a frontal assault. But Longstreet changed this plan to an infantry assault at dawn without an initial bombardment, hoping that the surprise would outweigh the benefits of an initial cannonade. But the Yankees were not surprised, having been alerted by the sight of enemy pickets hours before. Without scaling ladders, line after grey line poured into the ditch fronting the fort in attempts to scale the parapet, and the mud trough quickly became a slaughter pen. The attack, which had lasted no more than a half hour, resulted in 813 Confederate casualties, including 129 dead, 458 wounded, and 228 missing. On the south side of the Holston, the Texans had only one killed and one wounded in their diversionary demonstration.[38]

After recalling his battered men, Longstreet learned Grant had routed the Confederates at Chattanooga in a series of engagements November 23-25, forcing Bragg back to northern Georgia. A message from Bragg requested Longstreet to join him in Georgia "if practicable." Old Pete quickly concluded that marching south was "not practicable." Indeed, he relished the opportunity for independent command and later rejoining Lee. And despite the recent debacle, he intended to continue operations against Knoxville to relieve pressure on Bragg. However, he soon learned from a captured Federal courier that three armies were marching to Burnside's relief.

Longstreet hastily changed plans. On December 2, he issued orders to withdraw from the city, first north around Knoxville and then northeast along the north bank of the Holston. The assignment of guarding the army's trains fell to the 5th Texas, under Lt. Col. King Bryan, and the rest of the brigade, Law's men and a battery of Alexander's artillery. This force left their entrenchments on December 3, forming the advance echelon of Longstreet's movement east. The remainder of the army moved north the next day taking up a line of march behind the Texans. Maj. Gen. W. T. Martin's and Brig. Gen. W. E. Jones' cavalry guarded the rear and gathered stragglers.

38 Alexander, "Longstreet at Knoxville," in *B&L*, 3:748-50; Poe, "The Defense of Knoxville," in *B&L*, 3:743, 748-49; *OR* 31, pt.1, 341-45 ,466, 475, 490-91, 521; Freeman, *Lee's Lieutenants*, 3:293-94; Chicoine, *Confederates of Chappell Hill*, 116; J. A. H. Granberry, "Longstreet Before Knoxville," *CV* (1923), 31:372.

Before withdrawing from south of the Holston on December 3, Law and Robertson aggressively attacked the Federals in their front to help conceal the withdrawal. The Federals ultimately fell back to a secondary line of entrenchments closer to the river, allowing the two Confederate brigades to quietly withdraw westward, cross the Holston on the ferry early that evening, and march around Knoxville. As they led the march on December 4, the 5th Texas and the rest of the brigade, believing that they were finally rejoining the Army of Northern Virginia, began singing endless choruses of "Carry Me Back to Ole Virginny"—blissfully unaware of the travail awaiting them before they again saw Marse Robert and trod the soil of The Old Dominion.[39]

After leaving Knoxville, the Texans followed the East Tennessee and Virginia Railroad along the north bank of the Holston River for 10 miles, crossing to the south bank on the railroad bridge at Strawberry Plains. They encamped one mile from the river that evening. For the next four days, the regiment, still guarding the baggage and ordnance trains with the brigade and Law's, continued to follow the railroad along the western slope of the Bays Mountains passing through New Market, Mossy Creek, Morristown, and Russellville. There the column turned and followed the Rogersville and Jefferson Railroad to Rogersville, arriving there on December 8. They had marched about 60 miles.[40]

Longstreet's main body followed the trains east for a short distance, then marched along the river's north bank hoping, in vain, it turned out, to intercept Maj. Gen. John G. Foster's Union army, approaching Knoxville from the Cumberland Gap. Reaching Blain's Crossroad on December 5, it moved to Rutledge the next day, where the army encamped for two days, accumulating food and forage. On December 8, the column left Rutledge, marched through Bean's Station, and arrived at Rogersville on December 9, a day after the Texans got there with the trains. On December 10, Longstreet received a telegram from President Davis informing him that he had been accorded sole authority over the troops in his department, the Department of East Tennessee. As his first official act, Longstreet countermanded Bragg's order for the return of Martin's cavalry to the Army of Tennessee.[41]

On December 14, a Union force under Maj. Gen. J. G. Parke that had been following Longstreet along with three cavalry brigades and one infantry, with artillery

39 *OR* 31, pt. 1,461-62, 466; Longstreet, *Manassas to Appomattox*, 435-37; DiNardo, *James Longstreet*, 35; Polley, *Hood's Texas Brigade*, 223.

40 Polley, *Hood's Texas Brigade*, 223-24; Simpson, *Lee's Grenadier Guard*, 359.

41 *OR* 31, pt. 1, 454, 459, 462-63; Longstreet, *Manassas to Appomattox*, 439. Wheeler had been ordered back to Bragg's command on November 24, ceding command of Longstreet's cavalry to Martin.

support, was enticed into battle near Bean's Station, 17 southwest of Rogersville. There, the Confederates drove the Federals back through Bean's Station toward Knoxville but were unsuccessful in cutting off and capturing Parke's force. Longstreet was quick to blame Law and McLaws for Parke's escape. While the Confederates failed to snare the Federals, the engagement still proved profitable. Brig. Gen. Jones's cavalry captured a huge supply of coffee and sugar, both scarcities in Longstreet's army for some time. The 5th Texas took some occasional artillery fire but otherwise took no part in the fighting. Ordered to the vicinity with Law's command, but delayed by the cold high winds, it joined Longstreet on the 15th after a 16-mile march. So many of his men were barefooted, Robertson voiced his concern over their plight.[42]

The regiment remained at Bean's Station with the brigade until December 19. Once Parke evinced no more aggressive signs, the Texans crossed the Holston with the rest of Longstreet's artillery and on December 22, went into winter quarters at Morristown, some 40 miles northeast of Knoxville.[43]

Morristown sits aside the East Tennessee and Virginia Railroad in the fertile valley between the Holston and French Broad rivers, some 40 miles northeast of Knoxville. Atop a wooded hill, a mile north of the town, the 5th Texas set up its winter camp. And despite the wretched condition of their clothing and shoes, the troops anticipated a pleasant respite, for water was abundant and forage opportunities plentiful. Uncertain how long they would stay, the men initially remained in tents instead of constructing semi-permanent structures as they had in past winters. When it became clear Morristown would be a relatively permanent location—about two months was general belief—the Texans were soon busy "chopping logs and splitting boards for cabins." As the weather grew increasingly colder and military activity diminished, the tent encampment gave way to the more comfortable and warmer combinations of canvas and log structures.[44]

Maj. Gen. Gordon Granger, commander of the Union IV Corps, emerged from the Knoxville with a large force in early January, 1864. Following the French Broad River, he approached Morristown from the south through Dandridge, 30 miles east of Knoxville. Longstreet responded by ordering his infantry to the Strawberry Plains vicinity, about 25 miles to his southwest. The regiment received orders on January 10

42 *OR* 31, pt. 1, 463, 470, 480; Longstreet, *Manassas to Appomattox*, 439-40, 534; Boatner, *Civil War Dictionary*, 53-54; Freeman, *Lee's Lieutenants*, 3:299; West, *Texan in Search of a Fight*, 135; Alexander, *Military Memoirs*, 490.

43 Polley, *Hood's Texas Brigade*, 224; Granberry, "Longstreet Before Knoxville," *CV* 31:372; Moore, *Men of the Bayou City Guards*, 77; *OR* 31, pt. 1, 463.

44 *OR* 32, pt. 2, 210; Polley, *Hood's Texas Brigade*, 244; Granberry, "Longstreet Before Knoxville," *CV*, 31:372; West, *Texan in Search of a Fight*, 137.

to pack up and prepare to move westward. Reluctantly departing their snug huts, the Texans marched through Russellville on January 11, and then on to Panther Springs where they remained several days. On January 15, they marched south to Dandridge, only to discover the Federals gone. But later Union cavalry hit portions of Jenkins' Division at Kimbrough's Crossroads on the Morristown Road. Attacked and outgunned by Longstreet's cavalry, the Yankee horsemen eventually fell back to Dandridge. Longstreet also deployed his two infantry divisions trying to cut off Granger's line of communications and isolate him. But the Federal commander discovered the flanking maneuver in time, withdrew from Dandridge, and started back to Knoxville with Longstreet's cavalry closely on his heels.[45]

As darkness fell, all Federal units had retreated to the safety of their main line, pushed from the hills before Dandridge. Longstreet and his staff halted at the same house Granger had used for his headquarters a couple of hours before. The retreating Federals had left behind an unexpected memento: a flask of whiskey with which the jubilant Confederates toasted Granger— "May his shadow never grow less!"—and then continued their pursuit. The muddy roads bogged down pursuit considerably, thus allowing Granger to return to Knoxville without serious loss. Although the Federals destroyed the bridge across the Holston, Brig. Gen. Frank C. Armstrong's cavalry division, following closely, still managed to capture 800 head of beef cattle and 31 wagons. The Federals lost 100 men in the fighting and the Confederates 150. The regiment had taken no part in the fighting and by January 19, it was back in winter quarters at Morristown.[46]

Once the regiment returned to winter quarters, the Texans had the "opportunity" to enlist for the duration of the war. As inducement to re-enlist a furlough home would be awarded to every tenth man who "re-upped." Almost the entire brigade re-enlisted, despite their past or and ongoing sufferings or their disenchantment with the current state of the Confederate operations in East Tennessee. Captain Watson Williams of Company F reported that everyone in his command had re-enlisted but one. This did not disturb Williams, since the lone holdout had never been in a fight or seen "a day's duty since the company went into winter quarters on the Potomac in December 1861." Williams was glad to be rid of this malcontent.[47]

45 J. W. Minnich, "That Affair at Dandridge, Tenn.," *CV*, (1922) 30:297; Longstreet, *Manassas to Appomattox*, 451-53; Polley, *Hood's Texas Brigade*, 225-26.

46 Longstreet, *Manassas to Appomattox*, 451-53; Minnich, "That Affair at Dandridge, Tenn.," *CV*, 30:297; Parker, *Touched By Fire*, 85; Polley, *Hood's Texas Brigade*, 226; Polley, *Letters to Charming Nellie*, 221.

47 *OR* 36, pt. 2, 1019; Watson Williams to Laura Jesse Bryan, February 20, 1864, in CRC; Winkler, *Confederate Capital*, 152; Polley, *Hood's Texas Brigade*, 226; Polley, *Letters to Charming*

By late January, the railroads to Richmond were again in good repair, allowing limited shipments of food, forage, clothing, and mail to reach the army. The long awaited pontoons and flatboats for bridging the Holston also arrived, allowing a second effort to take Knoxville. Old Pete planned a mid-winter offensive to demonstrate "the strategic strength of the field, and persuade the authorities that an army of twenty thousand in that zone could be of greater service than double that force on the enemy's front or elsewhere." Longstreet planned to bridge the Holston at Strawberry Plains, then proceed south and west along the East Tennessee and Virginia Railroad to Knoxville. With the Fort Sanders fiasco fresh in his mind, he wanted to ensure a sufficient number of infantry to successfully storm the city's defenses. On February 17, 1864, Lee approved 10,000 infantry reinforcements, including Pickett's Division, to prosecute this campaign. Longstreet's enlarged army would pose a serious threat to the Federals at Knoxville.[48]

Jenkins' Division was ordered to Strawberry Plains on February 10 to lay the pontoon bridge across the Holston. The 5th Texas departed with the brigade, assisted in the bridge construction, and then crossed over to the north bank of the Holston on February 14. Thereafter, it trailed McLaws' Division westward along the railroad in support of the Confederate cavalry demonstrating in front of Knoxville. The next day the men were bivouacked 17 miles east of Knoxville, with a picket line at Flat Creek, four miles to their front. Here they remained on picket duty from February 15-20. Texas scouts, beyond the outer line, skirmished every day with Federal pickets posted three miles from the city.[49]

Longstreet's winter offensive ended almost before it started. On February 19, the Confederate war department cancelled the movement of Lee's promised 10,000 infantrymen, and Martin's cavalry was ordered back to the Army of Tennessee at Dalton, Georgia. Deprived of his cavalry, and with no prospects for additional reinforcements, Longstreet reluctantly withdrew from his advanced positions east of Knoxville, falling back toward the mountains. The retreat began on February 22, with Jenkins' Division and the cavalry protecting the withdrawal. The force made it safely to the Bays Mountains without Federal pressure, camping at Bull's Gap about 12 miles east of Morristown, between the Holston and Nolichucky rivers. Beginning on

---

Nellie, 221; Robertson, *Touched With Valor*, 60. The Confederate Congress later formally recognized the Texans' display of patriotism by passing a joint resolution of thanks to the brigade on May 17, 1864.

48 Longstreet, *Manassas to Appomattox*, 454, 456, 462-63; Simpson, *Lee's Grenadier Guard*, 364; Polley, *Hood's Texas Brigade*, 224.

49 *OR* 32, pt. 2, 334; Watson Williams to Laura Jesse Bryan , February 20, 1864, in CRC; Polley, *Hood's Texas Brigade*, 226; Longstreet, *Manassas to Appomattox*, 461-62; Parker, *Touched By Fire*, 85.

February 26, the regiment occupied a position at Bull's Gap, in what Capt. Williams described as "a miserable, hilly, mountaineous no account country." He was unfamiliar with the name of the mountains and was "inclined to think they were never named on account of their ugliness." The regiment remained here until Longstreet's entire force was ordered back to Virginia in late March.[50]

As they had the previous winter, the regiment's men suffered terribly from food, clothing, and shoe shortages throughout the winter of 1863-1864. The severity of the Tennessee winter compounded the suffering. When first encamped at Morristown, they enjoyed fruitful foraging in the area. Fertile land and prosperous local farms characterized the East Tennessee region. While picked over by the armies of both sides, there was still food to be had, particularly in the valley of the French Broad River, a source of food for the army for some period of time. But as mid-winter approached, with its freezing temperatures and deep snow, food became scarce and foraging extremely difficult. Consequently, large foraging parties were required to scour many miles thorough the region to sustain the army. These foraging parties were normally accompanied by a large guard detail, as they had to range far and wide and remained isolated from the main force for days at a time.[51]

Guarding the forage trains was dangerous and unpopular duty, even though it guaranteed better quality of food. Much of East Tennessee was pro-Union territory, and the area was loaded with bushwhackers, guerrillas, and desperate deserters from both sides. Moxley Sorrel described the local area citizens as "without pity or compassion—generosity and sympathy were strangers to them; but hatred and revenge made their homes in the breasts of these farmers." One Texan referred to the area as "a mountainous country full of 'bushwhackers,' 'moonshine stills' and 'jay hawkers.' It was a rough country and a tough set of people, men and women, and we had to fight all of them." The foraging wagons were overtaken on numerous occasions, and several men killed. These bushwhackers "seldom fought," Porter Alexander wrote, "but they [would] cut off small parties and took no prisoners."[52]

The Texans, of course, refused to suffer such indignities lying down. Tired of being ambushed as they plodded along with the foraging wagons, they often conducted offensive forays against the most notorious of these outlaws. Private A. N.

50 Watson Williams to Laura Jesse Bryan , March 4, 1864, in CRC; West, *A Texan in Search of a Fight*, 142; Parker, *Touched By Fire*, 85; Robertson, *Touched With Valor*, 60.

51 Polley, *Letters to Charming Nellie*, 195-96; Simpson, *Lee's Grenadier Guard*, 366-67.

52 Sorrel, *Confederate Staff Officer*, 221; Hamilton, *History of Company M*, 38; Simpson, *Lee's Grenadier Guard*, 367; Alexander, "Longstreet at Knoxville," in *B&L*, 3:751. A "bushwacker" referred to men who hid in the woods and thus could attack from the bush. A "jayhawker' was one skilled in guerrilla warfare tactics. Fletcher, *Rebel Private*, 116.

Vaughn of Company F described an experience of hunting down bushwhackers and deserters in the area. His detail cautiously approached the cabin of a local desperado of nefarious reputation. As they burst through the door, they found the scoundrel under a bed with cocked guns. His wife "yelled out saying all the rough, derisive words at her command and that if they were going to shoot him, to take him from under the bed and out of the house, and to leave her no nasty mess to clean up." The Texans were happy to oblige her.[53]

Clashes between foraging parties and renegades continued throughout the regiment's stay in northeastern Tennessee. The potential for losing forage wagons, teams, and men became part of the price of their continued presence. Food had to be procured locally, since supplying the demands of an army in such a remote area lay totally beyond the abilities of the Confederate commissary. Even with regular foraging, troops that winter were often times reduced to short and unpalatable rations. Before leaving as a forage train guard on New Year's Day in 1864, Polley reported he had eaten a breakfast of "blue beef and flour [biscuits] made of sick wheat just issued to us." John West claimed that the brigade "lived on corn issued to us in the ear from the wagons —three or four ears for man per day; that we shelled, parched and ate it and received nothing else. Parched corn, a pipe of good tobacco, [and] clear water, was the menu for several days." Members of the brigade also wrote that much of their flour was "sour." While it produced "nice looking biscuits," the taste "would nauseate the stomach like ipecac—sometimes would produce vomiting. We could not eat it ." Nicholas Pomeroy of Company A, after describing his usual fare of "bread and beef of the very poorest quality and deficient in quantity," apologized "if my letter is uninteresting, it is attributable to something else than overeating."[54]

Besides authorized foraging expeditions under the direction of Longstreet's quartermaster and commissary officers, considerable illicit moonlight requisitioning by individuals and small groups also thrived. Naturally, the regiment's men figured prominently in these unauthorized and generally successful forays. Occasionally, however, even they returned empty handed. By mid-March, so little food was available for both men and horses that Longstreet had to request immediate aid from Richmond. On March 19, he wrote pointedly to Adjutant General Cooper:

> We shall not be able to keep our animals alive more than a week or two [without corn] . . . our rations, too, are getting short, so that we will hardly be able to march. . . .

53 Fletcher, *Rebel Private*, 108.

54 Polley, *Letters to Charming Nellie*, 195; West, *Texan in Search of a Fight*, 140-41; Pomeroy, "War Memoirs," 71. Hanks, *History of Captain Benton's Company*, 25, 27; Simpson, *Lee's Grenadier Guard*, 369.

> I beg that you will send us supplies at once, in sufficient quantity at least to enable us to march. . . . These are perhaps the best troops in the Confederate armies and should not be left where they must starve.

Four days later, Longstreet was forced to cut the already scant bread and meat ration for his troops.[55]

The chronic lack of shoes, clothing, and blankets had even more deleterious effects on the men of the 5th Texas. The weather that winter was extremely harsh. As much as 16 inches of snow blanketed the ground, with temperatures frequently hovering around zero. A great many men in the ranks were barefooted, and had been in that condition for some weeks, and as always, shoes and socks were scarce. West wrote his wife December 25: "I shall leave you now and see what a Christmas our soldiers are enjoying with their bare feet and ragged clothes." Joe Joskins (Campbell) of Company A wrote of surviving most of the winter with only one shoe. Soldiers often tied pieces of shoes together to provide ersatz footwear. Footwear was so scarce that some of the men detailed to the brigade quartermaster section, which was responsible for issuing shoes, had to wear brogans from which their toes protruded. A Houston newspaper pleaded with its readers to send socks to the newspaper offices, where they could be gathered, organized, and "issued directly to needy applicants or placed in the hands of the Quartermaster of any regiment or Captain of any company as desired."[56]

Moxley Sorrel related that when the army advanced toward Dandridge, in the bitterly cold weather "not less than 2,000 of our little army were without shoes. Their bleeding feet left marks at every step." A number of the officers likened these bloody bare footprints in the snow to the similar situation the Continental soldiers faced at Morristown, NJ, in 1777. Longstreet observed that many of the "rough angles of mud as firm and sharp as so many freshly-quarried rocks" caused the troops on the march to leave these "bloody marks along the road." A local woman later recalled that she "never forgot those barefooted ragged Texas boys, who left bloody footprints in the snow as they marched past her home on their retreat" from Knoxville.[57]

55 *OR* 32, pt. 2, 655, 669.

56 Joskins, "A Sketch of Hood's Texas Brigade," in UTSA 152-53; Hanks, *History of Captain Benton's Company*, 26; West, *Texan in Search of a Fight*, 135-36; Polley, *Letters to Charming Nellie*, 183; Simpson, *Lee's Grenadier Guard*, 372; Hamilton, *History of Company M*, 40-41; Pomeroy, "War Memoirs," 86.

57 Joskins, "A Sketch of Hood's Texas Brigade," in UTSA 152-53; Hamilton, *History of Company M*, 40-41; Longstreet, *Manassas to Appomattox*, 450; West, *Texan in Search of a Fight*, 141; Simpson, *Lee's Grenadier Guard*, 372.

This sizeable body of barefooted men greatly reduced the combat readiness of Longstreet's army. Due to the frozen condition of the ground and the heavy snow, the shoeless men of Texas could not be relied upon for any type of offensive movement or even to perform regular picket duty. They were forced to "wallow around the camp fire and make lye hominy." And shoeless soldiers suffered in yet another manner: they could not forage and so missed the opportunity to add variety to their diet of "parched corn, sick wheat, blue beef and lye hominy." Old Pete tried to remedy the shortage of shoes in several ways. He established a makeshift shoe factory at Morristown, for example, and manned it with professional cobblers and tanners from the army. He also encouraged the men to make "Longstreet Moccasins" from green hides as they had the previous winter at Fredericksburg. He also pressed the quartermaster general in Richmond about this critical problem and urged emergency action to remedy it.[58]

The Longstreet Moccasin, though universally unpopular and seldom widely adopted the previous winter in Virginia, was readily accepted in Tennessee. Moccasins "were not gaudy footwear but many thousands in Longstreet's Corps blessed their good fortune when they were able to get them." This simple, effective, and relatively easy-to-produce footwear was formed by first cutting wet rawhide into the shape of a man's foot. The cutout piece of hide was then tied with rawhide laces to the foot, with the hair inside. To fit properly and comfortably, the hide moccasin had to be dried on the wearer's foot. If it dried naturally and slowly, the rawhide would tighten just enough to fit and be reasonably comfortable, like skin. If, however, it dried too rapidly, too close, or too long over the open fire, the rawhide shrunk dramatically, pinching and binding the foot. Unfortunately, improper fits were common, and soldiers had no recourse but to sleep in the footwear. It was said that "[o]nce they were put on they 'stayed put.' There was a binding obligation between the moccasin and the man that they would never part so long as life lasted—for the moccasin."[59]

Shoe and moccasin production at Morristown was only a temporary expediency. The footwear famine remained critical until late February, 1864, when the Quartermaster General finally provided 3,000 pairs of shoes. This shipment saw that all the men were finally shod while the army remained in East Tennessee.[60]

Clothing was also critically short during that harrowing winter. Many Texans had to fight half-naked, or, at best, in ragged and threadbare uniforms. Campaigning and

58 Longstreet, *Manassas to Appomattox*, 446; Moore, *Men of the Bayou City Guards*, 82; Hanks, *Captain Benton's Company*, 26. Hamilton, *History of Company M*, 45; Simpson, *Lee's Grenadier Guard*, 373.

59 Hamilton, *History of Company M*, 34; Simpson, *Lee's Grenadier Guard*, 373-74.

60 Longstreet, *Manassas to Appomattox*, 446.

foraging in inclement weather had reduced their uniforms to rags. Uncomfortable enough marching or fighting in a Virginia summer, the thin, tattered clothing simply would not work for campaigning in the dead of harsh winter in the Tennessee mountains. Letters from the men reported that many in their ranks had next to no clothing. Joe Joskins of Company A said it was altogether "a common sight to see . . . men with no pants and some without shirts," in winter camp; Nicholas Pomeroy, also of Company A, wrote that "our clothes and shoes were in a dilapidated condition." Underclothing, too, wore out during the campaign. While some new uniforms were finally shipped from Richmond in January when the railroads were repaired, undershirts and drawers were not included. In fact, underclothing became the Texans' greatest need that bitter winter. Letters and newspaper articles sent to numerous agencies and papers throughout the South publicized the dire need. Moved by the Texans' sorry plight, women from Georgia and Virginia shipped voluminous boxes of underclothing.[61]

Added to all of these great tribulations that winter, the dreadful, ubiquitous "grayback" (louse) maintained and even increased its irksome presence. Not since that first winter at Dumfries had lice been as bad. By wearing the same filthy rags day in and day out, rolling up in the same dirty blanket and sleeping in the same pallet of straw every night—not that they had a choice—the troops greatly spurred propagation of the dreaded pest. Washing oneself or one's clothes was a luxury few indulged in given the weather conditions; small quantities of water heated over the campfire did little to resolve the issue. One Texan recalled that "[s]ome of the boys said they [lice] had C. S. on them." The men described these pests as "exceedingly husky" ones. The evidence suggested the "Tennessee cooties were a larger specie than the Virginia variety."[62]

Official inspections of the Texas troops at Bull's Gap confirmed the impact the weather, the shortages of food and clothing and other trials had on the moral and well-being of the men. Discipline, military appearance, and clothing, ranked the lowest of the entire war. The men complained that because of their home being west of the Mississippi, they were denied lengthy furloughs accorded troops living in Virginia and

61 Joskins, "A Sketch of Hood's Texas Brigade," 152; Pomeroy, "War Memoirs," 71-72; Winkler, *Confederate Capital*, 153. Evander Law wrote of "one hardy fellow whose trousers were literally 'worn to a frazzle' and would no longer adhere to his legs even by dint of the most persistent patching. Unable to buy, beg or borrow another pair, he wore instead a pair of thin cotton drawers. By nursing these carefully he managed to get through the winter." Evander Law, "From the Wilderness to Cold Harbor," in *B&L*, 4:118-19. Joskins (Campbell) himself was relatively fortunate. He had a pair of pants, although one of its legs was missing.

62 Simpson, *Lee's Grenadier Guard*, 375-76; Hamilton, *History of Company M*, 40; Hanks, *Captain Benton's Company*, 27.

Georgia. Preparedness suffered as well: the roll numbers versus present for duty dipped below 50 percent in many units. Many of those "present for duty" were in fact still unfit for any kind of marching. The desertion rate was its highest in East Tennessee as any time during the war, with the exception of its final months. Still, morale remained reasonably good for those who remained. Longstreet claimed the "little army was bright and cheerful and ready for any work to which it could be called. West indicated that he "heard little murmuring and *saw* no signs of revolt" among the Texans.[63]

Even under these adverse conditions and their potential impact on morale at Bull's Gap that winter, the men of the 5th Texas still found time to pursue some amusements. Many spent considerable time chasing rabbits through the snow-covered ground. Once a rabbit was sighted, the cry would go up and hordes of men would chase the animal until it was stowed in a lucky soldier's knapsack. Snowball fights were also much in vogue, as they had been at Dumfries and Fredericksburg in winters past. Hundreds of Texans participated in these throwing duels, although none reached the magnitude of the Great Snowball Fight of January 23, 1863.[64]

That winter Texans had considerable concern that, if not quickly augmented, their shockingly depleted brigade might be consolidated with one or two other brigades. On December 10, Robertson reported to Hood that the brigade carried on its rolls 784 "present for duty," with many of that number being men unable to stand an "arduous march." The 5th Texas itself now totaled only 196 (18 officers and 178 men). Indeed, after two years enduring brutal fighting, disease, poor diet, and arduous weather in shabby clothing, the brigade had been reduced to the size of an under-strength regiment. Consequently, Robertson proposed that his whole command be furloughed to return to Texas and Arkansas in January 1864, to recuperate and conduct a mass recruiting drive, "making each officer and man a recruiting officer." Then his men, augmented by their recruits, would rendezvous at some pre-determined location west of the Mississippi on April 1 for the march to rejoin Longstreet. Robertson assured Hood, still in Richmond recuperating from his Chickamauga wound, of his confidence that all his men would not only return promptly, but that each would bring with him one or more recruits—and enlisted his support.[65]

63 OR 32, pt. 2, 640-41; Robertson, *Touched With Valor*, 52; Mendoza, *Confederate Struggle for Command*, 197; West, *Texan in Search of a Fight*, 141; Longstreet, *Manassas to Appomattox*, 449.

64 West, *Texan in Search of a Fight*, 139; Robertson, *Touched With Valor*, 54; Hanks, *Captain Benton's Company*, 26.

65 Robertson, *Touched With Valor*, 52-54; OR 29, pt. 2, 869-70.

Brig. Gen. John Gregg
Generals in Gray

Precedent existed for the concept. During the winter of 1862-63, each company had sent a commissioned officer and one or two enlisted men back to its home county, and this effort produced hundreds of recruits. But the same idea tried the next winter brought only meager results. Robertson therefore sought permission, quickly granted, to brief the Texas delegation to the Confederate Congress on his proposal. Hood, who vowed to "never consent to the consolidation of this brigade" also lobbied the Texas delegation, telling Robertson how much it grieved him "to know that my old troops are not doing well."

On December 12, 1863, Robertson petitioned the Texas delegation, indicating that casualties had reduced the brigade "to so small a number that, unless some plan is adopted that will fill up its ranks with recruits, it must ere long lose its identity and be merged into other commands. . . . The memory of our common toils and sufferings, and that of our fallen comrades, alike forbid a course that would destroy our organization." The Texas congressmen agreed and endorsed the proposal, adding their request that some arrangement be made for the transfer of the three Lone Star regiments to Texas to recruit. They also endorsed the plan, lauding the regiments' extraordinary services and hardships which eminently commended them for this "special favor of the Government." In the end, however, nothing happened. The war department refused to consider it. Robertson subsequently sought to visit Richmond for personal consultation with the Texas delegation and Hood, and an in-person proposal to the secretary of war, but Longstreet refused his request for a 15-day leave. Hood later wrote Robertson on January 6, 1864, pretty much dismissing all hope the scheme would work. The war department wanted to fill vacancies with "exchanged prisoners," he said.[66]

On February 1, 1864, Hood was promoted to lieutenant general and assigned to serve as a corps commander under Gen. Joseph E. Johnston, the new commander of the Army of Tennessee. Longstreet was actively working now to secure permanent

66 Robertson, *Touched With Valor*, 52-57, 65-66; *OR* 29, pt. 2, 869-70. That Robertson's plan would have worked is highly doubtful. There were few volunteers left in Texas by the winter of 1863-64, and the brigade refused to accept conscripts.

command of Hood's Division for Micah Jenkins, its temporary commander and one of Longstreet's favorites. When this appeared unlikely to happen, Longstreet championed Maj. Gen. Robert Ransom or W. H. C. Whiting for the position, but neither was available. Lee had suggested Maj. Gen. Simon B. Buckner, but the war department disapproved him. Then on February 12, Maj. Gen. Charles W. Field, promoted that very day, was assigned to duty with Hood's Division and given command of the division. Jenkins returned to his old brigade. Longstreet did not approve of either assignment and argued with the war department about it, to no avail.[67]

Considerable turmoil roiled the brigade and Longstreet's command generally that winter. Robertson had already felt Longstreet's wrath in the fall of 1863, when he was temporarily relieved of command, and then reinstated by Bragg. Back at his command, Robertson's reinstatement gave only a brief respite from further difficulties. On December 18, Jenkins preferred charges against him, stemming from detrimental remarks Robertson had supposedly made regarding Jenkins' generalship and judgment. The issue arose from comments Robertson had made at Bean's Station during one of the largely unshod brigade's periodic winter chases after Federal cavalry over frozen ice and snow. Robertson had observed that "he didn't see any reason to have his men run after every cavalryman that came by."[68]

Robertson's "arrest," enraged the Texans according to A. B. Hood. Longstreet thereafter ordered his subordinate to Bristol, Tennessee, on December 23, 1863 to "await the assembling of the court for the trial of his case." On December 30, Longstreet forwarded the specific charges and specifications against Robertson for "conduct highly prejudicial to good order and military discipline." He requested the convening of a court martial, believing that he himself lacked the authority to convene one.[69]

In his letter of January 6, 1864, reporting the war department's decision denying a furlough for the brigade to Texas for recruiting, Hood told Robertson that he would likely be tried by court martial, and ended "I am sorry on account of your troubles with Genl. Jenkins." Special orders no. 8 on January 11, 1864, appointed Brig. Gen. John

67 *OR* 31, pt. 3, 735, 859, 866; *OR* 32, pt. 2, 518; Freeman, *Lee's Lieutenant's*, 3:310-13, 318-19, 361.

68 *OR* 31, pt. 1, 467; Robertson, *Touched With Valor*, 101; Winkler, *Confederate Capital*, 151; Freeman, *Lee's Lieutenants*, 3:310-305; Polley, *Hood's Texas Brigade*, 225.

69 *OR* 31, pt. 1, 470; William Garrett Piston, *Lee's Tarnished Lieutenant: James Longstreet and His Place in Southern History* (Athens, GA, 1990), 79; Parker, *Touched By Fire*, 84; Winkler, *Confederate Capital*, 151; A. B. Hood to Cousin Jennie, February 14, 1864, in CRC. The charges against Robertson are in the *OR* reference cited above.

Gregg to command of the brigade. Gregg's availability arose when his own brigade had been eliminated in the general reorganization of the Army of Tennessee in late September 1863. He was ordered to Russellville on January 11, 1864 "for assignment with the Texas Brigade." At that time, only one field grade officer, the 5th's Lt. Col. Bryan, was present for duty. Gregg had just recovered from grievous wounds he had suffered at Chickamauga, ironically saved there from certain capture and probable death by the men of the Texas Brigade under Robertson. And even more ironic: Gregg had recently been assigned as a member of the court sitting in judgment of Robertson.[70]

A court martial convened at Russellville, Tennessee on February 12, 1864, with Maj. Gen. Simon Buckner as its president. The court reached its decision on February 25, acquitting Robertson of "improper motives," but nonetheless disapproving of his "conduct." He was accordingly sentenced to be reprimanded by general order no. 24, resulting in his removal from command of the Texas Brigade. He was thereby forced to seek a transfer to the Trans-Mississippi Department to seek another command.[71]

Gregg ultimately became the last general to command the Texans. His initial assessment of the brigade declared matters in "a deplorable condition of affairs" and recommended that the entire brigade be sent to the Army of Tennessee and there consolidated with another Texas brigade. He thought the Texans would find the matter more palatable if they were combined with other units from their home state. The brigade would become "one subdivision of the brigade." Gregg saw the troops eventually transferring to a command in Texas.[72]

Word reached Robertson on March 30, 1864, that his request for a command in Texas could not be approved; no Texas brigades were available in the Trans-Mississippi Department. So on April 1, he requested 90 days' leave in Texas to visit family, "with authority to report to Genl. Edmund Kirby Smith should he have a command" available. The leave was granted with permission to report to Smith "if he

70 *OR* 31, pt. 1, 466-67, *OR* 32, pt. 2, 206, 536, 546, 778-79; Robertson, *Touched With Valor*, 57, 101-102; Piston, *Lee's Tarnished Lieutenant*, 79; Simpson, *Lee's Grenadier Guard*, 385.

71 Robertson, *Touched With Valor*, 14, 57-58, 101; Parker, *Touched By Fire*, 84; Longstreet, *Manassas to Appomattox*, 469-70.

72 *OR* 31, pt. 1, 466-67, 470; Robertson, *Touched With Valor*, 14, 57-58; Winkler, *Confederate Capital*, 150; Parker, *Touched By Fire*, 84. Gregg came with an impressive was portfolio; elected colonel of the 7th Texas Infantry in the summer of 1861, he was captured with his whole regiment at Fort Donelson in February, 1862. Following his exchange, Gregg was soon promoted to brigadier on August 29, 1862, and was subsequently involved in all the engagements of the Western army including Chickamauga, where he commanded a mixed Tennessee/Texas brigade. Wright, *Texans in the War*, 80; Fulmore, *History and Geography of Texas*, 247. For more on Gregg, see Appendix B, Volume 1.

so desired" Robertson's services. Robertson first traveled to Richmond, was detained in Virginia as a witness in a civil trial, and he then left for Texas in early April. On May 30, orders came for him to take command of the Reserve Forces of the State of Texas under Magruder, commander of the District of Texas, New Mexico, and Arizona. Soon after leaving for Texas, he penned a poignant letter of farewell to the brigade. He ended it with "a mind saddened by the remembrances of ties broken, and with a prayer that God, in his mercy, will guard, protect and bless you, I bid you farewell." Thus downcast, the man who had commanded the Texans longer than any other officer during the war sadly took leave of his beloved command.[73]

The 5th Texas and the rest of the brigade completely sympathized with Robertson, and the officers and men signed several petitions to retain him in command. Extremely popular with the rank and file, they were distraught to see him removed. "The Brigade is very anxious to have him back" Tacitus Clay wrote his wife, "and he is now and has ever since the battle of Chickamauga, by far the most popular Commander it has Ever had—His Enemies have signally failed in destroying his popularity & the Confidence of the Texas Brigade—on the Contrary it has Endeared him the More to them." Private Hood of Company I wrote home that the "Brigade was alarmed about the treatment of Robertson by the general officers of the corps, it has been of a villainous character. All hands are for him."[74]

Robertson, while perhaps lacking Napoleonic leadership characteristics, thoroughly understood and appreciated his men and tried his utmost to respond to their needs and wants. And he was courageous to a fault. True, he sometimes resisted what he perceived as unwarranted orders from his superiors, including the infamous wintertime order from Jenkins, and that entangled him in the system. He paid the price for his fealty to his troops.[75]

Robertson was also well-respected by Hood and the other brigade commanders in the Division, and he received a number of stout letters of recommendation from them when he left Virginia. Hood wrote on April 11, 1864, "I know him to be an officer of great energy and faithful in the discharge of his duties. He has great experience as an officer and has taken part in many battles. His troops are very much attached to him." Benning concurred on March 10: "the country will be proud to keep

73 Robertson, *Touched With Valor*, 57-59, 63-64, 101; *OR* 32, pt. 2, 777-79; A. B. Hood to Cousin Jennie, February 14, 1864, in CRC. Kirby-Smith was commander of the Confederate Trans-Mississippi Department.

74 Robertson, *Touched With Valor*, 57-58; A. B. Hood to Cousin Jennie, February 14, 1864, in CRC; Mendoza, *Confederate Struggle for Command*, 191; Tacitus Clay to Bettie Clay, March 25, 1864, in MSU.

75 Winkler, *Confederate Capital*, 151; Simpson, *Lee's Grenadier Guard*, 387.

alive the memory of one who has done his whole duty on more than a dozen battlefields, many of them the most important of the war." A month later Evander Law told Robertson: "I can ask nothing better for you in the future than that your happiness and prosperity may be commensurate with the gallantry, ability and patriotism that you have displayed in the service."[76]

Matters in Longstreet's command did not exude sweetness and light. Old Pete also removed both Law and McLaws from command and preferred charges against them. He accused McLaws of exhibiting "a want of confidence" in Longstreet's "efforts and plans" at Fort Sanders. McLaws requested a court of inquiry, and he was found guilty on one of the specifications, but the president later disapproved the findings and assigned him to another command in Georgia. Law, under considerable pressure from Jenkins and Longstreet, finally resigned from Old Pete's command on December 19, 1863. Jenkins had accused him of failing to cooperate at Wauhatchie and Campbell's Station, and Longstreet for "dragging his heels" at Bean's Station. However Law also had Davis' support, and he ultimately returned to the command of his brigade.[77]

The entire East Tennessee campaign had been one of frustration, disappointment, and extreme hardship. No significant engagements followed the move east from Knoxville in early December, and no gain compensated for the immense suffering of the troops. So when word arrived on March 27, 1864, that the Texas Brigade was moving back toward Virginia, the news was met with vigorous cheers. Morale immediately skyrocketed. On March 28, the division left the Bays Mountains vicinity through Howard's Gap and then marched northeast along the East Tennessee and Virginia Railroad to Greenville, where it bivouacked for the evening. The regiment, after a four-day march through the mud in driving rain and snow, finally reached Zollicoffer, Tennessee, ten miles south of Bristol, on April 1, 1864. There, within one day's march of Virginia, it went into camp.[78]

While encamped near Zollicoffer, once again Mollie Bailey and Hood's Minstrels treated the Texans to a "musical and dancing program" on April 5, 1864. Mollie

76 Mendoza, *Confederate Struggle for Command*, 191; Simpson, *Lee's Grenadier Guard*, 386-87.

77 Longstreet, *Manassas to Appomattox*, 476-77; Sorrel, *Confederate Staff Officer*, 209-210; Warner, *Generals in Gray*, 204-205; Simpson, *Lee's Grenadier Guard*, 383; Freeman, *Lee's Lieutenants*, 3:337-38; *OR* 31, pt. 1, 219, 233, 474-75,467-68, 501-02, 505-506, pt. 3, 866-87, *OR* 33, pt. 1, 1291.

78 Joskins. "A Sketch of Hood's Texas Brigade, 153; Winkler, *Confederate Capital*, 154-55; *OR* 32, pt. 3, 756; *OR* 33, pt. 1, 1266. For information on Zollicoffer, TN, see Ned Jilton, "Bluff City/Zollicoffer, TN?," *Hardtack and Hard Times*, accessed November 5, 2009, http://www.timesnews.net/blogger.php?id=10239&postid+5918.

Arlene Kirkland had eloped in 1858 with James A. "Gus" Bailey, a cornet player in his father's circus band. With Mollie's sister and Gus's brother, the quartet formed the Bailey Family Troupe, which traveled through Alabama, Mississippi, and Arkansas acting, dancing, and singing. During the war, Gus served as bandmaster for the 3rd Arkansas, and Mollie traveled with the brigade as a nurse and occasional spy for Hood. During this time, Gus penned the words for "The Old Gray Mare," about a horse which almost died after eating green corn at Second Manassas. The tune soon became a famous marching song for the brigade. A makeshift stage was fashioned from cars for shipping horses "under the broad canopy of heaven," and General Anderson's headquarters furnished a tent forming the back curtain. The shows the makeshift troupe put on provided the troops much needed recreation and relief from the harsh winter's hardships. And it also mercifully kept them from thinking about the mayhem awaiting them in Virginia that spring.[79]

On April 7, 1864, President Davis directed Longstreet to move McLaws' and Fields' divisions and Alexander's artillery to Charlottesville, Virginia, to report there to Lee. The orders reached Old Pete at Bristol on April 11. Brigadier General John B. Kershaw, then commanding McLaws' Division, led the way, and Field's Division brought up the rear of the command. Typically, the regiment, as part of the Texas Brigade, was the last of Longstreet's units to leave Tennessee, boarding the trains at Zollicoffer on April 20, 1864, and arriving at Lynchburg, Virginia, on April 22. The spring campaign for the Army of Northern Virginia was finally grinding into motion, and the 5th Texas would again play an integral and fateful part in it.[80]

79 Diana J. Kleiner, "Bailey, Mollie Arline Kirkland," *Handbook of Texas Online*, Accessed November 4, 2009, https:// tsha.utexas.org/handbook/online/articles/ fba12; John Troesser, "Mollie Bailey: Born Mollie Arline Kirkland 'Circus Queen of the Southwest', " Texas Escapes.com, http://www.texasescapes.com/They-Shoe-Horses-Dont-They/Mollie-Bailey.htm; Narcissa Martin Boulware, "Mollie Bailey's Circus, Part III" *Montgomery County News*, March 12, 2005, accessed November 5, 2009, http://montgomerycountynews.net/mollie-baileys-circus-part-iii-p277-125.htm.

80 *OR* 32, pt. 3, 756; *OR* 33, pt. 1, 1054, 1255-56, 1266; Freeman, *Lee's Lieutenants*, 3:336-37.

Chapter 5

The Battle of the Wilderness

On April 26, following a brief rest in Charlottesville, the regiment marched northeast toward Cobham Station (Depot) on the Virginia Central Railroad, 16 miles away. It bivouacked in the nearby hamlet of Mechanicsville, about eight miles below Gordonsville. Within a few days, new uniforms and shoes arrived for the men. Along with ample rations, these additional supplies worked wonders for morale. Along with the food and clothing, however, came the inevitable camp requirements of reviews and inspections. Rumors circulated that Lee would soon arrive from his headquarters at Orange Court House to review the entire corps. Maj. Gen. Charles W. Field anticipating such a visitation, held an inspection and review of his five brigades on April 28.[1]

The next day, Lee arrived to officially welcome Longstreet and his men back to Virginia. Consequently in honor of the occasion, another review was held in a broad-pastured valley near Mechanicsville. As Lee approached, Porter Alexander's guns roared forth in a salute and the Rebel yell erupted from 10,000 energetic throats. Saluting them, Lee bared his gray head to the men. Elated at seeing their beloved Marse Robert again, the men cheered lustily as he moved down through their ranks on his favorite mount, Traveler. As he moved among Field's Division, he singled out the Texans, referring to them "as the best fighting brigade in the corps." One of the Texans recounted that afterwards: "The men hung around him and seemed satisfied to lay their hands on his gray horse or to touch the bridle, or the stirrup, or the old

1 *OR* 31, pt. 1, 446; Winkler, *Confederate Capital*, 155-56; Skoch, *Lone Star Confederate*, 102; Alexander, *Military Memoirs*, 493; Pomeroy, "War Memoirs," 72; Simpson, *Lee's Grenadier Guard*, 389. The Texans had already been "exposed to four days of ceremony when . . . [they] arrived at Cobham's Station." Simpson, *Lee's Grenadier Guard*, 389 n39.

general's leg—anything that Lee had was sacred to us fellows, who had just come back." Soon "[t]ears were seen tracing down Lee's cheeks . . . at the affection these returning veterans showed him."[2]

On April 30, the third inspection and review of Longstreet's returning troops in three days, brought the Texans to near-peak frustration. This particular "mustering of all hands" was a regular bi-monthly inspection of individual companies. It was not without its compensations, for the men signed the payroll records and collected their pay. Sadly, however, this would be the last pay for many of the Texans. The deadly battle of the Wilderness loomed within a week.[3]

On May 1, the regiment moved from Cobham Station a few miles north of Gordonsville on the road to Orange Court House. Lee's army, anticipating the Union's impending spring offensive, spread out along an extremely wide front. Longstreet's Corps was near Gordonsville, with Ewell's along the Rapidan above Mine Run, and A. P. Hill's posted on Ewell's left, higher up the river. Lee maintained his headquarters about two miles northeast of Orange Court House. The Confederates were generally situated along a 40-plus mile front south of the Rapidan, in position to concentrate wherever and whenever Grant moved toward Richmond. Uncertain about where the Union attack might come, Lee positioned his troops to cover the likely possibilities. Hill and Ewell covered the river across from Meade, while Longstreet was positioned to support Lee's main line or shuttle reinforcements to Richmond and the Shenandoah Valley. The Confederate cavalry kept a close watch on the Rappahannock east of Lee's main line, from Mine Run to Fredericksburg.[4]

Lieutenant General Grant, with his headquarters then at Culpeper Court House, commanded an army of almost 120,000 fully equipped, well-fed and clad men, comprising 40 full brigades of infantry, seven brigades of cavalry and 358 guns. Over 4,000 wagons accompanied the Army of the Potomac—a train that extended along some 70 miles of road during moves. Opposing this extraordinary force, Lee could muster but 65,000 men, in 35 under-strength brigades of infantry, seven of cavalry, and 224 guns. Notwithstanding this overwhelming disparity in numbers, Lee had three distinct advantages: he fought on known terrain, on interior lines and was less encumbered by trains and baggage (though this was a mixed blessing, at best). If Grant tried to turn his right flank, he would have to do so through the forbidding Wilderness,

2 *OR* 31, pt. 1, 1320-21; Gordon C. Rhea, *The Battle of the Wilderness*, May 5-6, 1864 (Baton Rouge, LA, 1994), 21-22; Freeman, *Lee's Lieutenants*, 3:342-43; Noah Andre Trudeau, *Bloody Roads South: The Wilderness to Cold Harbor, May-June, 1864* (Boston, MA, 1989), 20; John Cannon, *The Wilderness Campaign, May 1864* (Conshohocken, PA 1993), 19-20.

3 Simpson, *Lee's Grenadier Guard*, 389.

4 Rhea, *Battle of the Wilderness*, 22-24.

a tangled, heavily wooded, swampy terrain that would automatically neutralize his tremendous artillery advantage.[5]

Grant had dismissed advancing on Richmond from the east. He believed the Confederate capital a disadvantageous place to fight, as the Rebels held well-prepared earthworks nearer to their own supplies and reinforcements. The location also gave Lee room to maneuver. Instead, Grant determined to wage a war of attrition on the Rapidan. However, a frontal assault there would be costly, especially after the buildup of Lee's defenses following the Union debacle at Morton's Ford in February. So Grant believed the best plan was maneuvering Lee from behind his earthworks onto the open ground, where the Union's vastly superior numbers could be brought to bear. The only question was whether to cross the Rapidan above or below Lee's current position. Crossing upriver would shield Washington from Confederate raids and the surrounding farmland countryside would be quite suitable to maneuvering. But Lee would then be between Meade and Butler, and Meade would be dangerously dependent upon the Orange and Alexandria Railroad for supplies. Given the Union army's size, (close to 120,000 men and 50,000 horses), one rail line could not possibly supply all of Grant's transportation needs. Additionally, the railroad traversed "Mosby's Confederacy," country infested with John S. Mosby's highly effective irregular troops. If Grant failed to seize the line below the Rapidan, the campaign would fail. And the Yankees would have to march over 40 miles of open ground, with a series of hills, the Southwest Mountains running along the rail line, providing Lee an excellent defensive barrier.[6]

Alternatively, although pivoting around Lee's downriver flank avoided these issues, this course presented its own set of problems—especially the terrain. Once

5 *OR* 33, pt. 1, 1244-45; Rhea, *Battle of the Wilderness*, 18; Henry, *Story of the Confederacy*, 351-52; Alexander, *Military Memoirs*, 494; U. S. Grant, "Preparing For the Campaigns of '64," & E. M. Law, "From the Wilderness to Cold Harbor," in *B&L*, 4:110, 119, 125; Gordon, *Reminiscences of a Soldier*, 236; Longstreet, *Manassas to Appomattox*, 353-54; Alexander, *Military Memoirs*, 495; Sorrel, *Confederate Staff Officer*, 226.

6 Brooks Simpson, "'Great Expectations': Ulysses S. Grant, The Northern Press, and the Opening of the Wilderness Campaign," in *The Wilderness Campaign*, ed. Gary W. Gallagher (Chapel Hill, NC, 1997), 6-8; Rhea, *Battle of the Wilderness*, 49-51; Bruce Catton, *Stillness at Appomattox* (Garden City, NY, 1953), 57-58; Foote, *Civil War Narrative*, 3:127, 132-35. The Morton's Ford engagement resulted from a abortive surprise raid on Richmond. While the Army of the Potomac staged a diversion along the Rapidan, Maj. Gen. Benjamin Butler would push west to Richmond with his Army of the James. On February 6, the II Corps attacked Morton's Ford. When the Federals advanced toward the bluffs encircled with Confederate earthworks, they were repulsed and recrossed the Rapidan. They lost 200 killed and many more wounded in what turned out to be a wasted effort. Butler aborted his raid after a deserter disclosed his plans to the Confederates on the Peninsula. Salmon, *Virginia Battlefield Guide*, 260-62.

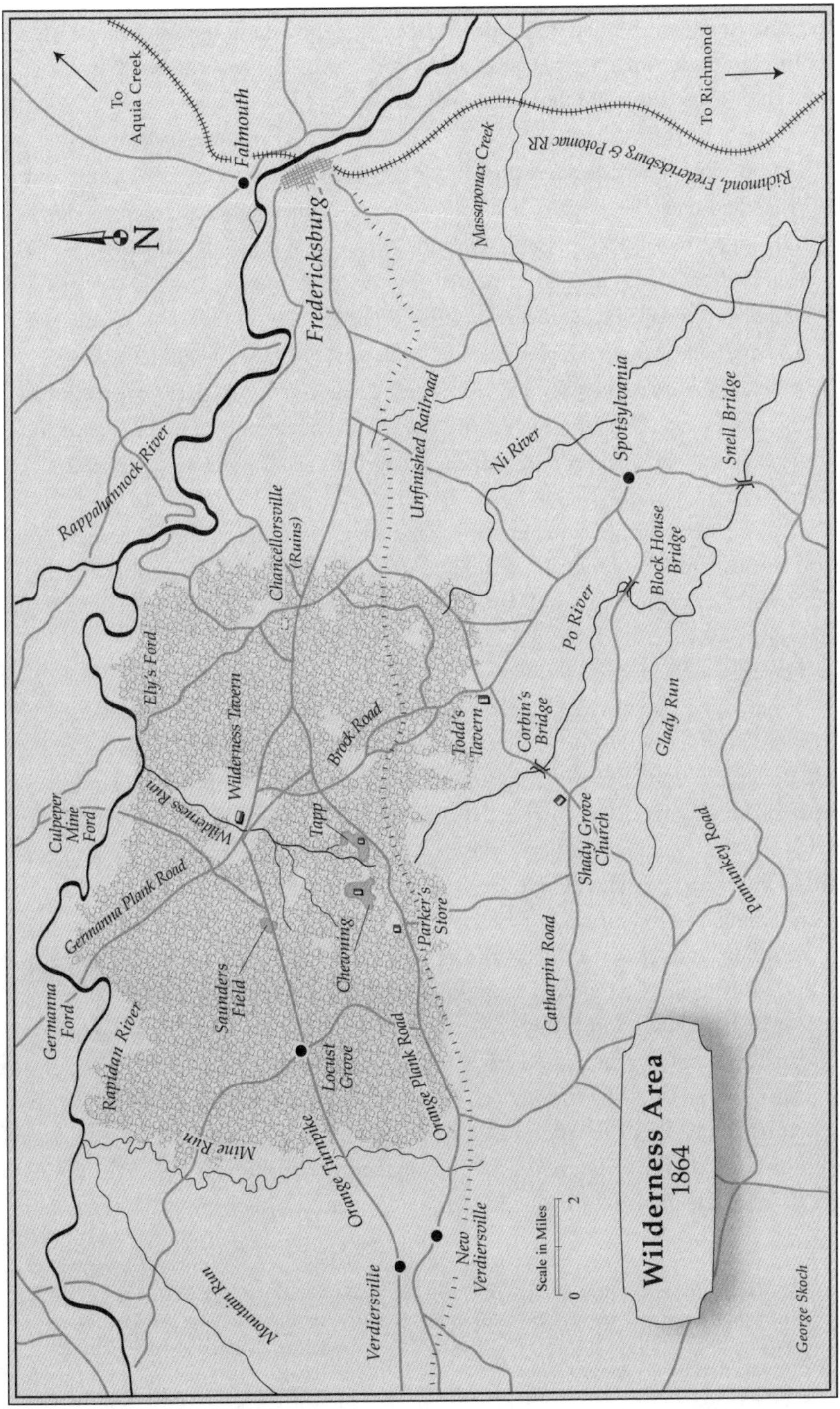

Wilderness Area
1864
N
To Aquia Creek
Falmouth
Fredericksburg
To Richmond
Richmond, Fredericksburg & Potomac RR
Massaponax Creek
Rappahannock River
Chancellorsville (Ruins)
Unfinished Railroad
Ni River
Spotsylvania
Snell Bridge
Block House Bridge
Po River
Ely's Ford
Wilderness Tavern
Brock Road
Todd's Tavern
Corbin's Bridge
Glady Run
Culpeper Mine Ford
Wilderness Run
Tapp
Germanna Plank Road
Shady Grove Church
Pamunkey Road
Chewning
Parker's Store
Catharpin Road
Germanna Ford
Saunders Field
Rapidan River
Locust Grove
Orange Plank Road
Mine Run
Orange Turnpike
Scale in Miles
0
2
New Verdiersville
Verdiersville
Mountain Run
George Skoch

across the Rapidan, the Federals would encounter the infamous Wilderness. Meade's veterans knew the area well: a year ago almost to the day, Stonewall Jackson had routed their army there at Chancellorsville. It was:

> a mean gloomy woodland, a dozen miles wide by half as deep, lying silent and forbidding along the southern bank of the river. Its virgin timber had been cut down years ago, mostly to provide fuel for small iron-smelting furnaces in the neighborhood, and a tangled second growth had sprung up—stinted pines, innumerable small saplings, dense underbrush, here and there a larger tree, vines and creepers trailing every which way through dead scrub pines with interlaced spiky branches; there were very few places in which a man could see as far as twenty yards. The soil was poor, and there were hardly any farms or clearings, and the land under the trees was like a choppy sea, broken by ridge and hillocks and irregular knolls.

This dense 15-mile square forest that lay between Orange Court House, Spotsylvania, and Fredericksburg had few clearings, fewer negotiable roads, and stinted visibility even on a good day. This terrain rendered cavalry practically useless, and artillery even less so.

Beyond the Wilderness, however, lay open country quite suitable for fighting. The key to maneuvering past Lee's right was to get through the Wilderness as quickly as possible. Considering all these factors, Grant chose to move left, where if the army made the appropriate progress, optimum, sea coast-based supply lines would sustain his offensive. A successfully executed plan would prevent Lee from ever taking the initiative again. It might not be possible to beat him, but he could be kept occupied, without the luxury of detaching troops to oppose Sherman, who was then on the brink of launching his campaign for Atlanta. Grant's army had one paramount responsibility: "get close to the enemy as soon as possible and . . . stay close until the war ended. If it did that, victory would come."[7]

Just before dawn on May 4, the Army of the Potomac began pouring across the Rapidan River at Germanna and Ely's fords, initiating the sixth "On to Richmond" campaign. After crossing the river, Grant planned to advance south down the Germanna Plank Road through dead center of the dense woodland. Once past the dark confines of the Wilderness, his immediate objective was Spotsylvania Court House about 20 miles south of the Rapidan and in a direct line with the capital in

7 Catton, *Stillness At Appomattox*, 57-58; Rhea, *Battle of the Wilderness*, 49-51, 56. See, generally, Bradley M. Gottfried, *The Maps of the Wilderness: An Atlas of the Wilderness Campaign, Including all Cavalry Operations, May 2-6, 1864* (Savas Beatie, 2016), for an outstanding grasp of the confused fighting during the campaign.

Richmond. General Lee quickly decided against disputing these crossings, or contesting Grant's entry into the Wilderness. In fact, this tangled morass was Lee's chosen field of battle.[8]

Early on May 4, with full knowledge of Grant's movements, Lee began concentrating his forces in the Wilderness. He ordered Ewell's and A. P. Hill's Corps east by way of the Orange Turnpike and the Orange Plank Road, respectively. These particular roads ran parallel to each other, from two to three miles apart, through the Wilderness, before merging at the Old Wilderness Church east of the thickest area. About noon that day, Ewell marched east on the Orange Turnpike, while A. P. Hill's Corps struck out in that same direction on the Orange Plank Road. Longstreet received orders also to move from Gordonsville at about 1:00 p.m. and follow Hill.[9]

The regiment and the rest of the brigade cooked three days' rations and left the bivouac area around Gordonsville late afternoon of May 4, proceeding northeast with Field's Division. Gregg's men marched steadily for 16 miles, reaching Brock's Bridge over the North Anna late that same night. Here the men rested while Longstreet arranged for a guide for the remainder of the march. Early the next morning, Longstreet's column marched to the northeast with the Texans in the lead. Via "swinging step" and "occasional rests," the Confederates marched hard for another 12 miles, reaching Richard's Shop on the Catharpin Road about 5:00 p.m. that afternoon, where they prepared to rest for the night.[10]

Meanwhile, Grant was so pleased with his initial progress that he responded to a newspaper reporter's inquiry as to when he expected to be in Richmond with the statement that: "I will agree to be there in about four days if General Lee becomes a party to the agreement. But if he objects, the trip will undoubtedly be prolonged." Unfortunately for Grant, Lee immediately objected.[11]

Major Generals Gouverneur K. Warren's V Corps and John Sedgwick's VI Corps arrived at the strategic crossroads near Wilderness Tavern on May 5, the place where the Germanna Plank Road leading southeast crossed the Orange Turnpike, running

8 Longstreet, *Manassas to Appomattox*, 476-77; Rhea, *Battle of the Wilderness*, 54-55, 60-64, 70; Foote, *Civil War Narrative*, 3:146-47; Trudeau, *Bloody Roads South*, 31-35; Catton, *Stillness at Appomattox*, 59-60: Alexander S. Webb, "Through the Wilderness," in *B&L*, 4:152-54.

9 Henry, *Story of the Confederacy*, 351; Rhea, *Battle of the Wilderness*, 88-90; John M. Priest, *Nowhere To Run: The Wilderness, May 4th and 5th, 1864* (Shippensburg, PA 1995), 20-21; Longstreet, *Manassas to Appomattox*, 556.

10 *OR* 36, pt. 1, 1054; Muster Roll, Field, Staff, and Band, and D. Company, 5th Texas, Apr. 30-June 30, 1864 in TSA; Longstreet, *Manassas to Appomattox*, 477; Pomeroy, "War Memoirs," 73; Winkler, *Confederate Capital*, 164.

11 Moore, *Men of the Bayou City Guards*, 84; Pomeroy, "War Memoirs," 73; Anders, *Hearts in Conflict*, 483; Foote, *Civil War Narrative*, 3:123, 148; Trudeau, *Bloody Roads South*, 36.

east and west. South of the turnpike, before meeting the Orange Plank Road, the Germanna Plank Road crossed Brock Road, the route of Stonewall Jackson's famous flanking movement the previous May. Indeed, Hancock's II Corps was encamped around the crossroads at Chancellorsville, where Ely's Ford Road met the Orange Turnpike. Burnside's IX Corps had still not crossed to south of the Rapidan. However, much closer than either Grant or Meade thought possible, a sizeable portion of Lee's army rested for the night. Ewell's Corps was on the Orange Turnpike, near Locust Grove, only six miles from the Wilderness Tavern and nine miles from Chancellorsville, while Hill's Corps was on the Orange Plank Road three miles south. Lee's front had changed to face east rather than north. It was now Grant whose right flank was exposed. That night, Lee dispatched orders for Ewell to be ready to move early in the morning, directing that "[i]f the enemy moves down the river [toward Fredericksburg], he [Lee] wishes you to push on after him. . . . The general's desire is to bring him to battle as soon now as possible."[12]

The Federals resumed their march about dawn. Hancock headed south from Chancellorsville and angled west to unite with Warren, moving south from Wilderness Tavern followed by Sedgwick's Corps. Warren left Brig. Gen. Charles Griffin's division on the turnpike to protect his right flank while starting his remaining two divisions south. Dawn was lightening the Virginia sky when Griffin's forward pickets spotted Rebel infantry forming a line of battle three-fourths of a mile to their front. A visibly shaken Warren ordered Griffin to "push a force out at once against the enemy." And thus Ewell's troops made first contact with the Federals that morning nudging the right flank of Grant's column. Though under orders not to engage until Longstreet arrived from his 42-mile marathon march, Ewell could not prevent a Union attack. Griffin advanced at 1:00 p.m., straddling the turnpike in a two-mile front. The entrenched Confederates withstood repeated Federal assaults across Saunders' Field. South of the field, Brig, Gen. John B. Gordon's Brigade counterattacked, crashing into and breaking the famous Iron Brigade. Sedgwick's men finally moved south, formed into line on Warren's right, and joined the fighting. Like it or not, a major engagement was underway on both sides of the turnpike and spreading south to the Orange Plank Road. Longstreet's Corps was still a good day's march away.[13]

12 Trudeau, *Bloody Roads South*, 40; Rhea, *Battle of the Wilderness*, 87-88, 90-91; Freeman, *Lee's Lieutenants*, 3:346-47; Law, "From the Wilderness to Cold Harbor," in *B&L*, 4:118-19.

13 Trudeau, *Bloody Roads South*, 40-45; Law, "From the Wilderness to Cold Harbor," in *B&L*, 121; U. S. Grant, "General Grant on the Wilderness Campaign," & Webb, "Through the Wilderness," in *B&L*, 4:145, 154-55; Rhea, *Battle of the Wilderness*, 100-104, 106-108, 160-62; *OR* 34, pt. 1, 1076-77.

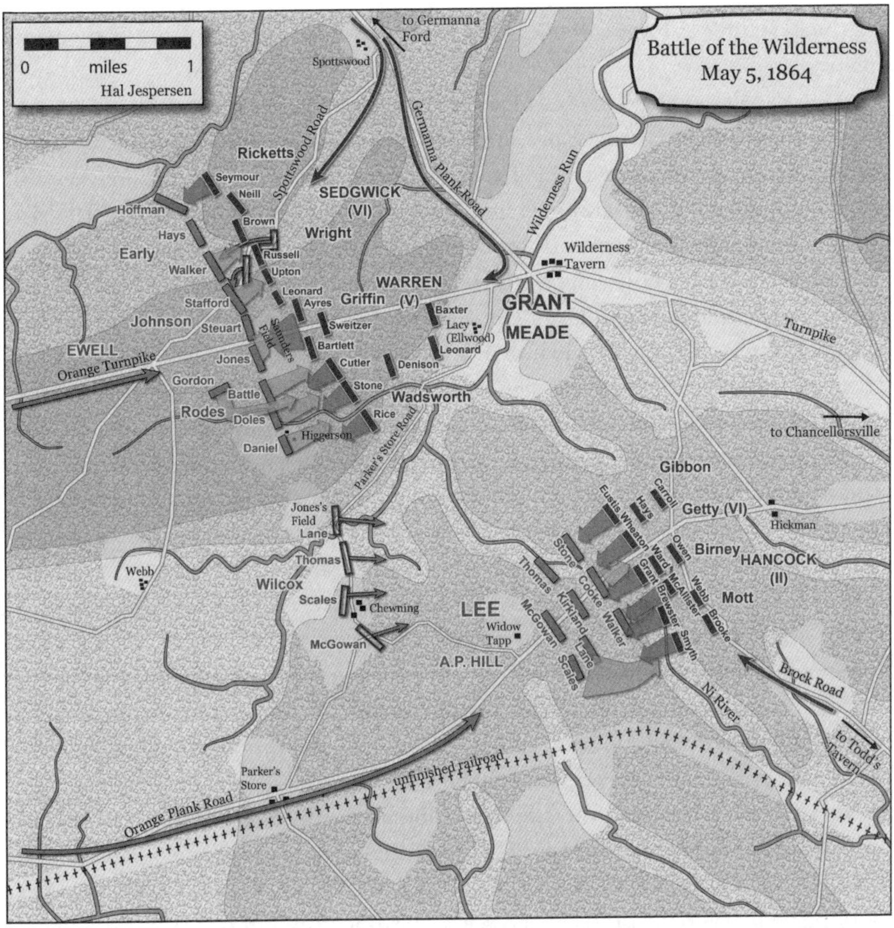

Soon after General Ewell became engaged on the turnpike, A. P. Hill's Third Corps advanced and struck Federal outposts on the Orange Plank Road at Parker's Store. Hill's Confederates drove in these Union pickets and followed up to their line of battle, posted to cover the junction of the Orange Plank Road with the Stevensburg and Brock roads, on which the Federals were marching in their effort to push through the tangled Wilderness to reach and hold Spotsylvania. Thus began the critically important fight between Brig. Gen. George W. Getty's Union division of Sedgwick's widely divided VI Corps and Maj. Gen. Henry Heth's Division, at the head of Hill's column. Meade recalled Hancock's II Corps, which was already marching hard for Spotsylvania by way of Chancellorsville, and ordered it to back up and link with Warren's left flank for form a solid front and prevent and sort of Rebel flanking operations. Maj. Gen. Cadmus M. Wilcox's Division pushed up to assist Heth embattled effort, and Lt. Col. William T. Poague's artillery battalion took up position in a small clearing on the north side of the Orange Plank Road behind the Confederate infantry.[14]

Getty's Division held the key intersection of the Orange Plank and Brock Roads. But the Meade-directed attack by Gerry down the Orange Plank Road wilted under horrific fire from Wilcox's Brigade in what amounted to sheer butchery. Lee had successfully linked his two corps when Hill's men eventually connected with troops of Gordon's brigade. Hancock finally arrived on the scene and rushed forward to support Getty's chewed up division. His troops met the same fate. A Confederate soldier described the scene: "Dead Yankees were *knee deep* all over about four acres of ground." Hancock eventually managed to rally the men behind a line of rifle pits, and Brig. Gen. John Gibbon's Division hurried over from Todd's Tavern to his support.[15]

After the battle was closely joined in the thickets in front, the artillery of both sides, whose guns might wreak as much carnage on friend as foe, fell silent. The two armies grappled on ground as grim and forbidding as the struggle itself. Officers could not see the whole length of their command's battle lines and could discern the location of their unseen troops only by the sound of the firing. Units became hopelessly intermingled. As night fell upon those tangled thickets, the troops struggled at close quarters since opposing lines could only be discerned by the noise of their passage through the underbrush or the flashing of their guns. The underbrush caught fire, making the horror all the worse, as hundreds of the severely wounded on both sides, their pitiful cries adding to the chaos and terror, burned to death in the crackling flames. As dusk fell, however, the tide began to turn, and the Confederates began having difficulty stemming the relentless Union attacks. Heth, whose division had fought all day, repeatedly requested Hill's permission withdraw some of his troops to regroup. But Hill refused, anticipating Longstreet's Corps early arrival the next morning to alleviate the problem and relieve his bone-tired troops.[16]

The fearsome fighting raged on unabated until after dark, ultimately ending in a stalemate. That night, Ewell's troops on the Confederate left built solid entrenchments to strengthen their position all along their line of battle. Hill, on the

14 Trudeau, *Bloody Roads South*, 63; Salmon, *Virginia Battlefield Guide*, 268-69; Rhea, *Battle of the Wilderness*, 117-18, 120-22, 126-29, 132-35; Freeman, *Lee's Lieutenants*, 3:350-55; Law & Webb, "From the Wilderness to Cold Harbor," "Through the Wilderness," in *B&L*, 4:122-24, 157.

15 Curt Anders, *Hearts in Conflict: A One Volume History of the Civil War* (New York, 1999), 484-85; Trudeau, *Bloody Roads South*, 75-82; Rhea, *Battle of the Wilderness*, 180-81, 242-45, 268; Salmon, *Virginia Battlefield Guide*, 268-69.

16 Trudeau, *Bloody Roads South*, 61, 74, 76-77; Rhea, *Battle of the Wilderness*, 252-5, 276-77; Law, "From the Wilderness to Cold Harbor," in *B&L*, 4:122-23; Alexander, *Military Memoirs*, 501-502; Freeman, *Lee's Lieutenants*, 3:350-52, 354.

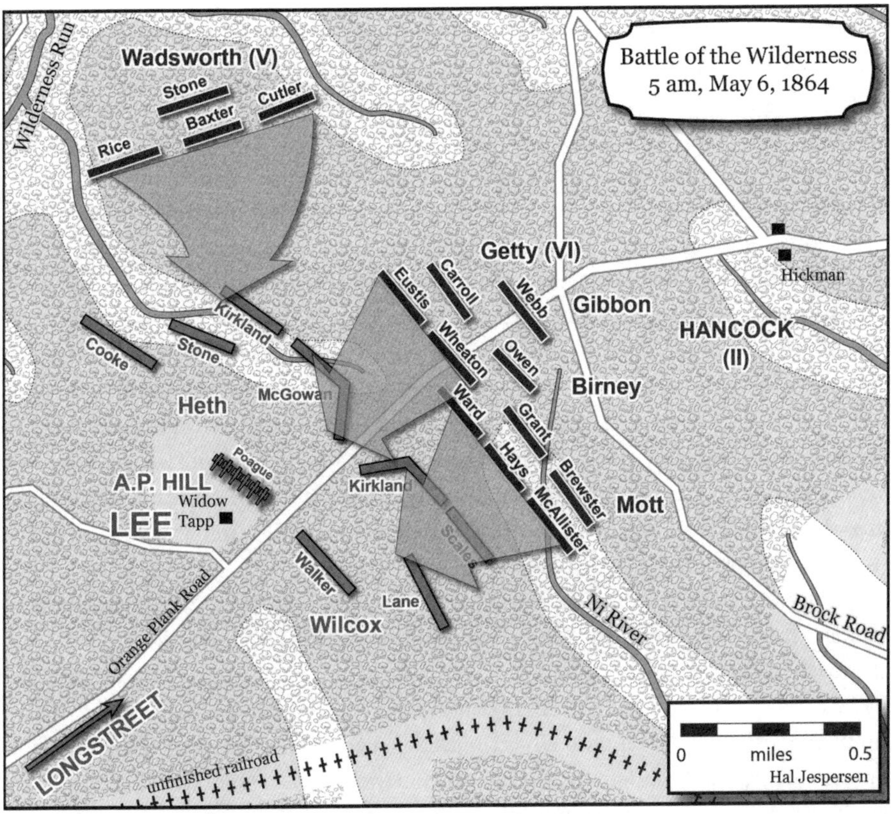

Confederate right, did not entrench, however, pleading fatigue and the expectation of being relieved before dawn by Longstreet's Corps, still hustling up from Gordonsville. This carelessness on Hill's part nearly cost Lee the battle, and the war the next day. Meanwhile, Lee, content that Grant would renew the fight early the next morning, dispatched his trusted aide, Col. C. S. Venable with a note to Longstreet "to make a night march, so as to arrive upon the field at daylight" on May 6.[17] Longstreet received Lee's order while at Richards' Shop, 10 miles from the fighting. He had intended to continue marching east on the Catharpin Road to strike Grant's vulnerable left flank. But with Hill's Corps heavily pressed, Lee told Longstreet to use the Orange Plank Road early the following morning. Longstreet had two objectives: first, continue Hill's attack eastward, while shifting Hill into the gap between his corps and Ewell's Corps. So Lee's order committed Old Pete to march six miles directly north of Parker's Store,

17 *OR* 36, pt. 1, 1054; Law, "From the Wilderness to Cold Harbor," in *B&L*, 4:123; Freeman, *Lee's Lieutenants*, 3:352-53; Longstreet, *Manassas to Appomattox*, 470-80; Rhea, *Battle of the Wilderness*, 240, 273-74.

and then east on the Orange Plank Road. This would place his two divisions directly in the rear of Hill's lines. Under a bright moon in the early hours of May 6, Longstreet's veterans marched north from Richards' Shop toward the Orange Plank Road. Field's Division, with the Texans at the front, took the lead[18]

Grant placed added significance on Longstreet's impending approach. Consequently, at 5:00 a.m. on the 6th, he launched a massive large-scale assault against Lee's entire line from north of the Orange Turnpike all the way south to the Orange Plank Road. Ewell's firmly entrenched men had brought up artillery for close support, and were well prepared to meet such an attack. On the Confederate right, however, five of Hancock's divisions viciously struck Hill's exhasted men, who were not well entrenched or fully prepared. The attack knocked them back to the west to the edge of the Widow Tapp Farm. In a clearing on a rise behind that farm house, close to Poague's guns were Lee and his staff, who nervously watched the onslaught as men of Heth's and Wilcox's divisions gave ground in great confusion. In less than another mile, Hancock would have Lee flanked and be among his supply trains, leaving the fate of the entire army in the balance.[19]

Longstreet's march through the fields and byways west of the Wilderness moved steadily from its inception and accelerated as time grew critical. As the men approached Parker's Store, sounds of a fierce battle to their front filled their ears. Field's Division struck out cross-country to reach the Orange Plank Road simultaneously with Kershaw's Division, using a parallel road. As both converged on Parker's Store near dawn, they were still an hour away from the rest of Lee's hard-pressed army. The two division commanders reached a crucial accommodation: they would rush eastward on that same road with two divisions abreast. Thus, side by side in columns of fours, Field's and Kershaw's men marched toward the "grand roars of musketry & quick thunders of artillery" down the road. The Texas Brigade led on the left and Barksdale's old Mississippi brigade under Brig. Gen. Benjamin G. Humphreys on the right. The men, noticing the blood-red sunrise, "predicted a hot

18 *OR* 36, pt. 1, 1054; Skoch, *Lone Star Confederate*, 102; Freeman, *Lee's Lieutenants*, 3:353-54; Law, "From the Wilderness to Cold Harbor," in *B&L*, 4:123; Commager, *The Blue and the Gray*, 2:983.

19 Freeman, *Lee's Lieutenants*, 3:355-56; Trudeau, *Bloody Roads South*, 85, 87-92, 97; Rhea, *Battle of the Wilderness*, 267, 281-82; Salmon, *Virginia Battlefield Guide*, 268. Grant and Meade learned of Longstreet's approach from interrogation of a Confederate prisoner. Grant had ordered Burnside's IX Corps to move up opposite Hancock's attack column on the Plank Road to support the offensive. But it took Burnside almost five hours to advance two miles and develop an attack on the Confederate left. Salmon, *Virginia Battlefield Guide*, 268.

time . . . today, for there is blood in the sun." General Gregg noticed too, pointing and declaring to his staff: "There is the sun of Austerlitz."[20]

Under the reddening dawn sky, Longstreet's parallel columns, still eight abreast, thereby filled the Plank Road as they advanced rapidly toward the roar of the guns ahead of them. Meanwhile, a greatly anxious Lee had dispatched his staffer Col. Venable back once again to tell Longstreet to come up with all speed. Following his orders, Longstreet increased the tempo of the advance. Thus his men "came the last mile and a half at the double quick." Inevitably, troops of the two divisions mingled together in their haste.[21]

Longstreet rode ahead of the men to confer with Lee and his staff. As he approached the huddle of Lee's command in the Widow Tapp's farmyard, Lee exclaimed: "Ah, General, we have been looking for you since 12 o'clock last night. We expect to be attacked at any moment, and are not in any shape to resist." Longstreet replied: "My troops are not up. I've ridden ahead." At that point, the roar of Hancock's ongoing attack erupted out of the brush, and Old Pete quickly wheeled his mount and galloped back, to spur his troops forward, leaving Lee heartened with the knowledge that help was close by. Just then, troops of Brig. Gen. Samuel McGowan's South Carolina Brigade of Wilcox's Division began streaming back through Poague's guns headed for the rear. A shaken Lee shouted to the harried commander: "My God, General McGowan! Is this splendid brigade of yours running like a flock of geese?" Stung by this public rebuke, the harried McGowan responded: "General, these men are not whipped, they only want a place to form and they will fight as well as they ever did."[22]

The 5th Texas advanced the last two miles at the double quick, surging down the road with their tattered flags flying, ready for action. Near Parker's Store, they passed A. P. Hill's field infirmary with its huge stack of bloody, amputated arms and legs, a harvest of the previous day's fight. One brigade officers admitted that this "hideous sight, fractured limbs and bloody clothing, did not add much to our courage." As Longstreet's men neared the day's killing field, a spectacle of mass confusion lay

20 Charles W. Field, "Campaign of 1864 and 1865," in *SHSP* (1886), 14:543; Robert Krick, "'Lee to the Rear,' the Texans Cried," *The Wilderness Campaign*, Gary Gallagher, ed. (Chapel Hill, NC, 1997), 164-65. Austerlitz was Napoleon's great victory over the combined Austrian and Prussian armies on December 2, 1805.

21 Polley, *Hood's Texas Brigade*, 280; Winkler, *Confederate Capital*, 166; Freeman, *Lee's Lieutenants*, 3:354; Rhea, *Battle of the Wilderness*, 297; Longstreet, *Manassas to Appomattox*, 479-50; Law, "From the Wilderness to Cold Harbor, in *B&L*, 4:123-24.

22 Foote, *Civil War Narrative*, 3:168-69; Rhea, *Battle of the Wilderness*, 293; Trudeau, *Bloody Roads South*, 91; Law, "From the Wilderness to Cold Harbor," in *B&L*, 123-24.

before them. Hundreds of Hill's men, wagons, horses, and mules clogged the road and fields; men were swarming rearward through the woods, heedless of their officers' attempts to halt them. Stragglers "without number were flocking to the rear with tales of distress, annihilation and defeat— all these signs betokened that a bloody and desperate work was going on, and not too many yards distant," Campbell related. Ambulances were flying to the rear accompanied by hundreds of wounded soldiers, some on litters, many supported by comrades. As the Texans sped through the midst of this demoralized, retreating mass, they chided their retreating comrades: "Do you belong to General Lee's army? You don't look like the men we left here. You are worse than Bragg's men."[23]

The horrifying distractions never slowed the Texans' onward rush. Law later observed that they came on "[i]n perfect order, ranks well closed, and no stragglers . . . regardless of the confusion on every side, pushing their steady way onward like 'a river in the sea' of confused and troubled human waves around them." Venable, who met up with Longstreet west of the Widow Tapp farm to hasten him along, years later recorded that the Texans' orderly movement into this utter chaos "was superb, and my heart beats quicker to think about it even at this distance of time."[24]

Until Longstreet's men arrived, the 16 guns of Poague's artillery battalion, entrenched in hastily constructed breastworks in the Widow Tapp's field, were all that stood in the face of the Federal advance but for remnants of Hill's broken corps falling back and still between the guns and approaching Union troops. As the shattered ranks of Wilcox's Division cleared their front, Poague's cannoneers, desperately playing for time, began blasting the oncoming Federals to retard their onslaught. Joe Kershaw's lead element, the veteran Mississippians under Ben Humphreys, arrived on the field at a key moment and were immediately directed to move south of the Orange Plank Road. A few minutes later Charles Field's men began forming below the road, with the Texans leading the way. Poague's cannons and Hill's beleaguered men cheered when they realized the First Corps had finally reached the field.

"Here's Longstreet. The old warhorse is up at last. It's all right now," they cheered. Gregg and Humphreys quickly brought their brigades into line of battle and established themselves near the brow of the hill with the Texans on the left and Humphreys on the right. "'Load and cap your pieces, men,'" the command rang out. "'Hold them well up.' The jingle of the hundreds of iron ramrods up and down the line

23 Field, "Campaign of 1864 and 1865," in *SHSP*, 14:543; Cannon, *Wilderness Campaign*, 158; Skoch, *Lone Star Confederate*, 104-105; Rhea, *Battle of the Wilderness*, 298.

24 Law, "From the Wilderness to Cold Harbor," in *B&L*, 4:124; Longstreet, *Manassas to Appomattox*, 490.

denoted that something horrible was soon to take place. Besides every old soldier knew from experience what was in store for him."[25]

While the rest of the division was still forming, the Texas Brigade was advanced to protect Poague's guns and blast the enemy. The balance of Longstreet's oncoming troops could not be thrown into the fray without reorganization: they needed time to reform and place themselves in a proper line of battle. So the brigade halted near the brink of a hill which sloped gradually downward for 200 yards to where the dense undergrowth of the Wilderness began. As the Texans approached the hastily prepared breastworks of the artillerymen, they found the area populated with a sizeable group of stragglers from Hill's Corps who had been rallied. They and Poague's guns were both firing into the dense Wilderness below. The scene was mayhem. "The cannon thundered, musketry rolled, stragglers were fleeing, couriers riding here and there in post-haste, minnies began to sing, the dying and wounded were jolted by the flying ambulances, and filling the road-side, adding to the excitement the terror of death."[26]

The Texans soon spotted General Lee and his staff near these breastworks. Never had they seen their beloved leader so agitated or "[s]o disturbed – never did anxiety or care manifest itself before so plainly upon his countenance." His concern was clearly understandable, though, with Hill's two divisions then grasping defeat from the jaws of yesterday evening's victory. The Federals currently were not far from the Confederate rear. Unless checked, and soon, they would be out of the Wilderness, in possession of the strategic hill, and thus prepared to strike a deathblow to the Army of Northern Virginia. Immediate and determined action was therefore essential to stem the Federal onslaught. Such action could not be delayed for a minute, as in less than five, the Federals would definitely be up upon that hill.[27]

As the Texans moved up to Poague's guns and formed, Lee, having never before met Gregg, promptly rode up and inquired, "General what brigade is this?" Gregg quickly responded "The Texas Brigade." The Southern commander exclaimed "I am glad to see it." Lee immediately ordered Gregg to form the brigade north of the Plank Road, and instructed him that "when you go in there, I wish you to give those men the cold steel— they will stand and fight all day, and never move unless you charge them." Gregg quickly responded "That is my experience." At that point, one of Longstreet's aides came up rapidly and ordered Gregg to "advance your command." Gregg called his troops to order: "Attention Texas Brigade, the eyes of General Lee are upon you,

25 Hanks, *Captain Benton's Company*, 28; Cannan, *Wilderness Campaign*, 159; Rhea, *Battle of the Wilderness*, 299; Foote, *Civil War Narrative*, 3:169.

26 Skoch, *Lone Star Confederate*, 106-07; Rhea, *Battle of the Wilderness*, 299.

27 Ibid., 104; Cannan, *Wilderness Campaign*, 159-60.

forward, march." At this point, Lee could no longer contain his emotions. Raising high in the stirrups, face contorted with excitement, he tore off his hat and waving it overhead, shouting, "Texans always move them!"[28]

A Texan in the front ranks later recalled that "[a] yell rent the air that must have been heard for miles around, but few eyes in that old brigade of veterans and heroes of many a bloody field was undimmed by honest, heartfelt tears." Brigade courier Pvt. Leonard G. Gee of Company E, mounted on his horse a few feet from Lee, uttered in a choking voice with tears streaming down his face: "I would charge hell itself for that old man." Campbell said later that "[i]t was not what Gen. Lee said that so infused and excited the men, as his tone and look, which each one of us knew were born of the dangers of the hour."[29]

As the brigade shifted into a line of battle at the edge of the woods behind Poague's guns, it was required to move through the artillery without losing its tactical cohesion. Leaping over the breastworks, the Texans quickly moved forward, under intense fire, with the skirmishers soon falling back into their places in the line. Poague's two guns on the far right, despite the advance, were still able to continue firing diagonally past the right of the 5th Texas and Kershaw's left front across the road.[30]

At the same time, Joe Kershaw's force had moved through the thick growth south of the Orange Plank Road to meet the advanced Federals. Some guns of Poague's artillery continued to blast the road and the woods beyond them. The Texans moved leftward into "the dense thicket of underbrush," advancing swiftly into and through ditches, many filled with stagnant water. Bullets began whistling past, felling small branches and leaves and occasionally men. As ordered, the Texans performed a well-executed general right wheel, swinging into position at right angles to their original line of advance down the Orange Plank Road and formed a strong line of battle. Longstreet endeavored to keep order in this process, riding through the woods

28 Joskins, "A Sketch of Hood's Texas Brigade," UTSA 158-60; Hanks, *Captain Benton's Company*, 28; Skoch, *Lone Star Confederate*, 106; Rhea, *Battle of the Wilderness,* 299-300.

29 R. C. [Robert Campbell], "Gen. Lee at the 'Wilderness'," *The Land We Love*, (1868), 5:485; Rhea, *Battle of the Wilderness*, 300; Campbell, *Lone Star Confederate*, 106-07. Leonard Groce Gee was born on March 5, 1838 in Independence, Texas. At the outbreak of the war, he enlisted in the Dixie Blues, which became Company E of the regiment. For more on Gee, see Appendix B, Volume 1.

30 Yeary, *Reminiscences of the Boys in Gray*, 1:13; Krick, "'Lee to the Rear,' the Texans Cried," *The Wilderness Campaign*, 176; Dayton Kelley, *General Lee and Hood's Texas Brigade at the Battle of the Wilderness* (Hillsboro, TX, 1969), 49.

and urging the men to "keep cool, men, we will straighten out in a short time—keep cool."[31]

The Texans began moving "steadily on to the slaughter pen" in their advance on Hancock's men. At first, they failed to notice that Lee had continued along with them, in their immediate rear. A still highly agitated Lee had impulsively spurred his horse through Poague's positions and continued advancing with the Texans. Halfway across the field, the troops realized that their beloved commander intended to lead the charge himself. Given the intensity of the fire and the enemy's overwhelming numerical superiority, everybody also realized that "[a]head was death, especially for a man on horseback."[32]

The men could not countenance the sight of their beloved leader so exposing himself to certain injury or death. Thus, the Texans slowed their pace to confront Lee, now bareheaded in his fervor to lead them into battle. A number of officers gathered around him, entreating him to retire, trying to seize his horse's reins, "but he shook them off and moved forward." Becoming fearful of their leader's fate, a cry rose across the entire Texas column, "Lee to the Rear, General Lee to the Rear!" Private John T. Allison of Company C heard someone shout that the country could not afford to lose him. The rank and file continued entreating Lee, saying "We won't go forward until you go back." Finally, the ragged regimental courier, Pvt. Gee, took Traveler by the bridle, while at the same time a living barrier of other Texans halted Lee's further progress as the bullets fell around them like rain.[33]

31 Krick, "'Lee to the Rear,' the Texans Cried," *The Wilderness Campaign*, 173-75; Polley, *Letters to Charming Nellie*, 231; Polley, *Hood's Texas Brigade*, 231, Winkler, *Confederate Capital*, 166; Hanks, *Captain Benton's Company*, 28. Despite several accounts to the contrary, Field later wrote that it was at the front of his division's column as it approached the fighting. It was leading to the right, Field said, but "before it could be followed up by the other brigades a second order was received from Longstreet to form in the quickest order I could and charge with any front I could make. Throwing the Texas brigade, which was second, on the left of the road and in line perpendicular to it . . . led by its gallant General Gregg, dashed forward as soon as it formed, without waiting for those in its rear to get ready." Field, "Campaign of 1864 and 1865," *SHSP*, 11:543.

32 Krick, "'Lee to the Rear,' the Texans Cried," *The Wilderness Campaign*, 180-81; W. C. Lockhart, "Lee at Orange C H," *CV* (1903), 11:268; R. C., "Gen. Lee at the 'Wilderness'," *The Land We Love* 5:481-83.

33 W. C. Lockhart, "Lee at Orange C H," *CV*, 11:268; R. C., "Gen. Lee at the 'Wilderness'," *The Land We Love*, 5: 481-83; Polley, *Hood's Texas Brigade*, 231; Yeary, *Reminiscences of the Boys in Gray*, 1:13; Winkler, *Confederate Capital*, 167; Chicoine, *Confederates of Chappell Hill*, 131. Another witness recounted hearing Lt. John Kerr, the brigade's adjutant, try to convince Lee that his presence constituted an obstacle to the counterattack—"You are about to spoil everything; the Texas brigade will not charge with you in front; they will not see you killed." Wood, *Partial List of Officer and Men Raised in Leon County*, 14-15; Moore, *Men of the Bayou City Guards*, 85; Cannon,

If Lee would "not expose himself, we pledge ourselves to drive the enemy back," the Texans promised. Soon Gregg came up to Lee, begging him to extricate himself from this deadly situation. Lee, perhaps finally recognizing the sheer folly of his noble actions, told the Texans: "I'll go my men, if you will drive back those people." Venable rode up to Lee's side and indicated that Longstreet was on the field to the Texans' right. At this the general reluctantly moved back toward the relative safety of the rear to confer with Longstreet on troop dispositions. When Lee had moved away following the discussion, Venable told Longstreet about what had happened, noting that something had to be done to prevent him from further risking his life. Longstreet immediately rode over to Lee and assured him that he could restore the line if given a free hand. If not needed, however, he intimated a desire to move back further "as it was not quite comfortable where we were." Lee acquiesced, and the matter was resolved.[34]

The Texans approached the fierce fighting with the 5th Texas on the right flank, the 4th Texas on its left, and the 1st Texas and the 3rd Arkansas extending the line northward. The officers, despite the loud and bloody chaos of the moment, had thrown out skirmishers from each of the regiments, many of whom had been almost immediately shot. The brigade's line moved forward somewhat to the left, with the 5th Texas on the far right refused a bit toward the rear. This alignment resulted in an advance that slanted across the open space as it moved toward the enemy. As the line

---

Wilderness Campaign, 163; Evans, *Confederate Military History*, 11:220. Numerous renditions of the "Lee to the Rear" episode exist, with at least 38 "eye witness" accounts. Several soldiers claim to have been the one to finally halt Lee's horse. The best evidence from a study of these sources indicates Gee as that individual, although Capt. Kerr is also cited in that role. Some additional validity is accorded to Gee's role through his selection by artist Harry A. McArdle, who recreated the scene right after the war following exhaustive research with the participants. See Kelley, *General Lee and Hood's Texas Brigade*, 11-19; Krick, "Lee to the Rear', the Texans Cried," 175-76, 183, 197n64; Chicoine, *Confederates of Chappell Hill*, 131. As a member of the brigade later wrote "I am confident that no one man is entitled to the credit or honor of causing General Lee to go to the rear; every man there would have gladly died to save one drop of his precious blood, and I am confident that General Lee saw a determination in the faces of his men to conquer or die." E. J. Parrent, "General Lee to the Rear," *CV* (1894), 2:14. Polley, *Hood's Texas Brigade*, 231, for a similar sentiment. Private Ben S. Fitzgerald of Company I said he had "heard as many different stories, as men asked. No two tell the same. . . . In a battle I know that the same thing will make different impressions upon the minds of men." Kelley, *General Lee and Hood's Texas Brigade*, 51-52.

34 Moore, *Men of the Bayou City Guards*, 85; Dallas *Morning News*, October 12, 1909; 85; Skoch, *Lone Star Confederate*, 108;. Charles S. Venable, *The Campaign from the Wilderness to Petersburg* (Richmond, VA, 1879), 5; Krick, "'Lee to the Rear', the Texans Cried," *Wilderness Campaign*, 183-84.

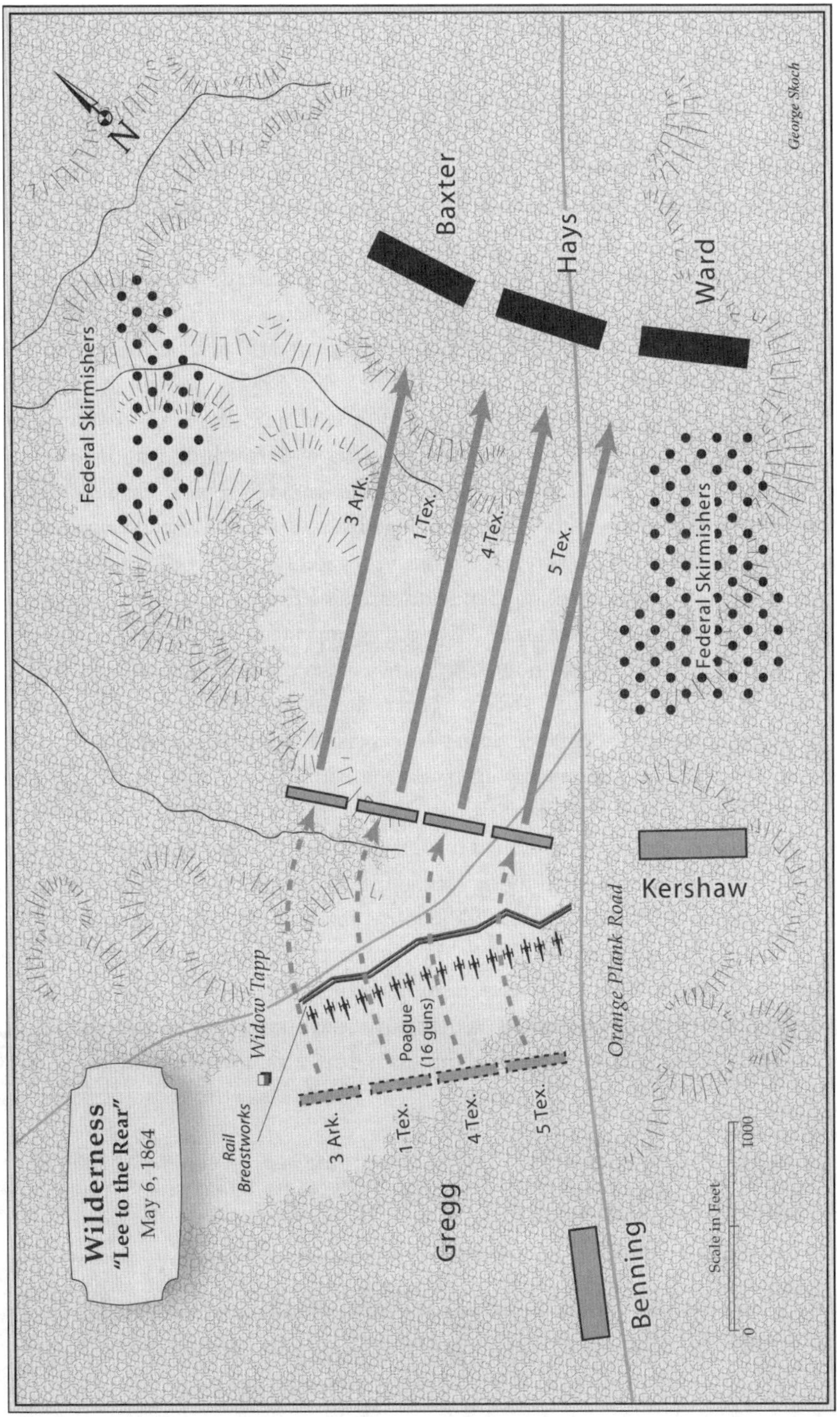
Wilderness
"Lee to the Rear"
May 6, 1864
N
Federal Skirmishers
Federal Skirmishers
Baxter
Hays
Ward
3 Ark.
1 Tex.
4 Tex.
5 Tex.
Rail Breastworks
Widow Tapp
Poague (16 guns)
3 Ark.
1 Tex.
4 Tex.
5 Tex.
Gregg
Orange Plank Road
Kershaw
Benning
Scale in Feet
0
1000
George Skoch

was then formed, the 5th Texas had its right firmly anchored on the Orange Plank Road as a guide.[35]

Here in the Wilderness, on what later observers considered the autumn of the Confederacy, the regiment and the whole brigade reached the zenith of their heralded, unparalleled service record. "Reduced to a hard core of some 800 battle-hardened and dedicated combat soldiers—the weak, the maligners and the sick . . . [having] long [ago] been dropped from the rolls," the Texans were committed to fulfilling their recent pledge to General Lee. As the brave Texans advanced, Yankee sharpshooters began picking off the men in front. Undeterred, and screaming like Comanches while increasing their pace to a double-quick, the Texans rapidly advanced into the thick brush in front of them.[36]

With flags flying high, the Texans surged forward into the fire of the oncoming enemy. Across the Widow Tapp's fields, the Union skirmish line, some 300 yards distant, opened fire from a stand of pine trees and undergrowth. Pushing past this heavy line of skirmishers, the Texans plunged ahead toward the far woods. "We reached the undergrowth—entered it with a yell, and in less than 100 yards came face to face with the advancing, triumphant, and sanguine foe," Campbell reported, "who could only fire and yield their ground." Soon, galling sheets of musketry and canister began to thin their ranks considerably, killing or wounding "many of our best and bravest before they had fired a shot," a Texan later lamented.[37]

Gregg quickened the brigade's pace as its men continued falling. About 200 yards beyond this point, another enemy line soon came into view. The Texans maintained their rapid pace, despite the intensified enemy fire and their diminishing numbers. As they closed on Hancock's entrenched troops, there was "a terrific crash, mingled with wild yells, which settled down into a steady roar of musketry." A Confederate later wrote home that "[t]he storm of battle became terrific." "We were confronted by a line of blue," another commented, "which, however, fled before us without firing a single volley." Soon Hancock's veteran troops broke and fled, with the 5th Texas and the rest of the brigade in pursuit. The men advanced across the field into a firestorm soon disintegrating into a deadly firefight. Each time a man fell, another stepped into

35 Parrent, "General Lee to the Rear," *CV*, 2:14; Field, "Campaigns of 1864 and 1865," *SHSP*, 14:543; Kelley, *General Lee and Hood's Texas Brigade*, 16-18; Krick, "'Lee to the Rear,' the Texans Cried," *The Wilderness Campaign*, 175.

36 Morris Schaaf, "The Battle of the Wilderness," *Atlantic Monthly*, 105 (1910), 99. Morris Schaaf, a West Point Graduate and classmate of many officers on both sides of the battle, wrote that "[t]he onset of Gregg's Texans was savage—it could not have been less after asking Lee to go back."

37 Skoch, *Lone Star Confederate*, 107; Polley, *Hood's Texas Brigade*, 231.

heavy fire to take his place in order to fill the gap. The brave Texans could not be stopped.[38]

Continuing to advance under extremely heavy fire, Gregg finally halted the brigade 100 yards from a line of log breastworks erected the previous evening. In less than ten minutes, over a half of that 800 were lying upon the field, dead or wounded; however, in the process "they had delivered a staggering blow, and broken the force of the Federal advance." Within a few minutes, Lt. Col. Bryan, leading the 5th Texas into battle for the first time, went down with a serious, permanently-disabling wound in his arm. Command of the regiment devolved upon Capt. Tacitus Clay, who had already been wounded in the hand. By this point, the brigade had advanced over 500 yards, totally unsupported and under constantly heavy fire. This remarkable achievement, however, had been accomplished only with a staggering thinning of its ranks. Since the Federals here outnumbered the Texans at least five or six to one, "death [thus] seemed to be our portion," wrote one of the Texas men.[39]

Hancock had posted a strong force south of the Orange Plank Road, which had opened a heavy enfilading fire on the 5th and 4th Texas. This attack on the flank occurred as the Texans were initiating a further assault of the Federal line of entrenchments north of the road. The 4th and 5th Texas therefore changed fronts and charged across the road into the thickets on its southern shoulder to thwart this new threat.[40]

As the 4th and 5th Texas crossed the Orange Plank Road, they came under additional fire from two artillery batteries as their line swept diagonally across their front. The double-shotted canister caused further carnage among the men. But the regiment and its companion continued across the road, discovering yet another line of entrenchments. Within 20-30 yards of this line, the Texans stood their ground in the face of overwhelming small arms and cannon fire. Campbell recalled that "[w]ith only 15 to 20 paces separating us, the contest waxed hat and deadlier. We gave a cheer and tried a charge, but with our handful of men our only success was to rush up to them, shoot them down, and shove them back some 10 to 15 yards." Alone, the Texas Brigade had "no support on our right, and not only none on our left, but a terrible

38 Polley, "Simple Justice Asked," *CV*, 3:317; Pomeroy, "War Memoirs," 76; Polley, *Hood's Texas Brigade*, 231-32; Simpson, *Lee's Grenadier Guard*, 398; Polley, *Letters to Charming Nellie*, 232-33.

39 R. C., "Gen. Lee at the 'Wilderness'," The Land We Love, 5:484; Polley, "Texas in the Battle of the Wilderness," *CV* 5:290; Polley, "Simple Justice Asked," *CV*, 3:317; Skoch, *Lone Star Confederate*, 108; Polley, *Hood's Texas Brigade*, 232.

40 Rhea, *Battle of the Wilderness*, 302-303; Polley, "Simple Justice Asked," *CV*, 3:317; Polley, "Texas in the Battle of the Wilderness," *CV*, 5:290; Polley, *Hood's Texas Brigade*, 232.

enfilading fire poured on us from that direction," Joseph Polley recalled. During the intense fighting, many Federals pulled the trigger before extracting their ramrods. John T. Allison of Company C proudly stated that "[h]ere I did my best fighting. I fired thirty shots and was drawing my cartridge box for more ammunition when I was shot through the right arm." Soon intermixed with Kershaw's advance, and facing steadfast enemy resistance, Longstreet's momentum finally began to dissipate.[41]

Brigade commander Gregg appeared wherever the action was the hottest in that desperate fight. He was nearly killed several times and had two mounts shot out from under him. His third horse, pierced by five separate bullets, each a mortal wound, was dying on its feet. The brigade had by then been reduced to little more than a skirmish line, with well over half its soldiers down— "dead, dying or wounded, and the few survivors could stand it no longer." After about 25 minutes of fighting, word arrived that a column of Federal reinforcements double-quicking from the left would soon have the Texans south of the Plank Road surrounded. Gregg decided it was time to withdraw. "I bore the order to the 5th and 1st Texas to fall back in order" to the north side of the Plank Road, Campbell wrote. The Texans withdrew, but they had accomplished their objective "to hold the enemy in check, to give Longstreet time to reform his corps." They had rocked the Federal assault "back on its heels."[42]

As the regiment, along with the 4th Texas, began falling back, the brigade's other two regiments north of the woods had already begun to retreat. The reunited brigade withdrew to a line about 300 yards in front of Poague's batteries near the Widow Tapp field, having lost 70 percent of its strength in casualties, whereupon they reformed and replenished their ammunition. Some of the Texas wounded walked back without aid to the field hospital; others were carried on litters by friends, and many continued to lie on the field awaiting succor.[43]

41 Rhea, *Battle of the Wilderness*, 302-303; Trudeau, *Bloody Roads South*, 92-93; Skoch, *Lone Star Confederate*, 108; Chicoine, *Confederates of Chappell Hill*, 131. The wound disabled Allison for the remainder of the war; however, he remained with the command until the surrender at Appomattox. Yeary, *Reminiscences of the Boys in Gray*, 1:13.

42 Rufus Felder to Sister, July 14, 1864, in CRC; Polley, "Texans in the Battle of the Wilderness," *CV*, 5:290; Skoch, *Lone Star Confederate*, 108. Campbell was probably referring to the 4th Texas rather than the 1st. Polley, *Letters to Charming Nellie*, 232-33; Polley, "Simple Justice Asked," *CV*, 3:317; Simpson, *Lee's Grenadier Guard*, 403. Other sources infer that Gregg was only mounted on one horse during the battle. Joskins, "A Sketch of Hood's Texas Brigade," UTSA 164-65; Polley, *Hood's Texas Brigade*, 232; Simpson, *Lee's Grenadier Guard*, 399-400; Pomeroy, "War Memoirs," 76.

43 Skoch, *Lone Star Confederate*, 109; Polley, *Hood's Texas Brigade*, 236. Besides Colonel Bryan and Clay, Captain D. C. Farmer, acting major, and Adjutant W. P. McGowan were all wounded, along with Lt. B. Pugh Fuller (Company A), Capt. J. J. McBride (Company C), Capt. W. T. Hill

The remainder of Field's Division had arrived on the ground by 6:30 a.m. and began sweeping past the withdrawing Texans. First came Benning's Brigade, which flew into the Federals still reeling from the Texans' onslaught. But soon his right flank became exposed to deadly fire from the Federals below the Orange Plank Road, as well as considerable fire from its left. Within minutes, the Georgians were badly cut up, and Benning himself fell wounded. These were hardly encouraging events. In a short period of time, his brigade was "badly cut up," Field later reported. A Confederate soldier in the rear observed the Texans and Georgians coming back from the assaults: "What a chill and horror to us—enough to unnerve and unman us! The groans and shrieks of the men lying by the side of the road; the rattle of musketry and then here comes the wounded of the Texas and Benning's brigades, and two men on each side of a horse carrying Benning to the rear."[44]

Benning was carted away on a litter, the thinned remnants of his brigade slowly staggering back, Law's Alabama Brigade, then commanded by Col. William F. Perry, moved into place. Noticing this, Lee ventured over to them and inquired "What troops are these?" A soldier quickly called back, "Law's Alabama brigade." A still agitated Lee exclaimed, "God bless the Alabamians. Alabama soldiers, all I ask of you is to keep up with the Texans." The Alabamians quickly completed their battle formation "at a double-quick step" and then swept along the northern shoulder of the Orange Plank Road to where the Texans and Georgians had just retired. Perry divided his force into two separate wings, one to traverse the Widow Tapp's field well above the Plank Road, cross a narrow swamp, and then move up a hill which Brig. Gen. James S. Wadsworth's division had just occupied. The right wing would proceed up the Plank Road. After some initial success, the left wing had to halt when hit with heavy enfilading fire from the north.

Fighting "seesawed in a protracted battle ,but the thinly-manned Confederate right wing proved too weak to drive the heavily reinforced Federals from their low hill north of the Plank Road. And so despite its staggering losses, the Texas Brigade was soon sent back into the battle to help the Alabamians. Gregg was ordered to attack a second time along the Plank Road to arrest this new threat presented by Federal reinforcements. A serious firefight soon erupted on the right along the part of Plank Road General Wadsworth occupied. The Texans, already bled nearly white by its first attack, advanced at a right angle to the general line of battle. Moving down a slight

(Company D), 2nd Lt B. Eldridge (Company E). Lts. W. Robinson (Company H) and Thomas Nash (Company K) were killed.

44 Field, "Campaigns of 1864 and 1865," in *SHSP*, 11:544; Polley, "Texans in Battle of the Wilderness," *CV*, 5:291; Rhea, *Battle of the Wilderness*, 303-04; Cannan, *Wilderness Campaign*, 163; Law, "From the Wilderness to Cold Harbor," in *B&L*, 4:125.

elevation, they crossed a swamp to the crest of another rise, where, along with the 15th Alabama under Col. Oates, they dispersed a heavy line of Federal skirmishers. Together, this force then outflanked and scattered the Union force then harassing the Alabama brigade's left. Lee's men finally regained the high ground east of the Widow Tapp's field. At this point, other units of Field's Division relieved the Texans and they saw no more action that day save a brief encounter with skirmishers toward dusk.[45]

Outnumbered, and having outpaced the Confederate forces below the Plank Road and under severe fire, Perry was finally forced to withdraw. As Field soon arrived on the scene, not only was Wadsworth's division was no longer a functioning combat force, but all three of Perry's brigades thrown into the battle had been wrecked. Disheartened, he remarked that "[t]his is all of my command that I can find," and decided against another attack. He then busied himself reorganizing the scattered and shattered remnants of his division. Nonetheless, by then his division had all but obliterated the northern half of the Federal assault column. The Yankees were in scarcely better shape. Badly scattered, masses of them were still fleeing toward the Lacy House.[46]

Once the enemy retired out of range, having left their dead and wounded on the field, a Texan observed that "[e]verything looked like destruction beyond measure." Battle's detritus— guns, iron ramrods, and myriad kinds of military equipment—were strewn everywhere. Every limb in the woods seemed to have been cut by bullets. Many trees as big around as a man's body had two to three dozen bullets in them, as well as many Federal ramrods, some shot into trees so deeply that they could not be extracted. That night, once the fighting ceased, Pvt. Pleasant K. Goree of Company H went to fill his canteen in the stream of the nearby ravine they had used during the day, and found the water "well mixed with blood."[47]

45 Polley, *Hood's Texas Brigade*, 232; Pomeroy, "War Memoirs," 76; Simpson, *Lee's Grenadier Guard*, 400; Joskins, "A Sketch of Hood's Texas Brigade," 164-65; Rhea, *Battle of the Wilderness*, 304-308.

46 Field, "Campaign of 1864 and 1865," *SHSP*, 11:544; William F. Perry, "Reminiscences of the Campaign of 1864 in Virginia," *SHSP* (1878), 7:52-57; George McRae, "With Benning's Brigade in the Wilderness," *Atlanta Journal*, August 17, 1901; Rhea, *Battle of the Wilderness*, 303-307; Polley, *Hood's Texas Brigade*, 232-33; Cannan, *Wilderness Campaign*, 163-66; Winkler, *Confederate Capital*, 164.

47 Hanks, *Captain Benton's Company*, 29; Yeary, *Reminiscences of the Boys In Gray*, 1: 274. The ramrods all came from the Federal side, doubtless fired by troops so excited and nervous that they forgot to remove them before discharging their weapons. While exploring the battlefield, the author personally found one of these ramrods still firmly affixed to a tree in 1975, 111 years later. For more on Goree, see Appendix B, Volume 1.

The Goree brothers, left to right: Langston, Edwin and Pleasant Kittrell Goree
Historical Research Center, Hill College

After turning back the Federal assaults, the initiative passed to Lee. Longstreet, leading four brigades of infantry down an unfinished railroad to the southeast later on May 6, struck Grant's exposed left flank. Just as the surprise assault appeared to be succeeding, Longstreet fell badly wounded in the throat and shoulder. Soon thereafter, a bullet to the temple instantly killed Brig. Gen. Jenkins, one-time commander of Hood's Division. With Old Pete out of the action, the Confederate assault bogged down and finally stalled. Before it could be resumed, Hancock had erected breastworks and the potential for an all-out victory virtually evaporated. Ewell now attempted a similar maneuver on the Union right flank; however, Lee's late attempt at a double envelopment failed and concluded the bloody fighting of May 6.[48]

48 Freeman, *Lee's Lieutenants*, 3:360-72; Law, "From the Wilderness to Cold Harbor," in *B&L*, 4:125-27; Alexander, *Military Memoirs*, 505-08; Longstreet, *Manassas to Appomattox*, 483-84; Rhea, *Battle of the Wilderness*, 372-73. A late afternoon attack by Brigadier General John Gordon's troops against Sedgwick, also came up short in the darkness. Gordon, *Reminiscences of*

The attack on its right flank spread panic throughout the Union lines though. Two Union generals had been captured and the Yankees were shoved back a full mile. The strain had even gotten to Grant. He had smoked over 20 cigars that day and had worn holes in the fingers of his gloves. The near collapse of his right wing was the last straw. Once the danger passed, he withdrew to his tent and "throwing himself face downward on his cot . . . gave vent to his feelings in a way which left no room to doubt that he was deeply moved." This display greatly disturbed his staff who had never before seen their chief betray the slightest apprehension or sense of danger. The stakes for Grant now were much higher, though: retreat would be a great calamity to his country and the president, not to mention his own career. However, he reverted to form soon enough, telling a war correspondent headed back to Washington that if he were to see Lincoln "tell him, from me, that, whatever happens, there will be no turning back." [49]

The Texans with their impetuous charge into Hancock's advance had dealt a staggering blow to that offensive and saved Lee's army that day. The brigade, without support, halted Hancock's attack down the Orange Plank Road and regained the ground Hill's men had lost the previous day. Lee's objective had been achieved, and his trust in the Texans again reinforced. But the Texas Brigade's counteroffensive extracted a typically horrendous cost. Of the more than 800 soldiers who charged that early morning under Lee's watchful gaze, 565 fell dead or wounded in 25 minutes of fighting. The 5th Texas itself entered the action with 180 men and officers, according to acting commander Captain Tacitus T. Clay. Those brutal 25 minutes killed or wounded 111 of them. The regiment lost its commanding officer, Lt. Col. King Bryan, every one of its regimental officers, including Clay, acting lieutenant colonel, Capt. D. C. Farmer, acting major, as well as Adjutant W. P. McGowan—all to grievous wounds. Six of ten company commanders were also casualties. Every officer but two had horses shot from under them. The redoubtable Texas Brigade might have saved Lee's army, but it would never again be the same.[50]

---

the Civil War (New York, NY, 1904), 243-57, 261; Rhea, *Battle of the Wilderness*, 424-25; Foote, *Civil War Narrative*, 3: 182-83.

49 Rhea, *Battle of the Wilderness*, 425-26; Anders, *Hearts in Conflict*, 490; Foote, *Civil War Narrative*, 3:385-86; Simpson, "Ulysses S. Grant, The Northern Press, and the Opening of the Wilderness Campaign," *The Wilderness Campaign*, 15.

50 Robertson, *Touched With Valor*, 95-96; Field, "Campaigns of 1864 and 1865," 544; Simpson, *Lee's Grenadier Guard*, 402n120, 403; Rhea, *Battle of the Wilderness*, 303; Muster Rolls, Field, Staff and Band, 5th Texas, April 30–June 30, 1864, in TSA; Joskins, "A Sketch of Hood's Texas Brigade," UTSA 164-65. Given that the brigade fought three separate actions on May 6, Simpson suggests a Galveston *Daily News* article (lost 565 out of 811 engaged) some ten years after the fight and in the wake of a brigade reunion, may well be correct. See *Galveston Daily*

On May 7, both armies remained behind their breastworks, far too exhausted and depleted for any renewal of hostilities. Special details patrolled no man's land in between the lines retrieving the dead and wounded, and the men of the regiment spent much of the day searching the field for their own casualties. Goree of Company H ventured out in search of a new mount. He reported "the dead and dying of both armies . . . so thickly strewn that we had to be careful where we rode." The unpleasant task of dealing with the dead was particularly repulsive in the Wilderness. Artillery rounds had set large areas of the woods ablaze, and many of the wounded, lying unseen or undiscovered in the thick underbrush, were burned to death before assistance could arrive. While searching for a fresh horse, Goree heard someone calling his name, and "found it to be the Lieutenant of my company, William Robinson, of San Jacinto, Tex." He was mortally wounded and begged "most piteously to be taken out, which Gen. Field was prompt to have done, as some litter bearers were near at hand."[51]

Joskins, also searching for a new mount, "beheld the dead faces of many familiar of the Brigade as they lie on the Plank road where we had fought." There he discovered the "dead and stiff body" of Lt. Whit Randall of Company C, who was acting on Gregg's staff that day, shot though the head. Five bullets had penetrated his body, and another his horse. He had been robbed of his hat, coat, watch and boots. Searchers found many others in the regiment severely injured or worse. Sergeant Major George J. Robinson of Company A had been hit in the face, the ball passing through both cheeks, shattering his jaw and nearly severing his tongue. He would be unable to take solid nourishment for the rest of his life.[52]

Private Edwin King Goree of Company H, Pleasant's brother, took a ball in the knee early in the action and was left for dead in the dense undergrowth. There he lay in the rain through May 6 until discovered by a burial party the next morning. Still alive, he was placed behind a soldier on horseback and on the way to the field hospital, fell from the horse. The rider thought he had died and left him for a burial detail. But Goree, still alive, lay there on the wet ground for several more hours before again

---

News, May 8, 1874. No official report of losses for the brigade was ever made or preserved. Other brigade sources reported losses at variance with these.

51 Polley, *Hood's Texas Brigade*, 236; Freeman, *Lee's Lieutenants*, 3: 375-80. Pleasant Goree was the brother of Edwin K. Goree, Langston J. and Thomas J., originally all from the regiment's Company H. Yeary, *Reminiscences of the Boys in Gray*, 274. Robinson died of his wounds the next day.

52 Joskins, "A Sketch of Hood's Texas Brigade," UTSA 166-67; Skoch, *Lone Star Confederate*, 72; Moore, *Men of Bayou City Guards*, 88, 172; Simpson, *Compendium*, 227; Robertson, *Touched With Valor*, 94. For more on Robinson, see Appendix B, Volume 1.

Edwin King Goree
Historical Research Center, Hill College

being discovered and carried to the hospital. Though seriously wounded, he survived the war following an amputation of his leg. Five men of the regiment had been shot through both legs, including Capt. J. J. McBride, commander of Company C. These multiple injuries undoubtedly resulted from the regiment's being positioned on the brigade's right flank, and thus most exposed to enfilading fire from Hancock's men south of the Orange Plank Road. Also among the regiment's dead that fateful day was Pvt. Thomas P. Bryan, of Company A, the regiment's newest recruit who had just enlisted at Enterprise, Mississippi on February 2. He was a native Texan, and the last of four brothers, all of whom (including his twin) had already been killed serving in the Confederate army.[53]

Sergeant Mark Smither's mess went into the battle that morning with five members; two were killed and one wounded. First Sergeant William H. Lewis and William E. Lewis, both of wealthy families in Waverly, Texas, were killed. Smither described them as "brave, noble hearted boys as ever took up arms in the Confederate cause." "Will" (William H.) had been "a general favorite," whom Smither "loved . . . as if he were a Brother." They were both the same age, and Smither had hoped Lewis would survive the war and "become an ornament to society as he was the pride of his family & friends." R. H. Griffin, "a promising young man and a gallant soldier," was yet another friend in Smither's company killed that day.[54]

53 Edwin Sue Goree, *A Family Mosaic*, 15, 17-18, 24; Joskins, "A Sketch of Hood's Texas Brigade," UTSA 166-67; Wood, *Partial Roster of the Officers and Men Raised in Leon County*, 14-15; Moore, *Men of the Bayou City Guards*, 84, 86; Simpson, *Compendium*, 175; Pomeroy, "War Memoirs," 75; Robertson, *Touched With Valor*, 95; Simpson, *Lee's Grenadier Guard*, 402-04; Houston *Daily Telegraph*, July 15, 1864; Yeary, *Reminiscences of the Boys in Gray*, 1:274. For more on Goree, and McBride, see Appendix B, Volume 1.

54 Fragment, Mark Smither to ___, June, 1864, in SHSU. For more on William H. and William E. Lewis, see Appendix B, Volume 1.

Among others of the regiment either killed in the morning attack that morning or soon died from mortal wounds were: John Francis McKee, T. W. Henry, T. W. McCrorey, and Nelson Wiley of Company K; William George, William Baldwin, John Davis, and J. W. Powell of Company I; Lt. Thomas Nash and C. E. Farquhar of Company E; W. W. Peeks of Company G; and Emil Auerbach of Company B, a Jewish immigrant from Mechlenburg, Germany, who lived in Columbus, and worked as a saddler.[55]

Lieutenant Nash had been one of the leaders of that infamous skirmish immediately after Seven Pines resulting in the prediction that "the Texas Brigade will kill more Yankees, storm more batteries, and capture fewer prisoners than any in the service." He had previously been wounded at Gaines' Mill and Second Manassas. Among the severely wounded either discharged or furloughed immediately following the battle as a result of their grievous wounds were: Edwin A. Keeble, W. B. Rome (leg amputated) and Alex H. Traylor, all of Company D; E. T. Tucker of Company F; James W. Evans and M. D. Garrett of Company G; Edward King Goree of Company H (leg amputated); and W. R. Barlow and A. B. Hood of Company I. James Edward Landes from Chappell Hill, a close friend and comrade-in-arms of Rufus King Felder, lost a finger in the action but still returned to the regiment and finished out the war.[56]

The Texans gathered their fallen comrades together in a central location for a dignified, mass burial. They chose a cleared area just north of the Orange Plank Road, adjacent to a large oak tree, and near the place where the brigade had halted Hancock's advance the previous morning. There, in the shade of a wide, spreading, stately oak tree, they excavated a long, wide trench, 18 inches deep, to inter the bodies of the fallen. Blankets, clothing, and canvas carefully lined the trench before the dead were placed side by side therein "as they had fought." Pieces of clothing, haversacks, and other articles to hold back the dirt were laid on top of the bodies, and at the head of each body a carved, wooden headboard with the fallen's name and organization. Once the massive grave was entirely covered, a board was nailed to the large oak tree with

55 Richmond *Dispatch*, "The Daily Dispatch," June 11, 1862; Stein, "Consider the Lily,"; Simpson, *Compendium*, 167-250; Hollace Ava Weiner and Kenneth Roseman, *Lone Star of David: The Jews of Texas* (Hanover, NH, 2007), 40-43.

56 Richmond *Dispatch*, "The Daily Dispatch," June 11, 1862; Stein, "Consider the Lily,"; Polley, *Hood's Texas Brigade*, 331-47; Simpson, *Compendium*, 167-250; Hollace Ava Weiner and Kenneth Roseman, *Lone Star of David*, 40-43; Simpson, *Compendium*, 167-250. For more on Keeble, see Appendix B, Volume 1.

these simple, but eloquent words: "Texas Dead—May 6, 1864." The brigade spent the balance of May 7 resting quietly, until evening, when the troops started south again.[57]

William P. Hopkins of the 7th Rhode Island Volunteers recalled encountering a huge mass of Confederate prisoners in the Union rear on May 7. These men were "lank, yellow, long-limbed, weather beaten, rough-haired fellows, but they were terrible soldiers, possessing the hardihood of wild animals." Hopkins observed their attire: "homespun, drab, gray or butternut predominated, the intermingling of raiment half-citizen, half military was so absolute, it could scarcely be affirmed that any uniform was possessed by them." He noted "it was pathetic, to note their knapsacks of woven carpets with coverlets and patchwork quilts and braided carpets used as blankets." Augustus Buell of Battery B, 4th U. S. Artillery, recounted an interesting incident involving one of these captured Confederates. Their captives were generally convinced the Federals were whipped and had to retreat, since Hancock's Corps had been totally cut off below the Plank Road.

> One old fellow was brought up out of the brush at the south edge of the Lacy Clearing. He belonged to the 5th Texas, of Gregg's Brigade. He had been hit in the shin by a bullet, which had temporarily paralyzed his leg . . . at the extreme point of the advance in the afternoon of the 6th, and so was left in our hand when they fell back. Some of the boys asked him what he thought of the battle. He was a comical old cuss, and his reply was, 'Battle be ______! It ain't no battle! It's a worse riot than Chickamauga was!' . . . 'You Yanks don't call this a battle, do you? At Chickamauga there was at least a rear, but here there ain't neither front nor rear. It's all a mess! And our two armies ain't nothin' but howlin' mobs!'[58]

The "*sang froid* of this grizzly old Texan was superb," Buell marveled. While the old Texan was eating, one of the battery's newest recruits stopped to chide him a little: "Say, Uncle Johnny," he inquired, "Haven't you fellows made up your minds that one Southerner can't whip five Yankees?" Then the "venerable Rebel replied," asking the youngster whether he had personally heard a Southern man say he could whip five Yankees. Upon obtaining a negative response, the Texan then inquired "well, then, whar did you git that notion?" The recruit indicated he heard the alleged boast in

57 Polley, *Hood's Texas Brigade*, 234; Polley, *Letters to Charming Nellie*, 233; Pomeroy, "War Memoirs," 77; Rhea, *Battle of the Wilderness*, 452.

58 William Palmer Hopkins, *The Seventh Rhode Island Regiment, Rhode Island Volunteers in the Civil War 1862-1865* (Providence, R. I, 1903), 167; Augustus Buell, *"The Cannoneer": Recollections of Service in the Army of the Potomac by "A Detached Volunteer" in the Regular Artillery* (Washington, DC, 1890), 168-69; Chicoine, *Confederates of Chappell Hill*, 131.

speeches back home given by recruiting officers, and he then surmised that the speeches were told "to get our dander up!" The Texan replied "Now let me tell you, Sonny, that that story, like a good many other things which helped to bring on this war, wasn't nothin' but a ____ Abolition lie!" Buell then observed that "You couldn't phase that old rooster much. He won our hearts by telling us that he had been in the 2nd Kentucky in the Mexican War, and had helped support the old Battery at Buena Vista." They were therefore guarding a former brother in arms.[59]

The fighting in the Wilderness, as fierce as any during the entire war, left on the battlefield a perfect portrait of destruction, death and desolation. Bullets had severed and pocked virtually everything in the woods. Surprisingly, the Federals had made no effort to bury their dead or to collect their arms. A Texan visiting the battlefield a week later, reported that

> [t]he stench from the putrefying corpses and carcasses of the thousands of men and horses that lay in every conceivable shape and position on the ground, pervaded the air and made impossible any long stay . . . . All the Confederate dead that could be found had been buried, but the Yankees had not buried a tenth of their dead. Vast quantities of clothing, ammunition and arms lay strewn over acres of ground.

The area "became so foul from the stench that the people, unable to undertake so huge an attempt, were forced to move away from the vicinity of the battlefield." Upon revisiting the site two weeks later, that same Texan observed that the road and paths "were alive with worms, and above them swarmed myriads of flies. The flesh had rotted from the corpses and only bones marked the spots where brave spirits, had taken leave of their tenements of clay." By then, the local residents had reclaimed the field, and all arms and ammunition had been carted away by the Confederate army.[60]

The battle of the Wilderness marked the first step in Grant's grand strategy to isolate Lee from Richmond. From this point until the middle of June, Grant undertook a number of "sidling" movements to his left trying to turn the Confederates' right flank and interpose his army between Lee and Richmond. Lee would successfully counter all of these movements. But the end was coming. Still

59 Hopkins, *The Seventh Rhode Island Regiment*, 167; Buell, *"The Cannoneer,"* 168-69; Chicoine, *Confederates of Chappell Hill*, 131. Robinson reported one member of the regiment captured. Another source reported two, J. E. Gilbert and Robert Stanton, both of Company D. Robertson, *Touched With Valor*, 96 : Simpson, *Compendium*, 199, 202.

60 Polley, *Hood's Texas Brigade*, 233-34; Winkler, *Confederate Capital*, 175; Freeman, *Lee's Lieutenants*, 3: 376; Parker, *Touched By Fire*, 86; Polley, "Texans in the Battle of the Wilderness," 290-91.

more fearsome fighting awaited the Texans the remainder of that spring and then grueling, perilous months of trench warfare. The severely thinned ranks of the 5th Texas had more yet to bleed.[61]

61 Polley, *Hood's Texas Brigade*, 233; Freeman, *Lee's Lieutenants*, 3:376; Winkler, *Confederate Capital*, 175.

Chapter 6

Spotsylvania, North Anna, and Cold Harbor

Spotsylvania Court House

Lee requested Brig. Gen. Gordon to accompany him on May 7th for a debriefing on his previous evening's offensive on the Federals' right flank. On the ride, Gordon asked Lee what he expected from Grant, as reports had circulated that the Union army was in retreat. Lee scoffed at the rumors. "General Grant is not going to retreat. [Rather,] he will move his army to Spotsylvania." Had Lee received information to that effect, Gordon asked. "[N]ot at all; but that is the next point at which the armies will meet. Spotsylvania is now General Grant's best strategic point. I am so sure of his next move that I have already made arrangements to march by the shortest practicable route, that we may meet him there."[1]

Indeed, Grant had issued orders at 6:30 a.m. for a night march toward Spotsylvania Court House. Lee made his prediction at about this same time, hours before Jeb Stuart's cavalry reported Federal wagons moving southward.

> This notable prophecy of General Lee and its fulfillment by General Grant show that the brains of these two foemen had been working at the same problem. The known quantities in that problem were the aims of Grant to crush Lee and capture Richmond, to which had been added the results of the last two days' fighting. The unknown quantity which both were endeavoring to find was the next movement

1 Gordon, *Reminiscences of the Civil War*, 268-69; Burke Davis, *The Gray Fox* (New York, NY, 1956), 296-97.

> which the aggressor would probably make. Grant stood in his own place and calculated from his own standpoint; Lee put himself in Grant's place and calculated from the same standpoint: and both found the same answer—Spotsylvania.[2]

Lee further opined that Grant was held in such high esteem by the Federal administration that he could command the country's massive resources in men and materials without limitation, while the Confederacy by then had exhausted both these categories. Lee's hope that spring, or as Gordon expressed it, his "conviction," was that if he could just keep the Confederate army between Grant and Richmond, checking him for several months more, some crisis in governmental affairs or a further change in public opinion and confidence in the North would induce the authorities in Washington to allow the South to go its own way, "rather than force their retention in the Union at so heavy a cost." Given the current public mood and the difficulties Lincoln was having within his own party, as well as the ever-mounting political opposition to the administration, there was certainly a basis for this belief.[3]

By 8:30 p.m. on May 7, Grant started his infantry down the Brock Road toward Spotsylvania Court House, preceded by Sheridan's cavalry; the Confederates could clearly hear the sounds of their movement. Lee promptly ordered his army south toward the same objective. Major General Richard H. Anderson, Longstreet's successor as commander of the First Corps, led the way, taking up the march toward the courthouse at 11:00 p.m. on May 7, out of the Wilderness and onto the river bottoms to the south. His troops were to march to Shady Grove Church Road, while his artillery would move south from Parker's Store later to join that same road. The two elements would unite there and continue marching east to Spotsylvania village. While Warren and Anderson's corps were marching in the dark of May 7, neither was aware of the other as they trudged down parallel roads less than a mile or two apart, toward the same objective. A desperate race for Spotsylvania Court House, some 12 miles distant, was on in deadly earnest.[4]

Warren's V Corps had begun to pull out of line and proceed toward Spotsylvania Court House at about 9:00 p.m., passing behind Burnside's and Hancock's corps, to be followed by Sedgwick and Burnside, on separate roads, and finally, Hancock, behind Warren on the Brock Road. It was an altogether hard march in the dark over unfamiliar roads, with entangling underbrush, treacherous ditches, overhanging tree

2 Gordon, *Reminiscences of the Civil War*, 270.

3 Ibid., 268.

4 Law, "Wilderness to Cold Harbor," in *B&L*, 4:128; Salmon, *Virginia Battlefield Guide*, 270-71; *OR* 36, pt. 1, 1056; Sorrell, *Confederate Staff Officer*, 240-41; Freeman, *Lee's Lieutenants*, 3:379.

limbs, sloshy areas, plus choking clouds of dust kicked up from the bone-dry roads. All this and for those passing through last spring's Chancellorsville battlefield, grisly reminders of that horrible carnage—bones and skulls, whole skeletons stripped white by the buzzards, and acres of battlefield wreckage.[5]

Despite their travails, once the blue-coated veterans sensed they were not headed north, as had done so often after closing with Lee in past campaigns, they began to cheer. "If we were under any other General except Grant I should expect a retreat," Elisha Hunt Rhodes of the 2nd Rhode Island, wrote, "but Grant is not that kind of soldier, and we feel that we can trust him."[6]

Following supper, the men of the 5th Texas were issued an extra day's rations, a pound of corn meal and a half pound of bacon, for their night march. Kershaw's Division moved first, soon followed by Field's, both of them on a road cut through the woods earlier during the day. Lee had ordered Brig. Gen. William N. Pendleton, chief of the artillery, to construct this trail south from Anderson's lower flank, so as to strike Carpathian Road west of Todd's Tavern. But in the black of night, with the road full of tree stumps and jammed with troops and wagons, stops proliferated. This went on for hours, and "if one sat down he was sure to go to sleep, we were so near worn out," a Texan recalled. Finally, the roads cleared and the Texans advanced more quickly. Anderson's infantry and artillery columns converged at Shady Grove Church, and continued down Shady Grove Church Road toward Spotsylvania Court House. At daybreak, Anderson selected a suitable bivouac down the road where the Block House Bridge crossed the Po River. There, the Texans consumed a hasty breakfast of cold rations amid the roar of musketry to their north.[7]

About 8:00 a.m. Anderson sent Law's Brigade north up Old Court House Road to join Humphreys' and Kershaw's Brigades at Laurel Hill, there to confront Warren's corps. He then dispatched Field's and Kershaw's remaining brigades, including the Texas Brigade, east toward Spotsylvania Court House itself to confront Brig. Gen. James H. Wilson's cavalry which they soon forced to evacuate the village. With Wilson's threat removed, Anderson recalled the units he had diverted to Spotsylvania

5 Trudeau, *Bloody Roads South*, 127-29; David W. Blight, *When This Cruel War Is Over* (Amherst, MA, 1992), 295.

6 Robert Hunt Rhodes, ed., *All For The Union* (New York, 1985), 146; Commager, *The Blue and the Gray*, 987.

7 *OR* 36, pt. 1, 1041, 1056; Polley, *Hood's Texas Brigade*, 237; Field, "Campaign of 1864 and 1865," in *B&L*, 4:547; Robert T. Coles, *From Huntsville to Appomattox*, Jeffery D. Stocker, ed. (Knoxville, TN, 1996), 167; Rhea, *The Battles for Spotsylvania Court House and the Road to Yellow Tavern May 7-12, 1864* (Baton Rouge, LA, 1997), 50, 60; Hanks, *Captain Benton's Company*, 30, 39; Law, "Wilderness to Cold Harbor," in *B&L*, 4: 128; Moore, *Men of the Bayou City Guards*, 86.

Court House. These, including the Texans, marched across Kershaw's position, coming up on his left flank, thus creating an unbroken half-mile line stretching from the Po River across Brock Road on the right. After a welcoming "shower of bomb shells" from the enemy, Anderson's divisions had formed a line of battle north of Spotsylvania Court House by mid-morning, Kershaw's Division on the right and Field's, the left. Ewell arrived north of the village the afternoon of May 8, drawing up on Anderson's right. Despite all the obstacles, Lee's able and less encumbered veterans had won the all night "race" to the key intersection. Grant's latest attempt to reach Richmond had been thwarted yet again.[8]

By the end of May 8, Anderson's Corps occupied Laurel Hill and its vicinity, its left flank resting on the Po River. Ewell's Corps on Anderson's right extended the Confederate line north and east. Immediately following their arrival the 5th Texas, employing tin cups, boards, plates and knives, as well as shovels and pick axes, labored throughout the night till dawn constructing entrenchments, traverses, artillery emplacements, and fields of fire. Luckily, the area's ample fence rails made for strengthening the works considerably. The men worked without rest until dawn on May 9 building these stout works. The Texans' line at Spotsylvania ran along Laurel Hill, a high ridge cleared of undergrowth in its front to give "a tolerably unobstructed view" for 150 yards. Beyond the clearing, "forbiddingly frowned a forest of heavy timber" and small growth, a murky *terra incognita* that concealed the enemy somewhere in its dark depths.[9]

Sunrise on May 9 revealed a distressing surprise to Ewell's Corps. All their hard work in the darkness following the natural contours of the terrain and the tree line building their formidable line had resulted in a salient projecting northward toward the Federal line. As with any salient, this one dubbed the "Mule Shoe" due to its shape, it was gravely exposed to enfilading Union fire. A breech in the lower line would isolate the Mule Shoe, exposing it to attacks from front and rear. However, Lee's chief engineer, Maj. Gen. Martin Smith, appraised the position as vital. It encompassed high ground that had to be kept out of Union hands at all costs. Almost nothing could be done to remedy the defensive nightmare in any case, since the Federals had already dug in opposite the Confederate position.

Lee, however, had frustrated Grant's attempt to occupy Spotsylvania Court House and successfully reunited his army. Hill's Corps, the wagon train's rear guard, reached the Confederate position early that day. With all three corps now in place, Lee

8 *OR* 36, pt.1, 1065-66; Field, "Campaigns of 1864 and 1865," in *SHSP*, 14:547; William M. Dame, *From the Rapidan to Richmond and the Spotsylvania Campaign* (Baltimore, MD, 1920), 108-11; Rhea, *Battles for Spotsylvania*, 68-69.

9 Polley, *Hood's Texas Brigade*, 292.

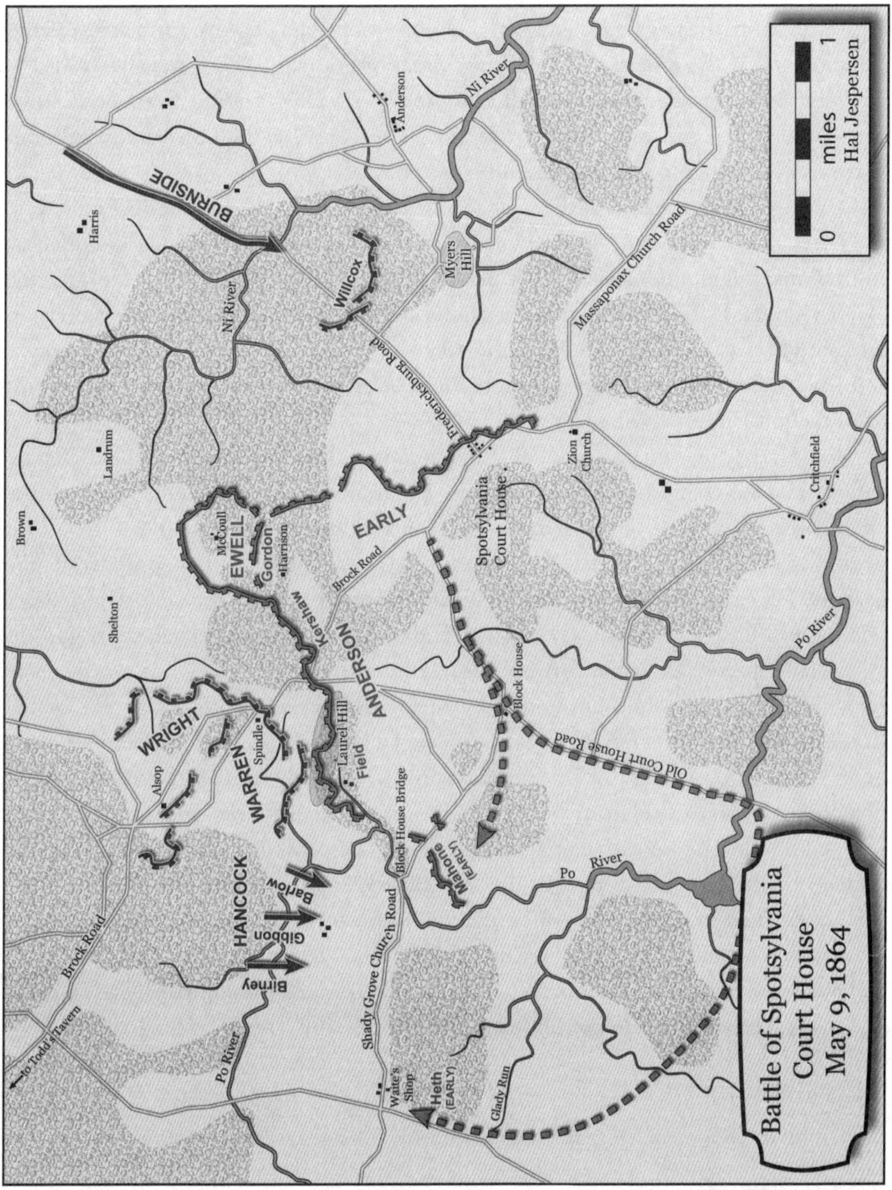

arranged his defenses across Grant's lines of approach. The Confederate left, Anderson's Corps, still rested on the Po River, opposite Warren's Corps and Wright's division of Sedgwick's corps; Ewell's Corps held the center, with Hill's newly arrived Third Corps with Jubal Early's Division positioned on the right, across the Fredericksburg Road opposite Burnside's IX Corps. Sedgwick's VI Corps confronted the Mule Shoe's left flank, with Warren's V Corps on the right facing the Rebel left. By early afternoon, the advance elements of Union troops had deployed and attacked the Confederates with artillery and small arms fire. For hours on May 8 and all day May 9, the "dull but incessant roar of small arms and the wicked boom of artillery told of repeated assaults on Ewell's lines on its right." The Texans in their breastworks farther to the left "felt slighted" at this point.[10]

Ewell's entrenchments at the U-shaped Mule Shoe were about one-half mile wide and jutted out nearly a mile, well beyond the rest of the Confederate lines. Naturally as an obvious, vulnerable weak spot it presented an inviting target to Meade's forces. Major General Robert E. Rhode's Division on the left (west) and Johnson's division on the right (east) actually occupied the salient. Gordon's division stood as a reserve and had constructed yet another reserve line of entrenchments extending eastward from the left-center of the salient.[11]

On May 10, Grant made an all-out attempt to break through the Confederate defenses by attacking the Confederate left. The multiple Union assaults fell upon the Texas Brigade among many others. Grant had positioned over 40,000 men to assault Anderson's and Ewell's Corps. The Texans' works, anchoring the Confederate line near the Po River, projected forward slightly forming a semicircular fort. A battery under Capt. Basil C. Manly had been attached to the brigade and arranged its guns to sweep all approaches to the fortifications. Three full Federal divisions attacked the trenches left of the Mule Shoe held by Field's Division on the left center of the Confederate line, and a fierce battle soon raged all along the line. The Federals came on in "perfect fury," and the Texans "slayed them with all our might," said one. With dreadfully accurate fire from behind the fortified breastworks and trenches, they stopped the first two massive attacks with relative ease. With their ranks significantly thinned by the horrific fighting at the Wilderness, however, the men were so thinly spread they had to stand at five-foot intervals to protect their sector of the line. After the first two assaults, Gregg had his men collect rifles and ammunition from the dead and wounded in front of their breastworks to prepare for another onslaught. So many Texans had multiple loaded weapons in their possession to repel a final assault.[12]

10 Parker, *Touched By Fire*, 86; Hanks, *Captain Benton's Company*, 30, 39; Polley, *Hood's Texas Brigade*, 236-37; Joskins, "A Sketch of Hood's Texas Brigade," in UTSA, 166-67; Winkler, *Confederate Capital*, 171.

11 *OR* 36, pt. 2, 582, 609; William D. Matter, *If It Takes All Summer: The Battle of Spotsylvania* (Chapel Hill, NC, 1988), 103, 129-30; Lowry, *No Turning Back*, 282-83.

12 Muster Roll, Company D, 5thTexas, April 30-June 30, 1864, in TSA; Law. "Wilderness to Cold Harbor," 4:128-29; Polley, *Hood's Texas Brigade*, 237; Hanks, *Captain Benton's Company*, 30; Ltr fragment, Mark Smither to ___, June 1864, in SHSU; Smith, *Reminiscences*, 52; Simpson, *Lee's Grenadier Guard*, 410.

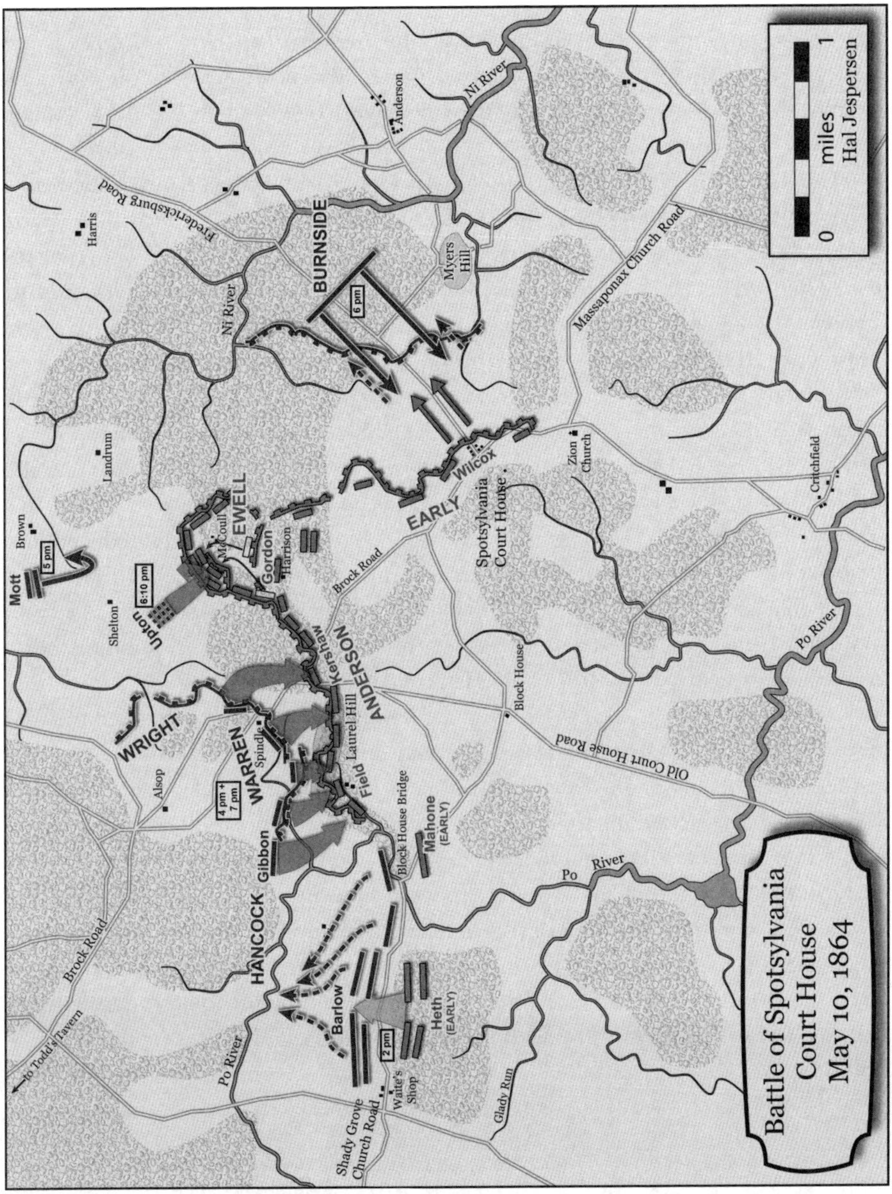

The Federals formed for a third and final attack around 7:00 p.m. in a thick wood 100 yards in front of the 5th Texas' position. Breaking from that cover with hearty huzzahs, they came on in an ever-increasing rush as they neared the Southern works. The Texans' line absorbed the full force of this attack. Pouring out of the woods, "yelling like madmen came the Federal infantry, fast as they could run, straight upon our lines," a Texan later remembered. "The whole field was blue with them!" For a moment, it appeared the Yankees might gain the breastworks. Then "a sheet of flame and a yell of defiance burst from the entrenchment, the bullets mowing the assailants down by the hundreds, and in front of the 4th and 5th Texas and the 3rd Arkansas this onset was soon checked."[13]

The 1st Texas fared worse. The massed Union front poured into their works through a narrow opening. A Yankee officer leaped on the works, according to Joe Joskins, "swinging his sword over his head . . . [crying] 'No Quarter'." The Yankees rushed onward demanding "Surrender; Surrender!" and killing numerous Texans with bayonets. "Squawk, damn you, I like to hear you squawk," a frenzied Yankee screamed as he drove his bayonet deep into a Texan. Fearsome, bloody, hand-to-hand fighting soon dominated the trenches, the Yankees still demanding surrender and the members of the 1st Texas forced to fight with clubbed muskets. The Federals pouring through the breach, however, were soon exposed to a fierce enfilading fire from the 3rd Arkansas on the left and the 4th and 5th Texas on the right, along with Anderson's brigade of Georgians. "These gallant fellows," Law later wrote, "now reduced to a mere handful by their losses in the Wilderness, stood manfully to their work.[14]

Unable to withstand this heavy flanking fire, the Federals soon withdrew in confusion from the Confederate works. Word went out: "They are running, boys, shoot them as fast as you can." O. T. Hanks later wrote "[y]ou may be assured that every fellow did that very thing and from the number of wounded and killed they did pretty good work." Confederate artillery and small arms fire raked the Federals mercilessly as they fled in disorder, and many ditches were "piled with dead and wounded Yanks," according to Joskins. So effective was the fire the Texans poured on the fleeing Yankees, a large number jumped into one large gulley, and trapped there, pledged to surrender if the Texans stopped shooting. Soon, in came 300-400 prisoners, along with a number of Texans they had captured. "It had been a vicious assault and a gallant repulse." The field in front of the breastworks, as well as the 1st Texas area inside the works, was littered with arms, clothing and accouterments, as well as dozens of dead and wounded Federals. In the several attacks by the II and V

13 *OR* 36, pt. 1, 470; Dame, *From the Rapidan to Richmond*, 164-65; Polley, *Hood's Texas Brigade*, 238. Colonel Robert S. Taylor of the 3rd Arkansas, taken by surprise while in the process of preparing his supper, showered the attackers with hot grease. J. B. Minor, "Rallying with a Frying Pan," *CV* (1905), 13:72-73.

14 Joskins, "A Sketch of Hood's Texas Brigade," in UTSA, 169; Dame, *From the Rapidan to Richmond*, 165; Hanks, *Captain Benton's Company*, 40; W. P. Johnson "Third Arkansas and Richmond Howitzers," *CV*, (1905), 13:210; Law, "Wilderness to Cold Harbor," in *B&L*, 4:129. Polley later claimed there was a 40 foot gap in the breastworks in the middle of the 1st Texas's line. Polley, *Hood's Texas Brigade*, 238.

Corps against Laurel Hill that day, the Federals lost over 5,000 men with fewer than 1,000 casualties for the Confederates.[15]

Although Joskins exaggerated when he claimed there were not 12 bayonets "in the whole brigade," indeed most of the 1st Texas, (and a significant number of the brigade's other regiments) had discarded their bayonets in East Tennessee, generally believing they could march more comfortably without the additional weight of a weapon they purportedly never used. The close, heavy individual combat at Spotsylvania, however, quickly induced the men to procure all the bayonets they could find. After a number of its members "felt the points of bayonets in the hands of the enemy," Joskins observed, "they 'saw the point' that such weapons were very good things to have." He noted "[t]he Texans were now [thoroughly] convinced that when fighting at close quarters cold steel had its advantages."[16]

Smither wrote home after the battle describing a close call he had experienced that day. Confronting the Federals near their breastworks, his position had come under intense artillery fire from a battery to its front. Absent his own musket, Smither sat behind Pvt. Samuel Bailey of Company A loading his gun for him after each shot. Close by Smither's other side was Pvt. John J. Pridgen of Company C, who had been caught out beyond the line skirmishing when the Federal assault hit. He was still attempting to catch his breath from running back in to his lines. Smither related that:

> I had just loaded Bailey's Gun and was in the act of passing it to him when a shell passed through our breastworks knocking down 4 or 5 men with the dirt and rocks before it came to us, took off Bailey's head took the gun out of mine and his hands, knocked me senseless and passed through Pridgens body carrying the gun barrel in with it, when I came to my senses I was covered nearly up with dirt and rails dead and wounded men &c I was knocked down by dirt driven through the breastwork before the shell came through or I would have been killed.

15 *OR* 36, pt. 1, 1057, 1065, *OR* 51, pt. 2, 911; Joskins, "A Sketch of Hood's Texas Brigade," in UTSA, 168-69; Ltr fragment, Mark Smither to ____, June, 1864, in SHSU; Law, "Wilderness to Cold Harbor," in *B&L*, 4:129; Pomeroy, "War Memoirs," 79; Simpson, *Lee's Grenadier Guard*, 411; Hanks, *Captain Benton's Company*, 30-31, 40. The prisoners were primarily from the 86th and 124th New York and the 3rd Maine regiments of Brig. Gen. J. H. Hobart Ward's brigade of Hancock's II Corps.

16 Houston *Daily Telegraph*, July 15, 1864; Skoch, *Lone Star Confederate*, 110; Polley, *Hood's Texas Brigade*, 238-39, 253; Simpson, *Lee's Grenadier Guard*, 413. Soon, Polley reported, the Texans "well-equipped" with bayonets, securing many abandoned by the Yankees and "borrowing, 'unbeknownst' to the owners, others from an Alabama brigade of another division." Following Spotsylvania, the 1st Texas soldiers became "experts in the use of them, defensively and offensively."

Joskins soon thereafter penned, "In Sam Bailey's death I lost one whom I loved—he was as brave—as noble and as generous as man can be – and none ever died who was better loved by his comrades than Sam Bailey—'Peace to his ashes.'"[17]

Earlier in the day's fight, Smither related that his company had been harassed by sharpshooters while working to improve their breastworks. Soon a sharpshooter's bullet instantly killed one of Smither's comrades to his front. Others in the line who heard the crack of the shot and its impact did not know for certain who had been hit, but knowing Smither to be in that general location, passed the word that he had been killed. "I was not aware that such a report was circulating and laid down and went to sleep and it was not till morning that I found that Madam Rumor had killed me the night before." Smither's comrades thus were rather astonished in daylight to discover him still very much alive.[18]

In addition to Pvts. Bailey and John J. Pridgen, the regiment also lost John T. Alverson and J. J. Shaw (Company D). Both young men had enlisted together in Huntsville in March, 1862, a pair of "poor, hardworking men, with families living on the Trinity River in the upper edge of Walker county."[19]

During the battle, an unusual incident occurred involving Levi Miller, a body servant belonging to Capt. J. J. McBride and Lt. J. E. Anderson, both of Company C. McBride had sustained injuries considered fatal at the Wilderness. Miller, who was with the wagon train, did not know of McBride's wounding until arriving at Spotsylvania, and on the morning of May 10, set out to bring Anderson a haversack of rations. To reach Anderson in the unit's temporary ditch and breastworks, the young black had to dodge Yankee sharpshooters, trying earnestly to "pick him off." When he finally arrived, Anderson told him how to find McBride and ordered the servant to leave after dark and "go and nurse the captain until he died and then return to me." When the Yankees attacked the Texans in full force later that day, Miller requested a gun and ammunition. Anderson obliged and later reported that the slave stood by his side, and no man ever fought "harder and better than he did and when the enemy tried to cross our little breastworks and we clubbed and bayoneted them off, no one used his bayonet with more skill, and effort, than Levi Miller." Miller was heard during the

17 Joskins, "A Sketch of Hood's Texas Brigade," in UTSA, 170.

18 Ltr fragment, Mark Smither to_____, June1864, in SHSU. Bailey had been wounded at Gaines' Mill, Second Manassas, and Gettysburg, as well as having been taken prisoner at Second Manassas. His wounds at Gettysburg earned him a discharge certificate which he kept in his pocket thereafter while continuing in service and fighting with his company. Pomeroy, *War Memoirs*, 79; Simpson, *Compendium*, 174; Moore, *Men of the Bayou City Guards*, 86-87; Leon County Historical Book Survey, *History of Leon County, Texas*, 19.

19 Ltr fragment, Mark Smither to ____, June, 1864, in UTSA, 1864.

hand-to-hand fighting to shout "Give 'em hell, Lee!" Soon thereafter, the 5th Texas supposedly "voted" Miller into the regiment by a unanimous vote of the men "as a full-fledged soldier, and for the remainder of the war saw active combat in Virginia."[20]

After the action on May 10, the Texans, though not directly involved in any heavy fighting, remained constantly under fire of the Federal sharpshooters throughout the 12 days of fighting in the area. They remained prudently under cover behind their works while the fury of the fight raged elsewhere along the Confederate lines. A third of the command always stood watch at night, while the rest slept fully clothed and geared up, guns in hand. O. T. Hanks of the brigade reported that "[w]e were not allowed to take off our shoes, notwithstanding it had been days and days since we had had them off." The circumstances dictated that the dead be buried immediately behind the breastworks, their shallow graves scraped out by comrades lying flat on the ground.[21]

On May 11, the Confederate forces watched the Union wounded, trapped in no-man's land between the lines, suffer and die. Whenever they sent their ambulances out to aid these wounded, Yankee sharpshooters forced them back, leaving their own comrades to die in agony. "We have now ended the sixth day of very heavy fighting,"

20 When he arrived in Richmond in 1861, McBride wrote to his brother living in Rockbridge Country, Virginia, requesting he send him one of his servants. The brother sent Miller, who accompanied McBride during all the fighting around Richmond in 1862 and on the Maryland campaign. When McBride was wounded at Second Manassas, Miller stayed at the hospital and nursed him back to health. Both men rejoined the regiment in time for Fredericksburg. Miller went to Suffolk with the regiment that winter. During the Gettysburg campaign, Miller confronted a number of his relatives at New Castle, Pennsylvania, who had fled from bondage in Virginia. "They tried to get Levi to desert – but he would not." Miller endured Chickamauga and the severe winter in East Tennessee. After Spotsylvania, Miller found McBride and again nursed him back to health. He later received a Confederate pension from the State of Virginia for his service. Dying in 1921 at Opequon, Virginia, and buried at Lexington, his coffin was draped with the Stars and Bars "in a hero's funeral." The Winchester *Evening Star*, in a front page obituary wrote that Miller "was affectionately known among the white as well as colored people of this section as the grand old man of his race. He always had a deep love for everything southern, and although born a slave, it was his loyalty to his state that led him to enter the southern army and fight through the four entire years of war." [Obviously, given the circumstances, some poetic license was involved in the telling]. J. E. Anderson to B. C. Shull, June 6, 1907; Joe Henry Segars and Charles Kelly Barrow, *Black Southerners in the Confederate Army* (Gretna, LA, 2001), 194-96; Winchester *Evening Star*, November 11, 1921: Ervin L. Jordan, *Black Confederates and Afro-Yankees in Civil War Virginia* (Charlottesville, VA, 1995), 196; Vernon R. Padgett, "Black Confederates: Southern Fantasy or Historical Fact?" Part II, SCV California, accessed November 20, 2009, www.scvcalifornia.blogspot.com; Cenantua Blog, "Some Thoughts on Levi Miller," accessed November 22, 2009, https://cenantua.wordpress.com/2008/09/28/some-thoughts-on-levi-miller/. B. C. Shull was the chairman of the Confederate Pension Board of Frederick County, Virginia.

21 Pomeroy, "War Memoirs," 80-81; Hanks, *Captain Benton's Company*, 31, 41.

General Grant reported, "[and] the result up to this time is much in our favor. I intend to fight it out on this line if it takes all summer." His simple declaration spoke volumes about Grant's tenacity and the tenor of future operations in Virginia. Relentless, brutal combat lay ahead. He probably did not anticipate, however, that final victory in the campaign would not arrive for another eleven, blood-drenched months.[22]

Grant envisioned a massive, coordinated attack on May 12, with Burnside moving from the east, Hancock from the north, simultaneously hitting the Mule Shoe, with Wright's and Warren's corps in reserve. Recognizing the apex of the salient as his Achilles heel, Ewell placed 22 guns in that area. Then, before the attack, a grievous miscalculation had relocated the Confederate artillery to the rear. Just then the Federals hit, overwhelming the Confederates in the right of the Mule Shoe, and resulting in the capture of thousands. Only the Confederates on the extreme left and right of the salient held firm. As Brig. Gen. John Gordon moved to seal the breach, Lee rode to the front, prepared to lead the charge. Gordon insisted that his men would save the day, but Lee had to retire to the rear. Once he did, Gordon went forward, stemming the onslaught in brutal hand-to-hand fighting until Ewell could move in more reinforcements.[23]

Within two and a half hours, Grant's attack had run out of steam, and he then ordered in his reserves: Warren's V and Wright's VI Corps. Wright hit the western angle of the Mule Shoe, and continuous, bloody hand-to-hand combat ensued for hours in that "Bloody Angle" as it came to be called. Warren, ordered to attack Laurel Hill's breastworks where the 5th Texas stood, hesitated, with some of his troops refusing to advance. When his attack eventually proceeded, it failed. Meanwhile, Burnside attacked piecemeal and failed to link with Hancock. Thus the Confederate right maintained a foothold at the base of the Mule Shoe. By afternoon, the Confederate defenses proved so effective that Lee ordered a counterattack, disrupting Burnside's further advance. By 3:00 p.m., the two sides had fought to a stalemate.[24]

Grant responded by throwing still more divisions against the Bloody Angle to probe Lee's weak spot. By then, however, the disorganization of Federal troops

22 Law, "Wilderness to Cold Harbor, 4:129; Trudeau, *Bloody Roads South*, 164-65; Simpson, *Lee's Grenadier Guard*, 413.

23 M. S. Stringfellow, "Letter to Editor of Richmond Times," *SHSP*, (1893), 21:247; Catlett J. Gibson, "The Battle of Spotsylvania Court House, May 12, 1864," *SHSP*, (1904), 21:204; George Q. Peyton, *A Civil War Record for 1864-1865*, Robert A. Hodge, ed. (Fredericksburg, VA, 1981), 27; Gordon, *Reminiscences of the Civil War*, 278-79; Rhea, *Battle of Spotsylvania*, 250-51.

24 *OR* 36, pt. 1, 1057; Horace Porter, *Campaigning With Grant* (Bloomington, IN, 1961), 103-05; Lowry, *No Turning Back*, 313-17; W. W. Smith, "General Lee to the Rear," in *SHSP*, (1880), 8:562-66; Commager, *The Blue and the Gray*, 988.

already at the front meant that additional units just added to the confusion. Fighting raged at the Bloody Angle all afternoon. As the rain came down in sheets, the trenches literally ran red with blood. In some places, the wounded and dying were trampled into the mud in the frenzied fighting. Flags of both armies would often fly simultaneously over the same breastworks. Troops reached over the breastworks to fire on the enemy or spear him with bayonets. Federal artillery blasted men to pieces. Periodically, one side would get the order to "clear the trench," and the men hoisted corpses over the ramparts to fall on the enemy beyond. However, the Texans never despaired. Polley reported hearing the comforting words "All right on the left," and "All right on the right," and "We've had a desperate time of it in the center, but we're not whipped to hurt." The slaughter continued even after dark, until the Federals began falling back at midnight. Lee then ordered a new set of earthworks across the base of the salient and by daybreak on May 13, his men had fallen back to occupy them.[25]

Grant did not seek a truce to bury his dead or gather up the wounded. Given the proximity of the breastworks and the ubiquitous snipers, "no man could go into the no-man's land between the lines and live." Thus, many of the 3,000 Yankees killed at Spotsylvania lay between the lines, their bodies blackened and bloated by the hot Virginia sun. The stench became so unbearable that the Confederates finally had to set barrels of tar on fire in front of their breastworks "to modify the smell."[26]

That evening, with Lee still in front of Spotsylvania, Grant decided to try to maneuver him out from his works. He ordered the II, V, and VI Corps to shift eastward, lengthening his left flank and realigning the Union position from an east-west to a north-south direction along the Fredericksburg Road. These corps accomplished the shift on night of May 14 and 15.[27]

Late on May 14, Anderson reported to Lee that the enemy had disappeared from his extreme left flank. Lee ordered Field's Division on his extreme left at Laurel Hill to move to the Confederate right flank. By noon the next day, the 5th Texas filed onto Brock Road and began marching to Zion Church, where Lee had his headquarters on the Massaponax Church Road. After marching southeast across the rear of the

25 *OR* 36, pt. 2, 656-57; Commager, *The Blue and the Gray*, 988, 995-96; Peyton, *A Civil War Record*, 27; Blight, *When This Cruel War Is Over*, 296-98; Matters, *If It Takes All Summer*, 206-07; Law, "Wilderness to Cold Harbor," in *B&L*, 4:129-30.Gordon, *Reminiscences of the Civil War*, 285. The Smithsonian Institution in Washington, DC contains a 22 inch oak cut down by small arms fire at the Bloody Angle on May 12, 1864, testifying to the enormity of the small arms fire that day.

26 Pomeroy, "War Memoirs," 81; Henry, *Story of the Confederacy*, 356, 361.

27 Blight, *When This Cruel War Is Over*, 296; Rhea, *Battle for Spotsylvania*, 308; Polley, *Hood's Texas Brigade*, 241.

Confederate army to a position south of A. P. Hill's Third Corps, along the Brock Road, the Texans commenced digging new trenches by nightfall, securing Lee's right flank.[28]

Upon discovering that Hancock had vacated the Spotsylvania front on May 15, Lee pulled Kershaw's Division from the trenches, reuniting it with Field's on the army's southern flank and leaving Laurel Hill vacant. Anderson's men finished their new line by May 16. Field's Division manned the trenches extending from Zion Church to the Po River, with Gregg's Texans overlapping Early's right flank near Zion Church in order to block the Massaponax Church Road. A masterpiece of military engineering, the First Corps' line, situated on a ridge, looked across a mile of open ground toward the Federal line. One Texan boasted at the time that the fortifications were so strong he only regretted not being able to carry them with him when the army moved on![29]

Grant's attempts to break the stalemate at Spotsylvania had not ended, however. On May 17, when the roads had dried enough to support a movement, Meade ordered Hancock's and Wright's corps to attack Lee's second line behind the Bloody Angle. This attack began at around 4:00 a.m. on May 18 with a furious cannonade, followed up by a futile series of infantry assaults. The fighting diminished significantly after 9:00 a.m., when Hancock convinced Grant that the Confederate position was impregnable. "We found the enemy so strongly entrenched," Meade wrote, "that even Grant thought it was useless to knock our heads against a brick wall, and directed a suspension."[30]

The following day, May 19, General Ewell tried to locate and strike the Federal right flank by leading his corps out of the entrenchments in a turning movement to the north and east. The effort found the Union extreme right located on some high ground at the Harris farm near the Fredericksburg Road. Brig. Gen. Stephen D. Ramseur's Brigade, with Gordon's Division in support, met with strong resistance from Yankee "heavy artillery units" (artillery units turned infantry) recently moved into the field. Before long it became apparent that these "Heavies" came close to enveloping Ramseur's command on both flanks. After some sharp fighting, the Confederates slipped back into their entrenchments and by 10:00 p.m. the firing ceased. The heavy artillery regiments on the Harris farm lost 1,535 casualties and

28 *OR* 51, pt. 2, 929; Rhea, *To the North Anna River*, 87, 124-27.

29 Rhea, *To the North Anna River*, 124-25; Gallagher, *Fighting for the Confederacy*, 381; Coles, *From Huntsville to Appomattox*, 171.

30 *OR* 51, pt. 2, 939, 942, 1019; Coles, *From Huntsville to Appomattox*, 171; Gallagher, *Fighting for the Confederacy*, 381; Rhea, *To the North Anna River*, 124; Trudeau, *Bloody Roads South*, 196.

Ewell about 900. The combat was the final engagement in the long and bloody Spotsylvania campaign.[31]

The North Anna

On May 20, Grant, accepting the impossibility of moving through or over the Confederates here, instead sidled to his left yet again and maneuvered his army south around Lee's right toward the North Anna River. Lee had been alerted and first ordered Ewell to move south on the Telegraph Road to Hanover Junction at daybreak on May 20 to protect the junction of two railroad lines there. Ewell's Corps moved to Anderson's right, establishing a position along the Po River. Lee had ordered Anderson to be ready "at a moment's notice" to move south. On the evening of May 21, once it became clear the Federals had moved on, the 5th Texas, and the rest of the Texans, filed out of their trenches and hurried forward to catch up with Ewell's men. At 8:00 p.m., it fell into line and began its march south to Traveler's Rest, then east to Mud Tavern, and finally turned right down the Telegraph Road, past Harris's Store and Golansville toward Mt. Carmel Church.[32]

Lee gathered his generals at Southworth House near the Po River that evening to issue final orders. As the Confederates vacated their lines around Spotsylvania, their ordnance details collected over 125,000 pounds of Yankee lead shot at (and missing) Lee's army, an ironic gift from their enemy which would be melted down, recast, and shot right back at them.[33]

The 5th Texas continued moving south throughout the afternoon the next day. Except for a two-hour rest in the early morning of May 22, the Texans marched continuously for the next 20 hours. Smither noted that they "marched nearly 40 miles between 8 o'clock one night and 5 o'clock the next evening and lo! To Gen Grants surprise and discomfiture we were there to dispute his passage across the Anna River!" The head of the column reached the North Anna River at 12:15 p.m. on May 22, and the regiment crossed over to the south side, bivouacking on the Richmond, Fredericksburg and Potomac Railroad near Hanover Junction. By that evening, Lee's

31 *OR* 36, pt. 1, 1057-58, 1067; Field, "Wilderness to Cold Harbor," in *B&L*, 4:548; Polley, *Hood's Texas Brigade*, 241; Trudeau, *Bloody Roads South*, 213; Matter, *If It Takes All Summer* 315-23. Union losses at Spotsylvania were placed at 18,399; Confederate estimated at approximately 10,000. In the two weeks since the campaign had opened, Grant had lost over 36,000 men.

32 *OR* 36, pt. 1, 1067; Rhea, *To the North Anna River*, 230-31, 249-53; Gallagher, *Fighting for the Confederacy*, 387.

33 Matter, *If It Takes All Summer*, 340-41;Trudeau, *Bloody Roads South*, 213, 229-32; Henry, *Story of the Confederacy*, 361; Simpson, *Lee's Grenadier Guard*, 413-14.

entire army had crossed over. As Lee had once again anticipated, Grant appeared on the north side of the river the next morning, and both sides quickly dug in, preparing for battle. Taking full advantage of his interior lines, Lee had effectively blocked the Federals' southward movement a second time.[34]

The Rebels understood their situation, and morale remained solid. Captain Watson Williams of Company F wrote on May 18 that "[t]he victory so far is decidedly in our favor, though the enemy of course claim all advantage." The army, he added, "is in the finest condition and spirits and anxious for Grant to make another attack. A perfect enthusiasm prevails . . . and the men are so confident of a decisive victory that they exhibit a delight in fighting." Despite their soaring spirits, the troops were nonetheless physically worn out—Anderson's Corps particularly. Since making the forced march from Gordonsville on May 4-5, the Texans had not seen their wagon trains, and few of them had been able to change clothes in all that time.[35]

The battle for the North Anna River began the afternoon of May 23. Warren's V Corps crossed the river upstream at Jericho Mill without opposition, and the Federals spent the rest of the day building bridges. Wilcox's Division of Hill's Corps attacked Warren that evening, but superior Federal numbers ultimately forced his withdrawal. Warren eventually moved his whole corps south of the river and began entrenching on the Virginia Central Railroad, Lee's connection to the Shenandoah Valley. Meanwhile, Hancock's Corps overran a redoubt guarding Chesterfield bridge on Telegraph Road, which the Confederates had unsuccessfully attempted to burn. The 5th Texas held a sector on the right center of the line near the Richmond, Fredericksburg & Potomac Railroad. It engaged in moderate skirmishing on the picket line but was not heavily involved. Downstream, the Yankees successful destroyed the Richmond, Fredericksburg & Potomac Railroad bridge.[36]

Lee met with his commanding generals that evening. Warren's successful crossing had cancelled his hopes of contesting all Grant's anticipated moves. He felt

34 *OR* 36, pt. I, 1057-58; Ltr fragment, Mark Smither to ____, June, 1864, in SHSU; Field, "Campaigns of 1864 and 1865," 458; Joskins, "A Sketch of Hood's Texas Brigade," UTSA 172-73; Henry, *Story of the Confederacy*, 361; Polley, *Hood's Texas Brigade*, 241.

35 Watson Williams to Sister, May 18, 1864, in CRC; Winkler, *Confederate Capital*, 172; Hanks, *Captain Benton's Company*, 41; Law, "Wilderness to Cold Harbor," in *B&L*, 4:548.

36 Rhea, *To the North Anna River*, 306-10, 314-15, 318-19; Lowry, *No Turning Back*, 422-23, 443; Trudeau, *Bloody Roads South*, 228-235; Foote, *Civil War Narrative*, 3: 267-68; Freeman, *R. E. Lee*, 3:357; Law, "Wilderness to Cold Harbor," in *B&L*, 4:136; Sorrell, *Recollections of a Staff Officer*, 244-45; Freeman, *Lee's Lieutenants*, 3: 496-501. Lee upbraided Hill for not using his entire corps, using just Wilcox to engage 15,000 Yankees. The outburst was uncharacteristic of Lee and indicated his discomfort from illness and stress. The hot-headed Hill, who had fallen out with every superior he had served under, held his tongue. Hill was well aware Lee was right.

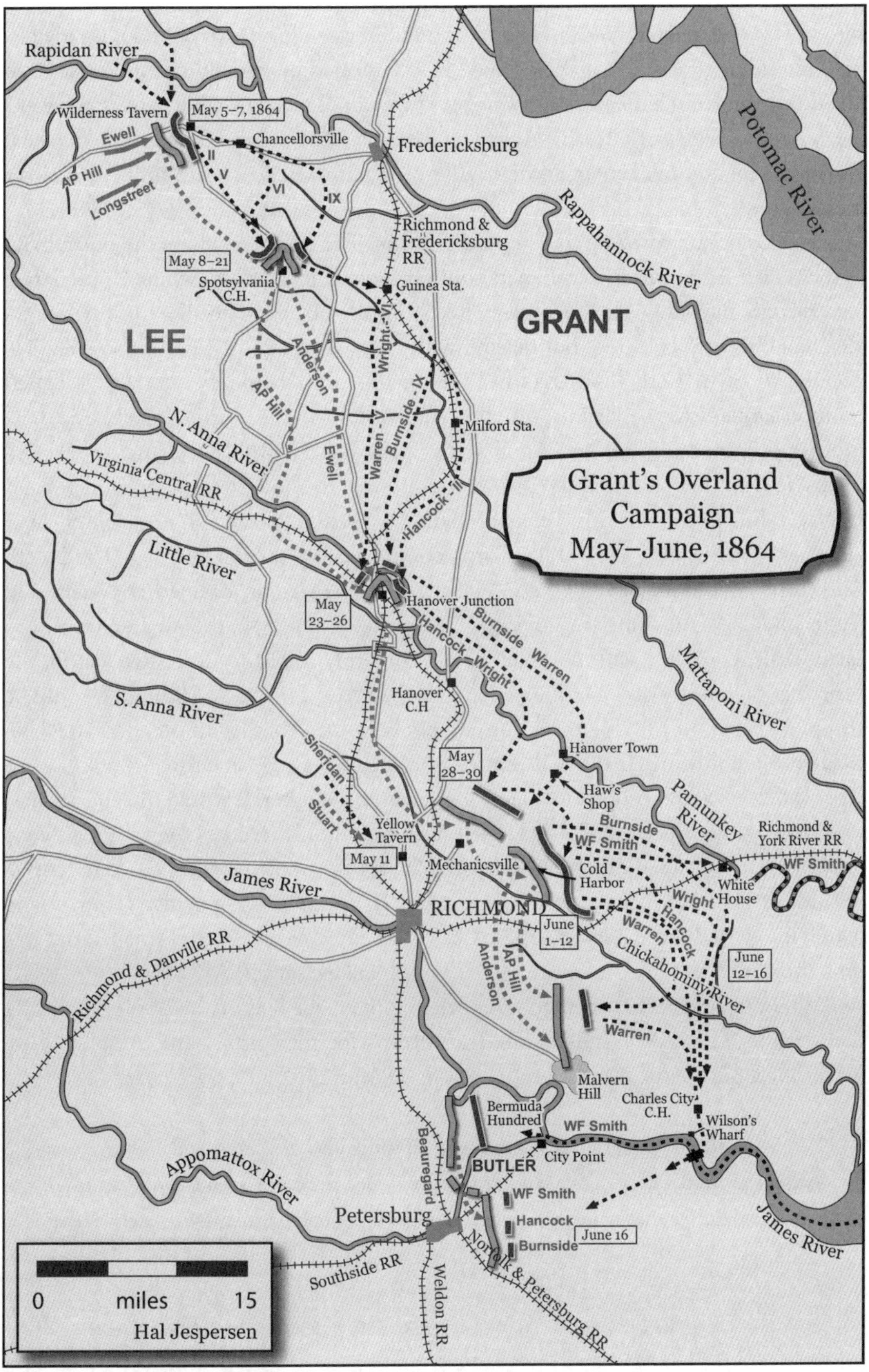
Grant's Overland Campaign
May–June, 1864
Rapidan River
Wilderness Tavern
May 5–7, 1864
Chancellorsville
Fredericksburg
Ewell
AP Hill
Longstreet
Potomac River
Rappahannock River
Richmond & Fredericksburg RR
May 8–21
Spotsylvania C.H.
Guinea Sta.
GRANT
LEE
Anderson
AP Hill
Wright - VI
Burnside - IX
Warren - V
Hancock - II
Ewell
Milford Sta.
N. Anna River
Virginia Central RR
Little River
May 23–26
Hanover Junction
Burnside
Warren
Hancock
Wright
Hanover C.H
Mattaponi River
S. Anna River
Sheridan
Stuart
Hanover Town
May 28–30
Haw's Shop
Pamunkey River
Richmond & York River RR
WF Smith
Yellow Tavern
May 11
Mechanicsville
Cold Harbor
White House
James River
RICHMOND
June 1–12
Chickahominy River
June 12–16
Richmond & Danville RR
Malvern Hill
Charles City C.H.
Wilson's Wharf
Bermuda Hundred
City Point
BUTLER
Beauregard
Appomattox River
Petersburg
Hancock
Burnside
June 16
Southside RR
Weldon RR
Norfolk & Petersburg RR
0 miles 15
Hal Jespersen

certain Hancock would cross over the captured bridge the next day. And if he tried to fight him along the riverbank, he would be outgunned by Federal cannon posted on the higher northern bank, as well as be outflanked by Warren moving eastward toward the Virginia Central Railroad. However, Lee was not about to abandon the vital Hanover Junction rail center, so he could not withdraw across the South Anna River either.

The Gray Fox came up with a bold solution. The one area where the north bank of the North Anna was lower than its south bank was at Ox Ford, where Confederate batteries definitely had the advantage. Lee's problem became not how to prevent an inevitable Federal crossing, but dealing with them once on his side of the river. He decided to pivot both his flanks back from the river in to an inverted V-shaped position similar to Spotsylvania, running southwest from the North Anna to one of its tributaries named Little River. Anderson's (including the 5th Texas) and Ewell's old Corps held the right leg of this V, running southeast to some swampy ground beyond Hanover Junction. The 5th Texas and Field's division posted in the center, with Kershaw's on its left. A. P. Hill's Corps comprised the shorter, left leg. The North Anna River, adjoining Brig. Gen. William Mahone's right, defined the apex and Anderson's left. All along this inverted V, five miles in length, the men erected deep earthworks, complete with complex abatis. Superbly suited to defensive action, the construction could also be employed as a springboard for attack. Either leg could be stripped of men to provide maximum numbers to the other leg in order to attack an isolated Federal wing. It did not matter *which* Federal wing, as either would have to cross the river *twice* in order adequately to reinforce the other. It would thus be unlikely to arrive in time, since the Confederates at most had only to cross the four mile wide base of their V-shaped defenses. Additionally, they occupied a formidable defensive position at Ox Ford. Lee was setting a massive trap, and he was positive Grant would march into it with his eyes wide open. Lee commented to a newspaperman about this time that "[i]f I can get one more pull at him, I will defeat him."[37]

While awaiting what seemed an inevitable fight, the Texans had time to ponder their plight. They were still required to sleep with their arms, and supplies were becoming a huge issue. One member wrote on May 23:

> We have had to undergo all in the way of watching, marching and fighting our natures are capable of, since we left Gordonsville. Have not seen our wagon train since, and during that time have had no changes of a single garment. We reached here

37 Lowry, *No Turning Back*, 423; Trudeau, *Bloody Roads South*, 236; Foote, *Civil War Narrative*, 3:272-73; Rhea, *To the North Anna River*, 321-24.

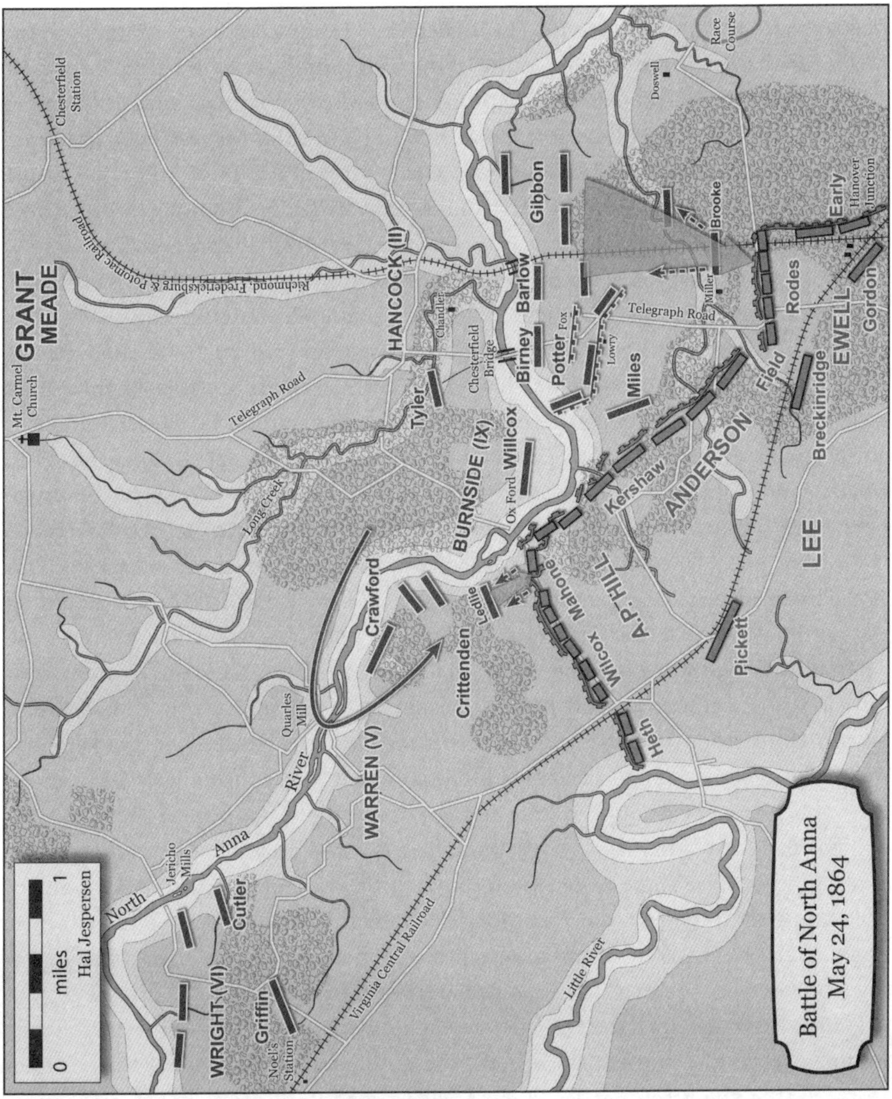

last night after a continuous march of over thirty hours, and I have seen my horse for the first time since the fight commenced.[38]

Grant, misreading Lee's pullback on May 24 as a retreat toward Richmond, ordered a general pursuit. He supplemented V Corps with Wright's VI Corps.

38 Winkler, *Confederate Capital*, 172.

Recognizing the heavy defenses at Ox Ford, he slowed his advance on the Confederate flanks awaiting the capture of the fortifications at the ford. Burnside's IX Corps in the Federal center faced Ox Ford. He pushed his corps forward seeking to cross the river, bringing his corps even with V and VI Corps. Major General Thomas L. Crittenden's division had crossed the North Anna above the ford by 3:00 p.m., establishing contact with Brig. Gen. Samuel Crawford's Division of V Corps. Brig. Gen. James H. Ledlie's brigade of Crittenden's division pushed forward alone in spite of cautionary orders, and attacked the western flank of the Ox Ford defenses. Ledlie, inebriated at the time, was pummeled first by a heavy artillery barrage, then ravaged by small arms fire once his troops came within range. Crawford's division attempted to provide support, but artillery fire halted the effort. Ultimately, the Confederates realized the attacking force was so small that a counterattack might surround and crush it. Several regiments advanced from the Rebel fortifications doing just that, while a sudden thunderstorm added to the impact of their charge. Soon, "[e]very man became his own general," and the Yankees scurried hastily back to their earthworks.[39]

Meanwhile, Hancock's II Corps, isolated from the rest of the army, with his back to the river, advanced cautiously from Chesterfield Bridge down Telegraph Road and the rail line toward Hanover Junction, the vital rail intersection. In the van, Col. Thomas A. Smyth's Brigade reconnoitered for the corps. Maj. Gen. Robert E. Rodes's Division of Ewell's corps and Field's division, of Anderson's Corps, guarded that junction, with Rodes' facing east along the railroad tracks and Field's, including the 5th Texas, facing north behind a farm road. The regiment held a position not far from the Richmond, Fredericksburg and Potomac Railroad.[40]

North of the farm road, some of Field's units formed a strong line of skirmishers and sharpshooters. These troops protected by rifle pits and trenches, and supported by a two-gun section of the Richmond Howitzers, arrested the Federal advance. Smyth then assaulted the skirmish line repeatedly, finally capturing its rifle pits. Just as the Confederates counterattacked, a thunderstorm broke loose. The opposing sides held their fire, concerned their powder would get wet by repeated firing. Fighting then resumed when the storm passed, with the Confederates recovering their former works. As Smyth retreated at dark, Grant called a halt for the day's offensive efforts.[41]

39 Rhea, *To the North Anna River*, 342-43, 252; Trudeau, *Bloody Roads South*, 240; Salmon, *Virginia Battlefield Guide*, 285-87; Lowry, *No Turning Back*, 324.

40 Rhea, *To the North Anna River*, 342-43, 352; Trudeau, *Bloody Roads South*, 240-41; Foote, *Civil War Narrative*, 3: 274-75; Salmon, *Virginia Battlefield Guide*, 285-87.

41 Rhea, *To the North Anna River*, 286-87, 352-53; Trudeau, *Bloody Roads South*, 240-41; Foote, *Civil War Narrative*, 3: 274-75; OR 36, pt. 1, 78-79; Ulysses Grant, *Personal Memoirs of U. S. Grant*, 2 vols. (New York, 1885-1886), 2:249-50.

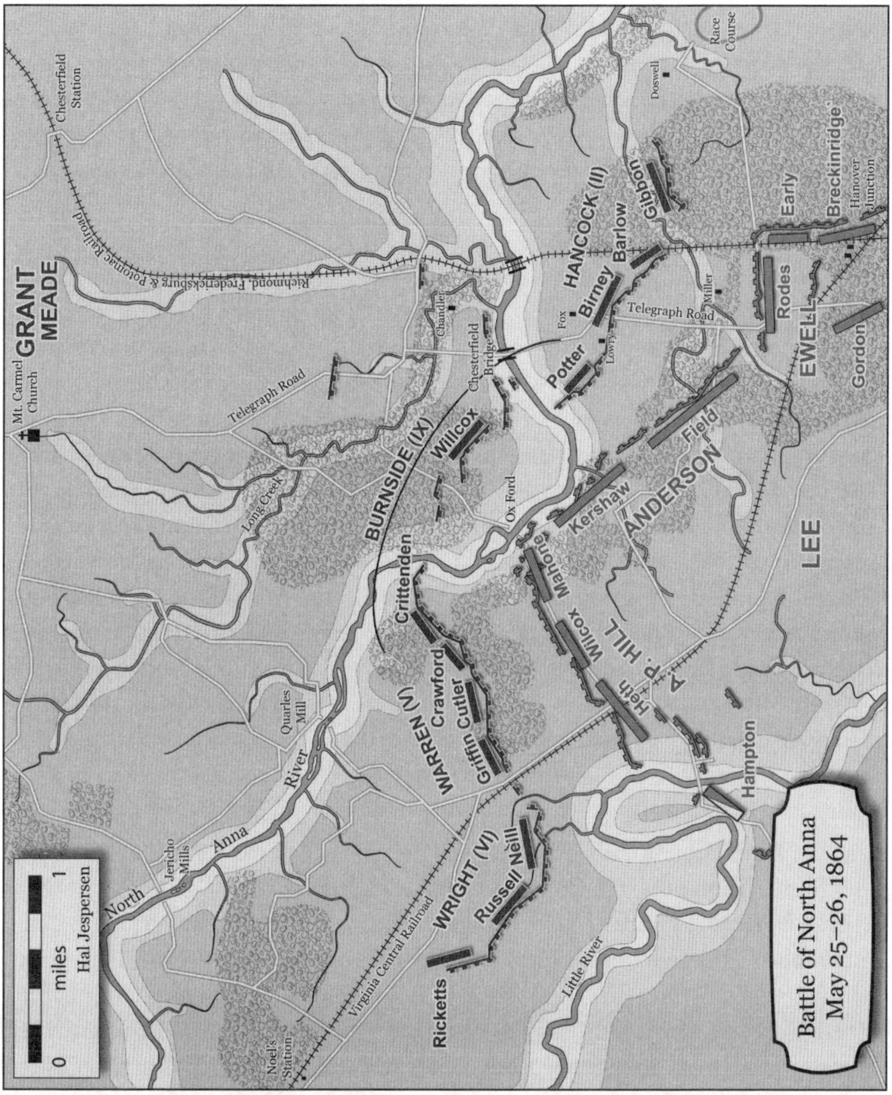

That evening and the next day, Grant discovered the strength and extent of Lee's defenses, and the mortal danger of his situation, with a large portion of his army separated and isolated from the remainder. He thus ordered his men to entrench, and spent May 25-26 skirmishing and probing for a weakness in the Southern defenses. Unable to discover one, Grant disengaged the army on May 26-27, and commenced maneuvering again on Lee's right flank. Lee, still indisposed from his illness, could do little to counter Grant's movement. However, the genius of Lee's inverted V had stopped Grant in his tracks, and displayed the Southern commander's skill at defensive warfare, as well as his overall engineering and military acumen.[42] Grant crossed the Pamunkey River around Hanovertown, some 17 miles from Hanover Junction, moving toward Totopotomoy Creek. Lee left the North Anna on the morning of May 27, shortly after Grant's absence was verified. He fell back south, traveling parallel with Grant's movements, remaining between the Federals and Richmond. The 5th Texas, with Field's Division, after three or four days of skirmishing and sharpshooting along the North Anna River, led the march of Anderson's Corps from Hanover Junction to Totopotomoy Creek. The Texans moved south, following the line of the Richmond, Fredericksburg and Potomac Railroad about eight miles to Ashland Station, then turned to the southeast and continued on another seven miles to Atlee's Station on the Virginia Central Railroad. The wagon trains were sent back across the South Anna and encamped between the Half Sink and Hughes' Cross-Roads, a few miles southwest of Ashland Station. On May 28, Early's Corps, ahead of the regiment on the same road, temporarily impeded its march. After crossing Totopotomoy Creek, they went into bivouac that evening between Hundley's Corners and the Walnut Grove Church, about four miles southeast of Atlee's Station, having marched over 28 miles in two days, ending their long trek within five miles of the capital.[43]

Totopotomoy Creek

The morning of May 29 crept in quietly. Lee positioned his army firmly on the south bank of Totopotomoy Creek, a swampy tributary of the Pamunkey River nine miles from Richmond. Hill's Corps formed the left, facing north to cover the Virginia Central and the road from Hanover Court House, with his right flank resting on high ground above the Pamunkey. Early's Corps took up the center from Pole Green Church and Opossum Creek east toward Polly Hundley's Corner. Here, the line curved to the south, where the 5th Texas and the rest of Anderson's Corps constituted the right flank, posted on Shady Grove Road. The Totopotomoy Creek line sliced across the main roads and rail lines leading south and southwest to the capital. Lee's "formation along Totopotomoy Creek was a masterpiece"—to attack it, Grant would

42 *OR* 36, pt. 1, 21, 78-79 1058; Rhea, *To the North Anna River*, 286-87, 353; Grant, *Personal Memoirs of U. S. Grant*, 2:249-50; Swinton, *Campaigns of the Army of the Potomac*, 477; Lowry, *No Turning Back*, 424; Foote, *Civil War Narrative*, 3:273-74; Law, "Wilderness to Cold Harbor," in *B&L*, 4:137-38; Freeman, *Lee's Lieutenants*, 3:498.

43 *OR* 36, Pt. 1, 1058; Simpson, *Lee's Grenadier Guard*, 417; Trudeau, *Bloody Roads South*, 248-49; Foote, *Civil War Narrative*, 3:277.

have to cross the creek and swampy lowlands and charge uphill across cleared ground and entanglements into "the teeth of the rebel entrenchments."[44]

That afternoon, with the Federals reported advancing, the Texans geared up for battle. The 5th Texas moved out with the rest of Field's Division, then turned around and occupied a marshy area behind Early, with Fields dispatching two regiments to fill in as skirmishers at intervals covering the swampy marshland between Early and Maj. Gen. John C. Breckinridge's lines.[45]

Following some probing, the Union troops under Burnside crossed the Totopotomoy the next day, forcing the Confederates back near Polly Hundley's Corner. Meanwhile, north of Strawhorn Creek, part of Hancock's corps captured Early's forward field works occupied by pickets, and then reversed the trenches there so they faced the main Confederate line to the west. However, the Federals made little headway against the stout Confederate defenses. Around noon, Lee, after reconnoitering the ground with Early, determined that Warren's corps on the Federal left was still moving into position near Bethesda Church near Shady Grove Church Road.[46]

Lee thus gained a reasonable impression of Grant's movements, and what they portended. Two whole Yankee corps had by then crossed the Totopotomoy and were positioned on the near bank, facing west. Lee explained to Richard Anderson that after fortifying their line, the enemy would make another move by their left flank toward the Chickahominy. His most trusted scout had recently reported the Federals appeared to be marching for Old Cold Harbor.[47]

Early on May 30, Lee spotted an opportunity in all of this maneuvering to possibly prevent Grant's movement by striking the part of his army already across the Totopotomoy in Early's front. Anticipating yet another swing southeast, Early had already had his corps cut cross-country traces from its Shady Grove Church Road lines all the way down to the Old Church Road, which ran from Mechanicsville through Bethesda Church. Cavalry reports indicated that the left flank of the Yankee line along Shady Grove Church Road barely touched that road to the south. Early contended this flank ripe for turning, and Lee agreed, and designated him to lead an

44 Gordon C. Rhea, *Cold Harbor: Grant and Lee, May 26-June 3, 1864* (Baton Rouge, 2002), 59-60, 91-92, 97-98, 108; Trudeau, *Bloody Roads South*, 122, 248-49; Salmon, *Virginia Battlefield Guide*, 290; Law, "From the Wilderness to Cold Harbor," in *B&L*, 4:137. Because of Ewell's illness, Early took over temporary command of Second Corps on May 27.

45 *OR* 36, pt. 1, 1058; Henry, *Story of the Confederacy*, 361; Simpson, *Lee's Grenadier Guard*, 417.

46 Salmon, *Virginia Battlefield Guide*, 290-91.

47 Rhea, *Cold Harbor*, 91-92, 97-98; Law, "From the Wilderness to Cold Harbor," in *B&L*, 4:137.

attack designed to discourage this latest edge around the Confederate right. With Bethesda Church on the Old Church Road secured, Early would be able to swing northward, interjecting his troops behind the forward elements of the Warren's V Corps.[48]

Anderson's Corps was designated to support this attack. Field's Division, including the 5th Texas, would move to the left of Early's position on Shady Grove Road and take his place on that line. Lee admonished Anderson to "[d]o everything for the grand object, the destruction of the enemy." To Early, his words were far blunter: "We must destroy this army of Grant's before he gets to the James River. If he gets there it will become a siege, and then it will be a mere question of time." If he did not stop Grant this time, Lee would confront the very circumstance he had fought so hard to avoid—the loss of all freedom to maneuver.[49]

Early delivered a disjointed and piecemeal attack at Bethesda Church, however. Rodes's Division, leading the assault, struck Warren's Corps at 2:00 p.m. but was quickly repulsed, and his promised support did not even show. Field's Division, including the regiment, did not arrive until almost nightfall and could not participate in the day's action. Lee's attack at Totopotomoy Creek melted away, and with it yet another opportunity. Unfortunately, Early had come closer to wrecking his *own* corps than to destroying a significant portion of Grant's army.[50]

Cold Harbor

Grant, having determined Lee's position at Totopotomoy Creek too strong to attack, decided instead to continue moving southeast toward the Chickahominy around Lee's right flank. He therefore continued to realign his men on an east-west axis in order to attack that flank directly. Brigadier General Alfred T. A. Torbert's division of Sheridan's cavalry reconnoitered to the south to locate Lee's right flank and secure the important intersection at Old Cold Harbor. This cavalry force, departing Haw's Shop on May 30, turned south at Old Church toward the

48 Lowry, *No Turning Back*, 440; Foote, *Civil War Narrative*, 3, 278-79; Trudeau, *Bloody Roads South*, 252-53.

49 Foote, *Civil War Narrative* 3: 279; Lowry, *No Turning Back*, 440. Lee saw the looming danger - beyond the Chickahominy was the James, where McClellan had sought sanctuary following Malvern Hill. There, Washington did not sustain him on the north bank of the river, nor in his plan to cross it and hit Richmond from the south astride its lines of supplies from Georgia and the Carolinas. Grant, however, was obviously held in much higher esteem than McClellan by Federal authorities.

50 Rhea, *Cold Harbor*, 124-25, 139-56; Trudeau, *Bloody Roads South*, 254-59; Foote, *Civil War Narrative*, 3:279.

Chickahominy, securing the crossing at Matadequin Creek. Around 2:00 p.m., Torbert's forces clashed with a smaller body of Rebel cavalry probing for the Federal left near Matadequin Creek and forced them back toward Old Cold Harbor. The Confederate troopers rallied near that village, and Torbert remained to the east of it that night.[51]

On the same day Grant dispatched Warren's Corps back through Haw's Shop on the Old Church Road and then southeast, behind the main line of the army and across the Totopotomoy Creek toward Cold Harbor. He ordered Maj. Gen. William F. "Baldy" Smith, commander of XVIII Corps, to link with the army near Cold Harbor on another road from White House Landing. Thus augmented, Grant's numbers would swell to 108,000 versus Lee's 62,000. Smith began his movement about 3:30 p.m. on May 31, but it took a wrong turn when he acted upon old orders that had never been rescinded directing him to the northwest toward New Castle.[52]

On May 31, part of Brig. Gen. Thomas L. Clingman's Brigade of Hoke's Division reached Old Cold Harbor and positioned itself to the left of the Confederate cavalry there. When Torbert's Federals charged with drawn sabers, however, the outnumbered Confederates fled back a mile to the west and quickly entrenched. Torbert called off the pursuit, content to consolidate his position at Cold Harbor by reversing the Confederate works to face west. Later that night, Sheridan, concerned with the Confederate buildup to his west, ordered Torbert to retire back to his camps east of Old Cold Harbor. Grant's interest in this area steadily grew, however, so he ordered Sheridan to hold this settlement "at all hazards." So back went Torbert at 1:00 a.m. and discovered the lucky fact that the Confederates had failed to detect his previous departure.[53]

Occupation of the intersection at Old Cold Harbor put Grant in position to turn the right flank of Lee's army. Lee, however, meant to block this latest Federal shift to the left by retaking Cold Harbor. So another race ensued—would Lee's army fortify their position there in time to resist an attack, or would Grant mount an assault before the Southerners could complete their works ? After the month's bloodbath, both sides needed reinforcements. Lee had dispatched numerous messages to Richmond, warning that if his operations failed for lack of reinforcements, the capital would fall,

51 Trudeau, *Bloody Roads South*, 259, 262; Rhea, *Cold Harbor*, 135, 138, 153; Foote, *Civil War Narrative*, 3:281-83; Salmon, *Virginia Battlefield Guide*, 292-94.

52 Foote, *Civil War Narrative*, 3:281-82; Rhea, *Cold Harbor*, 191-93, 197, 205; Trudeau, *Bloody Roads South*, 260, 267; Salmon, *Virginia Battlefield Guide*, 295.

53 Rhea, *Cold Harbor*, 184, 193-94; Trudeau, *Bloody Roads South*, 262-63; Edward G. Longacre, *Lee's Cavalrymen: A History of the Mounted Forces of the Army of Northern Virginia 1861-1865* (Mechanicsberg, PA, 2002), 296; Foote, *Civil War Narrative*, 3:282-83.

despite its formidable defenses. In response, Maj. Gen. Robert F. Hoke's Division quit the Howlett Line (the outer defenses of Richmond) moving by train on the Virginia Central, and marching from the Richmond depot through Mechanicsville, arriving in the afternoon of May 31. Anderson had orders to pass behind Early that night, connect with and take command of Hoke's Division.[54]

Grant continued "'sliding' to the left until he [was] . . . nearly into the position on the Peninsula that McClellan had in /62," Smither noted, but ironically with the loss of many thousands of men, "when he could have attained the same position without the loss of a thousand men." On June 1, the two armies faced each other near Cold Harbor, adjacent to the 1862 Gaines' Mill battlefield, where the Texans had fought so well two years before. Only this time, the opposing forces were reversed, with the Confederates facing northeast, instead of southeast. For the fifth time in less than a month, Lee had successfully thwarted Grant's effort to outflank him. To do this, however, he had been forced to yield valuable ground—Richmond now lay a mere twelve miles away.[55]

Cold Harbor was about to become "one of the hard and terrible names of the Civil War, perhaps the most terrible one of all." Though Grant probably never heard the name before, Sheridan had used it as a checkpoint following his Richmond raid. It was a vital, strategic location where five roads came together, halfway between Totopotomoy Creek and the Chickahominy River, both useful anchors for a line of defense. By holding this location, where the roads from Bethesda Church and White House Landing merged, Grant could extend his left to meet Smith's XVIII Corps (from Butler's Army of the James) advancing toward him from the east. The battle-hardened veterans of both armies knew the area well. As the Federals marched toward their fate at the little crossroads, one veteran remarked "There was where my brother was killed," pointing to a former skirmish line trench from the second battle of the Seven Days campaign two years prior—Gaines' Mill. As Anderson moved behind Early's corps that evening to connect with Hoke, the Federals could see and

54 Freeman, *Lee's Lieutenants*, 3:504; Rhea, *Cold Harbor*, 159-60, 162-64; Foote, *Civil War Narrative*, 3:280; Salmon, *Virginia Battlefield Guide*, 294-95. While Grant enjoyed a considerable numerical superiority, a month of bloody fighting had decimated and disorganized his regiments. Additionally, the terms of enlistment for many regiments would expire in the coming months. Thus, he felt a great need for reinforcements, regardless of his opponent's more desperate situation.

55 Ltr fragment, Mark Smither to ___, June, 1864, in SHSU. Rhea, *Cold Harbor*, 159-60, 162-63; Ernest B. Furgurson, *Not War But Murder: Cold Harbor 1864* (New York, 2000), 79-80; Thomas L. Clingman, "Second Cold Harbor," in Histories of the Several Regiments and Battalions from North Carolina in the Great War 1861-'65, ed. Walter Clark (Goldsboro, NC, 1901), 199-202.

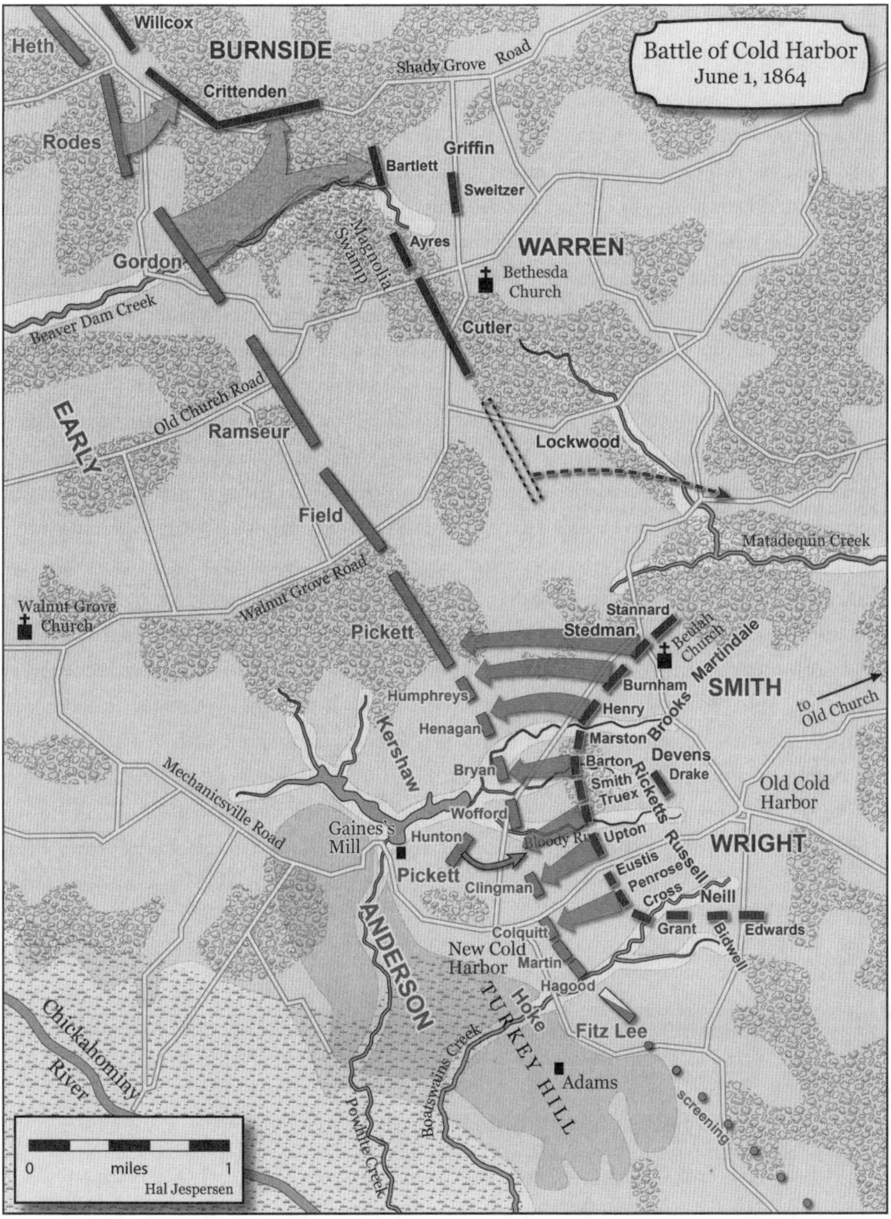
Battle of Cold Harbor
June 1, 1864
Heth
Willcox
BURNSIDE
Crittenden
Shady Grove Road
Rodes
Griffin
Bartlett
Sweitzer
Magnolia Swamp
Ayres
WARREN
Gordon
Bethesda Church
Beaver Dam Creek
Cutler
EARLY
Old Church Road
Ramseur
Lockwood
Field
Matadequin Creek
Walnut Grove Road
Walnut Grove Church
Stannard
Stedman
Beulah Church
Pickett
Martindale
Burnham
SMITH
Humphreys
Henry
to Old Church
Henagan
Brooks
Kershaw
Marston
Devens
Bryan
Barton
Smith
Drake
Truex
Ricketts
Old Cold Harbor
Mechanicsville Road
Wofford
Gaines's Mill
Hunton
Upton
Bloody Run
WRIGHT
Pickett
Eustis
Russell
Clingman
Penrose
Cross
Neill
Grant
Edwards
Colquitt
Bidwell
New Cold Harbor
Martin
ANDERSON
Hagood
Hoke
TURKEY HILL
Fitz Lee
Chickahominy River
Boatswains Creek
Adams
screening
Powhite Creek
0 miles 1
Hal Jespersen

hear both Field's and Pickett's men as they hurried toward Cold Harbor to join Kershaw.[56]

Anderson's planned to attack on June 1 with his lead divisions, Kershaw's and Hoke's, following up with Field's and Pickett's as they came on line. Hoke did not move out as ordered, however, and considerable delay and confusion ensued as the men formed into lines of battle that morning. Kershaw's attack did not start until near 8:00 a.m. Sheridan's 600-man front line, armed with either Sharps carbines or seven-shot Spencer magazine carbines, produced an hellish hail of lead at the oncoming Confederates. Severely mauled, Kershaw's force quickly fell back, a repulse so precipitous that the attack ended before Hoke's men on the right even realized it had begun.[57]

Kershaw withdrew his entire division out of range of the rapid-firing Union carbines, then launched a second attack about 10:00 a.m. that suffered a similar fate. By then, Wright's VI Corps began arriving from Grant's right flank on the Totopotomoy, taking over the breastworks from Sheridan's dismounted cavalry. After an all-night march, Wright's troops immediately began working to improve the Federal defenses. Ordered to advance, Wright withheld his attack until Smith arrived that afternoon. Meanwhile, Meade had decided the two corps insufficient for the impending attack and ordered Warren's V Corps to join, unless Warren deemed it "impracticable." Warren dispatched one division; however, faulty reconnaissance delayed it. Smith's road-weary troops now arrived and connected with Warren's line to the north. Grant became even more determined to shift the weight of his whole line down to Cold Harbor. At 3:30 p.m., he ordered Hancock to prepare for a withdrawal from the Union right at darkness, in order to extend the left flank where Sheridan's remaining two divisions were patrolling the space between Wright's line and the Chickahominy.[58]

56 Bruce Catton, *Grant Takes Command* (Boston, MA: Little Brown, 1968), 257-58; Furgurson, *Not War But Murder:* 77; *Trudeau, Bloody Roads South*, 269. Pickett's Division reunited with Lee's army on May 22.

57 *OR* 36, pt. 1, 1059, pt. 3, 446, 880; Joskins, "A Sketch of Hood's Texas Brigade, 173-74, in UTSA; Furgurson, *Not War But Murder*, 79-86; Polley, *Hood's Texas Brigade*, 241; Lowry, *No Turning Back*, 443-44, 450-51; Foote, *Civil War Narrative*, 3: 284-85; Rhea, *Cold Harbor*, 195-204, 209. The Sharps carbine was the best small arm of the decade. The Confederates often alluded to it as the one you could load on Sunday and fire it the rest of the week. An experienced soldier could fire 14 rounds per minute with it, as opposed to perhaps two or three with the 1861 Springfield or Enfield musket. Troops often saved their pay in order to buy a Sharps for their own use.

58 Furguson, *Not War But Murder*, 89-90, 94, 96-97, 112-13,121; Trudeau, *Bloody Roads South*, 268; Foote, *Civil War Narrative*, 3:285; Rhea, *Cold Harbor*, 191-93, 204-205, 208-209, 211-13, 226.

After his second repulse, Anderson's only remaining concern seemed to be defense. His battle line fell back to the west, taking a position northeast of Hoke's. By then, both Pickett and Field had their divisions in place and entrenching. The 5th Texas filled the space between Pickett's left and the right of Early's Corps. Lee also shifted troops across Warren's front, which he knew was strongly entrenched in his front. Somewhat surprisingly, Meade then suggested that Smith and Wright attack immediately. If Grant wanted a breakthrough the next morning, he argued, the chance of success would be greatly improved if his men could acquire positions closer to the Rebel lines. This would provide better jump-off positions for the next day's dawn attack. Grant agreed.[59]

By this time Anderson had finally connected with Hoke's Division along the Cold Harbor Road. Clingman's Brigade covered the road, while Brig. Gen. William T. Wofford's brigade from Kershaw's Division linked the line to the north. A stream and gully formed a gap some 50 to 75 yards wide between the flanks of the two brigades. Because this part of the line was considered impassible, neither troops nor breastworks guarded it. Clingman disagreed with this assessment, and tried unsuccessfully to extend his line into the gap. He had been informed, however, that Brig. Gen. Johnson Hagood's Brigade would be stationed in front of his left to cover the gap. What he did not know was that Hoke would later order Hagood to move to the right and leave the gap undefended.[60]

At 6:30 p.m., Wright and Smith finally advanced. After meeting stiff resistance, one of Wright's brigades found the gap and exploited it. The Federals forced their way through to Clingman's left-rear, firing when they stepped within 50 yards of the enemy troops. Taking advantage of the wooded ravine where the two divisions joined, the Federals broke through the Southern line. This penetration unhinged Wofford's Brigade on Clingman's left, as well as a large number of Clingman's own troops. Richard Anderson rose to the occasion. He detached Gregg's Texans, including the 5th Texas, from Field's Division, as well as Brig. Gen. Eppa Hunton's troops from Pickett's Division and sent both units forward in a spirited counterattack. After brutal fighting in the twilight, the Texans eventually steadied Wofford's line and pushed the Federals out of the gap, connected with Hunton's men, and permanently sealed the gap in the line. The savage fighting in the area finally died down around 10:00 p.m.

59 Furguson, *Not War But Murder*, 100-101; Trudeau, *Bloody Roads South*, 268; Foote, *Civil War Narrative*, 3:285; Rhea, *Cold Harbor*, 229-30, 233-34.

60 Furguson, *Not War But Murder*, 94, 107; Trudeau, *Bloody Roads South*, 265; Rhea, *Cold Harbor*, 202-204.

General Field came up later with three more of his brigades and personally supervised the layout of a new line behind Kershaw's original front.[61]

By the morning of June 2, both armies occupied strong defensive earthworks. Lee had constructed some of the most comprehensive such works of the entire war. Confederate parapets generally topped five feet in height, with a four-foot ditch in their immediate front. (And by the following day, they extended for nearly seven miles, from Totopotomoy Creek south to the Chickahominy River). In many places, the fortifications extended several trenches deep, with lateral works, or covered ways, connecting them to protect men moving to and from the front lines and any enfilading fields of fire. The enemy lines in the 5th Texas sector were so close that Gregg decided not to advance a picket line. He did, however, construct an abatis in front of the works to discourage surprise attacks. Although not under general attack that day, long range rifle fire peppered the regiment, as well as a heavy artillery barrage at dusk. At midnight, the Texans resumed working on still more breastwork improvements. According to Joskins, they had a "splendid line of works by the day of June 3rd."[62]

That night, Grant made final preparations for his grand assault against the Confederate center and right, an effort designed to pin Lee's army against the Chickahominy and annihilate it. While he had already postponed the attack for a day to give his commanders time to perfect the assault arrangements, the Yankee high command had not devised a coordinated plan. While the brass made their plans, the soldiers prepared also. Many of them were "calmly writing their names and home addresses on slips of paper and pinning them to the backs of their coats, so that their bodies might be recognized and their fate made known to their families at home." They knew what the generals' plans entailed for them.[63]

Lee, however, had carefully arranged to counter this impending attack. He strengthened his center and right with additional artillery and infantry and repositioned units so a heavy crossfire could be brought to bear against any advance there. His engineers constructed works along a chain of hills and ridges just low enough not to appear formidable, and yet high enough to give the troops a clear view

61 *OR* 36, pt. 3, 880; J. H. Cosgrove, "About the Attack at Cold Harbor," *CV*, (1912), 20:511; Law, "Wilderness to Cold Harbor," in *B&L*, 4:138; Trudeau, *Bloody Roads South*, 273-74; Furguson, *Not War But Murder*, 110.

62 Joskins, "A Sketch of Hood's Texas Brigade, in UTSA, 174-75; Polley, *Hood's Texas Brigade*, 240-42; Trudeau, *Bloody Roads South*, 274; Law, "From the Wilderness to Cold Harbor," in *B&L*, 4:138.

63 Polley, *Hood's Texas Brigade*, 241-42; Porter, *Campaigning With Grant*, 174-75; Lowry, *No Turning Back*, 451; Furgurson, *Not War But Murder*, 134-35; Rhea, *Cold Harbor*, 312, 314-15; Foote, *Civil War Narrative*, 3:290.

of the entire ground to their front. Intricate and zigzagged trenches protected the flanks and incorporated the lines with batteries inside built to enfilade an opposing force. The system was "a maze and labyrinth of works within works and works without works, each laid out with some definite design either of defense or offense."[64]

And the engineers had succeeded "beyond their wildest imaginings." Via a "combination of chance and design, Lee's men had created the perfect killing ground." In the process, they had perfected a way of laying out entrenchments with uncanny accuracy. They had used a long cord marked at intervals with small strips of white cotton cloth to mock up the trench lines along positions sited and plotted during the day. This prevented them from constructing any vulnerable, difficult-to-defend angles. The terrain in front of the Confederate works provided the soldiers a clear field of fire—flat, marshy in places, and relatively unobstructed for a considerable distance. Woe to an enemy that attempted to confront them there![65]

Early on June 3, the Federals appeared in heavy columns directly in front of Law and Anderson's Brigades, and partially in front of the 5th Texas. The Texans had been on alert early that morning, breakfasting on "clammy corn-bread and raw bacon" when the Yankees struck at 4:30 a.m. Union cannon began a fierce barrage, prompting a similar response from the Confederates. Richmond residents, 12 miles away, were jarred out of bed as the incessant thunder rained down on them. A heavy tramp began; commanders had synchronized their watches, and at precisely 4:40 a.m., three blue-jacketed corps, more than 60,000 men, moved forward, honing in on three points along the center and right center of the Rebel line, a line that "had fewer men defending its whole length than now were assaulting half of it."[66]

A force of over 40,000 men from Smith's, Wright's, and Hancock's corps advanced first against A. P. Hill and subsequently Anderson's men. They came on in heavy masses, "and with great spirit," only to be mercilessly mowed down. Row after row of Federal infantry rushed Lee's impregnable line, only to be quickly, devastatingly decimated by deadly frontal and enfilading fire. The artillery, blasting double-shotted canister, swept away scores with each blast. Law (who sustained a serious eye wound during the battle) later described the appalling carnage: "It was not war; it was murder," and confessed that his only concern was that his men might run

64 Charles A. Page, *Letters of A War Correspondent* (Boston, MA, 1899), 96; Lowry, *No Turning Back*, 450-51; Catton, *A Stillness At Appomattox*, 159.

65 Lowry, *No Turning Back*, 450-51; Trudeau, *Bloody Roads South*, 280-81; *OR* 36, pt. 1, 1059; Cosgrove, "About the Attack at Cold Harbor," in *CV*, 20:511; Polley, *Hood's Texas Brigade*, 240-41; Law, "From the Wilderness to Cold Harbor," in *B&L*, 4:138-39.

66 Trudeau, *Bloody Roads South*, 284; Rhea, *Cold Harbor*, 318-20; Foote, *Civil War Narrative*, 3:286, 290; Polley, *Hood's Texas Brigade*, 242.

out of cartridges before repelling the attack. William Oates, commanding the 15th Alabama, observed Union ranks enduring withering fire for several minutes then retreating "leaving the ground covered with their dead and dying" covering "more than five acres of ground about as thickly as they could be laid."[67]

"Men could not live in the fire poured on them from front and flanks," one veteran Texan later reported, "and although in the first rush a few came within several yards of our lines, they halted, about faced, and fled as fast as legs could carry them." In a little more than *twenty minutes*, Grant lost over 7,000 men, earning him the sobriquet "The Butcher." In all but a few instances, the attackers got no closer than 50 yards of the Confederate works. Lee suffered about 1,000 casualties.[68]

Brigadier General George T. Anderson's Georgia and Law's Brigades manned trenches between Kershaw's right and the Texans, who bore the brunt of this awesome Federal assault. The 5th Texas, positioned reasonably safe from direct attack, still played a direct role in repelling the Union assaults. One of the Federal columns, Smith's XVIII Corps, was directed against Law's position. The regiment, to Law's immediate right, with the rest of the Brigade, found that as the Federals came on, they exposed their left flank, and the Texans poured a destructive enfilading fire into them as fast as experienced soldiers "could load, aim and pull triggers." The Yankee advance "presented the fairest of targets for Texas and Arkansas marksmanship," according to Polley. D. H. Hamilton of the 1st Texas described the slaughter as "fearful" and "one of the most horrible sights of all the war of slaughter and suffering." The battle had ended in 30 minutes "and from the appearance of the field, it looked like we had killed or wounded most of the men who charged us." Joskins noted that by 7:00 a.m., although the Yankees had pounded the Confederate lines with grape, canister, and round shot while their men charged repeatedly "but 'No Go' we whipped them back with immense slaughter."[69]

At 7:40 a.m., Meade advised Hancock that "[n]o orders have been sent you suspending or rescinding the original order to attack." The II Corps commander, now thoroughly frustrated, quickly responded that "[u]nless success has been gained in other points, I do not advise persistence here." Wright and two other commanders

67 Field, "Campaigns of 1864 and 1865," 549; Commager, *The Blue and the Gray*, 1001; Trudeau, *Bloody Roads South*, 291.

68 Martin T. McMahon, "Cold Harbor," in *B&L*, 4: 217; Polley, *Hood's Texas Brigade*, 242; Hamilton, *History of Company M*, 60; Cosgrove, "About the Attack at Cold Harbor," *CV*, 20:511; Alexander, *Military Memoirs*, 540; Furgurson, *Not War But Murder*, 171, 188.

69 Hamilton, *History of Company M*, 60; Cosgrove, "About the Attack at Cold Harbor," 511; Polley, *Hood's Texas Brigade*, 242; Moore, *Men of the Bayou City Guard*, 87; Joskins, "A Sketch of Hood's Texas Brigade," in UTSA, 173-74.

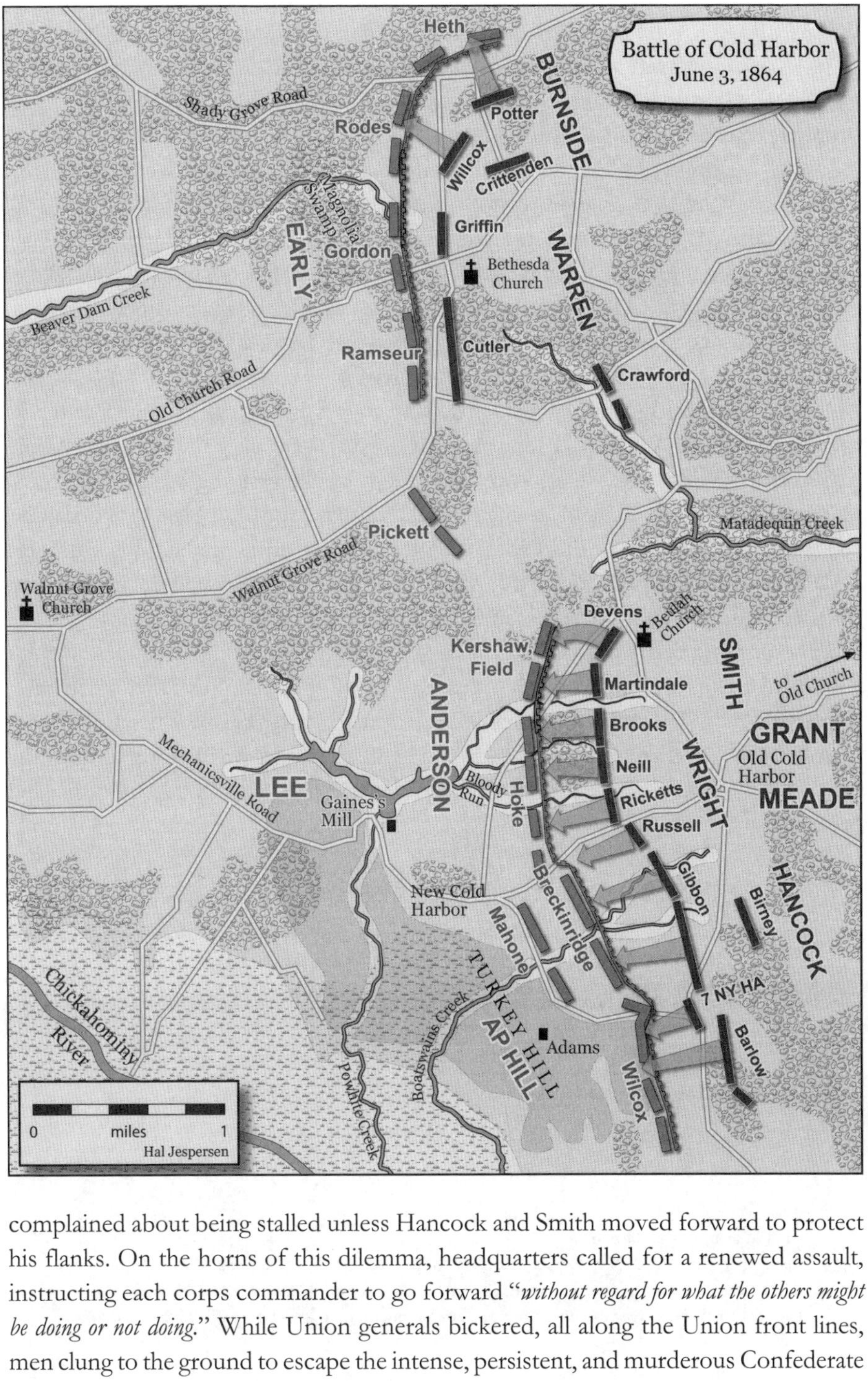

complained about being stalled unless Hancock and Smith moved forward to protect his flanks. On the horns of this dilemma, headquarters called for a renewed assault, instructing each corps commander to go forward "*without regard for what the others might be doing or not doing.*" While Union generals bickered, all along the Union front lines, men clung to the ground to escape the intense, persistent, and murderous Confederate fire. At 9:00 a.m., Grant ordered another assault. However, his men were having none of it, recognizing such a movement as absolutely suicidal. After visiting the front at 11:00 a.m., Grant issued orders at 1:30 p.m. suspending "[f]or the present all further offensive operations" for all three corps.[70]

The slaughter ceased, and Lee had won what his aide Venable deemed "perhaps the easiest victory ever granted to Confederate arms by the folly of Federal commanders." With relatively few losses in their ranks, the Rebel line looked out on a vast field covered with the Union dead. "Men lay in places like hogs in a pen," a soldier in Kershaw's Brigade later recalled, "some side by side, across each other, some two deep, while others with their legs lying across the head and body of their dead comrades." A young Georgian in Hoke's Division concurred: "I have been upon twenty battlefields, but the enemy's loss was greater on this field than I ever saw before." A veteran Texan later reported that the Yankees fought bravely, but "could not enter our works and were mowed down almost like grain before a cradle." The Federals retired from the field leaving their dead and wounded. A blood-stained diary, found in the pocket of a dead Federal soldier on the field there, had this gruesome final entry, typifying the day's horror: "June 3. Cold Harbor. I was killed." Once Grant assessed the day's reports and casualties, he informed his staff that evening—"I regret this assault more than any one I have ever ordered."[71]

One of the Confederates killed that day was Pvt. Columbus Dighton Seward, brother-in-law of Company I's commander, Tacitus T. Clay. The two men had been as close as blood brothers, and Tas always commented at length on Dighton's health and activities in his frequent letters to his wife Bettie. So Clay sadly reported that her brother:

> was shot through the head while going from Gen. Gregg's quarters to the breastworks by the enemies sharp shooters. . . . He had got about 20 feet from Gen. G's hut when he was struck. They heard him exclaim 'oh!' and on looking saw him fall. His death was instantaneous. I brought his remains in and bought a square of

70 Foote, *Civil War Narrative*, 3:292; Rhea, *Cold Harbor*, 379; Lowry, *No Turning Back*, 454.

71 Trudeau, *Bloody Roads South*, 295; Hanks, *Captain Benton's Company*, 31; Lowry, *No Turning Back*, 454; Furgurson, *Not War But Murder*, 178; Foote, *Civil War Narrative*, 3: 290. With this latest disaster, Grant had suffered 59,929 casualties in one month, a number which was greater than the total strength of the Army of Northern Virginia at that time. Foote, *Civil War Narrative*, 3:310.

ground in Hollywood Cemetery and had him properly interred. He was the most devoted friend that I ever had.[72]

The two armies remained in place, in some spots less than 100 yards from each other, for another 10 days. Heavy skirmishing occurred on June 4, but by that evening, the Federal line fell unusually quiet, and the lines stayed that way the next day. So for three days, Union corpses lay bloating in the hot Virginia sun. Though relatively quiet, "the stench of the unburied, rotting corpses of the Federal slain on the 3rd," was "constantly in the nostrils," one veteran remembered. Indeed, the stink got so intense that the Confederates found it difficult to man their breastworks. A deserter later related a common Rebel mock that Grant intended to "stink Lee out of his position, if nothing else will suffice." Grant was, in fact, loath to propose a truce, since at the time the side sending a flag of truce conceded loss of "the field of Battle." Grant attempted to finesse a request to tend to his dead and wounded, alluding to the wounded of both armies lying exposed and referencing humanitarian reasons, but Lee insisted on a strict protocol, including a flag of truce, "as is customary." So as the air remained "laden with the insufferable putrescence," Grant planned his move to the south of the James, sending officers to Bermuda Hundred in order to meet with Maj. Gen. Benjamin F. Butler, the commander of the Army of the James, and obtain available topographical information.[73]

On the afternoon of June 6th, Grant finally capitulated and agreed to a truce, seeking "a suspension of hostilities for sufficient time to collect them [the dead and wounded] in; say two hours." Grant did not receive Lee's response until midnight and was unable to reply until 10:30 a.m. on June 7th. A truce was then quickly granted to pick up the few wounded still alive after three days, as well as to inter the rotting dead lying thickly strewn in front of the Confederate works. During the truce, soldiers on both sides seized the opportunity to exchange newspapers and fraternize, and the respective bands of both armies struck up patriotic airs. Joskins of Company A reported that "Dixie" and "Yankee Doodle" elicited the most "cheers and hisses." When the truce expired, the soldiers quietly moved back to their respective

72 Tacitus Clay to Bettie Clay, October 26, 1864, in MSU. Columbus Dighton Seward as born March 7, 1831 in Quincy, Adams County, Illinois. Upon joining his brother-in-law's company, Dighton served as a nurse for him in June of 1862, and then as an aide to the brigade commander from October 1862 until June 3, 1864, when he was killed. Simpson, *Compendium*, 241.

73 Joskins, "A Sketch of Hood's Texas Brigade," UTSA174-75; Polley, *Hood's Texas Brigade*, 243.

breastworks, "the white flags came down, and the shooting commenced once again."[74]

The Federals began retiring from Early's and Field's front on June 6, and Lee quickly sensed Grant was preparing another withdrawal from their right. Gregg, then commanding Field's Division, was under orders to prepare his Texans and the rest of Field's Division to follow and support an attack by Pickett's division designed to deal a "sudden and disastrous blow to the enemy." The attack was called off, however, when pickets detected that the Yankees had not pulled back during the night. On the evening of June 7, the 5th Texas was relieved in the trenches and given a day's rest "in a camp in the woods." On June 9, it proceeded to the Totopotomoy and occupied Ewell's former position, while that corps was moving to the left. It saw some action there in a firefight with Federal cavalry, which it reportedly it dispatched "the worse for the wear." Thereafter, the field remained quiet from June 10-12.[75]

Capt. Watson Williams, then commanding Company F, wrote home that "[t]his is the 33rd day since fighting between these two armies has commenced and I'm quite sure not a single day has passed without fighting of some kind somewhere on the line, and many days have been characterized by bloody battles." He was correct in the assessment—casualties between the two armies exceeded 82,000 during May 1864. The war was now becoming one of attrition, and the North held all the advantages. Federal losses could be replaced in a matter of weeks, whereas Lee had no hope of augmenting his depleted ranks. Regardless, his men remained resolute and unshaken in their conviction that their cause was just and they would triumph in the end. Williams admitted his physical exhaustion but vowed he would never give up "as long as there [was] a Yankee south of the Rappahannock." Similarly, Smither wrote home that "[o]ur Army are in the "best possible" conditions with "the highest spirits" and "confident of our ability to whip the fight under any circumstances." He even allowed that the troops were "tolerably well clothed and are better fed than Grants Army."[76]

Following Cold Harbor, Gregg reported only 430 muskets in the whole brigade. He wrote to Richmond on June 11 regarding his unit's shrinking size, noting that many members of his brigade were across the Mississippi, and that all efforts to

74 Watson Williams to Wife, June 7, 1864, in CRC; Joskins, "A Sketch of Hood's Texas Brigade," in UTSA, 174-75; Simpson, *Lee's Grenadier Guard*, 421-22; McMahon, "Cold Harbor," 4: 219; Freeman, *Lee's Lieutenants*, 3:515; Alexander, *Military Memoirs*, 542; Henry, *Story of the Confederacy*, 363.

75 *OR* 36, pt. 1, 1059, pt. 3, 880; Joskins, "A Sketch of Hood's Texas Brigade," in UTSA, 174-75; Furgurson, *Not War But Murder*, 227; Polley, *Hood's Texas Brigade*, 243.

76 Watson Williams to Wife June 7, 1864, in CRC; Ltr fragment, Mark Smither to ____, June, 1864, in SHSU; Simpson, *Lee's Grenadier Guard*, 422.

procure their return thus far had failed. Indeed, the number of men fit for duty across the Mississippi probably exceeded those in Virginia. He proposed a "considerable force of the trans-Mississippi troops" be brought to Virginia—forcefully was the only way—along with much-needed horses, which could be procured in the West. Apparently, the fanciful proposal disappeared into the Richmond bureaucracy.[77]

After determining the impossibility of taking Richmond either by going over or around Lee's army, Grant decided to concentrate his efforts against the city of Petersburg, some 23 miles below Richmond. The key to the railroad system entering Richmond from the south, if it fell into Federal hands, Richmond would lose its ability to sustain an army and would fall without a fight. He thus pulled his army from the trenches northeast of the capital and began a rapid march south across the Chickahominy and James Rivers, ultimately arriving near Petersburg. Once Lee determined Grant had left his front, he too began moving toward the James.[78]

Anderson's entire corps, including the 5th Texas, left the trenches at Cold Harbor at 11:00 a.m. on June 13, passing within sight of the Gaines' Mill battlefield and crossed the Chickahominy on McClellan's Bridge. The Texans marched by way of Seven Pines over to the Charles City Road from whence they turned off at the Williams' house, bivouacking for the night just north of the old Frayser's Farm battlefield. They remained quietly there until June 16, when they marched to the James River, passing near Chaffin's Farm, crossing on a pontoon bridge below Drewry's Bluff, and moving south down the Petersburg Turnpike with the rest of Field's and Picket's Divisions. Once across the James in late evening of June 16, Field's Division, with the regiment, found itself near Walthall Station on the Richmond and Petersburg Railroad. Their immediate objective was to occupy the trenches recently abandoned by Gen. P. G. T. Beauregard around Bermuda Hundred, when the sudden appearance of Federal troops had forced him to shorten his lines to prevent the imminent fall of Petersburg. Upon passing the southern extension of the Confederate defenses from Richmond, the men encountered the right of Pickett's line along the road near the Appomattox River and took up position there. Butler's men had torn up the railroad and seized Beauregard's former lines. The same evening, an "awful & dreadful cannonading was heard in the direction of Petersburg—[some] 12 miles distant."[79]

77 *OR* 36, pt. 2, 874, 894.

78 Grant, *Personal Memoirs*, 2:279-80; Henry, *Story of the Confederacy*, 365, 368-72; Winkler, *Confederate Capital*, 178.

79 Field, "Campaign of 1864 and 1865," in *SHSP*,14:549; Joskins, "A Sketch of Hood's Texas Brigade," in UTSA, 175-77; Polley, *Hood's Texas Brigade*, 243.

Field's and Pickett's Divisions endured constant sharpshooting, skirmishing, and shelling from the Union forces facing their trenches. According to Polley, the men of Texas had never displayed greater solidarity than at Bermuda Hundred that June 17. They occupied an abandoned line of works in a hollow, and shortly determined that an immediate attack would recover the portion of the line Confederates had to abandon earlier that morning. After ducking all day in the trenches, without waiting for orders and "with one simultaneous impulse," the Texans and several other brigades of Pickett's Division spontaneously rushed from their breastworks "with one of the grandest rebel yells heard in a long time." One private shouted "[n]ow's the time, boys," and away they went. "The effect of the call seemed magical, for the words had scarce passed the speaker's lips when every member of the brigade sprang to his feet, gun in hand, and leaping over the breastworks, joined in a wild, reckless charge up the slope of the hill on the enemy." Halfway between the two lines the officers managed to overtake them and yell "Forward"—however, by then, every man of the regiment was already running full out.

The startled Yankees in front of the Texans quickly took to their heels, abandoning their position between Clay's and Howlett's houses. By dark, the brazen Rebels had succeeded in recovering Johnston's second line of defenses and reestablished Confederate control of the direct links between Richmond and Petersburg. Canister, grape, and round shot rained down upon the regiment until darkness fell. The brigade lost 30 men in the action, Joskins reported, including D. M. Sherrill of Company G, shot dead near Howlett's House. When the cannonade ceased, by working the remainder of the night, the men rebuilt the trenches.[80]

On June 18, Kershaw set out for Petersburg at 3:00 a.m., followed by Field's Division and the 5th Texas. The Texans, relieved by Pickett's troops, left Bermuda Hundred, marched west to the Richmond and Petersburg Railroad, and boarded cars for Petersburg just after dawn. Debarking about four miles from the city, the regiment crossed the Appomattox River and stopped long enough to enjoy a hogshead of coffee grateful citizens had hauled out on wagons. The refreshed Texans moved into trenches east of the city and south of the Appomattox late on June 18. Field formed to the right of Kershaw's Division, with the Texas Brigade holding the far left. Their initial position on the Petersburg front stood midway between the Norfolk and Petersburg Railroad and the Jerusalem Plank Road, about a mile and a half east of

80 *OR* 36, pt. 1, 1060, 1069-70; *OR* 40, pt. 1, 60, 661, 760; Watson Williams to Wife, June 16, 1864, in CRC; Joskins, "A Sketch of Hood's Texas Brigade," in UTSA, 176-78; Polley, *Letters to Charming Nellie*, 248; Polley, *Hood's Texas Brigade*, 244; Don Lowry, *Fate of the Country: The Civil War from June – September 1864* (New York, NY, 1992), 42; Moore, *Men of the Bayou City Guards*, 87; John Horne, *The Petersburg Campaign: June 1864 – April, 1865* (Cambridge, MA, 1993), 66. For more on Sherrill, see Appendix D.

Blandford Cemetery. The right side of the brigade anchored on Taylor's Branch. These trenches would double as home for the regiment for the next month. The men would be exposed here day and night to nearly incessant mortar shelling and sharpshooting, as well as to the peak anxiety they felt awaiting an assault that would never come.[81]

The opposing lines around Petersburg were exceptionally close, so at least a third of the men maintained watch around the clock. Petersburg's dangers were "worse than a big battle," Joskins said. Deadly accurate Federal sharpshooters killed at least one member of the brigade every day. A soldier could crouch to avoid having his head blown off, but there was no escaping the tremendous heat and choking dust caused by severe lack of rain. A Texas officer noted that:

> [d]uring the day the heat is oppressive, and not infrequently the Texan sighs for the refreshing breezes of his own prairie home. At night one-third of the officers and men are on the alert . . . and at the first indication of the approach of morning, all hands are up and in readiness to meet any attempt at a surprise—everybody literally living beneath the surface of the ground, and constantly on the *qui vive.*

The Texans constantly stood guard in the heat with only the shade from blankets and tent-clothes, stretched across such rails and planks for relief from the heat and glare. Nonetheless, the men of the regiment were in fine health, Smither reported, although the blazing sun "has melted us down to not much more then greasy spots." The men remained in or just behind the front lines east of Petersburg without relief until July 20.[82]

The Texas breastworks were "about seven feet high with a platform to step on while firing." Though well-constructed, they had to be manned with extreme caution. Yankee sharpshooters posted in trees and trenches anywhere from 100-600 yards away were alert to any part of a head showing about the ramparts. O. T. Hanks of the 4th Texas described hoisting his hat in a ramrod above the breastworks. Invariably, it

81 *OR* 40, pt. 1, 760; Parker, *Touched By Fire*, 90; Moore, *Men of the Bayou City Guards*, 87; G. T. Beauregard, "Four Days Of Battle at Petersburg," in *B&L*, 4: 543; Field, "Campaign of 1864 and 1865," in *SHSP*, 14:549; Hanks, *Captain Benton's Company*, 32. See Schmutz, *Battle of the Crater*, for a vivid account of the assault which occurred two days after the Texans left the lines at Petersburg.

82 Joskins, "A Sketch of Hood's Texas Brigade," 176; Winkler, *Confederate Capital*, 180; Polley, *Hood's Texas Brigade*, 246; Polley, *Hood's Texas Brigade*, 245-46; Mark Smither to Sister, July 15, 1864, in SHSU; Winkler, *Confederate Capital*, 180-83.

would return with "two quick holes made in it, one where the bullet went in and the other where it came out."[83]

Strong rumors of Union efforts to construct a mine under the Confederate lines circulated while the regiment manned these trenches. Confederate engineers developed a means to counter these tunneling efforts. The process involved sinking mines to discover the location of any Federal tunnels. They also drove pegs deep in the ground. A designated "peg biter" could supposedly detect the slightest vibration from underground excavation efforts when he clenched the peg in his teeth. Nothing was ever detected under the Texas sector with this technique, Hanks reported.[84]

The 5th Texas occupied its last position on the line at Petersburg in the immediate vicinity of an undetected Federal mine which was detonated on July 30 and spawned the infamous battle of the Crater. Had the brigade not relocated the evening of July 28, it would have experienced the fate of Brig. Gen. Stephen Elliott's South Carolinians, their replacements, instead. The massive explosion instantly obliterated over 230 of them. Some of the Federal prisoners captured in the failed assault following the explosion expressed bitter disappointment that the Texas Brigade had not been "extinguished" in that immense blast. The Texans were safely north of the James when they heard about the explosion and could reflect upon their good fortune. "Well, boys, hit's a d_ _d sight more comfortabler ter be stannin' here on good old Virginny terror firmer," one Texan said, "than ter be danglin,' heels up an' heads down, over that cussed mine, not knowin' whether you'd strike soft or hard groun' when you lit."[85]

At first the food at Petersburg—primarily corn meal bread, plus bacon or lean beef, occasionally supplemented with cow peas and rice—was adequate and was certainly much better than what the men ate last winter in Tennessee. Occasionally, a ration of coffee and sugar would make it into the lines. Coffee, "parched in a frying pan, beat in a cloth and then boiled in a tin cup," was especially favored. Routinely a man would issued one pound of corn meal per day which was baked into bread by a special cooking detail in the rear of the lines and brought up to the front every other day. A quarter of a pound per day per man of either bacon or "tough, lean" beef constituted the meat ration, which was borne to the front lines on the shoulders of the regimental commissary sergeants, then issued by each company to its men. Conditions

83 Hanks, *Captain Benton's Company*, 44-45; Winkler, *Confederate Capital*, 181.

84 Hanks, *Captain Benton's Company*, 44-45; Schmutz, *Battle of the Crater*, 72; Alexander, *Military Memoirs*, 561; Freemen, *Lee's Lieutenants*, 3:541.

85 *OR* 40, pt. 1, 787-93; Polley, *Hood's Texas Brigade*, 245-48; Winkler, *Confederate Capital*, 182, 185. Schmutz, *Battle of the Crater*, 373 n25.

on the ground at Petersburg virtually precluded foraging, so even the highly resourceful Texans had to make due exclusively with government issued rations. The 5th Texas remained in this area, defending Richmond, until the capital itself was evacuated in early April, 1865. The responsibility would not prove to be a tranquil one.[86]

86 Polley, *Hood's Texas Brigade*, 245; Winkler, *Confederate Capital*, 182.

Chapter 7

The Fighting for the Defense of Richmond

By July 29, according to Ewell, now commanding the Department of Richmond, the Confederate line north of the James extended from the New Market area toward the White Oak Swamp, with its right resting near Chaffin's farm. The Southerners were positioned to block any Federal thrust toward Richmond. Grant's plan was for Hancock's II Corps and Sheridan's cavalry to cross a newly constructed pontoon bridge from the northern tip of Jones' Neck to Deep Bottom, drawing Rebel troops away from Petersburg, thereby exploiting the impending explosion of the federal mine under Elliott's Salient on July 30 to the fullest. Brigadier General Robert S. Foster's division of the X Corps would cross over on a second pontoon bridge farther upstream and hold that bridgehead on the north bank of the James.[1]

At 3:00 a.m. on July 27, Hancock's force crossed the James on the new pontoon bridge to Deep Bottom. Moving against Fussell's Mill at dawn, it broke through the Confederate line on New Market Road. Meanwhile, Sheridan's cavalry moved from Darbytown Road to strike the Confederate left. The Confederate defenders had been reinforced by Kershaw's and Wilcox's Divisions, both moving east on the New Market Road behind the Confederate works atop the eastern face of New Market Heights. By that afternoon, a sharp artillery duel erupted on the heights to the north. Sheridan captured the high ground to the right of the Union infantry, near Fussell's Mill but was then driven off by one of Kershaw's Georgia brigades. Farther east, approaching Riddle's Shop, the Federal cavalry was slowed by one Confederate

1 John Horn, *Petersburg Campaign, June 1864-April 1865* (Cambridge Center, MA, 1993), 102, 105-07; Winkler, *Confederate Capital*, 177, 184; Freeman, *Lee's Lieutenants*, 3:542.

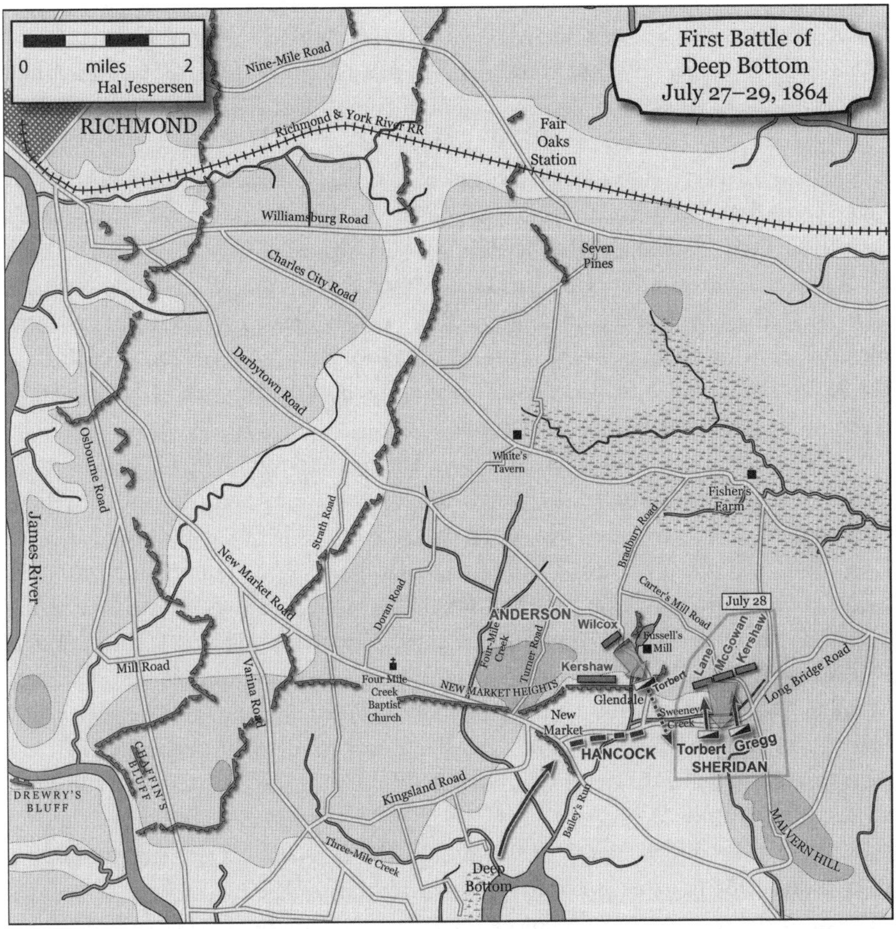

obstacle after another. That evening, the Confederates strengthened and extended their earthworks north from Fussell's Mill along the edge of a ravine and across Darbytown Road, and received yet more reinforcements from Petersburg.[2]

Recognizing Sheridan could no longer safely continue his raid toward Richmond and would most likely be prevented from returning through Deep Bottom, Grant ordered him to remain with Hancock. On July 28, Hancock left one division to hold his original position, and led the remainder northward to unite with Sheridan. As soon as the Federals had formed, however, the Confederates attacked, driving back the cavalry, until they dismounted, reformed, and finally halted the Confederates with a

2 *OR* 40, pt. 1, 309, 762, & pt. 3, 794, 813-15; Humphreys, *The Virginia Campaign of '64 and '65* (New York, 1916), 247-48; Freeman, *Lee's Lieutenants*, 3:542; Salmon, *Virginia Battlefield Guide*, 416-17; Winkler, *Confederate Capital*, 184-86; Polley, *Hood's Texas Brigade*, 247-49.

devastating fire. The Rebels retreated back to their defenses, losing 250 prisoners and two stands of colors. By then, however, Grant's main objective of surprising and destroying the Confederates "out to the South Anna," had vanished.[3]

By late that afternoon, Grant lost hope of raiding the railroads, too. Consequently, part of Hancock's corps was ordered back to their trenches at Petersburg that night to support the Federal offensive push after the mine's detonation. That same night, Rooney Lee's cavalry arrived at Deep Bottom. Hancock made a final demonstration with Brig. Gen. Robert S. Foster's division of the X Corps in front of the Confederate lines. While the Yankees drove the Confederates from their main line of rifle pits, Foster's troops could not dislodge them and after shelling the Rebels for an hour, he withdrew. Grant ordered both Hancock and Sheridan to return to Petersburg after dark that evening.[4]

Richard Anderson had received orders in the afternoon of July 27 to move his corps' "headquarters north of the James." So, on July 29, as part of Field's Division, the regiment joined the Confederate forces north of the James at Fussell's Mill near Deep Bottom, together with Fitzhugh Lee's cavalry. The Texans had left their trenches after dark on July 28, passing through Petersburg at about midnight. Crossing to the north bank of the Appomattox, they marched along the Richmond and Petersburg Railroad tracks to Dunlap Station and bivouacked for the night. The next morning, the regiment rode train cars to Rice's Turnout opposite Drewry's Bluff. From there, it marched to the James, crossing on the same pontoon bridge they had used on June 16 going the other way, past Chaffin's Farm and by dusk was in position at Fussell's Mill near Malvern Hill overlooking Deep Bottom. They were situated about eight miles directly south of Richmond. The regiment was not engaged in the Deep Bottom fighting, except for minor skirmishing, as the main body of Federals had withdrawn to the protection of their gunboats before the brigade arrived.[5]

Following the bloody debacle of the Crater offensive, Grant withdrew most of his troops from north of the James. Consequently, most of the Confederate forces returned to Petersburg, leaving only the Texas Brigade, Benning's Brigade, and Martin Gary's South Carolina Cavalry north of the river. And there the 5th Texas remained

3 *OR* 40, pt. 3, 310-11, 809; John B. Gibbon, *Personal Reflections of the Civil War* (New York, 1928 [reprint Morningside Books, 1978]), 248-49; Francis A. Walker, *History of the Second Army Corps of the Army of the Potomac* (New York, 1886), 566; Schmutz, *Battle of the Crater*, 82-83.

4 *OR* 40, pt. 1, 2, 134, 388-89, 693, 762, & pt. 3, 815, 819; John S. Wise, *The End of an Era* (Boston, MA, 1899), 354; Humphreys, *Virginia Campaign*, 253-58; Horn, *Petersburg Campaign*, 108-09; Schmutz, *Battle of the Crater*, 83-84.

5 Mark Smither to "Uncle," July 24, 1864, in SHSU; Winkler, *Confederate Capital*, 184-85; Polley, *Hood's Texas Brigade*, 245-46.

until Richmond was evacuated in early April, 1865. The responsibility proved far from tranquil—in the eight months the regiment maintained this post, it engaged in six major skirmishes and battles and numerous other deadly encounters.[6]

After the dismal results of the battle at the Crater, Grant turned his attention to the area between the James and the Chickahominy Rivers, an area laced with a network of improved roads leading to the Southern capital. Assigned control of the road network running southeast from Richmond, Field's Division guarded it against rapid incursions from the Federals. The 5th Texas was positioned in a fortified camp at New Market Heights, near the intersection of Long Bridge and New Market Roads. Strategically important, these heights afforded an excellent view of the Confederate left flank and overlooked one of the probable crossing points a Union force from Petersburg would use at Deep Bottom.[7]

The James ran due south out of Richmond for seven miles to Drewry's Bluff on its western bank. Thereafter, it made a 90-degree turn eastward, flowing for another mile before turning south again at Chaffin's Bluff on the eastern bank, and then again continuing to the southeast. The Chickahominy River also ran southeasterly through this area from at a point two or three miles from the capital. The two streams thus produced a small strip of land between them that became a major focus of Federal efforts to take Richmond.[8]

A series of roads radiated south and east from Richmond in this area. The Osborne Turnpike, farthest west, ran due south out of the capital, paralleling the James. Then came Varina Road, which split off from New Market Road two or three miles south of the city and ran southeasterly until it crossed the James at Aiken's Landing. The New Market Road, in turn, also split off Osborne Turnpike and ran generally southeast from the capital past New Market Heights and Deep Bottom. The Long Bridge Road split to the east-northeast from New Market Road approximately nine miles from the city, and ran east-northeasterly to Long Bridge on the Chickahominy. The Darbytown or Central Road paralleled the New Market Road some two miles north of it. Both the Darbytown and Charles City Roads terminated at Long Bridge Road. The Charles City Road paralleled the Darbytown Road at approximately one and a half miles to its north, running ran east-southeast to an area

6 *OR* 40, pt. 1, 762; Winkler, *Confederate Capital*, 185-86; Polley, *Hood's Texas Brigade*, 247-49; Alexander, *Military Memoirs*, 567; Moore, *Men of the Bayou City Guards*, 88. The six major engagements were: White Oak Swamp or Second Deep Bottom, Chaffin's Farm or New Market Heights, two engagements at Darbytown Road, Williamsburg Road, and New Market Road.

7 Field, "Camapaign of 1864 and 1865," in *SHSP*, 14:552.

8 Ibid., Field, 552; Simpson, *Lee's Grenadier Guard*, 432; Polley, *Hood's Texas Brigade*, 249.

east of Malvern Hill. Still farther north the Williamsburg Road, running almost due east through Seven Pines, tracked to Williamsburg itself.[9]

The Confederates constructed several rough lines of fortifications north of the James River for the defense of the capital. The outer line had begun in July, 1862, and anchored on the James River at Chaffin's Bluff. Fort Harrison, a nearby fortress, controlled Varina Road. From there, the line ran northeasterly, crossing Varina Road a mile and a half from Chaffin's Bluff and a quarter mile from Fort Harrison. It then bowed north-northeasterly, continuing two miles past Darbytown Road, and then another mile and a half, crossing the Charles City Road, and finally crossing Williamsburg Road after yet another mile and a half. This outer line incorporated all the major roads leading to the city. A fortified interior line was also constructed, paralleling the outer line but at considerably closer to the city by a quarter-mile to a mile in distance. Yet another set of works, referred to as "The New Market Line" was begun in 1864. Also anchored on the right at Chaffin's Farm, these works stretched almost due east to New Market Heights, then bent northeast for approximately another mile, until terminating at the intersection of Long Bridge and Darbytown Roads.[10]

Kershaw's entire division departed for the Shenandoah Valley with Jubal Early's force on August 9, accompanied by First Corps acting commander, Richard Anderson. This left Field's Division alone to hold the vital New Market Heights area—the most exposed portion of the army, furthest from any other division's support. With Anderson gone, and Lee preoccupied at Petersburg, Field operated virtually as an independent commander. Until mid-August, the 5th Texas itself existed in relative peace and quiet in its shaded camp, "with nothing to disturb its rest," as one veteran wrote, "the Texas command felt that its lines were cast in pleasant places." Black and "poor white" truck farmers of the area provided vegetables in relative abundance. Having just been paid, the men "fared as sumptuously as their wretchedly small allowance of bread and meat permitted." Obviously, this idyllic environment could not last long.[11]

9 Accessed May 27, 2008, www.home.comcast.net/~benningsbrigade/Andrew Johnson.

10 Ibid.

11 Early's Second Corps left Petersburg for the Shenandoah Valley on June 13 to clear that vital farmland of Union occupation and threaten Washington, thus relieving pressure on the main body of Lee's army. By July 11, Early's force got within sight of Washington, forcing Grant to send significant reinforcements from Petersburg. This in turn compelled Lee to send Kershaw's division through Culpeper Court House and threaten the rear of any Union force advancing on Early from Washington. These Confederate reinforcements reached Early in the Valley on August 13. *OR* 43, 1:783; Horn, *Petersburg Campaign*, 124; Lowry, *Fate of the Country*, 314, 335-36; Polley, *Hood's Texas Brigade*, 249, Hanks, *Captain Benton's Company*, 34.

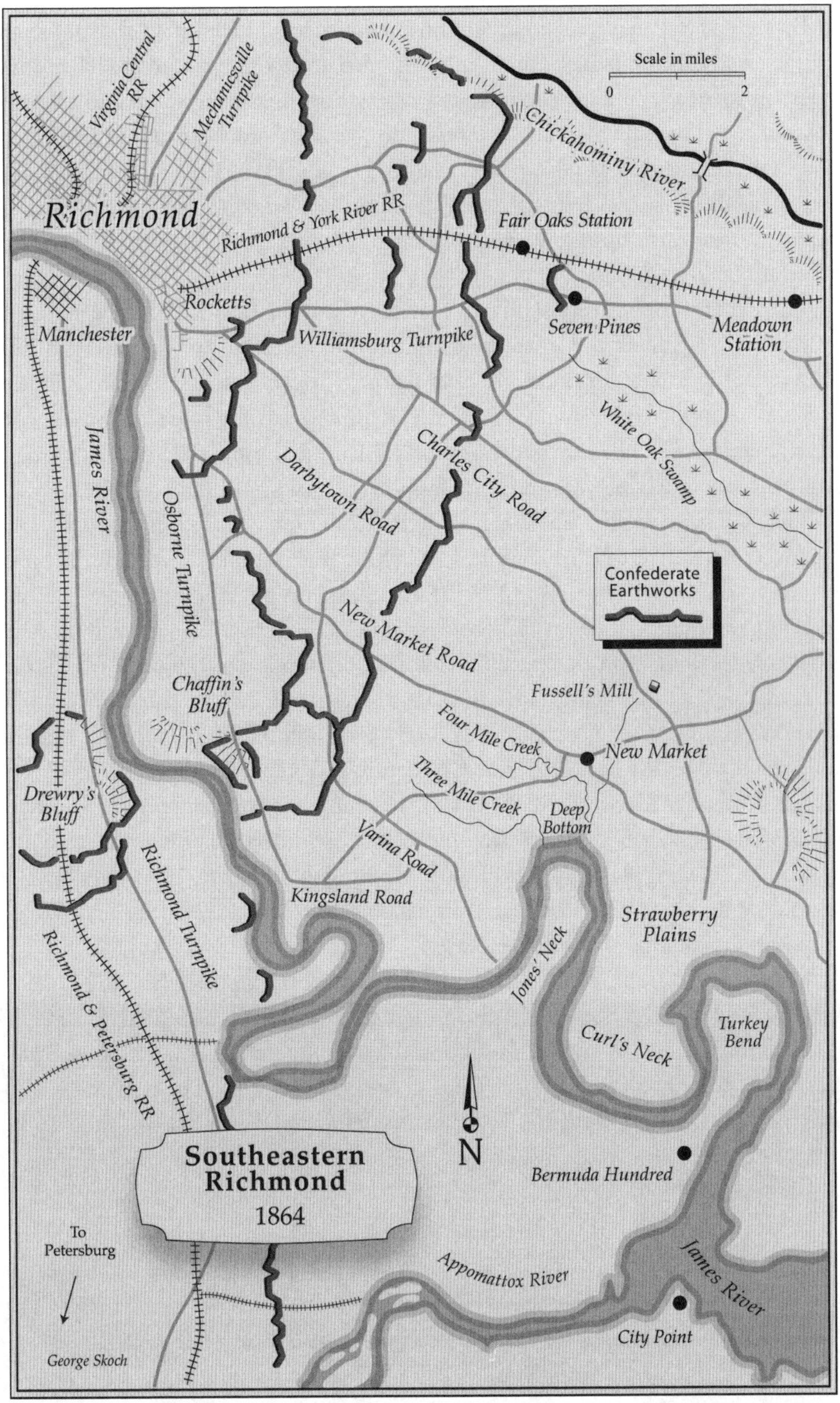
Southeastern Richmond
1864
Scale in miles
0
2
Confederate Earthworks
Richmond
Virginia Central RR
Mechanicsville Turnpike
Chickahominy River
Richmond & York River RR
Fair Oaks Station
Rocketts
Manchester
Seven Pines
Meadown Station
Williamsburg Turnpike
White Oak Swamp
Charles City Road
Darbytown Road
James River
Osborne Turnpike
New Market Road
Fussell's Mill
Chaffin's Bluff
Four Mile Creek
New Market
Three Mile Creek
Deep Bottom
Drewry's Bluff
Varina Road
Richmond Turnpike
Kingsland Road
Strawberry Plains
Jones' Neck
Richmond & Petersburg RR
Curl's Neck
Turkey Bend
N
Bermuda Hundred
To Petersburg
Appomattox River
James River
City Point
George Skoch

By August 8, Grant was confident his intelligence had identified all Confederate positions north of the James. Field was positioned around New Market Heights, with Anderson's Brigade holding the extreme eastern portion, facing south and east from its location at Fussell's Mill, at the intersection of the New Market and Darbytown Roads. Law's Brigade was next in line, followed by the Texas Brigade, with Benning's west of the Texans, and Bratton's next to it on the Division's right flank. Lane and Conner's Brigades, temporarily borrowed from Wilcox's Division of the Third Corps, backed up Field's Division, joining it to the James.[12]

The Federals planned to send two corps across the James River at Deep Bottom to turn Field's left flank and threaten Richmond similar to the previous Deep Bottom excursion. Rebel lines extended east and north of Anderson's Brigade and were supposedly supported by Brig. Gen. Martin W. Gary's cavalry brigade, but the works were unmanned. Grant's plan had Hancock's II Corps, Birney's X Corps, and Gregg's cavalry division, carrying out a movement similar to that implemented on July 27-29.

The X Corps was to break through the Confederate defenses opposite Deep Bottom and advance toward Chaffin's Bluff. Brigadier General Gershom Mott's II Corps division would advance up New Market Road on the right of Birney's division, while the reminder of Hancock's corps would attack Confederate defenses near Fussell's Mill. Gregg, on the extreme Union right, supported by part of Brig. Gen. Francis C. Barlow's division under Brig. Gen. Nelson A. Miles, would press toward Richmond as soon as Hancock's force broke through the Confederate lines. Hancock would travel down the James on steamboats, turn up river at midnight, and disembark at Deep Bottom at daybreak on August 14. The movement was intended to convince the Confederates that II Corps was moving to reinforce Sheridan in the Valley. Simultaneously with Hancock's operation, Grant would launch yet another attack to the south under Warren's overall command against the Petersburg and Weldon Railroad running south from Petersburg.

On August 13, the Confederates detected a river crossing when the II and X Corps crossed at Deep Bottom. Early on August 14, Field's men spotted Federal units to their front. Hancock's force was supposed to advance along Bailey's Creek by 5:00 a.m.; however, only half of it was off the steam boats by then. The remainder of the corps did not land until well after 7:40 a.m. Nonetheless, fighting began at daylight as the X Corps pressed slowly toward New Market Heights.[13]

12 Andre Noah Trudeau, *The Last Citadel: Petersburg, Virginia, June 1864–April 1865* (Boston, MA, 1991), 150-52; Field, "Campaign of 1864 and 1865," in *SHSP*, 14:551.

13 Horn, *Petersburg Campaign*, 126-28; Salmon, *Virginia Battlefield Guide*, 421-23; Trudeau, *Last Citadel*, 146-48, 151-56; Lowry, *Fate of the Country*, 338-39.

That day, several assaults were attempted but were "handsomely repulsed, with loss" to Hancock's troops. Then Hancock attempted to turn Field's left flank through the woods toward Fussell's Mill, but ran into Gary's cavalry, which skirmished on foot, and was quickly repulsed when Anderson's Brigade arrived with artillery support. By day's end, both sides had settled into strong defensive positions. The situation continued on August 15, with both sides receiving considerable reinforcements. Hancock had ordered Birney to march to the mill at 6:00 a.m. that day. However, the X Corps failed to advance up from Deep Bottom until 9:00 a.m., and then spent four more hours settling into its position at Fussell's Mill. Thus no significant offensive along the II Corps line occurred at all that day. In the meantime, Lee personally arrived north of the James, establishing his headquarters at Chaffin' Bluff. He dispatched two more infantry brigades from Petersburg to Field, as well as one from Pickett's Bermuda Hundred force, all reaching Field "at intervals during the 15th." This assistance nearly doubled Field's force, allowing him to extend his line considerably beyond Fussell's Mill, though even with those reinforcements, the Federals maintained an almost two-to-one advantage.[14]

Early on August 16, heavy firing erupted some 600 yards east of Fussell's Mill at a weak spot in the Confederate line running through rough, densely forested ground. Confederate troops there on the left at Fussell's Mill were primarily reinforcements under Brig. Gen. Victor Girardey that had only arrived within the last 24 hours. In their limited time there, they had been able to clear a field of fire only 50 yards deep in their front. This poorly prepared ground facilitated the X Corps' overrunning of their position, flanking and breaking a North Carolina regiment in the process, splitting the New Market Line wide open. Colonel Oates, commanding Law's Brigade, positioned on the line just south of the breakthrough, immediately refused his left hand regiments, a maneuver that temporarily stifled the Federal breakthrough. Meanwhile, Field ordered three of his brigades to hold their own lines with skirmishers, and double-quicked the bulk of that force to Fussell's Mill, with Benning's Brigade and a portion of Bratton's getting there first.[15]

The situation in the hills, swamps, and forests behind the Confederate lines became quite confused. There was considerable uncertainty about where the fight was actually located and where the Confederates were supposed to attack. Most of the men could thus see little in front of them through thick woods. Girardey was killed

14 Trudeau, *Last Citadel*, 152-53; Horn, *Petersburg Campaign*, 129-30; Field, "Campaign of 1864 and 1865," in *SHSP*, 14:552; Polley, *Hood's Texas Brigade*, 249; Salmon, *Virginia Battlefield Guide*, 423.

15 Freeman, *Lee's Lieutenants*, 3:547-48; Horn, *Petersburg Campaign*, 130-31; Field, "Campaign of 1864 and 1865," in *SHSP*, 14:552-53.

attempting to rally some of his men as Benning's Brigade deployed under Col. Dudley M. DuBose. But DuBose soon organized a counterattack with Bratton's Brigade that allowed Confederates to flank the enemy, and after about 90 minutes heavy fighting, they drove the Federals back half a mile to the first line of captured works, and then beyond that line entirely.[16]

Meanwhile, Gregg's Federal cavalry had begun a sweep around the battlefield at 6:00 a.m., moving northeast on New Market and Willis Church Roads to Glendale, and then northwest on Charles City Road toward Richmond. Initially, he was able to press forward almost as far as White's Tavern. Field ordered Wade Hampton's cavalry to meet the Federal threat along the Charles City Road while still attempting to close the breach. And he also detached the Texas Brigade, currently commanded by Col. Frederick Bass of the 1st Texas, from the division at Fussell's Mill, ordering it to the left with Hampton. The Texans set out after the Federal cavalry under a hot, cloudless sky with no water to be had except at the "slow-flowing wells of the few denizens of the section." "Rooney" Lee's cavalry division was advancing against Gregg and Miles's infantry just as Hampton arrived, taking his command around to the left. As the Confederate cavalry advanced, the Union center broke and fled rapidly back to the east. However, Hampton could not drive the Federals past their support until the 5th Texas and the rest of the brigade and Gary's cavalry arrived from Fussell's Mill and hit the Union flank at 11:00 a.m. This combined Confederate force proved overwhelming, and Gregg's cavalry and Miles' infantry receded faster than they had advanced earlier that morning. While Miles was recalled to assist with Birney's attack, Rooney Lee pressed forward again, pushing Gregg back into White Oak Swamp.[17]

The Federals left a regiment as a rear guard, but the Texans cornered it at sunset on Fisher's Farm, cut off their only passage through White Oak Swamp, and killed, wounded, or captured several hundred of them. Joskins proudly exaggerated the fruits of this victory over a cavalry division, claiming that "nearly every man had got a horse—a six shooter and sabre." Half again as many Federal troopers rode their mounts into the swamp hoping for a miracle escape, but few of those troopers escaped capture. And not a one escaped "submersion, head and ears, in the

16 Field, "Campaign of 1864 and 1865," in *SHSP*, 14:552-54. Girardey, born in Lauw, France, a captain two weeks before at the battle of the Crater, was the only officer of such rank promoted directly to general on the Southern side during the war. He was killed near Fussell's Mill on the Darbytown Road August 16, 1864. Schmutz, *Battle of the Crater*, 209-10, 235, 390n69.

17 Polley, *Hood's Texas Brigade*, 249-50; Trudeau, *Last Citadel*, 154-57; Salmon, *Virginia Battlefield Guide*, 421-23; Trudeau, *Last Citadel*, 158. During the engagement, Brig. Gen. John R. Chambliss, one of "Rooney" Lee's division commanders, was killed on Charles City Road two miles north of the infantry battleground. Gregg, a West Point classmate early in the 1850s, took charge of his body, later sending it through the lines to his widow.

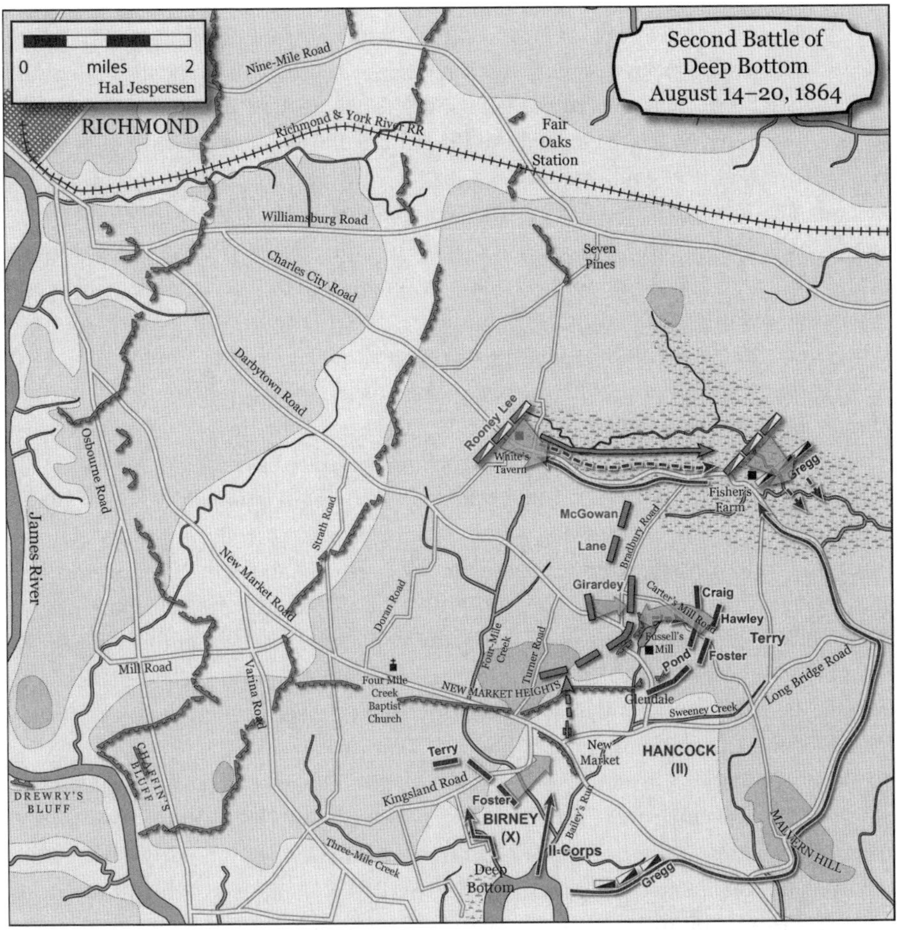

foul-smelling ooze into which they and their steeds sank." Most of the Federal troopers got rescued, but most of their valuable mounts were abandoned to die of starvation. First Lt. W. J. Terry of Company G and Sgt. J. C. Nobles of Company F were killed, and at least seven others were wounded in the engagement, and a number lost to sunstroke and overheating on this "hot and sultry" day.[18]

18 Polley, *Hood's Texas Brigade*, 249-50; Joskins, "A Sketch of Hood's Texas Brigade," UTSA 186; Field, "Campaign of 1864 and 1865," in *SHSP*, 14:554-55. Among the wounded were E. W. James (Co. C), T. H. Mullins (Co. E), Pleasant K. Goree, Jacob Hemphill (Co. H), and R. A. Ashby (Co. K). Simpson, *Compendium*, 208, 215, 219, 229, 231, 243-44. Polley reported none of the men were killed and few wounded. The battle is known various names, among them Second Deep Bottom, Fussell's Mill, Bailey's Creek, White's Tavern, Charles City Road, Strawberry Plains, and White Oak Swamp. The 5th Texas consistently referred to the engagement as "White Oak Swamp."

While the Federal attacks at Deep Bottom ultimately foundered, they did succeed in preventing Lee from sending reinforcements to the Shenandoah Valley and necessitated his keeping part of the Petersburg force north of the James. Meanwhile, south of the river, Warren attacked the Petersburg and Weldon Railroad around the Globe Tavern at 9:00 a.m., August 18. Opposed by only a weak body of cavalry, he successfully destroyed the tracks in the area in short order. Follow-up Confederate attacks halted the destruction, but they could not dislodge Warren that day. On the next, however, Confederate forces rushed through a gap in Warren's line, killing and wounding over 400 and capturing another 2,500 Federals. But neither this nor subsequent attacks were able to recapture the vital rail line. It was lost for good.[19]

The regiment returned with the rest of the brigade to its former position on New Market Heights the evening of August 16, and spent the next day "in desultory, long-distance sharpshooting," until Hancock requested for a cease fire. Then for the rest of the day, litter bearers scoured the field removing the human debris of battle. The Federals began withdrawing south of the James the following day, and the situation quieted down except for some cavalry engagements on the Confederate left, and artillery fire and spirited sharpshooting around New Market Heights, one of whom killed Pvt. W. L. Burton of Company B. Finally, on the night of August 20, Hancock disengaged completely and recrossed to the south side of the James. The Federals had lost some 2,900 men in the engagement, a sizeable number to heatstroke. Confederate casualties amounted to about 1,300.[20]

The Texans were ordered to a position at the Phillips house on August 21 to monitor the movements of Butler's U.S.C.T. brigades at Deep Bottom and detect attempts to reinforce them. The regiment remained there for a full five weeks. Felder reported the regiment "still on the north side of the James . . . [with] only three skeleton brigades on this side of the river. The consequence is our picket duty is very hard. We are on duty every other night & some times every day." On August 21, Anderson's and Law's brigades were transferred back to the Petersburg front, followed by Bratton's brigade on August 22. Only the Texas Brigade, Benning's

19 Trudeau, *Last Citadel*, 161-80; Horn, *Petersburg Campaign*, 132-51; Salmon, *Virginia Battlefield Guide*, 424-28. While further destruction of the line ended with the Federal defeat at Second Ream's Station on August 25, Union troops would control this railroad for the remainder of the campaign, forcing the Confederates to offload supplies from North Carolina at the Stoney Creek station, 18 miles south of Petersburg. Wagons moved supplies to Dinwiddie Court House and then up the Boydton Plank Road into Petersburg.

20 Field, "Campaign of 1864-1865," in *SHSP*, 14:550; Salmon, *Virginia Battlefield Guide*, 424; Polley, *Hood's Texas Brigade*, 251; Simpson, *Compendium*, 183. The actions are often collectively referred to as the second battle of Deep Bottom.

Brigade, and Gary's cavalry remained in front of Richmond, with Gregg in overall command.[21]

During the five weeks the Texans remained near the Phillips House at New Market Heights behind substantial breastworks, approximately a third of its men were required to serve picket duty covering the U.S.C.T.'s front. But life at the Phillips House was "not unenjoyable," as one Texas put it. It was actually "a quiet—happy—peaceful time," Joskins later reflected with ready access to vegetables and fruits in season, expensive but quickly purchased with the men's last two months' pay. In addition to the Richmond papers, the Texans could get the New York *Herald*, other Northern newspapers, and numerous journals from Yankee pickets, all in exchange for tobacco, the one abundant commodity from Rebel sutlers.[22]

But by now, most Texans were sorely homesick for their state and their loved ones. Felder of Company D responding to a 14-month-old letter he had just received from his sister, said: "It matters not how old your letters are . . . [it] gave me the greatest deal of pleasure. It carried my mind back to my dear home (which I almost forgot I had) & the memory of its dear loved ones always produce within me feelings of the most pleasant nature." Felder went on to inform his sister that her brother-in-law, George Elliott, had recently been "killed in one of the battles before Petersburg. I understand that Dr. Elliott takes his death very hard. The old man's recent bereavement must be almost insupportable in his declining years. OH! When will this dreadful contest end & put a stop to our troubles & suffering." Similarly, Capt. Tacitus Clay, Company I's commander, lamented to his wife Bettie, "I dislike this at all times, but particularly at this juncture of affair . . . I long for peace myself—and the blessings attending it. Home, my wife & children."[23]

Despite individual discouragement, spirits remained high in the 5th Texas. Felder remained fervent and optimistic, firmly patriotic and willing to sacrifice. A soldier recently killed at his side by a sharpshooter's bullet, "seemed not to think of himself or

21 Polley, *Hood's Texas Brigade*, 251; Rufus Felder to Emma Elliott, September 18, 1864, in Chicoine, *Confederates of Chappell Hill*, 133-34.

22 Polley, *Hood's Texas Brigade*, 252; Winkler, *Confederate Capital*, 189-90. Felder wrote about the Texans' first encounters with the emancipated black soldiers, saying that almost daily some would come over to the Confederate lines and ask to be sent back to their former masters. The "slaughter pen" at Petersburg had totally demoralized many of them, according to Felder, and they wanted out of this "white folks fight." Felder personally felt it "very humiliating . . . to fight & expose our lines to this mixed horde of black & white demons." Chicoine, *Confederates of Chappell Hill*, 133-34.

23 Rufus Felder to Emma Elliott, August 13, 1864 in Chicoine, *Confederates of Chappell Hill*, 132-33; Joskins, "A Sketch of Hood's Texas Brigade," UTSA 188. Emma had lost her husband, Thomas, in battle less than a year before. Tacitus Clay to Bettie Clay, August 23, 1864 in MSU.

the agony he suffered," he observed, "but prayed to God to spare his life that he may defend his beloved country & avenge himself on dastard foe. Such exhibitions of patriotism from a humble private is of daily occurrence & makes one proud to know he belongs to such an army." Felder confided that while he personally could have sought rank and the comforts it bestowed, "it will be to the private that the honor will be given . . . if our independence is achieved. . . . All that I want on this earth to make me happy is independence & a safe return to our once happy home."[24]

By September 28, Confederate forces north of the James amounted to just a few scattered units. A small brigade of Tennesseans, formally under Bushrod Johnson, watched the river crossing near the terminus of Varina Road at Aiken's Landing from less than a mile away. Gary's cavalry and the Texas brigade at New Market Heights kept watch for any crossings at Deep Bottom. Grant ordered yet another offensive for September 29 to induce Lee to further weaken his Petersburg garrison and to discourage his sending additional reinforcements to the Shenandoah. It followed the familiar pattern: a thrust toward Richmond from the Peninsula, followed by an attack on Confederate supply lines along the South Side Railroad. While still aspiring that Richmond might be taken, Grant remained content with the prospects of cutting the railroad, or at least diverting Lee from further reinforcing Early in the Shenandoah Valley.[25]

Unlike earlier efforts, Benjamin Butler, not Hancock, commanded this latest offensive. The attacking force north of the James comprised the Army of the James, including X Corps under David Birney, the XVIII Corps, now under Maj. Gen. Edward O. C. Ord, and Brig. Gen. August Kautz's cavalry division. To the south, two divisions of of V Corps and two from IX Corps with Gregg's cavalry division would simultaneously attack the rail lines.[26]

The elaborate network of Confederate breastworks south of Richmond extended from Chaffin's Farm on the James across to New Market Road, on both sides of Four Mile Run Creek. On the Varina Road, Fort Harrison stood at the extreme southeastern limit of the main Confederate line of fortifications around the capital commanding a broad plateau where the works angled squarely west to Chaffin's Bluff on the James River. Fort Harrison and Fort Gilmer, a mile and a half to the north on New Market Road, were the primary targets of this latest Federal attack. Fort Harrison

24 Rufus Felder to Emma Elliott, September 18, 1864, in CRC; Chicoine, *Confederates of Chappell Hill*, 133-34.

25 Trudeau, *Last Citadel*, 206-207; Field, "Campaign of 1864 and 1865," in *SHSP*, 14:555; Horn, *Petersburg Campaign*, 158-59; Salmon, *Virginia Battlefield Guide*, 427-28.

26 Horn, *Petersburg Campaign*, 158-59; Trudeau, *Last Citadel*, 207; Foote, *Civil War Narrative*, 3:560-61.

guarded the outer line of defenses and Fort Gilmer anchored the inner line. From Fort Harrison, entrenchments ran north for about 1,300 yards, and then turned west again for a like distance. The large redoubt of Fort Gilmer stood at the angle. Beside these main lines yet another shallow, straggling ditch ran due east from Fort Harrison toward New Market Heights, for a distance of two or three miles, intended only for a temporary defense in emergencies. On September 29, only some 400 Georgians, a remnant of Benning's old brigade and the Texas Brigade on the extreme left occupied this trench. Gary's cavalry supported it farther to the left. The 5th Texas and the other Texans were still encamped near the Phillips House, "a large, commodious, white painted residence" standing right on the line. The Texans by then had been idly occupying their current position for about two weeks and were bored by the inactivity.[27]

Butler's battle plan called for shifting the axis of movement on the capital upriver from the site of all previous efforts launched from Deep Bottom with no attempt contemplated to envelop the Confederate left flank. Instead, Butler's force would deliver swift assaults on its right and center. Major General O. C. Ord's XXIV Corps would cross the James at Aiken's Landing on a newly erected pontoon bridge, while Birney's force used the upper Deep Bottom pontoon bridge, followed by Brig. Gen. August V. Kautz's cavalry. Ord would then attack north on the Varina Road, with Birney storming New Market Heights to the east, and Kautz's force ready to exploit any success with a determined drive for Richmond.[28]

Butler's army crossed the James from the Bermuda Hundred on September 29 for its third attempt that year against Richmond. Butler planned a two-pronged attack: Birney's X Corps, including its U.S.C.T. brigade augmented by Brig. Gen. Charles J. Paine's division, detached from XVIII Corps, another three brigades of black troops, formed the right wing of the offensive. Its mission was to assault and breach the Confederate line south of New Market Road and capture New Market Heights and the Rebel artillery posted on its bluff. They would also protect the right flank of Ord's XVIII Corps, the Federal left wing, which would simultaneously attack Fort Harrison, the stronghold of the Confederate line. After neutralizing the New Market Road line,

27 A. C. Jones, "Texas and Arkansas at Fort Harrison," in *CV*, (1917), 25:24; Winkler, *Confederate Capital*, 187; Polley, *Hood's Texas Brigade*, 252. With Anderson still in the Valley, Gregg remained senior officer of the forces north of the James. Bass temporarily commanded the brigade itself, and Col. Dudley DuBose of the 15th Georgia commanded the Benning remnant. The Phillips', still inhabiting the house, had given the two first story rooms for use as regimental headquarters.

28 Horn, *Petersburg Campaign*, 158-59; Trudeau, *Last Citadel*, 209; Foote, *Civil War Narrative*, 3:560; Field, "Campaign of 1864 and 1865," in *SHSP*, 14:555.

the Union troops there would assist Ord's assault by hitting both Forts Gregg and Gilmer to the north of Fort Harrison.[29]

Ord's corps crossed the James on a hastily constructed pontoon bridge at Aiken's Landing upstream from Deep Bottom early on September 29 before dawn, without a shot being fired. But the Deep Bottom crossing had not been an easy one. Paine's division led the way, but Birney's corps straggled badly marching up Jones's Neck. Despite Butler's precautions, Confederate pickets observed and reported the crossing. Alerted, Lee began rushing reinforcements north from both the Howlett line and Richmond. At the time, however, only a hodgepodge force of 1,800 men manned all the defenses, the Texas Brigade and Benning's Georgia Brigade among them. Gregg chose to defend the ground around New Market Heights on his command's left. His force there consisted of the 5th Texas and the Texas Brigade on the left, and Benning's Georgia Brigade deployed on the New Market Line between New Market Heights and Fort Harrison, north of Kingsland Road near the Phillips House. Ewell, on the right, commanded a force of reservists and Fulton's Tennessee Brigade. Despite the lack of Federal coordination, Butler's force still benefitted from the divided Confederate command, because without coordination between Ewell and Gregg, the Confederates remained unaware that the Varina Road leading to Aiken's Landing had been left totally undefended.[30]

The 5th Texas and the rest of the brigade was posted near a strong line of breastworks in the valley of Deep Bottom at Bailey's Creek, a mile and a half north of Fort Harrison and a similar distance east of Fort Gilmer. The 3rd Arkansas rested on a creek, flanked on its left by the 5th, 4th, and 1st Texas. Three regiments of Gary's dismounted cavalry were situated to the brigade's left. Two guns of the 3rd Richmond Howitzers anchored the right while five guns of the Rockbridge Artillery secured the

29 Horn, *Petersburg Campaign*, 158-60; Lowry, *Dark and Cruel War*, 160-61; Salmon, *Virginia Battlefield Guide*, 429; J. D. Pickens, "Fort Harrison," *CV* (1913), 21:484; Moore, *Story of a Cannoneer*, 263-65; Richard J. Sommers, *Richmond Redeemed: The Seige of Petersburg* (Garden City, NY, 1981), 75; Charles Johnson, "Attack on Fort Gilmer, September 29, 1864,"in *SHSP* (1876), 13:40.

30 Johnson, "Attack on Fort Gilmer," 439-40; Horn, *Petersburg Campaign*, 159; Trudeau, *Last Citadel*, 208-09; Don Lowry, *Dark and Cruel War: The Decisive Months of the Civil War—September—December, 1864* (New York, 1995), 164. Brigadier General Martin Gary, known as "The Bald Eagle" by his men, at the time commanded the 7th South Carolina Cavalry, the 24th Virginia Cavalry, and the Hampton Legion's cavalry. James S. Price, *The Battle of New Market Heights: Freedom Will Be Theirs by the Sword* (Charleston, SC, 2011), 25. Other Confederate defenders on the New Market line were: Fulton's Tennessee Brigade, 300 strong, the City Battalion, some battalions of "Department" troops—clerks and attaches of various government departments—Gary's cavalry brigade, the Louisiana Guard Artillery, Hardaway's Battalion (four batteries), the Rockbridge Artillery, Third Company Richmond Howitzers, the Powhatan Artillery, and the Salem Artillery.

left. The Texas Brigade was entrenched on a rise overlooking a 300-yard field of fire the Federals would have to cross in order to reach these earthworks. The fortifications here strong. They topped five feet and were fronted by a ten-foot ditch beyond the earthworks. Fifty feet in front of that, an elaborate defensive network of sharpened stakes and felled trees with sharpened limbs ran out another 150 yards or so. This effective *chevaux-de-frise* amply protected a brigade with only one man for every five yards in the works, and since the line could not be manned for its entire length, troops had to await enemy activity and then shift troops to threatened points as they occurred.[31]

The Federals struck soon after dawn under cover of an early morning fog and the heavy woods. While the left wing attacked Fort Harrison, the right surged against the New Market Road works. Besides their formidable abatis, other natural obstacles at New Market Road considerably aided the besieged Confederates. Four Mile Creek, a boggy stream the Federals had to cross, presented a sizeable problem. Added to this was a dense, concealing ground fog that day, which both helped and hindered both sides.[32]

Immediately after sunrise, a U.S.C.T. brigade of Paine's division, under the command of Col. Samuel Duncan, led an initial, uncoordinated attack on the Confederate left. As the black regiments charged, the fog in the creek valley was "so thick as to render large objects, a hundred feet distant indistinguishable." The Federals forded Four Mile Creek, quickly driving in the pickets, and attacked the New Market Road line. While the Texans could hear the Union officers barking commands, they could see nothing until the enemy was only 100 feet away. The Texans formed a single line six feet apart and awaited their enemy with their muskets loaded but uncapped, and held their fire until the Federals reached the first line of abatis. They quickly sprang to the top of the low breastworks without awaiting orders and commenced firing, "shooting at shadows." When they reached the abatis 30 or 40 yards in front of the works, the blue-clad blacks, hopelessly entangled in the obstructions, were met with a horrific and galling fire of lead and iron that mowed them down with a terrible

31 Polley, *Hood's Texas Brigade*, 249, 252; J. H. Martin, "Forts Gilmer and Harrison Forces," *CV* (1906), 14:409; Winkler, *Confederate Capital*, 189; Chicoine, *Confederates of Chappell Hill*, 134; Lowry, *Dark and Cruel War*, 166; Nabours, "Active Service of a Texas Command," *CV*, 24:70; Pickens, "Fort Harrison," in *CV*, 21:484. On September 28, the day before the battle, the Texas Brigade hosted twelve belles from the capital at a dinner dance at their campsite near the Phillips House. Winkler, *Confederate Capital*, 191-92.

32 Trudeau, *Last Citadel*, 208-209; Salmon, *Virginia Battlefield Guide*, 432; Field, "Campaign of 1864 and 1865," in *SHSP*, 14:555-56. Other accounts placed the number of defenders in the vicinity at 2,900. See Price, *The Battle of New Market Heights*, 60.

slaughter. Additionally, one of Gary's cavalry regiments advanced to a position from which it could enfilade their right flank.[33]

The Confederates opened up on the entangled Yankees with small arms and artillery. Most of the unfortunate black soldiers able to extricate themselves from the first line of abatis were subsequently shot down before they could reach the next obstruction, a *chevaux-de-frise* (long rows of X-shaped, sharpened sticks attached to logs), but some actually crossed the parapet where they were soon surrounded and either killed or captured. Joskins of Company A exclaimed that "such slaughter my eyes never beheld." Dead black soldiers and their white officers covered the ground.[34]

The attackers had completely bogged down, unable to penetrate the massive obstructions the Confederates had prepared. And the accurate fire of the Texans behind strong breastworks was mowing them down mercilessly "in enthusiastic fashion." The entire black brigade, with many of its men massed within the confining banks of a dry creek bed, found itself totally helpless. "Not a dozen shots in all were fired" by the black soldiers, according to Polley, and not one member of the brigade was wounded. Many of the Texans believed the blacks blindly followed their leaders in some cases, rushing up to the very muzzles of their guns. Such breakthroughs were short-lived. The Yankees actually did break through the front line of the 1st Texas, but half of them were killed within three minutes. Elsewhere along the line, they could not get near the breastworks. Most halted between the lines, unsure where the most danger lay—many throwing down their rifles and fleeing for the rear, yet others dropped to the ground, lying there until captured. The entire struggle lasted only a few minutes, when, seized by a sudden panic, the blacks suddenly "broke and scattered to the winds," leaving a great many dead on the field, in addition to many prisoners.[35]

Remnants of the attacking force fled the field in great confusion, taking even more casualties as they got entangled in the brush. These desperate men clung to the ground just behind the abatis, hoping to shield themselves from the galling fire. But the Texans simply mounted the works and shot them "like sheep led to the shambles." The few remaining attackers withdrew to a ravine through which Four Mile Creek

33 Winkler, *Confederate Capital*, 192; Polley, *Hood's Texas Brigade*, 253; Jones, "Texas and Arkansas at Fort Harrison," 24; Lowry, *Dark and Cruel War*, 166. Gregg had ordered Benning's Brigade to the assistance of the Texans, but it did not arrive until the fight had ended.

34 Joskins, "A Sketch of Hood's Texas Brigade," UTSA 191-92; Polley, *Hood's Texas Brigade*, 253; Winkler, *Confederate Capital*, 192; Lowry, *Dark and Cruel War*, 24; Jones, "Texas and Arkansas at Fort Harrison," in *CV*, 25:24; Chicoine, *Confederates of Chappell Hill*, 134. Joskins reported that a number of black prisoners taken to the rear were "'lost,' in other words, killed."

35 Trudeau, *Last Citadel*, 208; Horn, *Petersburg Campaign*, 161; Field, "Campaign of 1864 and 1865," in *SHSP*, 14:556; Salmon, *Virginia Battlefield Guide*, 432.

flowed. Paine made little effort to support Duncan's attack, and Duncan himself was wounded four times in the assault. His troops sustained over 50 percent casualties in their half hour effort to carry the Confederate works. Over 1000 troops were lost in the brief first assault, including 194 black soldiers and 23 of their white officers, all killed in the span of five minutes. In some places, the dead had been stacked five deep. The Rebels captured two regimental colors along with hundreds of rifles, taken by the Texas soldiers. They also took 43 black soldiers prisoner, the majority of whom chose to serve their captors as orderlies, rather than face confinement in a Confederate prison. The Texans reportedly executed an unknown number of these brave black soldiers following their surrender.[36]

Paine decided to attempt a second piecemeal attack with Col. Alonzo G. Draper's brigade. Draper positioned his three regiments side by side, each deployed in a column two companies wide and five deep. This formation crossed Four Mile Creek, advancing through the same field as the previous attack, all the while being blasted by Confederate artillery. The black attackers nonetheless charged up the slope but floundered in the marshy creek tributary and the first line of abatis. There, the nearly impregnable Confederate rifle pits blistered them with lead. Pinned down by relentless shelling and shooting, the Yankees returned fire—violating the conventional maxim that troops in the open could not win against soldiers protected by earthworks. They seriously attempted to do just that for well over half an hour. Finally, when the fire slackened somewhat, the U.S.C.T. brigade seized the opportunity to charge New Market Heights—across the earthworks and the slopes beyond—only to discover that almost all of the Confederate defenders had vanished.[37]

36 Jones, "Texas and Arkansas at Fort Harrison," in *CV*, 25:24; H. H. Perry, "Assault on Fort Gilmer," in *CV* (1906), 13:414; Trudeau, *Last Citadel*, 209-11; T. J. May, "The Fight at Fort Gilmer," in *CV* (1905), 12:588; Yeary, *Reminiscences of the Boys in Gray*, 62; Polley, *Hood's Texas Brigade*, 252-54; J. H. Martin, "The Assault on Fort Gilmer," in *CV* (1905), 13:269; Hamilton, *History of Company M*, 62; Winkler, *Confederate Capital*, 192-94.

37 Lowry, *Dark and Cruel War*, 160, 166-67. Despite Confederate claims that the black units had to be prodded by bayonets to move forward, or that their "courage" was because they were "drunk on whiskey mixed with gunpowder," as several Texans later claimed, the black soldiers truly proved their meddle at this battle. Persevering despite being nearly cut to ribbons, their acts of heroism were so common that 14 of them were later awarded the Medal of Honor (along with two of their officers). Only16 black soldiers were so decorated during the entire war, a testament to their valor on this field. The Medal of Honor winners included: William H. Barnes, Powhatan Beatty, James H. Bronson, Christian A. Fleetwood, James Gardiner, James H. Harris, Thomas R. Hawkins, Alfred B. Hilton, Milton M. Holland, James Miles, Alexander Kelly, Robert A. Pinn, Edward Ratcliff, and Charles Veal. National Park Service, "African Americans at the Siege of Petersburg," accessed December 15, 2011, www.nps.gov/articles/african-americans-at-the-siege-of-petersburg.htm; The Civil War, "The Battle of New Market Heights," accessed December 15, 2011, www.mycivilwar.com/battles/ 604929.html.

While the Texans vigorously defended New Market Heights, the Federal left wing, two divisions of the XVIII Corps, advanced northwards around 6:00 a.m. toward Confederate Fort Harrison (or Fort Burnham). Home to Batteries No. 7, 8, and 9, Harrison commanded all the ground northeast of the outer Confederate defenses. On this particular morning, its defenders were painfully sparse, only seven companies of the 17th Georgia of Benning's Brigade. This diminutive force, along with the 1st Virginia Reserve Battalion, the small 63rd Tennessee regiment, and 200 artillerymen from the Department of Richmond, 800 men total, were the sole troops manning the entire exterior line from Jones's Salient, past Fort Harrison to Battery No. 11, against over 8,000 Federals.[38]

Gregg positioned himself to the west near the Varina Road and spotted yet another blue column advancing on the weak Confederate center up that road. He immediately recognized the grave danger to his main force of being cut off should it remain on New Market Heights, and he therefore dispatched orders for the Texans to abandon their current position and move at the double quick west toward Fort Harrison. From there he anticipated he could hold that portion of the exterior line. He then ordered the just arriving 2nd Virginia Reserve Battalion and DuBose's Georgia Brigade to counterattack and retake Fort Harrison, a mission utterly beyond their capabilities at this juncture. Instead, DuBose led the rest of his brigade northward to defend Fort Johnson. While the Texans were still in route, another courier arrived advising that Fort Harrison had already fallen, and that the Texans should therefore report to Gregg at once. When the Texans failed to arrive when he expected them, an impatient. Gregg rode eastward and found the wearied Texas Brigade and the 25th Virginia Battalion strung out in a long column heading west along the New Market Line. Following a 15-minute rest and regrouping break, the Texans double-quicked up to the outer line of entrenchments they had guarded weeks before. They used the broad, level ditch incorporated into the New Market Road defenses for their route west, which was both the shortest avenue and the best footing to reach these exterior lines.[39]

Butler later wrote that on September 29, 1864, "the capacity of the negro race for soldiers had then and there been fully settled forever." See Charles W. Hana, *African American Recipients of the Medal of Honor* (Jefferson, NC, 2002); *OR* 4, Series 3, 770-71; Dudly Cornish, *The Sable Arm: Black Troops in the Union Army, 1861-1865* (Lawrence, KA, 1987), 266.

38 Johnson, "Attack on Fort Gilmer," in *SHSP*, 13:439-40; Martin, "The Assault Upon Fort Gilmer," 269; Earl J. Hess, *In the Trenches at Petersburg: Field Fortifications & Confederate Defeat* (Chapel Hill, 2009), 162; Sommers, *Richmond Redeemed*, 38; Lowry, *Dark and Cruel War*, 168.

39 Sommers, *Richmond Redeemed*, 38; Lowry, *Dark and Cruel War*, 168-70, 184; Polley, *Hood's Texas Brigade*, 254-55. Fort Harrison ultimately fell at approximately 7:00 a.m. that morning.

Gregg accompanied his men west, and emerging from a woods along Three Mile Creek in view of Fort Harrison, he discovered significantly reinforced Federals there. The Federals were also bearing down on the Texans in line of battle, at right angles to the works to their right, effectively cutting them off. Faced with a superior force, the Texans also had the disadvantage of marching by the flank and were considerably strung out. As the Federals formed for a charge, the Texans rushed back north for a pine thicket to their right and rear, which offered ample cover. Then, skirting the enemy's left and rear, at a "dead run" they gained the position on the main line the enemy had occupied a few minutes before. It was, one veteran remembered "one of the neatest and most successful maneuvers" he saw during the war. Gregg now mulled launching a counterattack to retake Fort Harrison. But with the Federals on his left nearing the inner line of entrenchments, he altered his priorities. The pressure Benning's Brigade had already endured at Fort Johnson convinced him to use his Texans primarily to protect the intermediate defensive line. Richmond would be at the Federals' mercy if this line were lost. So he urged the Texans to make the best possible speed northwest to the inner line.[40]

Shortly before 2:00 p.m., the Federals made a flanking movement toward the Texans' left. Concealed by the broken terrain, the Yankees drawn close to Fort Gilmer and were about to attack, about a half mile to the Texans' left. Gregg galloped down the line pressing his men to double quick that half mile, which they immediately did "in about as short time as men ever passed over the same distance." The fleet Texans ultimately won the race with the onrushing enemy, arriving and lining up in the almost undefended works on Fort Gilmer's right just as the Federals appeared in force. The Texans had to hold a line of breastworks a mile and a half long; each soldier "had to be practically ubiquitous." Beset by artillery, infantry, and sharpshooters, the regiment "exhibited some as desperate fighting as was done anytime during the war," according to Nabours. Gregg dispatched a hasty message to Field, coming up from Petersburg—"for Gods sake to hurry up." With the numbers they faced "we could not hold our own," he pleaded. Soon remnants of other nearby brigades urgently sent to bolster the position joined the defense.[41]

Fort Gilmer stood on the tip of a fairly large salient in the intermediate line of Confederate defenses, where the north-south line turned 90 degrees to run east-west,

40 Jones, "Texas and Arkansas at Fort Harrison," *CV*, 25:24-25; Lowry, *Dark and Cruel War*, 168-70, 177.

41 *OR* 42, pt. 1., 331-34; Joskins, "A Sketch of Hood's Texas Brigade," in UTSA, 191-93, 199-200; Nabours, "Active Service of a Texas Command," in *CV*, 24:70; H. H. Perry, "Assault on Fort Gilmer," in *CV*, (1905), 13:24; Simpson, *Lee's Grenadier Guard*, 434-35; Polley, *Hood's Texas Brigade*, 254-55.

skirting around the headwater of a small tributary of Cornelius Creek with an "extensive flat in front, from which the trees had all been cut . . . [away]." Inside that fort were seven companies of the 15th Georgia, in addition to fragments of several others, and two heavy guns, including one heavy, 64-pounder. The men of two batteries of light artillery manned the line there between the fort and the creek.[42]

The oncoming Texans occupied the trenches left of the fort, previously held by 50 Georgians. Just as the men jumped into the earthworks, at least a full enemy brigade crested the brow of a hill some 200 yards away. Fortunately, the Federals failed to mount a coordinated, determined attack on the fort and surrounding fortifications. Their vastly superior force would have easily broken through. Instead, they punched at various sectors of the fortifications with unsupported, brigade level attacks. The huge disparity in numbers still pressured the defenders severely, however, compelling them "to hurry from one to another widely separated point, and there fight in single rank and far apart."[43]

Foster led three brigades of Birney's X Corps in on a long line that soon absorbed heavy Confederate artillery fire. Once the butternut infantry opened up and the artillery switched to canister, the Yankees quickly retreated to the cover of a ravine. U.S.C.T. troops from Paine's division sent in by Birney got bogged down and stalled in front of the *chevaux-de-frise* unable to work their way through. Defenders on the fort's left engaged with white units, while those in front faced this heavy force of black regiments. After emerging from a heavy wood several hundred yards east of Fort Gilmer, the Federals advanced under sporadic rifle and artillery fire until within 100 yards of the fort. At this point, the Confederate fire began to have a ruinous impact.[44]

At 10 paces, two Federal color bearers went down and the Union lines wavered, halted, and turned back, except for approximately 200 black soldiers who continued forward, dropping into a deep ditch surrounding the base of the fort. The 5th Texas and rest of the Texans' line poured in a deadly fire with many remaining attackers quickly falling, as others continued forward. These soldiers attempted to boost each other over the parapet, only to be methodically shot by the Texans when their heads appeared atop the breastworks. The Texans and Georgians easily repelled the swarming black troops, who were now trapped, with death beckoning from front and rear (from friendly fire). Refusing calls to surrender, the frantic bluecoats continued

42 Johnson, "Attack on Fort Gilmer," in *SHSP*, 13:441; Lowry, *Dark and Cruel War*, 183-84.

43 Jones, "Texas and Arkansas at Fort Harrison," in *CV*, 25:25; Polley, *Hood's Texas Brigade*, 252; Horn, *Petersburg Campaign*, 160-63; Trudeau, *Last Citadel*, 211-12.

44 *OR* 42, pt. 1, 795; Jones, "Texas and Arkansas at Fort Harrison," in *CV*, 25:24-25; Martin, "Assault on Fort Gilmer," in *CV*, 13:269-70; Sommers, *Richmond Redeemed*, 81-86; Lowry, *Dark and Cruel War*, 184-86.

boosting themselves up the wall, only to be killed by the well trained shots from the Confederate line. Upon a demand to surrender, several Texans heard one of their black soldiers yell to lift up "Corporal Dick," and the corporal was accordingly hoisted, only to fall back lifeless, a bullet through his head. Notwithstanding this loss, the Federals continued trying to climb the ditch. Many of those not shot trying to scale the wall were killed or crippled by makeshift grenades, lighted artillery shells thrown over the wall into the ditch which detonated with such effect that few attackers remained standing to surrender. Those men remaining finally begged for mercy, and the Texans took the few of them not dead or mortally wounded prisoner.[45]

This small band of Texas soldiers successfully held off attacks from Birney's sizeable units until 2:30 p.m., when the remainder of Field's men arrived, travelling by train from Drewry's Bluff and double-quicking across the bridge to Chaffin's Farm, a distance of five miles. These reinforcements were able to maintain the Confederate possession at this key fort and its supporting breastworks throughout the afternoon. By evening, still more reinforcements arrived to bolster the position.[46]

The fighting continued on September 30, including an unsuccessful Confederate attempt to retake Fort Harrison. Most of the Confederates engaged this day were reinforcements from the south side placed under Field's command. The 5th Texas was not engaged at all this second day. Miraculously, it had not lost one man in the

45 Joskins, "A Sketch of Hood's Texas Brigade," in UTSA, 192; Jess B. Lott, "Two Boys of the Fifth Texas Regiment," in *CV* (1905), 13:416-17; J. A. H. Granberry, "That Fort Gilmer Fight," in *CV* (1905), 13:413; May, "Fight at Fort Gilmer," in *CV*, 12:588; George Reese, "What Five Confederates Did at Petersburg [Richmond]," in *CV* (1904), 12:281. Joskins reported that the blacks captured at Fort Gilmer were taken some 300-500 yards to the rear and "lost," in other words, "executed." Joskins, "A Sketch of Hood's Texas Brigade," in UTSA, 192. Edward A. Pollard, *The Last Year of the War* (New York, 1866), 99-100. Here, as at New Market Heights, serious allegations arose of black soldiers being killed after surrendering or while trying to. A 17th Georgia soldier later wrote that "the Texans . . . killed niggers galore." However, as their foe at the time was predominantly black, this is not proof of an atrocity. George S. Burkhardt, *Confederate Rage, Yankee Wrath: No Quarter in the Civil War* (Carbondale, IL, 2007), 179. In fact, other sources say the Texans "bowed to black pluck when they refrained from killing the survivors" in the ditch, which was a departure from what happened elsewhere. Burkhardt, *Confederate Rage, Yankee Wrath*, 182. When Ewell received first hand reports of the slaughter of Birney's black infantry, he stopped the killings "instantly," reasoning that these men were now United States soldiers thus enjoying the same status accorded all enemy combatants. Paul D. Casdorph, *Confederate General R. S. Ewell: Robert E. Lee's Hesitant Commander* (Lexington, KY, 2004), 319-20. J. D. Pickens of the brigade later acknowledged the fighting qualities of the attackers, indicating "I want to say in this connection that, in my opinion, no troops up to that time fought us with more bravery than did those Negroes". Pickens, "Fort Harrison," in *CV*, 21:484.

46 Joskins, "A Sketch of Hood's Texas Brigade," in UTSA, 201-204; Perry, "Assault on Fort Gilmer," in *CV*, 13:24; Johnson, "Attack on Fort Gilmer," in *SHSP*, 13:441; Sommers, *Richmond Redeemed*, 81-86.

fighting on September 29 and suffered few wounded. One significant loss did occur, however, when brigade quartermaster Littlefield had to abandon many boxes of irreplaceable shoes and uniforms as Fort Harrison fell. In the two days of fighting, the Confederates lost 1,750 men, mostly on the second day, and the Federals 4,150, primarily on the first. The engagement thereafter was referred to variously as Chaffin's Farm, Laurel Hill, and New Market Heights, as well as Fort Gilmer and Fort Harrison.[47]

A dispatch from Ewell to Braxton Bragg, then military advisor to President Davis, reported that "the attack on Fort Gilmer was repulsed by Generals Field and Gregg, handsomely." The timid leadership of Birney and his subordinates squandered a golden opportunity that day for Grant to capture Richmond. Lesser witnesses said the same: "But for the pluck, the uncommon pluck of the heavy artillerists and of the privates of the Texas and Benning's Brigades," Polley wrote, "Fort Gilmer, the one place where the attack of the Federals seemed most determined, must have fallen, and had it, Richmond would have been in the grasp of the Union Army."[48]

Hardly reconciled to a permanent loss of Fort Harrison and its exterior line of fortifications, Lee remained determined to break the Union's possession. Federal gains on September 29, coupled with Southern manpower issues, required so many troops north of the James that he decided to make a virtue of necessity and retake the offensive. On October 7, he devised a plan to drive the Federals from a small portion of the outer defenses they had taken by capturing Fort Harrison on September 29. The left, or south flank of Butler's army, held by Bvt. Maj. Gen. Godfrey Weitzel's XVIII Corps was anchored near the James, assailable only from the front. However, beyond Weitzel's line, Kautz's cavalry division stretched away through Darbytown Road and the Charles City Road, some six miles southeast of the city. This Yankee force was insufficient to hold such a long line against a sizeable, determined enemy attack. Moreover, its flank was "in the air"—not abutting a natural obstacle as a safeguard and thereby subject to envelopment. It was the one vulnerable portion of Butler's line.[49]

In furtherance of this plan, Lee withdrew both Field's and Hoke's divisions from the Petersburg defenses, replacing them with local defense forces. Most of these new units were positioned on the Darbytown Road; Gary's cavalry brigade and one of Field's brigades formed on the Charles City Road, which ran parallel and north of the

47 OR 42, pt. 1. 136-7, 794-95, 876, 880; Johnson, "Attack on Fort Gilmer," 442; Pollard, *Last Year of the War*, 101-02; Salmon, *Virginia Battlefield Guide*, 433.

48 OR 42, pt. 1, 937; Polley, *Hood's Texas Brigade*, 255; Simpson, *Lee's Grenadier Guard*, 437.

49 Horn, *Petersburg Campaign*, 167-68; Lowry, *Dark and Cruel War*, 270-71.

Darbytown Road. The latter force was to attack down that road, breaking Kautz's thin line, then turn south to strike the primary objectivein the flank—a line of Federal entrenchments and barricades built across Darbytown Road some six miles southeast of the city—in its flank. Once that portion of the Union line was demolished, Field's entire infantry would wheel to its right and hit Butler's infantry in flank and rear, while Hoke simultaneously attacked its front. If the Union flank gave way, the entire enemy line could then be stripped away from the exterior line "like peeling the skin from a tangerine," forcing the Federals to evacuate Fort Harrison and retreat to Deep Bottom. Given its significance, Lee decided to command this operation in person. Darbytown Road was unfortunately to become a battle of uncoordinated Confederate attacks against a position of great strength. Unfortunately, the coming fight extracted a high cost from the Texas Brigade.[50]

At 3:00 a.m., the brigade was called into line and marched toward Darbytown Road, with Field's other brigades and several of Hoke's. The Texas Brigade was in position shortly after dawn on October 7. As the Texans passed Lee at dawn, the men observed him reading a Richmond newspaper. The Southern commander, astride Traveler, was alone, intently observing the battle preparations and awaiting reports from his staff about troop formations preparing for the assault. He got agitated a bit later when Porter Alexander told him that his guns had not been positioned for lack of local guides. He then rode off to near a fringe of woods where the 5th Texas was forming for the attack. Captain William T. Hill, the regiment's commander, related how

> [t]he Texas Brigade [had] formed in line about twenty yards from a dim road, on which, immediately in front of my company, General Lee, unattended, sat on his horse, obviously awaiting reports from members of his staff engaged in forming the troops in line. After quite a little while one of his aides approached him and saluted, and Lee asked if all the commands were ready for the advance. 'None but the Texas Brigade, General,' said the aide.

"The Texas Brigade is always ready," Lee retorted, and while he spoke in an ordinary tone, the clear, frosty air carried his words to the ears of whole regiment.[51]

50 *OR* 42, pt. 2, 142; Joskins, "A Sketch of Hood's Texas Brigade," in UTSA, 206-08; Freeman, *Lee's Lieutenants*, 3:592; Polley, *Hood's Texas Brigade*, 256-57; Simpson, *Lee's Grenadier Guard*, 438; 206-08; Sorrell, *Recollections of a Staff Officer*, 254-55; Salmon, *Virginia Battlefield Guide*, 436; Horn, *Petersburg Campaign*, 167-68.

51 Polley, *Hood's Texas Brigade*, 256-58; Sorrell, *Recollections of a Staff Officer*, 254-55; Simpson, *Lee's Grenadier Guard*, 438-39; Joskins, "A Sketch of Hood's Texas Brigade," in UTSA, 208-10.

The Federals discerned a growing movement against their line was underway. Deserters told them about the planned attack for that morning, and that the Federals prepared to receive it. However, Kautz had only 1,700 men to cover a line as long as the one the XVIII and X Corps combined covered. A great deal of work was still needed to reverse the captured Confederate exterior lines to make them suitable for attack from the west, with picks and shovels at a premium. A swamp incorporated into the design by Confederate engineers to impede an advance would now hamper any Federal retreat. Two Union brigades, both supported with batteries of four 3-inch guns of horse artillery manned the lines north and south of Darbytown Road, one on each side.[52]

Before dawn, Field's men moved into position opposite Kautz on the Darbytown Road, while Hoke's Division waited on New Market Road. Gary's cavalry opened the movement by driving in the Federal pickets on the Charles City Road then turning south toward Darbytown Road, where they clashed with Col. Samuel P. Spear's troopers. Field attacked Kautz at 9:00 a.m. with Bratton on the left of the road, facing Spear's brigade; Anderson's brigade to the right of the road confronted Col. Robert M. West's brigade, with the Texans in support on the road itself. The Confederates advanced with a strong skirmish line out front. Though Anderson's attack faltered, Bratton's men pushed through the heavy timber and drove off 400 of Spear's men, unused to "foot service." Some of Bratton's men then wheeled right and scattered West's troopers. Unable to be rallied, the Union formation soon disintegrated, and the men "took recourse to their legs," and the retreat became a rout when Gary's men charged into the Federal flank and rear. Freed from their encounter with Spear's attackers, Gary's cavalry then charged into the flank and rear of the retreating Federals. In short order, they overran an incomplete Federal fortification one-half mile in front of Kautz's main line, capturing eight pieces of artillery, several stands colors, and a sizeable number of prisoners.[53]

The din of battle to their immediate north alerted the X Corps at about 6:00 or 7:00 a.m. that a serious threat to their position was underway. Birney, who succumbed to malaria two weeks later, arose from his sickbed personally to direct the response to this threat on his right. He shifted units from his left to the northern portion of Fort Harrison so as to withdraw three brigades of Terry's division from the main line and place them in an east-west line facing north. Col. Francis B. Pond's brigade holding the left, connected the main line there in the strong works built to protect this flank

52 Lowry, *Dark and Cruel War*, 271-72.

53 Freeman, *R. E. Lee*, 3:508; Lowry, *Dark and Cruel War*, 271-73; Polley, *Hood's Texas Brigade*, 256-57; Horn, *Petersburg Campaign*, 168-69.

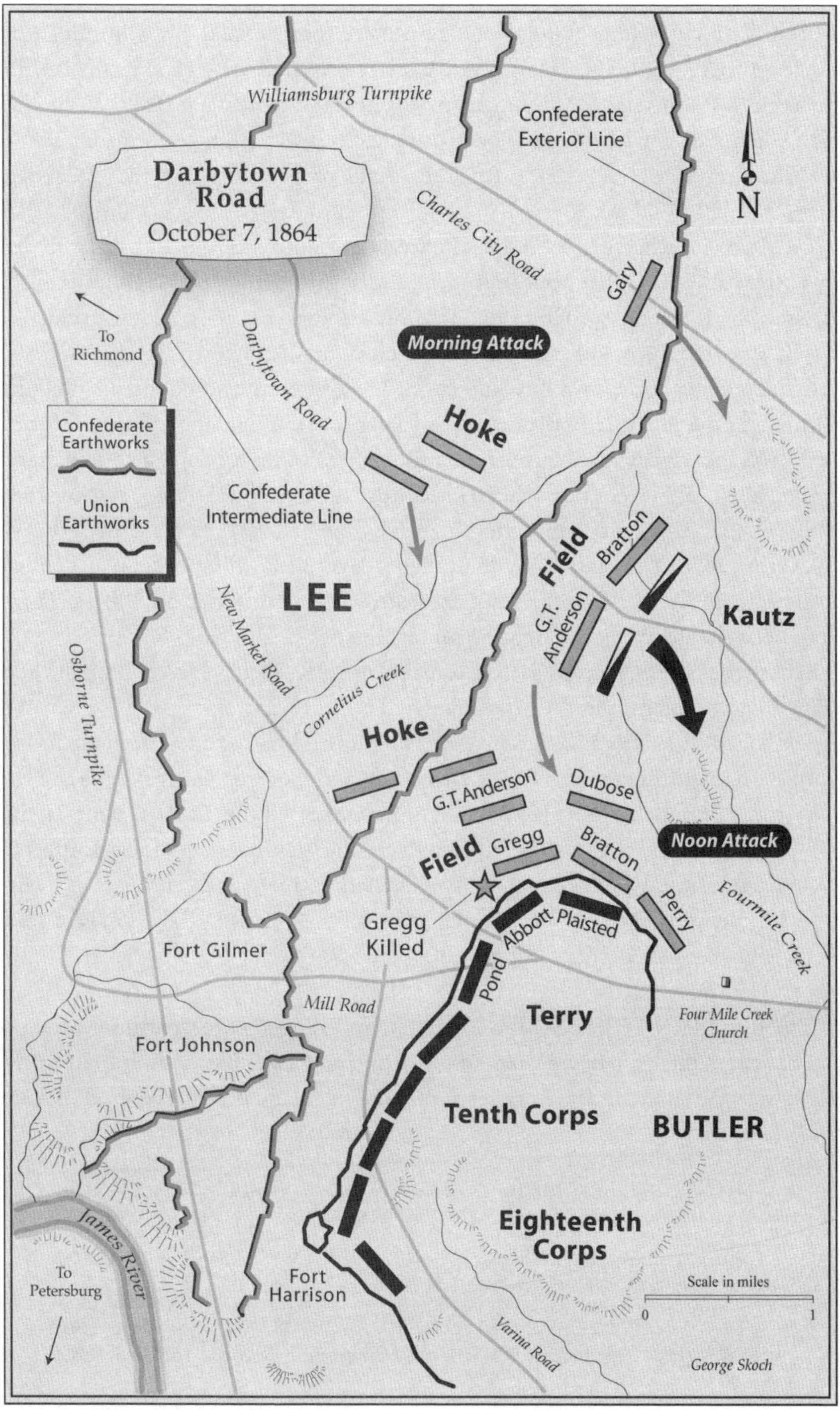
Darbytown Road
October 7, 1864
Williamsburg Turnpike
Confederate Exterior Line
N
Charles City Road
Gary
To Richmond
Morning Attack
Darbytown Road
Hoke
Confederate Earthworks
Union Earthworks
Confederate Intermediate Line
Field
Bratton
LEE
New Market Road
G.T. Anderson
Kautz
Osborne Turnpike
Cornelius Creek
Hoke
G.T.Anderson
Dubose
Noon Attack
Field
Gregg
Bratton
Fourmile Creek
Gregg Killed
Abbott
Plaisted
Perry
Fort Gilmer
Pond
Mill Road
Terry
Four Mile Creek Church
Fort Johnson
Tenth Corps
BUTLER
Eighteenth Corps
James River
To Petersburg
Fort Harrison
Scale in miles
0
1
Varina Road
George Skoch

north of the New Market Road. Pond's position, though solid, hung in the air until Cols. Joseph C. Abbott's and Harris M. Plaisted's brigades arrived and were placed at a right angle to Pond's right. Abbott's men then held the center, and Plaisted's the right, which consisted only of rifle pits located in deep woods. All three brigades sent out skirmishers, and at about 10:00 a.m. the sound of guns signaled the Confederate approach.[54]

Field's column had uncovered the Federal right, and with Kautz's cavalry in flight, they rushed ahead in what appeared to be the shortest route to turn that flank and push into the Federal rear. However, after great initial success, Field's attack lost its momentum amid the woods and streams south of the Darbytown Road. To continue against an enemy force in a new direction, Field's column took considerable time reforming into a line three brigades wide facing south. While the infantry reformed, Porter Alexander began maneuvering on the right with his artillery. The open terrain afforded him the ability to perform, in his words, "that beautiful manouevre in artillery drill of 'Fire advancing by half battery'" (half of the battery fires while the other half moves forward). The initial bombardment devastated the Federals. Eventually, however, their artillery found its range, destroying a gun less than 100 yards from where Lee was observing the fighting on his horse.[55]

After what Lee perceived as an excruciating delay, Field's Division finally began its new advance against the X Corps infantry. The 5th Texas, along with the rest of the brigade, spearheaded the assault down the Darbytown Road against formidable Union fortifications, with Anderson's Brigade on its left and the remaining brigades of Field's Division on Anderson's left. Hoke's Division supported the Texans' right. Initially, Lee's plan succeeded. Just as the infantry went in, Alexander's gunners fortuitously blew up one of the Federal caissons. Field's men "came tearing through the woods yelling like demons," one of Terry's men remembered. In fact, they came on so fast that Federal skirmishers could not get out of their way. Many of them "lay flat on their faces and let the charging column pass over them."[56]

The formidable Federal position featured imposing log breastworks on the crest of a hill, with a thick abatis 500 yards to its front, and a significant swamp in front of that. It was one of the most daunting fortifications the men were required to assault

54 Andre Noah Trudeau, "Darbytown Road Debacle," *America's Civil War* (1997), 5:36; Horn, *Petersburg Campaign*, 168-69; Lowry, *Dark and Cruel War*, 272-73.

55 Trudeau, "Darbytown Road Debacle," *America's Civil War*, 5:35; Salmon, *Virginia Battlefield Guide*, 436-37; Lowry, *Dark and Cruel War*, 273-74.

56 Joskins, "A Sketch of Hood's Texas Brigade," in UTSA, 211-18; Winkler, *Confederate Capital*, 195; Polley, *Hood's Texas Brigade*, 257-58; Field, "Campaign of 1864 and 1865," in *SHSP*, 14:556-57.

since Gaines' Mill. The strongest trenches bisected Darbytown Road, and the Texans' attack plunged directly down this road. Approaching within a quarter mile of the works, the Texans came under heavy artillery fire, forcing them to take cover and regroup. Following a brief pause, the men again advanced steadily onward and waded through the swamp, and then encountered the thick abatis at the other end. "[E]very tree of the many lying on the ground over which we charged pointed its sharpened branches at our eyes, faces, bodies and clothing," a Texan related. "No sooner was a fellow out of the detaining clutch of one, than another presented itself, and taking hold of flesh or clothing, held him captive a while." Staying in line simply proved impossible, yet the Texans bravely pressed forward until a heavy enfilading fire from the right roared from the enemy. Many Yankees were armed with Spencer repeating carbines, and their fire was withering on the regiment. Its effect was magnified because Hokes's Division, failing to keep pace on the flank, had halted. Hoke "did such a poor job of it," a Texan recalled, "that the Yankees had abundant leisure and opportunity to concentrate their strength against us." Soon, most of the brigade came to a halt in a depression about 300 yards short of the enemy earthworks, but at least somewhat protected from the intense Federal fire.[57]

On the weaker, right side of the Federal line, Perry's Brigade got within 40 yards of the Union earthworks, but lacking reinforcements soon fell back. One young soldier streaked with blood had approached Lee pleading for reinforcements. A concerned Lee inquired as to his wounds: "I'm shot through both arms General," he replied, "but I don't mind that, General! I want you to send some more men down there to help our boys."[58]

It was too late by then. The Texas Brigade on the Confederate right had charged through the remaining abatis toward Pond's brigade, the forbidding Federal left, with the strongest defenses. Opening up on the gray column, the Federals with their Spencer repeating carbines produced a noise "like appalling peals of thunder," a Union cavalryman said, and "the Texans swayed to the earth like cut grain." Private Basil Brashear of Company F wrote that the men started up the hill "with the old Texas yell, but the enemy mowed us down like hay." Climbing over and around the fallen tree tops in the face of horrific fire, the Texans totally lost their alignment and

57 Joskins, "A Sketch of Hood's Texas Brigade," in UTSA, 211-18; Winkler, *Confederate Capital*, 195; Polley, *Hood's Texas Brigade*, 257-58; Simpson, *Lee's Grenadier Guard*, 439; Sorrell, *Recollections of a Staff Officer*, 255; J. B. Polley, "Polley Lost A Foot—A Furlough," in *CV* (1897), 5:570; Trudeau, "Darbytown Road Debacle," *America's Civil War*, 5:36. Porter Alexander later claimed Hoke never moved forward at all.

58 Polley, *Hood's Texas Brigade*, 257, 260; Freeman, *R. E. Lee*, 3:509; Field, "Campaign of 1864 and 1865," in *SHSP*, 14:557-58.

scattered. While bullets struck his gun and clothing, Polley spotted the 5th Texas flag to his left, some 50 yards ahead, and thinking it belonged to the 4th Texas, he made for it. Before he reached it, though, the flag bearer cast a look behind him and finding himself virtually alone, ducked away from the storm. "First one and than another of the Fourth and Fifth dropped in behind him, until seven or eight of us were strung out in single file, your humble servant, as last comer, standing at the trail-end."[59]

Only a few of the 5th Texas men got within 40 yards of the Federal barricade, where they were pinned down or shot. Joskins remarked as to how "few" of the men were still in line. "[W]ho can imagine what it cost us to come those last five hundred yards . . . and our work was not yet done." Soon overcome by a murderous fire, with retreat no longer an option, many Texans were forced to surrender. At this point a fatal bullet bored through General Gregg's neck, killing him instantly. Colonel Bass of the 1st Texas assumed command of the brigade until he fell wounded. Command devolved upon Lt. Col. C. M. Winkler of the 4th Texas, who led the remnants of the brigade away from the lethal fire from every side to the cover of a woods and hollows in its rear, some five miles southwest of the capital on the west bank of Cornelius Creek.[60]

The attack cost the Confederates approximately 700 casualties to 458 for the Federals, with casualties among the Texans their heaviest since the battle of the Wilderness. Joskins estimated that "fully 200 out of the 450 of the Brigade had fallen" at Darbytown Road/New Market Road or Four Mile Creek, as it was sometimes referenced by various accounts. Another contemporary source placed the casualties at 119, including 11 killed, 90 wounded, and 18 missing.[61]

The 5th Texas came away particularly hard hit during the battle. Captain Hill, then in command, reported 53 men killed, wounded, or missing during September and October. Since the Chaffin's Farm/New Market Heights fight had cost no casualties, almost all of this number came at this fight at Darbytown Road. Captain Williams reported losing 10 of the 14 men of Company F he had led into the battle, the highest casualty rate F Company had experienced in the entire war. Williams wrote home that his regiment had but a handful of officers and only 61 enlisted men then present for

59 Joskins, "A Sketch of Hood's Texas Brigade," in UTSA, 216-17; Winkler, *Confederate Capital*, 195; Polley, *Hood's Texas Brigade*, 257-58; Field, "Campaign of 1864 and 1865," in *SHSP*, 14:557.

60 Joskins, "A Sketch of Hood's Texas Brigade," in UTSA, 216-17; Polley, *Hood's Texas Brigade*, 257-58; Lowry, *Dark and Cruel War*, 274-75; Trudeau, "Darbytown Road Debacle," *America's Civil War*, 5:36; Parker, *Touched By Fire*, 96; Winkler, *Confederate Capital*, 195; Sorrell, *Recollections of a Staff Officer*, 255; Hanks, *Captain Benton's Company*, 46.

61 Joskins, "A Sketch of Hood's Texas Brigade," in UTSA, 217-18; Winkler, *Confederate Capital*, 196-98; Polley, *Hood's Texas Brigade*, 258-60.

duty. Joskins received two wounds himself: one "in the right breast passing through and [another one in] the left knee." Horrified of being captured, he "immediately turned and started back, but he soon fell with "blood spouting from" his chest "like water from a pump." His only remaining mess mate carried him from the field and "tenderly cared" for him. Polley, also wounded in the battle, later stated that "[h]istory will likely call it a reconnaissance in force, but to me and fifty or a hundred others of the Texas Brigade who lost their lives or were seriously wounded, it was a desperate assault by a small force upon well-manned earthworks."[62]

Also among the seriously wounded were Capt. Clay, commander of Company I and Robert Campbell (Joskins) of Company A, shot through the right lung and left knee. Furloughed, Campbell arrived in Huntsville in January 1865 to recuperate from his grievous wounds. In April 1865, he sought retirement because his wounds "rendered . . . [him] unfit for Field Duty." Clay, of Independence, had been shot in the right leg, which required its amputation above the knee.

In late October 1864, Clay wrote his wife Bettie from General Hospital at Howard's Grove in Richmond about his condition. "I bear the loss without repining." He also reported fellow 5th Texas officers Capt. Thomas A. Baber of Company E, after amputation of his arm above the elbow, and Lt. Ben I. Franklin were both recuperating satisfactorily, while family friend Drew F. Morgan of Clay's company had sustained "a hard wound," and had died. He was "a gallant soldier & an unpretending gentleman. I not only sorrow on his account, but his friends and relatives have my sincere sympathy."[63]

62 Muster Roll, Field, Staff and Band, 5th Texas, Aug. 31 – Oct. 31, 1864, in TSA; Joskins, "A Sketch of Hood's Texas Brigade," in UTSA, 217-18; Watson Williams to Laura Jesse Bryan, October 7, 1864, in CRC; Simpson, *Lee's Grenadier Guard*, 440-41; Lowry, *Dark and Cruel War*, 275; Polley, *Hood's Texas Brigade*, 258; Salmon, *Virginia Battlefield Guide*, 458. The regiment's casualty report indicates at least 41 men, including eight killed or mortally wounded and one missing. Company E alone took 15 casualties. Moore, *Men of the Bayou City Guards*, 88; Simpson, *Compendium*, 164-250. J. S. Norton, a "Yankee by birth with a noble & generous & brave a soul as ever beat in [a] breast," nursed Joskins. This was the third time he had been seriously wounded, and the third time Norton had cared for him. Joskins, "A Sketch of Hood's Texas Brigade," in UTSA, 223-25.

63 Skoch, *Lone Star Confederate*, 113-15; Tacitus Clay to Bettie Clay, October 21, 24, 26, 1864, in MSU. Campbell's horse had been killed at Chaffin's Farm, and the Confederate government awarded him $1000 in compensation. Following his injury, he empowered Capt. John Shotwell of the 1st Texas to collect the money due him. As Campbell was scheduled to return to Texas on furlough, Mark Smither entrusted his latest letter to his sister to Campbell's care. He would have Campbell call on the family and "tell you all about us," he wrote, and he also predicted that Bob [Campbell] would be "on his knees to Miss Semmons in less than no time after arriving home." Mark Smither to Sister, November 12, 1864 in SHSU. For more on Baber and Morgan, see Appendix B, Volume 1.

Capt. Tacitus T. Clay
Historical Research Center, Hill College

Clay had built a Greek Revival mansion in Independence locally known as Clay Castle, renowned for its glassed-in ballroom on the third floor overlooking his fields. Clay Castle had been the scene of numerous galas and social gatherings before the war. Clay never again got to use this beloved room as he had before. Clay returned to Texas after recuperating and retired from the service on January 9, 1865. He died in Independence three years later, never having fully recovered, and was buried in the Old Independence Cemetery there.[64]

The greatest loss that the Texans suffered that day, however, was their highly respected commander, John Gregg. Gregg, whom Lee regarded "as the best brigadier in the army," was the last general officer to command the Texas Brigade, and its only commander killed in action. When the Texans fell back, Gregg's body lay sprawled in a pool of blood about 100 yards "in front of their somewhat disorganized line." One of Gregg's staff, Lt. John Shotwell, sought permission to take three enlisted men, to recover Gregg's body. Crawling back on their hands and knees through a heavy rain of shot and shell, the brave quartet reverently wrapped the dead General in a blanket and dragged him back to their lines. Lee delivered the sad news of the death of "brave General Gregg . . . at the head of his men" to Secretary of War James Seddon after the battle.[65]

64 Gracy Bohner Toland, *Austin Knew His Athens* (San Antonio, TX, 1938), 16; Marc Mantrana, *Lost Plantations of the South* (Jackson, MS, 2009); 232-33; Betty Cantrell Plummer, *Historic Homes of Washington County, 1821-1860* (San Marcos, TX, 1971); James L. Hailey, "Clay Castle," *The Handbook of Texas Online*, http://www.tsha.utexas.edu/handbook/online/articles/CC/ccc3-html; Thad Sitton and Dan K. Utley, *From Can See to Can't: Texas Cotton Farmers on the Southern Prairie* (Austin, TX, 1997), 25.

65 W. L. Timberlake, "Last Days in Front of Richmond," in *CV* (1912), 20:199; Winkler, *Confederate Capital*, 195; Lowry, *Dark and Cruel War*, 275. General Bratton also was wounded, as was Colonel Alexander Haskell, commander of the 7th South Carolina Cavalry, of Gary's Brigade, who was shot though the eye. Haskell went through a long period with a "brain fever," and had to relearn to talk; yet within four months, he was back in command of his regiment. He

Placed in a casket and conveyed to Richmond, the general's body lay in state in the House of Representatives amid hundreds of floral tributes and massed Confederate and Texas flags. "The men were deeply grieved at the death of their commander," Lt. Col. Winkler stated, ". . . but felt relieved that his body had been recovered, even in the face of the enemy." All through October 9, thousands of citizens passed by the bier in silent tribute. The "funeral was the saddest I ever witnessed," Winkler remarked, with "genuine sympathy for the brigade all delighted to honor, and also for the wife detained in Federal lines." Surprisingly, the Texas Brigade itself was permitted to attend the funeral *en masse*, the only time in the war they were able to pay their respects to a dead comrade off the battlefield. From the capital square, the funeral cortege, including the Texans, wound its way through the streets to Hollywood Cemetery. Reverend James A. Duncan, a Methodist minister, read an impressive burial service. The casket was then deposited in a private vault awaiting word from Gregg's widow "whose wishes it was impossible to consult." The President and his entire cabinet attended in a body. Postmaster-General John H. Reagan, and Col. F. R. Lubbock of Davis's staff, both Texans and members of the Texas congressional delegation, acted as pall-bearers. "Never were sadder faces than those who turned away after the last rite was ended, and wearily made their way back to the city,—out to the fortifications beyond,—still prepared to endure all for the Southern cause, Col. Winkler added."[66]

The battle of Darbytown Road proved to be the last major offensive of the war for the 5th Texas, though its battles were far from over. After October 7, the 5th Texas took a position in the Richmond defenses about four miles southeast of the capital, between the Williamsburg and Charles City Roads, and remained in the trenches until the end of the month with the rest of the brigade. On October 13, Brig. Gen. Alfred H. Terry led two of his X Corps divisions from the Federal works north of New Market Road to reconnoiter new Confederate defensive positions. A fight

---

always referred to Darbytown Road as "the time I was killed." Trudeau, "Darbytown Road Debacle," *America's Civil War*, 5:35-36.

66 *OR* 42, pt. 1, 852; *OR* 46, pt. 2, 349; Watson Williams to Jessie Laura Bryan, November 13, 1864, in CRC; Winkler, *Confederate Capital*, 196; Pomeroy, "War Memoirs," Polley, *Hood's Texas Brigade*, 259; Hanks, *Captain Benton's Company*, 52. It was days before Mary Gregg learned her husband had been killed. She was staying with her father in Decatur, Alabama, when the war department brought her the news. For a time she was inconsolable and battled depression. Ultimately, she traveled to Virginia to claim the body. With the Confederacy crumbling, retrieving the body was not an easy task. Moreover, a trip through enemy lines in Virginia was considered quite risky. She finally obtained an escort, Sgt. E. L. Sykes, a Confederate soldier and family friend. A month later, she arrived in Virginia to claim the body. She suffered a nervous breakdown, however, and it took several more weeks for her to recover and return with the general's body to Mississippi. The return trip took another month. In April of 1865, Gregg was finally interred at the Odd Fellow Cemetery on the outskirts of Aberdeen.

ensued between opposing skirmish lines. Gary's dismounted cavalry brigade occupied the Confederate left flank against Kautz's cavalry, protecting the Federal right flank. The Yankees began deploying skirmish lines at 7:00 a.m., one regiment in front of each advancing brigade. Hoke's division formed the Confederate right flank, with Field's men occupying the center, facing most of the Union infantry. Between 8:00-10:00 a.m., the Federal advance drove Confederate skirmishers near the woods on the Charles City Road into their earthworks. Gary sent for the cavalry regiment he had posted on the Nine Mile Road. Then, a force of Federals pressed Field's left and made a serious effort to turn it. The 5th Texas, with the brigade, together with Law's Brigade, were thrown rapidly to the left of Darbytown Road. Field's remaining brigades moved up to that road, with Hoke's division closing in on Field's.[67]

The skirmishing continued until mid-afternoon, when the Federals attacked Field's position in strength, and were soon repulsed with heavy loss. Field then counterattacked an hour later with a series of probes against Plaisted's brigade to keep the Union divisions at bay. Sometime between 4:00-5:00 p.m., having "developed" the Confederate defenses to his satisfaction, Terry returned to his original line on New Market Road. By nightfall, all was quiet. Field then had four of his brigades on the left of Darbytown Road and Bratton's to the right, with Hoke touching him on the right. Winkler wrote his wife that night that the

> victorious Confederates once more lay aside the weapons with which they have, "from early morn till dewy eve," sent destruction into the ranks of the enemy, and congregating round the camp-fire, recount in gleeful mood, the transactions of the past day, which I, thankful for my preservation, and well satisfied with our day's work, am seated on the ground endeavoring by the dim light of the fire, to relieve your anxiety.

The well-entrenched Confederates suffered only about 50 casualties in that day's fight, which came to be known as the battle of Darbytown Road/Alms House, to the Federals' 435-plus.[68]

On October 19, General Longstreet, sufficiently recovered from his wounding at the Wilderness, returned to active duty. Lee assigned him to command of all Confederate forces north of the James. At that time, Field's Division was guarding the trenches extending from Fort Gilmer to the exterior line of the Charles City Road.

67 Winkler, *Confederate Capital*, 197; Salmon, *Virginia Battlefield Guide*, 438-40; Field, "Campaign of 1864 and 1865," in *SHSP*, 14:558.

68 Winkler, *Confederate Capital*, 197; *OR* 42, pt. 1, 681, 876; Salmon, *Virginia Battlefield Guide*, 438-40; Winkler, *Confederate Capital*, 197.

Hoke's Division held the line between the New Market and Darbytown Roads, Gary's cavalry picketed the left flank of the Confederate lines near White Oak Swamp, Ewell's local defense force held the sector of the line between Fort Gilmer and the James, while Pickett's Division stood in reserve.[69]

On October 25, Grant initiated another large, simultaneous movement north and south of the James. His plan required portions of the V and IX Corps to advance up the east side of Hatcher's Run, some 14 miles southeast of Petersburg, while II Corps crossed to the far side, with the objective once more being the destruction of the South Side Railroad. This Union force, 32,000 infantry and 3,000 cavalry, aimed at turning Lee's right at Hatcher's Run. Meanwhile, Butler's Army of the James would launch a largely diversionary attack on the Richmond defenses. The ambitious Butler envisioned much grander plans for himself: nothing less than the capture of Richmond and ending the war. His plan called for Terry's X Corps to demonstrate before the Confederate line as far north as the Charles City Road while Weitzel led his XVIII Corps around Terry's right flank to turn the Confederate left. Weitzel was to follow Kautz's cavalry north, then attacking west along the Williamsburg Road.[70]

A dreary rain poured from dark skies that October 27 all along the Petersburg/Richmond front. Butler's offensive got underway at 4:00 a.m. with Terry moving north from the Union works on New Market Road, an advance over the same ground covered during the Darbytown Road engagement the week before. Longstreet, the master of defensive strategy, quickly divined Butler's intentions in the pre-dawn hours and set his men in motion to counter the maneuver. The X Corps effectively executed its plan, despite being held up by woods and underbrush. The XVIII Corps, however, had no such initial success. Weitzel could not advance until Terry cleared his front, and thereafter had to cover several miles by a circuitous route. Kautz was supposed to continue to the Williamsburg Road but instead chose to halt on the Charles City Road, some two miles short of his objective, to skirmish with the Confederates and await further orders. Weitzel found Kautz blocking his path and sent to Butler inquiring if plans had changed. So it was 1:00 p.m. before he and his seven brigades in column reached Williamsburg Road near Seven Pines. From there, the Federals detected a line of Confederate fortifications a mile and a half to the west. The long delay between Terry's initiation of fire and subsequent Federal actions clued Longstreet that their primary objective was elsewhere. Hence he ordered Field to pull

69 *OR* 42, pt. 1, 871, *OR* 46, pt. 2, 349; Pomeroy, "War Memoirs," 85; Hanks, *Captain Benton's Company*, 52; Watson Williams to Jessie Laura Bryan, November 13, 1864, in CRC; Polley, *Hood's Texas Brigade*, 259.

70 Horn, *Petersburg Campaign*, 176-77; Trudeau, *Last Citadel*, 222-24; Salmon, *Virginia Battlefield Guide*, 443; Lowry, *Dark and Cruel War*, 407-08.

his division, including the 5th Texas, out of line and advance to the Williamsburg Road, with Hoke extending his line to cover Field's prior front.[71]

Weitzel spent the next two hours reconnoitering and deploying his divisions and discovered the Confederate works on Williamsburg Road lightly defended despite Longstreet's actions. In the process, however, he lost contact with Terry and came to a halt worrying about the security of his own left. He deployed one division north of the road with Col. Edgar M. Cullen's brigade in line of battle, supported by the remaining two brigades. He placed another division south of the road with Col. Harrison S. Fairchild's brigade, supported by that division's remaining brigades. Colonel John Holman received orders to cross the York River Railroad at Fair Oaks Station still further to the right with his brigade of U.S.C.T. and then turn the Confederate left by advancing up Nine Mile Road.[72]

In the afternoon, an advanced guard of Federals attacked, driving an advanced portion of Gary's cavalry back to their breastworks. Around 3:30 p.m., Weitzel launched two brigades forward to assault the Williamsburg Road line in an area being held being by a mere 20 men of the Virginia Home Guard. The minuscule force had so far deceived the Federals as to its strength by dispersing along the line, yelling and firing weapons. As Field's column approached the Williamsburg Road, enemy skirmishers were already halfway across the field approaching the Confederate lines. The 5th Texas, with the rest of the brigade, led the advance toward this point, arriving at the works just as the heavy Federal force approached over open ground on both sides of the Williamsburg Road. As the tiny "home front" force braced to receive a massive assault alone, the Texans appeared at the double quick. "Glory to God, we are saved!" shouted one of the Home Guards, throwing his hat in the air. The Texans remained concealed in a growth of pine trees until, the Federals drew near, then a line of sharpshooters stepped into the works surprising the Federal skirmishers and quickly forcing them back.[73]

While Bratton's Brigade covered north of the road and the Texas Brigade covered the south, Law's and Anderson's Brigades with Johnson's and Haskell's artillery battalions moved in and quickly positioned themselves at advantageous places along the Confederate line. The grey lines, with no reserves, had to spread themselves

71 David J. Eicher, *The Longest Night: A Military History of the Civil War* (New York, 2001), 742; Horn, *Petersburg Campaign*, 180; Salmon, *Virginia Battlefield Guide*, 443-45; Lowry, *Dark and Cruel War*, 412-13.

72 Longstreet, *From Manassas to Appomattox*, 495-97; Lowry, *Dark and Cruel War*, 414; Horn, *Petersburg Campaign*, 180.

73 *OR* 42, pt. 1, 871; Polley, *Hood's Texas Brigade*, 259; J. W. Trowbridge, "Conspicuous Feats of Valor," in *CV* (1916), 24:25; Simpson, *Lee's Grenadier Guard*, 443.

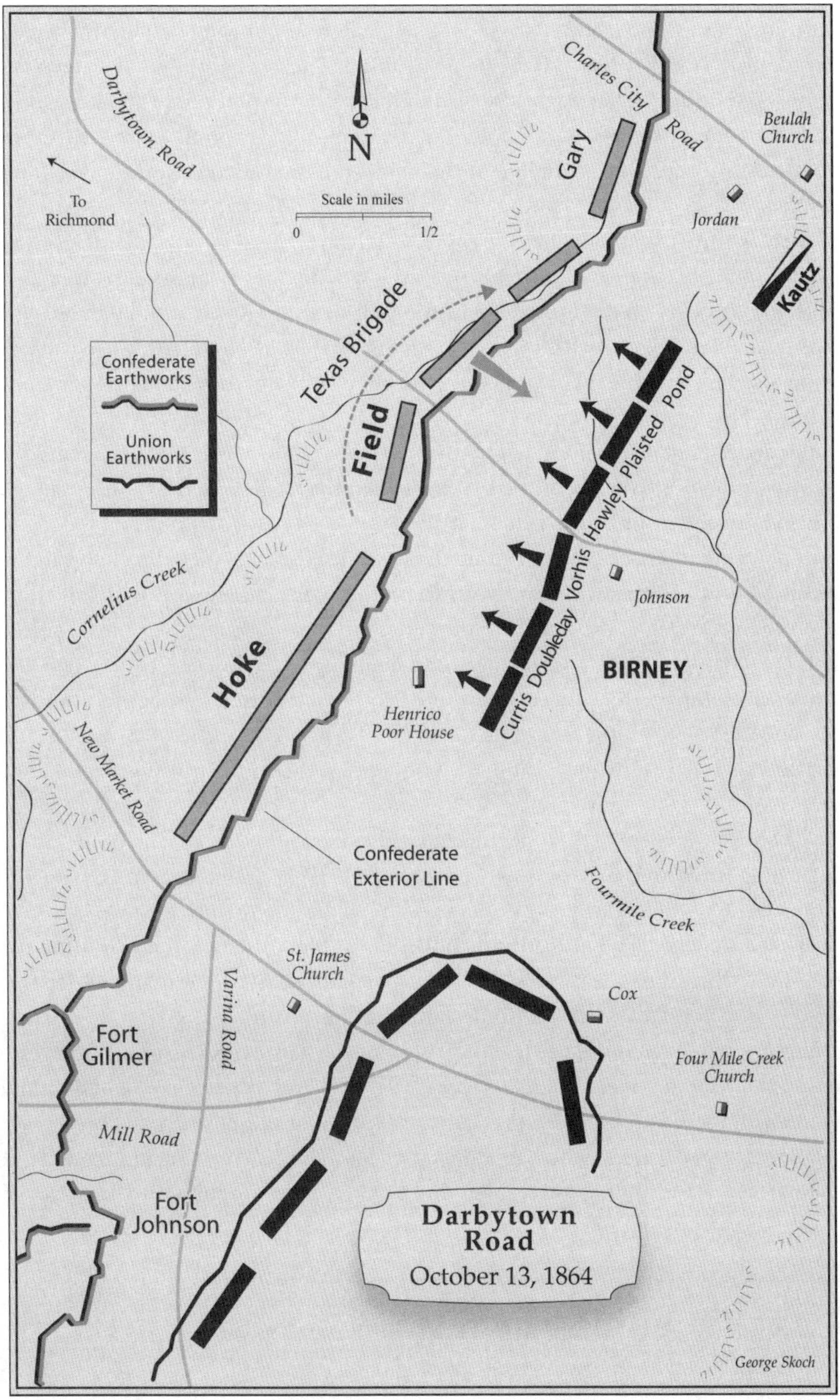
Darbytown Road
October 13, 1864
Charles City Road
Darbytown Road
To Richmond
N
Scale in miles
0
1/2
Beulah Church
Jordan
Gary
Kautz
Texas Brigade
Field
Confederate Earthworks
Union Earthworks
Pond
Plaisted
Hawley
Vorhis
Doubleday
Curtis
Johnson
BIRNEY
Henrico Poor House
Cornelius Creek
Hoke
New Market Road
Confederate Exterior Line
Fourmile Creek
St. James Church
Varina Road
Cox
Fort Gilmer
Four Mile Creek Church
Mill Road
Fort Johnson
George Skoch

exceedingly thin. The troops "stood in a single line, about eight feet apart," a Texan later recalled. But they held a formidable position. Their front was an open area some 600 yards wide and 1,200 yards long, extending from the York River Railroad on the north to a ditch draining into White Oak Swamp on the south. A five- to six-foot depression cut through the middle of the field, and it afforded the only cover for any attackers.[74]

Just as the Texans and their fellow Confederates got into line, a Federal battery and two infantry regiments emerged from the woods directly in their front, with the artillery positioned on the north side of the Williamsburg Road, and the infantry, the south side. The Texans with their devastating firepower handily thwarted the first Union assault led by the two regiments, one white and one black, advancing in double column. The attackers managed to approach to only about 200 yards of the Confederate trenches before being mowed down by a barrage of bullets. The survivors threw themselves on their stomachs in the shallow depression in the open field and refused to press the attack farther.[75]

The Federal artillery caused some damage in the attack, including several direct hits among the regiment operating north of the road. It blew up one Confederate cannon and compelled the Rebels to jump over to the outside of their breastworks to fight. Lieutenant Colonel Winkler, now commanding of the brigade, ordered two men from each company to concentrate their fire on the battery, especially its horses. Captain Hill described the fire of this detail as "so accurate and destructive . . . [that] the Federals hitched up and galloped away, leaving their infantry still recumbent on the ground."[76]

The prone Federals, now terrified of either retreating or advancing, continued exchanging fire with the Texans for approximately an hour. Finally, W. A. Traylor of Company D spontaneously sprang up and over the breastworks, began advancing toward the Federals. Hill immediately hollered for him to return; Traylor turned and protested: "But Captain, these slow-going generals of ours are going to let those Yankees out yonder get away," and started again toward the enemy. He had not advanced another 30 more yards, however, when, totally without orders, the rest of the regiment sprang over the breastworks, formed a line with Traylor, and continued closing with the Yankees. The line of advance led to a little gully near the breastworks sheltering a brave Federal who had done much harm by his constant and accurate fire. When Traylor got within 40 yards, the Yankee fired on him but missed. The

74 Trudeau, *Last Citadel*, 238-39.

75 Field, "Campaign of 1864 and 1865," in *SHSP*, 14:560; Trudeau, *Last Citadel*, 238-39.

76 Ibid.

courageous foe "paid for his gallantry with his life" as Traylor fired and did not miss. The Confederates ultimately captured 400-500 prisoners, but most of the Union soldiers finally crawled back into the protection of the woods.[77]

Meanwhile, the U.S.C.T. brigade Weitzel sent up Nine Mile Road had an eventful passage. After only a mile it spotted Rebel cavalry, and Col. Holman ordered the regiments into a square and charged. The 1st U.S.C.T. went in with a yell and took a battle position, while the 22nd U.S.C.T. got entangled in the underbrush and, raked by flanking fire, retired. While the Federals beat the Confederate cavalry for possession of the line on Nine Mile Road, a bold dash by Gary's men soon drove them off. The Yankees did get one benefit, though. Holman's movement drew enough attention to allow many of the trapped infantry in front of Field to escape.[78]

General Butler had over 30,000 men on the Peninsula, to Longstreet's 6,000. "Never before have I witnessed so large a disproportion," Winkler reported, "in fact it was a perfect frolic, so far as the Confederates were concerned. . . . Field's division accomplished wonders yesterday, though the papers to-day say little about it." The Federals had been repulsed "at all points," Winkler continued, and Grant's goal to garner favorable publicity for Lincoln's reelection had therefore failed miserably. "In a series of engagements, on the Richmond lines, Field's division had born a conspicuous part and deserves a distinct mention. For thirty days this division has stood at the gates of the capital against overwhelming odds; and almost unaided, has beaten back with sad havoc five of Grant's 'Ons to Richmond.'" Winkler also predicted that as soon as "we get through with General Grant's electioneering maneuvers . . . we will soon be quiet again."[79]

Longstreet later reported that Field's Division captured 11 stands of colors, and that his entire Confederate force captured 600 prisoners—not to mention a staggering quantity of war materiel. The fields and roads were thoroughly covered with clothing, small arms, knapsacks, and a massive quantity of ammunition (enough to last the entire Confederate army for a week.) When darkness arrived, Weitzel and Terry retired to the Union works on New Market Road, and the engagement ended. The Federal

77 Polley, *Hood's Texas Brigade*, 260; Trudeau, *Last Citadel*, 238-39.

78 Trudeau, *Last Citadel*, 240; Salmon, *Virginia Battlefield Guide*, 445.

79 *OR* 42, pt. 1, 877-78; Winkler, *Confederate Capital*, 198; Polley, *Hood's Texas Brigade*, 260-61. The mood in the North during this period was bleak—a "darkness had settled upon . . . [it] in the summer of 1864 . . . that was . . . difficult to endure." Several factors contributed to the grim mood: the Overland Campaign's apparent lack of success and its devastating cost in human lives, plus was a Lincoln's recent call for an additional 500,000 troops. Politically, Lincoln desperately needed military successes; Grant tried to oblige him. Doris Kearns Goodwin, *Team of Rivals: The Political Genius of Abraham Lincoln* (New York, 2005), 645, 648, 652-64; Schmutz, *Battle of the Crater*, 49, 319-20.

movement south of the James likewise failed. Hancock suffered a severe defeat at Hatcher's Run.[80]

The battle of Williamsburg Road (or Fair Oaks/Darbytown Road or Second Fair Oaks) resulted in 1,603 Federal casualties, while the Confederates lost fewer than 100 men. Although the engagement did not qualify as a major battle, artillery fire and skirmishing lasted for hours. The 5th Texas played a major role in the Confederate victory, leading Longstreet's force into battle and incurring the highest number of casualties in Field's Division, 19, including four killed and 15 wounded.[81]

With the cold and snow arriving in Virginia, the regiment soon settled down in its camp for yet another long winter—its fourth—miles and miles from home. So many of these brave men who marched so confidently from home years ago now lay in poorly marked graves in far-flung locations in Virginia, Maryland, Pennsylvania, North Carolina, and Georgia. Many others had returned Texas, no longer able to fight for their revered cause, but living with wounds which crippled their future lives. Yet their comrades remaining at the front in Virginia continued resolute—prepared to see this brutal fight through to its bitter end.

80 *OR* 42, pt. 1, 872; Polley, *Hood's Texas Brigade*, 259-60; Simpson, *Lee's Grenadier Guard*, 444; Salmon, *Virginia Battlefield Guide*, 445; Longstreet, *From Manassas to Appomattox*, 497.

81 *OR* 42, pt. 1, 872; Watson Williams to Jessie Laura Bryan, November 17, 1864, in CRC; Polley, *Hood's Texas Brigade*, 259-60; Simpson, *Lee's Grenadier Guard*, 444.

Chapter 8

Denouement: Winter and Spring, 1864-65

In mid-September, Felder took a few minutes to write home: "Autumn is upon us, but still the campaign goes on, nor do I see any probability of its ever coming to an end until the friendly snows of winter shall come & drop its shroud on the thousands of departed heroes, whose bones & bodys yet scarced decayed are still exposed to the gaze of man & at the sight of which the very angels weep." By the fall of 1864, protecting the capital and Petersburg required a Confederate line from the Chickahominy River east of Richmond to Hatcher's Run some 12 miles southwest of Petersburg, a distance of over 40 miles! To accomplish this, Lee had only 66,000 men to Grant's 110,000. North of the James, the long line required but a single file of men, standing five feet apart. The lines moved only when units transferred from one section to another to counter yet another Federal probe. Yet even under the dire circumstances of a prolonged, exhaustive siege, the Confederates struggled to make things as comfortable as possible.[1]

The 5th Texas together with the rest of Field's force occupied a line of works a mile and a half beyond the Richmond fortifications, whose trenches reached some three miles from the city. The Texans were camped near the Charles City Road, next to the John N. Davis house, located between the lines, one of the only residences in the area spared by McClellan in his Peninsula Campaign. Winkler, still commanding the brigade, used the house for a time. Every evening, the parlor would fill with soldier friends, music, and conversation. The Davis family later offered rental rooms in an

1 Rufus Felder to Sister, September 18, 1864, in CRC; "The Opposing Forces at Petersburg and Richmond," in *B&L*, 4:593-94; Simpson, *Lee's Grenadier Guard*, 445; Polley, *Hood's Texas Brigade*, 261.

outlying house in a nearby grove of trees, "with privileges of the parlor," and Winkler eventually moved in there.[2]

Winter came early that year; by late September, several frosts had already occurred, with nights cold enough to require "the old scraps of blankets" the men had nursed through yet another summer. All indications pointed toward yet another severe winter for the regiment, and so it was, particularly in central Virginia, buffeted by sleet and snow from December through February, 1865. The Texans once again constructed a shanty-town of crude huts, tents, and log cabins of varied architecture, whatever the paucity of material at their disposal allowed. Edifices either rose above or descended below the ground. Scant timber remained standing inside the Confederate lines, and that outside was jealously guarded by the enemy. The only available timber was reclaimed from deserted buildings and hauled by hand. The men ranged far and wide locating vacant houses, then carried everything from flooring to door frames back to the brigade campsite. The scarcity of axes (one per company) and the virtual absence of nails made actually using these scavenged materials for living quarters problematic. Nonetheless, crude dwellings framed with salvaged wood sprang up, with mud chimneys and fireplaces, sides of light logs, and roofs of canvas, thatched branches or blankets.[3]

Edifices ranged from a "tent for two covering a hole in the Virginia clay," to comfortable log cabins with three rooms. Pine logs "approximately six to eight inches in diameter, split in half, with the bark-side out" made the best shelters. Some men added a small pen 12 inches high, covering it with split pine poles to make a bed. As in past years, the men also built two large common-use structures for the entire brigade—a huge log theater and a 60x25-foot chapel.[4]

The first frost also spelled the end of fresh produce, until then readily obtainable from local farmers. So the regiment once again had to rely almost totally on the Confederate commissary system. By mid-winter, with the railroads impeded by the Yankees, the daily ration of a quarter-pound of meat and a pound of corn meal was cut in half, while immense quantities of provisions piled up in Georgia and the Carolinas. Sometimes molasses and sugar had to serve as a substitute for meat. Capt. Williams

2 Winkler, *Confederate Capital*, 200-01; Hanks, *Captain Benton's Company*, 39.

3 Polley, *Hood's Texas Brigade*, 261-63; Hanks, *Captain Benton's Company*, 39.

4 Watson Williams to Jesse Laura Bryan, September 22, 1864 & January 1, 1865, in CRC; Polley, *Hood's Texas Brigade*, 262-63; Pomeroy, "War Memoirs," 85; Hanks, *Captain Benton's Company*, 39; Winkler, *Confederate Capital*, 202-03; Simpson, *Lee's Grenadier Guard*, 447-48; James E. Hamer, Robert James Lowry Diary, Brooke Collection, United States Army Military History Institute, December 9, 25, 1864, January 18-28 & February 1-6, 14-15, 1865, 30. Hereinafter cited as USAMI.

sadly wrote home anticipating Christmas dinner from his cup—a mixture of bread and bacon—and traditional yuletide "eggnog" of "clean cold water from a well" right behind the breastworks. Aware of the soldiers' sorry plight, local residents worked tirelessly to provide Lee's army with an adequate, if not sumptuous, New Year's Day dinner, with sufficient food so that every soldier got well fed, at least for that day.[5]

On December 5, the assistant commissary general reported to a committee of the Confederate Congress that the army had only nine days' rations left on hand. On December 14, Lee telegraphed Davis that his army lacked meat entirely. Such scarcities led to an increase in the desertion figures. In January, Congress confirmed a lack of sufficient meat and bread for the armies. Meat had to be obtained from abroad, it reported, and by "a different system from which had hitherto prevailed." Bread could not be impressed, but rather had to be purchased at market rates, and often not with treasury script. Congress found the transportation system inadequate to meet the necessary demands of the service. Finally, it concluded that any ongoing supply of fresh meat to Lee's army was precarious, and if the army had to fall back from Richmond and Petersburg, a strong possibility existed that the supply would cease altogether. Defining this problem proved much easier for the politicians than remedying it. However, the "brave spirits who had borne so much, treated the matter rather as a joke," according to Mrs. Winkler, "and laughed at their own discomfiture, consoling themselves that 'Marse Bob', their hero, was sharing their privations, and were all devoted to a sublime cause—that of justice, and the right to govern themselves."[6]

Even with the food scarcity, the regiment chose to share what little they had with the impoverished citizens of Virginia. Smither reported that "the boys in our regiment are making arrangements to donate tomorrows rations to the poor of Richmond." On February 15, 1865, a letter ran in the Richmond *Dispatch* from the wife of a Confederate prisoner of war about having five small children and an orphaned sister to support, and they could not subsist given the exorbitant prices being charged for food. Several days later a letter from the 5th Texas in the paper reported that its members were sending $70 to the impoverished wife and mother, lamenting that it was "a small sum, but it is all we have."[7]

5 Watson Williams to Jesse Laura Bryan, September 29, November 17, 1864, 7 January 1, 1865, in CRC; Winkler, *Confederate Capital*, 187, 207, 240; Polley, *Hood's Texas Brigade*, 252, 261; Simpson, *Lee's Grenadier Guard*, 448-49.

6 Winkler, *Confederate Capital*, 234-35. See also, George Walsh, *Damage Them All You Can: Robert E. Lee's Army of Northern Virginia* (New York, 2002), 405-406.

7 Fragment, Mark Smither to __, 1864, in SHSU; Robertson, *Touched with Valor*, 41; Richmond *Dispatch*, February 15 & 27, 1865.

That winter, firewood itself, essential to the preparation of daily rations, got placed on the "rationed items list." Unfortunately, because the few horses remaining in the lines had been so broken down from overuse and lack of food they could not be employed to haul available wood from northwest of Richmond back to the troops. Thus, like building materials, fuel had to be carried at least a quarter-mile on the backs of the men. Organized scouting parties went after Yankee horses, breaching the Union lines and foraging for them. At least this activity relieved the monotony of camp life and well suited the Texans. "With no duty to perform save that of picketing our front," Hill, then commanding the regiment wrote, "time hung heavily on our hands, and to make it lighter, the men sought recreation and profit in scouting —the government offering $1500 for every horse captured from the enemy." Naturally, competition often became quite "heated" during the selection process for these forays.[8]

So depleted was the Confederate army that the defense of Richmond consisted of a single picket line, almost continuously manned by the few remaining men. The Confederates impressed several hundred blacks within the lines to work on adjacent fortifications, which soon became exceptionally strong and relieved the soldiers from yet another duty. To assume their picket lines, men of the 5th Texas had to wade through swampy ground only "to endure rain, frost, snow, and cold without fire for relief" after arriving there. Beside the constant tension of alerts, any activity sapped the physical strength of the ill-fed, weary men. The already scant rations continued to dwindle.[9]

Despite the numerous privations impacting Lee's army that winter, the most critical issue remained manpower—the crippling lack of soldiers present for duty. Troop levels by then proved insufficient to defend the entire Petersburg-Richmond front. Of the close to 120,000 men present and absent at the end of June, Lee could count on approximately 50,000 being "present for duty." Two months later, in September, field returns indicated about 100,000 troops present and absent, of which 38,000 were "present for duty." Lee added to the number of effectives by restricting details and aggressively pursuing absentees. By October 31, his army showed a total strength of 120,000 men, with 47,000 "present for duty," which was still woefully inadequate to man the front. "We are so small. We wouldn't even make a good Battalion," Smither observed of the Texas Brigade, "and I hardly think they would insult so much as to offer to put us in with a Reg. from another state." Frequently,

8 Polley, *Hood's Texas Brigade*, 261; Simpson, *Lee's Grenadier Guard*, 450; Moore, *Cannoneer Under Stonewall Jackson*, 266; Reichardt, *Forever the Cause*, 95.

9 Pomeroy, "War Memoirs," 85; Moore, *Men of the Bayou City Guards*, 93; Polley, *Hood's Texas Brigade*, 271.

regiments ended up half the size of decent companies and some companies with fewer than ten men remaining. "There are 8 men in my Company for duty including Lt. McKinnon and myself," Williams told his fiancé in October. "At inspection this morning there were 61 guns in the regiment."[10]

Many distinguished Texans visited the Texas troops occupying the trenches defending Richmond, including Senator W. S. Oldham; Judge John Reagan, Postmaster General; former governor Francis Lubbock, then serving on Davis' staff; as well as Texas congressmen Stephen F. Darden, Col. F. B. Sexton, and Col. John R. Baylor, frontiersman and Indian fighter, all contributing "their quota to the social life of camp." The Texans heartily enjoyed these visits with state dignitaries and relished the attention. Baylor particularly was a welcome relief. "His fund of anecdote was inexhaustible," Winkler later related, "and as he discussed congressional and military matters with the freedom of one familiar with all phases of life . . . [he was] at all times a valuable acquisition to any company." However, the utterances of another Texas notable, Senator Louis T. Wigfall, their former commander, greatly perturbed the men. Wigfall had publicly disagreed with Davis' decision to replace Joseph E. Johnston as commander of the Army of Tennessee in favor of John Bell Hood. Subsequent defeats suffered by the Army of Tennessee under Hood's command caused further denunciations from Wigfall, who had never been popular with the men. Declarations against their beloved Hood further relegated Wigfall's standing to a new low among the rank and file. The men detested criticism of their "patron saint," especially when "delivered by a politician."[11]

Given such hostile attitudes, maybe it was a good thing that a significant "revival of religion" swept through the ranks of the Army of Northern Virginia that winter, although living conditions certainly contributed to the new fervor. Services were conducted in the brigade chapel every Sabbath, with prominent ministers coming from Richmond and elsewhere to preach. Winkler related that:

> [t]he surroundings gave these occasions a weird interest, impossible to describe. The primitive building, rough seats, rude pulpit, the orderly crowd, attempted neatness of the faded grey jackets, the peculiar, careless grace of the manly forms, only acquired from daily contact with the world and its stirring events, and the deep silence where heart-beat answered to heart-beat, with a magnetic sympathy all their own—left an impression that the whispers of the eternal found here a response in every soul. . . . It

10 Mark Smither to Sister, January 7, 1865, in SHSU; Watson Williams to Jesse Laura Bryan, October 20, 1864, in CRC; J. Tracy Power, *Lee's Miserables: Life in the Army of Northern Virginia from the Wilderness to Appomattox* (Chapel Hill, NC, 2002), 212-15.

11 Winkler, *Confederate Capital*, 204, 208, 220, 239-40; Simpson, *Lee's Grenadier Guard*, 445.

> seemed as though the singers were back again, amidst scenes of the past, in peaceful company with those they loved, and to whom they drew nearer by this act of worship, while many an eye was dim with tears.

Consequently, many Texans began to measure "their eternal salvation" by services they attended in the brigade chapel that last winter of the war. The troops received religious literature, because each denomination had a publishing house in Richmond, producing "tracts, pocket editions of separate books of New Testament, Bibles, etc." While the paper quality for these was poor, it still "served as a medium for breaking the 'Bread of Life" to many a hungry soul."[12]

Still others in the regiment continued engaging in earthlier pursuits. Once settled in their quarters the troops ate, slept, laughed, joked, and played cards, checkers, cribbage, and chess. Strangely, Polley wrote, the men "were not altogether unhappy." The various brigade bands frequently serenaded the men while "a Texas sentinel" stood guard near the quarters. Smither observed a small settlement near the encampment "swarming with pretty girls, so you see we do not lack for amusement," he wrote home. And even when passes were unattainable, the men often risked punishment and "ran the blockade" availing themselves of the sights and temptations of the big city—"a big whoopee" and "painting the . . . [town] red," one veteran recalled.[13]

Besides revivals, theatricals, trips to Richmond, and quite often, female companionship broke the monotony of the trenches. The "Field Varieties" and "Hood's Minstrels," combined with some available professional talent, performed almost nightly in the brigade theater. The "Varieties," named for the division commander, again featured Mollie Bailey and her sister Pauline Kirkland both of whom had performed in Wilmington during the summers.[14]

On occasion, the unpleasant task of enforcing punishment for desertion was required, although "amnesty" had been Lee's long standing preference. On these rare occasions, an officer would march a six-man detail to a stack of six guns, half loaded with powder and ball, and half with blank cartridges. Each member of the detail would select a rifle, march up to within 10-12 yards in front of the already-kneeling

12 Winkler, *Confederate Capital*, 203-204.

13 Mark Smither to Sister, November 12, 1864 and January 7, 1865, in SHSU; Hanks, *Captain Benton's Company*, 39; Polley, *Hood's Texas Brigade*, 263; Winkler, *Confederate Capital*, 204. The settlement Smither referred to in his letter was most likely Rockett's.

14 Mark Smither to Sister, January 7, 1865, in SHSU; Simpson, *Lee's Grenadier Guard*, 450; Winkler, *Confederate Capital*, 203. Mollie was the wife of Gus Bailey of the 3rd Arkansas.

condemned man and fire simultaneously upon the officer's command. The offender would thus be dispatched, to desert no more.[15]

An unusual ceremony took place in early February at the Texas Brigade camp: gold stars, melted down from the jewelry of a "young lady in Texas" and sent to Lee, were presented to nine outstanding Texans for their bravery in action. The gold had supposedly been a gift from a "lost loved one she deemed sacred," who wanted to honor the bravest of the Texas Brigade. On January 21, Lee sent the stars—"about the size of a picayune"—to Col. Frederick S. Bass of the 1st Texas, then commanding the brigade, requesting him to pick the deserving recipients, as he could "with more certainty bestow them in accordance with the wishes of the donor." Bass passed the choice of recipients on to the soldiers, with each regiment allocated two stars, except the 4th Texas, which would receive three. Identifying nine men as being braver than all others in this fabled brigade was an impossible task, yet it was accomplished without dissention. Sgts. Cadmus Wilborn of Company F and Jacob Hemphill of Company H were selected as the 5th Texas honorees.[16]

As the men suffered through the last winter outside Richmond, two significant matters involving their future reached a crescendo. The first involved discussion of furloughing the entire brigade to Texas to undertake a mass recruiting campaign, which would then, rejuvenated and strengthened, rejoin the army in time for a spring campaign. The other matter involved a general reorganization of the Army of Northern Virginia. The men feared that their small brigade, now fewer than 600 present for duty, would be consolidated into another unit, forever losing its identity.

The war department had already disapproved a plan to furlough the brigade during the winter of 1863-64 for recruiting efforts. In May, 1864, Texas governor Pendleton Murrah signed and sent a state House and Senate joint resolution to the war department again requesting the mass furlough for the "purpose of recruiting their decimated ranks." When nothing came of this request, Robertson, though no longer connected to the brigade, tried again in October that year to have the mass recruiting plan approved. He encouraged Murrah to write the president directly about the

15 Hanks, *Captain Benton's Company*, 40; Powers, *Lee's Miserables*, 214-15.

16 Polley, *Hood's Texas Brigade*, 285-87; Hanks, *Captain Benton's Company*, 39-40; Yeary, *Reminiscences of the Boys in Gray*, 1:324. Unfortunately, the name of the donor was seemingly lost forever. Mamie Yeary, however, later published an account of Jacob Hemphill of Company H, who identified the donor as a Miss Fuller of Houston. He reported three gold stars and two silver. Hemphill received a star awarded to the "most meritorious Texas soldiers," and because he "had been a wicked young man, he had received a silver one instead of a gold." Yeary, *Reminiscences of the Boys in Gray*, 1:324. A Federal soldier took Hemphill's star from him when he was paroled at Appomattox.

matter. The governor, however, stung by rejection of his prior request, chose to drop the matter.[17]

In December, 1864, Col. Bass, still commanding the brigade, resurrected General Robertson's proposal in a letter to Secretary of War Seddon. All the brigade's noncommissioned officers and privates then present for duty endorsed the letter. Felder of Company E related that the brigade had:

> been using every exertion in our power to have the brigade transferred or furloughed to Texas this winter. We have drawn up a memorial to that effect, signed by all the officers & men of the brigade and presented it to the President. Many are confident that we will go home this winter, but I must confess that I think our chances are very slim. I could conceive of no event (except the establishment of our independence) that would create so much joy in the brigade than such a change.[18]

On January 2, 1865, Seddon referred the matter to Lee for advice. Two weeks later the Southern commander delicately demurred. While "[n]o brigade [had] done nobler service, or gained more credit for its State" than this one, and while "every indulgence" shown it pleased him greatly, with the spring campaign at hand, "I cannot recommend this." Seddon indorsed this correspondence back to Bass, reluctantly denying the application. In February, Senator Wigfall tried one more time, asking Lee to send the brigade "home to recruit." Lee had not changed his mind: "it is impossible for me to detach any men from this army now."[19]

Concern that the Texas Brigade might be consolidated with one or more smaller brigades began percolating near year's end. Major Littlefield, the brigade's quartermaster, feared that if that happened, "many will attempt to escape the army." Texas men and officers would certainly fight such an initiative to the end. They had gained a renowned reputation for battlefield aggressiveness, and although their ranks had been dramatically thinned by battlefield casualties and disease (the 5th Texas, for example, had only "61 guns" present for inspection on October 20, 1864), the name "Hood's Texas Brigade" still conjured immense pride and honor.[20]

17 *OR* 34, pt.4, 633-34, *OR* 36, pt. 3, 894-95; Robertson, *Touched With Valor*, 65-66.

18 Rufus Felder to Sister, December 18, 1864, in CRC.

19 Evans, *Confederate Military History*, 11:53; Winkler, *Confederate Capital*, 206-207; Simpson, *Lee's Grenadier Guard*, 453; Wright, *Southern Girl in '61*, 226.

20 Watson Williams to Jesse Laura Bryan, October 20, 1864, in CRC; Winkler, *Confederate Capital*, 207; Simpson, *Lee's Grenadier Guard*, 454. Smither wrote home on January 7, 1865, that

Lee appointed "consolidation committees" in each of the army's small brigades to consider their alternatives, and issue recommendations about possible consolidation. They were also charged with examining all company grade officers in their respective brigades to determine their fitness for further command. Colonel Winkler, 4th Texas commander, served as chairman of the brigade's committee. While it was hard at work on its task, the officers and men of the brigade held a mass meeting to protest any consolidation whatever. Private B. S. Fitzgerald of Company I was chosen chairman of this group, and the mass meeting appointed Maj. William K. "Howdy" Martin to present the brigade's case to President Davis. It also passed a series of resolutions reaffirming the brigade's strong faith in the Confederacy.[21]

Martin, taking his mission seriously, sought and got an appointment with the president through the good offices of Postmaster General Reagan. Lee was there with Davis when Martin made his strong "no merger" appeal. After the Texan's impassioned presentation, during which he displayed one of the battle-scarred regimental flags, Lee remarked to the President: "Mr. President, before you pass upon that request, I want to say I never ordered that Brigade to hold a place, that they did not hold it." Lee's testimonial, along with Martin's dramatic presentation, convinced Davis that merging the brigade with another would constitute a serious mistake. "Major Martin," he said, "as long as there is a man to carry that battle flag, you shall remain a brigade." And so, by executive order, the brigade remained a separate entity until the war's end.[22]

The only offensive movement the Texans participated in that winter—and incidentally, its last movement before pulling out to cover the army's retreat toward Appomattox—occurred on December 20. The objective was merely to harass the Federal lines, keeping "them in the open, and [to] disturb as much as possible their repose." The force set out early down the Charles City Road, then south on a smaller

---

"we wouldn't even make a good battalion [as the brigade is so small]." For more on Fitzgerald, see Appendix D.

21 Winkler, *Confederate Capital*, 208-209; Rufus Felder to Sister, December 18, 1864, in CRC. Other members of the Committee were Capt. Hill and Col. R. S. Taylor, 5th Texas and 3rd Arkansas commanders. Hill served as secretary. Due to the great loss of officers by 1864, many unqualified men from the ranks lacking the requisite leadership ability were still promoted to officer rank. Simpson, *Lee's Grenadier Guard*, 454. Smither wrote home on January 7 that everybody was "very anxiously awaiting" a Congressional decision about army consolidation. He had a personal stake in the game, for his promotion to first lieutenant was "now awaiting this decision." If consolidation did not happen, he would "most certainly" be promoted, he thought. Ultimately the brigade stayed intact, but Smither was not promoted. Mark Smither to Sister, January 7, 1865 in SHSU. For more on Fitzgerald, see Appendix B, Volume 1.

22 Winkler, *Confederate Capital*, 208-209.

road leading toward Deep Bottom. The day was overcast, gloomy, and bitterly cold, and "[m]urky clouds hung low and depressed the men's spirits." Their progress in the previous day's snow proved difficult, especially for the accompanying artillery. The Texans, having previously scouted the area, were on point with a force of 60-80 men, under the command of Maj. Martin. Just beyond New Market Road, the Confederates struck the Federal pickets, running in the reserves holding the position "with a rush and a yell." At noon, the men reached a plateau with a deep ravine beyond it. Two hundred yards away were the Federals, behind breastworks, with a fortified battery, in what appeared to be their main line, erected to protect their pontoon bridge and the lines along Deep Bottom. Martin led a force of about 40 men into the breastworks, and the Yankees broke and fled. Soon, however, a larger force returned and drove the Confederates back to the woods from which their assault had advanced. After an exchange of fire, the Rebels withdrew. The remainder of the force reunited with Martin as night fell. Field concluded it was too late for another charge, and with that, the engagement ended and the men returned to their huts and warm fires, to reflect on yet another Christmas season far from home.[23]

By late December, command of the 5th Texas, formally listed under the imprisoned Col. Robert M. Powell for so long, was finally, officially given to Capt. Hill, who had long been acting in such capacity. By special order No. 219, Maj. J. H. Littlefield became brigade quartermaster and Capt. W. N. Norwood of the regiment, assistant to the brigade quartermaster.[24]

Several weeks later, the regiment was overjoyed by news that Col. Powell had finally been paroled on February 6, 1865, after more than 16 months in prison at Johnson's Island in Ohio. Prisoner exchanges between the two armies having just been reinstituted after a long hiatus, and Powell, departing Johnson's Island on January 27, 1865, had been among the first Confederate prisoners exchanged. In early February, he finally arrived at the Texas Brigade's camp and was roundly welcomed by all. "Our 'beau ideal' of a soldier and gentleman, Col. R. Mike Powell, has returned to Dixie," Smither exulted. "I never saw boys in such exuberant spirits as when they heard [that] Col. Powell was in Richmond. In fact, the whole brigade almost shouted at the news."[25]

23 Polley, *Hood's Texas Brigade*, 263-68.

24 *OR* 42, pt. 2, 159, 1247-48, pt.3, 1188; *OR* 46, pt. 2, 1171, 1179.

25 Mark Smither to Elizabeth Smither, February 17, 1865, in SHSU; Reinhardt, *Forever the Cause*, 94; Parker, *Touched by Fire*, 103. By 1863, the prisoner exchange system ground to a halt. The Confederacy refused to recognize captured black soldiers as POWs, instead reducing them to slave status and threatening execution of Union officers who led them as insurrectionists. A retaliatory threat by the Union prevented the Confederacy from carrying out any executions but

Soon thereafter, Powell, as senior ranking officer, took command of the brigade. Colonel Bass returned to command the 1st Texas, and Hill retained command of the regiment, which he held for the remainder of the war. On March 18, 1865, the Texas congressional delegation recommended Powell for promotion to the rank of brigadier general, a request roundly endorsed by the rank and file. The war department got the request on March 21, as the Confederate government was unraveling, but never acted upon it. Smither, for example, reported that the men "are all anxious for him to be appointed Brig. General, and if we are not consolidated, I have no doubt but what he will be." In any event, the brigade had secured its final leader (a product of the 5th Texas) of the long, devastating war, now rapidly nearing its end.[26]

The prospects of success for the Southern cause faded rapidly during the winter of 1864-65. Early had been roundly whipped out of the Shenandoah Valley. Hood's foray into Tennessee fared disastrously, and after the battle of Nashville, his army had virtually ceased to exist. Sherman ravaged Georgia from Atlanta to Savannah and was marching northward trailing destruction through South Carolina. Fort Fisher, guarding Wilmington, NC, the last major Confederate seaport, fell, and the Union blockade was slowly strangulating the South. Grant tightened his choke hold around Petersburg with every passing day.

Meanwhile, the Confederate army holding on in Virginia dwindled slowly away, sapped by sickness, unrelieved trench warfare, starvation rations, and desertion. But despite it all, the Texans remained resolute and proclaimed to the world their ongoing fealty to the Confederate cause. On January 25, 1865, the brigade held a mass meeting, and five-man committees from every regiment drew up a prologue and eight resolutions subsequently adopted by the troops. Distributed to all Confederate civil and military high commands, as well as to state officials in Texas, and all interested Southern newspapers, the resolutions expressed continued confidence in President Davis and General Lee. They pledged the brigade to continue the war "to the last

---

did not restore the exchange program. Grant, with an abundance of soldiers at his disposal, was content to retain all captured Confederate soldiers in prison and away from any possible use to the Southern war effort.

26 Reichardt, *Forever the Cause*, 73-74, 94-95, 101-108; Mark Smither to Elizabeth Smither, February 17, 1865, in SHSU; Winkler, *Confederate Capital*, 232-34; Houston *Daily Telegraph*, April 21, 1865. After spending weeks recovering at Gettysburg's Lutheran Seminary from his wounds, Powell was transferred to the federal prison at Fort McHenry for five weeks, and then on September 28, to Johnson's Island military prison. He remained there for 16 months. While a prisoner at Fort McHenry, Powell became enamored with a young lady of the Confederate Relief Association of Baltimore, which helped tend the wounded. On January 30, 1865, in the presence of military officials and her friends, she was married at the Basilica of the Assumption of the Virgin Mary in downtown Baltimore "[t]o a man with whom she had never spoken until plighting their vow together."

extremity" and to rid the country "of the hated and despised foe" or otherwise "die in the attempt." Peace and independence would "come sooner or later. . . .and with it our independence. Our final triumph is certain and inevitable, and our subrogation is an impossibility." The Texans—always loyal to the Southern cause—remained defiant to the end.[27]

As 1865 dawned, the demise of the Confederacy appeared almost a certainty, exactly when was the only question. Meanwhile, Sherman cut a swath across Georgia, arriving triumphantly in Savannah on December 21, 1864, then began working his way north through South Carolina. What was left of the once-proud Army of Tennessee was clustered in northern Mississippi. Lee relieved Hood of command on January 23, 1865, and restored Joseph E. Johnston to active duty commanding the remnants of that army on February 22, the same day Wilmington, the South's last major port, fell.

Everywhere the Confederate system tottered. Texas and its supply of cattle had been cut off from the remainder of the Confederacy by Federal control of the Mississippi. Most of the rolling stock in the country had been worn beyond repair. Large quantities of meat, meal, and flour stored at Lynchburg and Danville, Virginia, could not reach Lee's army rapidly enough to feed it because the deplorable condition of the rail lines prevented their rapid transportation. Thus, "[i]t was not defeat that threatened the army—it was famine."[28]

Word of General Hood's crushing defeat outside Nashville arrived at the Petersburg-Richmond lines a few days after the mid-December battle, dealing a staggering blow to morale. Still, the men in butternut dutifully held their more than 40 miles of freezing lines "with a grip that neither cold nor hunger, nor shot nor shell, could loosen," wrote one. Still, the men had some inkling of what was happening. In this context, Rufus Felder wrote his sister on February 23:

> You are aware by this time all communication south cut & the man who carries this will have to walk a long ways to get around Sherman's army. Yes, my dear sister, the insolvent foe have dared to march through the very heart of South Carolina & I have no doubt committed depridations on the property, if not on the persons of our dear, but unfortunate relatives. God grant that they may have been spared and that the scenes of our childhood of our noble ancestors not desecrated by the ____ of our brutal enemy. Our cause looks gloomy indeed.

27 *OR* 46, pt.2, 1290, 1296; Robertson, *Touched with Valor*, 102-104; Simpson, *Lee's Grenadier Guard*, 456-57; Freeman, *Lee's Lieutenants*, 3:623-25.

28 Polley, *Hood's Texas Brigade*, 269-70; Trudeau, *Last Citadel*, 299-300; Foote, *Civil War Narrative*, 3:761-64.

Polley also wrote in a similar vein: "The hopes that had sustained and encouraged people and armies grew faint and to thinking men whose pride could humble itself to an abandonment of its dream of Southern independence and separate nationality, the one and only thing that seemed desirable, or even possible, [at this point] was an honorable peace."[29]

The fall of Petersburg appeared inevitable. Lee now had fewer than 40,000 men left in the field, a significant portion unfit for duty, and faced a Federal opponent with significantly more than twice that number. Petersburg had been under siege over six months, and the undermanned defenses spread ever thinner, barely one soldier every five feet to cover the entire line. The Federals continued resolutely pushing westward to turn the Confederate right flank and thereby cut off the South Side Railroad, the last rail line linking Lee's army to the south. To counter this westward shift, Lee launched a desperate, final offensive under the command of Maj. Gen. John Gordon against the Union's Fort Stedman east of Petersburg on March 25. While the initial assault seized the fort and many prisoners, a fierce counterattack forced the Confederates to withdraw. The action cost Lee 2,700 casualties, including 1,949 prisoners which he could ill afford to lose. Four days later, Sheridan's cavalry began a concerted attempt to turn Lee's flank. On March 31, Rooney Lee's cavalry and Pickett's infantry division met the Union vanguard northwest of Dinwiddie Court House, successfully pushing it back, and temporarily stalling Sheridan's momentum. However, with a host of Federal infantry fast approaching from the east, Maj. Gen. Pickett had to withdraw and entrench at the road junction of Five Forks, a crossroads village some 17 miles southwest of Petersburg, which Lee ordered him to hold at all costs.[30]

On April 1, the Confederate position at Five Forks completely collapsed when Union forces under Sheridan and Warren soundly routed Pickett. The Confederates suffered another 3,000 casualties, including almost 2,400 prisoners, while Federals' losses were only 830. Among the dead was the noted Rebel artillerist, twenty-three-year-old Col. Willie Pegram. Chief among those responsible for the disaster was Pickett who had chosen to attend a shad bake hosted by Maj. Gen. Thomas Rosser north of Hatcher's Run that day. Atmospheric conditions prevented them from hearing the roar of gunfire just two miles away. Pickett was astounded to learn he was under a fierce attack, and by the time he got to the field, it was too late.[31]

29 Rufus Felder to Sister, February 23, 1865, in CRC; Polley, *Hood's Texas Brigade*, 269.

30 Noah Andre Trudeau, *Out of the Storm: The End of the Civil War April—June 1865* (Boston, MA, 1994), 22-25; Reichardt, *Forever the Cause*, 95; Salmon, *Virginia Battlefield Guide*, 459-61.

31 Parker, *Touched By Fire*, 104; Salmon, *Virginia Battlefield Guide*, 449-50, 463-67; Trudeau, *Out of the Storm*, 23-45, 59; Don Lowry, *Toward An Indefinite Shore: The Final Months of the Civil War, December 1864—May 1865* (New York, 1995), 420-44.

With the capture of Five Forks, the last remaining artery connecting Petersburg with the South, the South Side Railroad lay wide open to a direct attack. Consequently, Grant ordered an all-out offensive to commence early on April 2, immediately following an immense artillery bombardment. At 4:30 a.m., Maj. Gen. John G. Parke's IX Corps, 18,000 men strong, attacked, capturing several batteries in the old Dimmock line four miles southeast of the city. Wright's VI Corps moved out west of Petersburg, and in short order compromised the breastworks manned by Lane's Brigade of Cadmus Wilcox's Division. Lee's heretofore impenetrable works had finally been broken. The Federals began to roll up the severely stretched Confederate line to the north and south. Lieutenant General A. P. Hill, following a hastily called meeting with Lee, ran into enemy soldiers while rushing back to his lines and was killed. To the west, II Corps moved against the Confederates west of Hatcher's Run, soon possessing a significant portion of the main Confederate line. By mid-morning, Lee realized the evacuation of Petersburg and ultimately, Richmond, was inevitable. He therefore dispatched an urgent telegram to President Davis, who was attending church services at St. Paul's Church in the capital at the time, which read: "I advise that all preparations be made for leaving Richmond tonight." Davis left immediately, and soon the whole church emptied.[32]

Given Lee's attention to detail, every Confederate command in those 40 miles of trenches received explicit instructions on exactly what route to pursue in an evacuation to ultimately link up with the main body of the army in its westward retreat. That night, with his right flank crushed and pressure all along his entire front, Lee ordered his exhausted, hungry men to evacuate the Richmond-Petersburg lines and rendezvous at Amelia Court House to the west. The retreat proceeded orderly apace.[33]

Federals overwhelmed the remaining Confederate defenders at Petersburg late that evening, inflicting 4,852 more casualties. Petersburg ultimately escaped much of

32 OR 46, pt. 1, 1264-65; Moore, *Men of the Bayou City Guards*, 93; Trudeau, *Out of the Storm*, 46-47, 52-57; Salmon, *Virginia Battlefield Guide*, 467-71; Freeman, *Lee's Lieutenants*, 3:646-74; Alexander, *Military Memoirs*, 591-94; Grant, *Personal Memoirs*, 2:430-49; Simpson, *Lee's Grenadier Guard*, 458-59.

33 The scattered remnants of Lee's army were to reconverge on Amelia Court House via four different routes. Mahone's Division, stationed at Bermuda Hundred, would move out toward Chesterfield Court House on County Road. Ewell, then commanding Kershaw's and Custis Lee's divisions and the naval Battalion, was to cross to the south side of the James River, and then take the Broad Rock Road to Goode's Bridge and cross the Appomattox. Pickett and Bushrod Johnson's Divisions and the rest of the cavalry, all positioned west of Petersburg, would move up the south bank of the Appomattox. The troops in Petersburg would cross the Appomattox at the bridges there and proceed west along its north bank. Fitzhugh Lee, *General Lee* (New York, 1894), 380; Polley, *Hood's Texas Brigade*, 273; Trudeau, *Out of the Storm*, 56; Lowry, *Towards An Indefinite Shore*, 459-60, 470-71.

Capt. William Traylor Hill
Historical Research Center, Hill College

the devastating fires that largely destroyed the capital. By morning, much of downtown Richmond had been totally engulfed by the great evacuation fire, and it took Federal troops several hours to extinguish the flames. Meanwhile the Confederates hurried westward through the Appomattox valley, toward a rendezvous at the Richmond & Danville Railroad depot at Amelia Court House, some 40 miles west of Petersburg, a place where Lee hoped to unite his scattered forces and acquire rations necessary for his famished army to continue the fight. Lee ultimately hoped to reach Danville, Virginia, some 125 miles from Petersburg, and at which point joining forces with Johnston's army, then retreating north under severe pressure from Sherman's thrust through the Carolinas. Lee's plan envisioned the merged Confederate force falling first on Sherman's army, then turning back to confront Grant.[34]

Lee ordered Longstreet early on the night of April 1 to immediately send a division from the Richmond defenses to Petersburg to prevent Federal passage to the Appomattox's north bank. Field's Division, which included the 5th Texas, then still in its winter quarters on the Williamsburg Road, received the assignment. This left only Kershaw's reduced division and Ewell's reservists covering Richmond. Field was to march into Richmond and board trains for Petersburg. The Texas Brigade and Law's, would bring up the Division's rear, while Ewell occupied the lines vacated by Field's men. Capt. Hill, then commanding the 5th Texas, wrote that the Texans received orders to be ready to march at daylight. Colonel Powell led the brigade out of the

34 Parker, *Touched By Fire*, 103-04; Polley, *Hood's Texas Brigade*, 273; Salmon, *Virginia Battlefield Guide*, 453-54, 470; Simpson, *Lee's Grenadier Guard*, 459; National Park Service, *Appomattox Court House National Historic Park, Virginia* (Washington, D. C, 1955), 6. Johnston concentrated the remnants of Hood's Army of Tennessee under Bragg, and those of Lt. Gen. William J. Hardee, into what became known as the Army of the South. Sherman ravaged the land as he slowly advanced, with Wheeler's and Hampton's cavalry constantly striking back and temporarily slowing the advance. Finally, the two forces met at Bentonville, North Carolina, on March 19 and 20, where Johnston achieved his objective of impeding Sherman's northern advance, and thereafter slipped away with his army intact as a fighting force. Chicoine, *Confederates of Chappell Hill*, 137; Reichardt, *Forever the Cause*, 96.

trenches at break of day., marching past Rocketts, then through the city to the intersection of Byrd and Eighth Streets, there boarding the rickety cars of the Richmond and Petersburg Railroad for the 16-mile trip south. By this time, flames engulfed much of the town including even the Texas Depot and the men's stored personal effects at 7th and Main Streets. Several veterans lamented the loss of the old weapons, possible "souvenirs." Total chaos prevailed. "The bridges were jammed almost beyond their capacity with a mass of living humanity, besides wagons, artillery and vehicles of various kinds."[35]

The 5th Texas arrived near Petersburg around noon, taking a position along the north side of the Appomattox, with orders to guard the crossings and fords to prevent the Federals from gaining the north side. The regiment remained there throughout the afternoon and evening of April 2. Most of Lee's army began crossing to the north bank of the Appomattox on four bridges—one railroad, two vehicular, and one pontoon. All but the pontoon bridge were subsequently burned behind the fleeing army. The Federals made no effort to cross as Lee's evacuation and westward retreat along the north bank of the Appomattox toward Amelia Court House began. His once mighty army by this time comprised only 30,000 exhausted, emaciated men. Far greater numbers of well-supplied, well-fed troops would soon be in hot pursuit.[36]

The 5th Texas remained near Petersburg throughout April 2, while the Lee's army retreated westward. The Texans could see long lines of Federals also marching that direction from the city. But since the Union troops made no effort to cross the river, the regiment's day passed quietly. Then, about 11:00 p.m. that evening, it commenced its own march westward, bringing up the rear of what remained of the Longstreet's Corps. Fires lit the sky in every direction; the Confederates seemed determined to destroy everything of potential service to the enemy. Near the 5th Texas' temporary station on the river, a house containing large quantities of bacon was deliberately burned. Captain Hill disgustedly, and doubtlessly with understatement, related that the famished Texans "felt it a hardship not to be allowed to fill our haversacks with

35 Hanks, *Captain Benton's Company*, 41; Moore, *Men of the Bayou City Guards*, 93; Polley, *Hood's Texas Brigade*, 274-75; Winkler, *Confederate Capital*, 248. A train wreck delayed the complete arrival of Field's Division. Only two regiments of Benning's Brigade arrived before the wreck, and they were placed as skirmishers in the crumbling defenses. Hours later, Bratton's Brigade reached the city, marching through to join Benning's men and the remnants of Wilcox's Division. The force held on for hours while the rest of the Army of Northern Virginia made its way out of the city. Marvel, *Lee's Last Retreat*, 22-23.

36 *OR* 46, pt. 1, 1293-93, pt. 3, 1372-77; Hanks, *Captain Benton's Company*, 41; Longstreet, *Manassas to Appomattox*, 521-24; Polley, *Hood's Texas Brigade*, 274-75; Pomeroy, "War Memoirs," 86; William Marvel, *Lee's Last Retreat: The Flight to Appomattox* (Chapel Hill, NC, 2002), 22-23; Reichardt, *Forever the Cause*, 96.

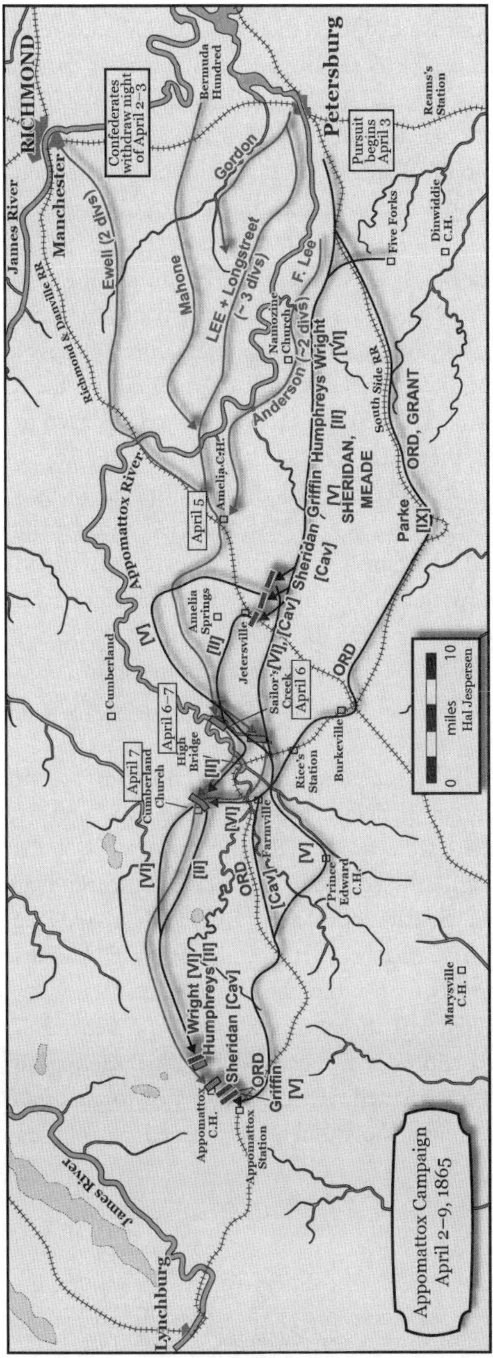
RICHMOND
Manchester
James River
Confederates withdraw night of April 2–3
Bermuda Hundred
Petersburg
Pursuit begins April 3
Reams's Station
Five Forks
Dinwiddie C.H.
Richmond & Danville RR
Ewell (2 divs)
Gordon
Mahone
LEE + Longstreet (~ 3 divs)
F. Lee
Namozine Church
Anderson (~2 divs)
Sheridan Griffin Humphreys Wright
[Cav] [V] [II] [VI]
SHERIDAN, MEADE
South Side RR
ORD, GRANT
Parke [IX]
Appomattox River
Amelia C.H.
April 5
Amelia Springs
Jetersville
Cumberland
Sailor's Creek
April 6
April 6–7
High Bridge
April 7
Cumberland Church
Rice's Station
Burkeville
Farmville
Prince Edward C.H.
Marysville C.H.
ORD
Wright [VI]
Humphreys [II]
Sheridan [Cav]
Griffin [V]
Appomattox C.H.
Appomattox Station
James River
Lynchburg
0 miles 10
Hal Jespersen
Appomattox Campaign
April 2–9, 1865

bacon before it was destroyed." Given their current position on the Confederate lines as well as past experience, the Texas Brigade now served as the rear guard of General Longstreet's force—the last time it would occupy this post of high honor. Petersburg burned as the Texans started pulling out that night, with flames and exploding ammunition lighting up the April sky for miles around. At precisely 4:28 a.m. on April 3, the United States' flag was raised from the tall courthouse clock tower in the city center.[37]

The night of April 2-3, Lee's forces made 20 miles, hampered the whole way by swollen watercourses and washed out bridges that constantly changed their assigned routes. For example, the vanguard of Longstreet's force discovered that rising river waters had washed out the approaches to Beville's Bridge on the River Road, and the column had to double back and stagger to a hastily constructed pontoon bridge near Goode's Bridge, where they finally crossed back to the right bank of the Appomattox. At this point some Confederate units began displaying signs of despondency; however, Field's with the Texans and Mahone's Divisions maintained outstanding morale and discipline. They actually formed the backbone of the army upon which the other units could rally. With 5,000 men, Field's Division was now the largest and most effective division in the entire army. It turned onto either side of the road, forming a battle line to engage any attack the Federals might make on Longstreet's column. By the evening of April 3, most of the Lee's army bivouacked just a few miles short of Amelia Court House.[38]

The 5th Texas itself had marched throughout the night of April 2 and all of April 3 without confronting any Federals. Extremely tired and ravished from hunger on their march, the Texans were awakened early on April 4, and trailing the rest of Longstreet's force south, crossed the Appomattox to Amelia Court House, a rather insignificant station on the Richmond and Danville Railroad. There, they once again crossed the river and marched west to the depot itself. About a mile beyond the village, the Texans spread out in a thin line of battle and scratching up their inevitable entrenchments with their left thrown back facing the Federal cavalry. Here, Lee's "anxious and haggard expression" betrayed his bitter disappointment at a recent discovery. Expecting and assured of vast supplies of foodstuffs for his men at the siding there, he found not the desperately needed 350,000 rations, but instead

37 Reichardt, *Forever the Cause*, 96; Polley, *Hood's Texas Brigade*, 274-75; Trudeau, *Out of the Storm*, 72 & *Last Citadel*, 403-08; Lowry, *Towards An Indefinite Shore*, 499-500.

38 Marvel, *Lee's Last Retreat*, 42-43.

hundreds of boxes of ammunition and harnesses for artillery horses, the result of some bureaucratic error.[39]

The army thus had to remain in the vicinity while the men desperately foraged for food. However, most of the wagons dispatched to convey bounty from the countryside returned almost empty, since the Confederate commissary department had already stripped the surrounding farms of their crops. The country was so destitute of subsistence for man and beast that many of the men were only allowed only three ears of corn apiece. Hill reported that the 5th Texas "had a little meal issued to it without salt, which was mostly boiled in tin cups, making a sort of gruel, which diseased the bowels of the soldiers."[40]

As if he needed more bad news, Lee learned the pontoon bridge his engineers were supposed to have constructed at Genito crossing had never arrived. Ewell's Richmond force would thus have to move south using Goode's Bridge, unless he could ford the swollen Appomattox elsewhere. Lee dispatched word of this change of plans to Ewell early on April 4, but his courier never located Ewell's command in time. Ewell used the railroad bridge at Mattoax, five miles north of Goode's Bridge for a crossing, though he did not reach the Appomattox until after nightfall on April 4. So, while Lee did ultimately concentrate his army at Amelia Court House pursuant to his plan, both lack of provisions and Ewell's tardy arrival caused a fatal delay. It allowed the Yankees to catch up and squandered the day's advance he so desperately needed. Indeed, Lee later cited this delay as *the* fatal event of his westward retreat, lost time that "could not be retrieved." The 5th Texas, as part of Longstreet's rear guard had skirmished heavily all that day with the pursuing Federals, while the tardy troops of Ewell's force were closing up from Richmond.[41]

The march of Lee's reunited army along the railroad south toward Danville continued in earnest on April 5, with Lee hoping to meet up with his supplies along the way. Once the wagons and artillery got under way, Longstreet proceeded with the infantry at 1:00 p.m. along the South Side Railroad. However, at Jetersville, the next stop on the line, six miles south of Amelia Court House, he discovered the enemy

39 Ibid., 48; Polley, *Hood's Texas Brigade*, 275; Field, "Campaign of 1864 and 1865," in *SHSP*, 14:560-61.

40 Polley, *Hood's Texas Brigade*, 275; Winkler, *Confederate Capital*, 258; Trudeau, *Out of the Storm*, 90-92. A. C. Jones, "Third Arkansas Regiment at Appomattox," *CV* (1915), 18:313; Marvel, *Lee's Last Retreat*, 33, 43, 48; Chilton, *Hood's Texas Brigade*, 182.

41 *OR* 46, pt. 1, 1265. Lee was not able to concentrate all the troops at Amelia Court House until midday on the April 5th, Ewell being the last to arrive. The small army was now contained four small infantry and one cavalry corps, under Longstreet, Ewell, R. H. Anderson, Gordon, and Fitzhugh Lee, respectively. Mahone's Division was assigned to Longstreet's Corps, and the naval battalion to Custis Lee's Division. Lee, *General Lee*, 380.

"square across . . . [his] route in force and entrenching." Sheridan had dispatched patrols north of Jetersville to reconnoiter Lee's left flank. And meanwhile, four miles beyond Paineville, the bluecoats attacked a Confederate wagon train, destroying the wagons and capturing large amounts of equipment and animals, and 600 men. A number of the prisoners turned out to be armed blacks in Confederate uniforms, the only known instance of combat in Virginia involving organized black Confederate soldiers. While Lee wished immediately to advance on the Union force blocking his passage, his son Rooney, commanding the advance cavalry force, cautioned that Sheridan's force was unfortunately more than they could "venture to attack."[42]

By this time, Grant had initiated a full-blown pursuit of the fleeing Confederates. One massive Union column pressed closely behind Lee's army, while a second swung to the southwest in an attempt to cut it off. Grant could sense his foe rapidly expiring, so he pressed in for the kill. Sheridan, commanding all Federal cavalry, pushed to head off Lee's "game but doomed" army. Seeing the route to Danville blocked, Lee decided to shift the line of march from south to west, striking for a still usable stretch of the South Side Railroad linking Farmville with the supply depot near Lynchburg. Unable to procure local guides, however, Lee had to rely solely on his dated maps. Though Farmville was still 23 miles away, scouts had reported a stockpile of food and grain there. The army therefore marched all night toward the town by way of Rice's Station, with the Federals in close pursuit.[43]

The 5th Texas, with Field's Division, passed through Deatonville at midnight on April 5. A mile beyond that village the road descended sharply into marshy terrain cut by Sandy Creek; two miles beyond this depression stood Holt's Corner, a locally known crossroads, and a mile and a half beyond that Sailor's Creek, where the house of James Hillsman overlooked the stream. Less than a half-mile farther on, the

42 Moore, *Men of the Bayou City Guards*, 94; Trudeau, *Out of the Storm*, 97-100; Salmon, *Virginia Battlefield Guide*, 476. Black troops were serving in the wagon train of the force then commanded by Custis Lee. They were apparently engaged in pulling down a rail fence for construction of defenses when attacked on April 5 at Paineville. These black soldiers symbolized the Confederacy's desperate straits. Not until February 1865 did the Confederate Congress authorize the raising of black regiments, and the majority of the Texas delegation opposed to the bill. Ralph A. Wooster, *Texas and Texans in the Civil War* (Austin, TX, 1995), 175; Proceedings of the Second Confederate Congress, Second Session, 331, 465, 470; Marvel, *Lee's Last Retreat*, 5.

43 Freeman, *Lee's Lieutenants*, 3:693-93, 4:58; Simpson, *Lee's Grenadier Guard*, 461; Lowry, *Toward An Indefinite Shore*, 524-30; Winkler, *Confederate Capital*, 258-59. Commissary General Isaac M. St. John, one of the last Confederates out of Richmond, informed Lee of the 80,000 rations waiting nearby. They had been on the way to the army via the South Side Railroad when the Yankees cut it at Burkeville, so they had to be brought back up the line to Farmville. Lowry, *Toward An Indefinite Shore*, 543.

regiment came to the intersection where the boundaries of Amelia, Nottaway, and Prince Edward Counties met. There, it was allowed to rest for an hour.[44]

As dawn broke on April 6, three Union Corps, the II, V, and VI, and Sheridan's cavalry were all concentrated at Jetersville, ready to advance east upon Amelia Court House, while the Army of the James, under Ord remained at Burkeville. Meanwhile, Lee marched west through Deatonville on three parallel roads. Soon outside that hamlet, however, the whole army had to take the same road, producing one, long, vulnerable procession of men and wagons. Longstreet's force took up the van after a brief hour's nap, with Field's Division and the regiment now in the lead, followed by Anderson, Ewell, and then Gordon guarding the rear. Longstreet crossed Little Sailor's Creek early that morning, heading toward Rice's Station, to prevent the Federals at Burkeville from seizing the depot on the South Side Railroad depot there. Just up from Rice's Station was Farmville, where 80,000 desperately needed rations were currently being stored for Lee's starving men.[45]

At Sailor's Creek, Longstreet later wrote, "the road 'forks,'—one road to the High Bridge crossing of Appomattox River, the other by Rice's Station to Farmville." Having intelligence that Ord was moving towards Rice's Station, Lee ordered Longstreet to make for that location to meet the enemy, while the other columns followed the wagon trains over the bridge. As soon as his men crossed the South Side Railroad tracks at Rice's Station on April 6, Longstreet sent scouts down the tracks toward Burkeville Junction. He had intelligence that several hundred Union infantry and a battalion of cavalry had already marched through the town on their way to High Bridge, which was the Confederates' sole escape route over the Appomattox should the Federals succeed in blocking the road past Rice's Station. Old Pete thus arranged his infantry facing east and south toward Burkeville Junction, across the anticipated route of Ord's march. Field's Division with the regiment occupied the east side of the South Side Railroad, with Wilcox's and Heth's Divisions to Field's right. All three divisions were ordered to entrench and deploy artillery in batteries. Longstreet then dispatched two cavalry divisions, those of Brig. Gen. Tom Rosser with his own and Brig. Gen. Thomas T. Munford's, north to secure High Bridge and capture or destroy any Federal raiders there. As soon as Gary arrived with several hundred additional cavalrymen, Longstreet sent him to follow Rosser.[46]

44 Marvel, *Lee's Last Retreat*, 68.

45 *OR* 46, pt. 3, 1386; Trudeau, *Out of the Storm*, 103-04.

46 Longstreet, *Manassas to Appomattox*, 525; Walsh, *Damage Them All You Can*, 422; Jones, "Third Arkansas at Appomattox," 18:314; Hanks, *Captain Benton's Company*, 42-43; Marvel, *Lee's Last Retreat*, 69-71; Lowry, *Toward An Indefinite Shore*, 545.

Ord had orders to cut the bridges along Lee's route if he continued west. The longest of these spans was High Bridge, five miles west of Sailor's Creek and three miles east of Farmville, a colossal engineering marvel on the South Side Railroad, some 2,500 feet long and 126 feet high, perched upon 60-foot brick piers. Along with an adjacent wagon bridge, it was the only river crossing in the area. As the Federal advance column neared this crossing around noon, Confederate pickets from the few mounted troops then in the area immediately engaged them. At 1:00 p.m., a cavalry force of about 1,200 troopers sent by Longstreet arrived, intercepted the raiders, captured 800 of them, and forced their retreat. For the time being, High Bridge remained a safe escape route for Lee's retreating army.[47]

But Lee's desperate effort to channel his forces along the single road from Deatonville to Rice's Station soon began to unravel. Longstreet's forced march to Rice's Station opened up a significant gap between his corps and Anderson's. The pace of the wagon trains had slowed Anderson's progress as well as did constant skirmishing with harassing detachments of Sheridan's cavalry. Longstreet, however, was not aware of either Anderson's delay or the resultant gap. Ewell's corps, next in line, had to hold a defensive position at Amelia Springs for three hours to allow the wagon train to move past. And it was not until 2:00 p.m. on April 6 that he was finally able to move onto the road, pass the wagons, and fall in behind Anderson. In the meantime, Gordon's corps, protecting the rear, had the most difficult experience of all, alternatively skirmishing, reforming, and retreating, in "one almost continuous shifting battle" at the Confederate rear.[48]

Then a fight then erupted at Holt's Corner. Anderson took a defensive position around the crossroads and was soon fending off the advance guard of an aggressive Yankee cavalry force. When Ewell arrived, Anderson reinstituted his move westward, leaving Ewell in command at the roadblock. This fracas had introduced yet more delay, and as Ewell deployed, the distance between these two corps and Longstreet only widened. Meanwhile George A. Custer's Yankee horsemen had discovered the gap and occupied the ground around Marshall's Cross Roads near the Harper farm athwart Anderson's path. As Anderson continued his march across Little Sailor's Creek and arrived near Marshall's Cross Roads, he sent word back to Ewell about the buildup of Federal cavalry to his front. Ewell decided to clear the wagons from his infantry's route, and sent them up the northern loop of the road. Rushing his 5,200

47 *OR* 46, pt. 1, 1302; Edward T. Bouve, "The Battle At High Bridge," *Civil War Papers*, MOLLUS (Boston, MA, 1900), 2:407-12; Trudeau, *Out of the Storm*, 102-06; Richard F. Welch, "Burning High Bridge: The South's Last Hope," *Civil War Times* (2007), 46:35-36.

48 Trudeau, *Out of the Storm*, 105-07; Salmon, *Virginia Battlefield Guide*, 479, 482-83; Lowry, *Toward An Indefinite Shore*, 546-48.

men to Anderson's support, Ewell positioned them on high ground southwest of the creek, with his rear guard positioned at the James M. Hillsman house.[49]

Wright's VI Corps soon engaged Ewell's rear guard at the Hillsman house, and around 5:00 p.m., Federal cannon opened up on Ewell's, followed in a short interval by a massive infantry attack. At 6:00 p.m., 7,000 of Sheridan's cavalry forded Little Sailor's Creek and attacked up the hill toward Ewell's position. The Confederates successfully broke up the initial attack and counterattacked, driving the Federals back across the creek. However, in a classic case of communications breakdown, Gordon's troops had followed the wagon trains toward Jamestown, without realizing the wagons were no longer following the rest of the army. Thus Gordon could not support Ewell's beleaguered force. The next Federal charge up the hill successfully turned both Ewell's flanks after a brutal fight. Among the 3,400 Confederates who ultimately surrendered were Maj. Gens. Custis Lee and Joseph B. Kershaw, brigadiers Seth M. Barton, Dudley M. DuBose, and James P. Simms, not to mention Ewell himself. Two miles away from the fight on the road to Farmville, the men of the 5th Texas could clearly hear the horrific fighting to their right around Sailor's Creek. "The roar of the muskets and cannon was beyond description," one Texas veteran exclaimed.[50]

A mile southwest of Ewell's force, Anderson's 6,300 men confronted three full cavalry divisions, about 8,500 troopers, at Marshall's Cross Roads. Brigadier General J. Irvin Gregg's dismounted brigade's attack forced Maj. Gen. Bushrod R. Johnson back on his wagons. Whereupon several charges led by Custer himself succeeded in routing Pickett's whole division. Anderson's line quickly collapsed, the disorganized soldiers fleeing through the woods toward Rice's Station. Approximately 2,600 more Confederates surrendered, including Brig. Gens. Eppa Hunton and Montgomery D. Corse.[51]

Meanwhile, Gordon and the wagon train came under intense attack from every hilltop west of Holt's Corner, which of course slowed his trailing infantry as well. At Double Bridges, crossing Little and Big Sailor's Creeks, a crisis developed when a wagon fell through the floor of one of those bridges. Gordon was forced to make a

49 Power, *Lee's Miserables*, 276.

50 Hanks, *Captain Benton's Company*, 43; Trudeau, *Out of the Storm*, 106-10; 478-79; Lowry, *Toward An Indefinite Shore*, 548-54. As Custer's "guest" following his capture at Sailor's Creek, Kershaw reported seeing 31 captured regimental banners from the previous day's fighting, "representing 31 of our regiments killed, captured or dispersed the day before. It was," said Kershaw, "not comforting to think of." Gregory J. W. Urwin, *Custer Victorious: The Civil War Battles of General George Armstrong Custer* (East Brunswick, NJ, 1983), 249-50. Many accounts refer to the stream and the battles in the vicinity as "Sayler's Creek." It is known as "Sailor's Creek" in current practice.

51 *OR* 46, pt. 1, 1288-91, 1294-98; Walsh, *Damage Them All You Can*, 421.

stand at the creek when confronted by Brig. Gen. Regis de Trobriand's division of Humphrey's II Corps at the Lockett farm around 5:00 p.m. Soon, Brig. Gen. Nelson A. Miles' division pushed in Gordon's left flank, forcing the Confederates back across the stream. Although a significant portion of Gordon's 7,000-man corps escaped, at least 1,700 more Confederate soldiers either surrendered or were killed as dusk fell on the valley, increasing the Confederates' total casualties that day to well over 7,700 men.[52]

Lee rode from Rice's Station toward the sound of the battle and watched as the ragged mob once constituting significant portions of his proud army fled haphazardly across Big Sailor's Creek. At this heart-wrenching sight, Lee despairingly exclaimed "My God! Has the army been dissolved?" Those who escaped continued on with yet another night march to Farmville, or crossed to the north bank over High Bridge. Later that night, Grant, still at Burkeville, received Sheridan's report on the day's successes, which concluded "If the thing is pressed I think that Lee will surrender." Grant forwarded Sheridan's message on to President Lincoln, who telegraphed back early the next morning "Let the thing be pressed."[53]

After dark that evening, after assuring that Gordon and Mahone's forces (which contained the remnants of Ewell's and Anderson's commands), would be able to successfully cross High Bridge, Longstreet disengaged his corps from the contest there. He began the march westward toward Farmville from Rice's Station where the 80,000 rations supposedly awaited. The 5th Texas and the rest of the brigade, in moving to Rice's Station to the south with Longstreet's Corps, now once again constituted the "rear guard of the rear guard" for Lee's westward movement. The miserable condition of the roads, together with inadequate bridges, caused the column to move at a snail's pace. Meanwhile, the regiment had to halt constantly, form a defense line, and thwart the probing maneuvers of Federal skirmishers closely dogging the retreat from Rice's Station to Farmville.

A mired battery on the road also caused Field's column to halt. Hundreds of wagons piled up at the Sandy River bridge, causing further delays. Late on April 6, Ord's advance force of Maj. Gen. John Gibbon's XXIV Corps also caught up to the Texans, deployed on the Farmville Road after they had left Rice's Station, where the brigade had already skirmished hotly with the enemy. In fact, the fighting became so fierce Powell had to call for reinforcements to drive the Federals off. Hill recalled that the Federal infantry "overtook the Texas Brigade, then the rear-guard of the rearguard

52 Walsh, *Damage Them All You Can*, 421; Salmon, *Virginia Battlefield Guide*, 479-80; Lowry, *Toward An Indefinite Shore*, 552-54.

53 Longstreet, *Manassas to Appomattox*, 527-28; Walsh, *Damage Them All You Can*, 422; Salmon, *Virginia Battlefield Guide*, 455-56, 480; Foote, *Civil War Narrative*, 3:915, 919.

of our army, on the evening of the . . . [6th], after we left Rice's Station, and the brigade skirmish line had a hot fight with them—so hot that it had to be heavily reinforced before it drove the enemy back." During this scrap, the regiment's fabled cockfighter, T. J. Boykin of Company C, fell mortally wounded and died in a Federal hospital weeks later. He had carried a rooster on his shoulder during the march and would occasionally pit his bird against another and pick both roosters up "when [the] contest got hot."[54]

By 9:00 a.m. on the 7th, Longstreet's leading element entered Farmville from the hills south of town, crossed a bridge to the north bank of the Appomattox, and were greeted by 40,000 rations of bread and 80,000 of cornmeal aboard the trains at the depot. The quartermasters quickly began culling Longstreet's wagon train of undependable wagons and excess baggage, putting them to the torch. Teamsters with sound wagons stopped at the depot to load up their vehicles, and as the first hungry troops entered the village, commissary details began tossing boxes of rations from the cars.[55]

The remainder of Mahone's decimated division served as a rear guard at High Bridge for what remained of Gordon's, Johnson's, and the remnants of Pickett's divisions as they began crossing the river sometime after midnight. Gordon's portion of the train crossed on the wagon bridge alongside High Bridge. By dawn, Mahone's men followed the remnants of Anderson's and Ewell's commands and Gordon's infantry force across the double-decker bridge, while Confederate engineers stood by to burn the structure once all the troops crossed. Unfortunately, confusion arose as to whether the engineers required Mahone's permission to fire the bridge.[56]

Mahone, under orders from Lee to destroy High Bridge and its companion span, pulled out without dispatching the order to the engineers to do so. The ensuing delay forced the engineers to engage in a fire fight with approaching bluecoats to set their torches. Once the bridges were set ablaze, High Bridge burned rapidly and four of its spans dropped into the water. But the oncoming Federals doused the flames on the low wagon or "common" bridge, and by late morning on April 7, Humphreys had his lead division over the river. The considerable Confederate force drawn up on the

54 Hanks, *Captain Benton's Company*, 56; Polley, *Hood's Texas Brigade*, 275; Simpson, *Lee's Grenadier Guard*, 462-63; Chilton, *Hood's Texas Brigade*, 182. Hill and Polley mistakenly refer to Boykin's being mortally wounded on the night of April 5. However, the Texans did not pass through Rice's Station on their way to Farmville until April 6. Records indicate Boykin was wounded at Farmville and subsequently died in a Federal field hospital there on April 29.

55 Alexander, *Military Memoirs*, 597-98; Salmon, *Virginia Battlefield Guide*, 483-84; Marvel, *Lee's Last Retreat*, 92-93, 122.

56 Marvel, *Lee's Last Retreat*, 119-20; Lowry, *Toward An Indefinite Shore*, 567.

heights opposite the bridge to oppose the crossing was soon driven off, and the Yankees crossed over. After brushing aside the Confederate rear guard, the Federals moved out rapidly in the direction of Farmville. Once on the same side of the Appomattox as Lee, the Yankees were able to push forward up the railroad almost unimpeded for a distance of at least two miles. With Mahone making straight for Cumberland Church from High Bridge, and Gordon marching on Farmville, Lee's army was now operating separately on three legs of a triangle with Union infantry dogging each one.[57]

Once Lee had crossed to the north bank with Longstreet's Corps, he learned that "someone" failed to carry out his orders to destroy both crossings at High Bridge, allowing the Federals to capture one of them nearly intact. He further learned that the scrambling Federals were already on the north bank of the river in strength. He flared with uncharacteristic anger at the news, speaking "of the blunder with a warmth and impatience which seemed to show how great a repression he ordinarily exercised over his feelings."[58]

As rations were being issued in Farmville to some of the troops, word arrived of the Federals' rapid approach, from both the south side of the river, and pressing upon Gordon and Mahone from the north side as well. With the enemy encroaching both from the east and south, Lee realized that he needed to march north at least to the vicinity of the Cumberland Presbyterian Church, about three miles north of town, to protect his vulnerable wagon train. Federals there were already closing in on Mahone. and he would need to stand and fight there before continuing westward toward Campbell Court House. Lee ordered the troops in Farmville to the north side of the river to prepare their breakfasts. He hoped by moving his entire army to the north side of the Appomattox and burning the spans Farmville, he might relieve his army from close enemy pursuit for a while, allowing him valuable time for his desperate flight west.[59]

Porter Alexander had been charged with destroying the railroad and highway bridges at Farmville, once the army had vacated the town. Alexander torched the

57 Longstreet, *Manassas to Appomattox*, 528-29; Lowry, *Toward An Indefinite Shore*, 556-57; Foote, *Civil War Narrative*, 3:921-23. Reports vary widely as to the time that the conflict on April 7 at High Bridge took place. Federal reports place it as early as daybreak to as late as 10:00 a.m. Confederate reports say their rear guard broke off at noon. The reports actually describe a moving skirmish from High Bridge toward Farmville. *OR* 46, pt. 1, 604, 631, 657, 674, 691, 701, 713, 751, 763-64, pt. 3, 622, 659, 687. On the post-war controversy over who was responsible for the Confederate lapse in destroying the bridges, see Marvel, *Lee's Last Retreat*, 121-22.

58 Trudeau, *Out of the Storm*, 118-19.

59 Marvel, *Lee's Last Retreat*, 123-24; Foote, *Civil War Narrative*, 3:922-23.

railroad bridge immediately, piling kindling inside the covered bridge on the country road, awaiting the approach of the enemy. The head of the Yankee advance soon reached Farmville, and heavy firing erupted downriver. Lee reconvened with Alexander and, with sharp memories of the High Bridge bungle, cautioned him not to hold his match too long. He also pointed out on a map where the Federals might intercept the army's line on a march to Cumberland Church, approximately four miles to the north.[60]

The 5th Texas had entered Farmville late that morning and marched north to the railroad bridge spanning the Appomattox to hold the enemy in check until that structure could be destroyed. They remained there until noon, when Powell received orders to retreat quickly, as the enemy threatened to cut off his brigade from the main army. "No time was lost in obeying the order," Powell recalled, and by marching along a blind road running parallel with the railroad, the Texans eluded the hard-pressing Federals. Crossing over the wagon bridge to the river's north bank, the Yankees were in plain view positioning a six-gun battery in front of the house of long-time area planter Hilary Richardson. But Hill also noticed that Lee had placed about 50 guns bearing on the Federal battery, thus solving "the mystery why the brigade was not fired on." Successfully over the bridge, the unit ascended the high hills toward Cumberland Church. Before crossing the river, Hill requested a local doctor to purchase all available bread in the town and hold it for the regiment. However, when the regiment reached the store, nary a loaf was to be had, and the men stayed hungry for a while longer. Finally, they received a little meat and corn meal issue in late afternoon; however, the march had to be resumed before any cooking could be undertaken.[61]

The Confederates constructed a line of earthworks near the Cumberland Church resembling a fishhook, with Mahone occupying the northern portion and Gordon the eastern face. Lt. Col. William T. Poague's artillery battalion occupied the ground between Mahone's right and Gordon's left. Farther along the line, Longstreet's corps comprised the line toward the south. As the regiment retreated west along the hills north of the river, they could see long lines of Federal infantry and cavalry following and paralleling their line of retreat. Field's Division now rested alongside Mahone's, and Wilcox's force followed Field's men into a position on his right, defining an entrenched, artillery studded arc over a mile long. Field maintained a tight grip on his men—his force and Mahone's probably amounted to over 8,000 men in line in the

60 Alexander, *Military Memoirs*, 597-98; Marvel, *Lee's Last Retreat*, 123-24; Trudeau, *Out Of the Storm*, 120-21.

61 Chilton, *Hood's Texas Brigade*, 182; Polley, *Hood's Texas Brigade*, 276.

area. Together with Wilcox's Division and Heth's brigades, the Confederates numbered approximately 12,000 men, thereby equaling Humphreys' strength. At 4:15 p.m., the Federals assaulted Mahone's flank; some of their force successfully reaching the Confederate defenses and began infiltrating the Confederate rear. A swift counterattack by "Tige" Anderson's Georgia Brigade soon succeeded in chasing the enemy back to its own lines. Brig. Gen. William G. Lewis' Brigade of Gordon's corps then turned back another Federal assault, and the bluecoats retreated across the river to Farmville as nightfall ended the day's fighting. Lee had seen his men win their last victory.[62]

Aided by Poague's cannon, Mahone had blunted the Federal assault. But when the young Poague went to congratulate Mahone on his victory, he found him sheltering from the rain under an apple tree, cursing the Yankees. He had just learned they had captured his headquarters wagon and with it, his cow. "It was a most serious loss," he lamented, "for he was not able, in the delicate condition of his health, to eat anything but tea and crackers and fresh milk."[63]

The Texans held position on a high hill in an open field where "everything could be plainly observed." As it grew dark, however, Polley noticed that the enemy's sharpshooters hidden behind trees at the foot of the hill "could see all we did and we could see nothing they did." To escape the bullets, the men had to dig little holes, build fires in them with small twigs, and cook more cornmeal gruel. "Each soldier had to crawl around like a lizard, as he did not dare raise his head," and present a Confederate silhouette to the Yankee sharpshooters. By then, so few Texas remained that the 5th Texas men had to perform double duty, often serving almost back-to-back 24-hour details on the skirmish line simply to maintain the army's security.[64]

From his headquarters at Farmville, Grant sent Lee a message that evening appealing for him to surrender. Lee and Longstreet were together in a cottage near Cumberland Church when the message arrived. Lee read it, then passed it to Old Pete, both a friend and distant in-law of Grant, who had served as a groomsman at his wedding. After reading the note, Longstreet returned it. "Not yet," he said. Lee scribbled an ambiguous response and upon dispatching the message, he gave orders for Longstreet's immediate withdrawal from the area.[65]

62 Chilton, *Hood's Texas Brigade*, 183; Salmon, *Virginia Battlefield Guide*, 486-87; Lowry, *Towards An Indefinite Shore*, 571-72; Polley, *Hood's Texas Brigade*, 276-77.

63 Walsh, *Damage Them All You Can*, 423.

64 Marvel, *Lee's Last Retreat*, 122-23, 130; *Chilton, Hood's Texas Brigade*, 183; Polley, *Hood's Texas Brigade*, 275-77; Reichardt, *Forever the Cause*, 98.

65 Marvel, *Lee's Last Retreat*, 130-31; Winkler, *Confederate Capital*, 259.

Though they could not break through the solid Confederate line at Cumberland Church, the Federals had succeeded in preoccupying the Southern army until darkness. To retreat further, the Confederates therefore had to strike out on a night march for the third night in a row. Beginning after 10:00 p.m., Lee planned to march west to Campbell Court House, just east of Lynchburg. He anticipated obtaining supplies en route at Appomattox Station on the South Side Railroad, approximately three miles southwest of Appomattox Court House, 38 miles distant. However, the route south of the river was a *full eight miles shorter*, offering the Federals an excellent opportunity to block the fleeing Southern army from its objective.[66]

Longstreet marched beyond the Lynchburg Stage Road to avoid the trains and troops already clogging it, then continued until reaching the parallel turn onto Buckingham Plank Road. As Old Pete's men and trains marched northward toward it, Gordon's column on the Lynchburg Stage Road pulled over to rest around midnight. Longstreet reached the Buckingham Plank Road at daylight on April 8. From there, he marched parallel to Gordon's, marching behind Walker's artillery. The rain clouds of the past few days finally parted, and a bright, welcomed sun arose. The pace and the heat soon had the men sweating. And there was little time for the regiment or brigade to rest; it halted only a few minutes at a time. There was little food, "no time to forage and no wagons up," one of the men recalled. The only available sustenance was hastily prepared dough kneaded on an oilcloth or bark, then baked on an iron ramrod or a spade.[67]

The regiment's march as the rear guard that day turned out to be a chaotic one characteristic of an army in full retreat, rapidly approaching its final demise along a road littered, clogged, and blocked by all manner of detritus: upended and burning wagons, vast assortments of camp equipment, personal effects, and weapons, broken and scattered medicine chests, disabled cannon and wrecked caissons, pots, pans cups and kettles. Dead horses and mules sprawled in the mud alongside the road. "Oh! The hardships, no tongue can tell; only the experienced," Hanks lamented, "[b]ut we knew this was war."[68]

Most of Lee's army remained relatively unmolested throughout April 8, though still doggedly pursued by the II and VI Corps. To the south, the V Corps, the Army of the James, and Sheridan's cavalry were rapidly outflanking Lee on their shorter

66 Davis, *To Appomattox*, 279-80, 284-85, 290-91; Moore, *Men of the Bayou City Guards*, 93; Jones, "Third Arkansas at Appomattox," 314.

67 Hanks, *Captain Benton's Company*, 41-42.

68 Ibid., 42; Polley, *Hood's Texas Brigade*, 277; Simpson, *Lee's Grenadier Guard*, 463; Winkler, *Confederate Capital*, 260.

approach toward Appomattox Station. The cavalry got there before the Confederate van, and Custer captured the supply trains and provisions awaiting Lee's famished troops. Later that same evening, the Yankees attacked the Confederate artillery and wagon trains. A large part of the Federal army now stood directly across Lee's front, then forming around Appomattox Court House. When the Confederates bivouacked for the night, the hundreds of campfires dotting the surrounding hillsides made it obvious to Grant that he had Lee bottled up. Confronted with the enemy infantry behind him and its cavalry across the line of march, Lee determined his only remaining, desperate option was a breakout through the Federal cavalry line early the next morning.[69]

Late that night of the 8th Powell led the Texas Brigade into bivouac between Holladay's and Fishpond Creeks, east of New Hope Church, approximately five miles northeast of Appomattox Court House. They "lay in a thicket near the highway upon the wet ground, without food. In our midst," Powell recalled, "stood silent and helpless two abandoned field pieces." Colonel Charles Marshall, Lee's military secretary, still awake despite the long march and late hour, heard the defiant Texans chanting a little Lone Star doggerel as they finally made their way into the Confederate lines that night: "The race is not to them that's got/ The longest legs to run,/ Nor the battle to that people/ That shoots the biggest gun." Meanwhile, Humphreys, closing on the Confederates' heels, received word that evening that the enemy had occupied the first high ground beyond his position, a least three miles away. This was Field's Division, including the regiment, Longstreet's rear guard.[70]

Throughout that night and early morning hours of April 9, the Union armies converged and all but surrounded Lee's beleaguered, exhausted, and famished army. Its only potential salvation remained a desperate breakout through the cavalry lines then straddling the road to Campbell Court House. Lee determined to mount such an attack at 5:00 a.m. to ascertain whether the Federal horse soldiers could be brushed aside. Gordon's divisions, along with Fitzhugh Lee's cavalry were to spearhead this assault, with Longstreet's Corps and the Confederate wagon train close on their heels. Gordon trudged into Appomattox Court House at around 4:00 a.m., just before

69 Wert, *General Longstreet*, 402; Salmon, *Virginia Battlefield Guide*, 456; Trudeau, *Out of the Storm*, 117-130; Freeman, *Lee's Lieutenants*, 3:693-95, 712-16.

70 Hanks, *Captain Benton's Company*, 56; Charles Marshall, "Occurrences at Lee's Surrender," in *CV* (1894), 2:44; Davis, *To Appomattox*, 341; Reichardt, *Forever the Cause*, 98; *OR* 46, pt. 3, 670. A Rebel deserter from Field's Division captured by Humphreys' men in late morning of April 9 indicated his division had camped "about four miles back from here" the previous night, i.e., between the two creeks. Marvel, *Lee's Last Retreat*, 266n25. Powell actually referred to Appomattox Station, southeast of Appomattox Court House, confusing the names of the two hamlets.

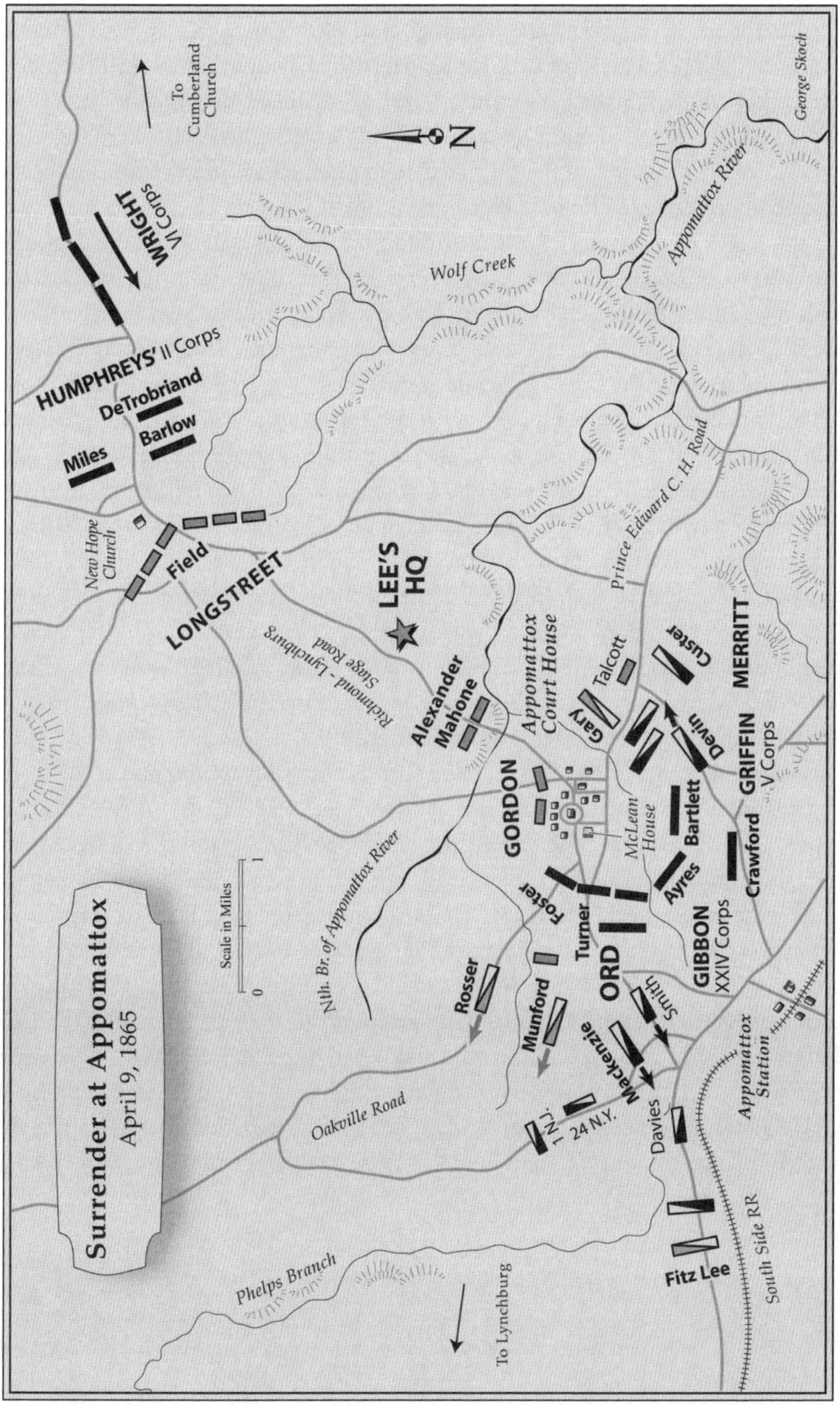
Surrender at Appomattox
April 9, 1865
Scale in Miles
0
1
To Cumberland Church
N
WRIGHT
VI Corps
HUMPHREYS' II Corps
DeTrobriand
Barlow
Miles
Wolf Creek
Appomattox River
George Skoch
New Hope Church
Field
LONGSTREET
LEE'S HQ
Richmond - Lynchburg Stage Road
Prince Edward C. H. Road
Alexander
Mahone
Appomattox Court House
GORDON
Talcott
Gary
Custer
MERRITT
Devin
GRIFFIN
V Corps
Bartlett
McLean House
Crawford
Ayres
GIBBON
XXIV Corps
Foster
Turner
ORD
Smith
Rosser
Munford
Mackenzie
Nth. Br. of Appomattox River
Oakville Road
1 N.J.
24 N.Y.
Davies
Appomattox Station
South Side RR
Fitz Lee
Phelps Branch
To Lynchburg

twilight. Johnson's Division and Fitzhugh Lee's cavalry lay all about the village, sleeping in disheveled lines of battle running through pastures, gardens, and across the intersection bordering the courthouse. Gordon marched beyond the cavalry line toward Oakville Road, about a quarter mile past Wilmer McLean's house to regroup.[71]

The 5th Texas, with the rest of Field's Division, sprawled out at the tail end of Lee's column, resting but ready. While most of the men dozed, pickets kept watch over the creeks beyond which Grant's army awaited. As rear guard and the largest and most effective division remaining, Field's troops had orders to move out last, once traffic ahead had cleared. He finally began moving out before dawn on what Powell described as a "damp, gloomy and foggy" morning and gained several miles on Humphreys, passing the same incinerated remains of the Confederate trains Mahone's men had smelled but not seen three hours earlier. The detritus of a retreating army was again scattered in great heaps on their route. Field's five brigades followed the serpentine course carved by stage roads, winding more than two miles from the turn at the Rose Bower house to the crude, wooden chapel known as New Hope Church. "Their route carried them through a countryside where empty chairs told the common story of the Confederacy. . . . In adjacent meadows and on distant ridges . . . [the men of the regiment] might have seen the flickering lights of breakfast candles in numerous other homes that had given sons or fathers to the cause." The regiment arrived at the church before midmorning, having marched "five or six miles" from their previous evening's campsite in one veteran's recollection.[72]

Longstreet ordered Field to halt and turn his division around and throw it into line of battle together with the residue of Heth's and Pickett's divisions below New Hope Church. In this spot the brigade prepared to make what it believed would be its last stand across from the old stage road, resigned to death and defeat rather than surrender. Powell reported reaching "the borders of an old field, lined on our side by a skirt of woods. . . . On entering this opening we formed a line of battle along the old fence row." Hill reported the regiment "found itself facing east, then north and then south to meet the threat of the enemy," and recognizing their situation, they thereafter "formed in a semi-circle across the road and began to build breastworks of whatever material was at hand," mostly fence railings. "Every man was immediately busied digging the 'last ditch' and, reportedly, "cheerfully preparing for the impending conflict." This movement became the very last operational march for the

71 Reichardt, *Forever the Cause*, 98-99; Marvel, *Lee's Last Retreat*, 161; Salmon, *Virginia Battlefield Guide*, 490; Lowry, *Toward An Indefinite Shore*, 591.

72 Polley, *Hood's Texas Brigade*, 277-78; Marvel, *Lee's Last Retreat*, 165; Reichardt, *Forever the Cause*, 98. Powell said they were within a mile of Appomattox Court House, but other authorities place the Texans about two and a half miles from the village.

regiment—the final mile of many hundreds that the Texans had traveled over the ravaged land from the plains of Manassas, to the hills of Maryland, Gettysburg, Chickamauga and the deadly trenches and breastworks of the Overland Campaign.[73]

Weakened from lack of food—the men had not eaten for over three days, save for a few scraps of hurriedly prepared bread and biscuits—and haggard "almost beyond words from the constant tension of being the rear guard and the nearly continuous marching" the regiment was in tenuous physical shape. While gathering branches and dissembling fence rails to construct their breastworks, the men of the regiment found scattered kernels of corn where officers had previously fed their horses, and brushing them off with some revulsion consumed them. Despite the apparent hopelessness of their plight, the 5th Texas, like most of Lee's veterans, prepared their defenses carefully, and determined to sell their lives dearly for their cause, anticipating a massive Federal attack from the east.[74]

Lee well knew the slim odds for a successful breakout were slim, and he anticipated that before the day was over, he could well be Grant's prisoner. But he launched the attack anyway. The Confederate line extended across the western edge of the village, with the cavalry on the right and Gordon's infantry on the left. The center of the line, with its left resting on the Richmond-Lynchburg Stage Road, was Johnson's old division. Gordon's men carried out the bulk of the attack, but after some initial success, their commander soon realized that he could not advance and withdrew his infantry to the ridges on the north side of the Appomattox River to avoid being outflanked. He informed Lee that the road ahead had been closed, and Lee promptly cancelled the offensive. Lee felt the offensive might have succeeded with Longstreet's support. However, Field and Mahone were holding Meade back in the Confederate rear and could not be spared.[75]

By mid-day on April 9, Hill reported that an "informal" truce had brought about an ominous silence that hung over the Appomattox valley. Word quickly spread among the Confederates that Lee had arranged an interview with Grant, an inconceivable idea to the men, as it could mean only one thing—Lee was considering surrender. In fact, Lee had been negotiating potential surrender terms with Grant since April 7, while he was still in Farmville with his situation desperate, but with a line of retreat still open to him. Now, he was practically surrounded and facing

73 Polley, *Hood's Texas Brigade*, 277; Reichardt, *Forever the Cause*, 98; Chilton, *Hood's Texas Brigade*, 183; Simpson, *Lee's Grenadier Guard*, 464.

74 Hamilton, *History of Company M*, 69; Hanks, *Captain Benton's Company*, 55; Polley, *Hood's Texas Brigade*, 277.

75 Polley, *Hood's Texas Brigade*, 277; Salmon, *Virginia Battlefield Guide*, 490-92; Winkler, *Confederate Capital*, 260-61.

annihilation. Although Longstreet and some other senior commanders argued for yet another attempt to fight their way through to Lynchburg and the mountains, Lee had seen more than enough bloodshed and recognized the futility of further resistance. He thus dispatched a final note to Grant late in that morning, requesting a meeting in order to arrange "the terms of a surrender for this army," the prospect of which he confessed he "would rather die a thousand deaths" than endure.[76]

While silence continued to prevail, the 5th Texas narrowly escaped fighting the army's last battle. Lee had sent a courier through Gordon's lines requesting a temporary truce, and Maj. Gen. Ord, Army of the James commander and the ranking Union officer near Appomattox Court House, quickly agreed to halt the Union advance. At this point, the Army of Northern Virginia had fired its last volley. However, Lee had not secured a truce at the other end of the line, and Meade intervened, fully aware of the equivocation in Lee's earlier correspondence with Grant. The only way a needless battle around New Hope Church could be avoided was Grant's ordering a truce before Humphreys came up on Field's breastworks. In fact, Humphreys' troops were already starting to overtake Longstreet's stragglers. Meanwhile, Longstreet had gone into the village with Gordon to meet Ord and Sheridan. Once Longstreet explained the tension still seething at the Confederate rear, Sheridan instructed his chief of staff, Col. James Forsyth, to ride through the Confederate lines under a protective escort toward New Hope Church and ensure the general truce was upheld. "After speaking with Forsyth, the suspicious Meade finally conceded to wait for two hours," and suggested that Lee send a second message to Grant. Longstreet went into the village with Gordon to meet with Ord and Sheridan bearing the second note.[77]

Lee surrendered to Grant that afternoon in Wilmer McLean's house—ironically, the same Wilmer McLean whose former residence, near Manassas, Virginia, had become part of the battlefield of two major engagements in 1861-62. Vowing then to move his family to a place "where the sound of battle would never reach them," he had obviously failed miserably.[78]

76 *OR* 46, pt. 1, 1266-67; Trudeau, *Out of the Storm*, 130-38; Freeman, *R. E. Lee*, 4:118-21; Grant, *Personal Memoirs*, 2:478-86.

77 Marvel, *Lee's Last Retreat*, 176-77; Freeman, *Lee's Lieutenants*, 3:734-38.

78 Rodick, *Appomattox*, 153; Lowry, *Towards An Indefinite Shore*, 615-16. The conduct of the Union officers after the surrender enraged McLean. Sheridan thrust $20 in gold into his hand and carted off the table upon which Grant had written out the terms of surrender. Ord paid $40 for the table where Lee sat, and other officers "bought" various mementoes, including the chairs, inkstand, brass candlesticks, and even a child's doll found in the room. Mclean, unwilling to part with any of these items voluntarily, supposedly threw the money down on his porch. He later told Porter Alexander, a relative by marriage: "These armies tore my place on Bull Run all

The surrender terms were generous—soldiers and officers paroled and allowed to return immediately to their homes, with officers retaining their side arms and other personal property. Grant additionally allowed the Confederates to keep their mounts, which were also personal property. He similarly offered 25,000 rations to feed Lee's hungry army, which Lee believed would be sufficient, not knowing exactly how many still remained in his depleted army. The meeting ended at 4:00 p.m., and Lee walked down the front steps, mounted Traveller, exchanged salutes with Grant, and rode off to face his men.[79]

News of the surrender spread rapidly through the ranks of both armies. Those Confederates who met Lee on the way back from the McLean House had only to look at his countenance to comprehend what had transpired. The grizzled, war-weary veterans gathered around their beloved leader, patting Traveller and touching Lee's leg; many took off their hats in deference to their commander. Fighting hard to maintain his dignity and composure, "the great Virginian was near tears" himself while he assured them he had done all he could do for them, and that now they must go home and become good citizens of the united country. Many openly wept, while still others sat stunned by the road.[80]

When word of the surrender finally reached the 5th Texas, in the far rear of Longstreet's Corps, the men at first refused to accept the shocking news. Teamsters who had come from the front first brought the news, and the incredulous Texans initially threatened them with bodily harm for spreading false rumors. Once finally convinced of the accuracy of the information, however, one of the Texans dropped his hands despondently and declared, "I'd rather have died than surrendered, but if 'Marse Bob' thinks that is best, then all that I have got to say is that Marse Bob is bound to be right as usual."[81]

Captain Hill reported that following confirmation of the surrender, the morale of the regiment never waned. On the contrary, "if Lee had but asked it, there was not a man but would have continued to fight as gamely as ever he had." Others did not accept the news philosophically, however. Determined that the Yankees not receive

---

to pieces, and kept running over it backward and forward until no man could live there, so I just sold out and came here, two hundred miles away, hoping I should never see a soldier again. And now just look around you! Not a fence rail is left on the place, the last guns trampled down all my crops, and Lee surrenders to Grant in my house."

79 Trudeau, *Out of the Storm*, 142-43; Freeman, *Lee's Lieutenants*, 737-39; Lowry, *Towards An Indefinite Shore*, 609-15.

80 Burleigh Cushing Rodick, *Appomattox: The Last Campaign* (New York, 1965), 152; Trudeau, *Out of the Storm*, 142-43; Henry, *Story of the Confederacy*, 466; Simpson, *Lee's Grenadier Guard*, 465.

81 Winkler, *Confederate Capital*, 268; Chilton, *Hood's Texas Brigade*, 183.

usable weapons, some members of the 5th Texas bent the barrels of their guns in the forks of oak trees, while others smashed their Enfields against rocks and trees. Hill quickly admonished against such senseless actions, indicating that unless the men surrendered their guns in good working order, they would not receive paroles. Almost immediately, although without much luck, the men were hard at work trying to straighten their damaged gun barrels. It did not matter. The brigade surrendered 348 rifles, and every Texan was paroled.[82]

Powell reported years later, perhaps with some embellishment and flavor forged by the passage of time, that Lee had been apprised of the total shock and indignation that many members of the Texas Brigade had felt regarding the surrender. And he

> hurriedly rode to our lines to counsel where he had so recently commanded. He was immediately surrounded. One glance of his eyes . . . revealed but too plainly what his lips hesitated to utter. . . . They pressed up to him to touch him, felt his horse, and secured as mementos of the sad ending of years of carnage and devotion, some hairs from the charger's mane and tail. . . . When Gen. Lee departed he left a sad and thoughtful multitude who retired to the line and took up their guns and caressed them lovingly and gently, talked to them and bid them farewell.[83]

Early on April 10, the regiment formed with the brigade on the color line to hear the officers read Lee's farewell address, General Orders No. 9, and to review the terms of surrender. Hill reported that as Lee's last address to the army was read on the color line, "the men listening to it in silence, but with tears in their eyes. All felt that he had done his best, all that could be done, and that he had surrendered the army only when every avenue of escape was closed and to struggle longer was to invite destruction." After the formation, the men of the regiment returned to the campsite to draw Federal rations and await further word on the surrender of their arms and flags.[84]

The date for the formal surrender at Appomattox Court House on Wednesday, April 12, dawned with a misty rain, overcast and chilly. The roads were still muddy from the rain that had been falling since April 9. Generals Grant and Lee had each appointed three general officers to establish the protocol of the surrender as well as the issuance of paroles for the Southerners. Neither leader attended the surrender itself. Grant had departed to catch a train to his headquarters at City Point on April 10.

82 Polley, *Hood's Texas Brigade*, 277-78; Winkler, *Confederate Capital*, 268; Chilton, *Hood's Texas Brigade*, 183.

83 *Missouri Republican*, July 10, 1886; Reichardt, *Forever the Cause*, 99.

84 Chilton, *Hood's Texas Brigade*, 183. Lee's farewell address is in *OR* 46, pt. 1, 1267.

Lee, while still in the vicinity, chose to remain at his field headquarters until the afternoon of the surrender, after which he left on Traveler for the lonely ride to his home in Richmond.[85]

At sunrise, the Confederate camp came to life as the men made ready for their final march as proud soldiers of the Texas Brigade. Early that morning, the columns began assembling on the high ground north of the Appomattox, with the remnant of Ewell's Corps, now commanded by Gordon, in front. Next, the remains of A. P. Hill's proud corps, now commanded by Henry Heth, formed. Longstreet's Corps, as it had so often throughout the war, marched last, with Field's Division and the Texans, bringing up its rear. Confederate battle flags flew in their appropriate positions, in the middle of each regiment.

Most of the regiments were now so small, however, that the column gave the appearance of being "crowned with red," so closely were the proud flags crowded together in the marching column. Not a single band marched with the column, and without the beat of a drum, Gordon set out through the thick mud and across the Appomattox toward the Federal lines. A large portion of these valiant warriors of four hard years of fighting were hobbled by sickness or injury as they filed down the road for the last time as soldiers in the Army of Northern Virginia; all were still weak from hunger. The Federally-issued rations had been their first substantial meal for several weeks.[86]

Brig. Gen. Joshua L. Chamberlain, commanding the 3rd Brigade of Maj. Gen. Joseph J. Barlett's division of the V Corps, was positioned in one row along the Richmond-Lynchburg Stage Road on the eastern outskirts of the hamlet, the northernmost portion of the Union line. When he spotted the head of the marching Confederate column, as he later recalled, Chamberlain gave the marching salute command "Carry, arms," out of respect for a longstanding and worthy adversary. Responding with an honor in return, Gordon dropped the point of his saber toward the ground, acknowledging Chamberlain's courtesy, and gave the command, "Carry,

85 Polley, *Hood's Texas Brigade*, 278; Freeman, *Lee's Lieutenants*, 3:741-42; Grant, *Personal Memoirs*, 2:494-95. Maj. Gen. John Gibbon and Brevet Maj. Gens. Wesley Merritt and Charles Griffin served as Union commissioners; James Longstreet, John Gordon, and William Pendleton made up their Confederate counterparts. W. T. Hill claimed the brigade was the last unit of the rear guard on the road Lee used when he passed out of his army's lines after the surrender. He passed within 70 yards of the 5thTexas, and in plain view with "an escort of four or five mounted men with him, whom we took to be his staff officers." Others contended Lee was alone, as depicted in a famous contemporary engraving. But, as Hill pointed out, it would have been unusual for him not to have an escort near. W. T. Hill, "Confederate Officers After Appomattox," in *CV*, (1911), 19:252.

86 Freeman, *Lee's Lieutenants*, 3:745-49; Chamberlain, *Passing of the Armies*, 259-60; Simpson, *Lee's Grenadier Guard*, 467; Grant, *Personal Memoirs*, 2:494-95.

arms" to his troops. With a final soldier's salute, the respective troops of the two armies honored each other and the four years of brutal fighting and death they had endured.[87]

Lee's ragged, gaunt soldiers stoically kept their composure until time came to stack their weapons and furl their revered, battle-stained banners. At this point came the realization that all they had been fighting and dying for through the brutal, four-year struggle—independence as a nation—as well as the camaraderie forged in bivouac and in battle had been fruitless. Many of these battle-hardened, undefeatable veterans sagged to their knees and wept while placing the ragged, blood-stained battle flags on the stacks of arms along the line of surrender. Chamberlain described the scene:

> [a]s each successive division masks our own, it halts, the men face inward towards us across the road, twelve feet away; then carefully 'dress' their line, each captain taking pains for the good appearance of the company, worn and half starved as they were. . . . They fix bayonets, stack arms; then, hesitantly, remove cartridge boxes and lay them down. Lastly, reluctantly, with agony of expression, they tenderly fold their flags, battle-worn and torn, blood-stained, heart-holding colors, and lay them down; some frenziedly rushing from the ranks, kneeling over them, clinging to them, pressing them to their lips with burning tears.[88]

General Gordon later wrote extensively about the event and offered similar reflections on the moving scene. As each Confederate unit marched forward to its assigned spot in the drama, he recalled,

> veterans . . . could no longer control their emotions, and tears ran like water down their shrunken faces. The flags which they still carried were objects of undisguised affection. . . . As we reached the designated point, the arms were stacked and the battle flags were folded. Those sad and suffering men, many of them weeping as they saw the old banners laid down upon the stacked guns . . . began to tear the flags from the staffs and hide them in their shirts.

87 John J. Pullen, *The Twentieth Maine: A Classic Story of Joshua Chamberlain and his Volunteer Regiment* (Philadelphia, PA, 1957), 273; National Park Service, *Appomattox Court House*, 7; Simpson, *Lee's Grenadier Guard*, 467; Freeman, *Lee's Lieutenants*, 3:744-45.

88 Gordon, *Reminiscences of the Civil War*, 443-48; Simpson, *Lee's Grenadier Guard*, 467-68; Chamberlain, *Passing of the Armies*, 258-65.

Longstreet's Corps, and the regiment with it, was among the last to surrender.[89] Colonel Powell described how:

> [a]rmed and equipped we marched in the direction of the federal headquarters, there to stack arms and receive our final dismissal. The road was on the hillside, on the right being high ground. There the field officers paraded in line. To the left was lower ground, where the troops were drawn up. Between these the Confederate forces passed. No word was spoken except the words of command to stack arms, which was done orderly and quietly, facing the line of federal troops.

In what had to be a dramatic and heartbreaking scene, he added that: "[h]uman lips were pressed to iron muzzles of guns and the men turned from them as sadly and sorrowfully as if they were moving from the graves of their first born. We passed on, never looking back to that national potter's field, where our young republic was buried."[90]

Of the 28,231 Confederates surrendering and subsequently paroled at Appomattox on April 12, the rolls listed only 7,892 considered capable of bearing arms at the time. The remainder, weakened by hunger or disease, or footsore, was unfit for duty, a pitiful sight as they limped along with their regiments. A total of approximately 5,300 men had enlisted in the Texas Brigade during the war. Of this number, a mere 617 remained to be paroled on April 12. Thus, some 4,700 members of the brigade, about 88 percent, had been killed in battle, died of disease, invalided home, or discharged for being over or under age. Only a few had ever deserted.[91]

The 5th Texas itself surrendered a total of 13 officers and 148 men on April 12, out of approximately 1,440 who served in the unit at some point during the war. Company A had no officers left; only Company I had more than one. Paroled from the 5th Texas that day were 161 men: seven regimental staff, nine from Company A, 10 from Companies B and C; 12 from Company F; 15 from Company G; 16 from Companies D and E; 21 from Companies I and K; and 24 from Company H. Of this

89 Major Henry Kyd Douglas commanded the final Confederate brigade to surrender, an honor he had requested from Gordon because his brigade had fired the last shot before the final truce on April 9. Henry Kyd Douglas, *I Rode With Stonewall: the War Experiences of the Youngest Member of Jackson's Staff* (Chapel Hill, NC, 1940), 318-19.

90 Gordon, *Reminiscences of the Civil War*, 443-48; Trudeau, *Out of the Storm*, 149; *Missouri Republican*, July 10, 1886, 1; Reichardt, *Forever the Cause*, 100.

91 Chilton, *Hood's Texas Brigade*, 183; Robertson, *Touched With Valor*, 65; Simpson, *Lee's Grenadier Guard*, 468-69; Freeman, *Lee's Lieutenants*, 3:744-45. Desertion figures for Longstreet's Corps from February 23-March 18, 1865 are in Appendix E.

total, 99 of these veterans had marched from their Texas communities with their respective companies on their formation that fateful summer of 1861.[92]

The war had finally ended for the men of the 5th Texas Infantry Regiment, after over three-and-a-half years of arduous service and untold sacrifice for their now defeated cause. All now left to them, after bidding farewell to their comrades-in-arms, was the promise of reclaiming a life for themselves in a reunited country. Thus, the thoughts of the men immediately turned to their loved ones and a renewed life in the Lone Star State. Most were extremely anxious to set out for Texas as soon as possible, however that might be accomplished.

92 *OR* 46, pt. 1, 1279, 1277; "Paroles of the Army of Northern Virginia," in *SHSP* (1887), 15:160-70. John A. Green of Company C is listed as 2nd Sergeant on the Roll of Officers and Men of the Brigade who surrendered. W. D. Wood later reported him as a second lieutenant in *Leon County CSA Sketches*, 19.

Chapter 9

The Long Road Home

On the afternoon of April 12, following the formal surrender, a mass meeting of the Texas companies assembled in "the pen," as the men had designated their campsite. With the formalities over, the paramount question for 5th Texas men now was how to get back to their Texas homes. Grant had generously allowed all of the Confederate parolees, officers and men, "to pass free on all Government transportation and military railroads." To these gallant veterans, who had little or no valid currency and were dead broke almost to the man, this directive appeared as a welcome concession. The meeting discussed a number of potential routes. Some men desired to travel to Yorktown, 150 miles to the east, and go by sea to either New Orleans or Galveston. Some preferred to remain in Virginia to recuperate before attempting the arduous journey home, while still others wanted to visit relatives in the various Southern states before making the difficult trek home to Texas. Most, however, decided to travel overland directly to Texas by way of the shortest, fastest route possible.[1]

Crippling wounds narrowed the choices for a considerable number of the regiment's veterans: Edwin King Goree of Company H, for example. One of three brothers in the 5th Texas, Goree had his leg so mangled in the Wilderness that it was a useless appendage. He had to hobble on a "forked peach tree" crutch all the way back to Texas, finally arriving there in May 1866. The journey home for others had to await their release from Federal prisons. Robert A. Brantley and William H. Mathews

1 *OR* 46, pt. 3, 687, 1392; Chilton, *Hood's Texas Brigade*, 184; Simpson, *Lee's Grenadier Guard*, 469. The issue was less difficult for the 3rd Arkansas, for it could return home by way of Chattanooga and Memphis, which it did. The Texans, however, had considerably farther to go. Sid S. Johnson, "H. A. Massey," *Texans Who Wore the Gray*, 8 vols., Tyler, TX (1907), 1:145.

remained in custody at Fort Delaware, for example, until mid-June, and Eli Yow of Company C, was not released from Point Lookout until June 22, 1865.[2]

Other men, such as William Ashford Nabours and Constantine Perkins Nance of Company G, chose to travel in small groups. As soon as they received their paroles, they set out for Lynchburg, immediately searching to acquire some bacon and hard tack. At Bristol, Tennessee, they received a hostile reception from the locals, and the next day, the companions encountered a squad of hostile Federal soldiers, who, after inspecting their paroles, relieved them of their blankets and canteens before allowing them to be on their way. Then, in Greenville, Tennessee, three Federal cavalrymen stopped the pair, and after examining their paroles, took every remaining personal item the two Texans still possessed. From there, the men boarded a train for Bull's Gap, and then rode atop a boxcar to Knoxville, where again, they received a hostile reception when seeking transportation west. They also witnessed the brutal beating of a returning local Confederate veteran on own his doorstep. The men quickly fled this unfriendly climate, finding a freight train bound for Chattanooga and climbed atop a boxcar. Their traveling companions on this ride, a group of former Confederate teamsters, advised then not to alight during stops along the way, because the local home guards were certain to harass them.[3]

In Chattanooga, Nabours and Nance remained on the boxcar until it started toward Murfreesboro the following morning. There, they arrived at the home of Nance's sister, whose husband was a Primitive Baptist minister. Family friends promptly donated clothing and shoes to the ragged men who resembled vagabonds more than former soldiers. After several days in Murfreesboro, the pair next visited Nance's parents on the Duck River in Lincoln County. Two of Nance's sisters accompanied them back to Murfreesboro and then on to the old homestead. The family's former slaves, who were caring for the family house, mistook Nabours for one of the sister's husband, and the young woman played along. "How do you like his

2 Jonathan Daniel Goree, *The Goree Boys, 1861-65* (Coolidge, AZ, 1965), 1; Edwin Sue Goree, *A Family Mosaic*, 17-18; Civil War Prisoner of War Records, 1861-1865, Provo, UT, 397; Simpson. *Compendium*, 175; Yeary, *Reminiscences of the Boys in Gray*, 1:76, 2:470.

3 Nabours, "Active Service of a Texas Command," in *CV*, 24:69-72. Born in Itawamba County, Mississippi, in 1839, to a Methodist preacher, Nabours (1839-1922) moved with his family to Milam County in the 1850s. Nance moved from Davidson County, TN, in 1860 and bought 500 acres in Milam County, Texas with his brother, James. He enlisted in what became Company G in 1861 at Cameron. He returned to Tennessee later in 1865 to care for his six younger sisters upon the death of his parents. See *Tennessee Civil War Questionnaire*, Genealogy Clearinghouse, accessed July 20, 2009, http://freepages.genealogy.rootsweb.ancestry.com/~nancegc/cp_nance.htm.

looks?" she inquired. The old black woman inspected Nabours carefully and replied "I 'spect he'll sorter do."[4]

The pair continued on to Nashville, where they boarded a steamboat headed down the Cumberland River. While the government-imposed transportation was steerage class, when the Texans reached Paducah and boarded the *St. Patrick* for New Orleans, the steamboat's other passengers insisted they be upgraded to berths in the cabins where they were accorded better treatment.[5]

About 100 miles south of Cairo, Illinois, the pair awoke in the middle of the night to a violent jarring and sizeable commotion. Panicked passengers were frantically rushing for the front of the boat. Dressing quickly, the Texans hurried out and saw deck hands securing the vessel to trees on the river bank. Another boat coming up the river had collided with theirs. The *St. Patrick* remained cabled to the bank until dawn, when its passengers transferred to another steamboat and resumed the trip to New Orleans. Two days thereafter, the men boarded the *Thomas Spark* in New Orleans, bound for Galveston, "a very slow and unpleasant experience," with "no shade, no shelter, just out on open deck" of the boat. From Galveston, the men then traveled north to Houston by rail, and from there to Navasota. And then they walked to Robertson County and rode mules to Fort Sullivan in Milam County. Finally, after another horseback ride, the two men finally reached Cameron on June 26, 1865.[6]

Sgt. Arter Berry Green of Company K wrote of a fellow Texan who decided to pay General Lee a visit at his Richmond residence on Franklin Street before departing for Texas. Lee's son, Custis, opened the door to the unannounced visitor, a tall soldier with one arm in a sling seeking an audience with the general. Custis explained that his father was extremely busy answering a panoply of correspondence and politely turned the soldier away. As the wounded veteran turned to leave, he mentioned that he had fought with Hood's Brigade, following Lee for four years. He just wanted to shake his old commander's hand before the long trek home, "but if he couldn't, he couldn't, and it could not be helped." Custis could no longer refuse the simple request and called his father. When Lee came downstairs, his hand extended "the soldier took him by the hand, struggled to say something and burst into tears." Quickly covering his face with his good arm, and quietly turning, he walked out of the room, and out of the house.

4 Nabours, W. A. "Active Service of a Texas Command," in *CV*, 24:69-72. The parents' former residence was outside Nashville, but the Federals had "banished" them during their occupation, loading them onto wagons without any of their personal belongings and unloading them by the roadside near the Duck River. The couple had lost two sons fighting for the Confederacy.

5 Ibid.

6 Ibid.

Arter Berry Green
Texas Heritage Museum

Lee gazed after him for a few moments, "his fine, deep, dark eyes suffused and darkened with emotion," and returned upstairs. "Not a single word was spoken during the meeting by any of the three participants." Greene also supposedly belonged to one of the groups that splintered from Captain Hill's main body on April 15. He decided upon a leisurely journey home, not reaching the Lone Star State until mid-July. He and Dennis A. Rowe, soon to be his brother-in-law, and one other Texan rode mules most of the way, stopping two or three days at a time to fish, pick berries and fruit, do farm chores, and "generally enjoyed themselves finely" on their way back to Greenville, Texas.[7]

Captain W. T. Hill and Maj. William H. "Howdy" Martin, commanders of the 5th and 4th Texas—original brigade members with impeccable combat records—assumed leadership at Appomattox for the largest group of Texans, about 300, planning to travel overland to Texas. These two men were well respected officers, original members of the brigade, with impeccable combat records. They decided to lead the Texans home by way of rail through Danville, Virginia, Charlotte, North Carolina, then Atlanta, Mobile, and New Orleans, and finally by steamboat to Galveston. This route made best use of the free rail and water transportation Grant afforded homeward bound Confederate soldiers. The Texans set out for home, "bidding [our] loved chieftain a farewell adieu, turning our backs with reluctance upon the Old Dominion State, a broad field of blood, and our loved lost comrades whose bones now mark the places of many hard fought battles." Hill's large group headed toward Danville the morning of April 13, and traveled nearly 20 miles that day. A local farmer gave them two ears of corn apiece that evening, and they ate parched corn that night. He "was so hungry," said one Texan, "that I could have eaten a piece of rubber

7 Richard M. Ketchum, "Faces From the Past—II" *American Heritage* (1961), 12:29; Harold B. Simpson, "Hood's Brigade at Appomattox," in Ralph Wooster, Lone Star Blue and Gray: Essays on Texas in the Civil War (Austin, TX, 1995), 338-40; "Sgt. Arter Berry Green," accessed June 1, 2009, www.findagrave.com/cgi-bin/fg.cgi?page=gr&GRid= 30678156.

boot." At noon the following day, the group bivouacked near Nowlin's Mill on Falling Creek. The availability of good clean water and corn meal there kept the Texans in place for the remainder of the day. Although lacking lard, soda, salt, and utensils, the men soon baked meal into some form of bread, the first the men had eaten since April 7. That evening, in a cold rain, was the last that the men would spend together as a group. Traveling in such large numbers had proven problematic for securing food and suitable campsites. Thus a number of smaller bodies splintered off, proceeding on their own along the same general route as the main body, southwest through the Carolinas.[8]

Their journey back to the Lone Star State was trying and tedious. The main group reached the environs of Danville on the April 15, where they rested for several days, allowing the stragglers to catch up. Their prospects of riding a train from Danville through Morgantown to Atlanta had been dashed by Federal cavalry and its recent destruction of considerable portions of the track. So the intrepid band of rugged, hungry Texans ultimately had to walk a large stretch of the way through the Carolinas, Georgia, and Alabama, the able bodied continually assisting their infirmed and wounded comrades.[9]

Near Greensboro they met with and joined a sizeable number of Texans from the Army of Tennessee, which had surrendered to General Sherman at Durham Station in North Carolina on April 26. This group included Maj. Moses B. George, who had served as General Hood's quartermaster in Virginia, and who had remained with the general in Georgia. Major George still had with him his Durham cow, which he had brought all the way from Texas in 1861. The animal had been a part of his wagon train through the brutal years of fighting. Surprising, given all she had been through and her inadequate food supply, she still provided milk. The major and his cow were a welcome addition to the famished band of Texans heading westward toward home. The band passed through Charlotte while President Davis, John H. Reagan, and other members of the Confederate cabinet and Congress were still there. According to Reagan, Martin, as senior officer among the Texans, gave the presidential party the first real details of the surrender and told them that a number of blank Federal parole forms had fortunately "fallen" into his hands. At Reagan's request, Martin gave him a

8 Polley, *Hood's Texas Brigade*, 278-80; Hanks, *Captain Benton's Company*, 44; Hamilton, *History of Company M*, 42. Col. Powell and Lt. Col. Winkler, both married during the war, arranged to travel back to Texas with their wives. Simpson, *Lee's Grenadier Guard*, 470-71; Chilton, *Hood's Texas Brigade*, 184.

9 Chilton, *Hood's Texas Brigade*, 184; Simpson, *Lee's Grenadier Guard*, 471. The Texans were only able to ride the rails toward Montgomery for four of the 30 days it took to get there. They walked some 360 miles.

sizeable number of parole forms, and later both Wigfall and Secretary of the Navy Mallory used them to pass through Federal lines.[10]

The men continued their journey southwestward through Chester and Abbeville, South Carolina, Washington, Atlanta, and West Point, Georgia, on to Auburn, Alabama. The advance portion of Hill's group finally reached Montgomery, Alabama, on May 7, and there assigned to temporary quarters in a large, two-story building near downtown. Over 400 Texans arrived there over the next five days to await water transportation to Mobile. On May 11, Martin learned that the steamer *Groesbeck*, scheduled to transport his men down the Alabama River to Mobile, had finally arrived. However, the vessel was still fully loaded with supplies and equipment for the Union garrison there. Learning that using the boat to go south would require that they first unload it, the Texans, working in shifts, accomplished this task in six hours, a job normally requiring a full 24-hour day for a 50-man crew of black laborers. Astounded at the massive stack of unloaded supplies and equipment, one Texan wearily declared "Boys, we could have never whipped the Yankees." Late that afternoon, the exhausted but relentless men were steaming toward Mobile. The passage proved a difficult one and not without incident. Only 50 miles out at Selma, the men were ordered ashore in order to allow a regiment of USCT to replace them. Following yet another day's layover, the men boarded the steamer *Lockwood*, again bound for Mobile. Once there the men spent five relaxing days in the city, enjoying suitable quarters and ample rations.[11]

On the morning of May 18, they embarked on the gulf steamer *Iberville* for New Orleans. This voyage proved to be was a rough one, during which the ship almost capsized on Lake Pontchartrain However, the group arrived safely in the Crescent City the next day. As soon as they disembarked, their paroles were duly endorsed by the local provost marshal, and they were shown to distressingly uncomfortable quarters in large cotton shed with no cots, mattresses, or blankets available. Only their ragged army blankets cushioned the men from the hard floor. Moreover, a company of black soldiers were assigned to "guard" them and one of their first actions was to forcibly attempt to cut the brass C.S.A. buttons off the Texans' tattered gray blouses. To avoid the humiliation, most Texans cut off their own buttons and concealed them. The men were detained in New Orleans nine days awaiting free sea transport to Galveston. But despite the guards, the accommodations, and their understandable impatience, the Texans still enjoyed a reasonably good time in the city. A number of

10 Chilton, *Hood's Texas Brigade*, 184; Wright, *Southern Girl in '61*, 243; Polley, *Hood's Texas Brigade*, 279.

11 Polley, *Hood's Texas Brigade*, 279; Chilton, *Hood's Texas Brigade*, 184-85; Simpson, *Lee's Grenadier Guard*, 473.

Irish women were particularly kind to the Texans, bringing baskets of food to the cotton shed and inviting some of them into their homes. These generous women also furnished each man with a suit of civilian clothes before he departed from the city.[12]

Transportation for the final leg of their journey to Galveston, Texas, had been arranged for May 29. The eager Texans, by now wearing a hodgepodge of civilian clothes and Confederate gray, duly presented themselves at the dock early that day, and boarded the steamer *Hendrick Hudson*, eager to embark on the final leg of their homeward odyssey. However, before the ship left the dock, fire bells clanged and a column of thick, black smoke arose adjacent to the home of one Colonel Henry, inducing the men to abandon ship and help subdue the fire. The Texans described Henry as a "grand old Rebel," who had just entertained them with a memorable dinner this past evening. They thus left the ship and assisted the "Colonel" in removing his belongings and guarding them against potential looters. After a six-hour delay, the thoroughly exhausted men trudged back to the riverfront and a livid ship's captain. The steamer finally got underway down the Mississippi by 4:30 p.m. that afternoon.[13]

As the *Hendrick Hudson* neared the mouth of the Mississippi at dawn on May 30, it ran fast aground on a mud flat at the Mouth of Passes, remaining stuck there despite the heroic efforts of two tugs to refloat her. For two days the men stayed in their crowded quarters, drenched in the steamy humidity of the Delta. Finally, on May 31, the *Exact*, a freighter already en route to Galveston, picked up the stranded Texans. The relief ship, however, turned out to be a filthy, poorly maintained transport. The stench of bilge water and human body heat, together with poor ventilation, soon drove the men out of the hold and onto the deck into the blistering sun. This sudden mass movement, in turn, almost capsized the freighter. The *Exact* reached Texas on June 2, proceeding slowly through the Federal blockade fleet still anchored off Galveston Island. The same day the Texans reached Galveston, General Edmund Kirby Smith, commander of the Army of the Trans-Mississippi, surrendered the last significant Confederate army to the Federals in that very city.[14]

As the *Exact* entered port, Brig. Gen. Edmund J. Davis, commanding the Federal troops there, initially refused to permit the Texans to dock, ordering the ship to

12 Chilton, *Hood's Texas Brigade*, 184-85; Polley, *Hood's Texas Brigade*, 280-81. Polley, Hill, and many locals referred to the black soldiers part of the "Corps d'Afrique," but since 1864 they had been consolidated into the U.S.C.T. See Jonathan Sutherland, *African Americans at War: An Encyclopedia* (Santa Barbara, CA.), 2 vols., 1:683-700.

13 Chilton, *Hood's Texas Brigade*, 185; Polley, *Hood's Texas Brigade*, 281; Simpson, *Lee's Grenadier Guard*, 474.

14 Chilton, *Hood's Texas Brigade*, 186; Simpson, *Lee's Grenadier Guard*, 474-75; Trudeau, *Out of the Storm*, 340-41; Lowry, *Towards An Indefinite Shore*, 805.

remain at anchor in the bay. Finally, around noon, he allowed the steamer to dock, the first "civilian" ship to enter the port since the end of hostilities there. Elated Texans rushed ashore with a yell, many grasping their native soil in their hands for the first time in four years. A delegation of Galveston's prominent citizens was on hand to welcomed them home. The spokesman for the group informed Martin and Hill that the citizens of Houston expected all of them to attend a series of dinners and balls welcoming them home that same evening. However, the tenuous, ongoing negotiations between Kirby Smith and Maj. Gen. Edward R. S. Canby, commander of the Federal Department of the Gulf, had kept Galveston in a state of suspended chaos, and Davis denied the returning veterans use of a Buffalo Bayou steamer for the trip north to Houston.[15]

The grateful citizens of Galveston, however, were not about to deny their returning heroes their richly deserved celebration. So they arranged a transportation package—a rusty railroad engine and several dilapidated cars of the Galveston, Houston, and Henderson Railroad—that could get the veterans to Houston in time for the festivities. Citizens and the Texas veterans soon had the engine in reasonable working condition, and just before sunset, the "Homecoming Special" readied for departure. Just as the Texans boarded, a group of Irish women came out from town and proceeded to thoroughly clean the cars. So well-known were the exploits of Hood's Texas Brigade, the grateful people of Texas almost fought one another to pay homage to these returning heroes of Texas and the Army of Northern Virginia.[16]

The train left Galveston around dusk for its 50-mile trip, a hectic journey for the vets on an uneven roadbed, under the unsteady hand of an amateur engineer, on the struggling locomotive, with its train of overcrowded flat cars. Though it was near midnight when the train arrived in Houston, a large contingent of citizens was on hand to greet the Texans and escort them to a series of welcome-home parties and festivities. The next day, June 3, after yet another gala dinner for the men, and the handclasps and farewells which followed, the brave band of 5th Texas survivors finally disbanded. Many of the men departed by themselves or in pairs or small groups, destined for their individual homes—now the shadows of history and legend. "There let us drop the curtain, for the great drama was over," Hill wrote.[17]

Other men connected with the regiment followed divers paths homeward. William Fletcher, late of Terry's Rangers, and formerly of the 5th Texas, found himself near Raleigh at war's end. He joined with about 150 Texans and started for home

15 Chilton, *Hood's Texas Brigade*, 186.

16 Ibid.; Simpson, *Lee's Grenadier Guard*, 475; Polley, *Hood's Texas Brigade*, 282.

17 Polley, *Hood's Texas Brigade*, 282; Chilton, *Hood's Texas Brigade*, 186.

without awaiting permission or paroles. By the time the men made it to Alabama, most had dropped out to visit friends or relatives, and Fletcher's organized party had diminished to a handful, and ultimately, to just three. In Mississippi, the men took advantage of the abundance of corn, moving slowly while feeding and resting their mounts. Near Natchez, the trio sold their mounts to a widow who was in the process of reestablishing her plantation. There, the men were paroled and furnished transportation; Fletcher chose to go to Alexandria, Louisiana, while his companions went on to New Orleans. From Alexandria, Fletcher walked to his sister's, a distance of some 40 miles. There he remained for a month before again setting out for Texas with his brother-in-law in a two-horse buggy.

On the way, Fletcher called on the mother of a former 5th Texas comrade near Lake Charles. The boy with his dying breath had made Fletcher promise to call on his mother and sisters when he returned. The mother was so out of sorts that he could not deliver the message. Instead, Fletcher's brother-in-law saw to it on his return home. The pair crossed the Sabine River by ferry near Nibletts Bluff. At the Neches River, they left the horses on the east side and crossed the river over the Texas and New Orleans Railroad trestle. Fletcher finally reunited with his aged father, half-brother and sisters in Beaumont. Soon after his arrival, Fletcher gathered up his father's old carpentry tools and took a job for $1.50 per day, "about one hundred feet from the place where I left off work [to enlist]." In the intervening months, Fletcher befriended a number of Yankee troops stationed in Beaumont, to the considerable consternation of local citizens. He would respond to their frequent admonitions by relating the story of his encounter with the North Carolina infantryman, ending by stating that "the war is over and I am following the North Carolinian's advice."[18]

Nicholas Pomeroy of Company A, sick at the time of the surrender, missed the formal ceremony. However, upon receiving his parole, he and two companions set out for Texas on their own. They traveled by train to Jackson, Mississippi, then "walked from there all the way to Texas." In the process, they crossed the Mississippi River in a "small row boat." Upon reaching the other side, they encountered a bottomland flooded over great areas. By wading, swimming, and floating on logs and sticks, they finally reached dry land.

18 Preceding paragraphs based on Fletcher, *Rebel Private*, 194-213. Fletcher never forgot the lesson he learned on the trip home. He had encountered a North Carolina infantryman who drawled "Boys, have you got any bacon?" To the affirmative reply, the Tarheel retorted: "Grease and slide back into the Union." After considerable reflection, Fletcher grasped the wisdom of the analogy and determined to "follow the lesson taught by the crude advice." Thereafter, in reflecting on his future civilian life, "day by day the sunshine of . . . [his] being grew brighter."

Thereafter, the group stopped at a planter's house, and, supplied with rations, they declined an offer of lodging, preferring to press on as they were so accustomed to camping outside. Their westward progress went well until an encounter with the pinewoods of western Louisiana and eastern Texas. Moving through the thick forests involved several days, with almost no roads, and no sources of food or water. Pomeroy arrived in Houston "none the worse for [his] . . . four years campaigning in . . . Virginia." He stayed in Houston where jobs were plentiful for two years following his homecoming. He finally went home and reunited with his aged parents, and, at his mother's urging, remained there.[19]

Powell likewise expressed the need to move forward to embrace a new life. He wrote of the need for the South to "organize and sustain the President and all will be done that is possible to save her from further distress and desolation." He confronted the obvious sentiment that these might seem as "strange sentiments to be advanced by one who was *first in the cause and the last to yield*—and now, heart broken, and stricken with grief, but I speak with the good of our people at heart, and fight no longer against Providence which, leagued with the heaviest battalions decreed against us."

Despite having to overcome enormous obstacles during Reconstruction, these veterans would become leaders of their communities and furnish Texas with merchants, physicians, lawyers, judges, legislators, clergymen, farmers, ranchers, and honest, hardworking tradesmen at a critical juncture in the state's history.[20]

* * *

> Although the sun of the Confederacy had set and the bloody experiment in states rights' government had come to an end, the world would long remember the soldiers of Hood's Texas Brigade. Few men in the history of modern warfare had fought so long and so well, with so little, and had suffered so many casualties. They were a credit to their American heritage, a credit to the famous army in which they fought and a credit to the states which they which they represented.[21]

19 Nicholas Pomeroy, "Reminiscences of the American War,1861-1865," (n.d.), 87-89 in Briscoe Center for American History, University of Texas, Austin, TX; Chicoine, *Confederates From Chappell Hill*, 141.

20 Simpson, *Lee's Grenadier Guard*, 476-77; Reichardt, *Forever the Cause*, 110.

21 Simpson, *Lee's Grenadier Guard*, 476-77.

Appendix A

Deaths From Disease or Accident

1861

Company A: Berry, M. F.; Fleming, D. N.; Sweeney, J. J.; Taylor, A. C. M.; Toole, H. P.; Zimmerman, T.

Company B: Byars, George C.; Cabaniss, Max; Haynes, B. W.; Higgs, J. F.; McCormick, J.

Company C: Alrick, H. L.; Brewer, J. H.; McGary, M. M.; Page, R. D.; Perry, W. B.; Thomas, Samuel P.

Company D: Alston, R. H.; Harper, W. E.

Company E: Gay, Milam; Muse, W. T.

Company F: Bostwick, J. A.; Fink, Charles; Frazier, Robert; Keith, Edmund N.; Lorisch, Albert; Miller, John J.; Read, A. J.; Reese, James; Simmons, Thomas; Wallace, W. W.

Company G: Blackman, W. J.; Converse, G. W.; Cross, Antonio; Ditto, Alex; Ford, G. M.; Ford, J. L.; Garrett, G. W.; King, B. D.; Ogden, Milton; Sherrill, James; Stedhan, Lewis

Company H: Byrd, A. B., Lt.; Carr, James; Connover, Charles; Dansby, Uriah; Floyd, W. R.; Foster, Milton; Grayless, J. A.; Hubert, M. D.; McAlexander, John; McGee, William; Mills, James H.; Ross, J. B.; Steel, A. J.; Steel, George

Company I: Banner, Thomas T.; Hill, Green W.; Hardy, John H.

Company K: Adams, J. J.; Allbritton, L.; Burch, Joseph; Hicks, A.; Killingsworth, J. M.; Lewis, J. M.; Nettles, J. H.; Ritter, Lewis; Simpson, L.; Speights, C. A.; Starling, John; Thornton, Sam B.; Walker, J. A.

1862

Company A: Netherly, James R.; Riley, W. J.; Williams, H. W.; Wright, R. F.

Company B: McCormick, Stephen; Rhodes, W. L.; Slayton, A. G.

Company C: Barbee, James B.; Boykin, William F.; Brashear, A. B.; Braim, William; Cosby, John S.; Deattey, James; Dezell, E. M.; Elkins, Benjamin P.; Graham, James R.; Graham, Strickling; Hayes, R. H.; Henry, William B.; Hough, William B.; Jones, A. A.; Moore, J. D.; Moore, William M.; Mulholland, B. E.; Murchison, William; Neighbors, John L.; Pruitt, W. A.; Rose, Joseph; Sawyers, Elbert H.; Underwood, James H.; Walker, Virgil J.; Welch, M. T.; Yeldell, J. R.

Company D: Brown, G. W.; Cunningham, F. M.; Elmore, J. F.; Estill, Black; Green, G. H.; Irvine, H. R.; Netherly, T. W.; Rose, J. D.; Smith, Rodum; Strayhorn, W. N.; Tomlinson, James

Company E: Cooper, George R.; Garrett, John T.; Goggans, D. Jack; Goodwin, C. S.; Hendley, F. M.; Hill, Anderson; Marshall, E. M.; Mayfield, John M.; Muir, W. A.; Randle, John A.; Reedy, W. S.; Ruark, W. A.; Stutsman, David; Traner, A. J.; Wilcox, John L.

Company F: Atchison, William; Benjamin, George; Bryan, Pryor L.; Bryan, W. M.; Dugat, Beasley; Gilman, John J.; Hart, Edwin; Howell, James; McCarty, William J.; Merriman, A. C.; Norton, Alonzo B.; Oxford, Isaac; Perryman, R. M.; Schultz, William

Company G: Bounds, J. H.; Evans, D. M.; Jones, H. E.; Langford, T. A.; Lester, Travis; Moore, G. W.; Munrow, John; Nabors, B. F.; Norman, P. W.; Price, Robert D.; Sharp, Robert; Sherrill, R. L.; Shirley, R. L.; Shirley, T. M.; Stiles, John; Thornton, J. E.; Watson, R. E.; Young, William

Company H: Bass, Nathan S.; Brinkley, Christian; Carter, G. M. T.; Daugherty, James; Hough, F. T.; Jackson, Benjamin; F. Jett, Valentine; Lewis, G. A.; Louis, James; Maxcy, W. S.; McCann, Washington; McLain, John; Obarr, G. D.; Simmons, Wiley W.; Stephenson, J. A.; Williams, D. R.

Company I: Banner, Martin A.; Boyles, Duff; Hill, John C.; Holmes, William H.; McKee, H.; Mitchell, John; Montgomery, T. Jeff; Sutherland, Tom N.

Company K: Butler, Aaron; Cochran, J. W.; Craig, Z. Q.; Calvert, Thomas; Clark, B. C; Crouch, Julius A.; DeWalt, N. B.; Dunn, John W.; Hendley, W. D. C.; Hobbs, James; Hudson, E. T.; Jones, J. F.; Knox, A. Z.; Lockheart, J. W. McClenny, Elijah C.; Myers, B. G.; Reese, J. F.; Slatter, Lewis W.; Treadway, Richard

1863

Company A: Emmanuel, T. S.; Patton, J. R.

Company B: Pratt, Henry

Company C: Bell, Edward; Bell, Zebulon P.; New, Joseph S.; Simmons, W. B. (accidently shot)

Company D: Allen, W. H.; Turner, William; Yoakum, George

Company E: Griffon, A. G.; Honea, Thomas S., Moore, L.P.

Company F: Johnson, James; Sanders, J. B.; Whitlock, Henry

Company G: Ansley, J. T.; Fleming, N. H.; Gould, E. Peter; McAlister, J. H.

Company H: Ferrel, W. B.; Lewis, G. A.; Lewis, James; Pinson, J. Wesley; Ruff, Allen; Serois, James

Company I: Flanagan, John W.; Weatherly, Sam S.

1864

Field and Staff: Leverett, S. P., Surgeon

Company A: Coffee, Cleveland; Lynch, Cornelius; Stroud, B. F.

Company B: Clark, W. A.

Company F: McCarty, Ed V.

Company G: Hairston, A. B.; Henderson, R. B.

Company H: Cunningham, Peter

Company I: Driscoll, Stephen S.

1865

Company A: Howe, William D.

Company C: Boykin, T. J.

Appendix B

Battle Deaths in the 5th Texas Regiment

Killed or Mortally Wounded

(Many wounded later succumbed to their wounds in hospitals or elsewhere and are not included here.)

Yorktown—April 24, 1862

Company C: Watson, William

Eltham's Landing—May 7, 1862

Field and Staff: Denney, W. D.
Company B: Scherer, Riley L.

Richmond Vicinity—June 8, 1862

Company C: Meredith, John L.

Gaines' Mill—June 27, 1862

Company A: Clute, J. E.; DeLesdenier, G. H.
Company B: Ganes, J. R.
Company C: Wallace, W. G.; Welch, M. T.; Williams, William King
Company D: Alston, Angus D.
Company E: Cooper, Moses K.; Pearson, R. W.
Company F: Hall, W. S.; Woods, George N.
Company G: Benge, J. J.; Lawrence, J. J.; McDonald, Sr., Elisha; Ward, Charles
Company H: Fitzgerald, Tilmon
Company I: Haynes (Haines), Richard J.
Company K: Butler, John T.

Malvern Hill—July 1, 1862

Company B: Koepke (Koepike), Fred
Company E: Sherman, Joseph W.
Company G: Sharp, S. W.

Freeman's Ford/Kelly's Ford—August 21-22, 1862

Field and Staff: Whaley, D. M.
Company B: Mathee, Fred

Company H: Wicks, William, (Kelly's Ford 8/21/62)
Company K: Wilson, J. B.

Thoroughfare Gap—August 28, 1862

Company H: Templeman, Madison Monroe

Second Manassas—August 29-30, 1862

Field and Staff: Upton, J. C.

Company A: McMurtry, John A.; Bell, John H.; Angel, Albert; DeLesdenier, John W.; DeYoung, John; Hefferan (Heffrin), J. H.; Massenburg (Massenberg), J. N. Walker, D. W.

Company B: Pinchback, William W.; Carter, A. V. L.; Carrigan, John; Doggett, Michael; Dunn, H. B.; Umbarger, John P.

Company C: Allen, Robert

Company D: Burden, Joseph C.; Estill, Ben P.; Estill, Black D.; Harris, James K. P.; Mass (Maas), Lewis; Nelms, W. M.; Pearce, W. T. C.; Ross, S. T.; Spivey, W. F.; Wynne, William L.

Company E: Pettey, V. E.; Allen, R. L.; Dean, Sam H.; Hutchinson, James S.; Hutchinson, J. H.; Moncrief, C. E.; Mullins, N. W.

Company F: Johnston, H. Blair;. Church, J. F.; Dugat, Albert G.; Fortescue, C G.; Little, John; Starnes, G. W. "Wash"; Pemberton, I. W.

Company G: Adams, C. J.; Bolinger, F. M.; McDonald Jr., Elisha P.; Ray, R. A.; Ray, Y. B.

Company H: Baines (Bains), R. R.; Freeman, Benjamin J.; Hall, C. L.; Pannel, David

Company I: Royston (Roysten), W. B.

Company K: Henry, B. W.; Easterling, H. A.; Ward, W. J.

Sharpsburg—September 17, 1862

Company A: Kossee (Kossen), Frank; Woolfe (Wolfe), A. F.; Hoffman, Joseph

Company B: Baker, A. Hicks; Kolbow, John; McNeillus (McNeillis), D.; Monroe, George

Company C: Stuart, Samuel; Boyd, Henry W.

Company D: Edwards, T. J.; Pirtle, Samuel; Ridgway, F. M. R.

Company E: Allen, Hardy; Hurt, James; Toland, R. S.

Company F: McColl, Thomas; Strickland, Mack

Company G: Walker, W. T.

Company H: McCormick, Maxley; Martin, D. G.

Company I: Baker, Bat; Drake, J. P.; Dunn, Edward H.

Company K: Walker, William A.

Suffolk—April 1863

Company K: Turner, Ike

Gettysburg Campaign—June 28-July 15, 1863

Company A: Cohen, S.; Diggs (Deggs), C. W.; Love, Joseph E.; McDowell, William

Company B: Henderson, D. H.; Carter, James T.; Howard, J. A.; Miller, John S.; Haynes, Henry; Hurley M.; Nelms, William F.; O'Neill, John Q.; Pratt, Henry; Sloan, A. G.; Smith, John; Wilson, W. B.; Wilson, J. C.

Company C: Dezell, Z. Y.; Douglas, N.; Lackman, E.; Pearce, W. J. C.; Poole, James H.

Company D: Abernathy, Henry; Douglas, N.; Eskridge, George W.; Henry, Z. P. (Williamsport - 7/6/63); Latchman, Earnest; McDade, J. A.; Murphy, M.; Ross, S. P.; Turner, William; Williamson, Peter

Company E: Boothe, John; Counts, George W.; Hudson, Richard S.; Lockett, S. S.; Sensebaugh, William; Stevens, W. E.; Walthall J. J.; Watson, Sam H.; Weathersby, Thomas

Company F: Baudwin, Albert; Brashear, Jr., Charles D.; Prue, Marshall

Company G: Anderson, W. P.; Blackman, M. W.; Clark, J. F.; Henderson, R. B.; Jackson, Andrew; Jolly, John A.; Jones, G. A.; Jones, W. C.; Locklin, J. D.; Webb, J. W.

Company H: Fitzgerald, Frank M.; McDonald, J. F.; Stevenson, S. V.; Weathers, J. R.

Company I: Bates, Thomas; Graham, C. A.; Haley, William; Holmes, James L.

Company K: Dunn, Simeon; Fields, W. H. H.; Hamm, George W.; Matthews, T. C.; Meece, J. P.; Meece, Calvin W.

Chickamauga—September 19-20, 1863

Company B: Hart, W. S.

Company C: Perry, Benjamin R.

Company D: Brown, M. C.; Skinner, John S.; Tomlinson, John; Watson, Thomas L.

Company E: Maddox (Mattox), T. E.; Spahn (Spann), James W.

Company F: Buxton, Pickney C.; Evans, W. S.; Toups, Demonsthenes, (French national-cousin of Capt. W. D. Williams)

Company G: Bagwell, C. L.; Griffin, Robert; Rowe, H. H.; Streetman, Sam

Company H: Jennings, J. A.; Simmons, T. J.

Company I: Crabtree, William; Driscol, S. S.; Graves, Junius K. ; Kilby, J. W.; Short, John

Company K: Beard, John C.; Oats, Nathan

Knoxville Campaign—November-December, 1863

Company C: Gough, John J.

Company D: Saunders, William

Company I: Spence, R. H.

Wilderness—May 6-7, 1864

Company A: Bryan, Thomas P.

Company B: Auerbach, E.; Hampton, T. L.

Company D: Griffin, Robert; Harris, W. E.; Lewis, William
Company E: Farquhar, C. E.; Nash, Thomas
Company G: Peeks, W. W.
Company H: Robinson, William
Company I: Baldwin, William George; Davis, John; Dean, John; Powell, J. W.
Company K: Henry, Thomas W.; McCrory, T.; McKee, John Francis; Wiley, Nelson

Spotsylvania Court House—May 8-21, 1864

Company A: Bailey, Samuel
Company C: Pridgen, John J.
Company D: Alverson, John T.; Shaw, James T.
Company H: Jones, W. J.

Cold Harbor—June 1-3, 1864

Company G: Tomlinson, J. B.
Company H: Woodall, L. H.
Company I: Seward, Columbus Dighton
Company K: Pierrot, Gustavus

Bermuda Hundred/Petersburg—June 16-July 29, 1864

Company A: Settle, H. G. "Ham"
Company B: Humphrey, R. J.
Company G: Sherrill, D. M.

White Oak Swamp—August 16, 1864

Company C: Copeland, J. M.
Company F: Nobles, J. C.
Company G: Terry, William J.

Chaffin's Farm/Fort Harrison/New Market Road—July 29, 1864

Company A: DeLoach, J. C.
Company B: Burton, W. H.

Darbytown Road/Williamsburg Road—October 7-27, 1864

Company F: Dillon, J. M.; Mallory, Peter; McKinnon, R. J.
Company H: Ball, William; Pinson, J. N.
Company I: Dudly, T. P.; Morgan, Drew F.
Company K: Boyles, W. N.

Appendix C

Head Count

Surviving muster rolls indicate that approximately 1,450 men served in the 5th Texas Regiment during the war in various capacities.

Company	
A	163
B	127
C	128
D	153
E	134
F	144
G	160
H	134
I	142
K	143
Total	**1,428**

Another 16 otherwise not accounted for were assigned to headquarters (Field, Staff, and Band), including Colonel James J. Archer, Major Paul J. Quattlebaum, Adjutant William H. Sellers, and Assistant adjutant John W. Kerr, as well as four surgeons, three assistant surgeons, a pair of hospital stewards, commissary and quartermaster officers, as well as color and ordnance sergeants.[1]

1 Muster Rolls, 5th Texas Regiment in Simpson, *Compendium*, 167-250; Polley, *Hood's Texas Brigade*, 296-347.

Appendix D

Interview with Author John F. Schmutz

SB: Tell us a little bit about yourself, and your background so readers can get a better sense about you, John.

JS: Sure. I am originally from Oneida, New York, and my wife and I are long-time residents of San Antonio, Texas. We have three adult children located in various parts of the US. I hold a B.A. from Canisius College, and law degrees from both The University of Notre Dame and George Washington University. Following a tour as a lawyer in the US Army, I enjoyed a rewarding career as a corporate attorney, initially in private practice, and then as general counsel and a member of the executive management team for several public companies.

SB: This is not your first rodeo when it comes to publishing . . .

JS: My first book was *The Battle of the Crater: A Complete History*, published in 2009. It enjoyed considerable success and got positive reviews from most readers and historians. I recall that *Civil War Times* magazine noted that "[f]or anyone who sees the Crater as the decisive battle that could and should have been, this book will provide the long-awaited answer to prayers." Another important outlet, *Civil War News*, wrote that the book "has set the standard for a study of this period of Civil War history." As you can imagine, that was very pleasing.

In addition to researching and writing about Civil War history, I enjoy genealogical research, and reading (particularly history). I still do pro bono legal work for charitable organizations, and I sit on several boards. I am an avid golfer and sports fan (especially the San Antonio Spurs) and enjoy international travel, which my wife and I indulge in whenever we can.

SB: What started you along on the path of researching the Civil War?

JS: I have always maintained a deep-seated interest in all aspects of the Civil War. I attribute this particular trait partially to my father and grandfather, both of whom were Civil War enthusiasts. Some of my earliest childhood memories are of trekking around the battlefields at Antietam and Gettysburg. In my formative years, I was fascinated by Bruce Catton's easily readable works, and later by Shelby Foote's magnificently written *The Civil War: A Narrative.*

Upon becoming a parent myself, family trips would often include at least one stop at a Civil War battlefield, regardless of the ultimate destination. While serving in the Army in Washington, DC, I was part of a group of Civil War enthusiasts that routinely walked the battlefields of Virginia, and legally hunted for relics. Those finds remain among my most prized possessions.

Throughout my career, I remained an avid reader of Civil War history, dreaming of the day I might find ample time to research and write for myself. In this regard, I was inspired early on by the example of a senior partner in the first law firm for which I worked, Alan Nolan, who published the influential book *The Iron Brigade* while still immersed in the practice of law. This encouraged me that choosing the law as a career did not preclude one from becoming a Civil War author.

SB: How did you become interested in the 5th Texas?

JS: The exploits of Hood's Texas Brigade—Lee's shock troops, if you will—have always fascinated me. Douglas Southall Freeman referred to that unit as "perhaps the most renowned of all" of Lee's army. (I generally refer to it as "Hood's" Texas Brigade, as this is a commonly utilized designation. However, the brigade had a number of commanders throughout the war, and is sometimes recognized by the names of other commanders.) Over the years, there have been a significant number of books on Hood's Texas Brigade as a whole, including Harold B. Simpson's seminal four-volume work from the 1970s. However, until *The Bloody Fifth*, there has never been a comprehensive, all-inclusive study of the 5th Texas Infantry Regiment, one of the units of that brigade. After considerable research on a number of the brave men who were a part of the 5th Texas Infantry, I made a decision to focus my efforts on a comprehensive book of the fabled unit.

SB: And yours is the first in-depth treatment of that organization?

JS: A number of authors, including members of the regiment, have written abbreviated works either about one of its companies, or personal memoirs of individual experiences during the war. However, there was no detailed history of this regiment as a whole, which was an integral part of Lee's most reliable, and I would argue favorite, brigade. Given the unprecedented contributions this entity made to

Hood's Texas Brigade, I came to realize that a book devoted to this remarkable unit was long overdue.

SB: The were few Texas troops in the Army of Northern Virginia, and its record of service was amazing . . .

JS: The story of the 5th Texas and its soldiers is a testament to brave Texans who always gave their all and never lost faith, despite overwhelming adversity and hardships. The 5th was one of only three Texas regiments to leave the state to fight in the East with Lee's Army of Northern Virginia.

SB: The first volume carried the regiment through the Suffolk Campaign, and the second from Gettysburg through the end of the war. Talk about that coverage a bit for us.

JS: Sure. Volume 1 follows the unit from the secession of the Lone Star State and the organization of ten independent companies from various counties of East/Central Texas through Suffolk—a fascinating and overlooked campaign, frankly. The entire work covers years of arduous fighting before culminating with Lee's surrender at Appomattox. The unit took part in 38 major engagements, including almost every significant battle in the East, in addition to a trip West to fight at Chickamauga, and elsewhere. The *Bloody Fifth* provides a detailed accounting of these conflicts, but pays special attention to the lives of the Texas soldiers themselves as they struggled through the war more than 1,300 miles from home. I included as much personal information about the men as possible to help readers feel close and familiar with these men.

SB: What does your book contribute to the literature on the 5th Texas Infantry?

JS: As I previously indicated, there has not been a full-length book on the 5th Texas Infantry covering the entire Civil War. Books such as *The Men of the Bayou City Guards*, by James Orville Moore (1988), *Lone Star Confederate*, edited by George Skoch (2003), R*ebel Private, Front and Rear*, by William A. Fletcher (1995), *A Texan in Search of a Fight*, by John C. West (1901), and *Reminiscences of the Civil War*, by John W. Stevens (1902) deal with a particular company, or one soldier's involvement in the unit, and are generally abbreviated accounts. *"The Bloody Fifth"* presents the entire scope of that regiment's experiences through almost four years of war. In my study, the main actor is the regiment. In dealing with a single regiment, The *Bloody Fifth* delves more deeply into the experiences of the battles, marches, encampments, hardships, and pastimes of one regiment of Hood's Texas Brigade than a brigade history could achieve. Similarly, it facilitates a study into the personal lives of the men as they struggled to survive a vicious war so far from home. *"The Fifth Texas"* established an exceptional combat record in an army known for its fighting capabilities.

SB: Let's talk more about Volume 1 for a moment. Takes us more in-depth there.

JS: Sure. As I noted earlier, Volume I commences with the secession of Texas and the organization of the various companies. It follows their training in Texas and Virginia, where they finally become the 5th Texas. The experiences of life that first winter are detailed, including encounters with the enemy and the horrific struggles with disease. The book thereafter follows the 5th Texas through the Peninsula Campaign, where it received its first real taste of fighting, and then the Seven Days' Battles, where the men gained real renown for their accomplishments at Gaines' Mill.

I go on to explore the breaking of John Pope's Union army before it could be reinforced and the resultant Battle at Second Manassas, where the regiment received its sobriquet "The Bloody Fifth." The march into Maryland is handled in detail, culminating in the bloody fighting at Sharpsburg, where the unit once again distinguished itself.

The volume covers the march to Fredericksburg at length, as it does the 5th Texas's involvement, and the soldiers' winter encampment thereafter. Next the reader follows the regiment as it leaves what it believed was to be its winter quarters for a movement to the Blackwater area of Virginia, near Suffolk. There, as part of Longstreet's corps, it was charged with gathering forage for Lee's army, which was nearly starving in the war-ravished portions of Virginia. In addition to foraging activities, several minor engagements took place. Rising star Major Isaac Newton "Ike" Turner was killed there in the final weeks of occupation in an effort to take some Federal works. The volume ends in April 1863, with Lee reuniting his army to fend off a Federal spring offensive.

SB: Throughout you focus on the men . . .

JS: I was cognizant that the history was about more than battles, and tried hard to describe camp life, an individual soldier's thoughts regarding the war, home and loved ones, relationships, and so forth.

SB: Volume 2 picks up in the same vein from Gettysburg through the end . . .

JS: It does. Gettysburg was especially hard on the regiment, as you can imagine, and the journey west on the rails to fight at Chickamauga, and then Chattanooga and the Eastern Tennessee operations was grueling as well. Retuning to Lee's army in the spring of 1864, the 5th served with distinction at the Wilderness, Spotsylvania, the North Anna, Cold Harbor, throughout the horrific siege of Petersburg, and finally during the retreat to Appomattox, where it surrendered 161 men.

SB: You make a number of references to the flags of the 5th Texas and those who carried them. Do any of the banners, in particular, stand out for you, and why?

JS: That's an interesting question. I think the regimental flag commissioned by the men early in the war patterned after the National colors, but with one large star replacing the circle of eleven smaller stars in its canton stands out. It was beloved by the men, who referred to it as the "Lone Star and Bars." Once Richmond disallowed the use of state flags, and the St. Andrews cross design was adopted as the exclusive Confederate battle flag, the men were rather disconsolate about it. After Longstreet rejected their entreaties to carry the "Lone Star and Bars," they surreptitiously switched flags at the last minute and carried only the Lone Star and Bars into the campaign of August 1862. Thus, that flag served as the regimental banner at Second Manassas and Sharpsburg. Seven color bearers fell carrying the flag at Second Manassas alone.

SB: What did you turn up in the process of researching your book that particularly struck you?

JS: As I mentioned, I was quite familiar with the history of Hood's Texas Brigade prior to my involvement with this work. Thus, I was cognizant of its exploits and achievements, and where it fought. However, in writing about the 5th Texas, I gained a deep seated appreciation for the individual fighting men of the unit. These men, from east central Texas, joined an army fighting for "independence" and their state's right to control its own destiny. They believed deeply in a cause for which they were willing to die to preserve (as many did). Rather than remain in Texas or its environs, they instead chose an opportunity to serve in Virginia, because they believed that was "where the heavy fighting would be." And weren't wrong.

SB: Why was it hard to fight so far from home?

JS: Most people don't stop to think about that. Being more than 1,300 miles from home created particular hardships that were not experienced at all, or in the same degree, by other troops. This was particularly true after the Mississippi River was firmly in Federal hands, and southern ports effectively blockaded. Food, clothing, sundries and even letters from home were hard to come by, which often left the men in worse shape than their neighbors. While the men grumbled, as all soldiers are prone to do, they remained a well-oiled fighting machine. They were always prepared to fight to the last measure, leading Lee to proudly proclaim that "the Texans are always ready."

SB: What particular exploits stand out?

JS: There were many. Three stand out more than others in my mind that demonstrate the mettle of the men. At Second Manassas, the Texans broke open the Federal left wing on Chinn Ridge and Bald Hill, opening the way for a devastating Federal defeat. Flushed with victory, they pressed through the disintegrating Federal lines and outdistanced not only the remainder of the brigade, but the rest of Lee's army. When wing commander (there were not yet formal "corps") James Longstreet questioned Hood as to the whereabouts of the 5th Texas, Hood replied that they had "slipped the bridle" and were "on their way to Washington." Longstreet nodded and replied, "If any men in the world can get there, those are the men." Their actions that day earned the regiment the sobriquet "the Bloody Fifth."

The regiment's victory there came with a frightening butcher's bill, however. The 5th Texas, the most engaged in the fighting, lost some 260 men, more than any other regiment in Lee's army. At the end of the fight, three of its companies had not a single officer remaining, and all field grade officers were casualties. Seven color bearers fell carrying the regiment's "Lone Star and Bars" that day, as I noted earlier.

Another exploit that stands out took place at Gettysburg, where the regiment faced the next-to-impossible task of taking Little Round Top. Venturing across a rocky field for a mile and then climbing a boulder-studded hill while being pummeled by shot and grape from cannon positioned to the left, sharpshooters to the immediate front, and Union troops protected by the steep heights, was more than anyone could stand.

SB: The losses must have been horrific . . .

JS: They were. The 5th Texas entered the battle with 409 men and lost 211 or 52 percent, including 112 men captured. The regiment never fully recovered from that slaughter.

SB: And the final exploit of the three?

JS: The Wilderness. Lee's army had its back to the wall on May 6, 1864, and was about to be hopelessly overrun. Longstreet's Corps, with the Texas Brigade in the lead, was desperately rushing toward the fighting to stem the tide. At the last moment, the Texans broke into the clearing in front of the oncoming Federals. A highly agitated Lee ordered the Texans forward, and to give the enemy "cold steel." As the men advanced, Lee attempted to lead them, shouting "Texans always move them." The men of the 5th Texas surrounded Lee and grasped the bridle of his mount, shouting "Lee to the rear!" Only after they pledged "to drive the enemy back," did Lee finally agree to retire.

SB: That is one of the legendary moments in Lee's entire career . . .

JS: And the 5th was in the thick of it. With Lee safely behind the lines, the Texans charged down the Plank Road, sweeping the enemy before them in a savage hail of lead and grape. The advance changed the tide of the battle. The regiment entered the combat with 180 officers and men, 111 of whom fell in 25 minutes. The 5th Texas lost its commander, along with every one of the regimental officers. Every officer but two had their horses shot out from under them.

SB: What were the total losses for the regiment in the war?

JS: It finally surrendered at Appomattox with 13 officers and 148 men. During the war, it suffered 303 men killed in battle, 506 wounded once, 138 wounded twice, and at least 19 hit three times. More than 140 died of disease.

SB: Can you describe your research and writing process, and the sources you consulted?

JS: Regarding research, there many valuable resources. I obviously went to the published accounts of members of the 5th Texas, some of which were mentioned earlier, as well as Harold Simpson, the trailblazer for any research project involving Hood's Texas Brigade. Articles contained in the *Confederate Veteran*, the *Southern Historical Society Papers*, MOLLUS, and of course the *Official Records* were invaluable. Beyond this, I refer you to the bibliography in Volume 2 of *"The Bloody Fifth"* [See page 322]. In delving into journals, letters, and miscellaneous unpublished papers, I obviously had to go to the source—the repository holding the particular collection of papers. As you can imagine, I traveled extensively, and of course, walked the ground where this fighting took place.

SB: What is your next project?

JS: My first book, *The Battle of the Crater*, covered a one-day battle. *"The Bloody Fifth"* took one regiment and followed it through the entire war. I am now going to attempt something a little different. I have done considerable research on the "Immortal Six Hundred," a group of Confederate officer-prisoners who were placed in front of the Federal batteries on Morris Island in Charleston harbor, effectively acting as human shields. I intend to tell the story of their imprisonment from Fort Delaware to their ultimate release, which will include their mistreatment at the hands of their Federal captors. Using their experiences as a starting point, I also intend to delve in some depth into the prisoner of war exchange process, and the prison systems of both sides.

SB: Thank you very much.

JS: You're welcome.

Bibliography

Abbreviations

B&L	*Battles and Leaders of the Civil War of the Civil War*
CHHS	Chappell Hill Historical Society, Chappell Hill, TX
CRC	Historical Research Center, Texas Heritage Museum, Hill College, Hillsboro, TX
CV	*Confederate Veteran Magazine*
DRTL	Daughters of the Republic of Texas Library, The Alamo, San Antonio, TX
DUL	Duke University, Special Collections Library, Durham, NC
GNMP	Gettysburg National Military Park Library
GHQ	*Georgia Historical Quarterly*
MOLLUS	War Papers Read before the Commandery of [State], Military Order of the Loyal Legions of the United States
OR	War of the Rebellion: A Compilation of the Official Records of the Union and the Confederate Armies
PM	Pearce Museum, Navarro College, Corsicana, TX
SHSP	*Southern Historical Society Papers*
SHQ	*Southwestern Historical Quarterly*
UNC	Southern Historical Collection, University of North Carolina, Chapel Hill
TSA	Texas State Archives, Austin, TX
USMAI	United States Army Military History Institute, Carlisle, PA
USTA	University of Texas at San Antonio, Special Collections, San Antonio, TX

Manuscripts, Letters, and Diaries

Antietam National Battlefield Library, Sharpsburg, MD

Henry Kyd Douglas Collection

Chappell Hill Historical Society Archives, Chappell Hill, TX

Thomas Bates, Letter

George Kelly File, Letter of July 20, 1864

Daughters of the Republic of Texas Library, San Antonio, TX

Campbell Wood Papers

Emory University, Manuscript, Archives and Rare Books Library, Atlanta, GA

Wood and Tabert Families Papers

Gettysburg National Military Park Library and Research Center, Gettysburg, PA

Gregory A. Coco Collection

Rufus K. Felder Letter

"Gettysburg Trip: The Lone Star Flag Over Devil's Den"

M. A. Hubert Diary

Military Order of the Loyal Legion of the US Papers
Robert M. Powell typescript, "Tales of the War—Graphic Sketch, from Missouri Republican, July 1886"
Southern Bivouac, August 1882-May 1887
Campbell Wood "Memoir"
Hill College, Harold B. Simpson History Center, Hillsboro, TX
Basil Brashear Letters
Arthur H. Edey Letter
Fifth Regiment Infantry Flag, Hood's Brigade, ANV
A. P. Hood Letter
Hood's Texas Brigade Letters
Wilson H. Lewis Letter
Smither Family Papers
Watson Dugat Williams Letters
Louisiana State University, Hill Memorial Library, Special Collections, Baton Rouge, LA
Goree Papers
Mississippi State University, Special Collection Department, Mitchell Memorial Library, Starkville, MS
Tacitus T. Campbell Letters
National Archives and Records Service, Washington, DC
Record Group 109
Compiled Service Records of Confederate Soldiers Who Served in Organizations from Texas
Navarro College, Pearce Civil War Collection, Corsicana, TX
W. B. Campbell Papers
Benjamin I. Franklin Papers
W. J. Terry Letters
Nesbitt Memorial Library, Columbus, TX
Benjamin Marshall Baker Letters
The New York Historical Society, New York, NY
Alfred Davenport Letters
Sam Houston State University, Newton Gresham Library, Huntsville, TX
Goree Family Papers 1833-1996
J. Mark Smither Civil War Letters
Texas Confederate Museum and Collection, Nita Stewart Haley Memorial Library, Midland, TX
Fifth Texas Rosters
John H. Roberts Letter, April 28, 1925
John S. Sellers Papers
Texas State Library and Archives Commission, Austin, TX
An Inventory of Texas Adjutant General's Civil War Records at the State Archives, 1855, 1860-1866
Seventeenth Brigade Correspondence Powell Letters to Adjutant General Byrd
Governor Edward Clark Records
United States Army Military History Institute, Carlisle, PA
Robert L. Brake Collection
Felder, Rufus K. Letter
Hubert, M. A. Diary

CWTI Collection
Moore, Fletcher B. Letters
Morrison, Henry Ruffner Letters
United States Command and General Staff College, Fort Leavenworth, KA
Foley, Kyle J., "John Bell Hood's Division in the Battle of Chickamauga: A Historic Analysis," 2003
University of Houston, Library-Special Collections, Houston, TX
Mrs. Anson Jones (Mary Smith McRory) Letters
Ella Smither Letters
University of North Carolina, Wilson Special Collection Library, Southern Historical Collection, Chapel Hill, NC
Edward Porter Alexander Papers
Henry L. Benning Papers, 1818-1897
Cobb-Hunter Family Papers, 1819-1904
James E. Cobb, 1835-1913
Diary of James Cobb, 1862-1864
James Longstreet Papers, 1875, 1904
Lafayette McLaws Papers, 1836-1897
Evander McIvor Law Papers, 1860-1864
University of South Carolina, South Carolinia Library, Manuscripts Collection, Columbia, SC
Micah Jenkins Letter
University of Texas at Austin, Briscoe Center for American History, Austin, TX
5th Texas Regiment, Muster Rolls, 1862-64
Henry Oldham Robertson Papers
University of Texas at San Antonio, Special Collections Library, San Antonio, TX
Joe Jenkins Manuscript, "A Sketch of Hood's Texas Brigade," 1865
Finney Family Papers, 1855-67
Virginia Historical Society, Richmond, VA

U. S. Government Sources

United States Federal Census 1860-1880
United States Federal Census 1880 Mortality Schedules
U. S. Congress, *Report of the Joint Committee on the Conduct of the War at the Second Session, Thirty-Eighth Congress, Army of the Potomac*, Washington, DC, 1865.
U. S. Congress, *Reports of the Senate of the United States for the Second Session of the Fifty-First Congress, 1890-1891, 3 vols., Washington, DC*, 1891.
U. S. War Department, *The War of the Rebellion: A Compilation of the Official Records of the Union and Confederate Armies, 128 vols., Washington, D. C.: U. S. Government Printing Office*, 1880-1901.
U. S. War Department, *Atlas to Accompany the Official Records of the Union and Confederate Armies.* Washington, D.C.: Government Printing Office, 1891-1895. New York, NY: Gramercy, 1983).

Published Primary Sources

Articles

"A Good Record." *Confederate Veteran*, (April 1904), 12:176.

"The Army of the James." *Harper's Weekly*, October 29, 1864: 693-94.

"The Battle In Georgia." *Harper's Weekly*, October 10, 1863: 642.

"Battle of Chickamauga." *Southern Historical Society Papers*, (January-December 1885), 13:367-415.

"Brig. Gen. James T. Archer." *Confederate Veteran*, (February 1900), 8:65-70.

"Colonel Robert C. Trigg, of Virginia." *Confederate Veteran*, (February 1909), 17:65.

"Confederate Officers After Appomattox." *Confederate Veteran*, (May 1911), 19:252.

"Constantine Perkins Nance." *Confederate Veteran*, (May 1925), 33:188.

"Dr. Campbell Wood." *Confederate Veteran*, (December 1914), 22:567.

"Finger Ring of Lieut. A. C. Graham, Seventh Texas." *Confederate Veteran*, (November 1903), 11:512.

"Heroes and Heroines In Virginia." *Confederate Veteran*, (September 1894), 2:267.

"Inquiries and Answers." *Confederate Veteran*, (April1906), 4:180.

"Judge J. N. Henderson." *Confederate Veteran*, (February 1908), 11:86.

"Judge James E. Cobb." *Confederate Veteran*, (December 1903), 11:563-64.

"Librarian of Congress to W. R. Hamby of Hood's Texas Brigade Association in 1908." *Confederate Veteran*, (December 1910)18:563.

"Regiments of Hood's Brigade." *Confederate Veteran*, (June 1923), 31:238.

"Reminiscences by Miss Sue Monroe." *Confederate Veteran*, (November 1896), 4:379.

"Reunion of Hood's Texas Brigade." *Confederate Veteran*, (Aug. 1909), 17:390.

"Saved By His Bible." *Confederate Veteran*, (March, 1905), 13:127.

"Sentiment of A Typical Confederate." *Confederate Veteran*, (October 1907), 15:459.

"Sidney Virgil Patrick." *Confederate Veteran*, (July1907), 15:322.

"Some South Carolina Boys Who Served in the Fifth Texas." *Confederate Veteran*, (December1901), 9: 554.

"The Opposing Forces at Petersburg and Richmond." in *Battles and Leaders of the Civil War, Being for the most part contributions by Union and Confederate officers. Based upon "The Century War Series." Edited by Robert Underwood Johnson and Clarence Clough Buel, of the Editorial Staff of "The Century Magazine."* 4 vols. reprint, New York, 1956, 4:590-94.

"The Opposing Forces at the Second Bull Run." *Battles and Leaders of the Civil War*, 2:497-500.

"The Opposing Forces in the Maryland Campaign." *Battles and Leaders of the Civil War*, 2:598-603.

"The Texans At Sharpsburg." *Confederate Veteran*, (December1914), 22:555.

"The Time of Longstreet's Arrival at Groveton." *Battles and Leaders of the Civil War of the Civil War*, 2: 527-28.

Alexander, E. P. "The Great Charge and Artillery Fighting at Gettysburg." *Battles and Leaders of the Civil War of the Civil War*, 3:359.

Alexander, E. Porter. "Longstreet at Knoxville." *Battles and Leaders of the Civil War of the Civil War*, 3: 745-51.

Allan, William. "A Reply To General Longstreet." *Battles and Leaders of the Civil War*, 3:355-56.

Ames, John W. "In Front of the Stone Wall at Fredericksburg." *Battles and Leaders of the Civil War*, 3: 122-25.

Aycock, B. L. "Dumfries Discovered." *Confederate Veteran*, (December 1924), 32:477.

Beauregard, G. T. "Four Days of Battle at Petersburg." *Battles and Leaders of the Civil War of the Civil War*, 4:540-44.

Belo, A. H. "The Battle of Gettysburg." *Confederate Veteran*, (April 1900), 8:165-68.

Bigbee, T. M. *Confederate Veteran*. (August 1899),7:357-58.

Blackford, William W. "An Incident of Lee's Surrender." *Southern Historical Society Papers*, (1885), 13: 454-55.

Bouve, Edward T. "The Battle of High Bridge." *MOLLUS-Massachusetts*, Boston, MA, (1900), 2: 403-12.

Bradfield, J. O. "At Gettysburg, July 3." *Confederate Veteran*, (June 1922), 30:225.

Brainerd, Wesley. "The Pontoniers at Fredericksburg." *Battles and Leaders of the Civil War*, 3:121-22.

Brown, William H. "On Gettysburg Field: A View from Little Round Top During the Progress of the Battle," Philadelphia *Weekly Times*, May 23, 1883.

Byers, S. H. M. "Sherman's Attack at the Tunnel." *Battles and Leaders of the Civil War*, 3:712-13.

[Campbell, Robert]. "Texans Always Move Them." in Henry Steele Commager, ed. *The Blue and the Gray*, 2 vols. Indianapolis, IN: Bobbs-Merrill, 1950: 2:983

Chicoine, Stephen. "'. . . Willing Never To Go in Another Fight': The Civil War Correspondence of Rufus King Felder of Chappell Hill." *Southwestern Historical Quarterly*, (2003), 104:575-97.

Cobb, James E. "Sentiments of a Typical Confederate." *Confederate Veteran*, (December 1903), 11:563-64.

Colgrove, Silas. "The Finding of Lee's Lost Order." *Battles and Leaders of the Civil War*, 2:603.

Colston, Frederick M. "Gettysburg as I Saw It." *Confederate Veteran*, (November 1897), 5:551-53.

Cooke, Philip St. George. "The Charge of Cooke's Cavalry at Gaines's Mill. *Battles and Leaders of the Civil War of the Civil War*, 2:344-46.

Cooper, J. "Pickett's Brigade at Gaines' Mill." *Confederate Veteran*, (August 1898), 6:472-73.

Cosgrove, J. H. "About the Attack at Cold Harbor." *Confederate Veteran*, (November 1912), 20:511.

Couch, Darius N. "Sumner's 'Right Grand Division'." *Battles and Leaders of the Civil War*, 3:105-20.

Cox, Jacob D. "Forcing Fox's Gap and Turner's Gap." *Battles and Leaders of the Civil War*, 2:583-90.

____. "The Battle of Antietam," *Battles and Leaders of the Civil War*, 2:630-60.

Coxe, John. "Chickamauga." *Confederate Veteran*, (August 1922), 30:291-94.

____. "In the Battle of Seven Pines." *Confederate Veteran*, (January1922), 30:25.

Crozier, Granville H. "A Private with General Hood." *Confederate Veteran*, (December 1917), 25:556.

Darrow, Caroline Baldwin. "Recollections of the Twiggs Surrender." *Battles and Leaders of the Civil War*, 1:33-38.

Douglas, H. T. "Hood's Messmates At Yorktown." *Confederate Veteran*, (February 1911), 19:78-79.

Douglas, Henry Kyd. "Stonewall Jackson In Maryland." *Battles and Leaders of the Civil War*, 2:620-29.

Field, Charles W. "Campaign of 1864 and 1865. Narrative of Major-General C. W. Field." *Southern Historical Society Papers*, (1886), 514:42-63.

Fleming, Elvis E, ed. "Some Hard Fighting: Letters of Private Robert T. Wilson, 5th Texas Infantry, Hood's Texas Brigade 1862-1864." *Military History of Texas and the Southwest*, Austin, TX, (1972), 9:299-302.

Floca, Samuel W., Jr. "Hood's Protest." *Confederate Veteran*, (January 1995), 6:27.

Franklin, William B. "Rear-Guard Fighting During the Change of Base." *Battles and Leaders of the Civil War*, 2:366-82.

____. "Notes on Crampton's Gap and Antietam." *Battles and Leaders of the Civil War*, 2:591-97.

Fullerton, Joseph S. "Reenforcing Thomas at Chickamauga." *Battles and Leaders of the Civil War*, 3: 665-67.

____. "The Army of the Cumberland at Chattanooga." *Battles and Leaders of the Civil War*, 3:719-27.

Gee, Leonard Grace. "The Texan Who Held Gen. R. E. Lee"s Horse." *Confederate Veteran*, (October, 1904), 12:478.

Gibson, J. Catlett. "The Battle of Spotsylvania Court House, May 12, 1864." *Southern Historical Society Papers*, (1904), 32:200-210.

Giles, Val. C. "The Flag of First Texas, A. N. Virginia." *Confederate Veteran*, (September 1907), 15:417.

Goldsmith, W. L. "Gen. Lee About to Enter Battle." *Confederate Veteran*, (February 1894), 2:36-37.

Gordon, John W. "Pleasant Days in Wartime." *Confederate Veteran*, (February 1929), 37:95.

Goss, Warren Lee. "Yorktown and Williamsburg." *Battles and Leaders of the Civil War*, 2:189-99.

Graham, Ziba B. "On to Gettysburg: Ten Days from My Diary of 1863." *War Papers read before the Michigan Commandery of the Military Order of the Loyal Legion of the United States.* 4 vols. Detroit, MI: Winn & Hammond 1893), 1:471-82.

Granberry, J. A. H. "Longstreet Before Knoxville." *Confederate Veteran*, (October 1923), 31:372.

____. "That Fort Gilmer Fight," *Confederate Veteran*, (September 1905), 13:413.

Grant, Ulysses S. "Chattanooga," *Battles and Leaders of the Civil War*, 3: 679-711.

____. "Preparing for the Campaigns of '64." *Battles and Leaders of the Civil War*, 4:97-117.

Grindlay, James G. "The 146th New York at Little Round Top." *Battles and Leaders of the Civil War*, 3: 315.

Guinn, R. A. "History of the Important Movements and Incidents of the Newton Rifles," *Confederate Letters, Diaries and Reminiscences, 1860-1865.* ed. Mrs. L. C. Bittick. Atlanta, GA: Dept. of Archives and History, 1946: 18.

Haight, Theron "Gainesville, Groveton, and Bull Run." *War Papers read before the Wisconsin Commandery of the Military Order of the Loyal Legion of the United States.* Milwaukee, WI: Burdick, Armitage & Allen, 1896, 2:357-72.

Hamby, William R. "Fourth Texas In Battle of Gaines' Mill." *Confederate Veteran*, (April 1906), 14: 183-85.

____. "Glory of Hood's Texas Brigade." *Confederate Veteran*, (December 1910), 18:563-66.

Hankins, Samuel W. "Simple Story of a Soldier." *Confederate Veteran*, (September 1912), 20:442-43.

Harding, R. J. "About the Gaines" Mill Battle." *Confederate Veteran*, (December 1898), 6:580.

____. "Lee to the Rear." in F. B. Chilton, ed. *Unveiling and Dedication of Monument to Hood's Texas Brigade.* Houston, TX: F. B. Chilton, 174-75.

Harrison, Constance Cary. "Richmond Scenes in '62." *Battles and Leaders of the Civil War*, 2:439-48.

Hawby, William R. "Fourth Texas in Battle of Gaines' Mill." *Confederate Veteran*, (April 1906) 14: 183-84.

Hazen, Samuel R. "'Fighting the Good Fight,': the 140th New York and Its Work on Little Round Top." *National Tribune*, September 13, 1894.

Henderson, Don E. "General Hood's Brigade." *Southern Historical Society Papers*, (1907), 35:185-200.

____. "General Hood's Brigade: Review of Its Glorious Achievements." *Southern Historical Society Papers*, (1901), 29:297-310.

Hill, Daniel H. "The Battle of Gaines's Mill." *The Century Magazine*, (1885) 30:294-309.

____. "The Battle of South Mountain, or Boonsboro." *Battles and Leaders of the Civil War*, 2:559-81.

____. "Chickamauga – The Great Battle of the West." *Battles and Leaders of the Civil War*, 3:638-62.

____. "Lee's Attacks North of the Chickahominy," *Battles and Leaders of the Civil War*, 2:347-362.

____. "McClellan's Change of Base and Malvern Hill." *Battles and Leaders of the Civil War*, 2:383-95.

Hill, W. T. "Confederate Officers After Appomattox." *Confederate Veteran*, (May 1911), 19:252.

____. "First Troops Through Thoroughfare Gap." *Confederate Veteran*, (December 1915), 23:544.

____. "Memories of Hood's Texas Brigade: From Winter Quarters to Appomattox and from Appomattox to Galveston." In Chilton, *Unveiling and Dedication of the Monument to Hood's Texas Brigade*, 181-86.

Hitchcock, W. H. "Recollections of a Participant in the Charge," *Battles and Leaders of the Civil War*, 2: 346.

Hood, John B. "Leading Confederates in the Battle of Gettysburg—Letter from General John B. Hood." *Southern Historical Society Papers*, (October 1877), 4:145-50.

____. "General Hood Wants to Outflank the Union Left." in Henry Steele Commager, ed. *The Blue and the Gray*. Indianapolis, IN: The Bobbs-Merrill Company, Inc., 1950, 608-12.

Hunt, Henry J. "The First Day at Gettysburg." *Battles and Leaders of the Civil War*, 3:255-84.

____. "The Second Day at Gettysburg." *Battles and Leaders of the Civil War*, 3:290-313.

Hunter, J. T. "A Thirty Days' Scout on the Potomac in '62." *Confederate Veteran*, (December 1916), 24:457-59.

____. "At Yorktown In 1862 And What Followed." *Confederate Veteran*, (March 1918), 26:112-15.

____. "Lieut. Gen. John B. Hood." *Confederate Veteran*, (June1916), 24:257-58.

____. "When Texas Seceded" *Confederate Veteran*, (August 1917), 25:362-63.

Imboden, John D. "Stonewall Jackson in the Shenandoah." *Battles and Leaders of the Civil War*, 2: 282-98.

____. "The Confederate Retreat From Gettysburg." *Battles and Leaders of the Civil War*, 3:420-29.

J. H. L. "Anecdotes of the Peninsular Campaign, II—Hood 'Feeling the Enemy.'" *Battles and Leaders of the Civil War*, 2:276.

Johnson, Charles. "Attack on Fort Gilmer, September 29, 1864." *Southern Historical Society Papers*, (June 1876), 1:438-42.

Johnson, Rev. J. Stoddard. "A Reminiscence of Sharpsburg." *Southern Historical Society Papers*, (October-December 1880), 8:526-29.

____. "General J. B. Hood and Chickamauga." *Confederate Veteran*, (December 1905), 13:550-52.

Johnson, W. P. "Third Arkansas and Richmond Howitzers." *Confederate Veteran*, (May 1905), 13:210.

Johnston, Joseph E. "Manassas to Seven Pines." *Battles and Leaders of the Civil War*, 2:202-18.

Jones, A. C. "Lee in the Wilderness." Philadelphia *Weekly Times*, May 8, 1880.

____."Texas and Arkansas at Fort Harrison." *Confederate Veteran*, (January 1917), 25:24-25.

____. "Third Arkansas Regiment At Appomattox." *Confederate Veteran*, (July 1915), 23:313-15.

Jones, J. William. "General Hood's Brigade," *Southern Historical Society Papers*, (1907), 35;185-200.

____."'General Lee to the Rear'—The Incident with Harris' Mississippi Brigade." *Southern Historical Society Papers*, (March 1903), 8:105-109.

____. "Reminiscences of the Army of Northern Virginia: Seven Days Around Richmond." *Southern Historical Society Papers*, (October-December 1881), 9:557-70.

Kilmer, George L. "The Army of the Potomac at Harrison's Landing." *Battles and Leaders of the Civil War*, 2:427-28.

Kriffin, Gilbert C. "Maneuvering Bragg Out of Tennessee." *Battles and Leaders of the Civil War*, 3: 635-37.

____. "The Battle of Stone's River." *Battles and Leaders of the Civil War*, 3:613-32.

Law, Evander M. "From the Wilderness to Cold Harbor." *Battles and Leaders of the Civil War*, 4: 118-44.

____. "Lookout Valley, October 28, 1863." *Southern Historical Society Papers*, (October- December 1880), 8:500-510.

____. "On the Confederate Right At Gaines's Mill." *Battles and Leaders of the Civil War*, 2:363-65.

____. "The Struggle For "Round Top'." *Battles and Leaders of the Civil War*, 3:318-330.

____. "The Virginia Campaign of 1862." Philadelphia *Weekly Press*, October 26-November 2, 1887.

Lippitt, Francis J. "Pope's Virginia Campaign, and Porter's Part in it." *Atlantic Monthly*, (September 1878), 42:349-66.

Lockhard, W. G. "Lee at Orange C. H." *Confederate Veteran*, (June 1903), 11:268.

Longstreet, James. "General James Longstreet's Account of the Gettysburg Campaign and Battle." *Southern Historical Society Papers*, (January 1878), 5:54-86.

____. "Lee in Pennsylvania," in *Annals of the War Written By Leading Participants North and South.* Alexander Kelly McClure, ed. Philadelphia, PA: Times Publishing Company, 1879, 414-66.

____. "Lee's Right Wing At Gettysburg." *Battles and Leaders of the Civil War*, 3:339-54.

____. "Our March Against Pope," *Battles and Leaders of the Civil War*, 2:512-26.

____. "The Battle of Fredericksburg." *Battles and Leaders of the Civil War*, 2:70-85.

____. "The 'Seven Days,' Including Frayser's Farm." *Battles and Leaders of the Civil War*, 2:396-405.

Lott, Jess B., "Two Boys of the Fifth Texas Regiment," *Confederate Veteran*, (September 1905), 13:416-17.

Marshall, Charles. "Occurrences at Lee's Surrender." *Confederate Veteran*, (December 1894), 2:42-44.

Martin, J. H. "Accurate Historic Records." *Confederate Veteran*, (March 1904), 12;113-15.

____. "The Assault Upon Fort Gilmer." *Confederate Veteran*, (June 1905), 13:269-270.

____."Forts Gilmer and Harrison Forces." Confederate Veteran, (September 1906), 14:409.

May, J. J. "The Fight at Fort Gilmer." *Confederate Veteran*, (June 1905), 12:588.

McClellan, George B. "The Peninsular Campaign." *Battles and Leaders of the Civil War*, 2:160-88.

McComb, William. "The Battle in Front of Richmond, 1862," *Confederate Veteran*, (April 1915), 23:161-62.

McLaws, Lafayette. "Gettysburg," *Southern Historical Society Papers*, (February 1879), 7:64-90.

____. "The Battle of Gettysburg," Philadelphia *Weekly Press*, April 21, 1886.

____. "The Confederate Left At Fredericksburg." *Battles and Leaders of the Civil War*, 2:86-94.

McMahon, Martin. "Cold Harbor." *Battles and Leaders of the Civil War*, 4:213-20.

Melcher, H. S. "The 20th Maine At Little Round Top." *Battles and Leaders of the Civil War*, 3:314-15.

Minnich, J. W. "That Affair at Dandridge, Tennessee." *Confederate Veteran*, (August 1922), 30:297.

Minor, J. B. "Rallying with a Frying Pan." *Confederate Veteran*, (February 1905), 13:72-73.

Mitchell, Mary Bedinger. "A Woman's Recollections of Antietam." *Battles and Leaders of the Civil War*, 2:686-94.

Monroe, Sue. "Reminiscences by Mrs. Sue Monroe." *Confederate Veteran*, (November 1896), 4:379.

Nabours, W. A. "Active Service of a Texas Command." *Confederate Veteran*, (February 1916), 24:69-71.

Nicolay, J. G. "Abraham Lincoln: A History of Pope's Virginia Campaign." *The Century Magazine*, (January 1889), 37:427-35.

"Organization of the Army of Northern Virginia (General R. E. Lee commanding), August 28 to September 1, 1862." *Southern Historical Society Papers*, (December 1882), 10:555-60.

"Organization of the Army of Tennessee, General Braxton Bragg, Confederate States Army, Commanding, at the Battle of Chickamauga." *Southern Historical Society Papers*, (April 1884), 12:145-60.

"Official Reports of the Battle of Gettysburg." *Southern Historical Society Papers*, (October 1877), 4:161-191.

"Official Reports of the Battle of Gettysburg." *Southern Historical Society Papers*, (January-December 1885), 13:173-216.

Opdycke, Emerson. "Notes on the Chickamauga Campaign." *Battles and Leaders of the Civil War*, 3:668-71.

Paris, Comte de. "History of the Battle of Gettysburg." *The Civil War in America*, 4 vols., Philadelphia, PA: Porter & Coates, 1886, 3:615-32.

Parrent, E. J., "General Lee to the Rear," *Confederate Veteran*, (January 1894) 2:14.

Parsons, H. C. "Farnsworth's Charge and Death." *Battles and Leaders of the Civil War*, 3:393-96.

Perry, D. M. "The Time of Longstreet's Arrival at Groveton." *Battles and Leaders of the Civil War*, 2:527-28.

Perry, H. H. "Assault on Fort Gilmer." *Confederate Veteran*, (September 1905), 13:414.

Perry, William F. "Reminiscences of the Campaign of 1864 in Virginia." *Southern Historical Society Papers*, (February 1879), 7:49-63.

Pickens, J. D. "Fort Harrison." *Confederate Veteran*, (October 1913), 21:484.

Platt, Philander. "On Little Round Top." *National Tribune*, April 11, 1907.

Poe, Orlando M. "The Defense of Knoxville." *Battles and Leaders of the Civil War*, 3:731-45.

Polley, J. B. "About All the Men In Hood's Texas Brigade." *Confederate Veteran*, (May 1911), 19:222-23.

____. "A Battle Above the Clouds." *Confederate Veteran*, (March 1897), 5:104-106.

____. "Brave Texans In the Virginia Army." *Confederate Veteran*, (May 1896), 4:158-59.

____. "Hood's Brigade and the 'Bucktails'." *Confederate Veteran*, (January 1916), 24:73-74.

____. "Hood's Texans Capture a Battery at Gaines' Mill" in Henry Steele Commager, ed., *The Blue and the Gray*. Indianapolis, IN: The Bobbs-Merrill Company, Inc., 1950, 136-38.

____. "Polley Lost a Foot—A Furlough," *Confederate Veteran*, (November 1897), 5:569-71.

____. "Second Manassas," *Confederate Veteran*, (October 1896), 4:218-20.

____. "Simple Justice Asked," *Confederate Veteran*, (July 1895), 3:317.

____. "Texans in the Battle of the Wilderness." *Confederate Veteran*, (1897), 5:290.

____. "The 'Charming Nellie' Letters." *Confederate Veteran*, (October 1896), 4:345-46.

Pope, John. "The Second Battle of Bull Run." *Battles and Leaders of the Civil War*, 2:449-94.

Porter, Fitz John. "Hanover Court House and Gaines's Mill." *Battles and Leaders of the Civil War*, 2:319-39.

____. "The Battle of Malvern Hill." *Battles and Leaders of the Civil War*, 2:406-27.

Porter, Horace. "Five Forks and the Pursuit of Lee." *Battles and Leaders of the Civil War*, 4:708-22.

____. "The Surrender At Appomattox Court House." *Battles and Leaders of the Civil War*, 4:729-46.

Powell, Robert Micajah. "Tales of the War—Graphic Sketch by Col. R.M. Powell of Hood's Texas Brigade," *The Missouri Republic* [St. Louis], July 10, 1886.

Purifoy, John W. "Farnsworth's Charge and Death at Gettysburg." *Confederate Veteran*, (August 1924), 32:307-309.

____. "The Lost Opportunity at Gettysburg." *Confederate Veteran*, (June 1923) 31:214-18.

R. C. "Texans Always Move Them." *The Land We Love*, (October 1868), 5: 481-86.

Ramsey, J. G. M. "Battle of King's Mountain." *The Land We Love*, (September 1867), 3:381-400.

Randolph, Janet H. Weaver. "James K. P. Harris, Of Fifth Texas Infantry." *Confederate Veteran*, (September 1905) 13:400.

Redwood, Allen C. "At Second Manassas with Jackson's 'Foot-Cavalry'." *The Century Magazine*, (February 1886), 31:614-21.

Reese, George. "What Five Confederates Did at Petersburg [Richmond]." *Confederate Veteran*, (June 1904), 12:286.

Rice, James R. "The Rebel Invasion of Pennsylvania: The Truth Regarding Some Important Historical Facts." *The New York Times*, November 28, 1863.

Robertson, Felix H. "Service with the Reserve Artillery." *Confederate Veteran*, (July1920), 28:251-52.

Robins, W. T. "Stuart's Ride Around McClellan." *Battles and Leaders of the Civil War*, 2:271-75.

Scott, James G. "The Texans at Gettysburg," *Sherman Register*, March 31, 1897.

Seilheimer, George O. "The Historical Basis of Whittier's 'Barbara Frietchie.'" *Battles and Leaders of the Civil War*, 2:618-19.

Smith, George E. "In the Ranks at Fredericksburg." *Battles and Leaders of the Civil War*, 3:142.

Smith, Gustavus W. "Two Days of Battle At Seven Pines (Fair Oaks)." *Battles and Leaders of the Civil War*, 2:221-263.

Smith, William Farrar. "Franklin's Left Grand Division." *Battles and Leaders of the Civil War*, 3:128-38.

Smith, W. W. "General Lee to the Rear." *Southern Historical Society Papers*, (October-December 1880) 8:562-66.

Soley, James Russell. "The Navy in the Peninsular Campaign." *Battles and Leaders of the Civil War*, 2:264-70.

Stevens, John K. "Of Mules and Men: The Night Fight at Wauhatchie Station," *The South Carolina Historical Magazine*, (1989), 90:282-98.

Stevens, John W., "Major J. H. Littlefield," Hillsboro *Reflector*, July 13, 1886.

Stringfellow, M. S. "Letter to Editor of Richmond Times." *Southern Historical Society Papers*, (Jan.-Dec. 1893), 21:245-51.

Strother, D. H. "Personal Recollections of the War By A Virginian." *Harper's New Monthly Magazine*, Vol. 36, No. 215, (April 1868), 586.

Sulivane, Clement. "The Fall of Richmond." *Battles and Leaders of the Civil War*, 4:725-28.

Taliaferro, W. B. "Jackson's Raid Around Pope." *Battles and Leaders of the Civil War*, 2:501-11.

Thompson, David L. "With Burnside At Antietam." *Battles and Leaders of the Civil War*, 2:660-62.

Thornton, M. E. "Fighting for Thoroughfare Gap." Philadelphia *Weekly Times*, December 14, 1881.

Thurston, Gates P. "The Crisis at Chickamauga." *Battles and Leaders of the Civil War*, 3:663-65.

Timberlake, W. L. "Last Days in Front of Richmond, 1864-1865." *Confederate Veteran*, (March 1912), 20:119.

Todd, George T. "Gaines's Mill–Pickett and Hood." *Confederate Veteran*, (December 1898), 6:565-67.

Trowbridge, J. W. "Conspicuous Feats of Valor." *Confederate Veteran*, (January 1916), 24:25-26.

[Untitled]. Confederate Veteran, (March 1906), 14:141.

Walker, I. B. "Chickamauga. Going Into Action with Hands Full of Bacon and Coffee." *National Tribune*, July 2, 1891.

Walker, John G. "Jackson's Capture of Harper's Ferry." *Battles and Leaders of the Civil War*, 2:604-18.

Walshe, Capt. B. T. "Recollections of Gaines's Mill." *Confederate Veteran*, (March 1899), 7:54-56.

Ward, W. C. "Incidents and Personal Experiences on the Battlefield at Gettysburg." *Confederate Veteran*, (August 1900), 8:345-49.

White, W. T. "First Texas Regiment at Gettysburg." *Confederate Veteran*, (May 1922), 30:185.

Willcox, Cadmus M. "Lee and Grant in the Wilderness" in The Annals of the War Written by Leading Participants *North and South*. Alexander K. McClure, ed. Philadelphia, PA: Times Pub. Co., 1879.

"Wilderness," *Atlanta Journal*, August 17, 1901.

Winder, J. R. "Judge Martin's Report Approved." *Confederate Veteran*, (September 1905), 13:417.

Wirsdorfer, George. "Louis Trezevant Wigfall." W. C. Nunn, ed., *Ten Texans in Gray*, Hillsboro, TX: Hillsboro Junior College Press, 1968.

York, R. W. "Gen. Hood's Release from Arrest: An Incident of the Battle of Boonesboro." *Our Living and Our Dead*, (June 1875), 2:420-23.

Young, M. J. "Fifth Texas Regiment Flag." *Confederate Veteran*, (March 1918) 11:105-06.

Books

103rd OVI Memorial Foundation. *Personal Reminiscences and Experiences by Members of the One Hundred and Third Ohio Volunteer Infantry: Campaign Life in the Union Army from1862 to 1865*. Sheffield Lake, OH: Fred Weidner & Sons Printers, Inc., 1984.

Abernathy, William M. *Our Mess: Southern Gallantry and Privations*. McKinney, TX: McKintex Press, 1977.

Acts and Resolutions of the Second Session of the Provisional Congress of the Confederate States, Held at Montgomery, Ala. Richmond, VA: Enquirer Books and Job Press, by Tyler, Wise, Allegre & Smith, 1861.

Alexander, E. Porter. *Fighting for the Confederacy: The Personal Recollections of General Edward Porter Alexander*, Gary W. Gallagher, ed. Chapel Hill, NC: University of North Carolina Press, 1989.

____. *Military Memoirs of a Confederate: A Critical Narrative*. New York: Charles Scribner's Sons, 1907.

Bartlett, Napier. *A Soldier's Story of the War: including the marches and battles of the Washington artillery, and of other artillery, and of other Louisiana troops*. New Orleans, LA: Clark & Hofeline, 1874.

Barziza, Decimus et Ultimus. *The Adventures of a Prisoner of War, 1863-1864*. R. Henderson Shuffler, ed. Austin, TX: University of Texas Press, 1964.

Belknap, Charles. *History of the Michigan Organizations at Chickamauga, Chattanooga and Missionary Ridge, 1863*. Lansing, MI: Robert Smith Printing Company, 1897.

Birney, William. "General William Birney's Answer to Libels Clandestinely Circulated by James Shaw, Jr., With a Review of the Military Record of the Said James Shaw, Jr." Washington, DC: Stanley Snodgrass, Printer, 1878.

Blight, Dwight W. ed., *When This Cruel War Is Over: The Civil War Letters of Charles Harvey Brewster*. Amherst, MA: The University of Massachusetts Press, 1992.

Buell, Augustus. *The Cannoneer: Recollections of Service in the Army of the Potomac by a Detached Volunteer in the Regular Army*. Washington, DC: *The National Tribune*, 1890.

Butler, Benjamin Franklin. *Autobiography and Personal Reminiscences of Major-General Benj. F. Butler: A Review of His Legal, Political and Military Career*. Boston, MA: A. M. Thayer, 1892.

Chamberlain, Joshua L. *The Passing of the Armies, an Account of the Final Campaign of the Army of the Potomac, Based Upon Personal Reminiscences of the Fifth Army Corps*. New York: Charles Scribner's Sons, 1915.

____. *Through Blood and Fire at Gettysburg: General Joshua L. Chamberlain and the 20th Maine*. Gettysburg, PA: Stan Clark Military Books, 1994.

Chesnut, May Boykin. *A Diary From Dixie*. New York: D. Appleton and Company, 1905.

Chilton, F. B. *Unveiling and Dedication of Monument to Hood's Texas Brigade on the Capitol Grounds at Austin, Texas Thursday, October Twenty-Seven, Nineteen Hundred and Ten*. Houston, TX: F. B. Chilton, 1911.

Coles, Robert T. *From Huntsville to Appomattox: R. T. Coles's History of the 4th Regiment, Alabama Volunteer Infantry, C. S. A., Army of Northern Virginia*. Jeffrey D. Stocker, ed., Knoxville, TN: University of Tennessee Press, 1996.

Colorado County Historical Commission. *Colorado County Chronicles: From the Beginning to 1923*. 2 vols., Austin, TX: Eakin Publications, Inc., 1986.

Commanger, Henry Steele, ed. *The Blue and the Gray*. 2 vols. Indianapolis, IN: Bobbs-Merrill, 1950.

____ and Erik A. Bruun, eds. "The Civil War Archive: The History of the Civil War in Documents," *The Southern Illustrated News*. New York: Leventhal Publishers, Inc., 2000.

Connolly, James Austin. *Three Years in the Army of the Cumberland: the Letters and Diary of Major James A. Connolly.* Bloomington, IN: Indiana University Press, 1959.

Cooke, John Easton. *Wearing the Gray.* New York: Appleton, 1876.

Cussons, John. *Jack Sterry; the Jessie Scout: an incident of the Second Battle of Manassas, on which turned the course of the campaign and the fate of the Southern army.* York, PA: Gazette Print, 1906.

____. *The Passage of Thoroughfare Gap And theAssembling of Lee's Army for the Second Battle of Manassas,* York, PA: Gazette Print, 1906.

Dabney, Robert L. *The Life and Campaigns of Lieutenant-General Thomas J. Stonewall Jackson*, Richmond, VA, 1866.

Dame, William M. *From the Rapidan to Richmond and the Spotsylvania Campaign.* Baltimore, MD: Green-Lucas Company, 1920.

Dana, Charles. *Recollections of the Civil War.* New York: Boughmans, 1898.

Davenport, Alfred. *Camp and Field Life of the Fifth New York Volunteer Infantry (Duryee Zouaves).* New York: Dick and Fitzgerald, 1879.

Davis, Nicholas A. *The Campaign from Texas to Maryland with the Battle of Fredericksburg.* Richmond, VA: Office of thePresbyterian Committee of Publication of the Confederate States, 1863.

Doubleday, Abner. *Chancellorsville and Gettysburg.* New York: C. Scibner's Sons, 1882.

Douglas, Henry Kyd. *I Rode With Stonewall: the War Experiences of the Youngest Member of Jackson's Staff.* Chapel Hill: University of North Carolina Press, 1940.

Dowdey, Clifford and Louis H. Manarin, eds. *The Wartime Papers of R. E. Lee.* New York: Little Brown, 1961.

Drum, Richard C. *Battle of Chickamauga, Ga., September 19-20,1863: I. Organization of the Army of the Cumberland (commanded by Major-General W.S. Rosecrans) and return of casualties. II. Organization of the Army of Tennessee (commanded by General Braxton Bragg).* Washington, DC: Adjutant General's Department, 1889.

Eby, Cecil D. ed., *A Virginia Yankee in the Civil War: the Diaries of David Hunter Strother.* Chapel Hill, NC: University of North Carolina Press, 1961.

Everett, Donald, ed. *Chaplin Davis and Hood's Texas Brigade: Being an Expanded Edition of the Reverend Nicholas A. Davis's "The Campaign from Texas to Maryland, with the Battle of Fredericksburg."* San Antonio, TX: Principia Press of Trinity University, 1962.

Fletcher, William A. *Rebel Private, Front and Rear: Memoirs of a Confederate Soldier.* New York: A Dutton Book, 1995.

Folsom, James Madison. *Heroes and Martyrs of Georgia: Georgia's Record in the Revolution of 1861.* Macon, GA: Burke, Boykin & Company, 1864.

Fowler, John D., ed. *The Confederate Experience Reader: Selected Documents and Essays.* New York: Routledge, 2007.

Freemantle, James A. L. *The Freemantle Diary, Being the Journal of Lieutenant Colonel James Arthur Freemantle, Coldstream Guards on His Three Months in the Southern States.* Walter Lord, ed. London: Andre Deutch, 1956.

Gibbon, John. *Personal Recollections of the Civil War.* New York: Putnam's, 1928.

Glover, Robert W., ed. *Tyler to Sharpsburg: The War Letters of Robert H. and William H. Gaston.* Waco, TX: W. M. Morrison, 1960.

Gordon, John B. *Reminiscences of the Civil War.* New York: Charles Scribner's Sons, 1904.

Goree, Thomas Jewett. *Longstreet's Aide: The Civil War Letters of Major Thomas J. Goree.* Thomas W. Cutrer, ed. Charlottesville, VA: University of Virginia Press, 1995.

Govan, Gilbert E. and James W. Livingood, eds. *The Haskell Memoirs: John Cheves Haskell.* New York: Putnam, 1960.

Grant, Ulysses S. *Memoirs and Selected Letters*. McFeely, Mary Drake and William S. McFeely, eds. New York, NY: Library of America, 1990.

____. *Personal Memoirs of U. S. Grant*. 2 vols. New York: C. B. Webster, 1866.

Hamilton, D. H. *History of Company M, First Texas Volunteer Infantry, Hood's Brigade*. Waco, TX: W. M. Morrison, 1962.

Hanks, O. Y. *History of Captain B. F. Benton's Company, Hood's Texas Brigade, 1861-1865*. Austin, TX: Morrison Books, 1984.

Hardin, Martin D. *History of the Twelfth Regiment Pennsylvania Reserve Volunteer Corps*. New York: M. D. Hardin, 1890.

Hood, John Bell. *Advance and Retreat: Personal Experiences in the United States & Confederate States Armies*. New Orleans, LA, P. G. T. Beauregard, 1880. Richard M. McMurry, ed., reprint New York, 1993.

Hopkins, William Palmer. *The Seventh Regiment Rhode Island Regiment, Rhode Island Volunteers in the Civil War 1862-1865*. Providence, RI: Snow & Farnham, Printers, 1903.

Hough, Alfred L. *Soldier in the West: The Civil War Letters of Alfred Lacey Hough*. Philadelphia, PA: University of Pennsylvania Press, 1957.

Humphreys, Andrew A. *The Virginia Campaign of '64 and '65*. New York: Scribner's, 1916.

Johnson, Richard N. *A Soldier's Reminiscences in Peace and War*. Philadelphia, PA: Lippincott Co., 1886.

Johnson, Robert U., and Clarence C. Buel, eds. *Battles andLeaders of the Civil War, Being for the most part contributions by Union and Confederate officers*. 4 vols. New York: Century Co., 1884-87.

Johnston, David E. *Four Years a Soldier*. Princeton, WV: n. p., 1887.

Jones, John B. *A Rebel War Clerk's Diary*. Earl Schenck Miers, ed. New York: Sagamore Press, 1958.

Jones, Tom. *Tom Jones' Hood's Texas Brigade Sketch Book*. Hillsboro, TX: Hill College Press, 1988.

Joyce, John A. *A Checkered Life*. Chicago, IL: S. P. Rounds, Jr., 1883.

Judson, Amos M. *History of the Eighty-Third Regiment Pennsylvania Volunteers*. Erie, PA: B. F. H. Lynn, 1865.

LaBree, Benjamin. *Camp Fires of the Confederacy: A Volume of Humorous Anecdotes, Reminiscences, Deeds of Heroism, Thrilling Narratives, Campaigns, Hand-to-hand Fights, Bold Dashes, Terrible Hardships Endured, Imprisonments . . . Etc*. Louisville, KY: Courier-Journal Print Co., 1898.

Ladd, David L. and Audrey J. Ladd, eds. *The Bachelder Papers*. 3 vols., Dayton, OH: Morningside, 1994-95.

Lasswell, Mary, ed. *Rags and Hope: The Recollections of Val C. Giles, Four Years With Hood's Brigade, Fourth Texas Infantry 1861-1865*. New York: Coward-McCann, Inc. 1961.

Lee, Fitzhugh. *General Lee*. New York: D. Appleton and Company, 1894.

Long, A. L. *Memoirs of Robert E. Lee: His Military and Personal History*. Marcus J. Wright, ed. New York: J. M. Stoddart and Company, 1886.

Longstreet, James *From Manassas to Appomattox: Memoirs of the Civil War in America*. Philadelphia, PA: J. B. Lippincott and Co., 1896.

McKee, John Francis and Joanne McKee Westmoreland, eds. *John Francis McKee, Pvt., Co. K, Fifth Texas Infantry, Hood's Brigade, Northern Army of Virginia, CSA: Letters Home, 1861-1863*. Nacogdoches, TX: Stephen F. Austin University, 2004.

McLaws, Lafayette. *A Soldier's General: the Civil War Letters of Major General Lafayette McLaws*. John C. Oeffinger, ed. Chapel Hill, NC: University of North Carolina Press, 2002.

Moore, Edward A. *The Story of a Cannoneer Under Stonewall Jackson*. New York, NY: The Neale Publishing Company, 1907.

Moore, Frank. *The Rebellion Record: A Diary of American Events, with Documents, Narratives, Illustrative Incidents, Poetry, Etc.*, 12 vols., New York: G. P. Putnam, 1864.

Nash, Eugene A. *A History of the Forty-Fourth Regiment, New York Volunteer Infantry in the Civil War, 1861-1865*. Chicago, IL: R. R. Donnelley & Sons, 1911.

Nesbitt, Mark, ed. *Through Blood and Fire: Selected Civil War Papers of Major General Joshua Chamberlain*. Mechanicsburg, PA: Stackpole Books 1996.

Norton, Oliver Willcox. *Army Letters, 1861-1865: Being Extracts from Private Letters to Relatives and Friends from a Soldier in the Field During the Civil War, With an Appendix Containing Copies of Some Official Documents, Papers and Addresses of Later Date*. Chicago, IL: O. L. Deming, 1903.

____. *Strong Vincent and His Brigade at Gettysburg, July 2, 1863*. Chicago, IL: [self published], 1909.

____. *The Attack and Defense of Little Round Top, Gettysburg, July 2, 1863*. New York: The Neale Publishing Company, 1913.

Oates, William C. *The war between the Union and the Confederacy and its lost opportunities, with a history of the 15th Alabama regiment and the forty-eight battles in which it was engaged : being an account of the author's experiences in the greatest conflict of modern times; a justification of secession, and showing that the Confederacy should have succeeded; a criticism of President Davis, the Confederate Congress and some of the general officers of the Confederate and Union Armies; praise of line officers and soldiers in the ranks for their heroism and patriotism, and including the author's observations and experiences as Brigadier-General in the war between the United States and Spain*. New York: Neale Publishing Company, 1905.

Page, Charles A. *Letters of a War Correspondent.* Boston, MA: L. C. Page, 1899.

Parker, Eddy R., ed. *Touched By Fire: Letters From Company D 5th Texas Infantry Hood's Brigade Army of Northern Virginia 1862-1865*. Hillsboro, TX: Hill College Press, 2000.

Peyton, George Q. *A Civil War Record for 1864-1865*. Robert A. Hodge, ed. Fredericksburg, VA: Robert A. Hodge, 1981.

Polk, J. M. *Memories of the Last Cause—Stories and Adventures of a Confederate Soldier in General R. E. Lee's Army, 1861-1865, and Ten Years in South America, Its Resources, Trade and Commerce, and Business Intercourse With Other Countries*. Austin, TX: n.p., 1905.

____. *The North and South American Review,* Austin, TX: Von Boeckmann-Jones Co., 1914.

Pollard, Edward A. The First Year of the War. Richmond, VA: West & Johnston, 1862.

____. *The Last Year of the War.* New York: Charles B. Richardson, 1866.

Polley, J. B. A Soldier's Letters to Charming Nellie. New York: The Neale Publishing Company, 1908.

____. *Hood's Texas Brigade: its marches, its battles, its achievements.* New York: The Neale Publishing Company,1910.

Pomeroy, Nicholas. *Reminiscences of the American War, 1861-1865*. n.p., n.d. in Briscoe Center for American History, University of Texas at Austin, Austin, TX.

Porter, Horace. *Campaigning With Grant.* Bloomington, IN: University of Indiana Press, 1961.

Powell, Robert M. "With Hood At Gettysburg, The Experiences of a Texas Officer in One of the Charges at Little Round Top." Philadelphia *Weekly Times*, December 13, 1884.

____. *Recollections of a Texas Colonel at Gettysburg.* Gregory A. Coco, ed. Gettysburg, PA: Thomas Publications, 1990.

Putman, Sallie Brock. *Richmond During the War: Four Years of Personal Observation.* New York: G. W. Carleton & Co.,1867.

Reagan, John H. *Memoirs with Special Reference to Secession and the Civil War.* New York: The Neale Publishing Company, 1906.

Regimental Committee. *History of the One-Hundred and Twenty-Fifth Regiment, Pennsylvania Volunteers 1862-1863*. Philadelphia, PA: Lippincott, 1906.

Reichardt, Robert E. *Forever the Cause: The Life and Legacy of Confederate Colonel Robert M. Powell, 5th Texas Infantry*. Robert M. Reichardt, 2007.

Rhodes, Robert Hunt, ed. *All For the Union: The Civil War Diary and Letters of Elisha Hunt Rhodes*. New York: Orion Books, 1985.

Robertson, Jerome B. *Touched With Valor: Civil War Papers and Casualty Reports of Hood's Texas Brigade.* Harold B. Simpson, ed. Hillsboro, TX: Hill Junior College Press, 1964.

Schaaf, Morris. *The Battle of the Wilderness*. Boston, MA: Houghton Mifflin Company. 1910.

Schaller, Mary M., Martin N. Schaller, eds. *Soldiering for Glory: The Civil War Letters of Colonel Frank Schaller, Twenty-second Mississippi Infantry*. Columbia: University of South Carolina Press, 2007.

Schmucker, Samuel M. *A History of the Civil War in the United States with a Preliminary View of its Causes and Biographical Sketches of Its Heroes*. Baltimore, MD: Jones Brothers & Co. 1862.

Schurz, Carl, Frederic Bancroft and William Archibald Dunning. *The Reminiscences of Carl Schurz*. New York: The McClure Company, 1907-1908.

Sears, Stephen W., ed. *The Civil War Papers of George B. McClellan: Selected Correspondence, 1860-1865.* New York: Ticknor & Fields, 1989.

Smith, Gustavus Woodson. *Confederate War Papers*. New York, NY: Atlantic Publishing and Engraving Co., 1884.

Snow, William Parker. *Southern Generals: Who They Are, And What They Have Done*. New York: C. B. Richardson, 1865.

Sorrell, G. Moxley. *At the Right Hand of Longstreet: Recollections of a Confederate Staff Officer*. New York: Neale Publishing Company, 1905.

Stevens, John W. *Reminiscences of the Civil War: A Soldier in Hood's Texas Brigade, Army of Northern Virginia*. Hillsboro, TX: Hillsboro Mirror Print, 1902.

Swinton, William. *Campaigns of the Army of the Potomac: A Critical History of Operations in Virginia, Maryland and Pennsylvania, From the Commencement to the Close of the War*. New York: C. B. Richardson, 1866.

Terrill, Thomas S. *The Boys From Brenham: The Letters of Virginius E. Petty*. Kerrville, TX: n.p., 2006.

Todd, George T. *Sketch of History, The First Texas Regiment, Hood's Brigade, A. N. Va.* Jefferson, TX: Jefferson Jimplecute, 1909, reprint, Waco, TX, 1963.

West, John C. *A Texan in Search of a Fight: A trip of a private soldier from Texas to Gettysburg and Chickamauga in 1863*. Waco, TX: Press of J. S. Hill & Co., 1901.

White, Russell C., ed. *The Civil War Diary of Wyman S. White, First Sergeant of Company F, 2nd United Sates Sharpshooter Regiment, 1861-1865*. Baltimore, MD: Butternut and Blue, 1993.

Winkler, Mrs. A. V. *Confederate Capital and Hood's Texas Brigade*. Houston, TX: Austin Eugene Von Boeckmann, 1894.

Winkler, Ernest W., ed. *Journal of the Secession Convention of Texas, 1861*. Austin, TX: Texas State Library, 1912.

Wise, John Sergeant. *The End of an Era*. Cambridge, MA: Houghton, Mifflin and Company, Riverside Press, 1899.

Wright, Louise Wigfall. *A Southern Girl in '61: The War-Time Memories of a Confederate Senator's Daughter.* New York: Doubleday, Page & Company, 1905.

Young, Dr. S. O. *True Stories of Old Houston and Houstonians: Historical and Personal Sketches*. Galveston, TX: Oscar Springer, 1913.

Secondary Sources

Articles

"Battle of the Wilderness." Augusta [Georgia] *Daily Constitutionalist*, May 31, 1864.

"Gettysburg Trip: The Lone Star Flag Over Devil's Den." *Gettysburg National Military Park*, 5th Texas Inf. Reg. file.

"Hood's Texas Brigade at Appomattox," *Texana* (Spring 1965), 3:1-19.

"Lookout Valley, October 28, 1863." *Southern Historical Society Papers*, (Oct.-Dec.1880), 8:500-511.

"Major-General Thomas." *Harper's Weekly*, October 10, 1863, 642.

"Paroles of the Army of Northern Virginia." *Southern Historical Society Papers*, (1887), 15:1-487.

"Relative Numbers at Gettysburg." *Southern Historical Society Papers*, (July, 1878), 6:10-36.

"The Battle of Chickamauga, 19th and 20th of September, 1863." *Southern Historical Society Papers*, (1888), 16:377-87.

"The Seven Days' Battle Before Richmond." T*he Confederate Military History*, Vol. 3, (1899).

"The Texas Brigade." Richmond *Times*, September 22, 1891.

"The Twentieth Maine at Gettysburg." [Portland, ME] *Eastern Argus*, December 20, 1865.

"Uncle John Cox." Nolan County [Texas] *Record*, February 15, 1894.

Allan, William. "Relative Strength at Second Manassas." *Southern Historical Society Papers*, (May 1880), 8:217-21.

Beverly, Trevia Wooster, ed. "Watson Dugat Williams." *Stripes*, No. 2 (June, 1982), Texas State Genealogical Society, 22:77-79

Block, W. T. "Civil War Comes to Jefferson County, Texas: The Road to Gettysburg, 1861-1863." *Blue & Gray Magazine*, (September, 1986), 4:10-18.

____. "G. W. O'Brien: Torchbearer of East Texas Civilization." Beaumont [Texas] *Sunday Enterprise-Journal*, November 9, 1980.

Boelt, Fred. "James City County Confederate Gravesites." *James City Cavalry Picket Lines*, Williamsburg, VA, (June 2010), 4-5.

Bohannon, Keith S. "One Solid Unbroken Roar of Thunder: Union and Confederate Artillery at the Battle of Malvern Hill." *The Richmond Campaign of 1862: The Peninsula & The Seven Days*, Gallagher, Gary, ed. Chapel Hill, NC: University of North Carolina, 2000, 217-19.

Breiner, Thomas L. "Pork Belly Politics or How Longstreet Brought Home the Bacon: James Longstreet and the Suffolk Campaign." *Cincinnati Civil War Round Table*, September 16, 1999.

Brooks, Charles E. "The Social and Cultural Dynamics of Soldiers in Hood's Texas Brigade." *The Journal of Southern History*, (August, 2001), 67:535-72.

Bruce, Susannah V. "The Fierce Pride of the Texas Brigade." *Civil War Times*, (September, 2007), 46:32-39.

Cameron, Steve. "In Defense of the Mountain Howitzer." *The Artilleryman*, (Spring, 2003), 24:1-3.

Dingus, Anne. "Grand Old Flags." *Texas Monthly*, March, 2002: 68-73.

East Texas Genealogical Society. *East Texas Family Records*. Vol. 2, No. 2 (Summer, 1978).

Eiserman, Rick. "The Winter That Made the Texas Brigade." *Civil War Times*, (August, 2011), 50:36-41.

Fink, Howard S. "The East Tennessee Campaign and the Battle of Knoxville in 1963." *The East Tennessee Historical Society Publications*, No. 29, 1957, 10.

Foley, Kyle J. "John Bell Hood's Division in the Battle of Chickamauga: A Historical Analysis," *U. S. Army Command and General Staff College*, Fort Leavenworth, KS, 2003.

Fox, William F. "The Chances of Being Hit In Battle." *The Century Magazine*, (May, 1888), 36:93-106.

Franks, Edward Carr. "The Detachment of Longstreet Considered: Braxton Bragg, James Longstreet, and the Chattanooga Campaign." *Leadership and Command in the American Civil War*, Woodworth, Steven, ed., Campbell, CA: Savas Woodbury Press, 1995.

Gage, Larry Joe. "The Texas Road to Secession and War—John Marshall And the Texas State Gazette, 1860-1861." *Southwestern Historical Quarterly*, (October, 1958), 62:194-95.

Gallagher, Gary W. "A Civil War Watershed: The 1862 Richmond Campaign in Perspective." *The Richmond Campaign*, Gallagher, Gary, ed., 3-27.

Hay, Thomas Robson. "The Campaign and Battle of Chickamauga." *Georgia Historical Quarterly*, (1923), 7:213-50.

Hubbell, John T. "The Seven Days of George Brinton McClellan." *The Richmond Campaign*, Gallagher, Gary, ed., 28-43.

Kelley, Dayton. "The Texas Brigade at the Wilderness May 6, 1864." *Texana*, (Spring, 1973), 11:103-23.

Ketchum, Richard M. "Faces From the Past—II." *American Heritage*, (June, 1961), 12:28-29.

Kingsbury, T. B. "Did Gen. Lee Offer to Lead Two Brigades?" *Our Living and Our Dead.* (March 1875), 2:46-51.

Krick, R. E. L. "The Men Who Carried This Position Were Soldiers Indeed: The Decisive Charge of Whiting's Division at Gaines's Mill." *The Richmond Campaign*, Gallagher, Gary, ed., 181-216.

Krick, Robert K. "If Longstreet Says So . . . It Is Not Likely True: James Longstreet and the Second Day at Gettysburg." *The Second Day at Gettysburg: Essays on Confederate and Union Leadership*, Gary W. Gallagher, ed., Kent, OH, Kent State University Press, 1993: 57-86.

____."Sleepless in the Saddle: Stonewall Jackson in the Seven Days" *The Richmond Campaign of 1862: The Peninsula Campaign and the Seven Days.* Gary W.Gallagher, ed., Chapel Hill, NC: University of North Carolina Press, 2000:66-95.

McAninoch, Frank. "McAninoch for the Confederacy. Eight Who Fought for Southern Independence." *McAninoch Family History Newsletter*, (November, 2001), 9:28.

Mendoza, Alex. "Machinations in the Confederate High Command: Gen. Braxton Bragg and his Campaign to Discredit Lt. Gen. James Longstreet." *North & South*, (2009), 11:43-48.

Miller, William J. "I Only Wait for the River: McClellan and His Engineers on the Chickahominy." *The Richmond Campaign of 1862: The Peninsula Campaign and the Seven Days.* Gallagher, Gary, ed., Chapel Hill, NC: University of North Carolina Press, 2000, 44-65.

Moore, Norma "The Flo News." *Buffalo Express*, May 28, 2003.

Pohanka, Brian C. "'Boys, Won't I Make a Fine Looking Corpse?' Duryee's Zouaves at Second Bull Run." *Civil War Regiments: A Journal of the American Civil War.* San Jose, CA, 1991), 1:29-41.

____. "Charge Bayonets: The 5th New York at the Battle of Gaines' Mill." *Civil War Times Illustrated*, (May/June, 1994), 33:30-39.

____. "Duryee's Zouaves: The 5th New York Volunteer Infantry." *Civil War Regiments: A Journal of the American Civil War*, (San Jose, CA, 1991), 1:7-28.

____. "Second Battle of Bull Run: Destruction of the 5th New York Zouaves." *America's Civil War*, (September, 2002), 15:46.

Robertson, William Glenn. "The Chickamauga Campaign: The Armies Collide." *Blue & Gray*, (Fall, 2007), 24:6-28.

Sandbo, Anna I. "The First Session of the Secession Convention in Texas." *Southwestern Historical Quarterly*, (October, 1914), 18:162-94.

____. "The First Session of the Secession Convention in Texas." Ch. XXXVI, *History of Texas*, Eugene Baker, ed., Dallas, TX: Southwest Press, 1929.

Schaaf, Morris. "The Battle of the Wilderness VIII." *Atlantic Monthly*, (January, 1910), 105:99-102.

Simpson, Harold B. "Hood's Texas Brigade at Appomattox." *Texana* (Spring, 1965), 3:1-19.

____. "Hood's Texas Brigade at Appomattox." *Lone Star Blue and Gray: Essays on Texas in the Civil War* (Austin, TX, 1995), 337-47.

Stein, William Mark. "'Consider the Lily: The Ungilded History of Colorado County, Texas. Pt. VI: 1861-1865". *Nesbitt Memorial Library Journal*, No. 2, (1977), 7:75-142.

____. "Civil War Letters of Benjamin Marshall Baker," *Nesbitt Memorial Library Journal*, No. 1, (1998), 8:33-37

Stinson, Dwight E., Jr. "Eltham's Landing – the End Run That Failed." *Civil War Times Illustrated*, (October, 1963), 1:38-41.

Teters, Kristopher. "'Sons of the Defenders of the Alamo' on America's Bloodiest Day." *Mid-Maryland History: Conflict, Growth and Change*, Barbara M. Powell and Michael A. Powell, eds., Charleston, SC: The History Press, 2008.

Toews, Ryan, "Flags of the Texas Brigade." unpublished ms., 2001, in author's possession.

Trudeau, Noah Andre. "Darbytown Road Debacle." *America's Civil War*, (May, 1992), 30-36.

Wooster, Ralph A. and Robert Wooster. "Ratin' for a Fight,": Texans in the Confederate Army." *The Southwestern Historical Quarterly*, (1981), 84:387-426.

Books

Adelman, Gary E. *Little Round Top: A Detailed Tour Guide.* Gettysburg, PA: Thomas Publications, 2000.

Allan, Francis D. *Allan's Lone Star Ballads: a collection of Southern patriotic songs, made during Confederate times.* New York, NY: Ayer Publishing, 1970.

Amann, William F. *Personnel of the Civil War.* 2 vols., New York,: Thomas Yoseloff, 1961.

Anders, Curt. *Hearts In Conflict: One Volume History of the Civil War.* New York: Barnes & Noble, 1999.

Andrew, Rod. *Wade Hampton: Confederate Warrior to Southern Redeemer.* Chapel Hill, NC: University of North Carolina Press, 2008.

Appomattox Court House. Washington, DC: National Park Service,1955.

Bakeless, John. *Spies of the Confederacy.* Mineola, NY: Courier Dover Publications, 1997.

Bates, Samuel P. *History of Pennsylvania Volunteers, 1861-1865.* 5 vols., Harrisburg, PA: B. Singerly, 1869.

Batte, Lelia M. *History of Milam County, Texas.* San Antonio, TX: The Naylor Company, 1956.

Black, Robert C., III. *Railroads of the Confederacy.* Chapel Hill, NC: University of North Carolina Press, 1952.

Boatner, Mark Mayo, III. *The Civil War Dictionary*, rev. ed. New York: Vintage Books, 1991.

Bonekemper, III, Edward H. *Grant and Lee: Victorious American and Vanquished Virginian.* Westport, CT: Praeger Publishers, 2008.

Boucher, John N. *History of Westmoreland County, Pennsylvania.* New York: The Lewis Publishing Company, 1906.

Bowden, Scott. *Last Chance for Victory: Robert E. Lee and the Gettysburg Campaign.* New York: Da Capo Press, 2003.

Bowers, John. *Chickamauga and Chattanooga: The Battles That Doomed the Confederacy*. New York: Harper Collins, 1994.

Boynton, H. V. *The National Military Park Chickamauga-Chattanooga: An Historical Guide*. Cincinnati, OH: The Robert Clark Company, 1895.

Bradley, Mark L. *Last Stand in the Carolinas: The Battle of Bentonville*. Mason City, IA: Savas Publishing Company,1996.

Buchanan, Roberdeau. *Genealogy of the Roberdeau Family Including a Biography of General Daniel Roberdeau of the Revolutionary Army, and the Continental Congress, and Signers of the Articles of Confederation*. Washington, DC: Joseph L. Pearson, Printers, 1876.

Burkhardt, George S. *Confederate Rage, Yankee Wrath: No Quarter in the Civil War*. Carbondale: Southern Illinois University Press, 2007.

Burleson, Georgia Jenkins. *The Life and Writings of Rufus C. Burleson, D. D., L.L. D.* Waco, TX: Georgia J. Burleson, 1901.

Burton, Brian K. *Extraordinary Circumstances: The Seven Days Battles*. Bloomington,: Indiana University Press, 2001.

Burton, Brian K. *The Peninsula and Seven Days: A Battlefield Guide*. Lincoln: University of Nebraska Press, 2007.

Cannan, John. *The Antietam Campaign: August-September 1862*. Conshohocken, PA: DaCapo Press, 1997.

____. *The Wilderness Campaign, May 1864*. Conshohocken, PA: Combined Books, 1993.

Carley, Kenneth. *Minnesota in the Civil War: An Illustrated History*. St. Paul, MN: Minnesota Historical Society Press, 2000.

Casdorph, Paul D. *Confederate General R. S. Ewell: Robert E. Lee's Hesitant Commander*. Lexington, KY: University ofKentucky Press, 2004.

Catton, Bruce. *A Stillness at Appomattox*. Garden City, NY: Doubleday & Company, Inc., 1953.

____. *Grant Takes Command*. Boston, MA: Little Brown, 1968.

Chicoine, Stephen. *The Confederates of Chappell Hill, Texas: Prosperity, Civil War and Decline*. Jefferson, NC: McFarland & Company, Inc., 2005.

Cisco, Walter Brian. Wade Hampton: *Confederate Warrior, Conservative Statesman*. Dulles, VA: Brassley's, Inc., 2004.

Clark, Lewis H. *Military History of Wayne County: The County in the Civil War*. Sodus, NY: Hulett & Graylord, 1883.

Coates, Earl J., and Dean S. Thomas. *An Introduction to Civil War Small Arms*. Gettysburg, PA: Thomas, 1990.

Coco, Gregory A. *Confederates Killed In Action at Gettysburg*. Gettysburg, PA: Thomas Publications, 2001.

____. *A Strange and Blighted Land: Gettysburg, The Aftermath of a Battle*. Gettysburg, PA: Thomas Publications,1995.

Coddington, Edwin B. *The Gettysburg Campaign: A Study in Command*. New York: Touchstone Books, 1997.

Collier, Calvin. They'll Do To Tie To: 3rd Arkansas Infantry Regiment, CSA. Little Rock, AR: James D. Warren, 1959.

Connelly, Thomas Lawrence. *Autumn of Glory: The Army of Tennessee, 1862-1865*. Baton Rouge, LA: Louisiana State University Press, 1971.

Cormier, Steven A. *The Siege of Suffolk: The Forgotten Campaign, April 11-May 4, 1863*. Lynchburg, VA: H. E.Howard, Inc., 1987.

Cornell, Saul, *The Other Founders: Anti-Federalism and the Dissenting Traditions in America, 1788-1828.* Chapel Hill, NC: University of North Carolina Press, 1999.

Cornish, Dudley Taylor. *The Sable Arm: Black Troops in the Union Army, 1861-1865.* Lawrence, KS: University Press of Kansas, 1956.

Cozzens, Peter. *The Shipwreck of Their Hopes: The Battles for Chattanooga.* Urbana, IL: University of Illinois Press, 1996.

____. *This Terrible Sound: The Battle of Chickamauga*, Urbana, IL: University of Illinois Press 1992.

Crews, D'Anne McAdams, ed. *Huntsville and Walker County, Texas: A Bicentennial History.* Huntsville, TX: Sam Houston State University Press, 1976.

Crouch, Howard R., *Relic Hunter: The Field Account of Civil War Sites, Artifacts and Hunting*, Oakpark, VA, 2006.

Crute, Joseph H. *Units of the Confederate States Army.* Midlothian, VA: Derwent Books 1987.

Cullen, Joseph P. *The Peninsula Campaign 1862 McClellan & Lee Struggle For Richmond.* New York: Bonanza Books, 1973.

Dameron, J. David. *Benning's Brigade: A History and Roster of the Fifteenth Georgia.* Westminster, MD: Heritage Books, Inc., 1997.

Davis, Archie K. *Boy Colonel of the Confederacy: The Life and Times of Henry King Burgwyn, Jr.* Chapel Hill: University of North Carolina Press, 1985.

Davis, Burke. *Jeb Stuart: The Last Cavalier.* New York: Bonanza Books, 1957.

____. *The Gray Fox.* New York: Rinehart & Co., 1956.

____. To *Appomattox, Nine April Days, 1865.* New York: Rinehart & Co., 1959.

Davis, George B. *The Official Military Atlas of the Civil War.* New York: Arno Press/Crown Publishers, Inc. 1978.

Davis, William C. *Breckinridge: Statesman, Soldier, Symbol.* Baton Rouge: Louisiana State University Press, 1973.

DiNardo, R. L. and Albert A. Nofi. *James Longstreet: The Man, the Soldier, the Controversy.* Conshohocken, PA: Da Capo Press, 1998.

Discorfano, Ken. *They Saved the Union at Little Round Top: Gettysburg—July 2, 1863.* Gettysburg, PA: Thomas Publications, 2002.

Dreese, Michael A. *Torn Families: Death and Kinship at the Battle of Gettysburg.* Jefferson, NC: McFarland Publishing Co., 2007.

Dyer, John Perry. *The Gallant Hood.* Indianapolis, IN: Bobbs-Merrill Company, 1950.

Earley, Gerald L. *The Second United States Sharpshooter: A History and Roster.* Jefferson, NC: McFarland & Company, Inc., 2009.

Eckenrode, Hamilton James & Conrad, Byron. *James Longstreet: Lee's War Horse.* Chapel Hill: University of North Carolina Press 1999.

Eicher, David J. *The Longest Night: A Military History of the Civil War.* New York: Simon and Schuster 2001.

Esposito, Vincent J. *The West Point Atlas of American Wars.* 2 vols., New York, NY: Frederick A. Praeger, 1959.

Evans, Clement A. ed., *Military History: A Library of Confederate States History, In Twelve Volumes Written By Distinguished Men of the South, and Edited By Gen. Clement A. Evans of Georgia.* 12 vols., Atlanta, GA: Confederate Publishing Company,1889.

Evans, June Banks. *Settlers Along the Shores of Virginia's York River.* New Orleans, LA: Bryn Ffyliaid Publications, 1989.

Faulk, J. J. *History of Henderson County, Texas.* Athens, TX: Athens Review Printing Co., 1929.

Fehrenbach, T. R. *Lone Star: A History of Texas and the Texans.* New York: Wings Books, 1968.

Field, Ron and Richard Hook. *The Confederate Army 1861-65*, 6 vols. Louisiana and Texas, vol. 3. Oxford: Osprey Publishing 2006.

____. *Uniforms of the Civil War: An Illustrated Guide for Historians, Collectors, and Reenactors*. Guilford, CT: The Lyons Press, 2005.

Fitch, Michael Hendrick. *The Chattanooga Campaign, With Especial Reference to Wisconsin's Participation Therein*. Madison, WI: Democratic Printing Co., 1911.

Flagel, Thomas R. and Ken Allers, Jr. *The History Buff's Guide toGettysburg*. Nashville, TN: Cumberland House, 2006.

Foote, Shelby. *The Civil War: A Narrative*. 3 vols. New York: Random House, 1958-74.

Fox, William F. *Regimental Losses in the American Civil War 1861-1865: A Treatise on the Extent and Nature of the Mortuary Losses in the Union Regiments, With Full and Exhaustive Statistics Compiled From the Official Records on File in the State Military Bureaus and at Washington*. Albany, NY: Albany Publishing Company, 1889.

Frassanito, William A. *Antietam: The Photographic Legacy of America's Bloodiest Day*. New York, Charles Scribner's Sons, 1978.

Freeman, Douglas Southall. *Lee's Lieutenants*. 3 vols., New York: Charles Scribner's Sons, 1942-44.

______. *R. E. Lee*. New York: 4 vols., Charles Scribner's Sons, 1934-35.

Friend, Llerena B. *Sam Houston: The Great Designer*. Austin, TX: University of Texas Press, 1954.

Fulmore, Z. T. *The History and Geography of Texas: As Told in County Names*. Austin, TX: Press of E. L. Stech, 1915.

Furgurson, Ernest B. *Not War But Murder: Cold Harbor 1864*. New York: Alfred A. Knopf, 2000.

Gallagher, Gary W. ed., *The Antietam Campaign*. Chapel Hill, NC: University of North Carolina Press, 1999.

____.*The Richmond Campaign of 1862: The Peninsula & The Seven Days*. Chapel Hill, NC: University of North Carolina Press 2000.

____. ed. *The Second Day At Gettysburg: Essays on Confederate and Union Leadership*. Kent, OH: The Ken State University Press, 1993.

____. *The Spotsylvania Campaign*. Chapel Hill, NC: University of North Carolina Press, 1998.

____. ed. *The Wilderness Campaign*. Chapel Hill: University of North Carolina Press, 1997.

Gallaway, B. P. Texas, the Dark Corner of the Confederacy: Contemporary Accounts of the Lone Star State in the Civil War. Lincoln, NE: University of Nebraska Press, 1994.

Gates, J. Y. & Fox, H. B. *A History of Leon County: With Informal Sketches and Interviews*. Centerville, TX: The Leon County News, 1936.

Gibbs, Joseph. *Three Years in the "Bloody Eleventh": The Campaigns of a Pennsylvania Reserves Regiment*. University Park, PA: Pennsylvania State University, 2002.

Goodwin, Doris Kearns. *A Team of Rivals: The Political Genius of Abraham Lincoln*. New York: Simon & Schuster, 2005.

Gordon, Lesley J. *General George E. Pickett in Life and Legend*. Chapel Hill, NC: University of North Carolina Press, 2002.

Goree, Edwin Sue. *A Family Mosaic: Fragmentary Sketches of Our Forebearers in America*. Coolidge, AZ: Jonathan Goree, 1961.

Goree, Jonathan Daniel. *The Goree Boys, 1861-1865*. Coolidge, AZ: privately printed, 1965.

Gottfried, Bradley M. *Brigades of Gettysburg: The Union and Confederate Brigades at the Battle of Gettysburg*. New York: Da Capo Press 2002.

____. *Kearny's Own: The History of the First New Jersey Brigade in the Civil War*. Piscataway, NJ: Rutgers University Press 2005.

Govan, Gilbert E. *The Chattanooga Country, 1540-1976: From Tomahawks to TVA.* Knoxville: University of Tennessee Press, 1977.

Grear, Charles D. *Why Texans Fought in the Civil War.* College Station, TX: Texas A & M University Press, 2010.

Greene, A. Wilson. *Civil War Petersburg: Confederate City in theCrucible of War.* Charlottesville: University of Virginia Press, 2006.

Groom, Winston. *Shrouds of Glory: From Atlanta to Nashville.* New York: Grove Press, 1995.

Guelzo, Allen C. *Gettysburg: The Last Invasion.* New York: Alfred A. Knopf, 2013.

Hanna, Charles W. *African American Recipients of the Medal of Honor.* Jefferson, NC: McFarland & Company, Inc., 2002.

Harvey, Bill. T*exas Cemeteries: The Resting Places of Famous, Infamous, and Just Plain Interesting Texans.* Austin: University of Texas Press, 2003.

Hasskarl, Robert A., Jr. *Brenham, Texas 1844-1958.* Brenham, TX: Banner-Press Publishing Company, 1958.

Hassler, William Woods. *A. P. Hill: Lee's Forgotten General.* Chapel Hill: University of North Carolina Press, 1962.

Hastings, Earl C. Jr., and David S. Hastings. *A Pitiless Rain: The Battle of Williamsburg, 1862.* Shippensburg, PA: White Mane, 1997.

Haynes, Emma. *The History of Polk County, Texas. Sam Houston Regional Library*, Liberty, TX, 1937.

Heidler, David Stephen, and Jeanne T. Heidler, eds. *Encyclopedia of the American Civil War: A Political, Social and Military History.* New York: W.W. Norton & Company, Inc., 2000.

Henderson, G. F. R., *Stonewall Jackson and the American Civil War.* 2 vols. (Secaucus, NJ: Blue and Gray Press, 1989).

Henderson, Harry McCorry. *Hood's Texas Brigade: An Address by Harry McCorry Henderson Before the Civil War Round Table*, February 2, 1955. n.p., 1955.

Hennessy, John J. *Return to Bull Run: The Campaign and Battle of Second Manassas.* New York: Simon & Schuster 1993.

Henry, Robert Selph. *The Story of the Confederacy.* Indianapolis, IN: Bobbs-Merrill Co., 1936.

Hess, Earl J. *Field Armies & Fortifications in the Civil War: The Eastern Campaigns, 1861-1864.* Chapel Hill, NC: University of North Carolina Press, 2005.

____. I*n the Trenches at Petersburg: Field Fortifications & Confederate Defeat.* Chapel Hill, NC: University of North Carolina Press, 2009.

____. *Pickett's Charge—The Last Attack at Gettysburg.* Chapel Hill, NC: University of North Carolina Press, 2001.

Horn, John. *The Petersburg Campaign: June 1864-April 1865.* Cambridge, MA: Da Capo Press, 1993.

Hunter, Alexander. T*he Women of the Debatable Land.* Washington, DC: Cobden Publishing Company, 1912.

James, Marquis. *The Raven.* New York, NY: Blue Ribbon Books, Inc., 1929.

Johnson, Clint. *In the Footsteps of Stonewall Jackson.* Winston-Salem, NC: John F. Blair, 2002.

Johnson, Curt and Richard C. Anderson. *Artillery Hell: The Employment of Artillery at Antietam.* College Station, TX: Texas A&M University Press, 1995.

Johnson, Frank W. *A History of Texas and Texans.* 4 vols. Chicago, IL: The American Historical Society, 1914.

Johnson, Sid S., "H. A. Massey," *Texans Who Wore the Gray.* Tyler, TX: self-published, 1907.

Jones, Wilmer L. *Generals in Blue and Gray: Lincoln's Generals.* Westport, CT: Praeger, 2004.

Jordan, Ervin L. *Black Confederates and Afro-Yankees in Civil War Virginia.* Charlottesville, VA: University of Virginia Press, 1995.

Kelley, Dayton. *General Lee and Hood's Texas Brigade at the Battle of the Wilderness.* Hillsboro, TX: Hill Junior College Press 1969.8

Konstram, Angus. *Seven Days Battles: Lee's Defense of Richmond.* Oxford, U.K.: Osprey Pub. Co., 2004.

Krick, Robert E. L. *Staff Officers In Gray: A Biographical Register of the Staff Officers In the Army of Northern Virginia.* Chapel Hill, NC: University of North Carolina Press, 2003.

Krick, Robert K. *The Smoothbore Volley That Doomed theConfederacy: The Death of Stonewall Jackson and Other Chapters on the Army of Northern Virginia.* Baton Rouge: Louisiana State University Press, 2002.

____. *Parker's Virginia Battery, C. S. A.* Berryville, VA: Virginia Book Company, 1975.

LaFantasie, Glenn W. *Twilight at Little Round Top: July 2, 1863—The Tide Turns at Gettysburg.* New York, NY: Random House, Inc., 2007.

Laine, J. Gary and Morris M. Penny. *Law's Alabama Brigade in the War Between the Union and the Confederacy.* Shippensburg, PA: White Mane Press, 1996.

Lamers, William. *The Edge of Glory: A Biography of General William S. Rosecrans, U. S. A.* New York: Harcourt, Brace and World, 1961.

Leon County Genealogical Society, Leon County Historical Committee, Leon County Historical Book Committee. *History of Leon County*, Texas. Dallas, TX: Curtis Media Corporation, 1986.

____. *Leon County, Texas, Historical Collections.* 3 vols., Centerville, TX: self-published, 1983.

Linton, Roger C. *Chickamauga: A Battlefield History in Images.* Athens, GA: University of Georgia, 2004.

Longacre, Edward G. *Joshua Chamberlain: The Soldier and the Man.* Cambridge. MA: Da Capo Press 2004.

Lonn, Ella. *Foreigners in the Confederacy.* Chapel Hill, NC: University of North Carolina Press, 2002.

Lossing, Benson John and Matthew Brady. *A History of the Civil War, 1861-65 and the causes that led up to the great conflict and a chronological summary and record of every engagement between the troops of the Union and of the Confederacy and showing the total losses and casualties together with war maps of localities, comp. from the official records of the War department.* New York: The War Memorial Association, 1912.

Lowry, Don. *Dark and Cruel War: The Decisive Months of the Civil War September—December 1864.* New York: Hippocrene Books 1993.

____. *Fate of the Country: The Civil War from June-September 1864.* New York: Hippocrene Books, 1992.

____. *No Turning Back: The Beginning of the End of the Civil War—March-June, 1864.* New York: Hippocrene Books, Inc., 1992.

____.*Towards An Indefinite Shore: The Final Months of the Civil War December 1864—May 1865.* New York: Hippocrene Books, 1995.

Maberry, Robert, Jr. *Texas Flags.* College Station, TX: Texas A & M University Press, 2001.

Mantrana, Marc. *Lost Plantations of the South.* Jackson: The University of Mississippi State Press, 2009.

Markham, James H. *The Diuguid Records 1861-1865 and Biographical Sketches.* Westminster, MD: Heritage Books, 2007.

Marvel, William. *Burnside.* Chapel Hill: University of North Carolina Press, 1991.

____. *Lee's Last Retreat: The Flight to Appomattox Courthouse.* Chapel Hill: University of North Carolina Press, 2002.

Matter, William D. *If It Takes All Summer: The Battle of Spotsylvania.* Chapel Hill: University of North Carolina Press, 1988.

McGrath, Thomas A. *Shepherdstown: Last Clash of the Antietam Campaign, September 19-20, 1862.* Lynchburg, VA: Schroeder Publications, 2007.

McMurry, Richard M. *John Bell Hood and the War for Southern Independence.* Lincoln: University of Nebraska Press, 1992.

McPherson, James M. *Antietam: The Battle That Changed the Course of the War.* New York: Oxford University Press, 2002.

____. *Battle Cry of Freedom: The Civil War Era*, New York: Oxford University Press, 1988.

Memorial and Biographical History of Navarro, Henderson, Anderson, Limestone, Freestone and Leon Counties, Texas. Chicago, IL: Lewis Publishing Company, 1903.

Memorial Record of Alabama: A Concise Account of the State's Political, Military, Professional and Industrial Progress, Together With the Personal Memoirs of Many of Its People. 2 vols. Madison, WI: Brant & Fuller, 1893.

Mendoza, Alexander. *Confederate Struggle for Command: James Longstreet and the First Corps in the West.* College Station, TX: Texas A&M University Press, 2008.

Miller, William J. *The Battles for Richmond 1862.* Conshohocken, PA: Eastern National Park and Monument Association,1996.

____. *The Peninsula Campaign of 1862: Yorktown to the Seven Days.* Campbell, CA: Savas Woodbury, 1997.

Mitchell, Thomas G. *Indian Fighters Turned American Politicians: From Military Service to Public Office.* Westport, CT: Praeger Publishers, 2003.

Moore, James Orville. *The Men of the Bayou City Guards (Company A, 5th Texas Infantry, Hood's Brigade).* Ann Arbor, MI: UMI, 1988.

Morton, Oren Frederic. *The Story of Winchester: The Oldest Town in the Shenandoah Valley.* Bowie, MD: Heritage Books, 2001.

National Park Service. *Antietam: National Battlefield Site–Maryland.* Washington, DC: U. S. Government Printing Office, 1961.

____. *Appomattox Court House.* Washington, DC: Government Printing Office, 1955.

____. *Gettysburg National Military Park, Pennsylvania.* National Park Service Historical Handbook Series No. 9, Washington, DC: U. S. Government Printing Office: 1954.

Nofi, Albert A. *A Civil War Treasury: Being a Miscellany of Arms & Artillery, Facts & Figures, Legends & Lore, Muses & Minstrels, Personalities & People.* Cambridge, MA: Da Capo Press, 1995.

O'Reilly, Francis Augustus. *The Fredericksburg Campaign: Winter War on the Rappahannock.* Baton Rouge: Louisiana State University Press, 2003.

Page, Thomas Nelson. *Robert E. Lee: Man and Soldier.* New York: Charles Scribner's Sons, 1911.

Partlow, Miriam. *Liberty, Liberty County and the Atascasito District.* Austin, TX: Jenkins Publishing Co., 1974.

Peebles, Ruth. *There Never Were Such Men Before: The Civil War Soldiers and Veterans of Polk County, Texas, 1861-1865.* Livingston, TX: Polk County Historical Commission, 1987.

Pennington, R. E. *History of Brenham and Washington County.* Houston, TX: Standard Printing & Lithographing Company, 1915.

Peterson, Dorothy Burns. *Daughters of the Republic of Texas: Patriot Ancestor Album.* Paducah, KY: Turner Publishing Company, 1995.

Pfanz, Harry W. *Gettysburg—Culp's Hill and Cemetery Hill.* Chapel Hill: University of North Carolina Press, 1993.

____. *Gettysburg: The Second Day.* Chapel Hill: University of North Carolina Press, 1987.

Pickett, Arlene. *Historic Liberty County.* Dallas, TX: Tardy Publishing Company,1936.

Piston, William Garrett. *Lee's Tarnished Lieutenant: James Longstreet and His Place in Southern History.* Athens: University of Georgia Press 1990.

Plummer, Betty Cantrell. *Historic Homes of Washington County, 1821-1860.* San Marcos, TX: Rio Fresco Books, 1971.

Pohanka, Brian. *Don Troinani's Civil War.* Mechanicksburg, PA: Stackpole Books, 1995.

Power, J. Tracy. *Lee's Miserables: Life in the Army of Northern Virginia from the Wilderness to Appomattox.* Chapel Hill: University of North Carolina Press, 2002.

Price, James S. *The Battle of New Market Heights: Freedom Will Be Theirs by the Sword.* Charleston, SC: The History Press, 2011.

Priest, John M. *Antietam: the Soldiers' Battle.* New York: Oxford University Press, 1993.

____. *No Where to Run: The Wilderness, May 4th and 5th, 1864.* Shippensburg, PA: White Mane Publishing Company, Inc., 1995.

____. *Stephen Elliott Welch of the Hampton Legion.* Shippensburg, PA: Burd Street Press 1994.

Pullen, John J. *The Twentieth Maine: A Classic Story of Joshua Chamberlain and His Volunteer Regiment.* Philadelphia, PA: J. B. Lippincott Co., 1957.

Rable, George C. *Fredericksburg! Fredericksburg!* Chapel Hill: University of North Carolina Press, 2002.

Rafuse, Ethan S. *McClellan's War: The Failure of Moderation in the Struggle for the Union.* Bloomington, IN: Indiana University Press, 2005.

Ramsdell, Charles. "Texas During the Civil War." *History of Texas.* Eugene C. Baker, ed. Dallas, TX: Southwest Press, 1929.

Reid, Thomas. *Spartan Band: Burnett's 13th Texas Cavalry in the Civil War.* Denton, TX: University of North Texas Press, 2005.

Rhea, Gordon C. *Cold Harbor: Grant and Lee May 26-June 3, 1864.* Baton Rouge: Louisiana State University Press, 2002.

____. *The Battles for Spotsylvania Court House and the Road to Yellow Tavern, May 7-12,* 1864. Baton Rouge: Louisiana State University Press, 1997.

____. *The Battle of the Wilderness, May 5-6, 1864.* Baton Rouge: Louisiana State University Press, 1994.

____. *To the North Anna River: Grant and Lee May 13-25, 1864.* Baton Rouge: Louisiana State University Press, 2000.

Richardson, Rupert *Norval, Texas, the Lone Star State.* Englewood Cliffs, NJ: Prentice-Hall, Inc., 1958.

Rister, Carl Coke. *Robert E. Lee in Texas.* Norman, OK: University of Oklahoma Press, 1946.

Roberts, O. M. *Confederate Military History, A Library of Confederate State History, In Twelve Volumes, Written By Distinguished Men of the South, and Edited by Gen. Clement A.. Evans of Georgia.* 12 vols. Atlanta, GA: Confederate Publishing Company, 1899.

Robertson, James I. *Stonewall Jackson: the Man, the Soldier, the Legend.* New York: McMillan, 1997.

Robertson, William Glenn, Edward P. Shanahan, John I. Boxberger and George E. Knapp. *The Staff Ride Handbook for the Battle of Chickamauga, 18-20 September 1863.* Ft. Leavenworth, KA: Combat Studies Institute, U. S. Army Command and General Staff College, 1992.

Rodick, Burleigh Cushing. *Appomattox: The Last Campaign.* New York: Philosophical Library, 1965.

Rowell, John. *Yankee Artillerymen: Through the Civil War With Eli Lilly's Indiana Battery.* Knoxville: University of Tennessee Press, 1975.

Rudisill, James J. *The Day of Our Abraham, 1811-1899.* York, PA: The York Publishing Company, 1936.

Salmon, John S. *The Official Virginia Civil War Battlefield Guide.* Mechanicsburg, PA: Stackpole Books, 2001.

Sandburg, Carl. *Abraham Lincoln: The War Years.* 4 vols., New York: Harcourt, Brace & Company, 1939.

Schaff, Morris. *The Battle of the Wilderness.* Boston, MA: Houghton Mifflin, 1910.

Schmidt, Charles F. *History of Washington County. San Antonio*, TX: The Naylor Company, 1949.

Schmutz, John F. *The Battle of the Crater: A Complete History.* Jefferson, NC: McFarland Publishing Co., 2009.

Scott, James, G., and Edward A. Wyatt. *Petersburg's Story: A History*. Petersburg, VA: Titmus Optical Company, 1960.

Sears, Stephen W. *Gettysburg*. Boston, MA: Houghton Mifflin Company, 2003.

____. *Landscape Turned Red: The Battle of Antietam*. New York: Houghton Mifflin Company, 1992.

____. *To the Gates of Richmond: The Peninsula Campaign*. New York: Houghton Mifflin Company, 1992.

Segars, Joe Henry and Charles Kelly Barrow. *Black Southerners in the Confederate Army*. Gretna, LA: Pelican Publishing Company, Inc., 2001.

Selby, John. *Stonewall Jackson As Military Commander*. New York: Barnes & Noble Books, 1999.

Seward, Frederick Whittlesey, Jr. *Obadiah Seward of Long Island, New York, and His Descendants*. Goshen, NY; self-published, 1948.

Seymour, Digby. *Divided Loyalties: Fort Sanders and the Civil War in East Tennessee*. Knoxville: The East Tennessee Historical Society, 1990.

Sheehan-Dean, Aaron Charles and Joseph T. Glatthaar. *The View from the Ground: Experiences of Civil War Soldiers*. Lexington, KY: University Press of Kentucky, 2007.

Simpson, Harold B., *Gaines'Mill To Appomattox: Waco and McLennon County In Hood's Texas Brigade*. Waco, TX: Texian Press, 1963.

____. *History of Hood's Texas Brigade*. Vol. 2, Hood's Texas Brigade: Lee's Grenadier Guard. Dallas, TX: Alcor Publishing Company, 1983.

____.ed. "Hood's Brigade at Appomattox," *Lone Star Blue and Gray: Essays on Texas in the Civil War* (Austin, TX, 1995), 338-40.

____. *Hood's Texas Brigade in Poetry and Song*. Hillsboro, TX: Hill Junior College Press, 1968.

____. *Hood's Texas Brigade: A Compendium*. Hillsboro, TX: Hill Junior College Press, 1977.

____. *The Recruiting, Training, and Camp Life of a Company of Hood's Brigade in Texas, 1861*. Austin, TX: National Guard Association of Texas, 1962.

Sitton, Thad and Dan Kutley. *From Can See to Can't: Texas Cotton Farmers on the Southern Prairies*. Austin: University of Texas Press, 1997.

Skoch, George & Mark W. Perkins, eds. *Lone Star Confederate: A Gallant and Good Soldier of the Fifth Texas Infantry*. College Station: Texas A & M University Press, 2003.

Smith, M. V. *Reminiscences of the Civil War*. n.p., n.d.

Smith, Robin, William Younghusband, and Bill Younghusband. *American Civil War Zouaves*. Oxford, U.K.: Osprey Publishing, 1996.

Sommers, Richard J. *Richmond Redeemed: The Siege of Petersburg*. Garden City, NY: Doubleday, 1981.

Southerland, Jonathan, *African-Americans at War: An Encyclopedia*, 2 vols. Santa Barbara, CA, ABC-CLIO, 2003.

Southwick, Thomas P. *A Duryee Zouave*. Washington, DC: Acme Printing, 1930.

Speer, William and John Henry Brown. *The Encyclopedia of the New West, containing fully authenticated information of the agricultural, mercantile, commercial, manufacturing, mining,. and grazing industries, and representing the character, development, resources, and present condition of Texas, Arkansas, Colorado, New Mexico, and Indian territory also biographical sketches of their representative men and women*. Marshall, TX: U.S. Biographical Pub. Co., 1881, reprint, Easley, SC, 1978.

Southerland, Jonathan. *African-Americans at War: An Encyclopedia*. Santa Barbara, CA: ABC-CLIO, 2003.

Spencer, John W. *The Confederate Guns of Navarro County*. Corsicana, TX: Texas Press, 1986.

Spruill, Matt and Matt Spruill IV. *Echoes of Thunder: A Guide to the Seven Days Battles*. Knoxville, TN: University of Tennessee Press, 2006.

Stackpole, Edward J. *Drama on the Rappahannock: The Fredericksburg Campaign*. New York: Bonanza Books, 1962.

____. *They Met At Gettysburg*. New York: Bonanza Books, 1956.

Stanard, Mary Newton. *Richmond: Its People and Its Story*. Philadelphia, PA: J. B. Lippincott, 1923.

Sullivan, James R. *Chickamauga and Chattanooga Battlefields*. Washington, DC: National Park. Service, 1956.

Sumerall, Alan K. *Battle Flags of Texans in the Confederacy*. Austin, TX: Eakin Press, 1995.

Sutherland, Jonathan. *African Americans at War: An Encyclopedia*. Santa Barbara, CA: ABC-CLIO, 2003.

Sword, Wiley. *Mountains Touched With Fire: Chattanooga Besieged*. New York: St. Martin's, 1997.

Tarpley, Webster G. and Aston Chartkin. *The Unauthorized Biography of George Bush*. Washington, D. C., Executive. Intelligence Review, 1992.

Taylor, Eugene G. *Gouveneur Kemble Warren: The Life and Letters of an American Soldier*. Boston, MA: Houghton Mifflin Company, 1932.

Toland, Gracey Booker. *Austin Knew His Athens*. San Antonio, TX: Naylor Co., 1938.

Trudeau, Noah Andre. *Bloody Roads South: The Wilderness to Cold Harbor, May—June 1864*. Boston, MA: Little, Brown and Company, 1989.

____. *Out of the Storm: The End of the Civil War, April—June 1865*. Boston, MA: Little, Brown and Company, 1994.

____. *The Last Citadel: Petersburg, Virginia, June 1864—April 1865*. Boston, MA: Little, Brown and Company, 1991.

Trulock, Alice Rains. *In the Hands of Providence: Joshua L. Chamberlain and the American Civil War*. Chapel Hill, NC: University of North Carolina Press, 1992.

Tucker, Glen. *Chickamauga: Bloody Battle in the West*. New York: Bobbs-Merrill, 1961.

Tucker, Phillip Thomas. *Burnside's Bridge: The Climatic Struggle of the 2nd and 20th Georgia at Antietam Creek*. Mechanicsburg, PA: Stackpole Books, 2000.

Turchin, John Basil. *Chickamauga*. Chicago, IL: Fergus Printing Company, 1888.

United States Department of the Interior. *Richmond National Battlefield Park*. Washington, DC: Government Printing Office, 1961.

Upton, Emory. *The Military Policy of the United States*. Washington, DC: Government Printing Office, 1912.

Urwin, Gregory, J. W. *Custer Victorious: The Civil War Battles of General George Armstrong Custer*. East Brunswick, NJ: Associated University Presses, 1983.

Venable, Charles S. *The Campaign from the Wilderness to Petersburg*. Richmond, VA: Geo. W. Gary, Printer, 1879.

Walker, Frances A. *History of the Second Army Corps of the Army of the Potomac*. New York: Scribner's, 1886.

Waller County Historical Survey Committee. *A History of Waller County, Texas*. Waco, TX: The Waller County Historical. Survey Committee, 1973.

Walsh, George *"Damage Them All You Can": Robert E. Lee's Army of Northern Virginia*. New York: McMillan, 2002.

Walther, Eric H. *The Fire-Eaters*. Baton Rouge: Louisiana State University Press, 1992.

Warner, Ezra. *Generals in Gray: Lives of the Confederate Commanders*. Baton Rouge: Louisiana State University Press, 1959.

Webb, Walker P. *The Handbook of Texas*. 2 vols., Austin: Texas State Historical Association, 1952.

Weigley, Russell Frank. *A Great Civil War: A Military and Political History, 1861-1865*. Bloomington: Indiana University Press, 2000.

Weiner, Hollace Ava, and Kenneth Roseman. *Lone Star of David: The Jews of Texas*. Hanover, NH: Brandeis University Press, 2007.

Wert, Jeffry D. *General James Longstreet: The Confederacy's Most Controversial Soldier: A Biography.* New York: Simon & Schuster, 1993.

____. *Gettysburg: Day Three.* New York: Simon & Schuster, 2001.

Wheeler, Richard. *On Fields of Fury: from the Wilderness to the Crater, An Eyewitness History.* New York: Harper Collins, 1991.

____. *Sword Over Richmond: An Eyewitness History of McClellan's Peninsula Campaign.* New York: The . Fairfax Press, 1986.

White, Gifford E. *1830 Citizens of Texas.* Austin, TX: Eakin, 1983.

Wiley, Bell Irvin. *The Life of Johnny Reb: The Common Soldier of the Confederacy.* Indianapolis, IN: The Bobbs-Merrill Company,1943.

Wilkenson, Warren. *A Scythe of Fire: Through the Civil War With One of Lee's Most Legendary Regiments.* New York: William Morrow, 2002.

Williams, James E. *Milam County, Texas in the Civil War.* Cameron, TX: self-published, 1993.

Wisehart, Marion K. *Sam Houston: American Giant.* Washington, DC: Robert B. Luce, Inc., 1962.

Wittenberg, Eric J., J. David Petruzzi, and Michael F. Nugent. *One Continuous Fight: The Retreat from Gettysburg and the Pursuit of Lee's Army of Northern Virginia, July 4-14, 1863.* New York: Savas Beatie, 2008.

Wood, William D. *A Partial Roster of the Officers and Men Raised in Leon County, Texas, for the Service of the Confederate States in the War between the States, with Short Biographical Sketches of Some of the Officers, and a Brief History of Maj. Gould's Battalion.* Waco, TX: W. M. Morrison, 1963.

Woodworth, Steven E. *A Deep Thunder: The Chickamauga and Chattanooga Campaigns.* Lincoln: NE: University of Nebraska Press, 1998.

____. *Chickamauga: A Battlefield Guide with a Section on Chattanooga.* Lincoln, NE: University of Nebraska Press, 1999.

____. *Six Armies in Tennessee: The Chickamauga and Chattanooga Campaigns.* Lincoln, NE: University of Nebraska Press, 1998.

Wooster, Ralph A. *Texas and Texans in the Civil War.* Austin, TX: Eakin Press, 1995.

Wooten, Dudley G. *History of Texas.* Dallas, TX: Texas History Company, 1889.

Wright, Marcus J. and Simpson, Harold B. *Texas in the War: 1861-1865.* Hillsboro, TX: The Hill Junior College Press, 1965.

Yeary, Mamie. *Reminiscences of the Boys in Gray, 1861-1865.* Dallas, TX: Smith & Lamar. 1912.

Young, Samuel O. *A Thumb-Nail Sketch of the City of Houston, Texas, from its founding in 1836 to the year 1912.* Houston, TX: Press of Rein and Sons Company, 1912.

Ziegler, Jesse A. *Wave of the Gulf.* San Antonio, TX: The Naylor Company, 1938.

Web Sources

Primary

"John Bell Hood's Post-War Recollections of Gettysburg." Accessed February 27, 2009, http://vcwsg.com/PDF%20Files/John%20Bell%20Hood's%20Post%20War%20Recollections%20of%20gettysburg%20.pdf.

Kemp, Mrs. Jeff T. "Obituary of William Ashford Nabours." Accessed March 5, 2009, http://homepages.rootsweb.ancestry.com/~mhmills/Holland/Sources-Holland/s-pages/text%20files/wa-nabours-obit.htm.

Willson, Gary. "Madison Ross Letter, 5th Texas Infantry vs 5th Zouaves." Accessed March 19, 2007, www.nycivilwar.us/ross.html.

Secondary

"African Americans at the Siege of Petersburg," Accessed December 15, 2015, http://www.nps.gov/articles/african-americans-at-the-siege-of-petersburg.htm.

Allers, Ken. "Compliments In Such A Damned Place As This: The Trans-Mississippi Units at Gettysburg." Accessed August 23, 2008, www.gdg.org/Research/Authorized/Items/allers.html.

Alton, Robert H. C. "Discovering the 2nd and 11th Mississippi Regiments of the Civil War's 'Camp Fisher'." August 2007. Accessed February 17, 2016, http://billriski.backpackit.com/pub/1191971.

"Baker and Botts History." Accessed May 18, 2008, http://www.bakerbotts.com/ about/history.

Barr, Alwyn. "Battle of Galveston," Handbook of Texas Online, Accessed, July 2, 2008, http://www.tshonline.org/handbook/online/articles/qeg01.

"Battle of Chickamauga, Staff Ride Tour, Day 1-Web Supplement." Accessed July 23, 2008, www.bluegraymagazine.com/Files/chick4supp.pdf.

"Battle of Wauhatchie." Georgia's Blue and Gray Trail Presents America's Civil War, Accessed July 20, 2008, www.blueandgraytrail.com/event/Battle_of_Wauhatchie.

Block, W. T. and Kevin Ladd. "Albert Gallatin Pradelles: Cotton Merchant of Wallisville, Texas." Accessed February 17, 2016, www.wtblock.com/wtblockjr/pradelles.htm.

Boulware, Narcissa Martin. "Mollie Bailey's Circus, Part III" Montgomery County News, March 12, 2005, Accessed November 5, 2009, http://montgomerycountynews.net/mollie-baileys-circus-part-iii-p277-125.htm.

Belinda's Burleson and Lancaster Family Home Page, Belinda Kay Pierce, Spokane, WA, Accessed October 2, 2009, cherokeebabe@comcast.net.

Brown, Jim. "Bunting of the Army of Northern Virginia Battle Flags." Accessed May 2, 2008, http://home.freeuk.com/gazkhan/blank_bunting.htm.

"Byran-Neyland Cemetery." Accessed March 5, 2009, www.rootsweb.ancestry.com/~txliberty/cemetery/bryanney/libcem2.htm#wdwilliams.

Chadwick, Rony. "CSA General Hood's Texans & the 140th New York." The American Civil War: The Battle of Gettysburg, Accessed May 13, 2008, http://www.brotherswar.com/Gettysburg-2t.htm.

"Charles Francis Hume." Hume Family Genealogy Base, Accessed February 20, 2009, http://homepages.rootsweb.ancestry.com/~hume/tree/3671.htm

Clarke, Daniel. "John Cussons: The Confederacy's Lincolnshire Scout," Accessed October 10, 2012, www.academia.edu/5775084/John_Cussons_The_Confederacys_Lincolnshire_Scout.

"Captain Isaac Newton Moreland Turner, C. S. A." Accessed March 23, 2008, http://www.stoppingpoints.com/texas/sights.cgi?marker=Captain+Isaac+newton+Moreland+Turner%2C+C.+S.+A.&cnty=polk.

"Cobb, James Edward, (1835-1903).", Accessed April 22, 2009, http://bioguide.congress.gov/scripts/biodisplay.pl?index=c000549.

Confederate Soldiers Buried in Colorado County." Colorado County and the Confederacy. Accessed May 2, 2008, http://www.coloradocountyhistory.org/confederacy/confederate soldiers burials.htm.

"The Court-Martial of Fitz John Porter, Part II," in Stories of the Civil War (2008), 2:8-10, Accessed February 24, 2009, http://www.thehistoricalarchive.com/ebooks/storiesofcw2.pdf.

"CSA Headstone Dedication Text." Dedication of Historic Texas Cemetery Marker and Confederate Headstone." Accessed June 25, 2008, http://magnoliacemeteryhouston.org/history/ Fuller.pdf.

Cutrer, Thomas W. "David Paul Smith Twiggs." David Emanuel, *Handbook of Texas Online*, Accessed March 12, 2008, http://www.tshaonline. http://www.tshaonline.org/handbook/online/articles/ftw03.

____. "Sion Record Bostick," *Handbook of Texas Online*, Accessed February 2, 2008, http://www.tshaonline.org/handbook/online/articles/fbo34.

____. "Wate, Carlos Adolphus." *Handbook of Texas Online*, http://www.tsaonline.org/handbook/online/articles/fwal2.

"Date of Issue: April 6, 1865." *Freedom by the Sword: A Historian's Journey through the American Civil War Era.* Accessed June 10, 2008, http://sablearm.blogspot.com/2010/04/date-of-issue-april-6-1865.html.

"Descendants of Isiah S. Fields." rootsweb, Accessed May 16, 2008, http://freepages.family.rootsweb.ancesrty.com/~polkcountytxconnections/Fields.html.

"Descendants of Obidiah Seward, Jr.," Accessed October 16, 2009, http://tangledwood.com/getperson.php?personID=I4747&tree=tree1.

"Dillard Cooper," *Handbook of Texas Online*, Accessed February 2, 2008, http://tshaonline.org/handbook/online/articles/fco58.

"The Flags of the Confederacy." Accessed October 22, 2008, www.americanrevival.org/csa/ref/flags.htm.

Gandy, William Harley. *A History of Montgomery County, Texas*, University of Houston 1952, Accessed July 7, 2008, http://www.countygenweb.com/txmontgomery/gandy a history of montgomerycounty.htm.

"Georgia's Blue and Gray Trail Presents America's Civil War," Accessed July 23, 2010, www.blueandgraytrail.com/event/Battle of Wauhatchie.

Haily, James L. "Clay Castle." *Handbook of Texas Online*, Accessed March 3, 2009, https://tshaonline.org/handbook/online/articles/ccc03.

Henson, Margaret Swett. "Matilda Jane Fuller Young." *Handbook of Texas Online*, Accessed August 2, 2008, http://www.tsaonline.org/handbook/online/articles/fyo10.

Hill, Randy. "A Southern Homecoming." USA *Deep South*, Accessed November 5, 2009, http://usads.ms11.net/randy.html.

Jilton, Ned. "Bluff City/Zollicoffer, TN?" *Hardtack and Hard Times*, Accessed September 29, 2009, www.timesnews.net/blogger.php?id=10239&postid+5918.

Johnson, Andrew, "Benning's Brigade." Accessed June 20, 2009, http://worldconnect.rootsweb.ancestry.com/cgi-bin/igm.cgi?op+GET&db+wjohnson&id+161527

Jones, James B., ed. *Tennessee Civil War Sourcebook*, Tennessee Historical Commission. Accessed March 2, 2008, www.tennessee.civilwarsourcebook.com.

Kaherl, John Burton. "Genealogy Report: Descendants of Francis Littlefield." Accessed September 29, 2009, http://www.genealogy.com/ftm/k/a/h/John-B-Kaherl/GENE15-0005. html.

King, Spurgeon. "Battle of Dandridge, January 16-17, 1863." *The Tennessee Encyclopedia of History and Culture*, Accessed March 2, 2008, www.tennesseeencyclopedia.net/entry.php?rec=1586.

____. "William Andrew Fletcher," *Handbook of Texas Online*, Accessed February 2, 2008, http://www.tshaonline.org/handbook/online/articles/ffldd.

Leon County History Collection, 3:60 "A Brief History of Bean Station." June 3, 2009, www.beanstationtn com/pages/history.html.

Livingston, Ronald Howard. "Benjamin Simms Fitzgerald: Pioneer Educator," *Brazoria County Genealogical Research*, Accessed April 20, 2009, http://history.brazoriaresearch.com/2010/02/18/ fitzcopy2 jpg.

Marler. J. C. "John Calhoun Cox: Battle Flag of the Fifth Texas Regiment, Hood's Brigade." Accessed March 12, 2010, http://gennotes.150m.com/batflag.html.

Martin, Mrs. John T. and Mrs. Louis C. Hill. Milam County, Texas, Accessed April 22, 2009, http://www.LKSFriday.com/MILAM/milam-820.htm.

Mayers, Gerald. "The First Maryland Campaign and Hood's Texans." Accessed March 2, 2009, http://www.civilwarhome.com/texansatantietam.htm.

Moore, Robert. "Some Thoughts on Levi Miller." Cenantua's Blog. Accessed November 22, 2009, www.cenantua.wordpress.com/2008/09/28/some-thoughts-on-levi-miller/.

Niemeyer, Stephanie P. "Paul J. Quattlebaum." *Handbook of Texas Online*, Accessed June 25. 2009, http://www.tshaonline.org/handbook/online/articles/fqu16.

____."Walter Browne Botts," *Handbook of Texas Online*, Accessed June 28, 2009, https://tshaonline.org/handbook/online/articles/fbobc.

"Opening the Cracker Line: The Battle of Wauhatchie Junction, October 29, 1863." *TAC News*, May-June 2009, 1-4, Accessed July 22, 2010, http://www.ghqmodels.com/newsletters/mayjun2009.pdf.

Padgett, Vernon R. "Black Confederates: Southern Fantasy or Historical Fact? Part II." Accessed November 20, 2009, SCVcalifornia.blogspot.com. July 20, 2008.

"Quantico," The Historical Marker Database, Accessed April 6, 2015, www.hmdb.org/Marker.asp?Marker=40092.

Rawls, Waite. "Untold Civil War stories: The Potomac Blockade," *A House Divided*, Accessed April 6, 2015; http://www.washingtonpost.com/blogs/house-divided/post/untold-civil-war-stories-the-potomac-blockade/2011/10/07/gIQAKMLcTL blog.html.

Robertson, William Glen. "Vignettes for the Staff Ride Tour." Web Supplement to "Chickamauga, Day 1," *Blue and Gray Magazine*, Vol. 24, No. 6, http://www.bluegraymagazine.com/Files/chick4supp.pdf.

Rogers, Marty. Book Review, *A Southern Girl in '61*. June, 2009, Accessed August 3, 2009, http://confederteprint.com/review.southern.girl in 61 php.

Rowe Cemetery. Accessed May 25, 2008, http://freepages.genealogy.rootsweb.ancestry.com/~polkcountytxconnections/RoweCem.html.

"Sgt. Arter Berry Green," Accessed June 1, 2009, http://findagrave.com/cgi-bin/fg.cgi?page=gr&GRid=30678156.

"Some Thoughts on Levi Miller." Accessed March 15, 2009, www.cenantua.wordpress.com/2008/09/28/some-thoughts-on- levi-miller/.

Smith, David Paul. "Twiggs, David Emanuel." *Handbook of Texas Online*, Accessed May 23, 2009, http://www.tshonline.org/handbook/online/articles/ftw03.

"Special Postal Routes Across the Lines During the American Civil War," Accessed April 5, 2008, http://www.rfajola.com/swlines/SWLines.pdf.

Spain, Charles A., Jr. "Flags of Texas." *The Handbook of Texas Online*, Accessed May 20, 2008, https://tshaonline.org/handbook/online/articles/msf01.

Swift, Eben. "The Fifth Regiment of Cavalry." http://www.history.army.mil/books/R&H/R&H-5CV.htm.

Tennessee Civil War Questionnaire of Constantine Perkins Nance. Accessed July 20, 2009, http://freepages.genealogy.rootsweb.ancestry.com/~nancegc/cp nance.htm.

"The Battle of Gettysburg—Thursday July 2, 1863." *The American Civil War: The Battle of Gettysburg*, Accessed August 3, 2009, www.brotherswar.com/Gettysburg-2t.htm.

The Battle of New Market Heights," Accessed December 15, 2015, http://www.mycivilwar.com/battles/640929.html.

Troesser, John. "Mollie Bailey: Born Mollie Arline Kirkland, Circus Queen of the Southwest." Accessed May 20, 2009, http://www.texasescapes.com/They-Shoe-Horses-Dont-They/Mollie- Bailey.htm.

The 26th Ohio Veteran Volunteer Infantry," Accessed January 23, 2009, http://www.oocities.org/ovi26th/onehundredfortyyearsoctober1863.html.

"Unnamed Chinese Prisoner of War, Union Civil War Veteran." *Association to Commemorate the Chinese Serving in the American Civil War*. Accessed October 3, 2009, https://sites.google.com/site/accsacw/Home/john-tommy.

"US Army Officers Who Joined the Confederate Army." Accessed July 27, 2008, http://www.angelfire.com/mi/robynn/indexpagesix.html.

Walden, Geoffrey R. "The Battle of Armstrong's Hill: The Sideshow of the Big Show," Accessed June 6, 2008, www.rootsweb.ancestry.com/~tnkcwr/KCWRT/Civil War History files/ARMSTRONG.pdf.

Newspapers

Athens [Georgia] *Banner-Herald*, September, 2001.

Atlanta *Century*, September, 1961.

Atlanta *Journal*, August, 1901.

Augusta [Georgia] *Daily Constitutionalist*, 1861-1864.

Austin [Texas] *Statesman*, September-October, 1905.

Beaumont *Enterprise*, November, 1980.

Bryan [Texas] *Daily Eagle*, June, 1925.

Buffalo [Texas] *Express*, May, 2003.

Byran [Texas] *Eagle*, June, 1925.

Calvert [Texas] *Picayune*, June 27, 1912.

Cameron [Texas] *Herald*, August 19, 1922.

Colorado [Texas] *Citizen*, 1861, 1899.

[Cortland, NY] *Gazette and Banner*, September, 1862.

Dallas *Morning News*, October, 1909.

Fredericksburg [Virginia] *Recorder*, March 25, 1862.

Galveston *Daily News*, March 14, 1874-1875, July, 1913.

Galveston *Tri-Weekly News*, 1863, 1875

Harper's Weekly, 1861-1875.

Hillsboro [Texas] *Reflector*, July 13, 1886.

Houston *Chronicle*, August, 1905.

Houston *Daily Telegraph*, 1864-1865.
Houston *Tri-Weekly Telegraph*,1861-1864.
Huntsville [Texas] *Item*, April 14, 1914.
Jasper [Texas] *News Boy*, May, 1911.
Missouri *Republican*, July, 1886.
Montgomery [Alabama] *Advertiser*, May,1889.
National Tribune 1890-1895.
New York *Herald*, September, 1862.
New York *Times*, 1863-1913
New York *World*, July, 1863.
Noland County [Texas] *Record*, February, 1894.
Philadelphia *Gazette*
Philadelphia *Weekly Times*, May, 1883.
Utica [New York] *Morning Herald*, September, 1862.
Richmond *Dispatch*, 1861-1865.
Richmond *Enquirer*, September, 1861.
Richmond *Times*, September, 1891.
Richmond *Whig*, October, 1864.
The Liberty [Texas] *Gazette*, January, 1861.
The Sherman [Texas] *Register*, March 31, 1897
The Shreveport *Journal*, October, 1929.
The [Austin] *State Gazette*, March, 1861.

Theses

Brockman, John Martin. "Port Sullivan, Texas: Ghost Town." (M.A. thesis), Texas A&M University, 1965.

Gandy, William Harley. "A History of Montgomery County, Texas." Department of History, University of Houston (M.A. Thesis), 1952.

Index

John F. Schmutz enjoyed a successful career as a corporate attorney and has maintained a lifelong fascination with all aspects of the Civil War. When he is not researching and writing, John enjoys playing golf and international travel. He is a veteran of the US Army. His first book was *The Battle of the Crater: A Complete History* (2009). He is also the author of *"The Bloody Fifth": The 5th Texas Infantry Regiment, Hood's Texas Brigade, Army of Northern Virginia. Vol. 1: Secession to the Suffolk Campaign* (2016), the winner of the 2017 Texas Association of Authors Book Award, Non-Fiction Military History.

A native of Oneida, New York, John lives with his wife in San Antonio, Texas.